Taking Sides: Clashing Views
on Social Issues, 18/e

by Kurt Finsterbusch

http://create.mcgraw-hill.com

ISBN-10: 1259161129   ISBN-13: 9781259161124

Contents

Preface

The English word *fanatic* is derived from the Latin *fanum,* meaning temple. It refers to the kind of madmen often seen in the precincts of temples in ancient times, the kind presumed to be possessed by deities or demons. The term first came into English usage during the seventeenth century, when it was used to describe religious zealots. Soon after, its meaning was broadened to include a political and social context. We have come to associate the term *fanatic* with a person who acts as if his or her views were inspired, a person utterly incapable of appreciating opposing points of view. The nineteenth-century English novelist George Eliot put it precisely: "I call a man fanatical when . . . he . . . becomes unjust and unsympathetic to men who are out of his own track." A fanatic may hear but is unable to listen. Confronted with those who disagree, a fanatic immediately vilifies opponents.

Most of us would avoid the company of fanatics, but who among us is not tempted to caricature opponents instead of listening to them? Who does not put certain topics off limits for discussion? Who does not grasp at euphemisms to avoid facing inconvenient facts? Who has not, in George Eliot's language, sometimes been "unjust and unsympathetic" to those on a different track? Who is not, at least in certain very sensitive areas, a *little* fanatical? The counterweight to fanaticism is open discussion. The difficult issues that trouble us as a society have at least two sides, and we lose as a society if we hear only one side. At the individual level, the answer to fanaticism is listening. And that is the underlying purpose of this book: to encourage its readers to listen to opposing points of view.

This book contains selections presented in a pro and con format. A variety of different controversial social issues are debated. The sociologists, political scientists, economists, and social critics whose views are debated here make their cases vigorously. In order to effectively read each selection, analyze the points raised, and debate the basic assumptions and values of each position, or, in other words, in order to think critically about what you are reading, you will first have to give each side a sympathetic hearing. John Stuart Mill, the nineteenth-century British philosopher, noted that the majority is not doing the minority a favor by listening to its views; it is doing *itself* a favor. By listening to contrasting points of view, we strengthen our own. In some cases, we change our viewpoints completely. But in most cases, we either incorporate some elements of the opposing view—thus making our own richer—or else learn how to answer the objections to our viewpoints. Either way, we gain from the experience.

Organization of the book   Each issue has an issue *Introduction,* which sets the stage for the debate as it is argued in the YES and NO selections. Accompanying *Learning Outcomes* further help the reader to focus on just what he/she should "take away" from the issue debate. Each issue concludes with a section that explores the issue further and suggests questions which should help you to consider the issues from different angles. In reading the issue and forming your own opinions, you should not feel confined to adopt one or the other of the positions presented. There are positions in between the given views or totally outside them, and the suggestions for further reading that appear within the *Exploring the Issue* section at the end of each issue should help you find resources to continue your study of the subject. *Internet References* that are relevant to the issue are also included.

A word to the instructor   An *Instructor's Resource Guide with Test Questions* (multiple-choice and essay) is available through the publisher for the instructor using *Taking Sides* in the classroom.

For more information on other McGraw-Hill Create™ titles and collections, visit www.mcgrawhillcreate.com.

Editor of This Volume

KURT FINSTERBUSCH is a professor of sociology at the University of Maryland at College Park. He received a BA in history from Princeton University in 1957, a BD from Grace Theological Seminary in 1960, and a PhD in sociology from Columbia University in 1969. He is the author of *Understanding Social Impacts* (Sage Publications, 1980), and he is the coauthor, with Annabelle Bender Motz, of *Social Research for Policy Decisions* (Wadsworth, 1980) and, with Jerald Hage, of *Organizational Change as a Development Strategy* (Lynne Rienner, 1987). He is the editor of *Annual Editions: Sociology* (McGraw-Hill/Contemporary Learning Series); *Annual Editions: Social Problems* (McGraw-Hill/Contemporary Learning Series); and *Sources: Notable Selections in Sociology,* 3rd ed. (McGraw-Hill/Dushkin, 1999).

Academic Advisory Board Members

Members of the Academic Advisory Board are instrumental in the final selection of articles for the *Taking Sides* series. Their review of the articles for content, level, and appropriateness provides critical direction to the editor(s) and staff. We think that you will find their careful consideration reflected in this book.

Rosalind Kopfstein
Western Connecticut State University

Rebecca Riehm
Jefferson Community College

Russ Ward
Maysville Community & Technical College

Correlation Guide

The *Taking Sides* series presents current issues in a debate-style format designed to stimulate student interest and develop critical-thinking skills. Each issue is thoughtfully framed with an issue summary, an issue introduction, and a postscript. The pro and con essays—selected for their liveliness and substance—represent the arguments of leading scholars and commentators in their fields.

Taking Sides: Clashing Views on Social Issues, 18/e, is an easy-to-use reader that presents issues on important topics such as *sex roles, stratification and inequality, political economy, crime,* and *social control.* For more information on *Taking Sides* and other Create™ titles and collections, visit www.mcgrawhillcreate.com.

This convenient guide matches the issues in *Taking Sides: Social Issues,* 18/e, with the corresponding chapters in our best-selling McGraw-Hill Sociology textbooks by Croteau/Hoynes, Witt, and Schaefer.

Taking Sides: Social Issues, 18/e	Experience Sociology, by Croteau/Hoynes	SOC 2013, 3/e by Witt	Sociology Matters, 6/e by Schaefer
Does the Media Have a Liberal Bias?	**Chapter 14:** Media and Consumption	**Chapter 5:** Social Structure and Interaction	**Chapter 3:** Social Interaction, Groups, and Social Structure
Is It Necessary to Become Less Consumerist?	**Chapter 16:** Politics and the Economy	**Chapter 9:** Government and Economy	**Chapter 9:** Social Institutions: Education, Government, and the Economy
Does Social Media Have Largely Positive Impacts on Its Users?	**Chapter 14:** Media and Consumption **Chapter 17:** Social Change: Globalization, Population and Social Movements	**Chapter 3:** Culture **Chapter 15:** Social Change	**Chapter 11:** Social Movements, Social Change, and Technology
Is the American Family in Trouble?	**Chapter 12:** Family and Religion	**Chapter 7:** Families	**Chapter 8:** Social Institutions: Family and Religion
Can Women Have It All?	**Chapter 1:** Sociology in Changing Times **Chapter 4:** Social Structure **Chapter 11:** Gender and Sexuality	**Chapter 5:** Social Structure and Interaction **Chapter 10:** Social Class **Chapter 12:** Gender and Sexuality	**Chapter 3:** Social Interaction, Groups, and Social Structure **Chapter 7:** Inequality by Gender
Is Same-Sex Marriage Harmful to America?	**Chapter 1:** Sociology in Changing Times **Chapter 11:** Gender and Sexuality	**Chapter 12:** Gender and Sexuality **Chapter 15:** Social Change	**Chapter 7:** Inequality by Gender **Chapter 8:** Social Institutions: Family and Religion
Is Increasing Economic Inequality a Serious Problem?	**Chapter 9:** Class and Global Inequality **Chapter 16:** Politics and the Economy	**Chapter 9:** Government and Economy **Chapter 10:** Social Class **Chapter 11:** Global Inequality	**Chapter 5:** Stratification in the United States and Global Inequality **Chapter 9:** Social Institutions: Education, Government, and the Economy
Is America Close to Being a Post-Racial Society?	**Chapter 10:** Race and Ethnicity	**Chapter 13:** Race and Ethnicity	**Chapter 5:** Stratification in the United States and Global Inequality **Chapter 6:** Inequality by Race and Ethnicity
Is the Gender Wage Gap Justified?	**Chapter 9:** Class and Global Inequality **Chapter 11:** Gender and Sexuality **Chapter 13:** Education and Work	**Chapter 10:** Social Class **Chapter 11:** Global Inequality **Chapter 12:** Gender and Sexuality	**Chapter 5:** Stratification in the United States and Global Inequality **Chapter 7:** Inequality by Gender **Chapter 9:** Social Institutions: Education, Government, and the Economy
Is Government Dominated by Big Business?	**Chapter 5:** Power **Chapter 16:** Politics and the Economy	**Chapter 9:** Government and Economy	**Chapter 9:** Social Institutions: Education, Government, and the Economy **Chapter 10:** Population, Community, Health, and the Environment
Does Capitalism Have Serious Defects?	**Chapter 16:** Politics and the Economy **Chapter 17:** Social Change: Globalization, Population and Social Movements	**Chapter 9:** Government and Economy	**Chapter 9:** Social Institutions: Education, Government, and the Economy **Chapter 10:** Population, Community, Health, and the Environment

Taking Sides: Social Issues, 18/e	Experience Sociology, by Croteau/Hoynes	SOC 2013, 3/e by Witt	Sociology Matters, 6/e by Schaefer
Is Stimulus the Best Way to Get the American Economy Back on Its Feet?	**Chapter 16**: Politics and the Economy	**Chapter 9**: Government and Economy	**Chapter 9**: Social Institutions: Education, Government, and the Economy
Was the Welfare Reform the Right Approach to Poverty?	**Chapter 4**: Social Structure **Chapter 16**: Politics and the Economy **Chapter 17**: Social Change: Globalization, Population and Social Movements	**Chapter 5**: Social Structure and Interaction **Chapter 9**: Government and Economy	**Chapter 9**: Social Institutions: Education, Government, and the Economy **Chapter 11**: Social Movements, Social Change, and Technology
Are Teachers the Key to Greatly Improving American Education?	**Chapter 13**: Education and Work	**Chapter 8**: Education and Religion	**Chapter 9**: Social Institutions: Education, Government, and the Economy
Will Biotechnology Have the Greatest Impact on the Next Half Century?	**Chapter 2**: Understanding the Research Process	**Chapter 2**: Sociological Research **Chapter 14**: Health, Medicine and Environment	**Chapter 1**: The Sociological View **Chapter 11**: Social Movements, Social Change, and Technology
Is the Crime Rate the Best Measure for Understanding and Treating Crime?	**Chapter 8**: Deviance and Social Control	**Chapter 6**: Deviance	**Chapter 4**: Deviance and Social Control
Should Laws Against Drug Use Remain Restrictive?	**Chapter 8**: Deviance and Social Control	**Chapter 6**: Deviance **Chapter 14**: Health, Medicine and Environment	**Chapter 4**: Deviance and Social Control
Are We Headed Toward a Nuclear 9/11?	**Chapter 16**: Politics and the Economy **Chapter 17**: Social Change: Globalization, Population and Social Movements	**Chapter 9**: Government and Economy **Chapter 15**: Social Change	**Chapter 9**: Social Institutions: Education, Government, and the Economy **Chapter 11**: Social Movements, Social Change, and Technology
Does Immigration Benefit the Economy?	**Chapter 16**: Politics and the Economy **Chapter 17**: Social Change: Globalization, Population and Social Movements	**Chapter 9**: Government and Economy **Chapter 15**: Social Change	**Chapter 9**: Social Institutions: Education, Government, and the Economy **Chapter 10**: Population, Community, Health, and the Environment **Chapter 11**: Social Movements, Social Change, and Technology
Is Humankind Dangerously Harming the Environment?	**Chapter 15**: Communities, the Environment, and Health **Chapter 17**: Social Change: Globalization, Population and Social Movements	**Chapter 14**: Health, Medicine and Environment	**Chapter 10**: Population, Community, Health, and the Environment **Chapter 11**: Social Movements, Social Change, and Technology
Is Economic Globalization Good for Both Rich and Poor?	**Chapter 15**: Communities, the Environment, and Health **Chapter 16**: Politics and the Economy **Chapter 17**: Social Change: Globalization, Population and Social Movements	**Chapter 9**: Government and Economy **Chapter 10**: Social Class **Chapter 15**: Social Change	**Chapter 9**: Social Institutions: Education, Government, and the Economy **Chapter 10**: Population, Community, Health, and the Environment **Chapter 11**: Social Movements, Social Change, and Technology
Should Government Intervene in a Capitalist Economy?	**Chapter 16**: Politics and the Economy **Chapter 17**: Social Change: Globalization, Population and Social Movements	**Chapter 9**: Government and Economy	**Chapter 9**: Social Institutions: Education, Government, and the Economy **Chapter 10**: Population, Community, Health, and the Environment

Topic Guide

This topic guide suggests how the selections in this book relate to the subjects covered in your course.

All the issues that relate to each topic are listed below the bold-faced term.

Biology

Will Biotechnology Have the Greatest Impact on the Next Half Century?

Business

Does Capitalism Have Serious Defects?
Is Government Dominated by Big Business?
Is the Crime Rate the Best Measure for Understanding and Treating Crime?

Capitalism

Does Capitalism Have Serious Defects?
Is Government Dominated by Big Business?
Should Government Intervene in a Capitalist Economy?

Crime

Is the Crime Rate the Best Measure for Understanding and Treating Crime?
Should Laws Against Drug Use Remain Restrictive?

Divorce

Is the American Family in Trouble?

Drugs

Should Laws Against Drug Use Remain Restrictive?

Economics

Does Capitalism Have Serious Defects?
Does Immigration Benefit the Economy?
Is Economic Globalization Good for Both Rich and Poor?
Is Increasing Economic Inequality a Serious Problem?
Is It Necessary to Become Less Consumerist?
Is Stimulus the Best Way to Get the American Economy Back on Its Feet?
Is the Gender Wage Gap Justified?
Should Government Intervene in a Capitalist Economy?

Education

Are Teachers the Key to Greatly Improving American Education?

Environment

Is Humankind Dangerously Harming the Environment?

Family

Is Same-Sex Marriage Harmful to America?
Is the American Family in Trouble?

Gender

Can Women Have It All?
Is Same-Sex Marriage Harmful to America?
Is the Gender Wage Gap Justified?

Government/Politics

Does the Media Have a Liberal Bias?
Is Government Dominated by Big Business?

Is Same-Sex Marriage Harmful to America?
Is Stimulus the Best Way to Get the American Economy Back on Its Feet?
Should Government Intervene in a Capitalist Economy?
Should Laws Against Drug Use Remain Restrictive?

Immigration

Does Immigration Benefit the Economy?

Inequality

Is America Close to Being a Post-Racial Society?
Is Increasing Economic Inequality a Serious Problem?
Is Same-Sex Marriage Harmful to America?

Legal Issues

Is Same-Sex Marriage Harmful to America?
Should Laws Against Drug Use Remain Restrictive?

Media

Does Social Media Have Largely Positive Impacts on Its Users?
Does the Media Have a Liberal Bias?

Nuclear War

Are We Headed Toward a Nuclear 9/11?

Poverty

Was the Welfare Reform the Right Approach to Poverty?

Racism

Is America Close to Being a Post-Racial Society?

Science

Will Biotechnology Have the Greatest Impact on the Next Half Century?

Society

Can Women Have It All?
Does Capitalism Have Serious Defects?
Is America Close to Being a Post-Racial Society?
Is Increasing Economic Inequality a Serious Problem?
Is Same-Sex Marriage Harmful to America?
Is the American Family in Trouble?

Technology

Will Biotechnology Have the Greatest Impact on the Next Half Century?

Welfare

Was the Welfare Reform the Right Approach to Poverty?

Women's Issues

Can Women Have It All?
Is the American Family in Trouble?

Introduction

Debating Social Issues

What Is Sociology?

"I have become a problem to myself," St. Augustine said. Put into a social and secular framework, St. Augustine's concern marks the starting point of sociology. We have become a problem to ourselves, and it is sociology that seeks to understand the problem and, perhaps, to find some solutions. The subject matter of sociology, then, is ourselves—people interacting with one another in groups and organizations.

Although the subject matter of sociology is very familiar, it is often useful to look at it in an unfamiliar light, one that involves a variety of theories and perceptual frameworks. In fact, to properly understand social phenomena, it *should* be looked at from several different points of view. In practice, however, this may lead to more friction than light, especially when each view proponent says, "I am right and you are wrong," rather than, "My view adds considerably to what your view has shown."

Sociology, as a science of society, was developed in the nineteenth century. Auguste Comte (1798–1857), the French mathematician and philosopher who is considered to be the father of sociology, had a vision of a well-run society based on social science knowledge. Sociologists (Comte coined the term) would discover the laws of social life and then determine how society should be structured and run. Society would not become perfect, because some problems are intractable, but he believed that a society guided by scientists and other experts was the best possible society.

Unfortunately, Comte's vision was extremely naive. For most matters of state there is no one best way of structuring or doing things that sociologists can discover and recommend. Instead, sociologists debate more social issues than they resolve.

The purpose of sociology is to throw light on social issues and their relationship to the complex, confusing, and dynamic social world around us. It seeks to describe how society is organized and how individuals fit into it. But neither the organization of society nor the fit of individuals is perfect. Social disorganization is a fact of life—at least in modern, complex societies such as the one we live in. Here, perfect harmony continues to elude us, and "social problems" are endemic. The very institutions, laws, and policies that produce benefits also produce what sociologists call "unintended effects"—unintended and undesirable. The changes that please one sector of the society may displease another, or the changes that seem so indisputably healthy at first turn out to have a dark underside to them. The examples are endless. Modern urban life

gives people privacy and freedom from snooping neighbors that the small town never afforded; yet that very privacy seems to breed an uneasy sense of anonymity and loneliness. Take another example: Hierarchy is necessary for organizations to function efficiently, but hierarchy leads to the creation of a ruling elite. Flatten out the hierarchy and you may achieve social equality—but at the price of confusion, incompetence, and low productivity.

This is not to say that all efforts to effect social change are ultimately futile and that the only sound view is the tragic one that concludes "nothing works." We can be realistic without falling into despair. In many respects, the human condition has improved over the centuries and has improved as a result of conscious social policies. But improvements are purchased at a price—not only a monetary price but one involving human discomfort and discontent. The job of policymakers is to balance the anticipated benefits against the probable costs.

It can never hurt policymakers to know more about the society in which they work or the social issues they confront. That, broadly speaking, is the purpose of sociology. It is what this book is about. This volume examines issues that are central to the study of sociology.

Culture and Values

A common value system is the major mechanism for integrating a society, but modern societies contain so many different groups with differing ideas and values that integration must be built as much on tolerance of differences as on common values. Furthermore, technology and social conditions change, so values must adjust to new situations, often weakening old values. Some people (often called *conservatives*) will defend the old values. Others (often called *liberals*) will make concessions to allow for change. For example, the protection of human life is a sacred value to most people, but some would compromise that value when the life involved is a 90-year-old comatose man on life-support machines, who had signed a document indicating that he did not want to be kept alive under those conditions. The conservative would counter that once we make the value of human life relative, we become dangerously open to greater evils—that perhaps society will come to think it acceptable to terminate all sick, elderly people undergoing expensive treatments. This is only one example of how values are hotly debated today.

The first issue examines a major institution that can be seen as responsible for instilling values and culture in people—the media. This issue focuses in particular on whether the news reporters and anchorpersons report and comment on the news with professional objectivity and relatively bias free. Fred Barnes argues that the major news outlets are liberal and hire liberal journalists. The selection and reporting of news, therefore, has a liberal bias. In contrast, Robert F. Kennedy Jr. counters that most people get their news from conservative sources and believe many conservative myths as a result.

The next issue concerns America's materialism and consumerism which Gary Gutting asserts has negative impacts on our characters and the shrinking of the common good. Michael Fisher, presenting James Livingston's thesis on the benefits of high consumption, challenges the theory that austerity is character building. Rather, we should enjoy life to the fullest.

The final issue deals with social media and discusses its positive and negative effects. The list of effects is quite long, and opinions differ on how beneficial it is overall. A major use of social media is to connect with friends and family. This positive benefit is tempered somewhat by the fact that heavy social media use is associated with fewer face-to-face interactions with these very people. Social media is also very useful for many instrumental purposes, including getting information and conducting one's affairs. The debate, however, arises over the many negative aspects of the social media and how much they subtract from the positive benefits. There is a debate over how much social media hurts social relations relative to how much it helps social relationships. We obtain much information from social media, but we also obtain much misinformation from it. It leads to social connections but also to social isolation and depression and even personality disorders in some people (though not often). Further, the loss of privacy has badly hurt some people. It is very hard to pull all the effects of social media together and come up with a clear view of its overall impact on individuals and society.

Sex Roles, Gender, and the Family

An area that has experienced tremendous value change in the last several decades is sex roles and the family. Women in large numbers have rejected major aspects of their traditional gender roles and family roles while remaining strongly committed to much of the mother role and to many feminine characteristics. Men have changed much less, but their situation has changed considerably.

The first issue examines the strength of the American family. Isabeth Sawhill points out that the family is strong only among the college educated and very weak among the noncollege educated. Bradford Wilcox directly counters the troubled family thesis which he calls a myth. He shows that the majority of marriages are happy and accepted as fair.

The next issue discusses the current debate about whether women can strongly pursue (lean in) a career and have a rich family life at the same time. Anne-Marie Slaughter says that they cannot and Gayle Tzemach Lemmon says they can. She admits it will be hard but it is doable and promises great rewards.

The final issue examines the positive and negative effects of same-sex marriage. Peter S. Sprigg identifies 10 negative effects of same-sex marriage which would produce horrific results. Some of these negative effects are based on his assumptions about how various governments, agencies, and institutions would change as a result of same-sex marriages. Liza Mundy cites research which shows that same-sex marriages are more intimate, less full of conflict, and happier than heterosexual marriages. Maybe same-sex marriages will improve heterosexual marriages by its positive example.

Stratification and Inequality

The first issue centers around a sociological debate about whether or not increasing economic inequality is a serious problem. James Kurth asserts that it is, while Gary S. Becker and Kevin M. Murphy argue that the increasing inequality is largely the result of the education premium, which, in turn, encourages young people to get more education and better themselves. Today one of the most controversial issues regarding inequalities is the position of blacks in American society. Is the election of Barack Obama an indicator that America is now a post-racial society, meaning that blacks and whites are essentially on equal footing?

In the next issue, Alvin Poussaint interprets the election of Barack Obama as a sign that America has turned a significant corner in race relations and that now young blacks have a role model that allows them to dream the highest dreams. Lawrence D. Bobo looks under the surface reality and explains the many subtle ways that racism still operates in America.

The final issue deals with the gender wage gap. Why do full-time women workers make only 72 percent of men measured by median income? J. R. Shackleton argues that the wage gap is justified because it is the outcome of women's free choices. To have time and energy to be good mothers and housewives, many of them seek less demanding jobs. Hilary M. Lips rejects the supposition that women's choices cause the gap but blames it largely on discrimination, prejudice, and stereotypes.

Political Economy and Institutions

Sociologists study not only the poor, the workers, and the victims of discrimination but also those at the top of society—those who occupy what the late sociologist C. Wright Mills used to call "the command posts." The question is whether the "pluralist" model or the "power elite" model is the one that best fits the facts in America. Does a single power elite rule the United States, or do many groups contend for power and influence so that the political process is accessible to all?

In the first issue, G. William Domhoff argues that the "owners and top-level managers in large income-producing properties are far and away the dominant power figures in the United States" and have a dominating influence in government decisions. Sheldon Kamieniecki's research tells a different story. He finds that business interests do not participate at a high rate in policy issues that affect them, have mixed results when they do, and often lose out to opposing interest groups.

Another major political economy issue is whether capitalism has serious defects. In the next issue, Jerry Z. Muller explains how capitalism greatly increases inequality which creates political imbalances that undermine democracy. It also causes commodification and erodes moral and cultural values. David Berg strongly praises capitalism on how it stimulates innovation and risk taking which greatly advances societies.

The following issue addresses a major debate of the day: how to get the economy growing again. One side argues that more stimulus is needed, and the other side argues that cutting government expenditures will get the country back on its feet. The stimulus view is promoted by Paul Krugman, who advocates the Keynesian view that until unemployment drops and idled assets are put back into production, government expenditures and tax cuts are needed to stimulate the economy. When the economy is healthy again, then the government must work on reducing the debt. The anti-Keynesian view, presented by Dwight R. Lee, believes the Krugman proposal is fiscally irresponsible and leads to slower economic growth over the long run. The Republicans generally support Lee's view, and the Democrats generally support Krugman's view. It looks like neither side will get its way, and both will be dissatisfied with the policies that will or will not be enacted.

The United States is a capitalist welfare state, and the role of the state in welfare is examined in the next issue. The government provides welfare to people who cannot provide for their own needs in the labor market. This issue debates the wisdom of the Work Opportunity Reconciliation Act of 1996, which ended Aid to Families of Dependent Children (which was what most people equated with welfare). David Coates presents the argument that the welfare reform was a great success because it greatly reduced welfare rolls and dramatically increased the employment of welfare mothers. Nicholas Eberstadt worries about how welfare causes dependency. Over time America has developed a vast empire of entitlements which is very expensive and constrains the economy. Welfare is out of hand and must be cut back.

Education is one of the biggest jobs of the government as well as the key to individual prosperity and the success of the economy. For decades the American system of education has been severely criticized. Such an important institution is destined to be closely scrutinized, and many reforms have been attempted. The main policy that is trying to improve public schools today is No Child Left Behind (NCLB), which is addressed by the next issue. Both authors judge NCLB a failure and propose reforms that will greatly improve K–12 schooling and make American schools competitive with European and Japanese schools. Jal Mehta criticizes American education for boring students and not making them creative and excited about learning. They are not ready for the complexities of the twenty-first century. Teachers must be highly trained and teaching must become a demanding profession. Jonathan Sackler places less emphasis on the teachers but just as much on radical change. Magnet and charter schools are a start in the right direction but the transformation will go further. Students will be creators and producers having access to vast learning materials through new technologies and practices.

The final issue in this section deals with a set of concerns about the use of present and soon-to-emerge biotechnologies and digital production technologies. The debate is about which set of miracle technologies will have the greatest impact on the twenty-first century. The value of biotechnologies for healing people is accepted by all.

It possibly could extend life significantly, engineer babies to be physically and mentally superior, and build immunity to most diseases into offspring. Digital production could also produce wonders. It might even produce unbelievable worldwide abundance.

Crime and Social Control

Crime is interesting to sociologists because crimes are those activities that society makes illegal and will use force to stop. Why are some acts made illegal and others (even those that may be more harmful) not made illegal? Surveys indicate that concern about crime is extremely high in America. Is the fear of crime, however, rightly placed? Americans fear mainly street crime, but the review of research on the costs of crime by Jacek Czabański in the first issue shows that the complete cost of white collar crime is much larger than the cost of street crime. His research shows that the full costs of crime are very high and constitute a significant portion of GDP. *The Economist* analyzes different statistics. It shows that crime has declined significantly throughout the developed world. These data justify major changes in the criminal justice system and how criminals should be treated.

A prominent aspect of the crime picture is the illegal drug trade. It has such bad consequences that some people are seriously talking about legalizing drugs in order to kill the illegal drug business. In the next issue, Herbert Kleber and Joseph Califano disagree. They think that drug laws should remain restrictive because legalization would result in increased use, especially by children. They contend that drug legalization would not eliminate drug-related violence but would increase the harm caused by drugs. Jacob Sullum points to all the problems which are caused by criminalizing drug use. It creates vast criminal organizations, expensive law enforcement, millions of people with criminal records, large prison populations, and inappropriate sentences.

The final issue deals with terrorism with weapons of mass destruction, perhaps the major problem in America today. According to Brian Michael Jenkins, a team of terrorists could easily be inserted into the United States and carry out a terrorist attack with a nuclear or radiological bomb. Graham Allison argues that we are not likely to experience a nuclear 9/11 because our counter-terrorist capacities have reduced the risk of nuclear terrorism to nearly zero.

The Future: Population/ Environment/Society

The first issue deals with population migration. Does the recent and current immigration into the United States benefit or harm our economy? Robert Lynch and Patrick Oakford show that immigrants help our economy when all costs and benefits are counted. The positive effect is greater if immigrants have a path to citizenship. Steven A. Camarota disagrees. He argues that immigration's benefit to the economy is too small to support a pro-immigration policy. Since immigration reduces the income of the poor with whom many immigrants compete for jobs, immigration should be minimized.

Many social commentators speculate on "the fate of the earth." The next issue on the state of the planet addresses this concern. Some environmentalists view the future in apocalyptic terms. They see the possibility that the human race could degrade the environment to the point that population growth and increasing economic production could overshoot the carrying capacity of the globe. The resulting collapse could lead to the extinction of much of the human race and the end of free societies. Other analysts believe that these fears are groundless. John Harte and Mary Ellen Harte criticize the attacks on the concerns of the environmentalists. The attackers point out a few false facts and some exaggerations but ignore the overwhelming evidence of serious environmental problems. They rely on market adjustments and new technologies to save the day, but they live by faith rather than science. Ramez Naam discusses both great progress and problems of the past century but argues that ideas and innovations will solve most of the identified problems and bring great prosperity.

The final issue assesses the benefits and costs of globalization. Staff members of the International Monetary Fund examine the effects of globalization and conclude that economic globalization contributes greatly to world prosperity. Ravinder Rena disagrees. Globalization does produce many benefits but also produces many negative impacts. The poor and poorer countries are the most harmed by globalization, so it should be restrained.

The Social Construction of Reality

An important idea in sociology is that people construct social reality in the course of interaction by attaching social meanings to the reality they are experiencing and then responding to those meanings. Two people can walk down a city street and derive very different meanings from what they see around them. Both, for example, may see homeless people—but they may see them in different

contexts. One fits them into a picture of once-vibrant cities dragged into decay and ruin because of permissive policies that have encouraged pathological types to harass citizens; the other observer fits them into a picture of an America that can no longer hide the wretchedness of its poor. Both feel that they are seeing something deplorable, but their views of what makes it deplorable are radically opposed. Their differing views of what they have seen will lead to very different prescriptions for what should be done about the problem.

The social construction of reality is an important idea for this book because each author is socially constructing reality and working hard to persuade you to see his or her point of view, that is, to see the definition of the situation and the set of meanings he or she has assigned to the situation. In doing this, each author presents a carefully selected set of facts, arguments, and values. The arguments contain assumptions or theories, some of which are spelled out and some of which are unspoken. The critical reader has to judge the evidence for the facts, the logic and soundness of the arguments, the importance of the values, and whether or not omitted facts, theories, and values invalidate the thesis. This book facilitates this critical thinking process by placing authors in opposition. This puts the reader in the position of critically evaluating two constructions of reality for each issue instead of one.

Conclusion

Writing in the 1950s, a period that was in some ways like our own, the sociologist C. Wright Mills said that Americans know a lot about their "troubles," but they cannot make the connections between seemingly personal concerns and the concerns of others in the world. If they could only learn to make those connections, they could turn their concerns into *issues*. An issue transcends the realm of the personal. According to Mills, "An issue is a public matter: some value cherished by publics is felt to be threatened. Often there is a debate about what the value really is and what it is that really threatens it." It is not primarily personal troubles but social issues that I have tried to present in this book. The variety of topics in it can be taken as an invitation to discover what Mills called "the sociological imagination." This imagination, said Mills, "is the capacity to shift from one perspective to another—from the political to the psychological; from examination of a single family to comparative assessment of the national budgets of the world. . . . It is the capacity to range from the most impersonal and remote transformations to the most intimate features of the human self—and to see the relations between the two." This book, with a range of issues well suited to the sociological imagination, is intended to enlarge that capacity.

Kurt Finsterbusch
University of Maryland, College Park

Unit 1

UNIT

Culture and Values

*S*ociologists *recognize that a fairly strong consensus on the basic values of a society contributes greatly to the smooth functioning of that society. The functioning of modern, complex urban societies, however, often depends on the tolerance of cultural differences and equal rights and protections for all cultural groups. In fact, such societies can be enriched by the contributions of different cultures. But at some point the cultural differences may result in a pulling apart that exceeds the pulling together.*

Selected, Edited, and with Issue Framing Material by:
Kurt Finsterbusch, *University of Maryland, College Park*

ISSUE

Does the Media Have a Liberal Bias?

YES: Fred Barnes, from "Is the Mainstream Media Fair and Balanced?" *Imprimis* (August 2006)

NO: Robert F. Kennedy Jr., from "The Disinformation Society," *Crimes Against Nature* (Harper Perennial, 2005)

Learning Outcomes
After reading this issue, you should be able to:
<ul><li>Understand how the media can be biased even when the writers or newscasters are trying to be fair and unbiased.</li><li>Assess the thesis that money controls the message in the media.</li><li>Explain how the professional value system of journalists affects their reporting.</li><li>Assess the importance of a media company or individual journalist having a reputation for unbiased reporting. In other words, how much do they lose by losing their professional reputation?</li><li>Comment on why people listen to reporters or programs with known ideological biases that obviously provide biased opinions. Does their audience care about the truthfulness of their reporting? If not, why not?</li><li>Analyze what forces make reporters accountable. How well do they work? What are the consequences when they do not work well?</li><li>Evaluate the arguments for the media being liberal.</li><li>Evaluate the arguments for the media being conservative.</li></ul>

ISSUE SUMMARY

YES: Fred Barnes, journalist, executive editor of *The Weekly Standard,* and TV commentator, argues that the mainstream media has a pronounced liberal bias. They do not hire conservatives, and an analysis of specific news stories shows their bias.

NO: Robert F. Kennedy Jr., environmentalist and political activist, agrees with Barnes that the media is biased but believes that it has a conservative bias. Surveys show that most Americans have many false beliefs that are fed to them by conservative talk radio shows and other conservative media outlets. Many media owners are very conservative and stifle investigative reporting.

"**A** small group of men, numbering perhaps no more than a dozen 'anchormen,' commentators and executive producers . . . decide what forty to fifty million Americans will learn of the day's events in the nation and the world." The speaker was Spiro Agnew, vice president of the United States during the Nixon administration. The thesis of Agnew's speech, delivered to an audience of midwestern Republicans in 1969, was that the television news media are controlled by a small group of liberals who foist their liberal opinions on viewers under the guise of "news." The upshot of this control, said Agnew, "is that a narrow and distorted picture of America often emerges from the televised news." Many Americans, even many of those who were later shocked by revelations that Agnew took bribes

while serving in public office, agreed with Agnew's critique of the "liberal media."

Politicians' complaints about unfair news coverage go back much farther than Agnew and the Nixon administration. The third president of the United States, Thomas Jefferson, was an eloquent champion of the press, but after 6 years as president, he could hardly contain his bitterness. "The man who never looks into a newspaper," he wrote, "is better informed than he who reads them, inasmuch as he who knows nothing is nearer to truth than he whose mind is filled with falsehoods and errors."

The press today is much different than it was in Jefferson's day. Newspapers then were pressed in hand-operated frames in many little printing shops around the country; everything was local and decentralized, and each paper averaged a few hundred subscribers. Today, newspaper chains have taken over most of the once independent local newspapers. Other newspapers, like *The New York Times* and *The Washington Post*, enjoy nationwide prestige and help set the nation's news agenda. Geographical centralization is even more obvious in the case of television. About 70 percent of the national news on television comes from three networks whose programming originates in New York City.

A second important difference between the media of the eighteenth century and the media today has to do with the ideal of "objectivity." In past eras, newspapers were frankly partisan sheets, full of nasty barbs at the politicians and parties the editors did not like; they made no distinction between "news" and "editorials." The ideal of objective journalism is a relatively recent development, tracing back to the early years of the twentieth century. Disgusted with the sensationalist "yellow journalism" of the time, intellectual leaders urged newspapers to cultivate a core of professionals who would concentrate on accurate reporting and who would leave their opinions to the editorial page. Journalism schools cropped up around the country, helping to promote the ideal of objectivity. Although some journalists now openly scoff at it, the ideal still commands the respect—in theory, if not always in practice—of working reporters.

These two historical developments, news centralization and news professionalism, play off against one another in the current debate over news "bias." The question of bias was irrelevant when the press was a scatter of little independent newspapers. Bias started to become an important question when newspapers became dominated by chains, and airwaves by networks, and when a few national press leaders like *The New York Times* and *The Washington Post*

began to emerge. Although these "mainstream" news outlets have been challenged in recent years by opinions expressed in a variety of alternative media—such as cable television, talk radio, newsletters, and computer mail—they still remain powerful conveyers of news.

Is media news reporting biased? The media constitutes a major socializing institution, so this is an important question. Defenders of the media usually hold that although journalists, like all human beings, have biases, their professionalism compels them to report news with considerable objectivity. Media critics insist that journalists constantly interject their biases into their news reports. The critics, however, often disagree about whether such bias is liberal or conservative, as is the case with this issue. In the following selections, Fred Barnes argues that the news media tilt to the left, whereas Robert F. Kennedy Jr. contends that the slant of the news media to which most people are exposed supports a conservative status quo.

Of course, a third possibility is that both views are right. Let's assume that there are biases on the left as Barnes argues and there are biases on the right as Kennedy argues. What is the net effect? One possibility is that biased people can find biased reporting to confirm their biases. That would make their biases stronger and people on opposite sides of issues would find it increasingly difficult to compromise with the other side. Ill will would also increase and possibly threaten the unifying forces that are essential to the survival of democracy. Many commentators today have expressed grave concerns about the level of hostility between Democrats and Republicans and between opponents on many issues. How much deeper can the chasms get? What can bring us back together and unite us?

YES ↵

Fred Barnes

Is the Mainstream Media Fair and Balanced?

Let me begin by defining three terms that are thrown around in debates about the media today. The first is objectivity, which means reporting the news with none of your own political views or instincts slanting the story one way or another. Perfect objectivity is pretty hard for anyone to attain, but it can be approximated. Then there's fairness. Fairness concedes that there may be some slant in a news story, but requires that a reporter will be honest and not misleading with regard to those with whom he disagrees. And finally there's balance, which means that both sides on an issue or on politics in general—or more than two sides, when there are more than two—get a hearing.

My topic today is how the mainstream media—meaning nationally influential newspapers like the *Washington Post*, the *New York Times*, the *Wall Street Journal* and *USA Today*; influential regional papers like the *Miami Herald*, the *Chicago Tribune* and the *Los Angeles Times*; the broadcast networks and cable news stations like CNN; and the wire services, which now are pretty much reduced to the Associated Press—stacks up in terms of the latter two journalistic standards, fairness and balance. In my opinion, they don't stack up very well.

Twenty years ago I wrote a piece in *The New Republic* entitled "Media Realignment," and the thrust of it was that the mainstream media was shedding some of its liberal slant and moving more to the center. This was in the Reagan years, and I pointed to things like *USA Today*, which was then about five years old and was a champion of the Reagan economic recovery. CNN was younger then, too, and quite different from the way it is now; Ted Turner owned it, but he wasn't manipulating it the way he did later, which turned it into something quite different. Financial news was suddenly very big in the midst of the 401(k) revolution, and the stock market boom was getting a lot of coverage. *The New Republic*, where I worked, had been pro-Stalin in the 1930s, but by the 1980s had become very pro-Reagan and anti-communist on foreign policy. I also cited a rise of new conservative columnists like George Will. But looking back on that piece now, I see that I couldn't have been more wrong. The idea that the mainstream media was moving to the center was a mirage. In fact, I would say that compared to what I was writing about back in the 1980s, the mainstream media today is more liberal, more elitist, more secular, more biased, more hostile to conservatives and Republicans, and more self-righteous.

Liberal and Impenetrable

Liberalism is endemic in the mainstream media today. Evan Thomas—the deputy editor of *Newsweek* and one of the honest liberals in the media—noted this very thing with regard to coverage of the 2004 presidential race, which I'll discuss later. It was obvious, he said, that the large majority in the media wanted John Kerry to win and that this bias slanted their coverage. And indeed, every poll of the media—and there have been a lot of them—shows that they're liberal, secular and so on. Polls of the Washington press corps, for instance, about who they voted for in 2004 always show that nine-to-one or ten-to-one of them voted Democratic. Peter Brown, a columnist who just recently left the *Orlando Sentinel*, conducted a poll a few years ago of newspaper staffs all around the country—not just at the big papers, but midsize papers and even some small papers—and found that this disparity existed everywhere.

Nor is this likely to change. Hugh Hewitt, the California lawyer and blogger and talk radio host, spent a few days recently at the Columbia Journalism School, supposedly the premiere journalism school in America. He spoke to a couple of classes there and polled them on who they had voted for. He found only one Bush voter in all the classes he spoke to. Steve Hayes, a fine young writer and reporter at *The Weekly Standard*, went to Columbia Journalism School and says that during his time there he was one of only two or three conservative students out of hundreds.

This is not to say that there aren't many fine young conservative journalists. But they aren't likely to be hired in the mainstream media. When I was at *The New Republic* for ten years—and *The New Republic* was quite liberal, despite its hawkish foreign policy—any young person who joined the staff and wrote stories that were interesting and demonstrated that he or she could write well was grabbed immediately by the *New York Times* or other big newspapers, *Newsweek*, *Time* or the networks. But that doesn't happen at *The Weekly Standard*, where I work now. Some of our young writers are the most talented I have ever met in my 30-plus years in journalism. But they don't get those phone calls. Why? Because they're with a conservative magazine. Of course there has been one famous exception—David Brooks, who is now the conservative columnist with the *New York Times*. But he was probably the least conservative person at *The Weekly Standard*.

Conservatives are tokens on most editorial pages, just as they are on the broadcast networks and on cable news stations like CNN and MSNBC. Of course, I have a vested interest, since I work for FOX News; but if you compare the number of liberal commentators on FOX—and there are a lot of them—with the number of conservatives on those other stations, you'll see what I mean.

The fact is that the mainstream media doesn't want conservatives. It doesn't matter whether they're good reporters or writers. They go out of their way not to hire them. This was true 20 years ago, and it's true today. This impenetrability is why conservatives have had to erect the alternative media—talk radio, the blogs, conservative magazines and FOX News. Together, these form a real infrastructure that's an alternative to the mainstream media. But it's still a lot smaller, it's not as influential and it's largely reactive. It's not the equal of the mainstream media, that's for sure.

Powerful and Unfair

One way to see the unequaled power of the mainstream media is in how it is able to shape and create the stories that we're stuck talking about in America. A good example is Cindy Sheehan last summer. The Sheehan story was a total creation of the mainstream media. And in creating the story, the media shamelessly mischaracterized Sheehan. It portrayed her as simply a poor woman who wanted to see President Bush because her son had been killed in Iraq. Well, in the first place, she had already seen President Bush once. Also, though you would never know it from the dominant coverage, she was in favor of the Iraqi insurgency—the beheaders, the killers of innocent women and children. She was on their side, and she said so. She was also filled with a deep hatred of Israel. Yet the media treated her in a completely sympathetic manner, failing to report the beliefs that she made little attempt to hide. In any case, the Cindy Sheehan story came to dominate the news for the latter part of the summer; only the mainstream media still has the power to *make* stories big.

To see how distorted the mainstream media's view of the world can be, one need only compare its coverage of the Valerie Plame "leak" story with its coverage of the NSA surveillance leak story. Plame is the CIA agent whose name was written about by reporter Robert Novak in a column, following which the media portrayed her as having been outed as an undercover CIA agent. The simple facts from the beginning were that she was not an undercover agent any more; she was not even overseas. The story had no national security repercussions at all—none. But that didn't stop the media, which built the story up to great heights—apparently in the groundless hope that it would lead to an indictment of Karl Rove—and kept it front page news, at least intermittently, for what seemed like forever. The NSA surveillance story, on the other hand, also created by the media—this time pursuant to a real leak, and one that was clearly in violation of the law—had tremendous

national security implications. After all, it revealed a secret and crucial program that was being used to uncover plots to bomb and massacre Americans and probably rendered that program no longer effective. Not only was this important story treated on an equal basis with the non-story of Valerie Plame, but the media was not interested, for the most part, in its national security repercussions. Instead the media mischaracterized the story as a "domestic spying scandal," suggesting constitutional overreach by the Bush administration. Well, a domestic spying story is exactly what the story was *not*. Those being spied on were Al-Qaeda members overseas who were using the telephone. If some of those calls were with people in the U.S., they were monitored for that reason only. But the media's stubborn mischaracterization of the story continued to frame the debate.

This brings me to the use of unfair and unbalanced labeling by the media. How often, if ever, have you heard or read the term "ultraliberal"? I don't think I've ever heard or read it. You'll hear and see the term "ultraconservative" a lot, but not "ultraliberal"—even though there are plenty of ultraliberals. Another widely used labeling term is "activist." If people are working to block a shopping center from being built or campaigning against Wal-Mart, they are called "activists." Of course, what the term "activist" means is *liberal*. But while conservatives are called conservatives by the media, liberals are "activists." For years we've seen something similar with regard to debates over judicial nominees. The Federalist Society, with which many conservative judicial nominees tend to be associated, is always referred to as the *conservative* Federalist Society, as if that's part of its name. But the groups opposing conservative nominees are rarely if ever labeled as liberal—giving the impression that they, unlike the Federalist Society, are somehow objective.

Related to this, I would mention that conservatives are often labeled in a way to suggest they are mean and hateful. Liberals criticize, but conservatives hate. Have you noticed that the media never characterizes individuals or groups as Bush haters? There are Bush critics, but there are no Bush haters—whereas in the Clinton years, critics of the president were often referred to as Clinton haters. I'm not saying that there weren't Clinton haters on the fringes in the 1990s. But far-left groups have been treated as acceptable . . . within the mainstream of American politics today by the media, while in truth they are as clearly animated by hatred as the most rabid anti-Clinton voices ever were.

Secular and Partisan Bias

With regard to religion, Christianity in particular—but also religious faith in general—is reflexively treated as something dangerous and pernicious by the mainstream media. Back in the early 1990s when I was still at *The New Republic*, I was invited to a dinner in Washington with Mario Cuomo. He was then governor of New York, and had invited several reporters to dinner because he was thinking about running for president. At one point that night he mentioned that he sent his children to Catholic schools in New York because he wanted them to be taught about a God-centered universe. This was in the context of expressing his whole-hearted support for public schools. But from the reaction, you would have thought he had said that one day a week he would bring out the snakes in his office and make policy decisions based on where they bit him. He was subsequently pummeled with stories about how improper it was for him, one, to send his kids to religious schools, and two, to talk about it. It was amazing. The most rigid form of secularism passes as the standard in mainstream journalism these days.

President Bush is similarly treated as someone who is obsessive about his religion. And what does he do? Well, he reads a devotional every day; he tries to get through the Bible, I think, once a year; and he prays. Now, I know many, many people who do this. Tens of millions of people do it. And yet the media treats Bush as some religious nut and pursues this story inaccurately. Again, it is clear that partisan bias is involved, too, because in fact, Bush talks publicly about his faith much less than other presidents have. There is a good book about Bush's religion by Paul Kengor, who went back to every word President Clinton spoke and found out that Clinton quoted scripture and mentioned God and Jesus Christ more than President Bush has. You would never get that from the mainstream media.

The partisan bias of the mainstream media has been at no time more evident than during the last presidential election. Presidential candidates used to be savaged equally by the media. No matter who—Republican or Democrat—they both used to take their hits. But that's not true any more. Robert Lichter, at the Center for Media and Public Affairs in Washington, measures the broadcast news for all sorts of things, including how they treat candidates. He's been doing it now for nearly 20 years. And would anyone care to guess what presidential candidate in all those years has gotten the most favorable treatment from the broadcast media? The answer is John Kerry, who got 77 percent favorable coverage in the stories regarding him on the three broadcast news shows. For Bush, it was 34 percent. This was true despite the fact that Kerry made his Vietnam service the motif of the Democratic National Convention, followed weeks later by 64 Swift Boat vets who served with Kerry in Vietnam claiming that he didn't do the things he said he did. It was a huge story, but the mainstream media didn't want to cover it and didn't cover it, for week after week after week.

There was an amazingly well documented book written by a man named John O'Neill—himself a Swift Boat vet—who went into great detail about why John Kerry didn't deserve his three Purple Hearts, etc. It might have been a right-wing screed, but if you actually read it, it wasn't a screed. It backed up its claims with evidence. Normally in journalism, when somebody makes some serious charges against a well-known person, reporters look into the charges to see if they're true or not. If they aren't, reporters look into the motives behind the false charges— for instance, to find out if someone paid the person making the false charges, and so on. But that's not what the media did in this case. The *New York Times* responded immediately by investigating the financing of the Swift Boat vets, rather than by trying to determine whether what they were saying was true. Ultimately, grudgingly— after bloggers and FOX News had covered the story sufficiently long that it couldn't be ignored—the mainstream media had to pick up on the story. But its whole effort was aimed at knocking down what the Swift Boat vets were saying.

Compare this with September 8, 2004, when Dan Rather reported on documents that he said showed not only that President Bush used preferential treatment to get into the Texas National Guard, but that he hadn't even done all his service. The very next morning, the whole story—because CBS put one of the documents on its Web site—was knocked down. It was knocked down because a blogger on a Web site called Little Green Footballs made a copy on his computer of the document that was supposedly made on a typewriter 30 years earlier and demonstrated that it was a fraud made on a modern computer. Then, only a few weeks after that embarrassment, CBS came up with a story, subsequently picked up by the *New York Times*, that an arms cache of 400 tons of ammunition in Iraq had been left unguarded by the American military and that the insurgents had gotten hold of it. Well, it turned out that they didn't know whether the insurgents had gotten that ammunition or not, or whether indeed the American military had possession of it. It was about a week before the election that these major news organizations broke this unsubstantiated story, something that would have been unimaginable in past campaigns. Why would they do that? Why would Dan Rather insist on releasing fraudulent documents when even his own experts recommended against it? Why would CBS and the *New York Times* come back with an explosive but unsubstantiated arms cache story only weeks later? They did it for one reason: They wanted to defeat President Bush for re-election. There is no other motive that would explain disregarding all the precautions you're taught you should have in journalism.

⋯⟨⊙⟩⋯

I'll wind up on a positive note, however. Forty years ago, John Kenneth Galbraith—the great liberal Harvard economist—said that he knew conservatism was dead because it was bookless. Conservatives didn't publish books. And to some extent, it was true at the time. But it's no longer true. Conservatives have become such prolific writers and consumers of books that Random House and other publishing companies have started separate conservative imprints. Nowadays it is common to see two or three or four conservative books—some of them kind of trashy, but some of them very good—on the bestseller list. Insofar as books are an indication of how well conservatives are doing—at least in the publishing part of the media world—I would say they're doing quite well. They're not winning, but they're much better off than they were before—something that can't be said about how they are faring in the unfair and unbalanced mainstream media.

FRED BARNES was the executive editor of *The Weekly Standard* from 1985 to 1995. He has a news TV talk show.

Robert F. Kennedy Jr.   → **NO**

The Disinformation Society

Many Democratic voters marveled at the election results. George W. Bush, they argued, has transformed a projected $5.6 trillion, 10-year Bill Clinton surplus into a projected $1.4 trillion deficit—a $7 trillion shift in wealth from our national treasury into the pockets of the wealthiest Americans, particularly the president's corporate paymasters. Any discerning observer, they argued, must acknowledge that the White House has repeatedly lied to the American people about critical policy issues—Medicare, education, the environment, the budget implications of its tax breaks, and the war in Iraq—with catastrophic results.

President Bush has opened our national lands and sacred places to the lowest bidder and launched a jihad against the American environment and public health to enrich his corporate sponsors. He has mired us in a costly, humiliating war that has killed more than 1,520 American soldiers and maimed 11,300. He has made America the target of Islamic hatred, caused thousands of new terrorists to be recruited to al-Qaeda, isolated us in the world, and drained our treasury of the funds necessary to rebuild Afghanistan and to finance our own vital homeland-security needs. He has shattered our traditional alliances and failed to protect vulnerable terrorist targets at home—chemical plants, nuclear facilities, air-cargo carriers, and ports. He has disgraced our nation and empowered tyrants with the unpunished excesses at Guantánamo and Abu Ghraib. These baffled Democrats were hard-pressed to believe that their fellow Americans would give a man like this a second term.

To explain the president's victory, political pundits posited a vast "values gap" between red states and blue states. They attributed the president's success in the polls, despite his tragic job failures, to the rise of religious fundamentalism. Heartland Americans, they suggested, are the soldiers in a new American Taliban, willing to vote against their own economic interests to promote "morality" issues that they see as the critical high ground in a life-or-death culture war.

I believe, however, that the Democrats lost the presidential contest not because of a philosophical chasm between red and blue states but due to an information deficit caused by a breakdown in our national media. Traditional broadcast networks have abandoned their former obligation to advance democracy and promote the public interest by informing the public about both sides of issues relevant to those goals. To attract viewers and advertising revenues, they entertain rather than inform. This threat to the flow of information, vital to democracy's survival, has been compounded in recent years by the growing power of right-wing media that twist the news and deliberately deceive the public to advance their radical agenda.

According to an October 2004 survey by the Program on International Policy Attitudes (PIPA), a joint program of the Center on Policy Attitudes, in Washington, D.C., and the Center for International and Security Studies at the University of Maryland:

- Seventy-two percent of Bush supporters believed Iraq had weapons of mass destruction (or a major program for developing them), versus 26 percent of Kerry voters. A seven-month search by 1,500 investigators led by David Kay, working for the C.I.A., found no such weapons.
- Seventy-five percent of Bush supporters believed that Iraq was providing substantial support to al-Qaeda, a view held by 30 percent of Kerry supporters. *The 9/11 Commission Report* concluded that there was no terrorist alliance between Iraq and al-Qaeda.
- Eighty-two percent of Bush supporters erroneously believed either that the rest of the world felt better about the U.S. thanks to its invasion of Iraq or that views were evenly divided. Eighty-six percent of Kerry supporters accurately understood that a majority of the world felt worse about our country.
- Most Bush supporters believed the Iraq war had strong support in the Islamic world. Kerry's supporters accurately estimated the low level of support in Islamic countries. Even Turkey, the most Westernized Islamic country, was 87 percent against the invasion.
- Most significant, the majority of Bush voters agreed with Kerry supporters that if Iraq did not have W.M.D. and was not providing assistance to al-Qaeda the U.S. should not have gone to war. Furthermore, most Bush supporters, according to PIPA, favored the Kyoto Protocol to fight global warming, the Mine Ban Treaty to ban land mines, and strong labor and environmental standards in trade agreements, and wrongly believed that their candidate favored these things. In other words, the values and principles were the same. Bush voters made their choice based on bad information.

It's no mystery where the false beliefs are coming from. Both Bush and Kerry supporters overwhelmingly believe that the Bush administration at the time of the 2004 U.S. election was telling the American people that Iraq had W.M.D. and that Saddam Hussein had strong links to al-Qaeda. The White House's false message was carried by right-wing media in bed with the administration. Prior to the election, Fox News reporters, for example, regularly made unsubstantiated claims about Iraq's W.M.D. Fox anchor Brit Hume, on his newscast in July 2004, announced that W.M.D. had actually been found. Sean Hannity repeatedly suggested without factual support that the phantom weapons had been moved to Syria and would soon be found. An October 2003 survey by PIPA showed that people who watch Fox News are disproportionately afflicted with the same misinformation evidenced by the 2004 PIPA report. The earlier study probed for the source of public misinformation about the Iraq war that might account for the common misperceptions that Saddam Hussein had been involved in the 9/11 attacks, that he supported al-Qaeda, that W.M.D. had been found, and that world opinion favored the U.S. invasion. The study discovered that "the extent of Americans' misperceptions vary significantly depending on their source of news. Those who receive most of their news from Fox News are more likely than average to have misperceptions."

Unfortunately for John Kerry, many Americans now do get their information from Fox—according to Nielsen Media Research, in February, Fox was the cable news leader, with an average of 1.57 million prime-time viewers, nearly 2.5 times CNN's average viewership in the same time slot—and from Fox's similarly biased cable colleagues, CNBC and MSNBC. Millions more tune to the Sinclair Broadcast Group—one of the nation's largest TV franchises. After 9/11, Sinclair forced its stations to broadcast spots pledging support for President Bush, and actively censored unfavorable coverage of the Iraq war—blacking out Ted Koppel's *Nightline* when it ran the names of the U.S. war dead. It retreated from its pre-election proposal to strong-arm its 62 TV stations into pre-empting their prime-time programming to air an erroneous and blatantly biased documentary about John Kerry's war record only when its stock dropped 17 percent due to Wall Street fears of sponsor boycotts and investor worries that Sinclair was putting its right-wing ideology ahead of shareholder profits.

Americans are also getting huge amounts of misinformation from talk radio, which is thoroughly dominated by the extreme right. A Gallup Poll conducted in December 2002 discovered that 22 percent of Americans receive their daily news from talk-radio programs. An estimated 15 million people listen to Rush Limbaugh alone, and on the top 45 AM radio stations in the country, listeners encounter 310 hours of conservative talk for every 5 hours of liberal talk. According to the nonprofit Democracy Radio, Inc., 90 percent of all political talk-radio programming is conservative, while only 10 percent is

progressive. All the leading talk-show hosts are right-wing radicals—Rush Limbaugh, Sean Hannity, Michael Savage, Oliver North, G. Gordon Liddy, Bill O'Reilly, and Michael Reagan—and the same applies to local talk radio.

Alas, while the right-wing media are deliberately misleading the American people, the traditional corporately owned media—CBS, NBC, ABC, and CNN—are doing little to remedy those wrong impressions. They are, instead, focusing on expanding viewership by hawking irrelevant stories that appeal to our prurient interest in sex and celebrity gossip. None of the three major networks gave gavel-to-gavel coverage of the party conventions or more than an hour in prime time, opting instead to entertain the public with semi-pornographic reality shows. "We're about to elect a president of the United States at a time when we have young people dying in our name overseas, we just had a report from the 9/11 commission which says we are not safe as a nation, and one of these two groups of people is going to run our country," commented PBS newsman Jim Lehrer, in disgust at the lack of convention coverage. CBS anchor Dan Rather said that "I argued the conventions were part of the dance of democracy. I found myself increasingly like the Mohicans, forced farther and farther back into the wilderness and eventually eliminated."

The broadcast reporters participating in the presidential debates were apparently so uninterested in real issues that they neglected to ask the candidates a single question about the president's environmental record. CBS anchor Bob Schieffer, who M.C.'d the final debate, asked no questions about the environment, focusing instead on abortion, gay marriage, and the personal faith of the candidates, an agenda that could have been dictated by Karl Rove.

Where is that dreaded but impossible-to-find "liberal bias" that supposedly infects the American press? The erroneous impression that the American media have a liberal bias is itself a mark of the triumph of the right-wing propaganda machine.

The Republican Noise Machine: Right-Wing Media and How It Corrupts Democracy, by David Brock—the president and C.E.O. of Media Matters for America, a watchdog group that documents misinformation in the right-wing media—traces the history of the "liberal bias" notion back to the Barry Goldwater presidential campaign, in 1964, in which aggrieved conservatives railed against Walter Cronkite and the "Eastern Liberal Press" at the Republican National Convention. In response to Spiro Agnew's 1969 attack on the networks as insufficiently supportive of Nixon's policies in Vietnam, conservatives formed an organization called Accuracy in Media, whose purpose was to discredit the media by tagging it as "liberal," and to market that idea with clever catchphrases. Polluter-funded foundations, including the Adolph Coors Foundation and the so-called four sisters—the Lynde and Harry Bradley Foundation, the

John M. Olin Foundation, Richard Mellon Scaife's foundations, and the Smith Richardson Foundation—all of which funded the anti-environmental movement, spent hundreds of millions of dollars to perpetuate the big lie of liberal bias, to convince the conservative base that it should not believe the mainstream, to create a market for right-wing media, and to intimidate and discipline the mainstream press into being more accommodating to conservatism.

According to Brock, right-wing groups such as the Heritage Foundation and Scaife's Landmark Legal Foundation helped persuade Ronald Reagan and his Federal Communications Commission, in 1987, to eliminate the Fairness Doctrine—the F.C.C.'s 1949 rule which dictated that broadcasters provide equal time to both sides of controversial public questions. It was a "godsend for conservatives," according to religious-right pioneer and Moral Majority co-founder Richard Viguerie, opening up talk radio to one-sided, right-wing broadcasters. (Rush Limbaugh nationally launched his talk show the following year.) Radical ideologues, faced with Niagara-size flows of money from the Adolph Coors Foundation, the four sisters, and others, set up magazines and newspapers and cultivated a generation of young pundits, writers, and propagandists, giving them lucrative sinecures inside right-wing think tanks, now numbering more than 500, from which they bombard the media with carefully honed messages justifying corporate profit taking.

Brock himself was one of the young stars recruited to this movement, working in turn for the Heritage Foundation, the Reverend Sun Myung Moon's *Washington Times,* and Scaife's *American Spectator.* "If you look at this history," Brock told me recently, "you will find that the conservative movement has in many ways purchased the debate. You have conservative media outlets day after day that are intentionally misinforming the public." Brock, who admits to participating in the deliberate deception while he was a so-called journalist on the right-wing payroll, worries that the right-wing media are systematically feeding the public "false and wrong information. It's a really significant problem for democracy.

"We're in a situation," continues Brock, "where you have 'red facts' and 'blue facts.' And I think the conservatives intentionally have done that to try to confuse and neutralize accurate information that may not serve the conservative agenda."

The consolidation of media ownership and its conservative drift are growing ever more severe. Following the election, Clear Channel, the biggest owner of radio stations in the country, announced that Fox News will now supply its news feed to many of the company's 1,240 stations, further amplifying the distorted drumbeat of right-wing propaganda that most Americans now take for news.

Sadly enough, right-wing radio and cable are increasingly driving the discussion in mainstream broadcasting as well. At a Harvard University symposium the day before the Democratic convention, three network anchors and a CNN anchor straightforwardly discussed the effects that right-wing broadcasters, conservative money, and organized pressure have on the networks. And in February 2005, Pat Mitchell announced her resignation as president of PBS, hounded from office by right-wing critics who felt her conciliatory efforts to conservatize the network—canceling a cartoon episode with a lesbian couple and adding talk shows by such right-wingers as Tucker Carlson and Paul Gigot—did not go far enough fast enough.

Furthermore, Fox's rating success has exerted irresistible gravities that have pulled its competitors' programming to starboard. In the days leading up to the Iraq war, MSNBC fired one of television's last liberal voices, Phil Donahue, who hosted its highest-rated show; an internal memo revealed that Donahue presented "a difficult public face for NBC in a time of war." CBS's post-election decision to retire Dan Rather, a lightning rod for right-wing wrath, coincided with Tom Brokaw's retirement from NBC. He was replaced by Brian Williams, who has said, "I think Rush [Limbaugh] has actually yet to get the credit he is due." According to NBC president Jeff Zucker, "No one understands this NASCAR nation more than Brian."

Conservative noise on cable and talk radio also has an echo effect on the rest of the media. One of the conservative talking points in the last election was that terrorists supported the candidacy of John Kerry. According to Media Matters, this pearl originated on Limbaugh's radio show in March 2004 and repeatedly surfaced in mainstream news. In May, CNN's Kelli Arena reported "speculation that al-Qaeda believes it has a better chance of winning in Iraq if John Kerry is in the White House"; in June it migrated to Dick Morris's *New York Post* column. Chris Matthews mentioned it in a July edition of *Hardball.* In September, Bill Schneider, CNN's senior political analyst, declared that al-Qaeda "would very much like to defeat President Bush," signaling that Limbaugh's contrivance was now embedded firmly in the national consciousness.

That "echo effect" is not random. Brock shows in his book how the cues by which mainstream news directors decide what is important to cover are no longer being suggested by *The New York Times* and other responsible media outlets, but rather by the "shadowy" participants of a Washington, D.C., meeting convened by Grover Norquist's Americans for Tax Reform, an anti-government organization that seeks to prevent federal regulation of business.

Every Wednesday morning the leaders of 80 conservative organizations meet in Washington in Norquist's boardroom. This radical cabal formulates policy with the Republican National Committee and the White House, developing talking points that go out to the conservative media via a sophisticated fax tree. Soon, millions of Americans are hearing the same message from cable news commentators and thousands of talk jocks across America. Their precisely crafted message and language then percolate through the mainstream media to form the underlying assumptions of our national debate.

This meeting has now grown to include more than 120 participants, including industry lobbyists and representatives of conservative media outlets such as *The Washington Times* and the *National Review*. According to Brock, columnist Bob Novak sends a researcher. *The Wall Street Journal*'s Peggy Noonan may attend in person. The lockstep coordination among right-wing political operatives and the press is new in American politics.

A typical meeting might focus on a new tax proposal released by President Bush. Following conference calls throughout the week, the decision will be made to call the plan "bold." Over the next 10 days, radio and cable will reiterate that it's "bold, bold, bold." The result, according to Brock, is that "people come to think that there must be something 'bold' about this plan."

This highly integrated network has given the right frightening power to disseminate its propaganda and has dramatically changed the way Americans get their information and formulate policy. In *The Republican Noise Machine*, Brock alleges routine fraud and systematically dishonest practices by his former employer the Reverend Sun Myung Moon's *Washington Times,* which is the primary propaganda organ for Moon's agenda to establish America as a Fascist theocracy. The paper doesn't reach more than a hundred thousand subscribers, but its articles are read on the air by Rush Limbaugh, reaching 15 million people, and are posted on Matt Drudge's Web site, to reach another 7 million people, and its writers regularly appear on *The O'Reilly Factor,* before another 2 million. Network TV talk-show producers and bookers use those appearances as a tip sheet for picking the subject matter and guests for their own shows. And so the capacity of the conservative movement to disseminate propaganda has increased exponentially.

This right-wing propaganda machine can quickly and indelibly brand Democratic candidates unfavorably—John Kerry as a flip-flopper, Al Gore as a liar. The machine is so powerful that it was able to orchestrate Clinton's impeachment despite the private and trivial nature of his "crime"—a lie about an extramarital tryst—when compared with President Bush's calamitous lies about Iraq, the budget, Medicare, education, and the environment. During the 2000 campaign, Al Gore was smeared as a liar—a charge that was completely false—by right-wing pundits such as gambling addict Bill Bennett and prescription-painkiller abuser Rush Limbaugh, both of whom the right wing has sold as moral paradigms. Meanwhile, George Bush's chronic problems with the truth during the three presidential debates that year were barely mentioned in the media, as Brock has noted. Americans accepted this negative characterization of Gore, and when they emerged from the voting booths in 2000, they told pollsters that Bush won their vote on "trust."

In the 2004 campaign, the so-called Swift Boat Veterans for Truth launched dishonest attacks which, amplified and repeated by the right-wing media, helped torpedo John Kerry's presidential ambitions. No matter who the Democratic nominee was, this machinery had the capacity to discredit and destroy him.

Meanwhile, there is a palpable absence of strong progressive voices on TV, unless one counts HBO's Bill Maher and Comedy Central's Jon Stewart—both comedians—or Fox's meek foil, Alan Colmes, who plays the ever losing Washington Generals to Scan Hannity's Harlem Globetrotters. There are no liberal equivalents to counterbalance Joe Scarborough, John Stossel, Bill O'Reilly, and Lawrence Kudlow. Brock points to the systematic structural imbalance in the panels that are featured across all of cable and on the networks' Sunday shows. Programs like *Meet the Press* and Chris Matthews's *Hardball* invariably pit conservative ideologues such as William Safire, Robert Novak, and Pat Buchanan against neutral, nonaligned reporters such as Andrea Mitchell, the diplomatic correspondent for NBC News, or *Los Angeles Times* reporter Ronald Brownstein in a rigged fight that leaves an empty chair for a strong progressive point of view.

There is still relevant information in the print media. But even that has been shamefully twisted by the pressures of the right. Both *The New York Times* and *The Washington Post*, which jumped on Scaife's bandwagon to lead the mainstream press in the Clinton-impeachment frenzy, have been forced to issue *mea culpas* for failing to ask the tough questions during the run-up to Bush's Iraq war.

Furthermore, America's newspapers, like most other media outlets, are owned predominantly by Republican conservatives. Newspapers endorsed Bush by two to one in the 2000 election. According to a recent survey, the op-ed columnists who appear in the most newspapers are conservatives Cal Thomas and George Will. Republican-owned newspapers often reprint misinformation from the right. And red-state journalists, whatever their personal political sympathies, are unlikely to offend their editors by spending inordinate energy exposing right-wing lies.

Print journalism is a victim of the same consolidation by a few large, profit-driven corporations that has affected the broadcasters. Today, a shrinking pool of owners—guided by big business rather than journalistic values—forces news executives to cut costs and seek the largest audience. The consolidation has led to demands on news organizations to return profits at rates never before expected of them. Last summer, just a few months after winning five Pulitzer Prizes, the *Los Angeles Times* was asked by its parent company to drop 60 newsroom positions.

The pressure for bottomline news leaves little incentive for investment in investigative reporting. Cost-cutting has liquidated news staffs, leaving reporters little time to research stories. According to an Ohio University study, the number of investigative reporters was cut almost in half between 1980 and 1995.

During the debate over the Radio Act of 1927, an early forerunner of the Fairness Doctrine, Texas congressman Luther Johnson warned Americans against the corporate and ideological consolidation of the national press that has now come to pass. "American thought and American politics will be largely at the mercy of those who operate these stations," he said. "For publicity is the most powerful weapon that can be wielded in a republic . . . and when a single selfish group is permitted to either tacitly or otherwise acquire ownership and dominate these broadcasting stations throughout the country, then woe be to those who dare to differ with them. It will be impossible to compete with them in reaching the ears of the American people."

The news isn't entirely bleak. Progressive voices are prevalent on the Internet, which is disproportionately utilized by the younger age groups that will exercise increasing influence in public affairs each year. The success of Air America Radio, the progressive network whose best-known host is Al Franken, offers great cause for optimism. Despite a shoestring budget and financial chaos at its inception, Air America has grown in one year to include 50 stations, from which it is accessible to half the American people. Most encouraging, a recent study shows that Air America personalities as a group rank second in popularity to Rush Limbaugh. Last fall in San Diego, a traditional Republican bastion, Air America was reported to be the No. 1 radio station among listeners 18 to 49 years old. But progressive activists need also to find a voice on television, and there the outlook is dark.

If there is a market for progressive voices, as the Air America experience suggests, why don't the big corporate owners leap in? A top industry executive recently told me that he was dead certain that there would be a large audience for a progressive TV news network to counterbalance the right-wing cable shows. "But," he said, "the corporate owners will never touch it. Multinationals, like Viacom, Disney, and General Electric, that rely on government business, contracts, and goodwill are not going to risk offending the Republicans who now control every branch of government."

This executive had recently spoken to Viacom chairman Sumner Redstone (a lifelong Democrat) about the corporation's open support of the Bush administration. "I said, 'Sumner, what about our children and what about our country?' He replied, 'Viacom is my life. I've got to do what's best for the company. I need to buy more stations, and the Republicans are going to let me do it. It's in the company's interest to support Republicans.'"

When veteran television journalist and former CBS news analyst Bill Moyers resigned as host of PBS's *Now* in December, he observed, "I think my peers in commercial television are talented and devoted journalists, but they've chosen to work in a corporate mainstream that trims their talent to fit the corporate nature of American life. And you do not get rewarded for telling the hard truths about America in a profit-seeking environment." Moyers called the decline in American journalism "the biggest story of our time." He added, "We have an ideological press that's interested in the election of Republicans, and a mainstream press that's interested in the bottom line. Therefore, we don't have a vigilant, independent press whose interest is the American people."

Moyers has elsewhere commented that "the quality of journalism and the quality of democracy are inextricably joined." By diminishing the capacity for voters to make rational choices, the breakdown of the American press is threatening not just our environment but our democracy.

ROBERT F. KENNEDY JR. is an environmental and political activist. He is an environmental lawyer and cohost of *Ring of Fire* on the Air America Radio Network and also serves as a senior attorney for the Natural Resources Defense Council.

EXPLORING THE ISSUE

Does the Media Have a Liberal Bias?

Critical Thinking and Reflection

1. Do you really want to hear both sides of hotly debated issues? What kind of media do you pay attention to and why? How unbiased are you in your selection of your news sources?
2. If you are biased in your selection of news sources, how do you justify your biased news gathering?
3. Evaluate the relative importance of information gathering versus entertainment in your choice of news sources.
4. How well does the current news system serve the public?
5. What changes in the current news system would serve the public better?
6. What is political correctness and are you for it or against it?
7. To what extent does money control the media and to what extent do professional norms have a strong influence on national media?

Is There Common Ground?

As the opposing arguments in this issue indicate, we can find critics on both the left and the right who agree that the media are biased. What divides such critics is the question of whether the bias is left-wing or right-wing. Defenders of the news media may seize upon this disagreement to bolster their own claim that "bias is in the eye of the beholder." But the case may be that the news media are unfair to both sides. If that were true, however, it would seem to take some of the force out of the argument that the news media have a distinct ideological tilt at all.

The problem of bias in news reporting has resulted in the emergence of fact checking groups that are used to determine what are the facts and the lies in the statements of politicians and sometimes commentators. Will they also become misused in biased ways?

Create Central

www.mhhe.com/createcentral

Additional Resources

A number of works tend to support Barnes's contention that the media slant leftward, including Ann Coulter in *Slander: Liberal Lies about the American Right* (Crown Publishers, 2002); Bernard Goldberg in *Bias: A CBS Insider Exposes How the Media Distort the News* (Regency Publishing, 2002); and *Arrogance: Rescuing America from the Media Elite* (Warner Books, 2003). On the other hand, those who think the media are biased rightward include Ben Bagdikian, *The Media Monopoly*, 6th ed. (Beacon Press, 2000); Eric Alterman, *What Liberal Media? The Truth about Bias and the News* (Basic Books, 2003); David Edwards and David Cromwell,

Guardians of Power: The Myth of the Liberal Media (Pluto Press, 2006); Jeffery Klaehn, ed., *Bound by Power: Intended Consequences* (Black Rose Books, 2006); and Robert Waterman McChesney, *The Problem of the Media: U.S. Communication Politics in the Twenty-First Century* (Monthly Review Press, 2004). In *South Park Conservatives: The Revolt Against Liberal Media Bias* (Regnery, 2005), Brian C. Anderson observes that the media were very liberal but America revolted and now conservative voices are being heard. Lies in the media have a long history as outlined by Eric Burns in *All the News Unfit to Print: A History of How Things Were—and How They Were Reported* (Wiley, 2009). Despite the prevalence of lies, Ronald N. Jacobs points out in *The Space of Opinion: Media Intellectuals and the Public Sphere* that objective journalism is also thriving (Oxford University Press, 2011).

There are many criticisms of the media besides its biases. Three interesting critiques are Chris Hedges, *Empire of Illusion: The End of Literacy and the Triumph of Spectacle* (Nation Books, 2009); Drew Curtis, *It's Not News, It's Fark: How Mass Media Tries to Pass Off Crap as News* (Gotham Books, 2007); and James Bowman, *Media Madness: The Corruption of Our Political Culture* (Encounter Books, 2008). Another connected issue is the concentration of the control of media outlets, which is addressed by C. Edwin Baker in *Media Concentration and Democracy: Why Ownership Matters* (Cambridge University Press, 2007). Several recent memoirs of journalists are very useful for the debate on media bias. See Tom Wicker's *On the Record* (Bedford/St. Martin's, 2002); Ted Koppel's *Off Camera* (Alfred A. Knopf, 2000); and Bill O'Reilly's *The No-Spin Zone* (Broadway Books, 2001). David Halberstam's *The Powers That Be* (Alfred A. Knopf, 1979), a historical study of CBS, *The Washington Post*, *Time* magazine, and the *Los Angeles Times*, describes some of the political and ideological struggles that have taken place within major media organizations.

Internet References . . .

Sociology—Study Sociology Online

http://edu.learnsoc.org/

Sociology Web Resources

www.mhhe.com/socscience/sociology/resources/index.htm

Sociosite

www.topsite.com/goto/sociosite.net

Socioweb

www.topsite.com/goto/socioweb.com

Selected, Edited, and with Issue Framing Material by:
Kurt Finsterbusch, *University of Maryland, College Park*

ISSUE

Is It Necessary to Become Less Consumerist?

YES: Gary Gutting, from "Less, Please," *Commonweal* (January 11, 2013)

NO: Michael Fisher, from "Review of James Livingston's *Against Thrift: Why Consumer Culture Is Good for the Economy, the Environment, and Your Soul*," Society for U.S. Intellectual History Blog, *U.S. Intellectual History* (March 22, 2012)

Learning Outcomes

After reading this issue, you should be able to:

- Assess whether consumption is contributing significantly to environmental deterioration.
- Consider both the positive and negative effects of modern consumption on the consumers.
- Look at the different types of consumption and evaluate what type of needs it typically meets: whether basic needs like food, or functional needs like automobile transportation, or social needs like taking care of a family, or symbolic needs like goods and services which enhance one's status.
- Discern which consumption strengthens character and which consumption weakens character.
- Analyze when consumption has an addictive aspect to it.
- Explain the meaning of insatiable with respect to consumption.

ISSUE SUMMARY

YES: Professor Gary Gutting, holder of the Notre Dame Endowed Chair in Philosophy, praises the modern economy for its amazing progress in production and consumer benefits but also recognizes its negative effects on our character and authentic well-being. It has led to economic insatiability and shrinking of the common good. Therefore, he favors less consumption.

NO: Michael Fisher, graduate student in American history at the University of Rochester, summarizes in this review article the thesis of James Livingston that the consumer culture is good, not bad. Though Fisher supports Livingston's thesis, he does not agree with Livingston's positive view of advertising. Nevertheless, he and Livingston favor more consumption.

There are two major concerns about consumption in America today. First, does it currently having net negative effects on the environment? Second, does it, on net, have positive or negative impacts on our character and moral fiber? If it has significant negative impacts on the environment, then the next question is whether these negative impacts will overcome the regenerative powers of the environment and thus limit the quality of life of future generations. Abundant data show that humans have been overexploiting croplands for decades leading to substantial worldwide soil loss and nutrient loss. Grasslands are overgrazed, forests are depleting, oceans are overfished, utilizable water is declining, and toxic pollution is increasing worldwide. Serious attention to these trends leads some analysts to give very pessimistic predictions for the future. For example, on October 29, 2013, I received an email which reported on an article by Naomi Klein in *The Statesman* arguing that we must make radical changes to prevent climate change impacts from destroying the planet. Others recognize these adverse environmental trends, argue that they are less severe than the pessimists claim, and believe that new technologies will overcome these problems. This aspect of consumption is a major focus of Issue 20. The impact of consumption on our character is treated in this issue.

What are the effects of modern consumption patterns on consumers, culture, and society? In 1960 Vance Packard wrote *The Waste Makers*, which tried to document the transformation of the frugal society to the wasteful society. In the frugal society people bought only what they needed. To keep the economy booming, however, they had to buy more. According to Packer, "What was needed was strategies that would make Americans in large numbers into voracious, wasteful, compulsive consumers." The producers succeeded, the economy roared ahead, and people's desires became insatiable. Packer had chapters on hedonism, planned obsolescence, throwaway spirit, commercialization of American life, and vanishing resources. His greatest concern was on the transformation of people's values to an emphasis on "pleasure-mindedness, self indulgence, materialism" and the decline of self-denial. In the half century since Packard's shock at the changing culture around him, a fairly large literature on consumption has confirmed his observations and expanded his critique. It generally asserts that consumption affects people at deep psychological levels and has become an important basis for one's self-esteem and the esteem of others.

The consumption literature from Packard to today emphasizes numerous negative aspects of this cultural change. First, since 1957 average consumption per capita has tripled but happiness has slightly declined. Happiness does not seem to be related to income except at a very low consumption level where survival is at stake. Second, the desire for consumer goods and services has become insatiable. No matter how much one has it is never enough. We always want more or better things. We are never satisfied. Third, this literature argues that the endless work required for high consumption and the consumption experiences themselves squeeze out close relationships and time with loved ones which are major causes of happiness.

Gary Gutting draws upon a book by Robert and Edward Skidelsky called *How Much Is Enough?* to address these issues. The Skidelskys tie excessive consumption to capitalism, which is an excellent system for providing basic needs but ends up pushing excessive consumption. The result is tragic because people are transformed in negative ways in the process. "The Skidelskys argue that this destructive spiral is not inevitable" and suggest ways to better achieve the good life. The reading by Michael Fisher presenting the analysis of James Livingston advocates the opposite view. For them the good life is the result of the myriad of benefits that affluence (high production and consumption) provide. They take issue with the puritanical view that we must not focus on enjoying ourselves but limit and control ourselves. That may be appropriate for eras of scarcity of centuries ago but today we should enjoy the benefits of prosperity.

YES ↵

Gary Gutting

Less, Please

Capitalism & the Good Life

Is capitalism an enemy of the good life? Marxists and other radicals think so. Toward the end of *How Much Is Enough?*, Robert and Edward Skidelsky (an economist father and his philosopher son) quote one such thinker:

> Working men have been surrendered, isolated and helpless, to the hard-heartedness of employ-ers and the greed of unchecked competition . . . so that a small number of very rich men have been able to lay upon the teeming masses of the labor-ing poor a yoke little better than that of slavery.

Readers of *Commonweal* will be more likely than most to recognize the firebrand cited as Leo XIII in *Rerum novarum.*

The Skidelskys' own rhetoric is usually more re-strained. The sober line of thought that underlies their engaging, informative, and stimulating book goes roughly as follows. Under capitalism, businesses sell us goods and service that are essential for living well, and most of us get the money to buy these things by working for businesses or, less often, profiting from investments in them. We need capitalism because no other economic system can produce sufficient goods to meet our essential material needs such as food, shelter, clothes, and medical care. But these goods are not enough. A good life mainly depends on intangi-bles such as love, friendship, beauty, and virtue—things capitalism cannot produce and money cannot buy. Given a sufficient minimum of material goods, the good life does not depend on the world of commerce.

Nonetheless, for most of us, work takes up the bulk of our time and energy, leaving comparatively little for liv-ing a good life. Some see their work itself as a pursuit of beauty, truth, or virtue. But most find what they do valu-able primarily as a means of earning money to buy mate-rial necessities. And capitalist society itself insists that a good life requires much more than a minimum of material goods. A truly good life, it urges, requires fine food, a large and well-furnished home, stylish clothing, and a steady diet of diverting and enriching experiences derived from sports, culture, and travel—all of which are expensive.

We all agree that there's a limit beyond which more material goods would make little difference to the good-ness of our lives. But almost all of us think we are consid-erably below that limit. In general, then, capitalism works against the good life from two directions. It requires us to engage in work that makes little contribution to our living well, beyond supplying our material necessities, and it urges us to believe, falsely, that a good life is mainly a mat-ter of accumulating material possessions. The Skidelskys sum it up this way: "The irony is that . . . now that we have achieved abundance [in advanced capitalist countries], the habits bred into us by capitalism have left us incapable of enjoying it properly."

Their view of capitalism is critical rather than revo-lutionary. They decry its tendency to sacrifice the human good to the goods of the market, but think we can curb this tendency and harness capitalism's productive power for our pursuit of the good life. For them, the core problem with capitalism is "economic insatiability"—the intrinsic drive for increasing production (and therefore profits) without limit. The limitless demand for more can even lead, as we have recently seen, to economic catastrophe. More important, capitalism is morally deficient because its drivers are the vices of "greed and acquisitiveness," which pile up "goods" that take us away from the good life.

The insatiability of capitalism exploits the corre-sponding insatiability of individual desires. No matter how much I possess, I find myself desiring more than I have. As I become rich enough to satisfy all my old desires, I develop new ones. Moreover, beyond a certain level of wealth, I begin to desire the best of everything, where the "best" (rare wines, exclusive resorts, the paint-ings of Old Masters) are in such limited supply that hardly anyone can afford them. And in addition to our sponta-neous individual desires, we develop other desires simply because there are things others have that we don't. Capi-talism's endless need to sell more and more is met by our need to buy more and more.

The Skidelskys argue that this destructive spiral is not inevitable. It has arisen only because we have moved away from a properly human ideal of a good life. Their positive project draws on the traditions of premodern thought for a viable contemporary account of what makes for a good life. Their discussion, perceptive if schematic, produces a plau-sible list of seven "basic goods": health, security, respect, personal freedom (which they refer to, somewhat oddly, as "personality"), harmony with nature, friendship, and leisure (not idleness but freedom from wage-labor for work that is satisfying in itself). Their list has the distinct merit of allowing for the wide range of current disagreement on moral questions such as sexuality and personal rights.

The authors also propose, with appropriate tentativeness, a variety of measures to curb capitalism's "insatiability." These include a basic wage (or personal endowment) for everyone, consumption taxes to curb excessive consumption, and severe restrictions on advertising.

This positive project has, of course, no point unless we accept the basic thesis that capitalism is a threat to a good life, and some of the Skidelskys' most crucial pages try to defuse two major objections to this claim. One objection comes from utilitarian thinkers, the other from liberal political theorists. I will assess the Skidelskys' position by reflecting on these two objections.

The first objection centers on a concept many readers will have found oddly absent from our discussion so far: happiness. Most modern people agree with utilitarian moral theorists that happiness is what everyone desires—and should desire—most. The Skidelskys would have no problem with this view if "happiness" were, like Aristotle's *eudaimonia,* merely a synonym for living a good life. But nowadays happiness is seen as a matter of subjective states of satisfaction, not objectively good achievements. The point of utilitarian morality is to maximize subjective satisfaction for everyone: "the greatest happiness for the greatest number." To do this, we need to find out what makes people happy and then supply them with whatever that is.

Economists and psychologists step forward for the first task, deploying "happiness surveys" to determine how various factors (health, wealth, sex, families, sports, reading, television, etc.) affect happiness. Once we know what we need to be happy, capitalist enterprises are ready to deliver the goods. To achieve their goal of maximizing profit, businesses must provide as many consumers as possible with as much satisfaction as they can. The capitalist is the merchant of happiness.

The Skidelskys are deeply skeptical of happiness science. They note that one of its most robust results is the "Easterlin paradox" (named for the economist Richard Easterlin, who formulated it in 1974). The paradox is that, in industrially advanced countries, major improvements in living standards have no long-term effect on happiness. This, the Skidelskys say, leads to a destructive dilemma. If the paradox is correct, then efforts to bring about improvements in living standards are futile. If it is not correct, then our best methods for discovering what makes people happy are inadequate. In either case, the utilitarian project of maximizing happiness is stymied.

This is an intriguing line of argument, but at best it undermines only the global project of producing happiness by altering the entire economic climate. It may still be possible to make numerous local improvements through actions focused on specific situations. In any case, the Skidelskys have a deeper critique of the happiness project: that the "supreme good" of humankind cannot be merely a succession of enjoyable psychological states. "We cannot think that all our suffering and labor has as its end something as trivial as a buzz or a tingle."

Although the Skidelskys don't mention him, Robert Nozick made the same point in *Anarchy, State, and Utopia*

with his thought experiment of the Experience Machine. Suppose neuroscientists develop a machine that would allow you to have any subjective experiences you like—a great romantic love, writing a brilliant novel, saving your nation from destruction. You could even program an entire life filled with the most enjoyable experiences possible. But plugging into such a machine would not give you a good life, because you would never have actually done anything; you would have spent your days sitting in a laboratory enjoying a succession of feelings. The Skidelskys describe such illusory satisfactions as "the mirage of happiness." "If happiness is a mere private sensation, with no intrinsic connection to living well . . . why not admit up front that our concern is with the good life—and let happiness look after itself?"

Their critique, however, succeeds against only the naive claim that a good life consists merely of a succession of felicific fizzes. They agree that pleasurable feelings produced by objective achievements contribute to the good life, referring, for example, to the "glad apprehension . . . that my daughter has got into university, that my country has been liberated." But then why not admit that subjective pleasure in its own right is one of the essential components of a good life? Imagine the inverse of Nozick's Experience Machine: a device that does not interfere with my achieving great things in the real world but deactivates the pleasure centers of the brain so that I never enjoy anything I do. The result would be a far cry from anything we would regard as a good life. Nor is it enough to allow only the "glad apprehension" that something objectively good has occurred. Enjoying the taste of food helps make for a good life, even if I don't also feel satisfaction at having partaken of healthy nourishment.

The Skidelskys have at best shown that pleasurable feelings cannot be all there is to a good life, but pleasure may still have a major role; it may even deserve a place on their list of what makes for such a life. If this is so—and common sense along with most philosophy and psychology supports the idea—our account of the good life cannot discount the pleasures provided by the capitalist system of production.

But I presume the Skidelskys could accept these points as friendly amendments. There remains the second objection, which the Skidelskys themselves recognize as "the last, and deepest, objection to our project." This is the claim that their view rejects the fundamental insight of liberalism put forward by John Rawls, Amartya Sen, and Martha Nussbaum, among others. Here is the Skidelskys own deft statement of the objection:

> A liberal state . . . embodies no positive vision but only such principles as are necessary for people of different tastes and ideals to live together in harmony. To promote, as a matter of public policy, a positive idea of the good life is by definition illiberal, perhaps even totalitarian.

Their brief initial response to this objection is that it "rests on a thorough misconception of liberalism," which, throughout most of its history, has been "imbued with classical and Christian ideals of dignity, civility, and tolerance." They also cite, from the twentieth century, such "prototypical liberals as Keynes, Isaiah Berlin, and Lionel Trilling," who "took it for granted that upholding civilization was among the functions of the state." They note that Rawls in particular allows for a category of "primary goods," including "civic and political liberties, income and wealth, access to public office and 'the social bases of respect.'" These are necessary conditions for, as Rawls puts it, "forming a rational plan of life" and so must be desired by all rational agents, regardless of what basic goods they hope to achieve by carrying out their life plan. (Rawls presents his basic goods as resources everyone should have. Sen and Nussbaum maintain that beyond Rawls's resources, people also need the capabilities to make use of them.)

The Skidelskys rightly point out that contemporary liberals insist on primary goods rather than basic goods because they see autonomy—the right of people to choose their own conception of the good life—as an overarching value. Basic goods specify the content of a good life; the primary goods merely tell us what is needed to choose and work for any conception of a good life. The liberal emphasis on autonomy restricts government to promoting primary goods, while remaining neutral regarding basic goods and the various conceptions of the good life they specify.

The Skidelskys cite an example from Nussbaum that nicely focuses the difference between them. "A person who has opportunities for play," she says, "can always choose a workaholic life"—her point being that, as long as this choice is free and does not harm others, the state has no reason to oppose it. Such opposition would, in fact, be a paternalistic interference with personal autonomy. The Skidelskys disagree, arguing that "if the workaholic life is an impoverished one, as most people who have thought about the matter agree it is, then its adoption over finer lives, whether freely chosen or not, is surely something to worry us." As to the charge of paternalism, they point out that all Western nations have laws limiting the use of drugs, pornography, and alcohol, and use taxation as an incentive to promote or discourage behaviors such as home ownership and energy conservation.

This is not a convincing response. For one thing, the fact that we deplore a behavior is not a reason for violating autonomy to discourage it. For another, allowing a paternalistic approach to some evils is consistent with refusing to put the power of the state behind a comprehensive view of the human good. (Also, as the Skidelskys note, an entirely rigorous liberalism would discourage only behavior that it sees as dangerous to others.) In any case, the Skidelskys agree that, precisely because "the good life is by any reasonable definition an autonomous or self-determined one, there is only so much that the state, as a coercive body, can do to promote it."

For a deeper grasp of what's at stake in the liberal objection, we need to return to the Skidelskys' starting point: the relation of capitalism to the good life. As proponents of a free society, they agree that in the end individuals must make their own choices about how to pursue a good life. They are also unwilling to reject capitalism as the engine of our economic system. The capitalist system claims to be the servant of free choice, producing whatever consumers desire, to the extent that they desire it. But the claim is disingenuous. The goal of capitalist enterprises is to maximize profit, and they are willing—and often well equipped—to form consumer desires and public policy to achieve this goal. Advertising, public relations, and lobbying are their most effective weapons.

How can we maintain capitalism as our means of economic production and yet not allow it to determine our conception of the good life? The Skidelskys' approach derives from Keynes's 1930 essay "Economic Possibilities for our Grandchildren," where he predicted that by 2030 the capitalist system would be able to meet all our material needs with the average employee working only about fifteen hours a week. This, he thought, would allow ample leisure time for people to pursue the good life. Keynes was right about the productive power of capitalism but wrong about the decrease in work hours, which have fallen only 20 percent since 1930. Why did Keynes go wrong about the balance of work and leisure? Because, the Skidelskys say, "a free-market economy both gives employers the power to dictate hours and terms of work and inflames our innate tendency to competitive, status-driven consumption."

In response, they propose their anti-insatiability conception of a good life and, as we have seen, suggest various legislative measures—primarily a guaranteed basic income that does not require employment (to make it easier for people to work less), as well as consumption taxes and strong restrictions on advertising (to reduce excessive consumption). But in a democracy such a legislative approach requires the support of most citizens, and that would be available only if the Skidelskys' goal were already achieved. The essential liberal objection to the Skidelskys is that their proposals are Utopian, given a population that overwhelmingly subscribes to the insatiability ethos of capitalism. The only people who would support their reforms are the small minority who have already renounced this ethos.

Let me suggest an alternative approach, one that is consistent with both the Skidelskys' appeal to traditional values and modern liberalism's emphasis on autonomy: a return to the weakened but still viable ideal of a liberal education.

We find enormous dissatisfaction with our educational system but there is still considerable respect for the idea that schooling should provide not so much vocational training as liberal learning. A liberal education forms citizens who have a broad understanding of the possibilities of human life as well as a critical ability to make informed choices among these possibilities. Such education will not necessarily inculcate the Skidelskys'—or any other—specific vision of the good life. But it will develop self-determining agents who can see through the blandishments of the market and insist that it provide what they have independently decided they need in order to lead a good life.

We cannot control the decisions of such agents, nor should we. They are free not only in the metaphysical sense of controlling their actions but also in the cultural sense of grasping, to some significant extent, the range of options available to them in their historical context. This latter freedom derives from access to our cultural history's enduring and ever-increasing legacy of literary, philosophical, political, religious, and scientific achievements. These achievements underlie the specific institutions and practices that define a person's world, but they also support radical critiques and alternatives to that world. Culture contains the seeds of revolution.

Here I am appealing to the same intellectual and moral heritage the Skidelskys draw on to formulate their conception of a good life. But they make the Utopian (ultimately Platonic) mistake of thinking that we can transform our world by legislating values from above. Rather, the transformation must come from below, forged by the very people it is meant to benefit. The liberal education I advocate is not that of old-world hereditary elites, bringing their inherited wisdom to the masses. It is inspired by the new-world ideal of an education equally open to everyone, limited only by one's ability and persistence. There is a risk that free citizens educated in this way will not arrive at the truth we have in mind. They may, free and informed, choose the material illusions of capitalism. But, in a democracy, an ideal of the good life has no force unless the people's will sustains it. Liberally educated consumers—and voters—are our only hope of subordinating capitalism to a humane vision of the good life.

GARY GUTTING holds the Notre Dame Endowed Chair in Philosophy and has authored seven books on philosophy.

Michael Fisher   **NO**

Review of James Livingston's *Against Thrift: Why Consumer Culture Is Good for the Economy, the Environment, and Your Soul*

Goods Aplenty: *Against Thrift* and the Question, "What For?"

Following on the heels of his contentious rereading of late twentieth-century American thought and culture,[1] James Livingston has written a new book that promises to provoke much more than historiographic controversy. As the title suggests, *Against Thrift* is an ethical indictment and a political argument against the Protestant work ethic; yet it also prophesies a new moral order that might be just around the corner.

Livingston wants us to be happier, more carefree and better able to enjoy the pleasures of this life. In no uncertain terms, he thinks we ought to abandon the last vestiges of Puritanism that constrain our bodies and our minds in favor of a wholehearted embrace of spending—vigorous spending. Instead of saving and delaying gratification, he goads us: we should be focusing our scarce psychic and material resources on satisfying desire in the here and now. Why? Because the age-old assumption that work should come before play, that self-discipline and restraint are preferable to immediate gratification, is based on a series of false premises. So Livingston says and, for much of *Against Thrift*, he presumes to demonstrate. As he puts it in the introduction, "In this book, I make the case for consumer culture: why it's actually good for the economy, the environment, and our souls, among other things. In this sense, I'm trying to heal the split in our personalities by demonstrating that less work, less thrift, more leisure, and more spending are the cures for what ails us."[2]

What ails us in Livingston's view is partly economic and partly psychological (hence the supposed split in our personalities). But the twin ailments stem from a common cultural root. At least in theory, most Americans still buy the Puritan premise that disciplined frugality begets virtue whereas giving in to one's instincts begets vice. Because we remain beholden to the resulting economic mindset, which assumes that saving and investing in the future are the best ways to ensure long-term growth and security,

we have trained ourselves psychologically to associate the deferral of emotional gratification—particularly the gratification that comes with buying consumer products—with goodness.

According to Livingston, this conventional wisdom informs everything from our personal morality to our response to the 2008 financial crisis; and the symmetry between the two examples is scarcely coincidental: "All adults—not just parents—have a powerful psychological urge to put their desires on hold, and that urge makes us receptive to the notion that we'd better be saving more and spending less, just like all the mainstream economists and reputable journalists keep telling us to. We know what will happen to our bank accounts, our waistlines, and our marriage vows if we stop listening to their insistent voice of reason."[3]

Against much popular (in fact Populist) opinion, Livingston argues quite convincingly that both the Great Depression and the Great Recession drew from this very thrift-centered mindset. We miss the connection, he says, only because we have yet to distance ourselves sufficiently from the late nineteenth century. Since the 1890s, when the original Populists almost succeeded in restructuring the existing relationship between labor and capital, American antimonopoly sentiment has gone hand in hand with the traditional argument against consumption; and the two have tended to reinforce each other. Particularly when the economy goes bust, as it did in 1929 and 2008, the majority of Americans blame corporate power and profligate consumers, and the underlying problem is said to be moral failings on the part of irresponsible individuals.

As Livingston documents throughout "Part One: Our Very Own Perestroika," this typical response—moral indignation against excessive spending, speculation, and greed—was especially widespread after the 2008 crisis. Yet it ignores several key pieces of historical evidence, most importantly the role of surplus capital, or what Livingston calls "redundant profits with no productive outlet, which eventually find their way into speculative markets that inflate bubbles." Here is his extended reading of both the Great Depression and the Great Recession:

> I explain <u>both</u> events as results of surplus capital generated by huge shifts in income shares away from labor, wages, and consumption, toward capital, profits, and corporate savings. And I draw the obvious conclusion from the historical comparison: if the New Deal succeeded by enfranchising working people and shifting income shares back toward wages and consumption—not by means of a 'financial fix'—then a massive <u>redistribution</u> of income away from capital, profits, and corporate savings is our best hope of addressing the causes of the recent crisis and laying the groundwork for balanced growth.[4]

In hardboiled form, this is Livingston's descriptive argument for why consumer culture is good for us, and it's difficult to refute. As Marx, Keynes, and even Milton Friedman all agree, he tells us, increasing aggregate consumption is the true handmaiden of long-term growth and security; it was what ended the Great Depression, and it is what will get us out of the current slump if we let it, that is if we give in to more of our desires and spend vigorously here and now. Our real obstacles are cultural and psychological, not economic, Livingston insists. But our atavistic resistance to instinctual gratification—in effect, our Puritan attraction to repression—runs deep. Without a total revaluation, or at least a major reshuffling, of values it's virtually immovable. Thankfully, Livingston is not one to shy away from ambitious intellectual tasks (his introduction is called "Waiting for Galileo"). In "Part Two: The Morality of Spending," he unveils his normative argument for consumer culture's goodness, this time with respect to our souls, and tries to redesignate consumption, instant gratification, and instinctual satisfaction as intrinsic moral goods.

As a self-described "radical empiricist,"[5] Livingston may object to this last claim. He doesn't believe in intrinsic moral goods the same way he doesn't believe in metaphysical ideals like Truth, Beauty, or Justice, he might say. Yet by employing the word "Good" in his subtitle, he slyly evades the hard edge of his radical empiricism. He wants to enter into the debate over values, and in true Nietzschean form, his epistemological hang-ups about what actually constitutes "truth" take a backseat to the argument he wants to make convincing, indeed appetizing.

Whether his language is a subtle pragmatist's[6] trick or not, we ought to take Livingston at his word: he aims to convince us that spending is "moral," that consumer culture is "good," and that learning these lessons "might produce a new human nature that is more at ease in the world . . . a human being informed by a constant awareness of the needs of others, whether animal, vegetable, or mineral." To be fair, he frames this last bit provisionally; Livingston admits that "we just don't know what will happen when the renunciation of desire and the deferral of gratification and the delay of satisfaction are no longer necessary to

organize society and build character."[7] But the reason he thinks this outcome is brightly possible is that he believes the liberation he prescribes is *intrinsically* good for us, not just pragmatically worthwhile. There is a difference, and Livingston's language makes his argument clear.

So how does his argument work? The first step involves what Livingston calls "the politics of more." Around the turn of the twentieth century, the Age of Scarcity passed into the Age of Abundance, and with this shift came a profound redefinition of American individualism. As Livingston describes it:

> Defenders of the old individualism, then and now, typically insisted that the site of self-discovery and self-determination—the address of autonomy—was <u>work</u>, where productive labor taught the moral lessons of punctuality, frugality, and honest effort, and meanwhile imposed external, objective, material limits on the imagination of the producer. Defenders of the new individualism moved this location, or rather scattered it, so that the site of self-discovery and self-determination could be <u>leisure</u>, the pleasurable scene of goods consumption, as well as work, the strenuous scene of goods production. Thus necessity and freedom, occupation and identity, even males and females, were now aligned at different angles.[8]

The Age of Abundance created the possibility for a new kind of self, a "social self" whose identity was primarily other-directed. For a social critic like Christopher Lasch, the erosion of traditional individual autonomy undermined psychic stability and led toward a culture of narcissism.[9] Yet Livingston sees the transition in more sanguine terms. "The politics of 'more' defined autonomy . . . as a *collective* result of association with others—fellow workers, to be sure, but also people gathered with purposes or interests reaching beyond any workplace." Redefined as such, American individuals enjoyed new political opportunities as well as new aesthetic ones. But the basic change was psychological: "This new individual's identity was anything but private. It wasn't an enduring inner self you discovered by retreating from the outer world; it was instead a social construction, the result of interaction with others."[10]

In Livingston's account, the movement beyond scarcity—in America, the first stirrings of a mature surplus economy that advanced rapidly after 1900—etched the contours of the new moral horizon of consumer culture. In doing so, it also laid the seeds for two of the most important social movements of the twentieth century. Pointing to the Civil Rights Movement and the revolutions in Eastern Europe between 1968–1989, Livingston identifies a common pattern of resistance in which the (social) desire to take part in the joys of consumption "produced revolutionary *political* change." In both cases, he argues, African American music—what he calls "the black aesthetic"—was "the crucial medium in the redistribution of representational power accomplished by the movement." It gave

African Americans and Eastern Europeans "the cultural credentials they needed to speak for the future, for the people, for the nation." And without the new technologies that allowed the black aesthetic to be mass distributed and mass consumed, neither movement could have succeeded. In short, Livingston thinks we owe both movements and their positive contributions to society to "the 'reification' or commodification of social life we (rightly) associate with consumer culture."[11] It goes without saying that this debt should make us more appreciative of the ways in which consumer culture is good for our souls.

Livingston is certainly right to point to the correlation between late twentieth-century social movements and expanding consumer consciousness. But he downplays the fact that Protestant Christianity was in many ways the deepest moral source of what came to pass in the American South between 1955–1963, and that Vaclav Havel had serious misgivings about the West's model of "consumer-led growth."[12] In Livingston's telling, it's as if the two movements arose from consumer longings alone, and *therefore* consumer culture stands acquitted of all the charges leveled against it. This curious logic points to a question Livingston never fully answers: independent of the ends to which people put them, is there a moral imperative embedded within consumer culture and the mass communication mediums that help diffuse it, or are these platforms morally neutral? Could they be used to produce any number of results, including the Civil Rights Movement? Or does some inherent moral property bend them toward manifesting greater respect for differences and deeper yearnings for democracy?

The question becomes especially pertinent when Livingston begins his defense of advertising, what he calls (again provisionally) "the thesaurus of our real feelings, the indispensable, vernacular language we use to plot our positions on the emotional atlas that is everyday life." By now it's clear what Livingston means by the eclipse of the former form of American individualism, and why he's glad about this as a radical empiricist. As he explains ever so delicately, there is not, and has never been, any "enduring, authentic, internal core of your self that you call your character." This is a myth we have inherited from history. In reality, "we all know that who we are depends, more or less, on what others make of us, how they see us, and that these others are mostly the absent causes we call strangers."[13] And we may as well embrace this. What David Riesman called the other-directed personality[14] is in fact the natural state of human existence, and this just happens to be good news for the advertising industry.

The reason Livingston calls advertising "the last utopian idiom of our time" is that he believes "it purveys a way of being in the world that is free of compulsion—free of necessary labor, the work you do because you have to—on the assumption that when at your leisure, you're free to choose an identity that might accord with the goods on offer." Yet what makes this way of being good for us? What about it furnishes the proper structure for our souls?

Presumably Livingston's answer to these questions is: "like it or not, we create identities by means of commodities, buying and selling what we want to be." But isn't this a shallow vision of what human life can be? Not to mention what it ought to be? The freedom to buy, to satisfy desire by clicking an icon after seeing an ad on TV, sets a low bar for Utopia, much less for the attainment of what any of us might call the good life. Still, Livingston seems willing to compromise: "what advertising invokes is more of an idea than a place, more like a map or a video game than something you can experience in three dimensions. But for now, that's utopian enough."[15] At this point one wants to cry out, "no, it isn't." Why should we be willing to settle for so little so late?

If, as Livingston believes, we have reached a condition of post-scarcity, advertising brings us no closer to lasting salvation. The surface depth and masked anxieties of the lives it depicts in its many varieties conjures something closer to hell: coercive visions of the good life achieved through proximity to certain products; silent invitations to mimic the elegant gestures of a person who exists only in a photograph or a set of moving images; how do these social messages offer anything resembling liberation from "compulsion, necessity, fear?"[16]

Following Livingston's logic, we end up mired in a wasteland of goods aplenty. He defends other-direction as the necessary and binding condition of our lives, but the only compass he offers is an endless stream of barely distinguishable commodities, of consumer "goods." This leaves him heralding a wild west version of American individualism in which nothing exists outside the market of changing circumstance, where insatiable desire is our only guide. Fortunately, Livingston doesn't have to worry whether some permutations of social selfhood are bad for us because he doesn't believe in any fixed human nature. Instead he says "we might as well buckle up and prepare for takeoff," letting "change, flux, the dissolution of everything we take for granted" carry us forward. But toward what? Where does the unstated "premise of advertising: 'All that is solid melts into air'" ultimately lead?[17] After how many purchases do we ask the question, "what for?"

We get a hint in Livingston's coda, "Bataille Made Me Do It." After describing in great detail the lead-up to his "hamburger experiment," the change in his life that he says is "most relevant to the arguments of this book," the morality of spending finally reveals itself. It took a lot for Livingston to eat a hamburger again. As a dutiful husband and father, he denied himself the pleasure of animal flesh for years. But then things changed, and he decided it was time to loosen up and live a little. He scoured the best restaurant guides he could find, settling on a place called The Homestead "where the Kobe beef hamburger goes for twenty-one dollars as a lunch special and thirty-nine dollars on the dinner menu." Livingston and his girlfriend went for dinner. He ordered a martini straight up to dull the pre-gratification anxiety, but it didn't help. Nothing did. All he could do was face the moment when the burger came. And come it did:

> It was delicious. Underdone, but delicious. All those fleeting bacon fumes from weekends past took up sudden residence in my mouth. But the meat was sliding around in there, as if the chef had somehow liquefied an honored part of a pampered, grass-fed cow. I was gargling beef. So I acceded to the unfreedom of my soul, took my girlfriend's advice, and sent the Kobe burger back to the kitchen. On its return, it was much more solid and no less delicious. Even so, the junior partner in the table's choices [his girlfriend's burger] was clearly superior in every respect: the smaller, cheaper burger got the better of us. The sheer excess of the bigger, ridiculously expensive burger was worth the price, but just this once.[18]

The lesson from Livingston's hamburger experiment is abundantly clear. But one wonders if he registers it. Although it's delicious, his break from renunciation, from all the hidden vestiges of Puritan morality, culminates in a moment of bleak insecurity punctuated by a powerful compensatory desire for more sensory experience. As soon as he finishes, he's "already descending that slippery slope, thinking ahead to another, maybe better hamburger."[19]

If this is where consumer culture leads, we need a better set of goods than James Livingston can buy, much less sell. Perhaps it's time to redefine American individualism, again?

References

[1] James Livingston, *The World Turned Inside Out: American Thought and Culture at the End of the Twentieth Century* (Lanham, MD, 2009).

[2] James Livingston, *Against Thrift: Why Consumer Culture Is Good for the Economy, the Environment, and Your Soul* (New York, 2011), x.

[3] Ibid., xi.

[4] Ibid., 7.

[5] Ibid., xviii.

[6] Livingston's unique interpretation of pragmatism can be found in his earlier books *Pragmatism and the Political Economy of Cultural Revolution, 1850–1940* (Chapel Hill, NC, 1994) and *Pragmatism, Feminism, and Democracy: Rethinking the Politics of American History* (New York, 2001).

[7] Livingston, *Against Thrift*, xii.

[8] Ibid., 90.

[9] Christopher Lasch, *The Culture of Narcissism: American Life in an Age of Diminishing Expectations* (New York, 1979). For related accounts of the new psychology engendered by twentieth-century social and economic developments, see: David Riesman, *The Lonely Crowd: A Study of The Changing American Character* (New Haven, 1950); Philip Rieff, *Freud: The Mind of a Moralist* (New York, 1961) and *The Triumph of the Therapeutic: Uses of Faith After Freud* (Chicago, 1966); Richard Wightman Fox and T. Jackson Lears, Ed., *The Culture of Consumption: Critical Essays in American History 1880–1980* (New York, 1983); Warren I. Susman, *Culture as History: The Transformation of American Society in the Twentieth Century* (New York, 1984); and Roland Marchand, *Advertising the American Dream: Making Way for Modernity 1920–1940* (Berkeley, 1985).

[10] Livingston, *Against Thrift*, 89.

[11] Ibid., 100, 104, 106. Surely Livingston would interpret Arab Spring along similar lines.

[12] Ibid., 114.

[13] Ibid., 115, 176, 177.

[14] In *The Lonely Crowd*.

[15] Livingston, *Against Thrift*, 116, 128.

[16] Ibid., 158.

[17] Ibid., 121.

[18] Ibid., 197, 207, 208.

[19] Ibid.

MICHAEL FISHER is a graduate student in American history at the University of Rochester who is working on his doctoral dissertation.

EXPLORING THE ISSUE

Is It Necessary to Become Less Consumerist?

Critical Thinking and Reflection

1. Evaluate your parents' consumption. Are most purchases sensible because they are very useful? Does the esteem of others influence much consumption?
2. Do you think that most people over consume and on what items?
3. What are the activities that interfere with family closeness?
4. What consumption activities are you most critical of?
5. What is the overall impact your family has on the environment?
6. Why not enjoy life to the fullest? Is the United States too puritanical?

Is There Common Ground?

No one advocates poverty over affluence. Affluence has made so many good things available to billions of people including better health, longer life, adequate and beneficial food and water, access to education and information, ease of communicating with loved ones, awareness of many different peoples and cultures, and greater oversight of economic and political leaders. On the other side no one approves of overconsumption. Gutting more thoroughly explores the negative effects of over consumption on people while Fisher and Livingston do not accept the premise that high consumption erodes character. It only erodes a puritanical viewpoint which equates abundance with loss of self control.

This issue is a classic example of how a situation can have both positive and negative impacts. High production and consumption solves many problems of survival but can weaken the moral character of society. Capitalist economies must grow or fall into recession and even depression which greatly reduces the quality of life for millions. The common belief is that even when economic growth causes problems it is far better than no growth or decline.

Create Central

www.mhhe.com/createcentral

Additional Resources

Benjamin R. Barber, *Consumed: How Markets Corrupt Children, Infantilize Adults, and Swallow Citizens Whole* (W. W. Norton, 2007)

Bill McKibben, "Reversal of Fortune," *Mother Jones* (March/April 2007)

Chris Hedges, "The Myth of Human Progress," *Truthdig* (January 20, 2013)

David Pearce Snyder, "A Rendezvous with Austerity: American Consumers Are About to Learn New Habits," *The Futurist* (July/August 2009)

Doug Brown, *Insatiable Is Not Sustainable* (Praeger, 2002)

Paul R. Ehrlich and Anne H. Ehrlich, Can a collapse of global civilization be avoided? Retrieved from rspb.royalsocietypublishing.org, accessed on August 7, 2013

Peter Dauvergne, "The Problem of Consumption," *Global Environmental Politics* (May 2010)

Ramez Naam, "How Innovation Could Save the Planet," *The Futurist* (March/April 2013)

Ronald Bailey, "How Free Markets and Human Ingenuity Can Save the Planet," A review of *The Infinite Resource: The Power of Ideas on a Finite Planet*, by Ramez Naam (April 12, 2013)

Worldwatch Institute, *2010 State of the World: Transforming Cultures from Consumerism to Sustainability* (W. W. Norton, 2010)

Internet References . . .

Sociosite

www.topsite.com/goto/sociosite.net

Sociology—Study Sociology Online

http://edu.learnsoc.org/

Sociology Web Resources

www.mhhe.com/socscience/sociology/resources/index.htm

Socioweb

www.topsite.com/goto/socioweb.com

Selected, Edited, and with Issue Framing Material by:
Kurt Finsterbusch, *University of Maryland, College Park*

ISSUE

Does Social Media Have Largely Positive Impacts on Its Users?

YES: Aaron Smith, from "Why Americans Use Social Media," *Pew Research Center Report* (November 14, 2011)

NO: Janna Quitney Anderson and Lee Rainie, from "Millennials Will Benefit *and* Suffer Due to Their Hyperconnected Lives," *Pew Research Center's Internet and American Life Project* (February 29, 2012)

Learning Outcomes

After reading this issue, you should be able to:

- Understand how multifaceted the impacts of social media on people and on society are.
- Be aware of the great variety of opinions that leading experts on social media have about its consequences.
- Understand the primary ways that people use social media.
- Be able to discern how different groups of users differ and are similar in their use of social media.
- Explain how social media affects the development of various intellectual and social skills of its users.
- Speculate on how social media might affect society in the future.

ISSUE SUMMARY

YES: Aaron Smith, senior research specialist of the Pew Research Center, presents the findings of his research project based on interviews in 2011 of 1,015 networking site users who reported on how they used social media. Their major use was for keeping in touch with family and current friends, and 87 percent also used it to connect with out-of-touch old friends.

NO: Janna Quitney Anderson of Elon University and Lee Rainie, research specialist of the Pew Research Center's Internet and American Life Project, report the findings of an opt-in online survey in 2011 of a diverse but nonrandom sample of 2,021 technology stakeholders and critics who report their expert opinion on the impacts of social media on the users. They report many positive and negative impacts.

We will briefly provide a survey of many of the positive and negative results of social media. On the positive side is the abundant use of social media to communicate with family and friends and increase connections and strengthen relationships. It facilitates face-to-face interaction. It especially helps people who are socially isolated or shy to connect with people. It helps seniors to feel more connected to society. Social networking has also increased life satisfaction and reduced health problems. Social media has become a main source of information for many people and they can get information very fast. On average its use also improves school performance, though it can also be a distraction. It has been used by businesses to great effect and it can be argued that it has helped the economy with products, services, profits, and jobs. Even law enforcement has used it positively. It has played a major role in recent elections and has helped many groups organize and accomplish things. It has contributed to significant social changes and there are many stories about its help to charities and noble social actions. I add as an academic that social media is being used to disseminate a great deal of academic knowledge.

Social media has also produced negative effects. It can negatively affect social relations. It causes people to spend less time in face-to-face interactions, especially in their homes (a small percent of young people even respond to social media during sex). Social networking has been found to make some children more prone to depression and loneliness and can lead to stress. It correlates with personality disorders like ADHD, difficulty in face-to-face conversations, self-centered personalities, anxiety, and addictive behaviors. It encourages people to waste time. Heavy social media users have lower grades. It can cause many troubles for users including inadvertently engaging in criminal behavior including some cases of "sexting," assisting criminal actions against users (e.g., travel plans informing criminals when to rob their house), loss of privacy, being targeted by scam artists or other criminals, use of the Internet by potential employers or universities who find reasons not to hire potential employees or admit potential students, having revealing pictures and unattractive information widely distributed, facilitating cyberbullying, and reducing some workers' productivity. It often provides misinformation and questionable and even dangerous amateur advice. It can facilitate and spread hate groups and organized crime. It is impossible to weigh these and other negative effects of social media against the positive effects, but most people are avid users in spite of the risks, so consumers believe the net effects are clearly positive.

The pros and cons of social media is a vast topic with many angles and vast changes in the past few years. The rapid speed of change of these phenomena has limited the lessons from empirical research on its effects. When empirical research is sparse, the opinions of experts provide useful guidance and that is what Anderson and Rainie provide us. Overall these 2,021 experts were positive but "were fairly evenly split as to whether the younger generation's always-on connection to people and information will turn out to be a net positive or a net negative by 2020." Aaron Smith is much more positive about the use of social media. His respondents used social media to increase social connections and facilitate their activities.

YES ⤶

Aaron Smith

Why Americans Use Social Media

Social networking sites are appealing as a way to maintain contact with close ties and reconnect with old friends.

Why Americans Use Online Social Media Tools

Two-thirds of online adults (66%) use social media platforms such as Facebook, Twitter, MySpace or LinkedIn.[1] These internet users say that connections with family members and friends (both new and old) are a primary consideration in their adoption of social media tools. Roughly two thirds of social media users say that staying in touch with current friends and family members is a major reason they use these sites, while half say that connecting with old friends they've lost touch with is a major reason behind their use of these technologies.

Other factors play a much smaller role—14% of users say that connecting around a shared hobby or interest is a major reason they use social media, and 9% say that making new friends is equally important. Reading comments by public figures and finding potential romantic partners are cited as major factors by just 5% and 3% of social media users, respectively.

Staying in touch with family members is a major factor across a range of social media users, but it's especially important to women.

Those who say that keeping up with family members is a major consideration in their use of social networking sites are a demographically diverse group. Two-thirds of all social media users cite family connections as a major reason for their use of these tools, and there are no major differences on this question in terms of age, income, education, race/ethnicity, parental status or place of residence. The primary difference on this topic pertains to gender, as female social media users are more likely than male users to cite family connections as a major reason for using these sites (72% vs. 55%).

Staying in touch with current friends and reconnecting with old friends is most relevant for those under the age of 50.

Compared with older adults, social media users under the age of 50 are especially likely to say that these tools help them keep up with existing friends and reconnect with old ones—roughly seven in ten users under the age of fifty say that staying in touch with current friends is a major reason they use online social platforms, and just over half say that connecting with old friends they've lost touch with is equally important. Each of these is significantly higher than comparable figures for users ages 50 and older, although a relatively large number of older adults point to connections with friends as a major reason for their social networking site usage as well.

In addition to age, gender and parental status are linked with users' attitudes towards social media as a way to maintain connections with friends. Women are slightly more likely than men to say that staying in touch with current friends is a major reason for using online social tools (70% vs. 63%) while parents are more likely than nonparents to say that connecting with old friends is a major reason behind their use of these sites (56% vs. 47%).

Compared with keeping tabs on current friends or old acquaintances, users place much less emphasis on using social platforms to make entirely new friends—just 9% say this is a major reason they use these sites, and 57% say that it is not a reason at all for their online social networking activity. Groups that are more likely than average to use social media to make new friends include men (12% say that making new friends is a major reason for using these sites), African Americans (15%), those who have a high school diploma but have not attended college (16%) and those with an annual household income under $30,000 (18%).

Middle-aged and older adults place a relatively high value on social media as a tool to connect with others around a hobby and interest.

Compared with maintaining or rekindling friendships, the ability to connect with others who share a hobby or interest using social media resonates with a slightly older cohort of users. Sixteen percent of 30–49 year olds and 18% of 50–64 year olds cite connecting with others with common hobbies or interests as a major reason they use social networking sites, compared with 10% of 18–29 year olds.

Additionally, men are a bit more likely than women to use these sites to connect around a hobby or

---

[1]Throughout this report the term "social media users" refers to individuals who "use a social networking site like MySpace, Facebook or LinkedIn" (65% of online adults do this) and/or "use Twitter" (13% of online adults).

Motivations for Using Social Networking Sites

Based on adults who use social networking sites such as Facebook, MySpace, Linkedin and/or Twitter

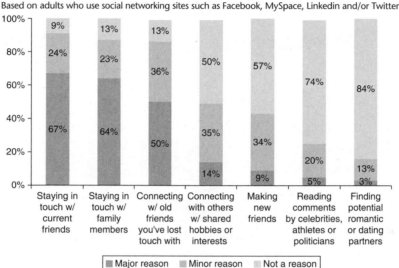

Source: The Pew Research Center's Internet & American Life Project, Aiprl 26–May 22, 2011 Spring Tracking Survey; n = 2,277 adults ages 18 and older, including 755 cell phone interviews. Interviews were conducted in English and Spanish. Margin of error is ±3 percentage points for SNS users (n = 1,015).

Staying in Touch with Current Friends and Reconnecting with Old Ones

% of social networking site users within each group who say the following are a "major reason" for their use of social networking sites

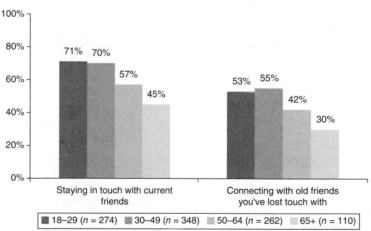

Source: The Pew Research Center's Internet & American Life Project, April 26–May 22, 2011 Spring Tracking Survey; n = 2,277 adults ages 18 and older, including 755 cell phone interviews. Interviews were conducted in English and Spanish. Margin of error is ±3 percentage points for SNS users (n = 1,015).

interest—56% of male users say that this is either a major or minor reason for their usage of these sites, compared with 44% of female users.

Connecting with public figures online is relatively popular among Twitter users, as well as African Americans and Latinos.

Among social media users as a whole, the ability to read comments by public figures such as politicians, celebrities or athletes does not come into play as a major factor—fully three quarters of users say that this plays no role whatsoever in their decision to use these sites. And while connecting with public figures has a relatively modest impact on users across a range of groups, both African Americans

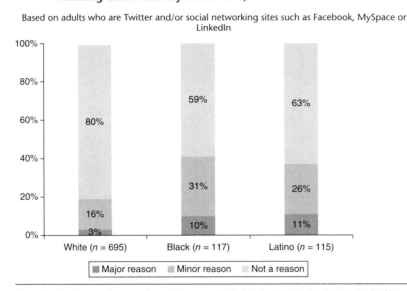

Reading Comments by Celebrities, Politicians or Athletes

Based on adults who are Twitter and/or social networking sites such as Facebook, MySpace or LinkedIn

Source: The Pew Research Center's Internet & American Life Project, April 26–May 22, 2011 Spring Tracking Survey; *n* = 2,277 adults ages 18 and older, including 755 cell phone interviews. Interviews were conducted in English and Spanish. Margin of error is ±3 percentage points for SNS users (*n* = 1,015).

and Latinos show more interest in this activity than white users. One in ten black social media users (10%) and 11% of Latinos say that reading comments from public figures is a major reason for using these sites (compared with just 3% of white users). Black and Latino social media users are also more likely to say that this is a minor factor (31% of blacks and 26% of Latinos say this, compared with 16% of whites).

Additionally, Twitter users are more interested in connecting with public figures than are social media users who do not use Twitter. One in ten Twitter users (11%) say that reading comments by politicians, celebrities or athletes is a major reason they use online social networks, and 30% say that this is a minor reason for their usage of these sites. Each of these is notably higher than the average for social media users who do not use Twitter (4% of these users say this is a major reason for using these sites, with 11% citing it as a minor reason).

Finding potential dating partners is at most a minor element of the social media experience.

Very few social media users say that finding potential romantic partners or people to date plays a role in their use of these sites—overall more than eight in ten (84%) do not use these sites for that purpose at all. Most of the remainder say that the prospect of romance is only a minor reason. Most differences on this question are quite modest—for example, men are twice as likely as women to say that finding potential dating or romantic partners is a minor reason

for using online social platforms (17% vs. 9%) but overall few men say that this is a major factor (just 4% do so).

To be sure, many Americans are currently in relationships or may not otherwise be seeking dating or romantic partners in any venue (on social networking sites or otherwise). Among those users who identify themselves as single, separated or divorced, 6% say that finding romantic or dating partners is a major reason why they use these sites (an additional 27% say that this is a minor reason for their social media usage).

About this survey

The results reported here are based on a national telephone survey of 2,277 adults conducted April 26–May 22, 2011. 1,522 interviews were conducted by landline phone, and 755 interviews were conducted by cell phone. Interviews were conducted in both English and Spanish. For results based on social networking site users, the margin of error is ±3 percentage points (*n* = 1,015).

AARON SMITH is a senior researcher for the Pew Research Center's Internet & American Life Project, whose primary areas of research with the Project include the role of the Internet in the political process, technology in civic life, and online engagement with government. He has also authored research on mobile Internet usage, the role of the Internet in family life, and demographic trends in technology adoption.

**Janna Quitney Anderson
and Lee Rainie**

 **NO**

Millennials Will Benefit *and* Suffer Due to Their Hyperconnected Lives

Analysts generally believe many young people growing up in today's networked world and counting on the internet as their external brain will be nimble analysts and decision-makers who will do well. But these experts also expect that constantly connected teens and young adults will thirst for instant gratification and often make quick, shallow choices. Where will that leave us in 2020? These survey respondents urge major education reform to emphasize new skills and literacies.

Overview

In a survey about the future of the internet, technology experts and stakeholders were fairly evenly split as to whether the younger generation's always-on connection to people and information will turn out to be a net positive or a net negative by 2020. They said many of the young people growing up hyperconnected to each other and the mobile Web and counting on the internet as their external brain will be nimble, quick-acting multitaskers who will do well in key respects.

At the same time, these experts predicted that the impact of networked living on today's young will drive them to thirst for instant gratification, settle for quick choices, and lack patience. A number of the survey respondents argued that it is vital to reform education and emphasize digital literacy. A notable number expressed concerns that trends are leading to a future in which most people are shallow consumers of information, and some mentioned George Orwell's *1984* or expressed their fears of control by powerful interests in an age of entertaining distractions.

These findings come from an opt-in, online survey of a diverse but non-random sample of 1,021 technology stakeholders and critics. The study was fielded by the Pew Research Center's Internet & American Life Project and Elon University's Imagining the Internet Center between August 28 and October 31, 2011.

The survey question about younger users was inspired by speculation over the past several years about the potential impact of technology on them. Looking toward the year 2020, respondents to this survey were fairly evenly split on whether the results will be primarily positive or mostly negative. They were asked to read two statements and select the one they believe that is most likely to be true and then explain their answers.

Some 55% agreed with the statement:

> In 2020 the brains of multitasking teens and young adults are "wired" differently from those over age 35 and overall it yields helpful results. They do not suffer notable cognitive shortcomings as they multitask and cycle quickly through personal- and work-related tasks. Rather, they are learning more and they are more adept at finding answers to deep questions, in part because they can search effectively and access collective intelligence via the internet. In sum, the changes in learning behavior and cognition among the young generally produce positive outcomes.

Some 42% agreed with the opposite statement, which posited:

> In 2020, the brains of multitasking teens and young adults are "wired" differently from those over age 35 and overall it yields baleful results. They do not retain information; they spend most of their energy sharing short social messages, being entertained, and being distracted away from deep engagement with people and knowledge. They lack deep-thinking capabilities; they lack face-to-face social skills; they depend in unhealthy ways on the internet and mobile devices to function. In sum, the changes in behavior and cognition among the young are generally negative outcomes.

While 55% agreed with the statement that the future for the hyperconnected will generally be positive, many who chose that view noted that it is more their hope than their best guess, and a number of people said the true outcome will be a combination of both scenarios. The research result here is really probably more like a 50-50 outcome than the 55-42 split recorded through survey takers' votes. Respondents were asked to select the positive or the negative, with no middle-ground choice, in order to encourage a spirited and deeply considered written elaboration about the potential future of hyperconnected people.

We did not offer a third alternative—that young people's brains would not be wired differently—but some of the respondents made that argument in their elaborations. They often noted that people's patterns of thinking will likely change, though the actual mechanisms of brain function will not change.

Survey participants did offer strong, consistent predictions about the most desired life skills for young people in 2020. Among those they listed are: public problem-solving through cooperative work (sometimes referred to as *crowdsourcing* solutions); the ability to search effectively for information online and to be able to discern the quality and veracity of the information one finds and then communicate these findings well (referred to as *digital literacy*); synthesizing (being able to bring together details from many sources); being strategically future-minded; the ability to concentrate; and the ability to distinguish between the "noise" and the message in the ever-growing sea of information.

Here is a sampling of their predictions and arguments:

- The environment itself will be full of data that can be retrieved almost effortlessly, and it will be arrayed in ways to help people—young and old—navigate their lives. Quick-twitch younger technology users will do well mastering these datastreams.
- Millennials' brains are being rewired to adapt to the new information-processing skills they will need to survive in this environment.
- "Memories are becoming hyperlinks to information triggered by keywords and URLs. We are becoming 'persistent paleontologists' of our own external memories, as our brains are storing the keywords to get back to those memories and not the full memories themselves," argued **Amber Case**, CEO of Geoloqi.
- There is evidence now that "supertaskers" can handle several complicated tasks well, noted communications expert **Stowe Boyd**. And some survey respondents noted that it is not necessarily only young adults who do this well.
- Young people accustomed to a diet of quick-fix information nuggets will be less likely to undertake deep, critical analysis of issues and challenging information. Shallow choices, an expectation of instant gratification, and a lack of patience are likely to be common results, especially for those who do not have the motivation or training that will help them master this new environment. One possible outcome is stagnation in innovation.
- Another possibility, though, is that evolving social structures will create a new "division of labor" that rewards those who make swift, correct decisions as they exploit new information streams *and* rewards the specialists who retain the skills of focused, deep thinking. New winners and losers will emerge in this reconfigured environment; the left-behind will be mired in the shallow diversions offered by technology.

- There are concerns about new social divides. "I suspect we're going to see an increased class division around labor and skills and attention," said media scholar **Danah Boyd.**
- A key differentiator between winners and losers will be winners' capacity to figure out the correct attention–allocation balance in this new environment. Just as we lost oral tradition with the written word, we will lose something big in the coming world, but we will gain as well. "As Sophocles once said, 'Nothing vast enters the life of mortals without a curse,'" noted **Tiffany Shlain**, director of the film *Connected* and founder of the Webby Awards.
- "The essential skills will be those of rapidly searching, browsing, assessing quality, and synthesizing the vast quantities of information," wrote **Jonathan Grudin**, principal researcher at Microsoft. "In contrast, the ability to read one thing and think hard about it for hours will not be of no consequence, but it will be of far less consequence for most people."
- Some argued that technology is not the issue as much as bedrock human behavior is. The "moral panic" over digital technology "seems to be wired into us,"—it parallels previous concerns about media that have not led to the downfall of civilization, noted **Christopher J. Ferguson**, a professor from Texas A&M whose research specialty is technologies' effects on human behavior.
- Reform of the education system is necessary to help learners know how to maximize the best and minimize the worst. Reform could start by recognizing that distractions of all kinds are the norm now. Educators should teach the management of multiple information streams, emphasizing the skills of filtering, analyzing, and synthesizing information. Also of value is an appreciation for silence, focused contemplation, and "lessons in ignoring people," as futurist **Marcel Bullinga** put it.
- Others noted research that challenges the idea that people can be "multitaskers." People really toggle between tasks and "time slice" their attention into ever-smaller chunks of time, argued Nikki Reynolds, director of instructional technology services at Hamilton College.

Futurist **John Smart**, president and founder of the Acceleration Studies Foundation, recalled an insight of economist Simon Kuznets about evolution of technology effects known as the Kuznets curve: "First-generation tech usually causes 'net negative' social effects; second-generation 'net neutral' effects; by the third generation of tech—once the tech is smart enough, and we've got the interface right, and it begins to reinforce the best behaviors—we finally get to 'net positive' effects," he noted. "We'll be early into conversational interface and agent technologies by 2020, so kids will begin to be seriously intelligently augmented by the internet. There will be many persistent drawbacks however [so the effect at this point will be net neutral]. The biggest

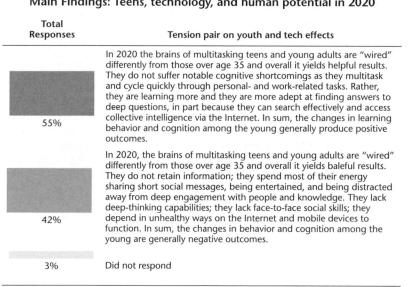

Main Findings: Teens, technology, and human potential in 2020

Total Responses	Tension pair on youth and tech effects
55%	In 2020 the brains of multitasking teens and young adults are "wired" differently from those over age 35 and overall it yields helpful results. They do not suffer notable cognitive shortcomings as they multitask and cycle quickly through personal- and work-related tasks. Rather, they are learning more and they are more adept at finding answers to deep questions, in part because they can search effectively and access collective intelligence via the Internet. In sum, the changes in learning behavior and cognition among the young generally produce positive outcomes.
42%	In 2020, the brains of multitasking teens and young adults are "wired" differently from those over age 35 and overall it yields baleful results. They do not retain information; they spend most of their energy sharing short social messages, being entertained, and being distracted away from deep engagement with people and knowledge. They lack deep-thinking capabilities; they lack face-to-face social skills; they depend in unhealthy ways on the Internet and mobile devices to function. In sum, the changes in behavior and cognition among the young are generally negative outcomes.
3%	Did not respond

problem from a personal-development perspective will be motivating people to work to be more self-actualized, productive, and civic than their parents were. They'll be more willing than ever to relax and remain distracted by entertainments amid accelerating technical productivity.

"As machine intelligence advances," Smart explained, "the first response of humans is to offload their intelligence and motivation to the machines. That's a dehumanizing, first-generation response. Only the later, third-generation educational systems will correct for this."

Another comprehensive insight came from **Barry Chudakov,** a Florida-based consultant and a research fellow in the McLuhan Program in Culture and Technology at the University of Toronto. He wrote that by 2020, "Technology will be so seamlessly integrated into our lives that it will effectively disappear. The line between self and technology is thin today; by then it will effectively vanish. We will think with, think into, and think through our smart tools but their presence and reach into our lives will be less visible. Youth will assume their minds and intentions are extended by technology, while tracking technologies will seek further incursions into behavioral monitoring and choice manipulation. Children will assume this is the way the world works. The cognitive challenge children and youth will face (as we are beginning to face now) is integrity, the state of being whole and undivided. There will be a premium on the skill of maintaining presence, of mindfulness, of awareness in the face of persistent and pervasive tool extensions and incursions into our lives. Is this my intention, or is the tool inciting me to feel and think this way? That question, more than multitasking or brain atrophy due to accessing collective intelligence via the internet, will be the challenge of the future."

Respondents' Thoughts

Hyperconnected. Always on. These terms have been invented to describe the environment created when people are linked continuously through tech devices to other humans and to global intelligence. Teens and young adults have been at the forefront of the rapid adoption of the mobile internet and the always-on lifestyle it has made possible.

The most recent nationally representative surveys of the Pew Internet Project show how immersed teens and young adults are in the tech environment and how tied they are to the mobile and social sides of it. Some 95% of teens ages 12–17 are online, 76% use social networking sites, and 77% have cell phones. Moreover, 96% of those ages 18–29 are internet users, 84% use social networking sites, and 97% have cell phones. Well over half of those in that age cohort have smartphones and 23% own tablet computers like iPads.

People are tuning in to communications technologies at an ever-expanding level. Some recent indicators:

- Nearly 20 million of the 225 million Twitter users follow 60 or more Twitter accounts and nearly 2 million follow more than 500 accounts.
- There are more than 800 million people now signed up for the social network Facebook; they spend 700 billion minutes using Facebook each month, and they install more than 20 million apps every day. Facebook users had uploaded more than 100 billion photos by mid-2011.
- YouTube users upload 60 hours of video per minute and they triggered more than 1 trillion playbacks in 2011—roughly 140 video views per person on earth.

When asked to choose one of the two 2020 scenarios presented in this survey question, respondents were asked to, "Explain your choice about the impact of technology on children and youth and share your view of any implications for the future. What are the positives, negatives and shades of grey in the likely future you anticipate? What intellectual and personal skills will be most highly valued in 2020?"

Following is a selection from the hundreds of written responses survey participants shared when answering this question. The selected statements are grouped under headings that indicate the major themes emerging from these responses. The headings reflect the varied and wide range of opinions found in respondents' replies.

This Is the Next Positive Step in Human Evolution: We Become "Persistent Paleontologists of Our External Memories"

Most of the survey respondents with the largest amount of expertise in this subject area said changes in learning behavior and cognition will generally produce positive outcomes.

One of the world's best-known researchers of teens and young adults—Danah Boyd of Microsoft Research—said there is no doubt that most people who are using the new communications technologies are experiencing the first scenario as they extend themselves into cyberspace. "Brains are being rewired—any shift in stimuli results in a rewiring," she wrote. "The techniques and mechanisms to engage in rapid-fire attention shifting will be extremely useful for the creative class whose job it is to integrate ideas; they relish opportunities to have stimuli that allow them to see things differently. . . ."

Negative Effects Include a Need for Instant Gratification, Loss of Patience

A number of the survey respondents who are young people in the under-35 age group—the central focus of this research question—shared concerns about changes in human attention and depth of discourse among those who spend most or all of their waking hours under the influence of hyperconnectivity.

Alvaro Retana, a distinguished technologist with Hewlett-Packard, expressed concerns about humans' future ability to tackle complex challenges. "The short attention spans resulting from the quick interactions will be detrimental to focusing on the harder problems, and we will probably see a stagnation in many areas: technology, even social venues such as literature," he predicted. "The people who will strive and lead the charge will be the ones able to disconnect themselves to focus on specific problems. . . ."

[Stephen] Masiclat said social systems will evolve to offer even more support to those who can implement deep-thinking skills. "The impact of a future 're-wiring' due to the multitasking and short-term mindset will be mostly negative not because it will reflect changes in the physical nature of thinking, but because the social incentives for deep engagement will erode," he noted. "We will likely retain deep-thinking capability if we just reward it sufficiently in many of our social institutions. . . ."

Dana Levin, a student at Drexel University College of Medicine, wrote, "The biggest consequence I foresee is an expectation of immediacy and decreased patience among people. Those who grow up with immediate access to media, quick response to email and rapid answers to all questions may be less likely to take longer routes to find information, seeking 'quick fixes' rather than taking the time to come to a conclusion or investigate an answer. . . ."

Many anonymous respondents focused their responses on what one referred to as "fast-twitch" wiring. Here's a collection of responses along those lines: "My friends are less interested in genuine human interaction than they are at looking at things on Facebook. People will always use a crutch when they can, and the distraction will only grow in the future."

"Parents and kids will spend less time developing meaningful and bonded relationships in deference to the pursuit and processing of more and more segmented information competing for space in their heads, slowly changing their connection to humanity. . . ."

"'Fast-twitch' wiring among today's youth generally leads to more harm than good. Much of the communication and media consumed in an 'always-on' environment is mind-numbing chatter. While we may see increases in productivity, I question the value of what is produced."

"There is less time for problems to be worked out, whether they are of a personal, political, economic, or environmental nature. When you (individual or collective) screw up (pollute, start a war, act in a selfish way, or commit a sexual indiscretion as a public person) everyone either knows very quickly or your actions affect many people in ways that are irreversible. . . ."

The Result Is Likely to Be a Wide-Ranging Mix of Positives and Negatives—and Not Just for Young People

. . . Youth expert Winograd said the Millennial generation will drive positive change in the next decade. "When Millennials remake our educational institutions so that they reflect this internet-based architecture, rather than the broadcast, 'expert in the center' framework of today's K-doctorate educational systems," he wrote, "then their ability to process, if not actually absorb, a greater amount of information will be used to produce positive outcomes for society. But that will take longer then eight years to accomplish."

"I made the optimistic choice, but in reality, I think that both outcomes will happen," noted Hal Varian, chief economist at Google. "This has been the case for every communications advance: writing, photography, movies, radio, TV, etc. There's no reason to believe that the internet is any different. It will provide ways to save time, and ways to waste time, and people will take advantage of both opportunities. In balance, however, I lean toward the more optimistic view since a larger fraction of the world's population will now be able to access human knowledge. This has got to be a good thing. . . ."

Jerry Michalski, founder and president of Sociate, asked, "What if we're seeing a temporary blip in behavior because an Aleph has suddenly opened in the middle of civilization, a Borges-like hole through which anyone can talk to anyone, and anyone can see everything that ever happened and is happening now? Because this has never existed, all the way back through prehistory, of course we're seeing addictive and compulsive behaviors. Naturally. The big question seems to me to be whether we'll regain our agency in the middle of all this, or surrender to consumerism and infotainment and live out a *WALL-E* world that's either Orwell's or Huxley's misanthropic fantasies in full bloom. I think we're figuring out how to be human again amid all this, and that we'll all learn how to use the new technologies to multitask as well as to dive deep into materials, weaving contexts of meaning that we haven't seen before. Call me an optimist."

Tiffany Shlain, director of the film *Connected* and founder of the Webby Awards, quoted Sophocles. "We are evolving and we are going to be able to access so much knowledge and different perspectives that we will come up with new ideas and new solutions to our world's problems," she responded. "The key will be valuing when to be present and when to unplug. The core of what makes us human is to connect deeply, so this always will be valued. Just as we lost oral tradition with the written word, we will lose something big, but we will gain a new way of thinking. As Sophocles once said, 'Nothing vast enters the life of mortals without a curse. . . .'"

Widening Divide? There's a Fear the Rich Will Get Richer, the Poor Poorer

Teens expert Danah Boyd raised concerns about a looming divide due to the switch in how young people negotiate the world. "Concentrated focus takes discipline, but it's not something everyone needs to do," she wrote, "unfortunately, it is what is expected of much of the workingclass labor force. I suspect we're going to see an increased class division around labor and skills and attention."

Barry Parr, owner and analyst for MediaSavvy, echoed Boyd's concern about a widening divide. "Knowledge workers and those inclined to be deep thinkers will gain more cognitive speed and leverage," he said, "but, the easily distracted will not become more adept at anything. History suggests that on balance people will adapt to the new order. The

greatest negative outcome will be that the split in adaptation will exacerbate existing trends toward social inequality. . . ."

No Matter What the Tech, It All Comes Down to Human Nature

Human tendencies drive human uses of technology tools. Many of the people participating in this survey emphasized the importance of the impact of basic human instincts and motivations.

Some survey respondents observed that all new tools initially tend to be questioned and feared by some segment of the public. Socrates, for instance, lamented about the scourge of writing implements and their likely threat to the future of intelligent discourse. In his response to this survey question, Christopher J. Ferguson, a professor from Texas A&M whose research specialty is technologies' effects on human behavior, noted, "The tendency to moralize and fret over new media seems to be wired into us."

He added, "Societal reaction to new media seems to fit into a pattern described by moral panic theory. Just as with older forms of media, from dime novels to comic books to rock and roll, some politicians and scholars can always be found to proclaim the new media to be harmful, often in the most hyperbolic terms. Perhaps we'll learn from these past mistakes? I think we may see the same pattern with social media. For instance the American Academy of Pediatrics claims for a 'Facebook Depression' already have been found to be false by independent scholarly review. New research is increasingly demonstrating that fears of violent video games leading to aggression were largely unfounded. Youth today are the least aggressive, most civically involved, and mentally well in several generations. Independent reviews of the literature by the US Supreme Court and the Australian Government have concluded the research does not support links between new technology and harm to minors. I think on balance we'll eventually accept that new media are generally a positive in our lives. . . ."

JANNA QUITNEY ANDERSON is an associate professor at Elon University's School of Communications and is the director of Imagining the Internet, a web-based foresight and history public-good project, which has won international acclaim. She is the lead author of the *Future of the Internet* book series published by Cambria Press. She is the author of *Imagining the Internet: Personalities, Predictions, Perspectives* (Rowman & Littlefield, 2005).

LEE RAINIE is the director of the Pew Research Center's Internet & American Life Project, which has studied the social impact of digital technologies since 2000. He is a co-author of *Networked: The New Social Operating System* and five books about the future of the Internet that are drawn from Pew Internet research. Prior to launching the Pew Internet Project, he was managing editor of *U.S. News & World Report*.

EXPLORING THE ISSUE

Does Social Media Have Largely Positive Impacts on Its Users?

Critical Thinking and Reflection

1. Should social media be considered simply a tool that users can use for either good or evil? Thus, it is neither good nor bad in itself.
2. How can the negative consequences of social media be reduced?
3. What role can education play in reducing the negative aspects of social media and increasing its positive aspects?
4. What have been the positive and negative results of your own use of social media?
5. What activities have been reduced by the time spent on social media?
6. How has social media impacted your community? Your nation?
7. Have you or your friends been embarrassed or harmed through your use of social media?

Is There Common Ground?

Both YES and NO selections recognize many of the benefits of social media. Anderson and Rainie also emphasize the many negative impacts of social media and Smith does not. Smith would not deny that social media does have negative impacts but treats them as less important than the positive impacts. Both selections consider the impacts on social connectedness as the key issue to examine, especially on family and close friends. Both agree that it is also useful for news, information, and helping conduct personal business. It also stimulates the economy and facilitates business, governments, and civil sector activities. For example, I just conveniently paid property taxes online 2 hours ago.

Create Central

www.mhhe.com/createcentral

Additional Resources

PEW Internet (pewinternet.org), a project of the PEW Research Center, produces many articles a year including the two articles selected for this issue. Another major resource is socialnetworking.procon.org. It is the most informative website on the pros and cons of social media with 173 footnotes, but it does not provide useful links. Its useful references include LexisNexis Risk Solutions, "Role of Social Media in Law Enforcement Significant and Growing," www.lexisnexis.com, July 18, 2012; Mary Wilks, "Online Social Networking's Effect on Adolescent Social Development," www.eckerd.edu (accessed December 5, 2012); Levi R. Baker and Debra L. Oswald, "Shyness and Online Social Networking Services," *Journal of Social and Personal Relationships* (November 2010); "Economist Debates: Social Networking," *The Economist*, www.economist.com, February 13, 2012; Tony Dokoupil, "Is the Onslaught Making Us Crazy?" *Newsweek*, July 16, 2012; Stephen Marche, "Is Facebook Making Us Lonely?" *Atlantic Monthly*, May 2012. Other useful references are José van Dijck, *The Culture of Connectivity: A Critical History of Social Media* (Oxford University Press, 2013); Tim Jordan, *Internet, Society and Culture [electronic resource]: Communicative Practices Before and After the Internet* (Bloomsbury Publishing, 2013); Francis L. F. Lee, ed., *Frontiers in New Media Research* (Routledge, 2013); Allison Cerra, *Identity Shift: Where Identity Meets Technology in the Networked-Community Age* (John Wiley & Sons, 2012); Andrew Keen, *Digital Vertigo: How Today's Online Social Revolution Is Dividing, Diminishing, and Disorienting Us* (Constable, 2012); Pamela Lund, *Massively Networked: How the Convergence of Social Media and Technology Is Changing Your Life,* 2nd ed. (PLI Media, 2012); Hana S. Noor, Al-Deen, and John Allen Hendricks, eds., *Social Media: Usage and Impact* (Lexington Books, 2012); Nora Young, *The Virtual Self: How Our Digital Lives Are Altering the World Around Us* (McClelland & Stewart, 2012).

Internet References . . .

Sociology—Study Sociology Online

http://edu.learnsoc.org/

Sociology Web Resources

www.mhhe.com/socscience/sociology/resources /index.htm

Sociosite

www.topsite.com/goto/sociosite.net

Socioweb

www.topsite.com/goto/socioweb.com

Unit 2

UNIT

Sex Roles, Gender, and the Family

*T*he modern feminist movement has advanced the causes of women to the point where there are now more women in the workforce in the United States than ever before. Professions and trades that were traditionally regarded as the provinces of men have opened up to women, and women now have easier access to the education and training necessary to excel in these new areas. But what is happening to sex roles, and what are the effects of changing sex roles? How have men and women been affected by the stress caused by current sex roles, the demand for the right to same-sex marriages, and the deterioration of the traditional family structure? The issues in this unit address these sorts of questions.

Selected, Edited, and with Issue Framing Material by:
Kurt Finsterbusch, *University of Maryland, College Park*

ISSUE

Is the American Family in Trouble?

YES: Isabel V. Sawhill, from "The New White Negro: What It Means That Family Breakdown Is Now Biracial," *Washington Monthly* (January/February 2013)

NO: W. Bradford Wilcox, from "Unequal, Unfair, and Unhappy: The 3 Biggest Myths about Marriage Today," *The Atlantic* Magazine (June 3, 2013)

Learning Outcomes
After reading this issue, you should be able to: • Estimate the general quality of marriages in America.   • Discern which groups have the least successful marriages generally.   • Know the major reasons due to which marriages fail.   • Be able to counter the myth that most marriages are bad.

ISSUE SUMMARY

YES: Isabel V. Sawhill, a senior fellow in Economic Studies at the Brookings Institution and director of the Budgeting for National Priorities Project and codirector of the Center on Children and Families, points out that marriages in college educated families are not declining but they are declining significantly for the non-college educated families, both white and black.

NO: W. Bradford Wilcox, associate professor of sociology and director of the National Marriage Project at the University of Virginia, describes the positive situation of families today. The majority of marriages are happy and are much more equal and fair than decades ago.

The state of the American family deeply concerns many Americans. About 40 percent of marriages end in divorce, and only 27 percent of children born in 1990 are expected to be living with both parents by the time they reach age 17. Most Americans, therefore, are affected personally or are close to people who are affected by structural changes in the family. Few people can avoid being exposed to the issue: violence in the family and celebrity divorces are standard fare for news programs, and magazine articles decrying the breakdown of the family appear frequently. Politicians today try to address the problems of the family. Academics have affirmed that the family crisis has numerous significant negative effects on children, spouses, and the rest of society.

But is the situation as bad as portrayed? Divorces are much easier to get than in the 1950s, and therefore, increased until the nineties. But is it not better to have a choice to stay or leave than to have no choice and be trapped in a bad marriage? Many of you reading this come from divorced homes and can evaluate how much you and your family suffered and whether you have been scarred for life. All of you can look around you and judge for yourselves how your acquaintances have been affected by divorce or other family issues.

One reason family strength is a very important issue is the important role that the family plays in the functioning of society. For a society to survive, its population must reproduce (or take in many immigrants), and its young must be trained to perform adult roles and to have the values and attitudes that will motivate them to contribute to society. Procreation and socialization are two vital roles that families traditionally have performed. In addition, the family provides economic and emotional support for its members, which is vital to their effective functioning in society. Stable, well-functioning families best perform these roles and divorce and family conflict jeopardize them.

Although most experts agree that the American family is in crisis, there is little agreement about what, if anything, should be done about it. After all, most of these problems result from the choices that people make to try to increase their well-being. People end unhappy marriages. When they do, most parents also carefully consider the best interests of their children. These considerations obviously prevent or delay many divorces and probably should prevent many more. Obviously, however, many situations are improved by divorce, especially if the divorce and aftermath arrangements are conducted in a compassionate manner. So which way is best is a judgment call, both by the potentially divorcing parents and by the academics who study the issue.

In the selections that follow, Isabel V. Sawhill shows that modern marriages have problems as divorce rates demonstrate. Her main point, however, is that marriage problems are much more prevalent in the lower class than in the middle or upper classes for both whites and blacks. In sum, Sawhill reports that marriage is in trouble but mainly in the lower class. W. Bradford Wilcox paints a brighter picture. He shows that "Most husbands and wives make about equal total contributions to the paid and unpaid work needed to sustain a family. Most judge their marriages to be fair and are happily married."

YES ⤶

Isabel V. Sawhill

The New White Negro: What It Means That Family Breakdown Is Now Biracial

In 1965, Daniel Patrick Moynihan released a controversial report written for his then boss, President Lyndon Johnson. Entitled "The Negro Family: The Case for National Action," it described the condition of lower-income African American families and catalyzed a highly acrimonious, decades-long debate about black culture and family values in America.

The report cited a series of staggering statistics showing high rates of divorce, unwed childbearing, and single motherhood among black families. "The white family has achieved a high degree of stability and is maintaining that stability," the report said. "By contrast, the family structure of lower class Negroes is highly unstable, and in many urban centers is approaching complete breakdown."

Nearly fifty years later, the picture is even more grim and the statistics can no longer be organized neatly by race. In fact, Moynihan's bracing profile of the collapsing black family in the 1960s looks remarkably similar to a profile of the average white family today. White households have similar—or worse—statistics of divorce, unwed childbearing, and single motherhood as the black households cited by Moynihan in his report. In 2000, the percentage of white children living with a single parent was identical to the percentage of black children living with a single parent in 1960: 22 percent.

What was happening to black families in the '60s can be reinterpreted today not as an indictment of the black family but as a harbinger of a larger collapse of traditional living arrangements—of what demographer Samuel Preston, in words that Moynihan later repeated, called "the earthquake that shuddered through the American family."

That earthquake has not affected all American families the same way. While the Moynihan report focused on disparities between white and black, increasingly it is class, and not just race, that matters for family structure. Although blacks as a group are still less likely to marry than whites, gaps in family formation patterns by class have increased for both races, with the sharpest declines in marriage rates occurring among the least educated of both races. For example, in 1960, 76 percent of adults with a college degree were married, compared to 72 percent of those with a high school diploma—a gap of only 4 percentage points. By 2008, not only was marriage less likely, but that gap had quadrupled, to 16 percentage points, with 64 percent of adults with college degrees getting married compared to only 48 percent of adults with a high school diploma. A report from the National Marriage Project at the University of Virginia summed up the data well: "Marriage is an emerging dividing line between America's moderately educated middle and those with college degrees." The group for whom marriage has largely disappeared now includes not just unskilled blacks but unskilled whites as well. Indeed, for younger women without a college degree, unwed childbearing is the new normal.

These differences in family formation are a problem not only for those concerned with "family values" per se, but also for those concerned with upward mobility in a society that values equal opportunity for its children. Because the breakdown of the traditional family is overwhelmingly occurring among working-class Americans of all races, these trends threaten to make the U.S. a much more class-based society over time. The well-educated and upper-middle-class parents who are still forming two-parent families are able to invest time and resources in their children—time and resources that lower- and working-class single mothers, however impressive their efforts to be both good parents and good breadwinners, simply do not have.

The striking similarities between what happened to black Americans at an earlier stage in our history and what is happening now to white working-class Americans may shed new light on old debates about cultural versus structural explanations of poverty. What's clear is that economic opportunity, while not the only factor affecting marriage, clearly matters.

The journalist Hanna Rosin describes the connection between declining economic opportunities for men and declining rates of marriage in her book *The End of Men*. Like Moynihan, she points to the importance of job opportunities for men in maintaining marriage as an institution. The disappearance of well-paying factory jobs has, in her view, led to the near collapse of marriage in towns where less educated men used to be able to support a family and a middle-class lifestyle, earning $70,000 or more in a single year. As these jobs have been outsourced or up-skilled, such men either are earning less or are jobless altogether, making them less desirable marriage partners. Other researchers, including Kathryn Edin at Harvard, Andrew Cherlin at Johns Hopkins, and Charles Murray of the American Enterprise Institute, drawing on close observations of other working-class communities, have made similar arguments.

Family life, to some extent, adapts to the necessities thrown up by the evolution of the economy. Just as joblessness among young black men contributed to the breakdown of the black family that Moynihan observed in the '60s, more recent changes in technology and global competition have hollowed out the job market for less educated whites. Unskilled white men have even less attachment to the labor force today than unskilled black men did fifty years ago, leading to a decline in their marriage rates in a similar way.

In 1960, the employment rate of prime-age (twenty-five to fifty-five) black men with less than a high school education was 80 percent. Fast-forward to 2000, and the employment rate of white men with less than a high school education was much lower, at 65 percent—and even for white high school graduates it was only 84 percent. Without an education in today's economy, being white is no guarantee of being able to find a job.

That's not to say that race isn't an issue. It's clear that black men have been much harder hit by the disappearance of jobs for the less skilled than white men. Black employment rates for those with less than a college education have sunk to near-catastrophic levels. In 2000, only 63 percent of black men with only a high school diploma (compared with 84 percent of white male graduates) were employed. Since the recession, those numbers have fallen even farther. And even black college graduates are not doing quite as well as their white counterparts. Based on these and other data, I believe it would be a mistake to conclude that race is unimportant; blacks continue to face unique disadvantages because of the color of their skin. It ought to be possible to say that class is becoming more important, but that race still matters a lot.

Most obviously, the black experience has been shaped by the impact of slavery and its ongoing aftermath. Even after emancipation and the civil rights revolution in the 1960s, African Americans faced exceptional challenges like segregated and inferior schools and discrimination in the labor market. It would take at least a generation for employers to begin to change their hiring practices and for educational disparities to diminish; even today these remain significant barriers. A recent audit study found that white applicants for low-wage jobs were twice as likely to be called in for interviews as equally qualified black applicants.

Black jobless rates not only exceed those of whites; in addition, a single-minded focus on declining job prospects for men and its consequences for family life ignores a number of other factors that have led to the decline of marriage. Male employment prospects can lead to more marriages, but scholars such as Harvard's David Ellwood and Christopher Jencks have argued that economic factors alone cannot explain the wholesale changes in the frequency of single parenting, unwed births, divorce, and marriage, especially among the least educated, that are leading to growing gaps between social classes. So what else explains the decline of marriage?

First, and critically important in my view, is the changing role of women. In my first book, *Time of Transition: The Growth of Families Headed by Women*, published in 1975, my coauthor and I argued that it was not just male earnings that mattered, but what men could earn relative to women. When women don't gain much, if anything, from getting married, they often choose to raise children on their own. Fifty years ago, women were far more economically dependent on marriage than they are now. Today, women are not just working more, they are better suited by education and tradition to work in such rapidly growing sectors of the economy as health care, education, administrative jobs, and services. While some observers may see women taking these jobs as a matter of necessity—and that's surely a factor—we shouldn't forget the revolution in women's roles that has made it possible for them to support a family on their own.

In a fascinating piece of academic research published in the *Journal of Human Resources* in 2011, Scott Hankins and Mark Hoekstra discovered that single women who won between $25,000 and $50,000 in the Florida lottery were 41 percent to 48 percent less likely to marry over the following three years than women who won less than $1,000. We economists call this a "natural experiment," because it shows the strong influence of women's ability to support themselves without marriage—uncontaminated by differences in personal attributes that may also affect one's ability or willingness to marry. My own earlier research also suggested that the relative incomes of wives and husbands predicted who would divorce and who would not.

Women's growing economic independence has interacted with stubborn attitudes about changing gender roles. When husbands fail to adjust to women's new breadwinning responsibilities (who cooks dinner or stays home with a sick child when both parents work?) the couple is more likely to divorce. It may be that well-educated younger men and women continue to marry not only because they can afford to but because many of the men in these families have adopted more egalitarian attitudes. While a working-class male might find such attitudes threatening to his manliness, an upper-middle-class man often does not, given his other sources of status. But when women find themselves having to do it all—that is, earn money in the workplace and shoulder the majority of child care and other domestic responsibilities—they raise the bar on whom they're willing to marry or stay married to.

These gender-related issues may play an even greater role for black women, since while white men hold slightly more high school diplomas and baccalaureate degrees than white women, black women are much better educated than black men. That means it's more difficult for well-educated black women to find black partners with comparable earning ability and social status. In 2010, black women made 87 percent of what black men did, whereas white women made only 70 percent of what white men earned. For less educated black women, there is, in addition, a shortage of black men because of high rates of incarceration. One estimate puts the proportion of black men who will spend some time in prison at almost one third.

In a forthcoming book, *Doing the Best I Can: Fatherhood in the Inner City,* Timothy Nelson and Edin, the Harvard sociologist, describe in great detail the kind of role reversal that has occurred among low-income families, both black and white. What they saw were mothers who were financially responsible for children, and fathers who were trying to maintain ties to their children in other ways, limited by the fact that these fathers have very little money, are often involved in drugs, crime, or other relationships, and rarely live with the mother and child.

In other words, low-income fathers are not only withdrawing from the traditional breadwinner role, they're staging a wholesale retreat—even as they make attempts to remain involved in their children's lives.

Normative changes figure as well. As the retreat from marriage has become more common, it's also become more acceptable. That acceptance came earlier among blacks than among whites because of their own distinct experiences. Now that unwed childbearing is becoming the norm among the white working class as well, there is no longer much of a stigma associated with single parenting, and there is a greater willingness on the part of the broader community to accept the legitimacy of single-parent households.

Despite this change in norms, however, most Americans, whatever their race or social class, still aspire to marriage. It's just that their aspirations are typically unrealistically high and their ability to achieve that ideal is out of step with their opportunities and lifestyle. As scholars such as Cherlin and Edin have emphasized, marriage is no longer a precursor to adult success. Instead, when it still takes place, marriage is more a badge of success already achieved. In particular, large numbers of young adults are having unplanned pregnancies long before they can cope with the responsibilities of parenthood. Paradoxically, although they view marriage as something they cannot afford, they rarely worry about the cost of raising a child.

Along with many others, I remain concerned about the effects on society of this wholesale retreat from stable two-parent families. The consequences for children, especially, are not good. Their educational achievements, and later chances of becoming involved in crime or a teen pregnancy are, on average, all adversely affected by growing up in a single-parent family. But I am also struck by the lessons that emerge from looking at how trends in family formation have differed by class as well as by race. If we were once two countries, one black and one white, we are now increasingly becoming two countries, one advantaged and one disadvantaged. Race still affects an individual's chances in life, but class is growing in importance. This argument was the theme of William Julius Wilson's 1980 book, *The Declining Significance of Race.* More recent evidence suggests that, despite all the controversy his book engendered, he was right.

To say that class is becoming more important than race isn't to dismiss race as a very important factor. Blacks have faced, and will continue to face, unique challenges. But when we look for the reasons why less skilled blacks are failing to marry and join the middle class, it is largely for the same reasons that marriage and a middle-class lifestyle is eluding a growing number of whites as well. The jobs that unskilled men once did are gone, women are increasingly financially independent, and a broad cultural shift across America has created a new normal.

Isabel V. Sawhill is a senior fellow in economic studies at the Brookings Institution and director of the Budgeting for National Priorities Project. She also codirects the Center on Children and Families and has authored several important books and many reports and articles.

the Baby Boom, and Social Change (University of Chicago Press, 2000); Barbara J. Risman's *Gender Vertigo: American Families in Transition* (Yale University Press, 1998); Ronald D. Taylor and Margaret C. Wang, eds., *Resilience across Contexts: Family, Work, Culture, and Community* (Lawrence Erlbaum, 2000); Linda J. Waite and Maggie Gallagher, *The Case for Marriage: Why Married People Are Happier, Healthier, and Better Off Financially* (Doubleday, 2000); Daniel P. Moynihan et al., eds., *Future of the Family* (Russell Sage Foundation, 2004); and Lynne M. Casper and Suzanne M. Bianchi, *Continuity and Change in the American Family* (Sage, 2002).

For counsel on how to strengthen marriages, see: David P. Gushee, *Getting Marriage Right: Realistic Counsel for Saving and Strengthening Relationships* (Baker Books, 2004).

For information on divorce among seniors, see: Deirdre Bair, *Calling It Quits: Late-Life Divorce and Starting Over*, 1st ed. (Random House, 2007).

For advice on handling divorce issues, see: Mark A. Fine and John H. Harvey, eds., *Handbook of Divorce and Relationship Dissolution* (Lawrence Erlbaum, 2006).

Finally, for information on the adjustment of children, see: Robert E. Emery, *Marriage, Divorce, and Children's Adjustment*, 2nd ed. (Sage, 1999).

Internet References . . .

National Council on Family Research

www.ncfr.com

Sociology—Study Sociology Online

http://edu.learnsoc.org/

Sociology Web Resources

www.mhhe.com/socscience/sociology/resources
/index.htm

Sociosite

www.topsite.com/goto/sociosite.net

Socioweb

www.topsite.com/goto/socioweb.com

Selected, Edited, and with Issue Framing Material by:
Kurt Finsterbusch, *University of Maryland, College Park*

ISSUE

Can Women Have It All?

YES: Gayle Tzemach Lemmon, from "Sheryl Sandberg's Radically Realistic 'And' Solution for Working Mothers," *The Atlantic* Magazine (February 20, 2013)

NO: Anne-Marie Slaughter, from "Why Women Still Can't Have It All," *The Atlantic* Magazine (July 2012)

Learning Outcomes

After reading this issue, you should be able to:

- Understand how people (in this case women) deal with the stress of situations involving the conflict between two very important values. Women have to make life-changing decisions regarding the balance of work and family responsibilities.
- Understand how the conditions affecting these choices have changed over time.
- Explore how the workplaces and family units are changing to accommodate women's needs in this set of conflicting demands.
- Explain, if possible, why these institutions are not more accommodating.
- Form an opinion about whether this issue is largely an individual problem or largely an institutional problem or is both.
- Evaluate what the role of husbands is in this situation.
- Discuss how men tend to handle the stress between work and family.

ISSUE SUMMARY

YES: Gayle Tzemach Lemmon, best-selling author, journalist, and a Senior Fellow with the Council on Foreign Relations' Women and Foreign Policy program, discusses the issues in Sheryl Sandberg's famous book, *Lean In*. Sandberg's advice to career women is not to opt out but to lean in, that is, to firmly choose both career and parenting. Unfortunately men still run the country so the societal changes that could facilitate *Lean In* are missing. Full commitment to both career and family will not be easy.

NO: Anne-Marie Slaughter, the Bert G. Kerstetter '66 University Professor of Politics and International Affairs at Princeton University and formerly dean of Princeton's Woodrow Wilson School of Public and International Affairs, explains why Sandberg is wrong and women cannot successfully pursue career and family at the same time. They must decide which to do well and which to do adequately but not avidly.

The fascinating aspect of social life is how many different trends and changes significantly affect how we live and the choices we make. For example, consider married women and their work–family choices. Ever since the 1950s, married women have increasingly participated in the labor force. Why? The reasons are numerous. Women want the money for themselves. Women need the money for the family. Women want the challenge of a career. Women want the social life that work provides. Women want independence. The list of reasons goes on and on. These reasons change, however, as the context changes.

For example, since 1965 the median price of the one-family home compared to the average income of private nonagricultural workers had doubled in real terms before the housing market crashed. Thus, the single earner family is having much more difficulty buying a house. This trend helps explain why married women increasingly enter or stay in the labor force. Attitudes have also changed. In 1968, a large survey asked young people what they expected to be doing at age 35. About 30 percent of the 20- to 21-year-olds said that they would be working. Seven years later, 65 percent of 20- to 21-year-olds said they would be working. That is an astounding change. The statistical result is that in 1900, women 16 and over constituted 18 percent of the labor force; in 1950, women constituted 30 percent; and since 1995, women constituted 45–47 percent of the labor force.

Educational changes in the past half century have also been dramatic. Females have overtaken males in most aspects of education. Women are now outnumbering men in college and currently earn 58 percent of all bachelor degrees, 60 percent of all master degrees, and 52 percent of PhDs. Women are also more focused on professional degrees while in college as demonstrated by their selection of majors. In 1966, 40 percent of college women graduates majored in education and 17 percent majored in English/literature, but only 2 percent majored in business. Women have stopped shying away from the business world. The percentage of female BA business degrees went from 9 percent in 1971 to 49 percent in 1997, while it went from 4 percent to 39 percent for MA business degrees and from 5 percent to 70 percent for law degrees. Another trend affecting choices and behaviors is the increasing scarcity of time. The percentage of males working more than 50 hours a week increased from 21.0 to 26.5 and for females from 5.2 to 11.3 during 1970–2000.

Two issues that have received major media attention explore the circumstances of the work–family choice. First, in the 1990s, employers talked about a mommy track for women employees who would be allowed an easier workload that would reduce the conflict between work and family but would slow down their advancement and hold down their income. Second, in the past decade investigators noticed that capable women with prosperous husbands "opted out" of the work world and stayed home with the kids. They had the circumstances that allowed them to make this choice. Could it be that if all women had such circumstances then the majority of them would make the same choice? This is the issue which is debated in the following selections. Gayle Tzemach Lemmon strongly supports Sheryl Sandberg's message in her famous book, *Lean In,* which advises career women not to opt out but to lean in, i.e., to firmly choose both career and parenting. It will not be easy but it is much better than the opt out alternative. Anne-Marie Slaughter attacks Sandberg thesis. She tries to show that women can not successfully pursue both career and family at the same time. They will fail at one or both objectives. They must decide which to do well and which to do adequately but not avidly.

YES ↵

Gayle Tzemach Lemmon

Sheryl Sandberg's Radically Realistic 'And' Solution for Working Mothers

At a wedding this summer, while I was eight months pregnant with twins, an older gentleman sitting next to me asked me whether I still worked in finance.

No, I told him, at the moment I was focused on my next book project, think-tank work, and several magazine pieces.

"Well," he said with a gentle, nearly sympathetic, smile, "in any case, soon you will be pushing three babies in a stroller, right? Won't leave time for much else."

Annoyance swelled up into my already enormous stomach. When our table rose to watch the bride cut the cake I scurried two seats over to my husband and fumed. "I was so irritated I couldn't even come up with a clever answer, other than to say that the kids have a father, too," I said. "No one would *ever* say something like that to you."

My husband laughed and told me not to pay any attention. "It's just because people think that women can only be one thing."

And therein lies the rub.

Somehow, today—even while women learn and earn in greater numbers than ever before—the idea that women live in an "either/or" world stubbornly hangs on. A woman can either be a mother or a professional. Career-driven or family-oriented. A great wife or a great worker. Not both. In other words, the choices are Donna Reed and Murphy Brown (pre-baby). Precious few Clair Huxtables out there.

That is the challenge Sheryl Sandberg's book sets out to tackle. In a women-in-the-workplace discussion consisting mostly of "either/ors," her argument in the upcoming book *Lean In* injects the word "and" into the conversation in a way that urges women to bring their "whole selves" to work. Choice is good, *and* so is aspiration. Ambition is great, and so is telling your boss that you want to have children. Working hard at your job is important, and so is finding a way to leave the office early enough to be home for dinner with your kids.

Already, weeks before the book's publication, criticism is within easy earshot. A 20-something friend told me that several women she respected greatly argued that Sandberg is hardly representative of others and that her advice is impractical for the non-wealthy. But it seems to me that this criticism misses the point. What Sandberg offers is a view that shows 20-somethings like my friend that choices and trade-offs surely exist, but that the "old normal" of blunting ambition so that you can fit in one category or another does not have to be the way it is. And that each of us has a say in what comes next. And that includes men.

We live in an era of immense change when it comes to what women do, how they do it, and with whom. 2011 marked the first year in which more women than men had advanced degrees. Between 1970 and 2009 the number of jobs held by women leapt from 37 percent to close to 48 percent. The boost in productivity resulting from women's increased labor participation accounts for 25 percent of U.S. GDP. Women own nearly 8 million businesses, enterprises that provide more than 20 million jobs. And as researcher Liza Mundy noted in her recent book, nearly 40 percent of wives in the U.S. now earn more than their husbands; Mundy predicts in a generation breadwinning wives will be the majority. Yet no real evolution in our expectations for women's lives and women's ambitions has accompanied these numbers, as Anne-Marie Slaughter's zeitgeist-channeling 2012 *Atlantic* story "Why Women Still Can't Have It All" points out.

Sandberg's proposition, though, looks a lot more like most women's lives than the "either/or" model into which women's lives get shoved. Many women navigate the "ands" every day, juggling a work life and a family life whose demands have meshed into one another in our constantly connected, 24/7-everything world. They don't have the luxury of choosing one or the other because they are too busy doing both. And as I have argued here at *The Atlantic*, all of these are undoubtedly high-class conversations the women I grew up with never had the chance to have.

Still, it is relevant to all women that, as Sandberg notes, "the blunt truth is that men still run the world." Women are fewer than 5 percent of all Fortune 500 CEOs and hold less than 20 percent of all executive board seats. Half the population accounts for barely 10 percent of all heads of state. And it was enormous progress for women to reach the 20-percent mark in the U.S. Senate last year. These dismal numbers and the lack of power they indicate are why it matters that the land of "and" is not only where women live now, but where they should want to stay and prosper. When 50 percent of the country has a kiddie seat at the head table, making room for others gets a whole lot harder. (Sandberg argues that women should, quite literally, sit "at the table" of power in which decisions get made.) Creating a world in which the next generation of talent gets to exercise its potential instead of bumping its head against career-stifling stereotypes or soul-crushing ceilings is in everyone's interest—and the American economy's.

Still, though, even when you succeed in winning fame and fortune in the world of "and", sometimes others make it "either/or" for you.

In a recent *Rolling Stone* piece on the end of the long-running television program *30 Rock*, show creator Tina Fey said the show had run its course, and dropping ratings meant no more. She wanted to do some movies and develop a multi-camera TV show while staying close to home and her two small children.

Her fellow *30 Rock* actor Alec Baldwin had a different and somewhat more detailed explanation.

Baldwin, the magazine wrote, is "convinced that having a second child, in 2011, may have been the breaking point for Fey. 'I saw a real difference in her,' says Baldwin. 'Tina always had her antenna up, but this year was the first time where she came in and laid down on the couch on set, and you could tell, she's a mom. She's fucking wiped out.'"

GAYLE TZEMACH LEMMON is a best-selling author, journalist, and a Senior Fellow with the Council on Foreign Relations' Women and Foreign Policy Program.

Anne-Marie Slaughter

Why Women Still Can't Have It All

It's time to stop fooling ourselves, says a woman who left a position of power: the women who have managed to be both mothers and top professionals are superhuman, rich, or self-employed. If we truly believe in equal opportunity for all women, here's what has to change.

Eighteen months into my job as the first woman director of policy planning at the State Department, a foreign-policy dream job that traces its origins back to George Kennan, I found myself in New York, at the United Nations' annual assemblage of every foreign minister and head of state in the world. On a Wednesday evening, President and Mrs. Obama hosted a glamorous reception at the American Museum of Natural History. I sipped champagne, greeted foreign dignitaries, and mingled. But I could not stop thinking about my 14-year-old son, who had started eighth grade three weeks earlier and was already resuming what had become his pattern of skipping homework, disrupting classes, failing math, and tuning out any adult who tried to reach him. Over the summer, we had barely spoken to each other—or, more accurately, he had barely spoken to me. And the previous spring I had received several urgent phone calls—invariably on the day of an important meeting—that required me to take the first train from Washington, D.C., where I worked, back to Princeton, New Jersey, where he lived. My husband, who has always done everything possible to support my career, took care of him and his 12-year-old brother during the week; outside of those midweek emergencies, I came home only on weekends.

As the evening wore on, I ran into a colleague who held a senior position in the White House. She has two sons exactly my sons' ages, but she had chosen to move them from California to D.C. when she got her job, which meant her husband commuted back to California regularly. I told her how difficult I was finding it to be away from my son when he clearly needed me. Then I said, "When this is over, I'm going to write an op-ed titled 'Women Can't Have It All.'"

She was horrified. "You *can't* write that," she said. "You, of all people." What she meant was that such a statement, coming from a high-profile career woman—a role model—would be a terrible signal to younger generations of women. By the end of the evening, she had talked me out of it, but for the remainder of my stint in Washington, I was increasingly aware that the feminist beliefs on which I had built my entire career were shifting under my feet.

I had always assumed that if I could get a foreign-policy job in the State Department or the White House while my party was in power, I would stay the course as long as I had the opportunity to do work I loved. But in January 2011, when my two-year public-service leave from Princeton University was up, I hurried home as fast as I could.

A rude epiphany hit me soon after I got there. When people asked why I had left government, I explained that I'd come home not only because of Princeton's rules (after two years of leave, you lose your tenure), but also because of my desire to be with my family and my conclusion that juggling high level government work with the needs of two teenage boys was not possible. I have not exactly left the ranks of full-time career women: I teach a full course load; write regular print and online columns on foreign policy; give 40 to 50 speeches a year; appear regularly on TV and radio; and am working on a new academic book. But I routinely got reactions from other women my age or older that ranged from disappointed ("It's such a pity that you had to leave Washington") to condescending ("I wouldn't generalize from your experience. *I've* never had to compromise, and *my* kids turned out great").

The first set of reactions, with the underlying assumption that my choice was somehow sad or unfortunate, was irksome enough. But it was the second set of reactions—those implying that my parenting and/or my commitment to my profession were somehow substandard—that triggered a blind fury. Suddenly, finally, the penny dropped. All my life, I'd been on the other side of this exchange. I'd been the woman smiling the faintly superior smile while another woman told me she had decided to take some time out or pursue a less competitive career track so that she could spend more time with her family. I'd been the woman congratulating herself on her unswerving commitment to the feminist cause, chatting smugly with her dwindling number of college or law-school friends who had reached and maintained their place on the highest rungs of their profession. I'd been the one telling young women at my lectures that you *can* have it all and do it all, regardless of what field you are in. Which means I'd been part, albeit unwittingly, of making millions of women feel that *they* are to blame if they cannot manage to rise up the ladder as fast as men and also have a family and an active home life (and be thin and beautiful to boot).

Last spring, I flew to Oxford to give a public lecture. At the request of a young Rhodes Scholar I know, I'd agreed to talk to the Rhodes community about "work-family balance." I ended up speaking to a group of about 40 men and women in their mid-20s. What poured out of me was a set of very frank reflections on how unexpectedly hard it was to do the kind of job I wanted to do as a high government official and be the kind of parent I wanted to be, at a demanding time for my children (even though my husband, an academic, was willing to take on the lion's share of parenting for the two years I was in Washington). I concluded by saying that my time in office had convinced me that further government service would be very unlikely while my sons were still at home. The audience was rapt, and asked many thoughtful questions. One of the first was from a young woman who began by thanking me for "not giving just one more fatuous 'You can have it all' talk." Just about all of the women in that room planned to combine careers and family in some way. But almost all assumed and accepted that they would have to make compromises that the men in their lives were far less likely to have to make.

The striking gap between the responses I heard from those young women (and others like them) and the responses I heard from my peers and associates prompted me to write this article. Women of my generation have clung to the feminist credo we were raised with, even as our ranks have been steadily thinned by unresolvable tensions between family and career, because we are determined not to drop the flag for the next generation. But when many members of the younger generation have stopped listening, on the grounds that glibly repeating "you can have it all" is simply airbrushing reality, it is time to talk.

I still strongly believe that women can "have it all" (and that men can too). I believe that we can "have it all at the same time." But not today, not with the way America's economy and society are currently structured. My experiences over the past three years have forced me to confront a number of uncomfortable facts that need to be widely acknowledged—and quickly changed.

Before my service in government, I'd spent my career in academia: as a law professor and then as the dean of Princeton's Woodrow Wilson School of Public and International Affairs. Both were demanding jobs, but I had the ability to set my own schedule most of the time. I could be with my kids when I needed to be, and still get the work done. I had to travel frequently, but I found I could make up for that with an extended period at home or a family vacation.

I knew that I was lucky in my career choice, but I had no idea how lucky until I spent two years in Washington within a rigid bureaucracy, even with bosses as understanding as Hillary Clinton and her chief of staff, Cheryl Mills. My workweek started at 4:20 on Monday morning, when I got up to get the 5:30 train from Trenton to Washington. It ended late on Friday, with the train home. In between, the days were crammed with meetings, and when the meetings stopped, the writing work began—a never-ending stream of memos, reports, and comments on other people's drafts. For two years, I never left the office early enough to go to any stores other than those open 24 hours, which meant that everything from dry cleaning to hair appointments to Christmas shopping had to be done on weekends, amid children's sporting events, music lessons, family meals, and conference calls. I was entitled to four hours of vacation per pay period, which came to one day of vacation a month. And I had it better than many of my peers in D.C.; Secretary Clinton deliberately came in around 8 a.m. and left around 7 p.m., to allow her close staff to have morning and evening time with their families (although of course she worked earlier and later, from home).

In short, the minute I found myself in a job that is typical for the vast majority of working women (and men), working long hours on someone else's schedule, I could no longer be both the parent and the professional I wanted to be—at least not with a child experiencing a rocky adolescence. I realized what should have perhaps been obvious: having it all, at least for me, depended almost entirely on what type of job I had. The flip side is the harder truth: having it all was not possible in many types of jobs, including high government office—at least not for very long.

I am hardly alone in this realization. Michèle Flournoy stepped down after three years as undersecretary of defense for policy, the third-highest job in the department, to spend more time at home with her three children, two of whom are teenagers. Karen Hughes left her position as the counselor to President George W. Bush after a year and a half in Washington to go home to Texas for the sake of her family. Mary Matalin, who spent two years as an assistant to Bush and the counselor to Vice President Dick Cheney before stepping down to spend more time with her daughters, wrote: "Having control over your schedule is the only way that women who want to have a career and a family can make it work."

Yet the decision to step down from a position of power—to value family over professional advancement, even for a time—is directly at odds with the prevailing social pressures on career professionals in the United States. One phrase says it all about current attitudes toward work and family, particularly among elites. In Washington, "leaving to spend time with your family" is a euphemism for being fired. This understanding is so ingrained that when Flournoy announced her resignation last December, *The New York Times* covered her decision as follows:

> Ms. Flournoy's announcement surprised friends and a number of Pentagon officials, but all said they took her reason for resignation at face value and not as a standard Washington excuse for an official who has in reality been forced out. "I can absolutely and unequivocally state that her

decision to step down has nothing to do with anything other than her commitment to her family," said Doug Wilson, a top Pentagon spokesman. "She has loved this job and people here love her."

Think about what this "standard Washington excuse" implies: it is so unthinkable that an official would *actually* step down to spend time with his or her family that this must be a cover for something else. How could anyone voluntarily leave the circles of power for the responsibilities of parenthood? Depending on one's vantage point, it is either ironic or maddening that this view abides in the nation's capital, despite the ritual commitments to "family values" that are part of every political campaign. Regardless, this sentiment makes true work-life balance exceptionally difficult. But it cannot change unless top women speak out.

Only recently have I begun to appreciate the extent to which many young professional women feel under assault by women my age and older. After I gave a recent speech in New York, several women in their late 60s or early 70s came up to tell me how glad and proud they were to see me speaking as a foreignpolicy expert. A couple of them went on, however, to contrast my career with the path being traveled by "younger women today." One expressed dismay that many younger women "are just not willing to get out there and do it." Said another, unaware of the circumstances of my recent job change: "They think they have to choose between having a career and having a family."

A similar assumption underlies Facebook Chief Operating Officer Sheryl Sandberg's widely publicized 2011 commencement speech at Barnard, and her earlier TED talk, in which she lamented the dismally small number of women at the top and advised young women not to "leave before you leave." When a woman starts thinking about having children, Sandberg said, "she doesn't raise her hand anymore . . . She starts leaning back." Although couched in terms of encouragement, Sandberg's exhortation contains more than a note of reproach. We who have made it to the top, or are striving to get there, are essentially saying to the women in the generation behind us: "What's the matter with you?"

They have an answer that we don't want to hear. After the speech I gave in New York, I went to dinner with a group of 30-somethings. I sat across from two vibrant women, one of whom worked at the UN and the other at a big New York law firm. As nearly always happens in these situations, they soon began asking me about work-life balance. When I told them I was writing this article, the lawyer said, "I look for role models and can't find any." She said the women in her firm who had become partners and taken on management positions had made tremendous sacrifices, "many of which they don't even seem to realize . . . They take two years off when their kids are young but then work like crazy to get back on track professionally, which means that they see their kids when they are toddlers but not teenagers, or really barely at all." Her friend nodded, mentioning the top professional women she knew, all of whom essentially relied on round-the-clock nannies. Both were very clear that they did not want that life, but could not figure out how to combine professional success and satisfaction with a real commitment to family.

I realize that I am blessed to have been born in the late 1950s instead of the early 1930s, as my mother was, or the beginning of the 20th century, as my grandmothers were. My mother built a successful and rewarding career as a professional artist largely in the years after my brothers and I left home—and after being told in her 20s that she could not go to medical school, as her father had done and her brother would go on to do, because, of course, she was going to get married. I owe my own freedoms and opportunities to the pioneering generation of women ahead of me—the women now in their 60s, 70s, and 80s who faced overt sexism of a kind I see only when watching *Mad Men,* and who knew that the only way to make it as a woman was to act exactly like a man. To admit to, much less act on, maternal longings would have been fatal to their careers.

But precisely thanks to their progress, a different kind of conversation is now possible. It is time for women in leadership positions to recognize that although we are still blazing trails and breaking ceilings, many of us are also reinforcing a falsehood: that "having it all" is, more than anything, a function of personal determination. As Kerry Rubin and Lia Macko, the authors of *Midlife Crisis at 30,* their cri de coeur for Gen-X and Gen-Y women, put it:

> What we discovered in our research is that while the empowerment part of the equation has been loudly celebrated, there has been very little honest discussion among women of our age about the real barriers and flaws that still exist in the system despite the opportunities we inherited.

I am well aware that the majority of American women face problems far greater than any discussed in this article. I am writing for my demographic—highly educated, well-off women who are privileged enough to have choices in the first place. We may not have choices about whether to do paid work, as dual incomes have become indispensable. But we have choices about the type and tempo of the work we do. We are the women who could be leading, and who should be equally represented in the leadership ranks.

Millions of other working women face much more difficult life circumstances. Some are single mothers; many struggle to find any job; others support husbands who cannot find jobs. Many cope with a work life in which good day care is either unavailable or very expensive; school schedules do not match work schedules; and schools themselves are failing to educate their children. Many of these women are worrying not about having it all, but rather about holding on to what they do have. And although women as a group have made substantial gains in wages, educational attainment, and prestige over the past three decades, the economists Justin Wolfers and Betsey Stevenson have shown that women are less happy today than their predecessors were in 1972, both in absolute terms and relative to men.

The best hope for improving the lot of all women, and for closing what Wolfers and Stevenson call a "new gender gap"—measured by well-being rather than wages—is to close the leadership gap: to elect a woman president and 50 women senators; to ensure that women are equally represented in the ranks of corporate executives and judicial leaders. Only when women wield power in sufficient numbers will we create a society that genuinely works for all women. That will be a society that works for everyone.

The Half-Truths We Hold Dear

Let's briefly examine the stories we tell ourselves, the clichés that I and many other women typically fall back on when younger women ask us how we have managed to "have it all." They are not necessarily lies, but at best partial truths. We must clear them out of the way to make room for a more honest and productive discussion about real solutions to the problems faced by professional women.

It's Possible If You Are Just Committed Enough

Our usual starting point, whether we say it explicitly or not, is that having it all depends primarily on the depth and intensity of a woman's commitment to her career. That is precisely the sentiment behind the dismay so many older career women feel about the younger generation. *They are not committed enough,* we say, to make the trade-offs and sacrifices that the women ahead of them made.

Yet instead of chiding, perhaps we should face some basic facts. Very few women reach leadership positions. The pool of female candidates for any top job is small, and will only grow smaller if the women who come after us decide to take time out, or drop out of professional competition altogether, to raise children. That is exactly what has Sheryl Sandberg so upset, and rightly so. In her words, "Women are not making it to the top. A hundred and ninety heads of state; nine are women. Of all the people in parliament in the world, 13 percent are women. In the corporate sector, [the share of] women at the top—C-level jobs, board seats—tops out at 15, 16 percent."

Can "insufficient commitment" even plausibly explain these numbers? To be sure, the women who do make it to the top are highly committed to their profession. On closer examination, however, it turns out that most of them have something else in common: they are genuine superwomen. Consider the number of women recently in the top ranks in Washington—Susan Rice, Elizabeth Sherwood-Randall, Michelle Gavin, Nancy-Ann Min DeParle—who are Rhodes Scholars. Samantha Power, another senior White House official, won a Pulitzer Prize at age 32. Or consider Sandberg herself, who graduated with the prize given to Harvard's top student of econom-

ics. These women cannot possibly be the standard against which even very talented professional women should measure themselves. Such a standard sets up most women for a sense of failure.

What's more, among those who have made it to the top, a balanced life still is more elusive for women than it is for men. A simple measure is how many women in top positions have children compared with their male colleagues. Every male Supreme Court justice has a family. Two of the three female justices are single with no children. And the third, Ruth Bader Ginsburg, began her career as a judge only when her younger child was almost grown. The pattern is the same at the National Security Council: Condoleezza Rice, the first and only woman national-security adviser, is also the only national-security adviser since the 1950s not to have a family.

The line of high-level women appointees in the Obama administration is one woman deep. Virtually all of us who have stepped down have been succeeded by men; searches for women to succeed men in similar positions come up empty. Just about every woman who could plausibly be tapped is already in government. The rest of the foreign-policy world is not much better; Micah Zenko, a fellow at the Council on Foreign Relations, recently surveyed the best data he could find across the government, the military, the academy, and think tanks, and found that women hold fewer than 30 percent of the senior foreign-policy positions in each of these institutions.

These numbers are all the more striking when we look back to the 1980s, when women now in their late 40s and 50s were coming out of graduate school, and remember that our classes were nearly 50–50 men and women. We were sure then that by now, we would be living in a 50–50 world. Something derailed that dream.

Sandberg thinks that "something" is an "ambition gap"—that women do not dream big enough. I am all for encouraging young women to reach for the stars. But I fear that the obstacles that keep women from reaching the top are rather more prosaic than the scope of their ambition. My longtime and invaluable assistant, who has a doctorate and juggles many balls as the mother of teenage twins, e-mailed me while I was working on this article: "You know what would help the vast majority of women with work/family balance? MAKE SCHOOL SCHEDULES MATCH WORK SCHEDULES." The present system, she noted, is based on a society that no longer exists—one in which farming was a major occupation and stay-at-home moms were the norm. Yet the system hasn't changed.

Consider some of the responses of women interviewed by Zenko about why "women are significantly underrepresented in foreign policy and national security positions in government, academia, and think tanks." Juliette Kayyem, who served as an assistant secretary in the Department of Homeland Security from 2009 to 2011 and now writes a foreign-policy and national-security column for *The Boston Globe,* told Zenko that among other reasons, the basic truth is also this: the travel sucks. As my youngest of three children is now 6, I can look back at the years when they were all young and realize just how disruptive all the travel was. There were also trips I couldn't take because I was pregnant or on leave, the conferences I couldn't attend because (note to conference organizers: weekends are a bad choice) kids would be home from school, and the various excursions that were offered but just couldn't be managed.

Jolynn Shoemaker, the director of Women in International Security, agreed: "Inflexible schedules, unrelenting travel, and constant pressure to be in the office are common features of these jobs."

These "mundane" issues—the need to travel constantly to succeed, the conflicts between school schedules and work schedules, the insistence that work be done in the office—cannot be solved by exhortations to close the ambition gap. I would hope to see commencement speeches that finger America's social and business policies, rather than women's level of ambition, in explaining the dearth of women at the top. But changing these policies requires much more than speeches. It means fighting the mundane battles—every day, every year—in individual workplaces, in legislatures, and in the media.

It's Possible If You Marry the Right Person

Sandberg's second message in her Barnard commencement address was: "The most important career decision you're going to make is whether or not you have a life partner and who that partner is." Lisa Jackson, the administrator of the Environmental Protection Agency, recently drove that message home to an audience of Princeton students and alumni gathered to hear her acceptance speech for the James Madison Medal. During the Q&A session, an audience member asked her how she managed her career and her family. She laughed and pointed to her husband in the front row, saying: "There's my work-life balance." I could never have had the career I have had without my husband, Andrew Moravcsik, who is a tenured professor of politics and international affairs at Princeton. Andy has spent more time with our sons than I have, not only on homework, but also on baseball, music lessons, photography, card games, and more. When each of them had to bring in a foreign dish for his fourth-grade class dinner, Andy made his grandmother's Hungarian *palacsinta;* when our older son needed to memorize his lines for a lead role in a school play, he turned to Andy for help.

Still, the proposition that women can have high-powered careers as long as their husbands or partners are willing to share the parenting load equally (or disproportionately) assumes that most women will *feel* as comfortable as men do about being away from their children, as long as their partner is home with them. In my experience, that is simply not the case.

Here I step onto treacherous ground, mined with stereotypes. From years of conversations and observations, however, I've come to believe that men and women respond quite differently when problems at home force them to recognize that their absence is hurting a child, or at least that their presence would likely help. I do not believe fathers love their children any less than mothers do, but men do seem more likely to choose their job at a cost to their family, while women seem more likely to choose their family at a cost to their job.

Many factors determine this choice, of course. Men are still socialized to believe that their primary family obligation is to be the breadwinner; women, to believe that their primary family obligation is to be the caregiver. But it may be more than that. When I described the choice between my children and my job to Senator Jeanne Shaheen, she said exactly what I felt: "There's really no choice." She wasn't referring to social expectations, but to a maternal imperative felt so deeply that the "choice" is reflexive.

Men and women also seem to frame the choice differently. In *Midlife Crisis at 30,* Mary Matalin recalls her days working as President Bush's assistant and Vice President Cheney's counselor:

> Even when the stress was overwhelming—those days when I'd cry in the car on the way to work, asking myself "Why am I doing this?"—I always knew the answer to that question: I believe in this president.

But Matalin goes on to describe her choice to leave in words that are again uncannily similar to the explanation I have given so many people since leaving the State Department:

> I finally asked myself, "Who needs me more?" And that's when I realized, it's somebody else's turn to do this job. I'm indispensable to my kids, but I'm not close to indispensable to the White House.

To many men, however, the choice to spend more time with their children, instead of working long hours on issues that affect many lives, seems selfish. Male leaders are routinely praised for having sacrificed their personal life on the altar of public or corporate service. That sacrifice, of course, typically involves their family. Yet their children, too, are trained to value public service over private responsibility. At the diplomat Richard Holbrooke's memorial service, one of his sons told the audience that when he was a child, his father was often gone, not around to teach him to throw a ball or to watch his games. But as he grew older, he said, he realized that Holbrooke's absence was the price of saving people around the world—a price worth paying.

It is not clear to me that this ethical framework makes sense for society. Why should we want leaders who fall short on personal responsibilities? Perhaps leaders who invested time in their own families would be more keenly aware of the toll their public choices—on issues from war to welfare—take on private lives. (Kati Marton, Holbrooke's widow and a noted author, says that although Holbrooke adored his children, he came to appreciate the full importance of family only in his 50s, at which point he became a very present parent and grandparent, while continuing to pursue an extraordinary public career.) Regardless, it is clear which set of choices society values more today. Workers who put their careers first are typically rewarded; workers who choose their families are overlooked, disbelieved, or accused of unprofessionalism.

In sum, having a supportive mate may well be a necessary condition if women are to have it all, but it is not sufficient. If women feel deeply that turning down a promotion that would involve more travel, for instance, is the right thing to do, then they will continue to do that. Ultimately, it is society that must change, coming to value choices to put family ahead of work just as much as those to put work ahead of family. If we really valued those choices, we would value the people who make them; if we valued the people who make them, we would do everything possible to hire and retain them; if we did everything possible to allow them to combine work and family equally over time, then the choices would get a lot easier.

It's Possible If You Sequence It Right

Young women should be wary of the assertion "You can have it all; you just can't have it all at once." This 21st-century addendum to the original line is now proffered by many senior women to their younger mentees. To the extent that it means, in the words of one working mother, "I'm going to do my best and I'm going to keep the long term in mind and know that it's not always going to be this hard to balance," it is sound advice. But to the extent that it means that women can have it all if they just find the right sequence of career and family, it's cheerfully wrong.

The most important sequencing issue is when to have children. Many of the top women leaders of the generation just ahead of me—Madeleine Albright, Hillary Clinton, Ruth Bader Ginsburg, Sandra Day O'Connor, Patricia Wald, Nannerl Keohane—had their children in their 20s and early 30s, as was the norm in the 1950s through the 1970s. A child born when his mother is 25 will finish high school when his mother is 43, an age at which, with full-time immersion in a career, she still has plenty of time and energy for advancement.

Yet this sequence has fallen out of favor with many high-potential women, and understandably so. People tend to marry later now, and anyway, if you have children earlier, you may have difficulty getting a graduate degree, a good first job, and opportunities for advancement in the crucial early years of your career. Making matters worse, you will also have less income while raising your children, and hence less ability to hire the help that can be indispensable to your juggling act.

When I was the dean, the Woodrow Wilson School created a program called Pathways to Public Service, aimed at advising women whose children were almost grown about how to go into public service, and many women still ask me about the best "on-ramps" to careers in their mid-40s. Honestly, I'm not sure what to tell most of them. Unlike the pioneering women who entered the workforce after having children in the 1970s, these women are competing with their younger selves. Government and NGO jobs are an option, but many careers are effectively closed off. Personally, I have never seen a woman in her 40s enter the academic market successfully, or enter a law firm as a junior associate, Alicia Florrick of *The Good Wife* notwithstanding.

These considerations are why so many career women of my generation chose to establish themselves in their careers first and have children in their mid-to-late 30s. But that raises the possibility of spending long, stressful years and a small fortune trying to have a baby. I lived that nightmare: for three years, beginning at age 35, I did everything possible to conceive and was frantic at the thought that I had simply left having a biological child until it was too late.

And when everything does work out? I had my first child at 38 (and counted myself blessed) and my second at 40. That means I will be 58 when both of my children are out of the house. What's more, it means that many peak career opportunities are coinciding precisely with their teenage years, when, experienced parents advise, being available as a parent is just as important as in the first years of a child's life.

Many women of my generation have found themselves, in the prime of their careers, saying no to opportunities they once would have jumped at and hoping those chances come around again later. Many others who have decided to step back for a while, taking on consultant positions or part-time work that lets them spend more time with their children (or aging parents), are worrying about how long they can "stay out" before they lose the competitive edge they worked so hard to acquire.

Given the way our work culture is oriented today, I recommend establishing yourself in your career first but still trying to have kids before you are 35—or else freeze your eggs, whether you are married or not. You may well be a more mature and less frustrated parent in your 30s or 40s; you are also more likely to have found a lasting life partner. But the truth is, neither sequence is optimal, and both involve trade-offs that men do not have to make.

You should be able to have a family if you want one—however and whenever your life circumstances allow—and still have the career you desire. If more women could strike this balance, more women would reach leadership positions. And if more women were in leadership positions, they could make it easier for more women to stay in the workforce. The rest of this essay details how.

Changing the Culture of Face Time

Back in the Reagan administration, a *New York Times* story about the ferociously competitive budget director Dick Darman reported, "Mr. Darman sometimes managed to convey the impression that he was the last one working in the Reagan White House by leaving his suit coat on his chair and his office light burning after he left for home." (Darman claimed that it was just easier to leave his suit jacket in the office so he could put it on again in the morning, but his record of psychological manipulation suggests otherwise.)

The culture of "time macho"—a relentless competition to work harder, stay later, pull more all-nighters, travel around the world and bill the extra hours that the international date line affords you—remains astonishingly prevalent among professionals today. Nothing captures the belief that more time equals more value better than the cult of billable hours afflicting large law firms across the country and providing exactly the wrong incentives for employees who hope to integrate work and family. Yet even in industries that don't explicitly reward sheer quantity of hours spent on the job, the pressure to arrive early, stay late, and be available, always, for in-person meetings at 11 a.m. on Saturdays can be intense. Indeed, by some measures, the problem has gotten worse over time: a study by the Center for American Progress reports that nationwide, the share of all professionals—women and men—working more than 50 hours a week has increased since the late 1970s.

But more time in the office does not always mean more "value added"—and it does not always add up to a more successful organization. In 2009, Sandra Pocharski, a senior female partner at Monitor Group and the head of the firm's Leadership and Organization practice, commissioned a Harvard Business School professor to assess the factors that helped or hindered women's effectiveness and advancement at Monitor. The study found that the company's culture was characterized by an "always on" mode of working, often without due regard to the impact on employees. Pocharski observed:

> Clients come first, always, and sometimes burning the midnight oil really does make the difference between success and failure. But sometimes we were just defaulting to behavior that overloaded our people without improving results much, if at all. We decided we needed managers to get better at distinguishing between these categories, and to recognize the hidden costs of assuming that "time is cheap." When that time doesn't add a lot of value and comes at a high cost to talented employees, who will leave when the personal cost becomes unsustainable—well, that is clearly a bad outcome for everyone.

I have worked very long hours and pulled plenty of all-nighters myself over the course of my career, including a few nights on my office couch during my two years in D.C. Being willing to put the time in when the job simply has to get done is rightfully a hallmark of a successful professional. But looking back, I have to admit that my assumption that I would stay late made me much less efficient over the course of the day than I might have been, and certainly less so than some of my colleagues, who

managed to get the same amount of work done and go home at a decent hour. If Dick Darman had a boss who clearly valued prioritization and time management, he might have found reason to turn out the lights and take his jacket home.

Long hours are one thing, and realistically, they are often unavoidable. But do they really need to be spent at the office? To be sure, being in the office *some* of the time is beneficial. In-person meetings can be far more efficient than phone or e-mail tag; trust and collegiality are much more easily built up around the same physical table; and spontaneous conversations often generate good ideas and lasting relationships. Still, armed with e-mail, instant messaging, phones, and videoconferencing technology, we should be able to move to a culture where the office is a base of operations more than the required locus of work.

Being able to work from home—in the evening after children are put to bed, or during their sick days or snow days, and at least some of the time on weekends—can be the key, for mothers, to carrying your full load versus letting a team down at crucial moments. State-of-the-art videoconferencing facilities can dramatically reduce the need for long business trips. These technologies are making inroads, and allowing easier integration of work and family life. According to the Women's Business Center, 61 percent of women business owners use technology to "integrate the responsibilities of work and home"; 44 percent use technology to allow employees "to work off-site or to have flexible work schedules." Yet our work culture still remains more office-centered than it needs to be, especially in light of technological advances.

One way to change that is by changing the "default rules" that govern office work—the baseline expectations about when, where, and how work will be done. As behavioral economists well know, these baselines can make an enormous difference in the way people act. It is one thing, for instance, for an organization to allow phone-ins to a meeting on an ad hoc basis, when parenting and work schedules collide—a system that's better than nothing, but likely to engender guilt among those calling in, and possibly resentment among those in the room. It is quite another for that organization to declare that its policy will be to schedule in-person meetings, whenever possible, during the hours of the school day—a system that might normalize call-ins for those (rarer) meetings still held in the late afternoon.

One real-world example comes from the British Foreign and Commonwealth Office, a place most people are more likely to associate with distinguished gentlemen in pinstripes than with progressive thinking about work-family balance. Like so many other places, however, the FCO worries about losing talented members of two-career couples around the world, particularly women. So it recently changed its basic policy from a default rule that jobs have to be done on-site to one that assumes that some jobs might be done remotely, and invites workers to make the case for remote work. Kara Owen, a career foreign-service officer who was the FCO's diversity director and will soon become the British deputy ambassador to France, writes that she has now done two remote jobs. Before her current maternity leave, she was working a London job from Dublin to be with her partner, using teleconferencing technology and timing her trips to London to coincide "with key meetings where I needed to be in the room (or chatting at the pre-meeting coffee) to have an impact, or to do intensive 'network maintenance.'" In fact, she writes, "I have found the distance and quiet to be a real advantage in a strategic role, providing I have put in the investment up front to develop very strong personal relationships with the game changers." Owen recognizes that not every job can be done this way. But she says that for her part, she has been able to combine family requirements with her career.

Changes in default office rules should not advantage parents over other workers; indeed, done right, they can improve relations among co-workers by raising their awareness of each other's circumstances and instilling a sense of fairness. Two years ago, the ACLU Foundation of Massachusetts decided to replace its "parental leave" policy with a "family leave" policy that provides for as much as 12 weeks of leave not only for new parents, but also for employees who need to care for a spouse, child, or parent with a serious health condition. According to Director Carol Rose, "We wanted a policy that took into account the fact that even employees who do not have children have family obligations." The policy was shaped by the belief that giving women "special treatment" can "backfire if the broader norms shaping the behavior of all employees do not change." When I was the dean of the Wilson School, I managed with the mantra "Family comes first"—any family—and found that my employees were both productive and intensely loyal.

None of these changes will happen by themselves, and reasons to avoid them will seldom be hard to find. But obstacles and inertia are usually surmountable if leaders are open to changing their assumptions about the workplace. The use of technology in many high-level government jobs, for instance, is complicated by the need to have access to classified information. But in 2009, Deputy Secretary of State James Steinberg, who shares the parenting of his two young daughters equally with his wife, made getting such access at home an immediate priority so that he could leave the office at a reasonable hour and participate in important meetings via videoconferencing if necessary. I wonder how many women in similar positions would be afraid to ask, lest they be seen as insufficiently committed to their jobs.

Revaluing Family Values

While employers shouldn't privilege parents over other workers, too often they end up doing the opposite, usually subtly, and usually in ways that make it harder for a primary caregiver to get ahead. Many people in positions of power seem to place a low value on child care in comparison with other outside activities. Consider the following proposition: An employer has two equally talented and productive employees. One trains for and runs marathons when he is not working. The other takes care of two children. What assumptions is the employer likely to make about the marathon runner? That he gets up in the dark every day and logs an hour or two running before even coming into the office, or drives himself to get out there even after a long day. That he is ferociously disciplined and willing to push himself through distraction, exhaustion, and days when nothing seems to go right in the service of a goal far in the distance. That he must manage his time exceptionally well to squeeze all of that in.

Be honest: Do you think the employer makes those same assumptions about the parent? Even though she likely rises in the dark hours before she needs to be at work, organizes her children's day, makes breakfast, packs lunch, gets them off to school, figures out shopping and other errands even if she is lucky enough to have a housekeeper—and does much the same work at the end of the day. Cheryl Mills, Hillary Clinton's indefatigable chief of staff, has twins in elementary school; even with a fully engaged husband, she famously gets up at four every morning to check and send e-mails before her kids wake up. Louise Richardson, now the vice chancellor of the University of St. Andrews, in Scotland, combined an assistant professorship in government at Harvard with mothering three young children. She organized her time so ruthlessly that she always keyed in 1:11 or 2:22 or 3:33 on the microwave rather than 1:00, 2:00, or 3:00, because hitting the same number three times took less time.

Elizabeth Warren, who is now running for the U.S. Senate in Massachusetts, has a similar story. When she had two young children and a part-time law practice, she struggled to find enough time to write the papers and articles that would help get her an academic position. In her words:

> I needed a plan. I figured out that writing time was when Alex was asleep. So the minute I put him down for a nap or he fell asleep in the baby swing, I went to my desk and started working on something—footnotes, reading, outlining, writing . . . I learned to do everything else with a baby on my hip.

The discipline, organization, and sheer endurance it takes to succeed at top levels with young children at home is easily comparable to running 20 to 40 miles a week. But that's rarely how employers see things, not only when making allowances, but when making promotions. Perhaps because people *choose* to have children? People also choose to run marathons.

One final example: I have worked with many Orthodox Jewish men who observed the Sabbath from sundown on Friday until sundown on Saturday. Jack Lew, the two-time director of the Office of Management and Budget, former deputy secretary of state for management and resources, and now White House chief of staff, is a case in point. Jack's wife lived in New York when he worked in the State Department, so he would leave the office early enough on Friday afternoon to take the shuttle to New York and a taxi to his apartment before sundown. He would not work on Friday after sundown or all day Saturday. Everyone who knew him, including me, admired his commitment to his faith and his ability to carve out the time for it, even with an enormously demanding job.

It is hard to imagine, however, that we would have the same response if a mother told us she was blocking out mid-Friday afternoon through the end of the day on Saturday, every week, to spend time with her children. I suspect this would be seen as unprofessional, an imposition of unnecessary costs on co-workers. In fact, of course, one of the great values of the Sabbath—whether Jewish or Christian—is precisely that it carves out a family oasis, with rituals and a mandatory settingaside of work.

Our assumptions are just that: things we believe that are not necessarily so. Yet what we assume has an enormous impact on our perceptions and responses. Fortunately, changing our assumptions is up to us.

Redefining the Arc of a Successful Career

The American definition of a successful professional is someone who can climb the ladder the furthest in the shortest time, generally peaking between ages 45 and 55. It is a definition well suited to the mid-20th century, an era when people had kids in their 20s, stayed in one job, retired at 67, and were dead, on average, by age 71.

It makes far less sense today. Average life expectancy for people in their 20s has increased to 80; men and women in good health can easily work until they are 75. They can expect to have multiple jobs and even multiple careers throughout their working life. Couples marry later, have kids later, and can expect to live on two incomes. They may well retire *earlier*—the average retirement age has gone down from 67 to 63—but that is commonly "retirement" only in the sense of collecting retirement benefits. Many people go on to "encore" careers.

Assuming the priceless gifts of good health and good fortune, a professional woman can thus expect her working life to stretch some 50 years, from her early or mid-20s to her mid-70s. It is reasonable to assume that she will build her credentials and establish herself, at least in her first career, between 22 and 35; she will have children, if she wants them, sometime between 25 and 45; she'll want maximum flexibility and control over her time in the 10 years that her children are 8 to 18; and she should plan to take positions of maximum authority and demands on her time after her children are out of the house. Women who have children in their late 20s can expect to immerse themselves completely in their careers in their late 40s, with plenty of time still to rise to the top in their late 50s and early 60s. Women who make partner, managing director, or senior vice president; get tenure; or establish a medical practice before having children in their late 30s should be coming back on line for the most demanding jobs at almost exactly the same age.

Along the way, women should think about the climb to leadership not in terms of a straight upward slope, but as irregular stair steps, with periodic plateaus (and even dips) when they turn down promotions to remain in a job that works for their family situation; when they leave high-powered jobs and spend a year or two at home on a reduced schedule; or when they step off a conventional professional track to take a consulting position or project-based work for a number of years. I think of these plateaus as "investment intervals." My husband and I took a sabbatical in Shanghai, from August 2007 to May 2008, right in the thick of an election year when many of my friends were advising various candidates on foreign-policy issues. We thought of the move in part as "putting money in the family bank," taking advantage of the opportunity to spend a close year together in a foreign culture. But we were also investing in our children's ability to learn Mandarin and in our own knowledge of Asia.

Peaking in your late 50s and early 60s rather than your late 40s and early 50s makes particular sense for women, who live longer than men. And many of the stereotypes about older workers simply do not hold. A 2006 survey of human-resources professionals shows that only 23 percent think older workers are less flexible than younger workers; only 11 percent think older workers require more training than younger workers; and only 7 percent think older workers have less drive than younger workers.

Whether women will really have the confidence to stair-step their careers, however, will again depend in part on perceptions. Slowing down the rate of promotions, taking time out periodically, pursuing an alternative path during crucial parenting or parent-care years—all have to become more visible and more noticeably accepted as a pause rather than an opt-out. (In an encouraging sign, *Mass Career Customization*, a 2007 book by Cathleen Benko and Anne Weisberg arguing that "today's career is no longer a straight climb up the corporate ladder, but rather a combination of climbs, lateral moves, and planned descents," was a *Wall Street Journal* best seller.)

Institutions can also take concrete steps to promote this acceptance. For instance, in 1970, Princeton established a tenure-extension policy that allowed female assistant professors expecting a child to request a one-year extension on their tenure clocks. This policy was later extended to men, and broadened to include adoptions. In the early 2000s, two reports on the status of female faculty discovered that only about 3 percent of assistant professors requested tenure extensions in a given year. And in response to a survey question, women were much more likely than men to think that a tenure extension would be detrimental to an assistant professor's career.

So in 2005, under President Shirley Tilghman, Princeton changed the default rule. The administration announced that all assistant professors, female and male, who had a new child would *automatically* receive a one-year extension on the tenure clock, with no opt-outs allowed. Instead, assistant professors could request early consideration for tenure if they wished. The number of assistant professors who receive a tenure extension has tripled since the change.

One of the best ways to move social norms in this direction is to choose and celebrate different role models. New Jersey Governor Chris Christie and I are poles apart politically, but he went way up in my estimation when he announced that one reason he decided against running for president in 2012 was the impact his campaign would have had on his children. He reportedly made clear at a fund-raiser in Louisiana that he didn't want to be away from his children for long periods of time; according to a Republican official at the event, he said that "his son [missed] him after being gone for the three days on the road, and that he needed to get back." He may not get my vote if and when he does run for president, but he definitely gets my admiration (providing he doesn't turn around and join the GOP ticket this fall).

If we are looking for high-profile female role models, we might begin with Michelle Obama. She started out with the same résumé as her husband, but has repeatedly made career decisions designed to let her do work she cared about and also be the kind of parent she wanted to be. She moved from a high-powered law firm first to Chicago city government and then to the University of Chicago shortly before her daughters were born, a move that let her work only 10 minutes away from home. She has spoken publicly and often about her initial concerns that her husband's entry into politics would be bad for their family life, and about her determination to limit her participation in the presidential election campaign to have more time at home. Even as first lady, she has been adamant that she be able to balance her official duties with family time. We should see her as a full-time career woman, but one who is taking a very visible investment interval. We should celebrate her not only as a wife, mother, and champion of healthy eating, but also as a woman who has had the courage and judgment to invest in her daughters when they need her most. And we should expect a glittering career from her after she leaves the White House and her daughters leave for college.

Rediscovering the Pursuit of Happiness

One of the most complicated and surprising parts of my journey out of Washington was coming to grips with what I really wanted. I had opportunities to stay on, and I could have tried to work out an arrangement allowing me to spend more time at home. I might have been able to get my family to join me in Washington for a year; I might have been able to get classified technology installed at my house the way Jim Steinberg did; I might have been able

to commute only four days a week instead of five. (While this last change would have still left me very little time at home, given the intensity of my job, it might have made the job doable for another year or two.) But I realized that I didn't just *need* to go home. Deep down, I *wanted* to go home. I wanted to be able to spend time with my children in the last few years that they are likely to live at home, crucial years for their development into responsible, productive, happy, and caring adults. But also irreplaceable years for me to enjoy the simple pleasures of parenting—baseball games, piano recitals, waffle breakfasts, family trips, and goofy rituals. My older son is doing very well these days, but even when he gives us a hard time, as all teenagers do, being home to shape his choices and help him make good decisions is deeply satisfying.

The flip side of my realization is captured in Macko and Rubin's ruminations on the importance of bringing the different parts of their lives together as 30-year-old women:

> If we didn't start to learn how to integrate our personal, social, and professional lives, we were about five years away from morphing into the angry woman on the other side of a mahogany desk who questions her staff's work ethic after standard 12-hour workdays, before heading home to eat moo shoo pork in her lonely apartment.

Women have contributed to the fetish of the one-dimensional life, albeit by necessity. The pioneer generation of feminists walled off their personal lives from their professional personas to ensure that they could never be discriminated against for a lack of commitment to their work. When I was a law student in the 1980s, many women who were then climbing the legal hierarchy in New York firms told me that they never admitted to taking time out for a child's doctor appointment or school performance, but instead invented a much more neutral excuse.

Today, however, women in power can and should change that environment, although change is not easy. When I became dean of the Woodrow Wilson School, in 2002, I decided that one of the advantages of being a woman in power was that I could help change the norms by deliberately talking about my children and my desire to have a balanced life. Thus, I would end faculty meetings at 6 p.m. by saying that I had to go home for dinner; I would also make clear to all student organizations that I would not come to dinner with them, because I needed to be home from six to eight, but that I would often be willing to come back after eight for a meeting. I also once told the Dean's Advisory Committee that the associate dean would chair the next session so I could go to a parent-teacher conference.

After a few months of this, several female assistant professors showed up in my office quite agitated. "You *have* to stop talking about your kids," one said. "You are not showing the gravitas that people expect from a dean, which is particularly damaging precisely because you are the first woman dean of the school." I told them that I was doing it deliberately and continued my practice, but it is interesting that gravitas and parenthood don't seem to go together.

Ten years later, whenever I am introduced at a lecture or other speaking engagement, I insist that the person introducing me mention that I have two sons. It seems odd to me to list degrees, awards, positions, and interests and *not* include the dimension of my life that is most important to me—and takes an enormous amount of my time. As Secretary Clinton once said in a television interview in Beijing when the interviewer asked her about Chelsea's upcoming wedding: "That's my real life." But I notice that my male introducers are typically uncomfortable when I make the request. They frequently say things like "And she particularly wanted me to mention that she has two sons"—thereby drawing attention to the unusual nature of my request, when my entire purpose is to make family references routine and normal in professional life.

This does not mean that you should insist that your colleagues spend time cooing over pictures of your baby or listening to the prodigious accomplishments of your kindergartner. It does mean that if you are late coming in one week, because it is your turn to drive the kids to school, that you be honest about what you are doing. Indeed, Sheryl Sandberg recently acknowledged not only that she leaves work at 5:30 to have dinner with her family, but also that for many years she did not dare make this admission, even though she would of course make up the work time later in the evening. Her willingness to speak out now is a strong step in the right direction.

Seeking out a more balanced life is not a women's issue; balance would be better for us all. Bronnie Ware, an Australian blogger who worked for years in palliative care and is the author of the 2011 book *The Top Five Regrets of the Dying*, writes that the regret she heard most often was "I wish I'd had the courage to live a life true to myself, not the life others expected of me." The second-most-common regret was "I wish I didn't work so hard." She writes: "This came from every male patient that I nursed. They missed their children's youth and their partner's companionship."

Juliette Kayyem, who several years ago left the Department of Homeland Security soon after her husband, David Barron, left a high position in the Justice Department, says their joint decision to leave Washington and return to Boston sprang from their desire to work on the *"happiness project,"* meaning quality time with their three children. (She borrowed the term from her friend Gretchen Rubin, who wrote a best-selling book and now runs a blog with that name.)

It's time to embrace a national happiness project. As a daughter of Charlottesville, Virginia, the home of Thomas Jefferson and the university he founded, I grew up with the Declaration of Independence in my blood. Last I checked, he did not declare American independence in the name of life, liberty, and professional success. Let us rediscover the pursuit of happiness, and let us start at home.

Innovation Nation

As I write this, I can hear the reaction of some readers to many of the proposals in this essay: It's all fine and well for a tenured professor to write about flexible working hours, investment intervals, and family-comes-first management. But what about the real world? Most American women cannot demand these things, particularly in a bad economy, and their employers have little incentive to grant them voluntarily. Indeed, the most frequent reaction I get in putting forth these ideas is that when the choice is whether to hire a man who will work whenever and wherever needed, or a woman who needs more flexibility, choosing the man will add more value to the company.

In fact, while many of these issues are hard to quantify and measure precisely, the statistics seem to tell a different story. A seminal study of 527 U.S. companies, published in the *Academy of Management Journal* in 2000, suggests that "organizations with more extensive work-family policies have higher perceived firm-level performance" among their industry peers. These findings accorded with a 2003 study conducted by Michelle Arthur at the University of New Mexico. Examining 130 announcements of family-friendly policies in *The Wall Street Journal*, Arthur found that the announcements alone significantly improved share prices. In 2011, a study on flexibility in the workplace by Ellen Galinsky, Kelly Sakai, and Tyler Wigton of the Families and Work Institute showed that increased flexibility correlates positively with job engagement, job satisfaction, employee retention, and employee health.

This is only a small sampling from a large and growing literature trying to pin down the relationship between family-friendly policies and economic performance. Other scholars have concluded that good family policies attract better talent, which in turn raises productivity, but that the policies themselves have no impact on productivity. Still others argue that results attributed to these policies are actually a function of good management overall. What is evident, however, is that many firms that recruit and train well-educated professional women are aware that when a woman leaves because of bad work-family balance, they are losing the money and time they invested in her.

Even the legal industry, built around the billable hour, is taking notice. Deborah Epstein Henry, a former big-firm litigator, is now the president of Flex-Time Lawyers, a national consulting firm focused partly on strategies for the retention of female attorneys. In her book *Law and Reorder*, published by the American Bar Association in 2010, she describes a legal profession "where the billable hour no longer works"; where attorneys, judges, recruiters, and academics all agree that this system of compensation has perverted the industry, leading to brutal work hours, massive inefficiency, and highly inflated costs. The answer—already being deployed in different corners of the industry—is a combination of alternative fee structures, virtual firms, women-owned firms, and the outsourcing of discrete legal jobs to other jurisdictions. Women, and

Generation X and Y lawyers more generally, are pushing for these changes on the supply side; clients determined to reduce legal fees and increase flexible service are pulling on the demand side. Slowly, change is happening.

At the core of all this is self-interest. Losing smart and motivated women not only diminishes a company's talent pool; it also reduces the return on its investment in training and mentoring. In trying to address these issues, some firms are finding out that women's ways of working may just be better ways of working, for employees and clients alike.

Experts on creativity and innovation emphasize the value of encouraging nonlinear thinking and cultivating randomness by taking long walks or looking at your environment from unusual angles. In their new book, *A New Culture of Learning: Cultivating the Imagination for a World of Constant Change*, the innovation gurus John Seely Brown and Douglas Thomas write, "We believe that connecting play and imagination may be the single most important step in unleashing the new culture of learning."

Space for play and imagination is exactly what emerges when rigid work schedules and hierarchies loosen up. Skeptics should consider the "California effect." California is the cradle of American innovation—in technology, entertainment, sports, food, and lifestyles. It is also a place where people take leisure as seriously as they take work; where companies like Google deliberately encourage play, with Ping-Pong tables, light sabers, and policies that require employees to spend one day a week working on whatever they wish. Charles Baudelaire wrote: "Genius is nothing more nor less than childhood recovered at will." Google apparently has taken note.

No parent would mistake child care for childhood. Still, seeing the world anew through a child's eyes can be a powerful source of stimulation. When the Nobel laureate Thomas Schelling wrote *The Strategy of Conflict*, a classic text applying game theory to conflicts among nations, he frequently drew on child-rearing for examples of when deterrence might succeed or fail. "It may be easier to articulate the peculiar difficulty of constraining [a ruler] by the use of threats," he wrote, "when one is fresh from a vain attempt at using threats to keep a small child from hurting a dog or a small dog from hurting a child."

The books I've read with my children, the silly movies I've watched, the games I've played, questions I've answered, and people I've met while parenting have broadened my world. Another axiom of the literature on innovation is that the more often people with different perspectives come together, the more likely creative ideas are to emerge. Giving workers the ability to integrate their non-work lives with their work—whether they spend that time mothering or marathoning—will open the door to a much wider range of influences and ideas.

Enlisting Men

Perhaps the most encouraging news of all for achieving the sorts of changes that I have proposed is that men are joining the cause. In commenting on a draft of this article,

Martha Minow, the dean of the Harvard Law School, wrote me that one change she has observed during 30 years of teaching law at Harvard is that today many young men are asking questions about how they can manage a work-life balance. And more systematic research on Generation Y confirms that many more men than in the past are asking questions about how they are going to integrate active parenthood with their professional lives.

Abstract aspirations are easier than concrete trade-offs, of course. These young men have not yet faced the question of whether they are prepared to give up that more prestigious clerkship or fellowship, decline a promotion, or delay their professional goals to spend more time with their children and to support their partner's career.

Yet once work practices and work culture begin to evolve, those changes are likely to carry their own momentum. Kara Owen, the British foreign-service officer who worked a London job from Dublin, wrote me in an e-mail:

> I think the culture on flexible working started to change the minute the Board of Management (who were all men at the time) started to work flexibly—quite a few of them started working one day a week from home.

Men have, of course, become much more involved parents over the past couple of decades, and that, too, suggests broad support for big changes in the way we balance work and family. It is noteworthy that both James Steinberg, deputy secretary of state, and William Lynn, deputy secretary of defense, stepped down two years into the Obama administration so that they could spend more time with their children (for real).

Going forward, women would do well to frame work-family balance in terms of the broader social and economic issues that affect both women and men. After all, we have a new generation of young men who have been raised by full-time working mothers. Let us presume, as I do with my sons, that they will understand "supporting their families" to mean more than earning money.

I HAVE BEEN BLESSED to work with and be mentored by some extraordinary women. Watching Hillary Clinton in action makes me incredibly proud—of her intelligence, expertise, professionalism, charisma, and command of any audience. I get a similar rush when I see a frontpage picture of Christine Lagarde, the managing director of the International Monetary Fund, and Angela Merkel, the chancellor of Germany, deep in conversation about some of the most important issues on the world stage; or of Susan Rice, the U.S. ambassador to the United Nations, standing up forcefully for the Syrian people in the Security Council.

These women are extraordinary role models. If I had a daughter, I would encourage her to look to them, and I want a world in which they are extraordinary but not unusual. Yet I also want a world in which, in Lisa Jackson's words, "to be a strong woman, you don't have to give up on the things that define you as a woman." That means respecting, enabling, and indeed celebrating the full range of women's choices. "Empowering yourself," Jackson said in her speech at Princeton, "doesn't have to mean rejecting motherhood, or eliminating the nurturing or feminine aspects of who you are."

I gave a speech at Vassar last November and arrived in time to wander the campus on a lovely fall afternoon. It is a place infused with a spirit of community and generosity, filled with benches, walkways, public art, and quiet places donated by alumnae seeking to encourage contemplation and connection. Turning the pages of the alumni magazine (Vassar is now coed), I was struck by the entries of older alumnae, who greeted their classmates with *Salve* (Latin for "hello") and wrote witty remembrances sprinkled with literary allusions. Theirs was a world in which women wore their learning lightly; their news is mostly of their children's accomplishments. Many of us look back on that earlier era as a time when it was fine to joke that women went to college to get an "M.R.S." And many women of my generation abandoned the Seven Sisters as soon as the formerly all-male Ivy League universities became coed. I would never return to the world of segregated sexes and rampant discrimination. But now is the time to revisit the assumption that women must rush to adapt to the "man's world" that our mothers and mentors warned us about.

I continually push the young women in my classes to speak more. They must gain the confidence to value their own insights and questions, and to present them readily. My husband agrees, but he actually tries to get the young men in his classes to act more like the women—to speak less and listen more. If women are ever to achieve real equality as leaders, then we have to stop accepting male behavior and male choices as the default and the ideal. We must insist on changing social policies and bending career tracks to accommodate *our* choices, too. We have the power to do it if we decide to, and we have many men standing beside us.

We'll create a better society in the process, for *all* women. We may need to put a woman in the White House before we are able to change the conditions of the women working at Walmart. But when we do, we will stop talking about whether women can have it all. We will properly focus on how we can help all Americans have healthy, happy, productive lives, valuing the people they love as much as the success they seek.

ANNE-MARIE SLAUGHTER is the Bert G. Kerstetter '66 University Professor of Politics and International Affairs at Princeton University and formerly dean of Princeton's Woodrow Wilson School of Public and International Affairs. She is currently the president and CEO of the New America Foundation, a public policy institute and idea incubator based in Washington and New York.

EXPLORING THE ISSUE

Can Women Have It All?

Critical Thinking and Reflection

1. The debate about leaning in is largely limited to professional women because that is the group that can afford to choose to lean in or opt out. What hypotheses would you make about the desires of nonprofessional women based on the behavior of professional women?
2. Note two facts. First, the percentage of mothers with at-home children that were working in the labor force increased until the 1990s and then leveled off. Second, a noticeable number of professional women who could afford to were opting out. Linda Hirshman concludes from these facts that "the belief that women are responsible for childrearing and homemaking was largely untouched by decades of workplace feminism." Do a critique of this conclusion.
3. How does the fact that many mothers return to the labor force when their children are of school age and more return when their children leave home impact your view of this debate?
4. What public policies would improve the lives of women with work/family tensions?
5. What is your judgment about the companies that have a "mommy track" policy?

Is There Common Ground?

Both authors want what is best for women and are upset about the situation that they analyze. Both would like societal arrangements to reduce the conflict between work and family. Both want women to be able to have it all. Their debate is over how possible it is to have it all. Gayle Tzemach Lemmon thinks they can have it all but it will not be easy. They will have to "lean in," which involves strength and determination. Anne-Marie Slaughter argues that the cost is generally too high. Women should put family first and career second. They can still have careers but must pursue them in ways that do not sacrifice too much for the family. I know that I would feel very deprived if I had to quit my professor's job to raise children even though children are a great joy. But I do not have to make this choice. This is what is obviously unfair about this issue. It is mostly a female problem. Men are not expected to quit their jobs and stay home and raise their children. Some, in fact, are doing just this since their wives are making far more money than they can, but this is rare. Society and religious groups generally preach that the wife should put family before work, so the stress is generally on women.

Create Central

www.mhhe.com/createcentral

Additional Resources

Women who quit careers to go home to raise a family are said to "opt out." For analyses of the opt out phenomenon look at: Pamela Stone, *Opting Out?: Why Women Really Quit Careers and Head Home* (University of California Press, 2007); Lisa A. Mainiero and Sherry E. Sullivan, *The Opt-Out Revolt* (Davies-Black, 2006); Phyllis Moen, *The Career*

Mystique (Rowan & Littlefield, 2005); Ann Crittenden, *The Price of Motherhood* (Metropolitan Books, 2001); and Susan Chira, *A Mother's Place: Choosing Work and Family Without Guilt or Shame* (Perennial, 1999).

Some who advocate for "leaning in" and against opting out are: Leslie Bennetts, who strongly advises women not to give up their careers in *The Feminine Mistake* (Voice/Hyperion, 2007), and Sylvia Ann Hewlett does the same in *Off-Ramps and On-Ramps: Keeping Talented Women on the Road to Success* (Harvard Business School Press, 2007).

For discussions of the demands of work and family on women, see: Suzanne M. Bianchi, John P. Robinson, and Melissa Milkie, *Changing Rhythms of Family Life* (American Sociological Association, 2006); Susan Thistle, *From Marriage to the Market* (University of California Press, 2006); Arlie Russell Hochschild, *The Second Shift* (Penguin Books, 2003); and Anna Fels, *Necessary Dreams: Ambition in Women's Changing Lives* (Pantheon Book, 2004). Mary Eberstadt is the major critic of the working mothers who leave much of the childrearing to others. See her *Home-Alone America: The Hidden Toll of Daycare, Behavioral Drugs, and Other Parent Substitutes* (Penguin, 2004).

On the issue of time scarcity and time use, which factors into the debate on the tension between work and family, see: *Fighting for Time: Shifting Boundaries of Work and Social Life*, edited by Cynthia Fuchs-Epstein and Arne L. Kalleberg (Russell Sage Foundation, 2004); Phyllis Moen, *It's About Time: Couples and Careers* (Cornell University Press, 2003); Harriet B. Presser, *Working in a 24/7 Economy: Challenges for American Families* (Russell Sage Foundation, 2003); John Robinson and Geoffrey Godbey, *Time for Life: The Surprising Ways Americans Use Their Time*, 2nd ed. (State University Press, 1999); Juliet Schor, *The Overworked American: The Unexpected Decline of Leisure* (Basic Books, 1991); and Jerry A. Jacobs and Kathleen Gerson, *The Time Divide: Work, Family, and Gender Inequality* (Harvard University Press, 2004).

Internet References . . .

National Council on Family Research

www.ncfr.com

Sociology—Study Sociology Online

http://edu.learnsoc.org/

Sociology Web Resources

www.mhhe.com/socscience/sociology/resources
/index.htm

Sociosite

www.topsite.com/goto/sociosite.net

Socioweb

www.topsite.com/goto/socioweb.com

Selected, Edited, and with Issue Framing Material by:
Kurt Finsterbusch, *University of Maryland, College Park*

ISSUE

Is Same-Sex Marriage Harmful to America?

YES: **Peter Sprigg**, from "The Top Ten Harms of Same-Sex 'Marriage,'" website of the *Family Research Council* (2013)

NO: **Liza Mundy**, from "The Gay Guide to Wedded Bliss," *The Atlantic* Magazine (June 2013)

Learning Outcomes

After reading this issue, you should be able to:

- Understand the potential force of traditions in delegitimizing proposed changes that counter them.
- Understand the importance of other traditions and strongly held values in supporting changes that seem to oppose accepted traditions.
- Observe how the way the issue is defined affects the success or failure of the change efforts.
- Analyze how the political system and its laws can be ahead of the public on changing institutions or can lag behind the public.
- Understand the arguments and the values that underpin the support for and the opposition against same-sex marriage.

ISSUE SUMMARY

YES: Peter Sprigg, Senior Fellow for Policy Studies at the Family Research Council, identifies 10 negative effects of same-sex marriages. Many of these worries concern how various institutions are likely to change as a result of same-sex marriages, and how authorities are likely to change their regulations and enforcement practices.

NO: Liza Mundy, a Bernard L. Schwartz Fellow at the New America Foundation and author of *The Richer Sex: How the New Majority of Female Breadwinners Is Transforming Our Culture,* reports on the numerous studies that show that same-sex marriages are more intimate, more egalitarian, less conflictful, and happier than heterosexual marriages.

In 1979, in Sioux Falls, South Dakota, Randy Rohl and Grady Quinn became the first acknowledged homosexual couple in America to receive permission from their high school principal to attend the senior prom together. The National Gay Task Force hailed the event as a milestone in the progress of human rights. It is unclear what the voters of Sioux Falls thought about it, because it was not put up to a vote. However, if their views were similar to those of voters in Dade County, Florida; Houston, Texas; Wichita, Kansas; and various localities in the state of Oregon, they probably were not pleased. In referenda held in these and other areas, voters have reversed decisions by legislators and local boards that banned discrimination by sexual preference.

Yet the attitude of Americans toward the rights of homosexuals is not easy to pin down. Voters have also defeated resolutions such as the one in California in 1978 that would have banned the hiring of homosexual schoolteachers, or the one on the Oregon ballot in 1992 identifying homosexuality as "abnormal, wrong, unnatural, and perverse." In some states, notably Colorado, voters have approved initiatives widely perceived as antihomosexual. But, almost invariably, these resolutions have been carefully worded so as to appear to oppose "special" rights for homosexuals. In general, polls show that a large majority of Americans believe that homosexuals should have equal rights with heterosexuals with regard to job opportunities. On the other hand, many view homosexuality as morally wrong. These developments prompted President Bush to propose a constitutional amendment limiting marriage to the union of a man and a woman, but this law did not pass Congress.

Since 2001, ten countries have legalized same-sex marriages nationwide, but currently, same-sex marriages are not legally recognized by Congress. In the Defense of

Marriage Act of 1996, Congress defined marriage as heterosexual. A state does not have to recognize another state's nonheterosexual marriage. The legal situation is constantly changing. The states that have legalized same-sex marriages are Connecticut, the District of Columbia, Iowa, Massachusetts, New Hampshire, New York, Vermont, and most recently, Maryland. However, 31 states have constitutional restrictions limiting marriage to one man and one woman. By the time this book is published the situation will probably change. Activists on both sides are constantly introducing legislation on same-sex marriages and gay rights. This is not only a civil rights issue but also a moral, religious, social, and political issue that can be sliced and diced in many ways. President Obama preferred to keep the term marriage for heterosexual couples but to legalize same-sex civil unions with almost all the rights of married couples. Recently he changed his view and approved same-sex marriages. There are many other positions on gay rights as people try to balance their moral, religious, and political values. On the other hand, the issue is a legal matter and new legislation for or against same-sex marriages must conform to the constitution and various standing civil rights laws.

One argument in support of same-sex marriage is that marriage conveys many important benefits on the couple, and denying same-sex couples legal access to marriage represents discrimination based on sexual orientation, which should violate our civil rights laws. They would be denied many financial, psychological, and physical well-being benefits and their children would grow up in a less conducive atmosphere. A serious question is whether legalized civil unions would convey all these benefits or whether the word marriage is necessary. Of course, those who think that even civil unions for same-sex couples are morally and religiously wrong would oppose such civil unions.

The issue of same-sex marriage fascinates sociologists because it represents a basic change in a major social institution and is being played out on several fields: legal, cultural/moral, and behavioral. The legal debate will be decided by courts and legislatures; the cultural/moral debate is open to all of us; and the behavioral debate will be conducted by the activists on both sides. In the selections that follow, Peter Sprigg argues that marriage must remain heterosexual while Liza Mundy presents the major arguments for same-sex marriages.

YES

Peter Sprigg

The Top Ten Harms of Same-Sex "Marriage"

Some advocates of same-sex "marriage" scoff at the idea that it could harm anyone. Here are ten ways in which society could be harmed by legalizing same-sex "marriage." Most of these effects would become evident only in the long run, but several would occur immediately.

Immediate Effects

Taxpayers, Consumers, and Businesses Would Be Forced to Subsidize Homosexual Relationships

One of the key arguments often heard in support of homosexual civil "marriage" revolves around all the government "benefits" that homosexuals claim they are denied. Many of these "benefits" involve one thing—taxpayer money that homosexuals are eager to get their hands on. For example, one of the goals of homosexual activists is to take part in the biggest government entitlement program of all—Social Security. Homosexuals want their partners to be eligible for Social Security survivors benefits when one partner dies.

The fact that Social Security survivors benefits were intended to help stay-at-home mothers who did not have retirement benefits from a former employer has not kept homosexuals from demanding the benefit.[1] Homosexual activists are also demanding that children raised by a homosexual couple be eligible for benefits when one of the partners dies—even if the deceased partner was not the child's biological or adoptive parent. . . .

Imagine, though, what the impact on employee benefit programs would be if homosexual "marriage" is legalized nationwide. Right now, marriage still provides a clear, bright line, both legally and socially, to distinguish those who receive dependent benefits and those who don't. But if homosexual couples are granted the full legal status of civil "marriage," then employers who do not want to grant benefits to homosexual partners—whether out of principle, or simply because of a prudent economic judgment—would undoubtedly be coerced by court orders to do so.

Schools Would Teach That Homosexual Relationships Are Identical to Heterosexual Ones

The advocates of same-sex "marriage" argue that it will have little impact on anyone other than the couples who "marry." However, even the brief experience in Massachusetts, where same-sex "marriage" was imposed by the state's Supreme Judicial Court and began on May 17, 2004, has demonstrated that the impact of such a social revolution will extend much further—including into the public schools. In September 2004, National Public Radio reported, "Already, some gay and lesbian advocates are working on a new gay-friendly curriculum for kindergarten and up." They also featured an interview with Deb Allen, a lesbian who teaches eighth-grade sex education in Brookline, Mass. Allen now feels "emboldened" in teaching a "gay-friendly" curriculum, declaring, "If somebody wants to challenge me, I'll say, 'Give me a break. It's legal now.'" Her lessons include descriptions of homosexual sex given "thoroughly and explicitly with a chart." Allen reports she will ask her students, "Can a woman and a woman have vaginal intercourse, and they will all say no. And I'll say, 'Hold it. Of course, they can. They can use a sex toy. They could use'—and we talk—and we discuss that. So the answer there is yes."[2] . . .

Freedom of Conscience and Religious Liberty Would Be Threatened

Another important and immediate result of same-sex "marriage" would be serious damage to religious liberty. . . .

Some of these threats to religious liberty can arise from "nondiscrimination" laws based on sexual orientation, even without same-sex "marriage." But when homosexual "marriage" becomes legal, then laws which once applied to homosexuals only as individuals then apply to homosexual couples as well. So, for example, when Catholic Charities in Boston insisted that they would stay true to principle and refuse to place children for adoption with same-sex couples, they were told by the state that they could no longer do adoptions at all.[3]

In other cases, a variety of benefits or opportunities that the state makes available to religious nonprofits could be withheld based on the organization's refusal to treat same-sex couples and "marriages" the same as opposite-sex marriages. Organizations might be denied government grants or aid otherwise available to faith-based groups; they might be denied access to public facilities for events; and they might even have their tax-exempt status removed.[4] That is what happened to the Ocean Grove Camp Meeting Association in New Jersey when they refused to rent facilities for a lesbian "civil union" ceremony.[5] . . .

Religious liberty is one of the deepest American values. We must not sacrifice it on the altar of political correctness that homosexual "marriage" would create.

Long-Term Effects

Fewer People Would Marry

Even where legal recognition and marital rights and benefits are available to same-sex couples (whether through same-sex civil "marriages," "civil unions," or "domestic partnerships"), *relatively few same-sex couples even bother to seek such recognition or claim such benefits.*

The most simple way to document this is by comparing the number of same-sex couples who have sought such legal recognition in a given state[6] with the number of "same-sex unmarried-partner households" in the most recent U.S. Census.[7]

When a relatively small percentage of same-sex couples—even among those already living together as partners—even bother to seek legal recognition of their relationships, while an overwhelming majority of heterosexual couples who live together are legally married, it suggests that homosexuals are far more likely than heterosexuals to *reject the institution of marriage* or its legal equivalent. . . .

These figures show that a large percentage, and possibly even an outright majority, of homosexuals—even those already living with a partner—neither need nor desire to participate in the institution of marriage. Legalizing same-sex "marriage" would be very effective in sending a message of endorsement of homosexual behavior. But the indifference of most homosexuals to "marriage" would send a message to society that marriage does not matter—that it is no longer the normative setting for sexual relations and child-rearing, but is instead nothing more than one relationship option among many, made available as a government entitlement program to those who seek taxpayer-funded benefits.

Couples who could marry, but choose instead to cohabit without the benefit of marriage, harm the institution of marriage by setting an example for other couples, making non-marital cohabitation seem more acceptable as well. If same-sex "marriage" were legalized, the evidence suggests that the percentage of homosexual couples who would choose cohabitation over "marriage" would be much larger than the current percentage of heterosexual couples who choose cohabitation over marriage. It is likely that the poor example set by homosexual couples would,

over time, lead to lower marriage rates among heterosexuals as well.[8]

Fewer People Would Remain Monogamous and Sexually Faithful

One value that remains remarkably strong, even among people who have multiple sexual partners before marriage, is the belief that marriage itself is a sexually exclusive relationship. Among married heterosexuals, having sexual relations with anyone other than one's spouse is still considered a grave breach of trust and a violation of the marriage covenant by the vast majority of people.

Yet the same cannot be said of homosexuals—particularly of homosexual men. Numerous studies of homosexual relationships, including "partnered" relationships, covering a span of decades, have shown that sex with multiple partners is tolerated and often expected, even when one has a "long-term" partner. Perhaps the most startling of these studies was published in the journal *AIDS*. In the context of studying HIV risk behavior among young homosexual men in the Netherlands (coincidentally, the first country in the world to legalize homosexual civil "marriage"), the researchers found that homosexual men who were *in partnered relationships* had an *average* of eight sexual partners *per year* outside of the primary relationship.[9] (It must be conceded that having such a partnership did have some "taming" effect upon such men—those without a "permanent" partner had an average of 22 sexual partners per year). This is an astonishing contrast to the typical behavior of married heterosexuals, among whom 75% of the men and 85% of the women report *never* having had extra-marital sex even once during the entire duration of their marriage.[10] . . .

Fewer People Would Remain Married for a Lifetime

Lawrence Kurdek, a homosexual psychologist from Ohio's Wright State University,[11] who has done extensive research on the nature of homosexual relationships, has correctly stated, "Perhaps the most important 'bottom-line' question about gay and lesbian couples is whether their relationships last."[12] After extensive research, he determined that "it is safe to conclude that gay and lesbian couples dissolve their relationships more frequently than heterosexual couples, especially heterosexual couples with children."[13]

Once again, abundant research has borne out this point. Older studies came to similar conclusions. In one study of 156 male couples, for instance, only seven had been together for longer than five years (and none of those seven had remained sexually faithful to each other).[14] . . .

How would this affect heterosexual couples? If the unstable nature of homosexual partnerships becomes part of the ideal of marriage that is being held up to society, it will inevitably affect the future behavior of everyone in society—heterosexuals included. Therefore, we can predict the following:

If homosexual "marriage" is legalized, the percentage of homosexual couples that remain together for a lifetime will always be lower than the percentage of heterosexual couples that do so; but the percentage of heterosexual couples demonstrating lifelong commitment will also decline, to the harm of society as a whole.

Fewer Children Would Be Raised by a Married Mother and Father

The greatest tragedy resulting from the legalization of homosexual "marriage" would not be its effect on adults, but its effect on children. For the first time in history, society would be placing its highest stamp of official government approval on the *deliberate* creation of *permanently* motherless or fatherless households for children.

There simply cannot be any serious debate, based on the mass of scholarly literature available to us, about the ideal family form for children. It consists of a mother and father who are committed to one another in marriage. Children raised by their married mother and father experience lower rates of many social pathologies, including:

- premarital childbearing;[15]
- illicit drug use;[16]
- arrest;[17]
- health, emotional, or behavioral problems;[18]
- poverty;[19]
- or school failure or expulsion.[20]

These benefits are then passed on to future generations as well, because children raised by their married mother and father are themselves less likely to cohabit or to divorce as adults.[21]

In a perfect world, every child would have that kind of household provided by his or her own loving and capable biological parents (and every husband and wife who wanted children would be able to conceive them together). Of course, we do not live in a perfect world. . . .

As scholar Stanley Kurtz says,

If, as in Norway, gay "marriage" were imposed here by a socially liberal cultural elite, it would likely speed us on the way toward the classic Nordic pattern of less frequent marriage, more frequent out-of-wedlock birth, and skyrocketing family dissolution. In the American context, this would be a disaster.[22]

More Children Would Grow Up Fatherless

This harm is closely related to the previous one, but worth noting separately. As more children grow up without a married mother and father, they will be deprived of the tangible and intangible benefits and security that come from that family structure. However, most of those who live with only one biological parent will live with their mothers. In the general population, 79% of single-parent households are headed by the mother, compared to only 10% which are headed by the father.[23] Among homosexual couples, as identified in the 2000 census, 34% of lesbian couples have children living at home, while only 22% of male couples were raising children.[24] The encouragement of homosexual relationships that is intrinsic in the legalization of same-sex "marriage" would thus result in an increase in the number of children who suffer a specific set of negative consequences that are clearly associated with fatherlessness.

Homosexual activists say that having both a mother and a father simply does not matter—it is having two loving parents that counts. But social science research simply does not support this claim. Dr. Kyle Pruett of Yale Medical School, for example, has demonstrated in his book *Fatherneed* that fathers contribute to parenting in ways that mothers do not. Pruett declares, "From deep within their biological and psychological being, children need to connect to fathers . . . to live life whole."[25]

Children—both sons and daughters—suffer without a father in their lives. The body of evidence supporting this conclusion is both large and growing.[26] For example, research has shown that "youth incarceration risks in a national male cohort were elevated for adolescents in father-absent households," even after controlling for other factors.[27] Among daughters, "father absence was strongly associated with elevated risk for early sexual activity and adolescent pregnancy."[28] Author David Blankenhorn puts these risks more succinctly: "One primary result of growing fatherlessness is more boys with guns. Another is more girls with babies."[29] Even researchers who are supportive of homosexual parenting have had to admit that "children raised in fatherless families from infancy," while closer to their mothers, "perceived themselves to be less cognitively and physically competent than their peers from father-present families."[30]

Some lesbian couples are deliberately *creating* new children in order to raise them fatherless from birth. It is quite striking to read, for example, the model "Donor Agreement" for sperm donors offered on the Human Rights Campaign website, and to see the lengths to which they will go to legally insure that the actual biological father plays no role in the life of a lesbian mother's child.[31] Yet a recent study of children conceived through sperm donation found, "Donor offspring are significantly more likely than those raised by their biological parents to struggle with serious, negative outcomes such as delinquency, substance abuse, and depression, even when controlling for socio-economic and other factors."[32] Remarkably, 38% of donor offspring born to lesbian couples in the study agreed that "it is wrong deliberately to conceive a fatherless child."[33]

Birth Rates Would Fall

One of the most fundamental tasks of any society is to reproduce itself. That is why virtually every human society up until the present day has given a privileged social status to male-female sexual relationships—the only type capable of resulting in natural procreation. This privileged social status is what we call "marriage."

Extending the benefits and status of "marriage" to couples who are intrinsically incapable of natural procreation (i.e., two men or two women) would dramatically change the social meaning of the institution. It would become impossible to argue that "marriage" is about encouraging the formation of life-long, potentially procreative (i.e., opposite-sex) relationships. The likely long-term result would be that fewer such relationships would be formed, fewer such couples would choose to procreate, and fewer babies would be born.

There is already evidence of at least a *correlation* between low birth rates and the legalization of same-sex "marriage." At this writing, five U.S. states grant marriage licenses to same-sex couples. As of 2007, the last year for which complete data are available, four of those five states ranked within the bottom eight out of all fifty states in both birth rate (measured in relation to the total population) and fertility rate (measured in relation to the population of women of childbearing age).[34] . . .

The contribution of same-sex "marriage" to declining birth rates would clearly lead to significant harm for society.

Demands for Legalization of Polygamy Would Grow

If the natural sexual complementarity of male and female and the theoretical procreative capacity of an opposite-sex union are to be discarded as principles central to the definition of marriage, then what is left? According to the arguments of the homosexual "marriage" advocates, only love and companionship are truly necessary elements of marriage.

But if that is the case, then why should *other* relationships that provide love, companionship, and a lifelong commitment not *also* be recognized as "marriages"—including relationships between adults and children, or between blood relatives, or between three or more adults? And if it violates the equal protection of the laws to deny homosexuals their first choice of marital partner, why would it not do the same to deny pedophiles, polygamists, or the incestuous the right to marry the person (or persons) of their choice?

Of these, the road to polygamy seems the best-paved—and it is the most difficult for homosexual "marriage" advocates to deny. If, as they claim, it is arbitrary and unjust to limit the *gender* of one's marital partner, it is hard to explain why it would not be equally arbitrary and unjust to limit the *number* of marital partners.

There are also two other reasons why same-sex "marriage" advocates have trouble refuting warnings of a slippery slope toward polygamy. The first is that there is far more precedent cross-culturally for polygamy as an accepted marital structure than there is for homosexual "marriage." The second is that there is a genuine movement for polygamy or "polyamory" in some circles. . . .

The "gay" oriented newspaper the *Washington Blade* has also featured this topic in a full-page article under the headline "Polygamy advocates buoyed by gay court wins." It quotes Art Spitzer of the American Civil Liberties Union acknowledging, "Yes, I think [the Supreme Court decision in *Lawrence v. Texas*] would give a lawyer a foothold to argue such a case. The general framework of that case, that states can't make it a crime to engage in private consensual intimate relationships, is a strong argument."[35]

This argument is already being pressed in the courts. Two convicted bigamists in Utah, Tom Green and Rodney Holm, have appealed to have their convictions overturned—citing the Supreme Court's decision in the *Lawrence* case as precedent.[36] And another attorney has filed suit challenging the refusal of the Salt Lake County clerk to grant a marriage license for G. Lee Cook to take a second wife.[37]

Make no mistake about it—if same-sex "marriage" is not stopped now, we will have the exact same debate about "plural" marriages only one generation from now.

References

1. One of the architects of Social Security, Abraham Epstein, said, "[T]he American standard assumes a normal family of man, wife, and two or three children, with the father fully able to provide for them out of his own income." Abraham Epstein, *Insecurity: A Challenge to America* (New York: Harrison Smith and Robert Haas, 1933), 101–102; cited in Allan Carlson, *The "American Way": Family and Community in the Shaping of the American Identity* (Wilmington, DE: ISI Books, 2003), 69. See generally Carlson's entire chapter on "'Sanctifying the Traditional Family': The New Deal and National Solidarity," 55–77.
2. "Debate in Massachusetts over how to address the issue of discussing gay relationships and sex in public school classrooms," *All Things Considered*, National Public Radio, September 13, 2004.
3. Maggie Gallagher, "Banned in Boston: The coming conflict between same-sex marriage and religious liberty," *The Weekly Standard* Vol. 11, Issue 33, May 15, 2006; online at: http://weeklystandard.com/Content/Public/Articles/000/000/012/191kgwgh.asp
4. Roger Severino, "Or for Poorer? How Same-Sex Marriage Threatens Religious Liberty," *Harvard Journal of Law and Public Policy* 30, Issue 3 (Summer 2007), 939–82.
5. Jill P. Capuzzo, "Group Loses Tax Break Over Gay Union Issue," *The New York Times*, September 18, 2007, p. B2. Online at: http://www.nytimes.com/2007/09/18/nyregion/18grove.html?_r=1&scp=1&sq=Ocean%20Grove%20Camp%20Meeting%20&%20civil%20union&st=cse
6. This is a matter of public record, although some states do not track same-sex "marriages" separately from opposite-sex ones.

7. The 2000 Census was the first in which cohabiting individuals (both opposite-sex and same-sex) were given the option of declaring themselves to be "partners." Since people who are merely roommates or housemates can still identify themselves as such, the presumption is that the term "partners" will only be used by those in a sexual relationship. See Tavia Simmons and Martin O'Connell, "Married-Couple and Unmarried Partner Households: 2000," *Census 2000 Special Reports* CENSR-5 (Washington, DC: U.S. Census Bureau). Online at: http://www.census.gov/prod/2003pubs/censr_5.pdf

8. For example, in the Netherlands, the percentage of heterosexual couples rejecting marriage jumped by more than a third, from 13% to 18%, between 1995 and 2004—during the very time period when same-sex "marriage" was legalized. "Types of households in the Netherlands 1995–2004," op. cit.

9. Maria Xiridou, et al., "The Contribution of Steady and Casual Partnerships to the Incidence of HIV Infection among Homosexual Men in Amsterdam," *AIDS* 17 (2003): 1031.

10. E. O. Laumann et al., *The Social Organization of Sexuality: Sexual Practices in the United States* (Chicago: University of Chicago Press, 1994): 216.

11. Peter Freiberg, "Couples study shows strengths," *The Washington Blade*, March 16, 2001.

12. Lawrence Kurdek, "What Do We Know about Gay and Lesbian Couples?" *Current Directions in Psychological Science* 14 (2005): 252.

13. Lawrence Kurdek, "Are Gay and Lesbian Cohabiting Couples *Really* Different from Heterosexual Married Couples?" *Journal of Marriage and Family* 66 (November 2004): 896.

14. David P. McWhirter and Andrew M. Mattison, *The Male Couple: How Relationships Develop* (Englewood Cliffs: Prentice-Hall, 1984): 252, 253.

15. Kristin A. Moore, "Nonmarital School-Age Motherhood: Family, Individual, and School Characteristics," *Journal of Adolescent Research* 13, October 1998: 433–457.

16. John P. Hoffman and Robert A. Johnson, "A National Portrait of Family Structure and Adolescent Drug Use," *Journal of Marriage and the Family* 60, August 1998: 633–645.

17. Chris Coughlin and Samuel Vucinich, "Family Experience in Preadolescence and the Development of Male Delinquency," *Journal of Marriage and the Family* 58, May 1996: 491–501.

18. Debra L. Blackwell, "Family structure and children's health in the United States: Findings from the National Health Interview Survey, 2001–2007," *Vital and Health Statistics*, Series 10, No. 246 (Hyattsville, MD: National Center for Health Statistics, December 2010). Online at: http://www.cdc.gov/nchs/data/series/sr_10/sr10_246.pdf

19. Federal Interagency Forum on Child and Family Statistics, *America's Children: Key Indicators of Well-Being 2001*, Washington, D.C., p. 14.

20. Deborah A. Dawson, "Family Structure and Children's Health and Well-Being: Data from the 1988 National Health Interview Survey on Child Health," *Journal of Marriage and the Family* 53, August 1991: 573–584.

21. Paul R. Amato and Alan Booth, *A Generation at Risk: Growing Up in an Era of Family Upheaval*, Cambridge, Massachusetts: Harvard University Press, 1997, pp. 111–115.

22. Stanley Kurtz, "The End of Marriage in Scandinavia: The 'conservative case' for same-sex marriage collapses," *The Weekly Standard* 9, No. 20 (February 2, 2004): 26–33.

23. Rose M. Kreider, "Living Arrangements of Children: 2004," *Current Population Reports* P70–114 (Washington, DC: U.S. Census Bureau), February 2008, Figure 1, p. 5.

24. Simmons and O'Connell, op. cit., Table 4, p. 9.

25. Kyle D. Pruett, *Fatherneed: Why Father Care Is as Essential as Mother Care for Your Child* (New York: The Free Press, 2000), p. 16.

26. A good recent summary is Paul C. Vitz, *The Importance of Fathers: Evidence and Theory from Social Science* (Arlington, VA: Institute for the Psychological Sciences, June 2010); online at: http://www.profam.org/docs/thc.vitz.1006.htm

27. Cynthia C. Harper and Sara S. McLanahan, "Father Absence and Youth Incarceration," *Journal of Research on Adolescence* 14(3), 2004, p. 388.

28. Bruce J. Ellis, John E. Bates, Kenneth A. Dodge, David M. Fergusson, L. John Horwood, Gregory S. Pettit, Lianne Woodward, "Does Father Absence Place Daughters at Special Risk for Early Sexual Activity and Teenage Pregnancy?" *Child Development* Vol. 74, Issue 3, May 2003; abstract online at: http://onlinelibrary.wiley.com/doi/10.1111/1467-8624.00569/abstract

29. David Blankenhorn, *Fatherless America: Confronting Our Most Urgent Social Problem* (New York: BasicBooks, 1995), p. 45.

30. Susan Golombok, Fiona Tasker, Clare Murray, "Children Raised in Fatherless Families from Infancy: Family Relationships and the Socioemotional Development of Children of Lesbian and Single Heterosexual Mothers," *Journal of Child Psychologyc and Psychiatry* Vol. 38, Issue 7 (October 1997); abstract online at: http://onlinelibrary.wiley.com/doi/10.1111/j.1469-7610.1997.tb01596.x/abstract

31. Human Rights Campaign, *Donor Agreement*; online at: http://www.hrc.org/Template.cfm?Section=Search_the_Law_Database&Template=/ContentManagement/ContentDisplay.cfm&ContentID=18669

32. Elizabeth Marquardt, Norval D. Glenn, and Karen Clark, *My Daddy's Name is Donor: A New Study of Young Adults Conceived Through Sperm Donation* (New York: Institute for American Values, 2010) p. 9.

33. Ibid., Table 2, p. 110.

34. Joyce A. Martin, Brady E. Hamilton, Paul D. Sutton, Stephanie J. Ventura, T. J. Mathews, Sharon Kirmeyer, and Michelle J. K. Osterman, U.S. Department of Health and Human Services, Centers for Disease Control and Prevention, National Center for Health Statistics, National

Vital Statistics System, "Births: Final Data for 2007," *National Vital Statistics Reports* Vol. 58, No. 24, August, 2010, Table 11. Rankings calculated by the author.

35. Joe Crea, "Polygamy advocates buoyed by gay court wins: Some see sodomy, marriage opinions as helping their cause," *Washington Blade* (December 26, 2003): 14.

36. Both appeals failed—but legalization of same-sex "marriage" would create a stronger argument than the one based on *Lawrence v. Texas*, which was not related to marriage. See: Warren Richey, "Supreme Court declines polygamy case: The husband of three wives claimed the court's landmark ruling on gays applies to polygamists," *The Christian Science Monitor*, February 27, 2007; online at: http://www.csmonitor.com/2007/0227/p25s01-usju.html; and

Brooke Adams, "Polygamist Green wants 'a private, quiet life' after Tuesday parole," *Salt Lake Tribune*, August 6, 2007. Online. Nexis

37. Alexandria Sage, "Attorney challenges Utah ban on polygamy, cites Texas sodomy case," *Associated Press* (January 12, 2004).

PETER SPRIGG serves as vice president for policy at the Family Research Council and oversees FRC research, publications, and policy formulation. He is also the author of the book *Outrage: How Gay Activists and Liberal Judges Are Trashing Democracy to Redefine Marriage* (Regnery, 2004) and the coeditor of the book *Getting It Straight: What the Research Shows about Homosexuality*.

Liza Mundy

→ **NO**

The Gay Guide to Wedded Bliss

Compared with straight marriages, research finds, same-sex unions tend to be happier, with less conflict, greater emotional intimacy, and more-equal sharing of chores and child-rearing. What gay and lesbian spouses can teach straight ones about living happily ever after.

It is more than a little ironic that gay marriage has emerged as the era's defining civil-rights struggle even as marriage itself seems more endangered every day. Americans are waiting longer to marry: according to the U.S. Census Bureau, the median age of first marriage is 28 for men and 26 for women, up from 23 and 20, respectively, in 1950. Rates of cohabitation have risen swiftly and sharply, and more people than ever are living single. Most Americans still marry at some point, but many of those marriages end in divorce. (Although the U.S. divorce rate has declined from its all-time high in the late '70s and early '80s, it has remained higher than those of most European countries.) All told, this has created an unstable system of what the UCLA sociologist Suzanne Bianchi calls "partnering and repartnering," a relentless emotional and domestic churn that sometimes results in people forgoing the institution altogether.

Though people may be waiting to marry, they are not necessarily waiting to have children. The National Center for Family and Marriage Research has produced a startling analysis of data from the Census Bureau and the Centers for Disease Control and Prevention showing that women's median age when they have their first child is lower than their median age at first marriage. In other words, having children before you marry has become normal. College graduates enjoy relatively stable unions, but for every other group, marriage is collapsing. Among "middle American" women (those with a high-school degree or some college), an astonishing 58 percent of first-time mothers are unmarried. . . .

Against this backdrop, gay-marriage opponents have argued that allowing same-sex couples to wed will pretty much finish matrimony off. This point was advanced in briefs and oral arguments before the Supreme Court in March, in two major same-sex-marriage cases. One of these is a constitutional challenge to a key section of the Defense of Marriage Act, the 1996 law that defines marriage as a union between a man and a woman, and bars the federal government from recognizing same-sex marriages. The other involves California's Proposition 8,

a same-sex-marriage ban passed by voters in 2008 but overturned by a federal judge in 2010. Appearing before the high court in March, Charles J. Cooper, the lawyer defending the California ban, predicted that same-sex marriage would undermine traditional marriage by eroding "marital norms."

The belief that gay marriage will harm marriage has roots in both religious beliefs about matrimony and secular conservative concerns about broader shifts in American life. One prominent line of thinking holds that men and women have distinct roles to play in family life; that children need both a mother and a father, preferably biologically related to them; and that a central purpose of marriage is abetting heterosexual procreation. During the Supreme Court arguments over Proposition 8, Justice Elena Kagan asked Cooper whether the essence of his argument against gay marriage was that opposite-sex couples can procreate while same-sex ones cannot. "That's the essential thrust of our position, yes," replied Cooper. He also warned that "redefining marriage as a genderless institution could well lead over time to harms to that institution." . . .

In mounting their defense, advocates of same-sex marriage have argued that gays and lesbians who wish to marry are committed to family well-being; that concern for children's welfare is a chief reason many do want to marry; that gay people are being discriminated against, as a class, in being denied rights readily available to any heterosexual. . . .

But what if the critics are correct, just not in the way they suppose? What if same-sex marriage does change marriage, but primarily for the better? For one thing, there is reason to think that, rather than making marriage more fragile, the boom of publicity around same-sex weddings could awaken among heterosexuals a new interest in the institution, at least for a time. But the larger change might be this: by providing a new model of how two people can live together equitably, same-sex marriage could help haul matrimony more fully into the 21st century. Although marriage is in many ways fairer and more pleasurable for both men and women than it once was, it hasn't entirely thrown off old notions and habits. As a result, many men and women enter into it burdened with assumptions and stereotypes that create stress and resentment. Others, confronted with these increasingly anachronistic expectations—expectations at odds with the economic and practical realities of their own lives—don't enter into it at all.

Same-sex spouses, who cannot divide their labor based on preexisting gender norms, must approach marriage differently than their heterosexual peers. From sex to fighting, from child-rearing to chores, they must hammer out every last detail of domestic life without falling back on assumptions about who will do what. In this regard, they provide an example that can be enlightening to all couples. Critics warn of an institution rendered "genderless." But if a genderless marriage is a marriage in which the wife is not automatically expected to be responsible for school forms and child care and dinner preparation and birthday parties and midnight feedings and holiday shopping, I think it's fair to say that many heterosexual women would cry "Bring it on!". . .

Rules for a More Perfect Union

Not all is broken within modern marriage, of course. On the contrary: the institution is far more flexible and forgiving than it used to be. In the wake of women's large-scale entry into the workplace, men are less likely than they once were to be saddled with being a family's sole breadwinner, and can carve out a life that includes the close companionship of their children. Meanwhile, women are less likely to be saddled with the sole responsibility for child care and housework, and can envision a life beyond the stove top and laundry basket.

And yet for many couples, as Bianchi, the UCLA sociologist, has pointed out, the modern ideal of egalitarianism has proved "quite difficult to realize." Though men are carrying more of a domestic workload than in the past, women still bear the brunt of the second shift. Among couples with children, when both spouses work full-time, women do 32 hours a week of housework, child care, shopping, and other family-related services, compared with the 21 hours men put in. Men do more paid work—45 hours, compared with 39 for women—but still have more free time: 31 hours, compared with 25 for women. Betsey Stevenson and Justin Wolfers, economists and professors of public policy at the University of Michigan, have shown that happiness rates among women have dropped even as women have acquired more life options. One possible cause is the lingering inequity in male-female marriage: women's at-home workload can become so burdensome that wives opt out of the paid workforce—or sit at the office making mental lists of the chores they do versus the chores their husbands do, and bang their heads on their desks in despair.

Not that everything is easy for fathers in dual-earner couples, who now feel afflicted by work-life conflict in even greater numbers than their wives (60 percent of men in such couples say they experience this conflict, versus 47 percent of women, according to a 2008 study by the Families and Work Institute). And men face a set of unfair expectations all their own: the Pew Research Center found in 2010 that 67 percent of Americans still believe it's "very important" that a man be ready to support a family before getting married, while only 33 percent believe the same about women.

This burden, exacerbated by the economic realities facing many men today, has undoubtedly contributed to marriage's recent decline. As our economy has transitioned away from manufacturing and industry, men with a high-school education can no longer expect the steady, well-paying union jobs that formerly enabled many to support their families. Outdated assumptions that men should bring something to the table, and that this something should be money, don't help. Surveying their prospects, many working-class mothers reject marriage altogether, perhaps reasoning that they can support a child, but don't want a dependent husband. . . .

What Schwartz and Blumstein found is that gay and lesbian couples were fairer in their dealings with one another than straight couples, both in intent and in practice. The lesbians in the study were almost painfully egalitarian—in some cases putting money in jars and splitting everything down to the penny in a way, Schwartz says, that "would have driven me crazy." Many unmarried heterosexual cohabitators were also careful about divvying things up, but lesbian couples seemed to take the practice to extremes: "It was almost like 'my kitty, your litter.'" Gay men, like lesbians, were more likely than straight couples to share cooking and chores. . . .

Lesbians also tended to discuss things endlessly, achieving a degree of closeness unmatched by the other types of couples. Schwartz wondered whether this might account for another finding: over time, sex in lesbian relationships dwindled—a state of affairs she has described as "lesbian bed death." . . . She posits that lesbians may have had so much intimacy already that they didn't need sex to get it; by contrast, heterosexual women, whose spouses were less likely to be chatty, found that "sex is a highway to intimacy." As for men, she eventually concluded that whether they were straight or gay, they approached sex as they might a sandwich: good, bad, or mediocre, they were likely to grab it. . . .

When It Comes to Parenting, a 50-50 Split Isn't Necessarily Best

Charlotte J. Patterson, a psychologist at the University of Virginia, has arresting visual evidence of the same egalitarianism at work in parenting: compared with husband-and-wife pairs, she has found, same-sex parents tend to be more cooperative and mutually hands-on. Patterson and a colleague, Rachel Farr, have conducted a study of more than 100 same-sex and heterosexual adoptive parents in 11 states and the District of Columbia; it is among the first such studies to include gay fathers. As reported in an article in a forthcoming issue of the journal *Child Development*, the researchers visited families in their homes, scattered some toys on a blanket, invited the subjects to play with them any way they chose, and videotaped the interactions. "What you see is what they did with that blank slate," Patterson says. "One thing that I found riveting: the same-sex couples are far more likely to be in there together, and the opposite-sex couples show the conventional pattern—the mom more involved, the dad playing with Tinkertoys by himself." When the opposite-sex couples did parent simultaneously, they were more likely to undermine each other by talking at cross-purposes or suggesting different toys. The lesbian mothers tended to be egalitarian and warm in their dealings with one another, and showed greater pleasure in parenting than the other groups did. Same-sex dads were also more egalitarian in their division of labor than straight couples, though not as warm or interactive as lesbian moms. (Patterson says she and her colleagues may need to refine their analysis to take into account male ways of expressing warmth.)

By and large, all of the families studied, gay and straight alike, were happy, high functioning, and financially secure. Each type of partner—gay, straight; man, woman—reported satisfaction with his or her family's parenting arrangement, though the heterosexual wife was less content than the others, invariably saying that she wanted more help from her husband. "Of all the parents we've studied, she's the least satisfied with the division of labor," says Patterson, who is in a same-sex partnership and says she knows from experience that deciding who will do what isn't always easy.

Even as they are more egalitarian in their parenting styles, same-sex parents resemble their heterosexual counterparts in one somewhat old-fashioned way: a surprising number establish a division of labor whereby one spouse becomes the primary earner and the [other] stays home. Lee Badgett, an economist at the University of Massachusetts at Amherst, told me that, "in terms of economics," same-sex couples with children resemble heterosexual couples with children much more than they resemble childless same-sex couples. You might say that gay parents are simultaneously departing from traditional family structures and leading the way back toward them. . . .

Don't Want a Divorce? Don't Marry a Woman

Three years after they first gathered information from the couples who received licenses in Vermont, Esther Rothblum and her colleagues checked back to evaluate the condition of their relationships. Overall, the researchers found that the quality of gay and lesbian relationships was higher on many measures than that of the straight control group (the married heterosexual siblings), with more compatibility and intimacy, and less conflict.

Which is not to say same-sex couples don't have conflict. When they fight, however, they fight fairer. They can even fight funny, as researchers from the University of Washington and the University of California at Berkeley showed in an article published in 2003, based on a study of couples who were navigating potentially tense interactions. Recruiting married straight couples as well as gays and lesbians in committed relationships, the researchers orchestrated a scenario in which one partner had to bring up an area of conflict to discuss with the other. In same-sex couples, the partner with the bone to pick was rated "less belligerent and less domineering" than the straight-couple counterpart, while the person on the receiving end was less aggressive and showed less fear or tension. The same-sex "initiator" also displayed less sadness and "whining," and more affection, joy, and humor. In trying to make sense of the disparity, the researchers noted that same-sex couples valued equality more, and posited that the greater negativity of straight couples "may have to do with the standard status hierarchy between men and women." Which perhaps boils down to something like this: straight women see themselves as being less powerful than men, and this breeds hostility. . . .

The Contagion Effect

Whatever this string of studies may teach us about marriage and gender dynamics, the next logical question becomes this: Might such marriages do more than merely inform our understanding of straight marriage—might their attributes trickle over to straight marriage in some fashion?

In the course of my reporting this year in states that had newly legalized same-sex marriage, people in the know—wedding planners, officiants, fiancés and fiancées—told me time and again that nuptial fever had broken out around them, among gay and straight couples alike. Same-sex weddings seemed to be bestowing a new frisson on the idea of getting hitched, or maybe restoring an old one. At the Gay and Lesbian Wedding Expo in downtown Baltimore, just a few weeks after same-sex marriage became legal in Maryland, Drew Vanlandingham, who describes himself as a "wedding planner designer," was delighted at how business had picked up. Here it was, January, and many of his favorite venues were booked into late summer—much to the consternation, he said, of his straight brides. "They're like, 'I better get a move on!'" It was his view that in Maryland, both teams were now engaged in an amiable but spirited race to the altar. . . .

There is some reason to suppose that attitudes about marriage could, in fact, be catching. The phenomenon known as "social contagion" lies at the heart of an increasingly prominent line of research on how our behavior and emotions affect the people we know. One famous example dates from 2008, when James H. Fowler and Nicholas A. Christakis published a study showing that happiness "spreads" through social networks. They arrived at this conclusion via an ingenious crunching of data from a long-running medical study involving thousands of interconnected residents—and their children, and later their grandchildren—in Framingham, Massachusetts. "Emotional states can be transferred directly from one individual to another," they found, across three degrees of separation. Other studies have shown that obesity, smoking habits, and school performance may also be catching.

Most relevant, in a working paper that is under submission to a sociology journal, the Brown University political scientist Rose McDermott, along with her co-authors, Fowler and Christakis, has identified a contagion effect for divorce. Divorce, she found, can spread among friends. She told me that she also suspects that tending to the marriages of friends can help preserve your own. McDermott says she readily sees how marriage could itself be contagious. Intriguingly, some of the Scandinavian countries where same-sex unions have been legal for a decade or more have seen a rise, not a fall, in marriage rates. In response to conservative arguments that same-sex marriage had driven a stake through the heart of marriage in northern Europe, the Yale University law professor William N. Eskridge Jr. and Darren Spedale in 2006 published an analysis showing that in the decade since same-sex partnerships became legal, heterosexual marriage rates had increased 10.7 percent in Denmark, 12.7 percent in Norway, and 28.8 percent in Sweden. Divorce rates had dropped in all three countries. Although there was no way to prove cause and effect, the authors allowed, you could safely say that marriage had not been harmed. . . .

Other experts question the idea that most gay males share a preference for non-monogamous relationships, or will in the long term. Savage's argument that non-monogamy is a safety valve is "very interesting, but it really is no more than a claim," says Justin Garcia, an evolutionary biologist at the Kinsey Institute for Research in Sex, Gender, and Reproduction. Garcia points out that not all men are relentlessly sexual beings, and not all men want an open relationship. "In some ways, same-sex couples are healthier—they tend to have these negotiations more," he says. But negotiating can be stressful: in many cases, Garcia notes, one gay partner would prefer to be monogamous, but gives in to the other partner.

So which version will prevail: non-monogamous marriage, or marriage as we conventionally understand it? It's worth pointing out that in the U.S., same-sex unions are slightly more likely between women, and non-monogamy is not a cause women tend to champion. And some evidence suggests that getting married changes behavior: William Eskridge and Darren Spedale found that in the years after Norway, Sweden, and Denmark instituted registered partnerships, many same-sex couples reported placing a greater emphasis on monogamy, while national rates of HIV infections declined.

Sex, then, may be one area where the institution of marriage pushes back against norms that have been embraced by many gay couples. Gary Hall of the National

Cathedral allows that in many ways, gay relationships offer a salutary "critique" of marriage, but argues that the marriage establishment will do some critiquing back. He says he would not marry two people who intended to be non-monogamous, and believes that monogamy will be a "critical issue" in the dialogue between the gay community and the Church. Up until now, he says, progressive churches have embraced "the part of gay behavior that looks like straight behavior," but at some point, churches also have to engage gay couples whose behavior doesn't conform to monogamous ideals. He hopes that, in the course of this give-and-take, the church ends up reckoning with other ongoing cultural changes, from unmarried cohabitation to the increasing number of adults who choose to live as singles. "How do we speak credibly to people about their sexuality and their sexual relationships?" he asks. "We really need to rethink this."

So yes, marriage will change. Or rather, it will change again. The fact is, there is no such thing as traditional marriage. In various places and at various points in human history, marriage has been a means by which young children were betrothed, uniting royal houses and sealing alliances between nations. In the Bible, it was a union that sometimes took place between a man and his dead brother's widow, or between one man and several wives. It has been a vehicle for the orderly transfer of property from one generation of males to the next; the test by which children were deemed legitimate or bastard; a privilege not available to black Americans; something parents arranged for their adult children; a contract under which women, legally, ceased to exist. Well into the 19th century, the British common-law concept of "unity of person" meant a woman *became* her husband when she married, giving up her legal standing and the right to own property or control her own wages.

Many of these strictures have already loosened. Child marriage is today seen by most people as the human-rights violation that it is. The Married Women's Property Acts guaranteed that a woman could get married and remain a legally recognized human being. The Supreme Court's decision in *Loving v. Virginia* did away with state bans on interracial marriage. By making it easier to dissolve marriage, no-fault divorce helped ensure that unions need not be lifelong. The recent surge in single parenthood, combined with an aging population, has unyoked marriage and child-rearing. History shows that marriage evolves over time. We have every reason to believe that same-sex marriage will contribute to its continued evolution.

The argument that gays and lesbians are social pioneers and bellwethers has been made before. Back in 1992, the British sociologist Anthony Giddens suggested that gays and lesbians were a harbinger of a new kind of union, one subject to constant renegotiation and expected to last only as long as both partners were happy with it. Now that these so-called harbingers are looking to commit to more-binding relationships, we will have the "counterfactual" that Gary Gates talks about: we will be better able to tell which marital stresses and pleasures are due to gender, and which are not.

In the end, it could turn out that same-sex marriage isn't all that different from straight marriage. If gay and lesbian marriages are in the long run as quarrelsome, tedious, and unbearable; as satisfying, joyous, and loving as other marriages, we'll know that a certain amount of strife is not the fault of the alleged war between men and women, but just an inevitable thing that happens when two human beings are doing the best they can to find a way to live together.

LIZA MUNDY is a Bernard L. Schwartz Fellow at the New America Foundation and author of *The Richer Sex: How the New Majority of Female Breadwinners Is Transforming Our Culture.*

EXPLORING THE ISSUE

Is Same-Sex Marriage Harmful to America?

Critical Thinking and Reflection

1. What is your theory about homosexuality? Do you think it is a choice or is there a biological basis for it? Can homosexuals be reprogrammed to be heterosexuals? (The research is not decisive on this point. No gene for homosexuality has been discovered yet, but people do vary considerably in their levels of various hormones.)
2. Does your theory influence your opinion on the debate issue?
3. Can the civil rights of homosexuals on the issue of unions be protected in any other way than by same-sex marriages?
4. No proposed law would require religious leaders to marry same-sex couples. Do you think this largely nullifies the religious objection to same-sex marriage?
5. Has the legalization of same-sex marriages in several states and foreign countries caused problems that give good reasons for opposing same-sex marriages in the United States?
6. Evaluate the argument that homosexual marriage is a threat to heterosexual marriage. Has it had negative effects on heterosexual marriages so far as you can tell?

Is There Common Ground?

The issue of the rights of homosexuals creates a social dilemma. Most people would agree that all members of society should have equal rights. However, the majority may disapprove of the lifestyles of a minority group and pass laws against some of their behaviors. The question is, when do these laws violate civil rights? Are laws against same-sex marriage such a violation?

Another common set of values is the right to life, liberty, and the pursuit of happiness. Life is not threatened in this issue but liberty and happiness are. Thus, the liberty and happiness of homosexuals should be promoted unless that would harm heterosexuals. We must ask, therefore, who is hurt by same-sex marriages? Are heterosexuals being hurt? As far as I know, I have not been hurt as a heterosexual. I know some people who are upset by same-sex marriage laws, but I know more who are upset by the lack of such laws. Do these feelings have any standing in the moral argument?

Create Central

www.mhhe.com/createcentral

Additional Resources

There is a considerable literature on homosexuality and the social and legal status of homosexuals. Recent works on gay marriage include: Craig A. Rimmerman and Clyde Wilcox, eds., *The Politics of Same-Sex Marriage* (University of Chicago Press, 2007); Daniel R. Pinello, *America's Struggle for Same-Sex Marriage* (Cambridge University Press, 2006); Donald J. Cantor et al., *Same-Sex Marriage: The Legal and Psychological Evolution in America* (Wesleyan University Press, 2006); R. Claire Snyder, *Gay Marriage and Democracy:*

Equality for All (Rowman & Littlefield, 2006); David Moats, *Civil Wars: A Battle for Gay Marriage* (Harcourt, 2004); Evan Gerstmann, *Same-Sex Marriage and the Constitution* (Cambridge University Press, 2004); Jonathan Rauch, *Gay Marriage: Why It Is Good for Gays, Good for Straights, and Good for America* (Times Books, 2004); Lynn D. Wordle et al., eds., *Marriage and Same-Sex Unions: A Debate* (Praeger, 2003); Martin Dupuis, *Same-Sex Marriage, Legal Mobilization, and the Politics of Rights* (Peter Lang, 2002); Kevin Bourassa, *Just Married: Gay Marriage and the Expansion of Human Rights* (University of Wisconsin Press, 2002); and a four-volume set: *Defending Same-Sex Marriage*, vol. 1; *"Separate But Equal" No More: A Guide to the Legal Status of Same-Sex Marriage, Civil Unions, and Other Partnerships*, vol. 2, edited by Mark Strasser; *Our Family Values: Same-Sex Marriage and Religion*, vol. 3, edited by Traci C. West; *The Freedom-to-Marry Movement: Education, Advocacy, Culture, and the Media*, vol. 4, edited by Martin Dupuis and William A. Thompson (Praeger, 2007).

Most works are pro-gay rights. For opposition to same-sex marriage, see: Jaye Cee Whitehead, *The Nuptial Deal: Same-Sex Marriage and Neo-Liberal Governance* (University of Chicago Press, 2012).

Recent works on the history of the gay rights movement include: Dudley Clendinen and Adam Nagourney, *Out for Good: The Struggle to Build a Gay Rights Movement in America* (Simon & Schuster, 1999); Ronald J. Hunt, *Historical Dictionary of the Gay Liberation Movement* (Scarecrow Press, 1999); JoAnne Myers, *Historical Dictionary of the Lesbian Liberation Movement: Still the Rage* (Scarecrow Press, 2003); and John Loughery, *The Other Side of Silence: Men's Lives and Gay Identities: A Twentieth-Century History* (Henry Holt, 1998).

For broad academic works on homosexuality, see: Kath Weston, *Long Slow Burn: Sexuality and Social Science* (Routledge, 1998), and Michael Ruse, *Homosexuality: A Philosophical Inquiry* (Blackwell, 1998).

Recent works that focus on homosexual rights include: David A. J. Richards, *Identity and the Case for Gay Rights* (University of Chicago Press, 1999); Daniel R. Pinello, *Gay Rights and American Law* (Cambridge University Press, 2003); Carlos A. Ball, *The Morality of Gay Rights: An Exploration in Political Philosophy* (Routledge, 2003);

Brette McWhorter Sember, *Gay and Lesbian Rights: A Guide for GLBT Singles, Couples, and Families* (Sphinx, 2003); and Nan D. Hunter, *The Rights of Lesbians, Gay Men, Bisexuals, and Transgender People: The Authoritative ACLU Guide to a Lesbian, Gay, Bisexual, or Transgender Person's Rights*, 4th ed. (Southern Illinois University Press, 2004).

Internet References . . .

Sociology—Study Sociology Online

http://edu.learnsoc.org/

Sociology Web Resource

www.mhhe.com/socscience/sociology
/resources/index.htm

Sociosite

www.topsite.com/goto/sociosite.net

Socioweb

www.topsite.com/goto/socioweb.com

Unit 3

UNIT

Stratification and Inequality

*W*hy is there so much poverty in a society as rich as ours? Why has there been such a noticeable increase in inequality over the past quarter century? Although the ideal of equal opportunity for all is strong in the United States, many charge that the American political and economic systems are unfair. Does extensive poverty demonstrate that policymakers have failed to live up to U.S. egalitarian principles? Are American institutions deeply flawed in that they provide fabulous opportunities for the educated and rich and meager opportunities for the uneducated and poor? Is the American stratification system at fault or are the poor themselves at fault? And what about the racial gap? The civil rights movement and the Civil Rights Act have made America more fair than it was, so why does a sizable racial gap remain? Various affirmative action programs have been implemented to remedy unequal opportunities, but some argue that this is discrimination in reverse. In fact, California passed a referendum banning affirmative action. Where should America go from here? Social scientists debate questions such as these in this unit.

Selected, Edited, and with Issue Framing Material by:
Kurt Finsterbusch, *University of Maryland, College Park*

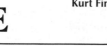

ISSUE

Is Increasing Economic Inequality a Serious Problem?

YES: Joseph Stiglitz, from "Joseph Stiglitz: The Price of Inequality," AlterNet.org (June 11, 2012)

NO: Robert Rector and Rachel Sheffield, from "Understanding Poverty in the United States: Surprising Facts about America's Poor," The Heritage Foundation, *The Heritage Foundation Backgrounder* (September 13, 2011)

Learning Outcomes

After reading this issue, you should be able to:

- Know the basic facts about the level of income inequality in America and how it compares with the degree of income inequality in other developed countries.
- Explain the high levels of inequality in America and predict whether those same forces will increase inequality in the future.
- Identify what commentators claim are the benefits of income inequality and what are the adverse effects.
- Present the pros and cons of the trickle-down theory.
- Understand what policies, institutions, or technologies can increase or decrease income inequality in America.
- Critique the thesis that the poor are to be blamed for their poverty.

ISSUE SUMMARY

YES: Nobel Laureate Joseph Stiglitz, professor of economics at Columbia University, demonstrates the vast inequality in America and argues that it makes the economic system less stable, less efficient, and less productive. It also endangers democracy and facilitates the capture of our political system by moneyed interests which leads to many other adverse consequences.

NO: Robert Rector is Senior Research Fellow in the Domestic Policy Studies Department, and Rachel Sheffield is a Research Assistant in the Richard and Helen DeVos Center for Religion and Civil Society at The Heritage Foundation. They argue that inequality is not so bad because the poor are rather well-off when we look at all the facts. The living conditions of the poor have improved for decades. Most of the poor have consumer items that were significant purchases for the middle class a few decades ago. They establish their thesis on countless facts such as "82 percent of poor adults reported never being hungry at any time in the prior year due to lack of money for food."

The cover of the January 29, 1996, issue of *Time* magazine bears a picture of 1996 Republican presidential candidate Steve Forbes and large letters reading: "DOES A FLAT TAX MAKE SENSE?" During his campaign, Forbes expressed his willingness to spend $25 million of his own wealth in pursuit of the presidency, with the major focus of his presidential campaign being a flat tax that would reduce taxes substantially for the rich. It seems reasonable to say that if the rich pay less in taxes, others would have to pay more. Is it acceptable for the tax burden to be shifted away from the rich in America? Forbes believed that the flat tax would benefit the poor as well as the rich. He theorized that the economy would surge ahead because investors would shift their money from relatively nonproductive, but tax-exempt, investments to productive investments. Although Forbes has disappeared from the political scene, his basic argument still thrives today. It is an example of the trickle-down theory, which states that helping the rich stimulates the economy, which in turn helps the poor. In fact, the trickle-down theory is the major rationalization for the view that great economic inequality benefits all of society.

Inequality is not a simple subject. For example, America is commonly viewed as having more social equality than do the more hierarchical societies of Europe and Japan, but America has more income inequality than almost all other industrial societies. This apparent contradiction becomes understandable when one recognizes that American equality is not in income, but in the opportunity to obtain higher incomes. The issue of economic inequality is further complicated by other categories of equality/inequality, which include political power, social status, and legal rights.

Americans believe that everyone should have an equal opportunity to compete for jobs and rewards. This belief is backed up by free public school education, which provides poor children with a ladder to success, and by laws that forbid discrimination. Americans, however, do not agree on many specific issues regarding opportunities or rights. For example, should society compensate for handicaps such as disadvantaged family backgrounds or the legacy of past discrimination? This issue has divided the country. Americans do not agree on programs such as income-based scholarships, quotas, affirmative action, or the Head Start compensatory education program for poor preschoolers.

America's commitment to political equality is strong in principle, although less strong in practice. Everyone over 18 years old gets one vote, and all votes are counted equally. However, the political system tilts in the direction of special interest groups; those who do not belong to such groups are seldom heard. Furthermore, as in the case of Forbes, money plays an increasingly important role in political campaigns.

The final dimension of equality/inequality is status. Inequality of status involves differences in prestige, and it cannot be eliminated by legislation. Ideally, the people who contribute the most to society are the most highly esteemed. To what extent does this principle hold true in the United States?

The Declaration of Independence proclaims that "all men are created equal," and the Founding Fathers who wrote the Declaration of Independence went on to base the laws of the land on the principle of equality. The equality they were referring to was equality of opportunity and legal and political rights for white, property-owning males. In the two centuries following the signing of the Declaration, nonwhites and women struggled for and won considerable equality of opportunity and rights. Meanwhile, income gaps in the United States have been widening.

In the readings that follow the fact of inequality is hotly debated. Joseph Stiglitz presents data showing the vast inequality in America and then argues that it is hurting America. It makes the economic system less efficient, less productive, and less stable. It also threatens democracy. Robert Rector and Rachel Sheffield, on the other hand, argue that American inequality may look bad but the reality is better than it looks. In fact, the poor are richer that we think. Most of them have most of the items that a middle class person would have several decades ago.

YES ↵

Joseph Stiglitz

Joseph Stiglitz: The Price of Inequality

The Failure of Markets

Markets have clearly not been working in the way that their boosters claim. Markets are supposed to be stable, but the global financial crisis showed that they could be very unstable, with devastating consequences. The bankers had taken bets that, without government assistance, would have brought them and the entire economy down. But a closer look at the *system* showed that this was not an accident; the bankers had incentives to behave this way.

The virtue of the market is supposed to be its efficiency. But the market obviously is *not* efficient. The most basic law of economics—necessary if the economy is to be efficient—is that demand equals supply. But we have a world in which there are huge unmet needs—investments to bring the poor out of poverty, to promote development in less developed countries in Africa and other continents around the world, to retrofit the global economy to face the challenges of global warming. At the same time, we have vast underutilized resources—workers and machines that are idle or are not producing up to their potential. Unemployment—the inability of the market to generate jobs for so many citizens—is the worst failure of the market, the greatest source of inefficiency, and a major cause of inequality.

As of March 2012, some 24 million Americans who would have liked a full-time job couldn't get one.

In the United States, we are throwing millions out of their homes. We have empty homes and homeless people.

But even before the crisis, the American economy had not been delivering what had been promised: although there was growth in GDP, *most citizens were seeing their standards of living erode*. For most American families, even before the onset of recession, incomes adjusted for inflation were lower than they had been a decade earlier. America had created a marvelous economic machine, but evidently one that worked only for those at the top.

So Much at Stake

This book is about why our economic system is failing for most Americans, why inequality is growing to the extent it is, and what the consequences are. The underlying thesis is that we are paying a high price for our inequality—an economic system that is less stable and less efficient, with less growth, and a democracy that has been put into peril. But even more is at stake: as our economic system is seen to fail for most citizens, and as our political system seems to be captured by moneyed interests, confidence in our democracy and in our market economy will erode along with our global influence. As the reality sinks in that we are no longer a country of opportunity and that even our long-vaunted rule of law and system of justice have been compromised, even our sense of national identity may be put into jeopardy.

In some countries the Occupy Wall Street movement has become closely allied with the antiglobalization movement. They do have some things in common: a belief not only that something is wrong but also that change is possible. The problem, however, is not that globalization is bad or wrong but that governments are managing it so poorly—largely for the benefit of special interests. The interconnectedness of peoples, countries, and economies around the globe is a development that can be used as effectively to promote prosperity as to spread greed and misery. The same is true for the market economy: the power of markets is enormous, but they have no inherent moral character. We have to decide how to manage them. At their best, markets have played a central role in the stunning increases in productivity and standards of living in the past two hundred years—increases that far exceeded those of the previous two millennia.

But government has also played a major role in these advances, a fact that free-market advocates typically fail to acknowledge. On the other hand, markets can also concentrate wealth, pass environmental costs onto society, and abuse workers and consumers. For all these reasons, it is plain that markets must be tamed and tempered to make sure they work to the benefit of most citizens. And that has to be done repeatedly, to ensure that they continue to do so. That happened in the United States in the Progressive Era, when competition laws were passed for the first time. It happened in the New Deal, when Social Security, employment, and minimum-wage laws were passed.

The message of Occupy Wall Street—and of so many other protesters around the world—is that markets once again must be tamed and tempered. The consequences of not doing so are serious: within a meaningful democracy, where the voices of ordinary citizens are heard, we cannot maintain an open and globalized market system, at least not in the form that we know it, if that system year after year makes those citizens worse-off. One or the other will have to give—either our politics or our economics.

Inequality and Unfairness

Markets, by themselves, even when they are stable, often lead to high levels of inequality, outcomes that are widely viewed as unfair. Recent research in economics and psychology has shown the importance that individuals attach to fairness. More than anything else, a sense that the economic and political systems were unfair is what motivates the protests around the world. In Tunisia and Egypt and other parts of the Middle East, it wasn't merely that jobs were hard to come by but that those jobs that were available went to those with connections.

In the United States and Europe, things seemed more fair, but only superficially so. Those who graduated from the best schools with the best grades had a better chance at the good jobs. But the system was stacked because wealthy parents sent their children to the best kindergartens, grade schools, and high schools, and those students had a far better chance of getting into the elite universities.

Americans grasped that the Occupy Wall Street protesters were speaking to *their* values, which was why, while the numbers protesting may have been relatively small, two-thirds of Americans said that they supported the protesters. If there was any doubt of this support, the ability of the protesters to gather 300,000 signatures to keep their protests alive, almost overnight, when Mayor Michael Bloomberg of New York first suggested that he would shut down the camp at Zuccotti Park, near Wall Street, showed otherwise. And support came not just among the poor and the disaffected. While the police may have been excessively rough with protesters in Oakland—and the 30,000 who joined the protests the day after the downtown encampment was violently disbanded seemed to think so—it was noteworthy that some of the police themselves expressed support for the protesters.

The financial crisis unleashed a new realization that our economic system was not only inefficient and unstable but also fundamentally unfair. Indeed, in the aftermath of the crisis (and the response of the Bush and the Obama administrations), almost half thought so, according to a recent poll. It was rightly perceived to be grossly unfair that many in the financial sector (which, for shorthand, I will often refer to as "the bankers") walked off with outsize bonuses, while those who suffered from the crisis brought on by these bankers went without a job; or that government bailed out the banks, but was reluctant to even extend unemployment insurance for those who, through no fault of their own, could not get employment after searching for months and months; or that government failed to provide anything except token help to the millions who were losing their homes.

What happened in the midst of the crisis made clear that it was *not* contribution to society that determined relative pay, but something else: bankers received large rewards, though their contribution to society—and even to their firms—*had been negative*. The wealth given to the elites and to the bankers seemed to arise out of their ability and willingness to take advantage of others.

One aspect of fairness that is deeply ingrained in American values is opportunity. America has always thought of itself as a land of *equal opportunity*. Horatio Alger stories, of individuals who made it from the bottom to the top, are part of American folklore. But, increasingly, the American dream that saw the country as a land of opportunity began to seem just that: a dream, a myth reinforced by anecdotes and stories, but not supported by the data. The chances of an American citizen making his way from the bottom to the top are less than those of citizens in other advanced industrial countries.

There is a corresponding myth—rags to riches in three generations—suggesting that those at the top have to work hard to stay there; if they don't, they (or their descendants) quickly move down. But this too is largely a myth, for the children of those at the top will, more likely than not, remain there.

In a way, in America and throughout the world, the youthful protesters took what they heard from their parents and politicians at face value—just as America's youth did fifty years ago during the civil rights movement. Back then they scrutinized the values *equality, fairness,* and *justice* in the context of the nation's treatment of African Americans, and they found the nation's policies wanting. Now they scrutinize the same values in terms of how our economic and judicial system works, and they have found the system wanting for poor and middle-class Americans—not just for minorities but for *most* Americans of all backgrounds.

If President Obama and our court system had found those who brought the economy to the brink of ruin "guilty" of some malfeasance, then perhaps it would have been possible to say that the system was functioning. There was at least some sense of accountability. In fact, however, those who should have been so convicted were often not charged, and when they were charged, they were typically found innocent or at least not convicted. A few in the hedge fund industry have been convicted subsequently of insider trading, but this is a sideshow, almost a distraction. The hedge fund industry did not cause the crisis. It was the banks. And it is the bankers who have gone, almost to a person, free.

If no one is accountable, if no individual can be *blamed* for what has happened, it means that the problem lies in the economic and political system.

From Social Cohesion to Class Warfare

The slogan "we are the 99 percent" may have marked an important turning point in the debate about inequality in the United States. Americans have always shied away from class analysis; America, we liked to believe, is a middle-class country, and that belief helps bind us together. There should be no divisions between the upper and the lower classes, between the bourgeoisie and the workers. But if by a class-based society we mean one in which the prospects of those at the bottom to move up are low, America may have become even more class-based than old Europe, and our divisions have now become even greater than those there. Those in the 99 percent are continuing with the "we're all middle class" tradition, with one slight modification: they recognize that we're actually not all moving up together. The vast majority is suffering together, and the very top— the 1 percent—is living a different life. The "99 percent" marks an attempt to forge a new coalition—a new sense of national identity, based not on the fiction of a universal middle-class but on the reality of the economic divides within our economy and our society.

For years there was a deal between the top and the rest of our society that went something like this: we will provide you jobs and prosperity, and you will let us walk away with the bonuses. You all get a share, even if we get a bigger share. But now that tacit agreement between the rich and the rest, which was always fragile, has come apart. Those in the 1 percent are walking off with the riches, but in doing so they have provided nothing but anxiety and insecurity to the 99 percent. The majority of Americans have simply not been benefiting from the country's growth.

Is Our Market System Eroding Fundamental Values?

While this book focuses on equality and fairness, there is another fundamental value that our system seems to be undermining—a sense of *fair play*. A basic sense of values should, for instance, have led to guilt feelings on the part of those who were engaged in predatory lending, who provided mortgages to poor people that were ticking time bombs, or who were designing the "programs" that led to excessive charges for overdrafts in the billions of dollars. What is remarkable is how few seemed—and still seem—to feel guilty, and how few were the whistleblowers. Something has happened to our sense of values, when the end of making more money justifies the means, which in the U.S. subprime crisis meant exploiting the poorest and least-educated among us.

Much of what has gone on can only be described by the words "moral deprivation." Something wrong happened to the moral compass of so many of the people working in the financial sector and elsewhere. When the norms of a society change in a way that so many have lost their moral compass, it says something significant about the society.

Capitalism seems to have changed the people who were ensnared by it. The brightest of the bright who went to work on Wall Street were like most other Americans except that they did better in their schools. They put on hold their dreams of making a lifesaving discovery, of building a new industry, of helping the poorest out of poverty, as they reached out for salaries that seemed beyond belief, often in return for work that (in its number of hours) seemed beyond belief. But then, too often, something happened: it wasn't that the dreams were put on hold; they were forgotten.

It is thus not surprising that the list of grievances against corporations (and not just financial institutions) is long and of long standing. For instance, cigarette companies stealthily made their dangerous products more addictive, and as they tried to persuade Americans that there was no "scientific evidence" of their products' dangers, their files were filled with evidence to the contrary. Exxon similarly used its money to try to persuade Americans that the evidence on global warming was weak, though the National Academy of Sciences had joined every other national scientific body in saying that the evidence was strong. And while the economy was still reeling from the misdeeds of the financial sector, the BP oil spill showed another aspect of corporate recklessness: lack of care in drilling had endangered the environment and threatened jobs of thousands of those depending on fishing and tourism in the Gulf of Mexico.

If markets had actually delivered on the promises of improving the standards of living of most citizens, then all of the sins of corporations, all the seeming social injustices, the insults to our environment, the exploitation of the poor, might have been forgiven. But to the young *indignados* and protestors elsewhere in the world, capitalism is failing to produce what was promised, but is delivering on what was not promised—inequality, pollution, unemployment, and, *most important of all*, the degradation of values to the point where everything is acceptable and no one is accountable.

Failure of Political System

The political system seems to be failing as much as the economic system. Given the high level of youth unemployment around the world—near 50 percent in Spain and 18 percent in the United States—it was perhaps more surprising that it took so long for the protest movements to begin than that protests eventually broke out. The unemployed, including young people who had studied hard and done everything that they were supposed to do ("played by the rules," as some politicians are wont to say), faced a stark choice: remaining unemployed or accepting a job far below that for which they were qualified. In many cases there was not even a choice: there simply were no jobs, and hadn't been for years.

One interpretation of the long delay in the arrival of mass protests was that, in the aftermath of the crisis, there was hope in democracy, faith that the political system would work, that it would hold accountable those who had brought on the crisis and quickly repair the economic system. But years after the breaking of the bubble, it became clear that our political system had failed, just as it had failed to prevent the crisis, to check the growing inequality, to protect those at the bottom, to prevent the corporate abuses. It was only then that protesters turned to the streets.

Americans, Europeans and people in other democracies around the world take great pride in their democratic institutions. But the protesters have called into question whether there is a *real* democracy. Real democracy is more than the right to vote once every two or four years. The choices have to be meaningful. The politicians have to listen to the voices of the citizens. But increasingly, and especially in the United States, it seems that the political system is more akin to "one dollar one vote" than to "one person one vote." Rather than correcting the market's failures, the political system was reinforcing them.

Politicians give speeches about what is happening to our values and our society, but then they appoint to high office the CEOs and other corporate officials who were at the helm in the financial sector as the system was failing so badly. We shouldn't have expected the architects of the system that has not been working to rebuild the system to make it work, and especially work for most citizens—and they didn't.

The failures in politics and economics are related, and they reinforce each other. A political system that amplifies the voice of the wealthy provides ample opportunity for laws and regulations—and the administration of them—to be designed in ways that not only fail to protect the ordinary citizens against the wealthy but also further enrich the wealthy at the expense of the rest of society.

This brings me to one of the central theses of this book: while there may be underlying economic forces at play, politics have shaped it in ways that advantage the top at the expense of the rest. Any economic system has to have rules and regulations; it has to operate within a legal framework. There are many different such frameworks, and each has consequences for distribution as well as growth, efficiency, and stability. The economic elite have pushed for a framework that benefits them at the expense of the rest, but it is an economic system that is neither efficient nor fair. I explain how our inequality gets reflected in every important decision that we make as a nation—from our budget to our monetary policy, even to our system of justice—and show how these decisions themselves help perpetuate and exacerbate this inequality.

Given a political system that is so sensitive to moneyed interests, growing economic inequality leads to a growing imbalance of political power, a vicious nexus between politics and economics. And the two together shape, and are shaped by, societal forces—social mores and institutions—that help reinforce this growing inequality.

What the Protesters Are Asking for, and What They Are Accomplishing

The protesters, perhaps more than most politicians, grasped what was going on. At one level, they are asking for so little: for a chance to use their skills, for the right to decent work at decent pay, for a fairer economy and society, one that treats them with dignity. In Europe and the United States, their requests are not revolutionary, but evolutionary. At another level, though, they are asking for a great deal: for a democracy where people, not dollars, matter; and for a market economy that delivers on what it is supposed to do. The two demands are related: unfettered markets do not work well, as we have seen. For markets to work the way markets are supposed to, there has to be appropriate government regulation. But for that to occur, we have to have a democracy that reflects the general interests—not the special interests or just those at the top.

The protesters have been criticized for not having an agenda, but such criticism misses the point of protest movements. They are an expression of frustration with the political system and even, in those countries where there are elections, with the electoral process. They sound an alarm.

In some ways the protesters have already accomplished a great deal: think tanks, government agencies, and the media have confirmed their allegations, the failures not just of the market system but of the high and *unjustifiable* level of inequality. The expression "we are the 99 percent" has entered into popular consciousness. No one can be sure where the movements will lead. But of this we can be sure: these young protesters have already altered public discourse and the consciousness of ordinary citizens and politicians alike.

Concluding Comments

In the weeks following the protest movements in Tunisia and Egypt, I wrote (in an early draft of my *Vanity Fair* article),

> As we gaze out at the popular fervor in the streets, one question to ask ourselves is this: when will it come to America? In important ways, our own country has become like one of these distant, troubled places. In particular, there is the stranglehold exercised on almost everything by that tiny sliver of people at the top—the wealthiest 1 percent of the population.

It was to be but a few months before those protests reached the shores of this country.

This book attempts to fathom the depths of one aspect of what has happened in the United States—how we became a society that was so unequal, with opportunity so diminished, and what those consequences are likely to be.

The picture I paint today is bleak: we are only just beginning to grasp how far our country has deviated from our aspirations. But there is also a message of hope. There are alternative frameworks that will work better for the economy as a whole and, most importantly, for the vast majority of citizens. Part of this alternative framework entails a better balance between markets and the state—a perspective that is supported, as I shall explain, both by modern economic theory and by historical evidence. In these alternative frameworks, one of the roles that the government undertakes is to redistribute income, especially if the outcomes of market processes are too disparate.

Critics of redistribution sometimes suggest that the cost of redistribution is too high. The disincentives, they claim, are too great, and the gains to the poor and those in the middle are more than offset by the losses to the top. It is often argued on the right that we could have more equality, but only at the steep price of slower growth and lower GDP. The reality (as I will show) is just the opposite: we have a system that has been working overtime to move money from the bottom and middle to the top, but the system is so inefficient that the gains to the top are far less than the losses to the middle and bottom. We are, in fact, paying a high price for our growing and outsize inequality:

not only slower growth and lower GDP but even more instability. And this is not to say anything about the other prices we are paying: a weakened democracy, a diminished sense of fairness and justice, and even, as I have suggested, a questioning of our sense of identity.

JOSEPH STIGLITZ is an economist and a professor at Columbia University. In 2001, he received the Nobel Memorial Prize in Economic Sciences. He is a former senior vice president and chief economist of the World Bank, and is a former member and chairman of the Council of Economic Advisers. In 2000, Stiglitz founded the Initiative for Policy Dialogue (IPD), a think tank on international development based at Columbia University.

Robert Rector and Rachel Sheffield  **NO**

Understanding Poverty in the United States: Surprising Facts about America's Poor

Today, the Census Bureau released its annual poverty report, which declared that 46.2 million (roughly one in seven) Americans were poor in 2010. The numbers were up sharply from the previous year's total of 43.6 million. Although the current recession has increased the numbers of the poor, high levels of poverty predate the recession. In most years for the past two decades, the Census Bureau has declared that at least 35 million Americans lived in poverty.

Yet what do these numbers actually mean? What does it mean to be poor in America? For most Americans, the word "poverty" suggests near destitution: an inability to provide nutritious food, clothing, or reasonable shelter for one's family. For example, the Poverty Pulse poll by the Catholic Campaign for Human Development in 2005 asked the general public: "How would you describe being poor in the U.S.?" The overwhelming majority of responses focused on homelessness, hunger or not being able to eat properly, and not being able to meet basic needs. Yet if poverty means lacking nutritious food, adequate warm housing, and clothing, relatively few of the 46 million people identified by the Census Bureau as being "in poverty" could be characterized as poor.

The Census Bureau's poverty report is widely publicized by the press. Regrettably, the report provides only a bare count of the number of Americans defined as poor by the government. It provides no data on or description of their actual living conditions. However, several other federal surveys provide detailed information on the living conditions of the poor. These surveys provide a very different sense of American poverty. They reveal that the actual standard of living of America's poor—in terms of amenities in the home, housing, food consumption, and nutrition—is far higher than expected.

These surveys show that most people whom the government defines as "in poverty" are not actually poor in any ordinary sense of the term. While material hardship does exist in the United States, it is restricted in scope and severity. Regrettably, the mainstream press rarely reports on these detailed surveys of living conditions.

TALKING POINTS

- The typical poor American lives in an air-conditioned house or apartment that is in good repair and has cable TV, a car, multiple color TVs, a DVD player, a VCR, and many other appliances. Half of the poor have computers, and one-third have wide-screen plasma TVs.
- Some 96 percent of poor parents report their chilldren were never hungry at any time in the prior year.
- A poor child is more likely to have cable TV, a computer, a wide-screen plasma TV, an Xbox, or a TiVo in the home than to be hungry.
- Poor Americans have more living space in their homes than the average non-poor Swede, Frenchman, or German.
- Sound anti-poverty policy must be based on accurate information and address the causes of poverty, not merely the symptoms. Exaggerating the extent and severity of hardships will not benefit society, the taxpayers, or the poor.

Amenities in Poor Households

Chart 1 shows ownership of property and consumer durables among poor households based on data from the 2009 American Housing Survey, which was conducted by the U.S. Department of Housing and Urban Development and the Census Bureau, and the 2009 Residential Energy Consumption Survey, which was conducted by the U.S. Department of Energy. These surveys show that:

- 80 percent of poor households have air conditioning. By contrast, in 1970, only 36 percent of the U.S. population enjoyed air conditioning.
- 92 percent of poor households have a microwave.
- Nearly three-fourths have a car or truck, and 31 percent have two or more cars or trucks.
- Nearly two-thirds have cable or satellite TV.
- Two-thirds have at least one DVD player, and 70 percent have a VCR.
- Half have a personal computer, and one in seven have two or more computers.

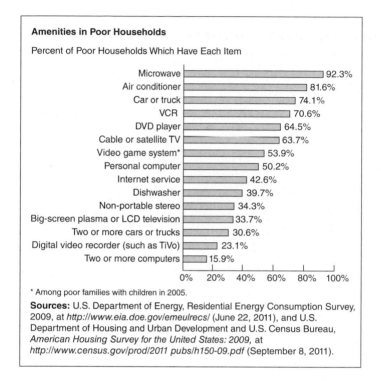

Amenities in Poor Households

Percent of Poor Households Which Have Each Item

Item	Percent
Microwave	92.3%
Air conditioner	81.6%
Car or truck	74.1%
VCR	70.6%
DVD player	64.5%
Cable or satellite TV	63.7%
Video game system*	53.9%
Personal computer	50.2%
Internet service	42.6%
Dishwasher	39.7%
Non-portable stereo	34.3%
Big-screen plasma or LCD television	33.7%
Two or more cars or trucks	30.6%
Digital video recorder (such as TiVo)	23.1%
Two or more computers	15.9%

* Among poor families with children in 2005.

Sources: U.S. Department of Energy, Residential Energy Consumption Survey, 2009, at *http://www.eia.doe.gov/emeulrecs/* (June 22, 2011), and U.S. Department of Housing and Urban Development and U.S. Census Bureau, *American Housing Survey for the United States: 2009,* at *http://www.census.gov/prod/2011 pubs/h150-09.pdf* (September 8, 2011).

- More than half of poor families with children have a video game system, such as an Xbox or PlayStation.
- 43 percent have Internet service.
- 40 percent have an automatic dishwasher.
- One-third have a wide-screen plasma or LCD TV.
- Around one-fourth have a digital video recorder, such as a TiVo.
- More than half have a cell phone.

Of course, nearly all poor households have commonplace amenities such as color TVs, telephones, and kitchens equipped with an oven, stove, and refrigerator.

In 2005, more than half of poor households had at least five of the following 10 conveniences: a computer, cable or satellite TV, air conditioning, Internet service, a large-screen TV, non-portable stereo, computer printer, separate freezer or second refrigerator, microwave, and at least one color TV. One-fourth of the poor had seven or more of these 10 items in their homes. . . .

Steady Improvement in Living Conditions

Are the numbers in Chart 1 a fluke? Have they been inflated by working-class families with lots of conveniences in the home who have lost jobs in the recession and temporarily joined the ranks of the poor? No. The data indicate that the broad array of modern conveniences in the homes of the poor is the result of decades of steady progress in the living standards of the poor. Year by year, the poor tend to be better off. Consumer items that were luxuries or signifi-

cant purchases for the middle class a few decades ago have become commonplace in poor households.

In part, this is caused by a normal downward trend in prices after a new product is introduced. Initially, new products tend to be expensive and therefore available only to the affluent. Over time, prices fall sharply, and the product saturates the entire population including poor households. As a rule of thumb, poor households tend to obtain modern conveniences about a dozen years after the middle class. Today, most poor families have conveniences that were major purchases or unaffordable to the middle class not too long ago.

Liberals use the declining relative prices of many amenities to argue that it is no big deal that poor households have air conditioning, computers, and cable TV. They contend that even though most poor families have houses full of modern conveniences, the average poor family still suffers from serious deprivation in basic needs, such as food, nutrition, and housing. While such an outcome is theoretically possible, this paper demonstrates that this is not the case. In fact, the overwhelming majority of poor households have an adequate and reasonably steady supply of food, are not hungry, and are well housed.

Poverty and Malnutrition

Malnutrition (also called undernutrition) is a condition of reduced health due to a chronic shortage of calories and nutriments. There is little or no evidence of poverty-induced malnutrition in the United States. It is often believed that a lack of financial resources forces poor people to eat low-quality diets that are deficient in nutriments and high in fat, but survey data show that nutriment density (amount of vitamins, minerals, and protein per kilocalorie of food) does not vary by income class. Nor do the poor consume higher-fat diets than do members of the middle class. The percentage of persons with high fat intake (as a share of total calories) is virtually the same for low-income and upper-middle-income persons. However, overconsumption of calories is a major problem among the poor, as it is in the general U.S. population.

Examination of the average nutriment consumption of Americans reveals that age and gender play a far greater role than income class in determining nutritional intake. For example, the nutriment intakes of adult women in the upper middle class (incomes above 350 percent of the poverty level—roughly $76,000 for a family of four in today's dollars) more closely resemble the intakes of poor women than those of upper-middle-class men, children, or teens. The average nutriment consumption of upper-middle-income preschoolers is virtually identical with that of poor preschoolers, but not with the consumption of adults or older children in the upper middle class.

This same pattern holds for adult males, teens, and most other age and gender groups. In general, children who are 0–11 years old have the highest average level of nutriment intakes relative to the recommended daily allowance (RDA), followed by adult and teen males. Adult and teen females have the lowest level of intakes. This pattern holds for all income classes.

Nutrition and Poor Children

Government surveys provide little evidence of widespread undernutrition among poor children. In fact, they show that the average nutriment consumption among the poor closely resembles consumption among the upper middle class. Children in families with incomes below the poverty level actually consume more meat than do children in upper-middle-class families. . . .

Poverty and Consistency of Food Supply

Most poor Americans are not undernourished, but experience an abundance of food over time rather than chronic shortfalls of food. However, even though the poor generally have an ample food supply, some do suffer from temporary food shortages. For example, even if a poor household has an adequate or good overall food supply when measured over a moderate period, it still might need to cut back meals or go without if food stamps run out at the end of the month. This problem of temporary food shortages leads some advocates to claim that there is widespread "hunger" in the United States.

The current deep recession and prolonged high levels of unemployment have made it much more difficult for families to have a steady supply of food. Many families have been forced to eat less expensive food than they are accustomed to eating. Nonetheless, USDA survey data show that most households, poor or non-poor, do not suffer even temporarily from food shortages. During the recession in 2009, 95 percent of all U.S. households report that they had "enough food to eat," although not always the kinds of food that they would have preferred. Some 3.9 percent of all households report they "sometimes" did not have enough food to eat, while 1 percent said they "often" did not have enough food.

Among the poor, the figures are slightly lower: 83.4 percent of poor households asserted that they always had "enough food to eat," although a full 38 percent of these did not always have the foods they would have preferred. Some 13 percent of poor households stated that they "sometimes" did not have enough food, and 3.7 percent said that they "often" did not have enough food. The bottom line is that, although a significant portion of poor households do report temporary food shortages, five out of six poor households stated that they had enough food to eat even in the middle of a recession.

Poverty and Temporary Food Shortages

The USDA also measures temporary food shortages within households, a condition it calls "very low food security." According to the USDA, in households with very low food security, the "eating patterns of one or more household members were disrupted and their food intake reduced, at least some time during the year, because they couldn't afford enough food."

At times, these households worried that food would run out, ate unbalanced meals, and relied on cheaper foods. In addition, adults usually cut back on the size of their meals or skipped meals to save money. In a majority of these households, adults reported feeling hungry at times but not eating due to a lack of food. In the overwhelming majority of households with very low food security, adults ate less while shielding children from reductions in food intake.

Very low food security is almost always an intermittent and episodic problem for families rather than a chronic condition. The average family with very low food security experienced disrupted food intakes in seven months of the year, for one to seven days per month. . . .

In 2009, the USDA also asked parents living in poverty the following question about their children: "In the last 12 months, were the children ever hungry but you just couldn't afford more food?" Some 96 percent of poor parents responded that their children had never been hungry during the previous year due to a lack of food resources. Only 4 percent of poor parents responded that their children had been hungry at some point in the year.

Poverty and Homelessness

The mainstream press and activist groups frequently conflate poverty with homelessness. News stories about poverty often feature homeless families living "on the street."

This depiction is seriously misleading because only a small portion of persons "living in poverty" will become homeless over the course of a year. The overwhelming majority of the poor reside throughout the year in non-crowded housing that is in good repair.

The *2009 Annual Homeless Assessment Report to Congress* published by the U.S. Department of Housing and Urban Development (HUD) states that on a given night in 2009, some 643,000 persons in the U.S. were homeless (without permanent domicile). This means that at any given time, one out of 470 persons in the general population or one out of 70 persons with incomes below the poverty level was homeless.

Moreover, two-thirds of the 643,000 homeless persons were residing in emergency shelters or transitional housing. Only 240,000 were without shelter; these "unsheltered" individuals were "on the street," meaning that they were living in cars, abandoned buildings, alleyways, parks, or similar places. At any point in 2009, roughly one person out of 1,250 in the general population or one out of 180 poor persons was homeless in the literal sense of being on the street and without shelter.

Homelessness is usually a transitional condition. Individuals typically lose housing, reside in an emergency shelter for a few weeks or months, and then reenter permanent housing. The transitional nature of homelessness means that many more people become temporarily homeless over the course of a year than are homeless at any single point in time. Thus, HUD reports that 1.56 million persons resided in an emergency shelter or transitional housing at least one night during 2009. The year-round total of individuals who ever stayed in a shelter or transitional housing was nearly four times larger than the 403,000 who resided in such facilities on an average night.

Based on the year-round data on shelter use, roughly one person in 195 in the general population resided in an emergency shelter or transitional housing for at least one night during a full 12-month period. Roughly one in 25 poor persons (4 percent of all poor persons) resided in an emergency shelter or transitional housing for at least one night during the full year.

Although news stories often suggest that poverty and homelessness are similar, this is inaccurate. In reality, the gap between the living conditions of a homeless person and the typical poor household are proportionately as great as the gap between the poor household and a middle-class family in the suburbs.

Housing Conditions and Poverty

When the mainstream media do not portray the poor as homeless, they will often present them as living in dismal conditions such as an overcrowded, dilapidated trailer. Again, government survey data provide a very different picture. Most poor Americans live in conventional houses or apartments that are in good repair. 49.5 percent of poor households live in single-family homes, either unattached single dwellings or attached units such as townhouses. Another 41 percent live in apartments, and 9.5 percent live in mobile homes.

Poverty and Crowding

Both the overall U.S. population and the poor in America live in very spacious housing. 71 percent of all U.S. households have two or more rooms per tenant. Among the poor, this figure is 65 percent.

Crowding is quite rare. Only 2.2 percent of all households and 6.2 percent of poor households are crowded with less than one room per person. By contrast, social reformer Jacob Riis, writing on tenement living conditions around 1890 in New York City, described crowded families living with four or five persons per room and some 20 square feet of living space per person. . . .

Conclusion

The living conditions of the poor as defined by the government bear little resemblance to notions of "poverty" promoted by politicians and political activists. If poverty is defined as lacking adequate nutritious food for one's family, a reasonably warm and dry apartment, or a car to go to work when one is needed, then the United States has relatively few poor persons. Real material hardship does occur, but it is limited in scope and severity.

In 2005, the typical poor household as defined by the government had a car and air conditioning. For entertainment, the household had two color TVs, cable or satellite TV, a DVD player, and a VCR. If children—especially boys—were in the home, the family had a game system, such as an Xbox or PlayStation. In the kitchen, the household had a refrigerator, an oven and stove, and a microwave. Other household conveniences included a clothes washer, clothes dryer, ceiling fans, a cordless phone, and a coffee maker.

The home of the typical poor family was not overcrowded and was in good repair. The family was able to obtain medical care when needed. By its own report, the family was not hungry and had sufficient funds during the previous year to meet all essential needs.

Poor families certainly struggle to make ends meet, but in most cases, they are struggling to pay for air conditioning and the cable TV bill as well as to put food on the table. While poor households certainly are not sitting in the lap of luxury, their actual living standards are far different from the images of dire deprivation promoted by activists and the mainstream media.

However, the average poor family does not represent every poor family. There is a range of living conditions within the poverty population. Although most poor families are well housed, a small minority are homeless. Although most poor families are well fed and have a fairly stable food supply, a sizeable minority experiences temporary shortages in food supply at various times during the year.

Nonetheless, the living standards of most poor households are far different from what the public imagines and differ greatly from the images of dramatic hardship conveyed by advocacy groups and the mainstream media. Why, then, does the Census Bureau routinely report that over 35 million Americans live in poverty? Its annual poverty report is inaccurate and misleading in part because nearly all of the welfare state is excluded from its poverty calculations. The Census Bureau identifies a family as "poor" if its income falls below specific thresholds; however, in counting a family's income, the Census Bureau omits nearly all welfare benefits. In 2010, government spent $871 billion on means-tested welfare programs that provided cash, food, housing, medical care, and social services to poor and low-income Americans. Virtually none of this assistance is counted as income for purposes of the Census Bureau's estimations of poverty or inequality.

In 2010, government means-tested assistance averaged nearly $9,000 for each poor and low-income American. Many "poor" families have higher than expected living standards in part because they receive considerable government aid that is "off the books" for purposes of counting poverty. Do the higher living standards of the poor mean that the welfare state has been successful?

The answer is: yes and no. Not even the government can spend $9,000 per person without having a significant effect on living conditions. But the original goal of the War on Poverty was not to prop up living standards artificially through an ever-expanding welfare state. President Lyndon Johnson intended for the War on Poverty to make Americans self-sufficient and prosperous through their own abilities, not through increased reliance on government aid. Ironically, Johnson actually planned to reduce, not increase, welfare dependence. His declared goal for the War on Poverty was "making taxpayers out of taxeaters."

Since the beginning of the War on Poverty, the U.S. has spent over $17 trillion on anti-poverty programs. In terms of its original goal of making poor Americans self-sufficient and prosperous through their own abilities, the War on Poverty has been a colossal failure. In many low-income communities, the work ethic has eroded and marriage has collapsed. As result, lower-income groups are less capable of self-sufficient prosperity today than they were when the War on Poverty began.

Congress should reorient the massive welfare state to promote self-sufficient prosperity rather than expanded dependence. As the recession ends, able-bodied recipients should be required to work or prepare for work as a condition of receiving aid. Even more important, the welfare system needs to abandon its 50-year-old tradition of ignoring, dismissing, and penalizing marriage. It should embark on a new course to strengthen and rebuild marriage in low-income communities.

ROBERT RECTOR is Senior Research Fellow in the Domestic Policy Studies Department and is a leading authority on poverty, welfare programs, and immigration in America for three decades.

RACHEL SHEFFIELD is a Research Assistant in the Richard and Helen DeVos Center for Religion and Civil Society, at The Heritage Foundation.

EXPLORING THE ISSUE

Is Increasing Economic Inequality a Serious Problem?

Critical Thinking and Reflection

1. How did a country with such a strong commitment to equality come to have such a high level of inequality?
2. What are the arguments for the trickle-down theory and what are the arguments against it?
3. How does the growing inequality in America affect the functioning of democracy? Does it further corrupt the election processes? Does it directly affect the legislative and administrative processes? If so, how?
4. How can the adverse effects of inequality be mitigated by policies or regulations?
5. Currently many activists are claiming that the 1 percent is screwing the 99 percent. What evidence supports this claim and what evidence contradicts it?
6. What should be done about the growing inequality, or should nothing be done?

Is There Common Ground?

There is not much common ground between the two selections. Stiglitz says the inequality is very bad and its consequences are very bad. Rector and Sheffield say that the inequality is not so bad and its consequences are not so bad. Both sides want America to be prosperous, and that includes a prosperous lower class. Stiglitz says that most Americans are worse off than a decade ago and especially the lower class. Rector and Sheffield say that the poor are far better off than most people realize because they actually own many things that were hard for the middle class to own decades ago. They back this point up with generous statistics. Most of the poor have cable, a car, DVD player, video player, personal computer, air conditioner, and a microwave. Their homes are filled with abundant possessions. In fact, they say that "for decades, the living conditions of the poor have steadily improved." They are also relatively well-off in the basics. "Most of the poor do not experience hunger or food shortages . . . 96 percent of poor parents stated that their children were never hungry at any time during the year because they could not afford food." They are well-off even in their housing. "The average poor American has more living space than the typical non-poor person in Sweden, France, or the United Kingdom." These and other statistics do not erase the vast inequality in incomes in America but they make a good case for seeing the inequality as not so bad.

Stiglitz has income inequality statistics on his side but does not focus on living conditions. Rather his concerns are with inequality's impacts on the economy and the government. It makes the economic system less stable, less efficient, grow less, and fail most citizens. It also threatens democracy, subordinates the government to moneyed interests, and erodes public support and global influence.

So both sides have very different views of America today and would probably disagree on what to do about

commonly recognized problems. Both want a strong and prosperous America and a well-off lower class but differ on what are the best ways to achieve it. All agree that they should get educational assistance. Do free public schools accomplish that. Some European countries make education free through college. Should America do the same? Are food stamps, free school lunches, Head Start, and welfare for the needy enough at their current levels to enable the poor young people to climb the ladder of success? Everyone recognizes that there is a danger that help can create dependency, so how much is enough and not too much?

Create Central

www.mhhe.com/createcentral

Additional Resources

Inequality, stratification, and social mobility are central concerns of sociology, and they are addressed by a large body of literature. Important discussions of income inequality include: Rebecca M. Blank, *Changing Inequality* (University of California Press, 2011); Nathan J. Kelly, *The Politics of Income Inequality in the United States* (Cambridge University Press, 2009); Robert H. Frank, *Falling Behind: How Rising Inequality Harms the Middle Class* (University of California Press, 2007); Thom Hartmann, *Screwed: The Undeclared War Against the Middle Class—And What We Can Do About It* (Berrett-Koehler Publishers, 2006); Lou Dobbs, *War on the Middle Class: How the Government, Big Business, and Special Interest Groups Are Waging War on the American Dream and How to Fight Back* (Viking, 2006); Allan C. Ornstein, *Class Counts: Education, Inequality, and the Shrinking Middle Class* (Rowman & Littlefield, 2007); John Hively, *The Rigged Game: Corporate America and a People Betrayed* (Black Rose Books, 2006); Barry Bluestone and Bennett Harrison, *Growing Prosperity: The Battle for Growth with Equity in the Twenty-First Century* (Houghton Mifflin, 2000); Richard B. Freeman, *When Earnings Diverge: Causes, Consequences, and Cures for the New Inequality in the U.S.* (National Policy Association, 1997); Andrew Hacker, *Money: Who Has How Much and Why* (Scribner's Reference, 1997); Chuck Collins and Felice Yeskel, *Economic Apartheid in America* (New Press, 2005); Paul Ryscavage, *Rethinking the Income Gap* (Transaction Publishers, 2009); Edward N. Wolff, *Top Heavy: The Increasing Inequality of Wealth in America and What Can Be Done about It* (New Press, 2002); Finis Welch (ed.), *The Causes and Consequences of Increasing Inequality* (University of Chicago Press, 2001); James Tardner and David Smith (eds.), *Inequality Matters: The Growing Economic Divide in America and Its Poisonous Consequences* (New Press, 2005); and Samuel Bowles et al. (eds.), *Unequal Chances* (Princeton University Press, 2005).

The survey coverage of the inequality is covered by: Benjamin I. Page in *Class War?: What Americans Really Think about Economic Inequality* (University of Chicago Press, 2009).

A big part of the inequality picture is the condition of the working poor, which is analyzed by: Lawrence Mishel et al., *The State of Working America, 2002–2003* (Cornell University Press, 2003); Eileen Appelbaum et al. (eds.), *Low-Wage America: How Employers Are Reshaping Opportunity in the Workplace* (Russell Sage Foundation, 2003); and David K. Shipler, *The Working Poor: Invisible in America* (Knopf, 2004).

For a poignant ethnographic study of the poor and their disadvantages, see: Elliot Liebow, *Tell Them Who I Am: The Lives of Homeless Women* (Free Press, 1993).

Internet References . . .

Sociology—Study Sociology Online

http://edu.learnsoc.org/

Sociology Web Resources

www.mhhe.com/socscience/sociology/resources
/index.htm

Sociosite

www.topsite.com/goto/sociosite.net

Socioweb

www.topsite.com/goto/socioweb.com

Selected, Edited, and with Issue Framing Material by:
Kurt Finsterbusch, *University of Maryland, College Park*

ISSUE

Is America Close to Being a
Post-Racial Society?

YES: **Alvin Poussaint**, from "Obama, Cosby, King, and the Mountaintop," *CNN.com* (November 13, 2008)

NO: **Lawrence D. Bobo**, from "Somewhere Between Jim Crow and Post-Racialism: Reflections on the Racial Divide in America Today," *Daedalus* (Spring 2011)

Learning Outcomes

After reading this issue, you should be able to:

- Apprehend the changes in the civil rights of blacks in America in the past half century.
- Evaluate the discrimination, biases, prejudices, stereotypes, and values that still hold blacks back.
- Know basic facts about current racial inequalities and a sense of the extent of change since the 1950s.
- Understand how change is resisted.
- Understand how public figures affect children's perceptions and thereby their lives.
- Discern what can be accomplished by new policies and what cannot be accomplished by them.
- Understand indirect victimization and judge its importance in current racial inequality.

ISSUE SUMMARY

YES: Alvin Poussaint is a professor of psychiatry at the Harvard Medical School with a focus on child psychiatry. He argues that the election of Barack Obama may indicate that America is approaching the mountaintop that King preached about.

NO: Lawrence D. Bobo, the W. E. B. Du Bois Professor of the Social Sciences at Harvard University, provides a scholarly analysis of racial inequalities. He explains how inequalities in America are constantly being recreated. Change occurs and is much celebrated, but change is successfully resisted in many subtle ways.

This debate analyzes interracial (and interethnic) relations, but our focus will be on black–white relations. Our starting point is the question, "What does the election of Barack Obama indicate about race relations in America today?" A black was elected to the highest position in America. This was impossible to imagine 50 years ago. Clearly America has changed. There were important precursors to the Obama presidency such as very popular Oprah Winfrey and many other popular black entertainers. Blacks have also become prominent political leaders such as Colin Powell and Condoleezza Rice. The public image of blacks has greatly improved. *The Cosby Show* had something to do with this. As a viewer I identified with Dr. Huxtable and his family as well as many other black actors and actresses in movies and TV shows over the years.

The images that young people see are quite different from what I saw when I was growing up. The first movie that I saw about interracial marriage was *Guess Who's Coming to Dinner* with Spencer Tracy, Katherine Hepburn, and Sidney Poitier. It came out in 1967, and was a bombshell at the time—very tense. Many people could not handle it.

Today the situation is totally different. Interracial and interethnic marriages are more common and thus more normal, and this reflects changes in interracial attitudes and laws. Interracial marriages were illegal in many states until the Supreme Court declared these laws unconstitutional in 1967. Change in interracial marriages has been slow, however, since only 2.9 percent of the population were interracial in 2010. On the other hand, 5.6 percent of the population under age 18 are interracial. According to the 2010 census, 8.5 percent of married black men and 3.9 percent of married black women had a white spouse. According to the 2008 Pew Research Center Report based on the Census Bureau's 2008 American Community Survey:

> Among all newlyweds in 2008, 9% of whites, 16% of blacks, 26% of Hispanics and 31% of Asians married someone whose race or ethnicity was different from their own. . . . Among all newlyweds in 2008, intermarried pairings were primarily White-Hispanic (41%) as compared to White-Asian (15%), White-Black (11%), and Other Combinations (33%). . . . Rates of intermarriages among newlyweds in the U.S. more than doubled between 1980 (6.7%) and 2008 (14.6%). . . . Most Americans say they approve of racial or ethnic intermarriage—not just in the abstract, but in their own families. More than six-in-ten say it would be fine with them if a family member told them they were going to marry someone from any of three major race/ethnic groups other than their own. More than a third of adults (35%) say they have a family member who is married to someone of a different race. Blacks say this at higher rates than do whites; younger adults at higher rates than older adults; and Westerners at higher rates than people living in other regions of the country.

These statistics demonstrate that considerable change has occurred, and also show that there is room for a great deal more change. The United States is moving toward a post-racial society, but it is debatable whether it is moving enough to get there this century.

Alvin Poussaint, an African American child psychiatrist, predicts that Barack Obama's election will have a major impact on race perceptions, especially of children. Black children will feel less like outsiders and more like full members of society. White children will also have different perceptions of blacks than their parents did. Lawrence D. Bobo focuses more on the resistance to change than the progress that appears on the surface. Discrimination and bias are subtle and often unseen. Whites are unaware of the extent of their advantages and are likely to assume that people get what they deserve. Bobo skillfully reveals the true story.

YES ↵

Alvin Poussaint

Obama, Cosby, King, and the Mountaintop

(**C**NN)—Rev. Martin Luther King Jr. told followers the night before he was killed that he had been "to the mountaintop" and seen the promised land of racial equality. Last week's election of Barack Obama was the equivalent of taking all African-Americans to that peak, says Dr. Alvin Poussaint.

In his view, Obama's victory last week wasn't just a political triumph. It was a seismic event in the history of black America.

Poussaint has made it his life's work to study how African-Americans see themselves and how the larger society sees them.

From the days of the civil rights movement through the 1980s, when he was a script consultant on "The Cosby Show," to today, he has been a leader in assessing how images of black people in the media shape perceptions. Poussaint, who is 74, is professor of psychiatry at Judge Baker Children's Center in Boston and at Harvard Medical School.

At a key point in the civil rights movement, Poussaint moved to Mississippi and worked for the Medical Committee for Human Rights, in Jackson, from 1965 to 1967, helping care for civil rights workers and aiding the desegregation of hospitals and other health care institutions.

Poussaint met Bill Cosby in the 1970s and has worked with him on a variety of books and shows, most recently co-authoring a book with Cosby. He was interviewed by CNN on Wednesday.

CNN: What do you think is the long-term impact of the election of Barack Obama as a symbol and a message to the black community in America?

Dr. Alvin Poussaint: We're going to have a generation of children—if he's in there for eight years—being born in 2009, looking at television and images, hearing before they can talk, absorbing it in their brain and being wired to see the visual images of a black man being president of the United States and understanding very early that that's the highest position in the United States.

So I think that's going to be very powerful in its visual imagery . . . and they're going to see these images constantly on television, probably offsetting a lot of the negative imagery that they may see in shows and videos and sometimes in stereotypic comedy.

These images will also make black parents proud. Although there are many barriers to this, it might put back on the table the importance of the two-parent family. . . . Maybe it will do something for couples and bring black men and black women closer together.

The sense of pride may carry over into family life, the same way it is being carried over now into the life of the church already. At black churches this past Sunday, all of them were talking about Obama and being ambassadors for Obama—in other words, suggesting that now that he's president, that black people should take the high road.

The big problem with all of this is that if there's high expectations that somehow the social ills that the black community faces will suddenly evaporate, they're going to be disappointed—because the economy, the economic crisis is a major issue that's going to affect the black community, making things worse. . . . So there's going to be more unemployment, more poor people, more black homeless and more poverty. . . .

Obama's also going to have a positive effect on the white community. Way back in the 1960s, I used to go to Atlanta when it was segregated and even after it started desegregating. When you went downtown to restaurants, you would walk in as a black person and they would kind of act like, "What are you doing here?" You weren't welcome, you know, you just felt it.

And Maynard Jackson became the first black mayor, and I felt a whole change in the tone of the city. You went places and when you walked in, people had to consider: "Is this someone who knows the mayor, this black person?" And so I think they began to treat all black people better because black people were now in power. . . . This may help to eradicate stereotypes that they hold. . . .

So this may have a spinoff effect . . . maybe more blacks will break through the glass ceiling in corporations, more blacks may, because of their newfound confidence, become more civically engaged, run for office.

CNN: What if he had lost, what would the impact have been then?

Poussaint: A lot of black people would have concluded that he lost because of his race, and the black people who had no faith in the system in the first place would have continued to feel that way, maybe even more strongly, and maybe even have more anger at the institutions that have authority over them and that they see as white-controlled.

CNN: Obama is taking over at a time of tremendous international and national challenges. Every president has setbacks. What would be the impact of setbacks on a political level?

Poussaint: Nearly everybody that you hear talk about it realizes that he's inheriting a horrible situation. In fact one of the black leaders joked about how, as soon as things are falling apart in the country, that they hand it over to a black person—"Here, you take it."

People are saying that he's just been dealt a terrible hand and is going to have to work very hard to be successful and they're rooting for him and hoping. There's a mindset right now of "What can we do to help Obama?" And I don't think it's just black people saying it, it's all the people who voted for him, young people and women, the workers, the unions—"What can we do to help him be successful, and undo the mess that we're in?"

CNN: What do you make of the idea that "The Cosby Show" made America more ready to vote for a black man to be president?

Poussaint: I don't know, you can't study this stuff scientifically. The intent when the Cosby show came on . . . was to present a black family that was not the old stereotypical family that white people laughed at in a sitcom. And we wanted the show to have a universality, in terms of a mother, a father, wonderful children, a lot of love being shown, an emphasis on education.

Today if you have 12 or 15 million viewers of a show a week, it's number one. Well, Cosby was bringing in about 60 million people a week. So this had a deep effect on white children, Latino children, and even many adults, what their images of black people were.

So that's why Karl Rove reached into the hat the other day and said this was the beginning of the post-racial era, because it made white people embrace this black family like a family of their own and fall in love with it.

It probably played some role at chipping away at those negative images, which made white people . . . more ready to embrace a lot of things, including Tiger Woods and Oprah Winfrey and Denzel Washington and Will Smith. Certainly when Obama gets on the scene, people don't say, "What kind of black family is that? We haven't seen any black family like that."

Because that's what they said about the Cosby show, . . . that this doesn't represent a black family, this is fantasy. And it wasn't fantasy, because there were black families like that in 1984, and there are many more black families like that in the middle class and upper-middle class today.

CNN: You were a consultant on the Cosby show. How did that come about?

Poussaint: I knew him and his wife. When the show was coming on, he called me and said he wanted me to . . . be a production consultant to keep this a positive show without stereotyping: "I want you to read and critique every single script before it goes into production, anything you want to say to make this family psychologically believable, living in reality." He wanted the story lines to have a plot that made sense. . . . He told me to weed out what he called put-down humor, which he felt was too prevalent, particularly on a lot of black shows where you make fun of people.

I was allowed to comment on anything, from the clothes to some of the people they were casting, to making sure there was a wide range of colors on the show in terms of complexion, what's on the reading table, what cultural activities the kids are going to, what colleges they're applying to. . . .

CNN: You co-authored a book with Bill Cosby. What's the message of that book?

Poussaint: It's called, "Come on People: On the Road from Victims to Victors." The message is, don't be helpless and hopeless and see yourself as a victim and wallow in failing and think that's your lot in life. What you have to do is take the high road and you have to work hard to try to achieve against the odds. . . .

Most of the black people are where they are today because we succeeded against the odds, we didn't allow the racism out there to totally squelch us. And we feel that spirit is being lost, particularly in low-income communities and sometimes among middle-income people too. And we felt they had to adopt more of an attitude of being victors.

And victors are active, they try to do their best, they take education very seriously. And Obama's a good example—if he took a victim's attitude and said, "Well, a black man could never get elected president of the United States," which a lot of us felt like, he wouldn't have run for the presidency. So he adopted what we call a victor's attitude—"I'm going to go for it, it may be a longshot, but it's possible."

CNN: What do you compare the Obama victory to in terms of significance?

Poussaint: The civil rights movement's success in getting the civil rights bill of '64 and the Voting Rights Act of '65, that opened things mightily for the black communities all over the country. Obviously getting those bills and those accomplishments—forget about The Cosby Show—the voting rights bill played a significant role in Obama's victory.

CNN: Does Obama's victory as a historical moment equal those?

Poussaint: It equals those but it has a more powerful visual symbolism. It's like people are going from [Martin Luther]

King, who was moving us toward the mountaintop . . . to Obama, people saying [we're] getting to the mountaintop and now being able to gaze down. So it's the fruition of a movement beginning in slavery. . . . We were in slavery for 250 years, and then Jim Crow segregation for another 100, and we've been struggling for freedom. Obama represents us winning our freedom—like "free at last, free at last, free at last."

But it's not really true. We still have racial discrimination in the country, we're still going to have racial injustice.

ALVIN POUSSAINT is a noted professor of Psychiatry at Harvard Medical School. He has authored several books on the subject of child psychiatry.

Lawrence D. Bobo   ➡ **NO**

Somewhere Between Jim Crow and Post-Racialism: Reflections on the Racial Divide in America Today

> In assessing the results of the Negro revolution so far, it can be concluded that Negroes have established a foothold, no more. We have written a Declaration of Independence, itself an accomplishment, but the effort to transform the words into a life experience still lies ahead.
>
> —Martin Luther King, Jr., *Where Do We Go from Here?* (1968)

> By the middle of the twentieth century, the color line was as well defined and as firmly entrenched as any institution in the land. After all, it was older than most institutions, including the federal government itself. More important, it informed the content and shaped the lives of those institutions and the people who lived under them.
>
> —John Hope Franklin, *The Color Line* (1993)

> This is where we are right now. It's a racial stalemate we've been stuck in for years. Contrary to the claims of some of my critics, black and white, I have never been so naive as to believe that we can get beyond our racial divisions in a single election cycle, or with a single candidacy—particularly a candidacy as imperfect as my own.
>
> —Barack H. Obama, "A More Perfect Union" (May 18, 2008)

The year 1965 marked an important inflection point in the struggle for racial justice in the United States, underscoring two fundamental points about race in America. First, that racial inequality and division were not only Southern problems attached to Jim Crow segregation. Second, that the nature of those inequalities and divisions was a matter not merely of formal civil status and law, but also of deeply etched economic arrangements, social and political conditions, and cultural outlooks and practices. Viewed in full, the racial divide was a challenge of truly national reach, multilayered in its complexity and depth.

Therefore, the achievement of basic citizenship rights in the South was a pivotal but far from exhaustive stage of the struggle.

The positive trend of the times revolved around the achievement of voting rights. March 7, 1965, now known as Bloody Sunday, saw police and state troopers attack several hundred peaceful civil rights protestors at the Edmund Pettus Bridge in Selma, Alabama. The subsequent march from Selma to Montgomery, participated in by tens of thousands, along with other protest actions, provided the pressure that finally compelled Congress to pass the Voting Rights Act of 1965. A triumphant Reverend Martin Luther King, Jr., and other activists attended the signing in Washington, D.C., on August 6, 1965. It was a moment of great triumph for civil rights.

The long march to freedom seemed to be at its apex, inspiring talk of an era of "Second Reconstruction." A decade earlier, in the historic *Brown v. Board of Education* decision of 1954, the U.S. Supreme Court repudiated the "separate but equal" doctrine. Subsequently, a major civil rights movement victory was achieved with the passage of the Civil Rights Act of 1964, which forbade discrimination in employment and in most public places. With voting rights now protected as well, and the federal government authorized to intervene directly to assure those rights, one might have expected 1965 to stand as a moment of shimmering and untarnished civil rights progress. Yet the mood of optimism and triumph did not last for long.

The negative trend of the times was epitomized by deep and explosive inequalities and resentments of race smoldering in many Northern, urban ghettos. The extent to which the "race problem" was not just a Southern problem of civil rights, but a national problem of inequality woven deep into our economic and cultural fabric, would quickly be laid bare following passage of the Voting Rights Act. Scarcely five days after then-President Johnson signed the bill into law, the Los Angeles community of Watts erupted into flames. Quelling the disorder, which raged for roughly six days, required the mobilization of the National Guard and nearly fifteen thousand troops. When disorder finally subsided, thirty-four people had died, more than one thousand had been injured, well over three thousand were arrested, and approximately $35 million in property

Bobo, Lawrence D. From *Daedalus*, Spring 2011. Copyright © 2011 by MIT Press Journals/American Academy of Arts and Sciences. Reprinted by permission. www.mitpressjournals.org/doi/abs/10.1162/DAED_a_00091

damage had been done. Subsequent studies and reports revealed patterns of police abuse, political marginalization, intense poverty, and myriad forms of economic, housing, and social discrimination as contributing to the mix of conditions that led to the riots.

It was thus more than fitting that in 1965, *Daedalus* committed two issues to examining the conditions of "The Negro American. . . ." Some critical observations stand out from two of those earlier essays, which have been amplified and made centerpieces of much subsequent social science scholarship. Sociologist and anthropologist St. Clair Drake drew a distinction between what he termed primary victimization and indirect victimization. Primary victimization involved overt discrimination in the labor market that imposed a job ceiling on the economic opportunities available to blacks alongside housing discrimination and segregation that relegated blacks to racially distinct urban ghettos. Indirect or secondary victimization involved the multidimensional and cumulative disadvantages resulting from primary victimization. These consequences included poorer schooling, poor health, and greater exposure to disorder and crime. In a related vein, sociologist Daniel Patrick Moynihan stressed the central importance of employment prospects in the wake of the civil rights victories that secured the basic citizenship rights of African Americans. Both Drake and Moynihan expressed concern about a black class structure marked by signs of a large and growing economically marginalized segment of the black community. Drake went so far as to declare, "If Negroes are not to become a permanent lumpen-proletariat within American society as a result of social forces already at work and increased automation, deliberate planning by governmental and private agencies will be necessary." Striking a similar chord, Moynihan asserted: "[T]here would also seem to be no question that opportunities for a large mass of Negro workers in the lower ranges of training and education have not been improving, that in many ways the circumstances of these workers relative to the white work force have grown worse." This marginalized economic status, both scholars suggested, would have ramifying effects, including weakening family structures in ways likely to worsen the challenges faced by black communities.

If the scholarly assessments of 1965 occurred against a backdrop of powerful and transformative mass-based movement for civil rights and an inchoate sense of deep but imminent change, the backdrop for most scholarly assessments today is the election of Barack Obama as president of the United States, the rise of a potent narrative of post-racialism, and a sense of stalemate or stagnation in racial change. Many meanings or interpretations can be attached to the term post-racial. In its simplest and least controversial form, the term is intended merely to signal a hopeful trajectory for events and social trends, not an accomplished fact of social life. It is something toward which we as a nation still strive and remain guardedly hopeful about fully achieving. Three other meanings of post-racialism are filled with more grounds for dispute

and controversy. One of these meanings attaches to the waning salience of what some have portrayed as a "black victimology" narrative. From this perspective, black complaints and grievances about inequality and discrimination are well-worn tales, at least passé if not now pointedly false assessments of the main challenges facing blacks in a world largely free of the dismal burdens of overt racial divisions and oppression.

A second and no less controversial view of post-racialism takes the position that the level and pace of change in the demographic makeup and the identity choices and politics of Americans are rendering the traditional black–white divide irrelevant. Accordingly, Americans increasingly revere mixture and hybridity and are rushing to embrace a decidedly "beige" view of themselves and what is good for the body politic. Old-fashioned racial dichotomies pale against the surge toward flexible, deracialized, and mixed ethnoracial identities and outlooks.

A third, and perhaps the most controversial, view of post-racialism has the most in common with the well-rehearsed rhetoric of color blindness. To wit, American society, or at least a large and steadily growing fraction of it, has genuinely moved beyond race—so much so that we as a nation are now ready to transcend the disabling racial divisions of the past. From this perspective, nothing symbolizes better the moment of transcendence than Obama's election as president. This transcendence is said to be especially true of a younger generation, what *New Yorker* editor David Remnick has referred to as "the Joshua Generation." More than any other, this generation is ready to cross the great river of racial identity, division, and acrimony that has for so long defined American culture and politics.

It is in this context of the first African American president of the United States and the rise to prominence of the narrative of post-racialism that a group of social scientists were asked to examine, from many different disciplinary and intellectual vantage points, changes in the racial divide since the time of the *Daedalus* issues focusing on race in 1965 and 1966.

The context today has points of great discontinuity and of great similarity to that mid-1960s inflection point. From the viewpoint of 1965, the election of Obama as the first African American president of the United States, as well as the expansion and the cultural prominence and success of the black middle class of which Obama is a member, speak to the enormous and enduring successes of the civil rights era. Yet also from the standpoint of 1965, the persistence of deep poverty and joblessness for a large fraction of the black population, slowly changing rates of residential segregation by race, continued evidence of antiblack discrimination in many domains of life, and historically high rates of black incarceration signal a journey toward racial justice that remains, even by superficial accounting, seriously incomplete.

In order to set a context for the essays contained in this volume, I address three key questions in this introduction. The first concerns racial boundaries. In an era of widespread talk of having achieved the post-racial society, do we have real evidence that attention to and the meaning of basic race categories are fundamentally breaking down? The second set of questions concerns the extent of economic inequality along the racial divide. Has racial economic inequality narrowed to a point where we need no longer think or talk of black disadvantage? Or have the bases of race-linked economic inequality changed so much that, at the least, the dynamics of discrimination and prejudice no longer need concern us? The third question is, how have racial attitudes changed in the period since the mid-1960s *Daedalus* issues?

To foreshadow a bit, I will show that basic racial boundaries are not quickly and inevitably collapsing, though they are changing and under great pressure. Racial economic inequality is less extreme today, there is a substantial black middle class, and inequality within the black population itself has probably never been greater. Yet there remain large and durable patterns of black–white economic inequality as well, patterns that are not overcome or eliminated even for the middle class and that still rest to a significant degree on discriminatory social processes. In addition, I maintain that we continue to witness the erosion and decline of Jim Crow racist attitudes in the United States. However, in their place has emerged a new pattern of attitudes and beliefs, variously labeled symbolic racism, modern racism, color-blind racism, or as I prefer it, laissez-faire racism. The new form of racism is a more covert, sophisticated, culture-centered, and subtle racist ideology, qualitatively less extreme and more socially permeable than Jim Crow racism with its attendant biological foundations and calls for overt discrimination. But this new racism yields a powerful influence in our culture and politics.

Consider first the matter of group boundaries. The 2000 Census broke new ground by allowing individuals to mark more than one box in designating racial background. Nearly seven million people exercised that option in 2000. . . . Despite Obama's electoral success and the press attention given to the phenomenon, some will no doubt find it surprising that the overwhelming majority of Americans identify with only one race. . . . Less than 2 percent of the population marked more than one box on the 2000 Census in designating their racial background. Fully 98 percent marked just one. I claim no deep-rootedness or profound personal salience for these identities. Rather, my point is that we should be mindful that the level of "discussion" and contention around mixture is far out of proportion to the extent to which most Americans actually designate and see themselves in these terms.

Moreover, even if we restrict attention to just those who marked more than one box, two-thirds of these respondents designated two groups other than blacks (namely, Hispanic-white, Asian-white, or Hispanic and Asian mixtures). . . . Some degree of mixture with black constituted just under a third of mixed race identifiers in 2000. Given the historic size of the black population and the extended length of

contact with white Americans, this remarkable result says something powerful about the potency and durability of the historic black–white divide.

It is worth recalling that sexual relations and child-bearing across the racial divide are not recent phenomena. The 1890 U.S. Census contained categories for not only "Negro" but also "Mulatto," "Quadroon," and even "Octoroon"; these were clear signs of the extent of "mixing" that had taken place in the United States. Indeed, well over one million individuals fell into one of the mixed race categories at that time. In order to protect the institution of slavery and to prevent the offspring of white slave masters and exploited black slave women from having a claim on freedom as well as on the property of the master, slave status, as defined by law, followed the mother's status, not the father's. For most of its history, the United States legally barred or discouraged racial mixing and intermarriage. At the time of the *Loving v. Virginia* case in 1967, seventeen states still banned racial intermarriage.

Formal, legal definitions of who was black, and especially the development of rules of "hypodescent," or the one drop rule, have a further implication that is often lost in discussions of race: these practices tended to fuse together race and class, in effect making blackness synonymous with the very bottom of the class structure. As historian David Hollinger explains: The combination of hypodescent with the denial to blacks residing in many states with large black populations of any opportunity for legal marriage to whites ensured that the color line would long remain to a very large extent a property line. Hence, the dynamics of race formation and the dynamics of class formation were, in this most crucial of all American cases, largely the same. This is one of the most important truths about the history of the United States brought into sharper focus when that history is viewed through the lens of the question of ethnoracial mixture.

Still, we know that today the ethnoracial landscape in the United States is changing. As of the 2000 Census, whites constituted just 69 percent of the U.S. population, with Hispanics and blacks each around 12 percent. This distribution represents a substantial decline in the percentage of whites from twenty or, even more so, forty years ago.

With continued immigration, differential group fertility patterns, and the continued degree of intermarriage and mixing, these patterns will not remain stable. . . . Forecasts predict that somewhere between 2040 and 2045, whites will cease to be a numerical majority of the population. (This change could possibly happen much sooner than that.) The relative size of the Hispanic population is expected to grow substantially, with the black, Asian, Native Hawaiian and other Pacific Islander, American Indian, and Alaska Native groups remaining relatively constant. [This] strongly implies that pressure to transform our understanding of racial categories will continue.

Does that pressure for change foretell the ultimate undoing of the black–white divide? At least three lines of research raise doubts about such a forecast. First, studies of the perceptions of and identities among those of mixed racial backgrounds point to strong evidence of the cultural persistence of the one-drop rule. Systematic experiments by sociologists and social psychologists are intriguing in this regard. For example, sociologist Melissa Herman's recent research concluded that "others' perceptions shape a person's identity and social understandings of race. My study found that part black multiracial youth are more likely to be seen as black by observers and to define themselves as black when forced to choose one race."

Second, studies of patterns in racial intermarriage point to a highly durable if somewhat less extreme black–white divide today. A careful assessment of racial intermarriage patterns in 1990 by demographer Vincent Kang Fu found that "one key feature of the data is overwhelming endogamy for blacks and whites. At least 92 percent of white men, white women, black women and black men are married to members of their own group. . . ."

Third, some key synthetic works argue for an evolving racial scheme in the United States, but a scheme that nonetheless preserves a heavily stigmatized black category. A decade ago, sociologist Herbert Gans offered the provocative but well-grounded speculation that the United States would witness a transition from a society defined by a great white–nonwhite divide to one increasingly defined by a black–non-black fissure, with an in-between or residual category for those granted provisional or "honorary white" status. . . .

If basic racial categories and identities are not soon to dissolve, then let me now address that second set of questions, concerning the degree of racial economic inequality. I should begin by noting that there has been considerable expansion in the size, security, and, arguably, salience and influence of the black middle class.

Turning to the question of income, we find a similar trend. . . . At the very bottom are those who the Census would designate as the "very poor": that is, having a family income that is 50 percent or less of the poverty level. At the very top are those in the "comfortable" category, having family incomes that are five times or more the poverty level. The proportion of whites in this upper category exceeded 10 percent in 1960 and rose to nearly 30 percent by 2008. For blacks, the proportion was less than 5 percent in 1968 but about 12 percent in 2008. Likewise, the fraction in the middle class (those with family incomes more than twice the poverty level) grows for both groups. But crucially, the proportion of blacks in the "poor" (at the poverty line) or "very poor" categories remains large, at a combined figure of nearly 40 percent in 2008. This contrasts with the roughly 20 percent of whites in those same categories.

The official black poverty rate has fluctuated between two to three times the poverty rate for whites. Recent trend analyses suggest that this disparity declined during the economic boom years of the 1990s but remained substantial. As public policy analyst Michael Stoll explains:

"Among all black families, the poverty rate declined from a 20 year high of about 40 percent in 1982 and 1993 to 25 percent in 2000. During this period, the poverty rate for white families remained fairly constant, at about 10 percent." That figure of 25 percent remains true through more recent estimates. In addition, the Great Recession has taken a particularly heavy toll on minority communities, African Americans perhaps most of all. As the Center for American Progress declared in a recent report: "Economic security and losses during the recession and recovery exacerbated the already weak situation for African Americans. They experienced declining employment rates, rising poverty rates, falling home ownership rates, decreasing health insurance and retirement coverage during the last business cycle from 2001 to 2007. The recession that followed made a bad situation much worse."

Overall trends in poverty, however, do not fully capture the cumulative and multidimensional nature of black economic disadvantage. Sociologist William Julius Wilson stresses how circumstances of persistently weak employment prospects and joblessness, particularly for low-skilled black men, weaken the formation of stable two-parent households and undermine other community structures. Persistent economic hardship and weakened social institutions then create circumstances that lead to rising rates of single-parent households, out-of-wedlock childbearing, welfare dependency, and greater risk of juvenile delinquency and involvement in crime. Harvard sociologist Robert Sampson points to an extraordinary circumstance of exposure to living in deeply disadvantaged communities for large segments of the African American population. This disadvantage involves living in conditions that expose residents to high surrounding rates of unemployment, family breakup, individuals and families reliant on welfare, poor-performing schools, juvenile delinquency, and crime. As Sampson explains:

> [A]lthough we knew that the average national rate of family disruption and poverty among blacks was two to four times higher than among whites, the number of distinct ecological contexts in which blacks achieve equality to whites is striking. In not one city of 100,000 or more in the United States do blacks live in ecological equality with whites when it comes to these basic features of economic and family organization. Accordingly, racial differences in poverty and family disruption are so strong that the "worst" urban contexts in which whites reside are considerably better than the average context of black communities.

Recent work published by sociologist Patrick Sharkey assesses race differences in the chances of mobility out of impoverished neighborhoods. The result is a very depressing one. He finds evidence of little upward social mobility for disadvantaged blacks and a fragile capacity to maintain advantaged status among even the most well-off African Americans. He writes: "[M]ore than 70% of black children who are raised in the poorest quarter of American neighborhoods will continue to live in the poorest quarter of neighborhoods as adults. Since the 1970s, more than half of black families have lived in the poorest quarter of neighborhoods in consecutive generations, compared to just 7% of white families." Discussing the upper end, Sharkey writes: "Among the small number of black families who live in the top quartile, only 35% remain there in the second generation. . . . White families exhibit a high rate of mobility out of the poor neighborhoods and a low rate of moving out of the most affluent neighborhoods, and the opposite is true among black families."

The general labor market prospects of Americans have undergone key changes in the last several decades. Three loom large. There is far more internal differentiation and inequality within the black population than was true at close of World War II. . . . The fortunes of men and women have recently diverged within the black community. Black women have considerably narrowed the gap between themselves and white women in terms of educational attainment, major occupational categories, and earnings. Black men have faced a growing problem of economic marginalization. Importantly, this is contingent on levels of education; education has become a far sharper dividing line, shaping life chances more heavily than ever before in the black community.

Several other dimensions of socioeconomic status bear mentioning. Even by conservative estimates, the high school dropout rate among blacks is twice that of whites, at 20 percent versus 11 percent. Blacks also have much lower college completion rates (17 percent versus 30 percent) and lower advanced degree completion rates (6 percent versus 11 percent). These differences are enormously consequential. . . . [E]ducational attainment and achievement increasingly define access to the good life, broadly defined.

One of the major social trends affecting African Americans over the past several decades has been the sharply punitive and incarceration-focused turn in the American criminal justice system. Between 1980 and 2000, the rate of black incarceration nearly tripled. The black-to-white incarceration ratio increased to above eight to one during this time period. . . . The reach of mass incarceration has risen to such levels that some analysts view it as altering normative life-course experiences for blacks in low-income neighborhoods. Indeed, the fabric of social life changes in heavily policed, low income urban communities.

Processes of racial residential segregation are a key factor in contemporary racial inequality. Despite important declines in overall rates of segregation over the past three decades and blacks' increasing suburbanization, blacks remain highly segregated from whites. Some have suggested that active self-segregation on the part of blacks is now a major factor sustaining residential segregation. A number of careful investigations of preferences for neighborhood characteristics and makeup and of the housing search process strongly challenge such claims. Instead, there is substantial evidence that, particularly among white

Americans, neighborhoods and social spaces are strongly racially coded, with negative racial stereotypes playing a powerful role in shaping the degree of willingness to enter (or remain) in racially integrated living spaces. Moreover, careful auditing studies continue to show lower, but still significant, rates of antiblack discrimination on the part of real estate agents, homeowners, and landlords.

Lastly, I want to stress that wealth inequality between blacks and whites remains enormous. Recent scholarship has convincingly argued that wealth (or accumulated assets) is a crucial determinant of quality of life. Blacks at all levels of the class hierarchy typically possess far less wealth than otherwise comparable whites. Moreover, the composition of black wealth is more heavily based in homes and automobiles as compared to white wealth, which includes a more even spread across savings, stocks and bonds, business ownership, and other more readily liquidated assets. Whereas approximately 75 percent of whites own their homes, only 47 percent of blacks do. Looking beyond home ownership to the full range of financial assets, analyses from sociologists Melvin Oliver and Tom Shapiro put the black-to-white wealth gap ratio in the range of ten or eleven to one. . . .

What do we know about changes in racial attitudes in the United States? The first and most consistent finding of the major national studies of racial attitudes in the United States has been a steady repudiation of the outlooks that supported the Jim Crow social order. Jim Crow racism once reigned in American society, particularly in the South. Accordingly, blacks were understood as inherently inferior to whites, both intellectually and temperamentally. As a result, society was to be expressly ordered in terms of white privilege, with blacks relegated to secondary status in education, access to jobs, and in civic status such as the right to vote. Above all, racial mixture was to be avoided; hence, society needed to be segregated. The best survey data on American public opinion suggest that this set of ideas has been in steady retreat since the 1940s.

This picture of the repudiation of Jim Crow is complicated somewhat by evidence of significant social distance preferences. To be sure, low and typically declining percentages of whites objected when asked about entering into integrated social settings—neighborhoods or schools—where one or just a small number of blacks might be present. But as the number of blacks involved increased, and as one shifts from more impersonal and public domains of life (workplaces, schools, neighborhoods) to more intimate and personal domains (intermarriage), expressed levels of white resistance rise and the degree of positive change is not as great.

There is low and decreasing support among whites for the overtly racist belief that blacks have less inborn ability. The most widely endorsed account among whites points to a lack of motivation or willpower on the part of blacks as a key factor in racial inequality, though this attribution declines over time. . . . Blacks are generally far more likely than whites to endorse structural accounts of racial inequality, particularly the strongest attribution of discrimination. However, like their white counterparts, a declining number of blacks point to discrimination as the key factor, and there is actually a rise in the percentage of African Americans attributing racial inequality to a lack of motivation or willpower on the part of blacks themselves. . . .

To the extent that unfavorable beliefs about the behavioral characteristics of blacks have a bearing on levels of support for policies designed to benefit blacks, these data imply, and much evidence confirms, that negative beliefs about blacks' abilities and behavioral choices contribute to low levels of white support for significant social policy interventions to ameliorate racial inequality.

Judged by the trends considered here . . . , declarations of having arrived at the post-racial moment are premature. Much has changed—and unequivocally for the better—in light of where the United States stood in 1965. Indeed, I will speculate that none of the contributors to the 1965/1966 *Daedalus* volumes would have considered likely changes that have now, a mere four or so decades later, been realized, including the election of an African American President of the United States, the appointment of the first black Chair of the Joint Chiefs of Staff, and the appointment of two different African American Secretaries of State. Similarly, the size and reach of today's black middle class were not easy to forecast from the scholarly perch of mid-1960s data and understandings. At the same time, troublingly entrenched patterns of poverty, segregation, gaps in educational attainment and achievement, racial identity formation, and disparaging racial stereotypes all endure into the present, even if in somewhat less extreme forms. And the scandalous rise in what is now termed racialized mass incarceration was not foreseen but now adds a new measure of urgency to these concerns. . . .

These results underscore why discussions of race so easily and quickly become polarized and fractious along racial lines. The central tendencies of public opinion on these issues, despite real increasing overlap, remain enormously far apart between black and white Americans. When such differences in perception and belief are grounded in, or at least reinforced by, wide economic inequality, persistent residential segregation, largely racially homogeneous family units and close friendship networks, and a popular culture still suffused with negative ideas and images about African Americans, then there should be little surprise that we still find it enormously difficult to have sustained civil discussions about race and racial matters. Despite growing much closer together in recent decades, the gaps in perspective between blacks and whites are still sizable.

LAWRENCE D. BOBO is the Martin Luther King Jr. Centennial Professor at Harvard University, where he is also director of the Center for Comparative Study in Race and Ethnicity and director of the Program in African and African-American Studies.

EXPLORING THE ISSUE

Is America Close to Being a Post-Racial Society?

Critical Thinking and Reflection

1. What criteria should a scholar use to judge a social movement's success?
2. What are the advantages and disadvantages of movement leaders setting movement goals higher than it is possible to achieve?
3. Can civil rights equity be legislated? Can integration be legislated? If integration can be legislated in the economy, can it also be legislated in the churches?
4. Does complete integration require that intermarriages become as common as intramarriages?
5. Are black self-images on a par with white self-images? If not, why not?
6. Consider the power of symbols in national life.
7. The election of Obama had the potential to unite our country racially and ethnically. Why are we more divided than ever?

Is There Common Ground?

Both authors agree that much progress has been made in the civil rights of blacks. The main difference in their opinions regards how far this country has come and how far it has yet to go. According to Lawrence D. Bobo's title, America is somewhere between Jim Crow and post-racialism. According to Alvin Poussaint, America is closer to King's mountaintop than Jim Crow. It comes down to what you emphasize: half empty or half full. I went to Princeton University in 1953 and there was only one black in my class. In fact the first African American undergraduate to enter Princeton during peacetime arrived only 6 years earlier. According to an article in the *Princeton Alumni Weekly* in 2010, "The percentage of minority students—defined by Princeton University as Asian-Americans, African-Americans, Hispanics, Native Americans, and those who self-identify as multiracial—make up 37 percent of students in the Class of 2013. Asian-American students are the largest ethnic minority in the freshman class (17.7 percent), followed by African-Americans (7.3 percent), Hispanics (6.8 percent), and Native Americans (0.5 percent). In recent years, the University has allowed students to identify themselves as multiracial, and more than 5 percent of freshmen do so." Check the history of your college or employer and you will see a dramatic story. The story of your neighborhood will probably also involve racial changes but in several different directions. The story of your church or other religious body will probably show the least change, and that is a story in itself. From what has happened around you, how much do you think America has moved toward a post-racial society?

Create Central

www.mhhe.com/createcentral

Additional Resources

The following books bitterly proclaim that the treatment of blacks is definitely unfair: Gregory S. Parks and Matthew W. Hughey, eds., *12 Angry Men: True Stories of Being a Black Man in America Today* (New Press, 2010); Molefi K. Asante, *Erasing Racism: The Survival of the American Nation* (Prometheus Books, 2009); Michael C. Dawson, *Not in Our Lifetimes: The Future of Black Politics* (University of Chicago Press, 2011); Joe R. Feagan, *Racist America: Roots, Current Realities, and Future Reparations* (Routledge, 2010); John Hartigan, *What Can You Say?: America's National Conversation on Race* (Stanford University Press, 2010); Roy H. Kaplan, *The Myth of Post-Racial America: Searching for Equality in the Age of Materialism* (Rowman & Littlefield Education, 2011); Robert E. Pierre, *A Day Late and a Dollar Short: High Hopes and Deferred Dreams in Obama's "Postracial" America* (Wiley, 2010); and Tim J. Wise, *Colorblind: The Rise of Post-Racial Politics and the Retreat from Equity* (City Lights Books, 2010). The historical perspective is presented in Greta De Jong, *Invisible Enemy: The African American Freedom Struggle After 1965* (Wiley-Blackwell, 2010); Cynthia Griggs Fleming, *Yes We Did?: From King's Dream to Obama's Promise* (University of Kentucky Press, 2009); and Emilye Crosby, ed., *Civil Rights History from the Ground Up: Local Struggles, a National Movement* (University of Georgia Press, 2011). *The Obamas and a (Post) Racial America?* edited by Gregory S. Parks and Matthew W. Highey (Oxford University Press, 2011) focuses on the role of the Obamas in altering racial relations.

This debate connects strongly with black politics, which is the focus of several books including: Manning Marable, *Beyond Black and White: Transforming African-American Politics* (Verso, 2009); Desmond S. King, *Still a House Divided: Race and Politics in Obama's America* (Princeton University Press, 2011); Gwen Ifill,

The Breakthrough: Politics and Race in the Age of Obama (Doubleday, 2009); Theodore James Davis, *Black Politics Today: The Era of Socioeconomic Transition* (Routledge, 2012); and Manning Marable and Kristen Clarke, eds., *Barack Obama and African American Empowerment: The Rise of Black America's New Leadership* (Palgrave Macmillan, 2009). The broader issue of racism is analyzed in George Lipsitz, *How Racism Takes Place* (Temple University Press, 2011) and Roy L. Brooks, *Racial Justice in the Age of Obama* (Princeton University Press, 2009).

Internet References . . .

Sociology—Study Sociology Online

http://edu.learnsoc.org/

Sociology Web Resources

www.mhhe.com/socscience/sociology/resources/index.htm

Sociosite

www.topsite.com/goto/sociosite.net

Socioweb

www.topsite.com/goto/socioweb.com

Selected, Edited, and with Issue Framing Material by:
Kurt Finsterbusch, *University of Maryland, College Park*

ISSUE

Is the Gender Wage Gap Justified?

YES: J. R. Shackleton, from "Explaining the Overall Pay Gap" in *Should We Mind the Gap? Gender Pay Differentials and Public Policy* (Institute of Economic Affairs, 2008)

NO: Hilary M. Lips, from "The Gender Wage Gap: Debunking the Rationalizations" and "Blaming Women's Choices for the Gender Pay Gap," *Expert Advice for Working Women,* www.womensmedia.com (2009)

Learning Outcomes

After reading this issue, you should be able to:

- Explain why women earn less money than men, or at least know the main theories that explain these differences.
- Understand the various possible meanings of "equal pay" and understand the difficulties of legislating equal pay for comparable work.
- Understand the motives that underlie women's work/family choices.
- Have insights into the consequences for society of women's work/family choices.
- Debate the pros and cons of women's work/family choices.

ISSUE SUMMARY

YES: J. R. Shackleton, a professor of economics and dean of the Royal Docks Business School at the University of East London, argues that the gender wage gap is not largely due to discrimination. It is largely due to the differential value of male and female workers in the employment market. Employers want profits, so they pay differently for different skills, commitment, and performance, and women choose less profitable training and limit their commitment.

NO: Hilary M. Lips, professor and chair of psychology and director of the Center for Gender Studies at Radford University, documents the continuing gender gap in wages and blames it largely on discrimination based on stereotypes and prejudice.

According to the 2012 *Statistical Abstract,* the median income of full-time women workers was 71.8 percent of median income of full-time men workers. This is a troubling fact that needs to be explained. It calls into question the success of the feminist movement. It calls into question the effectiveness of the antidiscrimination laws and their enforcement. It may not be the result of discrimination but may indicate that women are choosing to limit their participation in the labor force to less demanding and less stressful jobs. It may be driven by the same forces that lead to the "opting out" phenomena debated in Issue 4. Another possibility is that the discrimination against women that still exists makes women want to reduce their participation in the labor force.

Most commentators approach this issue in agreement on several basic issues. First, discrimination is wrong. Equal pay for equal work has been a feminist demand from the beginning and very few would argue against this principle today. Second, both work and family are important to most adults. Third, most married persons experience tension between work and family. Fourth, the "traditional" family value system resulted in less tension between work and family than today's value system. Traditionally, the husband was the provider and the wife was the homemaker. Today, both tend to be providers and active parents. In spite of these agreements, commentators today provide very different judgments about the gender wage gap. The argument starts with the meaning of equal work. Feminists argue that it should include equal pay for comparable work, but many object to this standard. Many argue that the market should determine what different occupations should be paid. The Equal Pay Act states, "Employers may not pay unequal wages to men and women who perform jobs that require substantially equal skill, effort, and responsibility, and that are performed under similar working conditions within the same establishment." It therefore proposes the comparable work rule. It also states, "Pay differentials are permitted when they are based on seniority, merit, quantity or quality of production, or a factor other than sex." This provision provides the grounds for more definitional debates. Another issue is how willing should the employer be to facilitate various special considerations that wives might need to accommodate their family role such as a greater use of sick days or unavailability for out-of-town travel? So what is fair? This is a matter of values, not science.

One side argues that the wage gap is justified because it is the outcome of women's free choices to work at less demanding jobs. The other side argues that it is not justified because the wage gap largely results from discrimination, prejudice, and stereotypes. J. R. Shackleton presents the first view and Hilary L. Lips presents the second view.

YES ↵

J. R. Shackleton

Explaining the Overall Pay Gap

In this chapter various possible explanations for the differences in male and female earnings are examined.

We should begin by asking what determines pay, in general terms, in a competitive market. In such a market we would not expect everybody to earn the same. In the short run, wages are determined simply by supply and demand. If there is a sudden increase in the demand for construction workers because a new underground line is being built, and a limited supply of those with the necessary skills, wages will rise. But in the longer term, more workers will be attracted into construction, perhaps from abroad, or workers in other occupations will retrain. Longer term, it is possible that big pay differentials can persist if people possess unique skills or talents in high demand. . . .

Compensating Differentials

Even where people are free to enter a well-paid field of employment, however, they may not choose to do so. Long ago Adam Smith, in his *Wealth of Nations,* spelled out several reasons why some workers consistently earn more than others. His reasoning forms the basis for the modern idea of "compensating differentials"—where jobs that are unattractive may have to be rewarded with higher pay if they are to attract sufficient workers.

One factor is what Smith called "the difficulty and expense" of learning a job. Some forms of employment require years of training, education, and work experience—generically classed as human capital. The acquisition of human capital typically involves some cost to the trainee in terms of time and forgone earnings, even if the direct costs are paid by the state or the employer, and the worker will expect to be compensated by higher pay. This is clearly relevant to discussion of the gender pay gap, because women are likely to differ from men in relation to their human capital.

Note, however, that the amount of extra pay required will vary, Smith argues, with the "agreeableness or disagreeableness" of the job. Apparently an academic job in a high-ranking research department at Oxford carries sufficient kudos to offset the higher salary obtainable in other universities. By contrast, a cook on a North Sea oil rig, for example, will normally be paid more than a similarly skilled cook working in a city. But whether a premium is paid, and its size, will depend on the tastes and preferences

of individuals. If, over time, Oxford becomes overcrowded and less attractive as a city, the university will have to pay more to attract the best academics. If lots of cooks develop a taste for working at sea, their premium will diminish or disappear. This is pertinent to discussion of the pay gap, for women's preferences in relation to jobs may differ systematically from those of men, as we shall see.

It is rarely discussed in the debate over the pay gap, but part of the explanation for men's higher average pay could well be that there is a compensating differential for less attractive working conditions. Men are more likely to work outside in all weathers. They are more likely to work unsocial hours. Thirty-six percent of male managers work more than 48 hours a week; the figure for women managers is only 18 percent. Men suffer much higher rates of industrial injury.

Looking at the economy as a whole, we see that women's jobs are less at risk: in the three months from November 2007 to January 2008, there were 3.4 redundancies per thousand female employees; the figure for men was 5.3. Women are more likely to get employer-provided training: 13.6 percent of females had received job-related training in the last four weeks in the third quarter of 2007, as against 11.3 percent of males. They have a shorter commuting time to work and take more time off work. No wonder, perhaps, that they report greater job satisfaction than men.

The implication of this is that the "true" gender pay gap may be less than the measured one, as male pay may include an element of compensation for less attractive working conditions. This is ignored in many empirical studies, and it is a serious omission.

Discrimination

Discrimination is often seen as an important explanation of the gender pay gap. The concept needs some clarification before we assess this belief.

Discrimination is a word that has changed its common meaning. Whereas once it was seen as something worthy of praise—as in somebody displaying "a fine discrimination" between paintings or pieces of music—it now usually means something unfair, unacceptable, and, in an increasing number of cases, illegal.

Economic analysis of the subject effectively began with the work of Gary Becker in the 1950s. In Becker's analysis, employers, fellow employees, and governments may engage in discrimination, which he interprets as an economically unjustified preference for one group over another, such that members of the favoured group would be more likely to be given a job, to be paid more, or otherwise treated better than another group or groups. Becker's particular insight was that this preference, this "taste for discrimination," could be seen as an end in itself, something that therefore entailed a "cost" to the discriminator. For example, employers might prefer to hire male rather than female workers even if this were more expensive. In this respect Becker differed fundamentally from Marxists and other critics of capitalism who saw discrimination as a means of exploiting subordinate groups to the benefit of the discriminator.

If this taste for discrimination exists, it *may* be manifested in the existence of a pay gap. This is not necessarily the case, however. If rigorous laws prevent women being paid less than men, discriminating firms may simply hire fewer women, but they will be paid the same as men. So Becker's analysis supports the point made earlier in relation to Italy and Spain: the size of the pay gap in itself does not say very much about the extent of discrimination.

From Becker's analysis, originally applied to racial differences, it followed that discriminating firms would hire white workers, or pay them a higher wage, rather than black workers of identical or superior productivity characteristics. But, he reasoned, this behaviour would raise costs. If other employers who were "colour-blind" entered the market, they would be able to undercut the discriminators and gain a competitive edge.

From this, Becker argued that, in a competitive market where non-discriminators were free to enter, discrimination would be unlikely to persist for long. It could be found where firms had monopsony power;[1] it could also be found where trade unions exercised power to protect white workers against blacks, or, in our context, men against women. But Becker, as a Chicago economist, argued that market power to sustain discrimination is unlikely to persist for any extended period if free entry of firms is allowed and union power is limited. Therefore any sustained discriminatory power is to be attributed to government interference in the free market. Apartheid South Africa is an obvious example. And in the USA, the so-called "Jim Crow" laws in the South sustained labour market discrimination for many years: when they were abolished there was a big increase in the relative pay of black workers—the reduction in the white/black pay gap since then has been relatively modest.

In our current context, it should be remembered that government discrimination against women was often quite explicit in the UK until the mid-twentieth century, with different pay rates for men and women civil servants and teachers, requirements to resign on marriage, and prohibitions on working at all in certain jobs.

A quite different approach to the economics of discrimination was taken by Arrow and Phelps. In their view, employer discrimination was not the result of "tastes" or simple prejudice. Rather, it was a rational response to imperfect knowledge about the characteristics of individual job applicants. This led risk-averse employers to operate with stereotypes, which might be accurate or inaccurate, of common group characteristics. Suppose—and this is true, whatever its cause—that women on average take more time off work than men for sickness, employers might hold this against a female job applicant even if, unknown to the employer, she as an individual had a low sickness risk. Such "statistical discrimination" would be economically rational even if unfair to individuals in particular cases.

As in Becker's reasoning, however, free competition ought to reduce discrimination. Some firms might find it easier than others to acquire more information about individuals, or would be prepared to take a chance on them, because they faced different cost and demand conditions. Not all firms, therefore, will behave in the same way. Furthermore, individuals are not passive. They can signal more information about themselves and market themselves more effectively to potential employers. One way they could in principle do this is to offer to work for less pay during a trial period. In most developed countries, however, such trial arrangements are difficult if not impossible because of legislation on equal pay, minimum wages, and employment protection. Again, governments may be part of the problem.

Some support is given to the common Becker and Arrow/Phelps thesis that free competition tends to eliminate discrimination, while some forms of government intervention assist it, countries with greater economic competition, as measured by the Economic Freedom Index, display lower gender pay gaps. The OECD has recently reached similar conclusions, with the added insight that product market regulation may be an important factor, by protecting disproportionately male "insiders" from new entrants. It finds that "regulatory barriers to competition explain between 20% and 40% of the cross country/time series variation in the gender wage gap."

As overt discrimination is now illegal, direct evidence of its existence is hard to come by. Some studies have used "correspondence tests," where there is some limited evidence that matched job applications from females and males elicit more interview offers for males. Another example is that of "blind" musical auditions which suggest women do better if only their playing is heard. And careful documentation of practices in, for instance, construction indicates prejudice against female employees. But this sort of evidence is sparse.

Those seeking evidence of discrimination might also point to the large number of employment tribunal cases over sex discrimination and equal pay issues as evidence of the problem. It is certainly true that the number of such cases has risen recently: between 2004/05 and 2006/07, the number of sex discrimination cases accepted by tribunals rose from 11,726 to 28,153, while equal pay cases rose from 8,229 to a massive 44,013. There has been little detailed analysis of the growth of these cases, but it is known that there were special factors associated with changes in the law, and with the advent of "no-win, no-fee" lawyers. It is interesting, incidentally, that a disproportionate number of these cases are against public sector employers, although as we have seen, the gender pay gap is much smaller in the public sector. The majority of these claims were multiple claims brought against local authorities and the NHS, paradoxically as a result of the introduction of Job Evaluation Schemes aimed at closing the pay gap.

Looking at the private sector, though, it is clear that only a small proportion of equal pay and sex discrimination claims succeed. The Women and Work Commission examined all private sector equal pay claims from 2000 to 2004 and found that only 25 reached the decision stage, with applicants winning in only five cases.

Despite their growing numbers, tribunal cases are brought by only a tiny proportion of the workforce and cannot really do much to explain the aggregate phenomenon of the overall gender pay gap. They often concern procedural issues rather than more fundamental matters: in the case of sex discrimination tribunal claims, they are often about issues such as sexual harassment, bullying, and other offences rather than issues directly related to pay.

Econometric Analysis of the Pay Gap

Given the limited evidence of direct discrimination, in trying to analyse pay inequality researchers have increasingly concentrated on econometric work.[2] A substantial literature is concerned with separating out that part of the overall gender pay gap that can be accounted for by relevant economic characteristics and that residual part which could possibly be attributable to discrimination—defined as paying different amounts to men and women for identical skills and abilities, and usually seen as conscious or unconscious behaviour by misguided employers.

The large number of studies that have been made of pay gaps in many different countries vary considerably in methodology and conclusions, but there are some common threads. Most studies use a statistical technique first developed more or less simultaneously by Oaxaca and Blinder. This decomposes the gender pay gap into two parts. The first component is the difference in pay associated with differences in observable characteristics such as experience and education. The second is the "residual," which may partly result from discrimination.

The procedure involves first estimating a wage equation, which relates the logarithm of wages to years of education, work experience, and a range of other productivity-related characteristics that are available in the particular dataset the researcher is using. . . .

Variations in rates of return might reflect discrimination or the systematic undervaluing of the jobs of graduates in areas where women dominate. But there are some obvious structural factors at work. One is the sector in which different types of graduates are likely to work. Over a quarter of all women in higher education are studying nursing or education. The vast majority of graduates in these areas will work in the public sector: there are relatively few highly paid jobs in government employment.

Lifestyles, Preferences, Attitudes, Expectations

After allowing for these factors, is that part of the pay gap left unexplained attributable to discrimination, as many claim? Well, possibly, but in addition to [various] factors [such as amount of full-time experience; interruption in employment; education; years of part-time experience, etc.] there is also what econometricians call "unobservable heterogeneity." Here this means differences in attitudes, preferences, and expectations which can cause apparently similarly qualified and experienced individuals to behave very differently.

Catherine Hakim, a sociologist whose work on "preference theory" has created some controversy, claims that, in countries such as the UK, women now have a wide range of lifestyle options and that they can be classified into three relatively distinct groups by their preferences—those who are home-centred, those who are work-centred, and those who are "adaptive."

The first group, which she estimates to be approximately 20 percent of UK women, prioritise family life and children, and prefer not to work in the labour market (though they do so, they are not career-driven). Work-centred women, again about 20 percent, are likely to be childless, committed to their careers, and with a high level of investment in qualifications and training. The largest group, the "adaptives," around 60 percent of UK women, want to work, but they also want families. Their careers tend to be more erratic.

Hakim carried out a national survey which indicated that women's expressed preferences were good predictors of their employment status, whereas, perhaps surprisingly, their educational qualifications were not: some well-qualified women were in the "home-centred" camp. She argues that her preference theory "explains continuing sex differentials in labour market behaviour (workrates, labour turnover, the choice of job etc.) and hence also in the pay gap." . . .

[Another study] includes information on the values that graduates attach to jobs and their career expectations. Men and women differ significantly with regard to these characteristics: men are more likely to state that career development and financial rewards are very important, and are much more likely to define themselves as very ambitious, while women emphasise job satisfaction, being valued by employers and doing a socially useful job. Two-thirds of women in this sample expect to take career breaks for family reasons; 40 percent of men expect their partners to do this, but only 12 percent expect to do it themselves.

When these attitudinal variables are added to the specification, the result is that 84 percent of the wage gap can now be explained. This suggests that many of the models that generate large "unexplained" wage gaps, and from which non-specialists frequently infer a significant element of employer discrimination, are simply misspecified. They just don't incorporate sufficient explanatory variables for a satisfactory analysis of the causes of the gender pay differential. . . .

So the conclusion we can draw from empirical analysis of the full-time pay gap is that a high proportion of this gap can be accounted for, given sufficient information on individual and job characteristics and the attitudes and expectations of employees. Males and females make different choices in the labour market, in terms of the trade-off between pay and other job characteristics, choice of education, choice of occupation, and attitudes to work. These strongly influence earnings. Employer attitudes and discrimination seem not to be nearly as important as politicians and lobbyists have suggested.

Summary

There is a sizeable gap between the average hourly earnings of UK men and women working full time: this is the gender pay gap. The gap has, however, declined over time and is expected to decline further given demographic trends and changes in women's qualifications. It could even go into reverse.

The view that the UK has a particularly large gender pay gap by international standards is misleading. The gap is anyway only one indicator of women's economic status. Its size is not necessarily related to other indicators of sex discrimination and it can increase or decrease for reasons that have nothing to do with employers' behaviour.

The pay gap may partly reflect compensating differentials: men's jobs may typically have disadvantages that are reflected in higher pay. Women report greater job satisfaction than men.

There is little evidence of direct discrimination by employers against women. Discrimination is often inferred from the unexplained residual in econometric analyses of the causes of the gender pay gap.

When attitudes and preferences, as well as objective characteristics such as work experience and qualifications, are brought into the picture, however, most of the pay gap can be explained without reference to discrimination.

Notes

1. Where a firm is the dominant employer in an area, it may be able to segment the job market and pay different rates to different groups of workers without being undercut by other firms. Such a situation could also arise if gender segregation occurred as a result of employee job choice.
2. Econometrics uses statistical methods to analyse and test relationships between economic variables.

J. R. Shackleton is a professor of economics at the University of East London. He was previously dean of the Royal Docks Business School at the University of East London and prior to that was dean of the Westminster Business School. His research interests are primarily in labor economics. He has over a hundred publications to his name and is a frequent commentator on TV and radio.

Hilary M. Lips

 **NO**

The Gender Wage Gap: Debunking the Rationalizations

Last year, a labor economist from the Economic Policy Institute made the widely-quoted estimate that the gender pay gap would be closed within 30 years. Other commentators state confidently that the gap does not reflect discrimination, but other factors, such as the high wages of a few white men, and gendered patterns of occupational and educational choice and work experience. The effect of such assertions is to make women feel complacent about the wage gap—and perhaps to feel that they can avoid its impact by making the right educational, occupational, and negotiation-related choices. Such complacency is unwarranted.

The Wage Gap Exists within Racial/Ethnic Groups

White men are not the only group that out-earns women, although the wage gap is largest between white men and white women. Within other groups, such as African Americans, Latinos, and Asian/Pacific Islanders, men earn more than women (Source: U.S. Census Bureau).

What Difference Does Education Make?

Higher levels of education increase women's earnings, just as they do for men. However, there is no evidence that the gender gap in wages closes at higher levels of education. If anything, the reverse is true: at the very highest levels of education, the gap is at its largest.

The Wage Gap Exists within Occupations

Some people think that if women move into male-dominated occupations in larger numbers, the wage gap will close. However, there appears to be a gender-related wage gap in virtually every occupational category. In researching this issue at the Center for Gender Studies, we found only four occupational categories for which comparison data were available in which women earned even a little more than men: special education teachers, order clerks, electrical

and electronic engineers, and miscellaneous food preparation occupations (Source: Bureau of Labor Statistics).

The movement of women into higher paid occupations, whether male-dominated or not, may not have the impact of narrowing the earnings gap. Social psychologists have demonstrated repeatedly that occupations associated with women or requiring stereotypically feminine skills are rated as less prestigious and deserving of less pay than occupations associated with men and masculine skills. Thus, as more and more women enter an occupation, there may be a tendency to value (and reward) that occupation less and less.

Do Women Earn Less Because They Work Less?

Women are more likely than men to work part-time. However, most gender wage comparisons leave out part-time workers and focus only on full-time, year-round workers. A close look at the earnings of women and men who work 40 hours or more per week reveals that the wage gap may actually widen as the number of hours worked increases. Women working 41 to 44 hours per week earn 84.6% of what men working similar hours earn; women working more than 60 hours per week earn only 78.3% of what men in the same time category earn (Source: Bureau of Labor Statistics). Furthermore, women may work longer to receive the promotions that provide access to higher pay. For example, among school principals, women have an average of 3 years longer as teachers than men do (Source: National Center for Education Statistics). So it is hard to argue that women's lower earnings are simply a result of women putting in fewer hours per week, or even fewer years than men.

Is the Wage Gap Closing?

The U.S. Census Bureau has made available statistics on women's and men's earnings for several decades. By examining this time series of data, it is possible to get a feel for the changes and trends in earnings. One thing revealed by a simple visual examination of the series since 1960 is how closely the shapes of the two lines parallel each other. The dips and bumps in women's and men's earnings seem to move in tandem. Clearly, similar economic and social forces are at work in influencing the rise and fall of earnings for both sexes. Men's earnings do not stand still and wait for women's to catch up.

Another thing that is apparent is that there is some minor fluctuation in the size of the wage gap. For example, the gap widened in the 1960s, closed a little in the 1980s, and widened slightly in the late 1990s. Thus, depending on which chunk of years one examines, it may be possible to conclude that the gap is either widening or narrowing. The only way to get a clear picture of what is happening is to examine the whole series rather than a few years at a time.

The series of data points from 1960 onward provides a basis for a forecast of the future, although such forecasts are always estimates rather than hard certainties. When we used forecasting analyses to project the earnings of women and men into the future, to the year 2010, we found no evidence on which we could base a prediction for a closing (or widening) wage gap. The forecast was, in essence, for the two lines to remain parallel, although the 90% confidence intervals (the range within which we are 90% certain the actual future earnings will fall) do overlap a little.

A Question of Value

As women and men left their jobs this spring because they were called up for military duty, employers scrambled to make sure that these workers did not suffer losses of salary and benefits. In a number of cases, organizations made up the difference between their employees' military pay and their normal pay, held jobs open, and made sure that benefits continued during workers' absence. At the same time, the media made a hero out of a father who chose to ship out with his military unit rather than stay home with his infant son who was awaiting a heart transplant. The message about what we as a society consider important is clear:

- When something perceived as very important needs to be done outside of the workplace, employers feel obligated to provide support for their employees to go and do it.
- In the eyes of society, or at least many employers, family concerns and the care of children do not fall into the category of "very important"— certainly not as important as military duty.

Are these the values we want to live by? If women and men continue to accept the notion that the domestic and caretaking work traditionally classified as "women's work" is not important enough for employers to accommodate, the gender gap in wages will never close. A few individual women may be able to evade the gap by choosing to be childfree, being fortunate enough to have a supportive spouse, and carefully following a model of career advance-

ment that was developed to fit men's needs. However, to make the wage gap disappear will require that we stop buying into the idea that the rules are gender-neutral and that men just follow them better than women do. One by one, employers must be convinced to re-examine assumptions that unwittingly place higher value on the type of work men do than on the type of work women do. The most important step in closing the wage gap is for all of us to give up the notion that, to be paid fairly, a woman must "make it in a man's world."

Blaming Women's Choices for the Gender Pay Gap

A 2006 article in the *New York Times* cited Labor Department statistics that, for college-educated women in middle adulthood, the gender pay gap had widened during the previous decade. The phenomenon was attributed partly to discrimination, but also to "women's own choices. The number of women staying home with young children has risen . . . especially among highly educated mothers, who might otherwise be earning high salaries."

A 2007 report from the American Association of University Women sounded the alarm about a continuing wage gap that is evident even in the first year after college graduation. The authors noted, however, that individual choices with respect to college major, occupation, and parenthood have a strong impact on the gap. Accepting the idea that much of the pay gap can be accounted for by such neutral factors as experience and training, they concluded that, in the first year after college graduation, about 5 percent of the pay gap is unexplained by such factors—and it is that 5 percent that represents the impact of discrimination.

The language attributing women's lower pay to their own lifestyle choices is seductive—in an era when women are widely believed to have overcome the most serious forms of discrimination and in a society in which we are fond of emphasizing individual responsibility for life outcomes. Indeed, it is possible to point to a variety of ways in which women's work lives differ from men's in ways that might justify gender differences in earnings. Women work in lower-paid occupations; on average they work fewer paid hours per week and fewer paid weeks per year than men do; their employment is more likely than men's to be discontinuous. As many economists with a predilection for the "human capital model" would argue, women as a group make lower investments in their working lives, so they logically reap fewer rewards.

At first blush, this argument sounds reasonable. However, a closer look reveals that the language of "choice" obscures larger social forces that maintain the wage gap and the very real constraints under which women labor. The impact of discrimination, far from being limited to the portion of the wage gap that cannot be accounted for by women's choices, is actually deeply embedded in and constrains these choices.

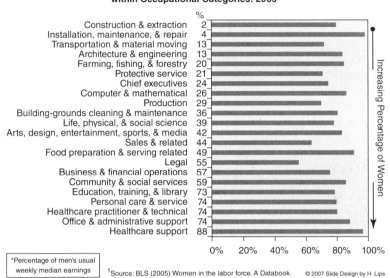

U.S. Women's Earnings as a Percent of Men's*
within Occupational Categories: 2005[1]

Category	%
Construction & extraction	2
Installation, maintenance, & repair	4
Transportation & material moving	13
Architecture & engineering	13
Farming, fishing, & forestry	20
Protective service	21
Chief executives	24
Computer & mathematical	26
Production	29
Building-grounds cleaning & maintenance	36
Life, physical, & social science	39
Arts, design, entertainment, sports, & media	42
Sales & related	44
Food preparation & serving related	49
Legal	55
Business & financial operations	57
Community & social services	59
Education, training, & library	73
Personal care & service	74
Healthcare practitioner & technical	74
Office & administrative support	74
Healthcare support	88

*Percentage of men's usual weekly median earnings

[1]Source: BLS (2005) Women in the labor force. A Databook.   © 2007 Slide Design by H. Lips

Do Women Choose Lower-Paid Occupations?

Women continue to be clustered in low-paid occupational categories: office and administrative support and various service jobs. While they now make up a majority of university students, they are concentrated in academic specialties that lead to lower paid occupations: education rather than engineering, for example. If women persist in choosing work that is poorly paid, shouldn't the responsibility for the wage gap be laid squarely at their own doorstep?

Actually, within groups graduating with particular academic majors, women earn less than men, as illustrated in the AAUW report cited above. And within occupational categories, women earn less than their male counterparts, as revealed in this chart.

Furthermore, there is a catch-22 embedded in women's occupational choices: the migration of women into an occupation is associated with a lowering of its status and salary, and defining an occupation as requiring stereotypically masculine skills is associated with higher prestige, salary, and discrimination in favor of male job applicants. So convincing women in large numbers to shift their occupational choices is unlikely to obliterate the earnings gap.

As well, using the language of choice to refer to women's career outcomes tacitly ignores the many subtle constraints on such decisions. From childhood onward, we view media that consistently portray men more often than women in professional occupations and in masculine-stereotyped jobs. Not surprisingly, researchers find that the more TV children watch, the more accepting they are of occupational gender stereotypes. Why does the acceptance of gender stereotypes matter? Gender-stereotyped messages about particular skills (e.g., "males are generally better at this

than females") lower women's beliefs in their competence—even when they perform at exactly the same level as their male counterparts. In such situations, women's lower confidence in their abilities translates into a reluctance to pursue career paths that require such abilities.

So, there are many problems with treating women's occupational choices as based purely on individual temperament and as occurring within a static occupational system that is unaffected by such choices. Women's employment choices are systematically channeled and constrained—and when women elude the constraints and flow into previously male-dominated jobs, the system apparently adapts to keep those jobs low-paid.

If Women Chose to Work More Hours, Would They Close the Gap?

Women work fewer paid hours per week than men do, but among workers who labor more than 40 hours per week, women earn less than men. Indeed, among workers working 60 hours or more per week at their primary job, women earned only 82% of men's median weekly earnings in 2006. Furthermore, women do not necessarily choose to work fewer hours than men do. One researcher found that 58% of workers want to change their work hours in some way—and that 19% of women report they want the opportunity to work more hours. Also, women have recently brought lawsuits against corporations such as Boeing and CBS claiming discrimination in access to overtime. Thus, in the realm of hours worked for pay, it is probably a mistake to use the number of hours worked as a simple indicator of women's (or men's) choices. As in the case of occupational segregation by gender, the number of hours worked reflects some systematic constraints.

Choosing Parenthood Means Lower Wages Only for Women

For women, having children has a negative effect on wages, even when labor market experience is taken into account. This may be due to mothers' temporary separation from the workforce and/or the loss of the benefits of seniority and position-specific training, experience, and contacts. Among married persons working full-time, the ratio of women's to men's median weekly earnings is 76.4% for those with no children under the age of 18, but only 73.6% for those with children. And when women and men of all marital statuses are considered together, women with children under 18 earn 97.1% of what women without children earn, whereas men with children under 18 earn 122% of what men without children earn.

So, the choice to have children is associated with very different earnings-related outcomes for women and men. In terms of children, it is not that women and men are making different choices, but that the same choices have very different consequences for the two groups. Those consequences reflect society's failure to value the work of parenting. Yet, if most women decided to forego motherhood, the declining birthrate already causing concern in some parts of the developed world would soon become catastrophic.

Women's Choices Are Not the Problem

Individual women can sometimes evade the effects of the gender pay gap by making certain kinds of choices, such as selecting male-dominated occupations, working more hours, avoiding parenthood. However, these choices occur in an environment suffused with subtle sexism and discrimination: there are more barriers for women than for men to making certain choices, and the consequences of some choices are starkly different for women and men.

Moreover, these individual solutions are not effective on a societal level; they work only if the women enacting them remain in a minority. For example, if most women moved into jobs that are now male-dominated, signs are that the salaries associated with those jobs would likely drop. But, by making it difficult to go against the tide, the forces of discrimination ensure that most women don't move into such jobs. And as long as a few women get past the barriers, the illusion persists that any woman could do it if she wanted to—it's a matter of free choice. However, women's choices will not be free until their abilities and their work are valued equally with men's, and until women and men reap equivalent consequences for their choices in the realm of work and family.

HILARY M. LIPS is professor and chair of the Department of Psychology and director of the Center for Gender Studies at Radford University.

EXPLORING THE ISSUE

Is the Gender Wage Gap Justified?

Critical Thinking and Reflection

1. How can any inequality be justified? Does the gender wage gap fit under one of these justifications of inequality?
2. Why are current values about gender roles better than traditional values which were more patriarchial?
3. Are values entirely relative or are there logical standards that can justify some values and actions and condemn other values and actions? God can make some values absolute but can secular reasoning also make some values superior to others?
4. What obligations do women have? What obligations do men have? Why do women have more obligations to childrearing and housework than men? Do men have more obligations to work outside the home than women, and if so, why?
5. What work/family arrangements best serve the general good (good of society)?

Is There Common Ground?

Equality is a commonly held value in America. Very few would argue against different groups getting equal pay for equal work. That agreement breaks down when the equality formula is equal pay for comparable work. Many think that "comparable" is used politically and often is unfair. There is also general agreement that disadvantaged people should be given some assistance such as Head Start to make their competition with advantaged people more fair. There is vehement disagreement, however, over how much assistance is fair. The assistance principle is the basis for affirmative action programs that had more support in the past because many whites now claim that affirmative action has gone too far and is putting whites at too great a disadvantage. This may be true in specific cases but on the whole, I as a white would not want to trade all the advantages whites currently have for the supposed advantages that blacks have.

Another area of agreement in America is that women are on a par with men as having moral value. In some societies, women are the property of their husband or father and have very few rights. Here they have rights and supposedly equal value. Nevertheless, in the 1950s, they did not have equal rights in the workplace and few paid attention. As women went to college in large numbers and young people spoke out against the war, traditions, authorities, and injustices in the 1960s, a new women's movement developed that changed the political landscape. Equal treatment in the workplace became a hot issue with no strong moral arguments against it. The progress of women has been impressive except for the "glass ceiling" that limited women's promotions at the highest levels. Now this is part of the present debate about the justice or injustice of the gender wage gap.

Create Central

www.mhhe.com/createcentral

Additional Resources

Gender discrimination has been greatly reduced in the last several decades, but it still remains. Several works that research this problem include Barbara A. Gutek and M. S. Stockdale, "Sex Discrimination in Employment," in F. Landy, ed., *Employment Discrimination Litigation: Behavioral, Quantitative, and Legal Perspectives* (Jossey-Bass, 2005); Cecilia L. Ridgeway, *Framed by Gender: How Gender Inequality Persists in the Modern World* (Oxford University Press, 2011); Robert L. Kaufman, *Race, Gender, and the Labor Market: Inequalities at Work* (Lynne Rienner Publishers, 2010); Louise Marie Roth, *Selling Women Short: Gender Inequality on Wall Street* (Princeton University Press, 2006); and Lis W. Wiehl, *The 51% Minority: How Women Still Are Not Equal and What You Can Do about It* (Ballantine Books, 2007). Robert L. Nelson focuses on the legal aspects of this issue in *Legalizing Gender Inequality: Courts, Markets, and Unequal Pay for Women in America* (Cambridge University Press, 1999). Two books look at a number of issues in addition to pay inequality: International Labor Office, *Gender Equality and Decent Work: Good Practices at the Workplace* (Brookings Institution Press, 2005), and Jeanette N. Cleveland, Kevin R. Murphy, and Margaret Stockdale, eds., *Women and Men in Organizations: Sex and Gender Issues at Work* (Lawrence Erlbaum Associates, 2001). Two works that focus on gender inequality at the manager level are Kjell Erik Lommerud and Steinar Vagstad, *Mommy Tracks and Public Policy: On Self-Fulfilling Prophecies and Gender Gaps in Promotion* (Centre for Economic Policy Research, 2000), and Linda Wirth, *Breaking Through the Glass Ceiling: Women in Management* (International Labour Organization, 2001). Works that examine theoretical and historical aspects of the gender pay gap include Sonya O. Rose, *What Is Gender History?* (Polity, 2010), and Joan Huber, *On the Origins of Gender Inequality* (Paradigm Publishers, 2007).

Internet References . . .

Sociology—Study Sociology Online

> http://edu.learnsoc.org/

Sociology Web Resources

> www.mhhe.com/socsclence/sociology/resources/index.htm

Sociosite

> www.topsite.com/goto/sociosite.net

Socioweb

> www.topsite.com/goto/socioweb.com

Unit 4

UNIT

Political Economy and Institutions

*W*hat is the proper role of government in the economy? Some believe that the government must correct for the many failures of the market, while others think that the government usually complicates the workings of the free market and reduces its effectiveness.

Selected, Edited, and with Issue Framing Material by:
Kurt Finsterbusch, *University of Maryland, College Park*

ISSUE

Is Government Dominated by Big Business?

YES: G. William Domhoff, from *Who Rules America? Power, Politics, and Social Change,* 5th ed. (McGraw-Hill, 2006)

NO: Sheldon Kamieniecki, from *Corporate America and Environmental Policy: How Often Does Business Get Its Way?* (Stanford Law and Politics 2006)

Learning Outcomes

After reading this issue, you should be able to:

- Know which groups have been identified as the ones with the greatest influence over the U.S. government and the main evidence supporting the thesis of their inordinate influence.
- Understand the tactics that are used to influence government policies and the administration of these policies.
- Understand the concept of negative power and use it to explain how minority groups can stop policies that are perceived as likely to adversely affect them.
- Identify the limits to the power of big corporations in influencing government policies.
- Analyze the recent bank bailout and its aftermath on the one hand and the stimulus package to generate jobs on the other. Comment on the rebound of the stock market (although still fragile) and the continued high unemployment.
- Analyze the consequences of the current structure of power in America.

ISSUE SUMMARY

YES: Political sociologist G. William Domhoff argues that the "owners and top-level managers in large income-producing properties are far and away the dominant power figures in the United States" and that they have inordinate influence in the federal government.

NO: Political scientist Sheldon Kamieniecki's research finds that business interests do not participate at a high rate in policy issues that affect them, "and when they do, they have mixed success in influencing policy outcomes." In fact, environmental and other groups often have considerable influence vis-à-vis business interests.

Since the framing of the U.S. Constitution in 1787, there have been periodic charges that America is unduly influenced by wealthy financial interests. Richard Henry Lee, a signer of the Declaration of Independence, spoke for many Anti-Federalists (those who opposed ratification of the Constitution) when he warned that the proposed charter shifted power away from the people and into the hands of the "aristocrats" and "moneyites."

Before the Civil War, Jacksonian Democrats denounced the eastern merchants and bankers who, they charged, were usurping the power of the people. After the Civil War, a number of radical parties and movements revived this theme of antielitism. The ferment—which was brought about by the rise of industrial monopolies, government corruption, and economic hardship for Western farmers—culminated in the founding of the People's Party at the beginning of the 1890s. The Populists, as they were more commonly called, wanted economic and political reforms aimed at transferring power away from the rich and back to "the plain people."

By the early 1900s, the People's Party had disintegrated, but many writers and activists have continued to echo the Populists' central thesis: that the U.S. democratic political system is in fact dominated by business elites. Yet the thesis has not gone unchallenged. During the 1950s and the early 1960s, many social scientists subscribed to the pluralist view of America.

Pluralists argue that because there are many influential elites in America, each group is limited to some extent by the others. There are some groups, like the business elites, that are more powerful than their opponents, but even the more powerful groups are denied their objectives at times. Labor groups are often opposed to business groups; conservative interests challenge liberal interests, and vice versa; and organized civil libertarians sometimes fight with groups that seek government-imposed bans on pornography or groups that demand tougher criminal laws. No single group, the pluralists argue, can dominate the political system.

Pluralists readily acknowledge that American government is not democratic in the full sense of the word; it is not driven by the majority. But neither, they insist, is it run by a conspiratorial "power elite." In the pluralist view, the closest description of the American form of government would be neither majority rule nor minority rule but minorities rule. (Note that in this context, "minorities" does not necessarily refer to race or ethnicity but to any organized group of people with something in common—including race, religion, or economic interests—not constituting a majority of the population.) Each organized minority enjoys some degree of power in the making of public policy. In extreme cases, when a minority feels threatened, its power may take a negative form: the power to derail policy. When the majority—or, more accurately,

a coalition of other minorities—attempts to pass a measure that threatens the vital interests of an organized minority, that group may use its power to obstruct their efforts. (Often cited in this connection is the use of the Senate filibuster, which is the practice of using tactics during the legislative process that cause extreme delays or prevent action, thus enabling a group to "talk to death" a bill that threatens its vital interests.) But in the pluralist view, negative power is not the only driving force: When minorities work together and reach consensus on certain issues, they can institute new laws and policy initiatives that enjoy broad public support. Pluralism, although capable of producing temporary gridlock, ultimately leads to compromise, consensus, and moderation.

Critics of pluralism argue that pluralism is an idealized depiction of a political system that is in the grip of powerful elite groups. Critics fault pluralist theory for failing to recognize the extent to which big business dominates the policymaking process. In the selections that follow, G. William Domhoff supports this view, identifies the groups that compose the power elite, and details the way they control or support social, political, and knowledge-producing associations and organizations that advance their interests. Sheldon Kamieniecki, in opposition, argues that, thanks to new consumer, environmental, and other citizen groups, big business has a much more limited influence on Washington policymakers than Domhoff claims.

YES ↵

G. William Domhoff

Who Rules America? Power, Politics, and Social Change

Introduction

Using a wide range of systematic empirical findings, this book shows how the owners and top-level managers in large companies work together to maintain themselves as the core of the dominant power group. Their corporations, banks, and agribusinesses form a *corporate community* that shapes the federal government on the policy issues of interest to it, issues that have a major impact on the income, job security, and well-being of most other Americans. At the same time, there is competition within the corporate community for profit opportunities, which can lead to highly visible policy conflicts among rival corporate leaders that are sometimes fought out in Congress. Yet the corporate community is cohesive on the policy issues that affect its general welfare, which is often at stake when political challenges are made by organized workers, liberals, or strong environmentalists. The book therefore deals with another seeming paradox: How can a highly competitive group of corporate leaders cooperate enough to work their common will in the political and policy arenas?

Partly because the owners and high-level managers within the corporate community share great wealth and common economic interests, but also due to political opposition to their interests, they band together to develop their own social institutions—gated neighborhoods, private schools, exclusive social clubs, debutante balls, and secluded summer resorts. These social institutions create social cohesion and a sense of group belonging, a "we" feeling, and thereby mold wealthy people into a *social upper class*. In addition, the owners and managers supplement their small numbers by financing and directing a wide variety of nonprofit organizations—e.g., tax-free foundations, think tanks, and policy-discussion groups—to aid them in developing policy alternatives that serve their interests. The highest-ranking employees in these nonprofit organizations become part of a general leadership group for the corporate community and the upper class, called the *power elite*.

Corporate owners and their top executives enter into the electoral arena as the leaders of a *corporate-conservative coalition*, which they shape through large campaign contributions, the advocacy of policy options developed by their hired experts, and easy access to the mass media. They are aided by a wide variety of middle-class patriotic, antitax, and single-issue organizations that celebrate the status quo and warn against "big government." These opinion-shaping organizations are funded in good part by the corporate community, but they have some degree of independence due to direct-mail appeals and modest donations by a large number of middle-class conservatives. The corporate leaders play a large role in both of the major political parties at the presidential level and succeeded in electing a pro-corporate majority to Congress throughout the twentieth century. Historically, this majority in Congress consisted of Northern Republicans and Southern Democrats, but that arrangement changed gradually after the Voting Rights Act of 1965 made it possible for a coalition of African-Americans and white liberals to push the most conservative Southern Democrats into the Republican Party.

Since the last quarter of the twentieth century, the corporate-conservative coalition has been joined by the Christian Right, which consists of a wide range of middle-class religious groups concerned with a variety of social issues, including abortion, prayer in schools, teenage sexual behavior, homosexuality, gay marriage, and pornography. The alliance is sometimes an uneasy one because the corporate community and the Christian Right do not have quite the same priorities, yet they work together because of their common mistrust of government power.

The corporate community's ability to transform its economic power into policy influence and political access, along with its capacity to enter into a coalition with middle-class social and religious conservatives, makes it the most important influence in the federal government. Its key leaders are appointed to top positions in the executive branch and the policy recommendations of its experts are listened to carefully by its allies in Congress. This combination of economic power, policy expertise, and continuing political success makes the corporate owners and executives a *dominant class*, not in the sense of complete and absolute power, but in the sense that they have the power to shape the economic and political frameworks within which other groups and classes must operate. They therefore win far more often than they lose on the issues of concern to them.

Who Wins?

There are many issues over which the corporate-conservative and liberal-labor coalitions disagree, including taxation, unionization, business regulation, foreign trade, the outsourcing of jobs, and the funding of Social Security. Power can be inferred on the basis of these issue conflicts by determining who successfully initiates, modifies, or vetoes policy alternatives. This indicator, by focusing on relationships between the two rival coalitions, comes closest to approximating the process of power contained in the formal definition. It is the indicator preferred by most social scientists. For many reasons, however, it is also the most difficult to use in an accurate way. Aspects of a decision process may remain hidden, some informants may exaggerate or downplay their roles, and people's memories about who did what often become cloudy shortly after the event. Worse, the key concerns of the corporate community may never arise as issues for public discussion because it has the power to keep them off the agenda through a variety of means that are explained throughout later chapters.

Despite the difficulties in using the *Who wins?* indicator of power, it is possible to provide a theoretical framework for analyzing governmental decision-making that mitigates many of them. This framework encompasses the various means by which the corporate community attempts to influence both the government and the general population in a conscious and planned manner, thereby making it possible to assess its degree of success very directly. More specifically, there are four relatively distinct, but overlapping processes (discovered by means of membership network analysis) through which the corporate community controls the public agenda and then wins on most issues that appear on it. These four power networks, which are discussed in detail in later chapters, are as follows:

1. The *special-interest process* deals with the narrow and short-run policy concerns of wealthy families, specific corporations, and specific business sectors. It operates primarily through lobbyists, company lawyers, and trade associations, with a focus on congressional committees, departments of the executive branch, and regulatory agencies.
2. The *policy-planning process* formulates the general interests of the corporate community. It operates through a policy-planning network of foundations, think tanks, and policy-discussion groups, with a focus on the White House, relevant congressional committees, and the high-status newspapers and opinion magazines published in New York and Washington.
3. The *candidate-selection process* is concerned with the election of candidates who are sympathetic to the agenda put forth in the special-interest and policy-planning processes. It operates through large campaign donations and hired political consultants, with a focus on the presidential campaigns of both major political parties and the congressional campaigns of the Republican Party.
4. The *opinion-shaping process* attempts to influence public opinion and keep some issues off the public agenda. Often drawing on policy positions, rationales, and statements developed within the policy-planning process, it operates through the public relations departments of large corporations, general public relations firms, and many small opinion-shaping organizations, with a focus on middle-class voluntary organizations, educational institutions, and the mass media.

Taken together, the people and organizations that operate in these four networks constitute the political-action arm of the corporate community and upper class.

How the Power Elite Dominate Government

The power elite build on their structural economic power, their storehouse of policy expertise, and their success in the electoral arena to dominate the federal government on the issues about which they care. Lobbyists from corporations, law firms, and trade associations play a key role in shaping government on narrow issues of concern to specific corporations or business sectors, and the policy-planning network supplies new policy directions on major issues, along with top-level governmental appointees to implement those policies.

However, victories within government are far from automatic. As is the case in the competition for public opinion and electoral success, the power elite face opposition from a minority of elected officials and their supporters in labor unions and liberal advocacy groups. These liberal opponents are sometimes successful in blocking the social initiatives put forth by the Christian Right, but the corporate-conservative coalition itself seldom loses when it is united.

Appointees to Government

The first way to see how the power elite shapes the federal government is to look at the social and occupational backgrounds of the people who are appointed to manage the major departments of the executive branch, such as state, treasury, defense, and justice. If the power elite are as important as this book claims, they should come disproportionately from the upper class, the corporate community, and the policy-planning network.

There have been numerous studies of major governmental appointees under both Republican and Democratic administrations, usually focusing on the top appointees in the departments that are represented in the president's cabinet. These studies are unanimous in their conclusion that most top appointees in both Republican and Democratic administrations are corporate executives and corporate lawyers, and hence members of the power elite. Moreover, they are often part of the policy-planning network as well, supporting the claim that the network plays a central role in preparing members of the power elite for government service.

The Special-Interest Process

The special-interest process consists of the many and varied means by which specific corporations and business sectors gain the favors, tax breaks, regulatory rulings, and other governmental assistance they need to realize their narrow and short-run interests. The process is carried out by people with a wide range of experiences: former elected officials, experts who once served on congressional staffs or in regulatory agencies, employees of trade associations, corporate executives whose explicit function is government liaison, and an assortment of lawyers and public-relations specialists. The process is based on a great amount of personal contact, but its most important ingredients are the information and financial support that the lobbyists have to offer. Much of the time this information comes from grassroots pressure generated by the lobbyists to show that voting for a given measure will or will not hurt a particular politician.

Corporations spend far more money on lobbying than their officers give to PACs, by a margin of ten to one. In 2000, for example, the tobacco industry, facing lawsuits and regulatory threats, spent $44 million on lobbyists and $17 million on the Tobacco Institute, an industry public relations arm, but gave only $8.4 million to political campaigns through PACs. More generally, a study of the top 20 defense contractors showed that they spent $400 million on lobbying between 1997 and 2003, but only $46 million on campaign contributions.

The trend toward increasingly large tax breaks continued from 2001 to 2003, with the effective tax rate on corporations declining from 21.7 percent during the last years of the Clinton Administration to 17.2 percent in 2003. Forty-six of 275 major companies studied for 2003 paid no federal income taxes, a considerable increase from a similar study in the late 1990s. A new tax bill in October 2004 added another $137 billion in tax breaks for manufacturing and energy companies, with General Electric, which spent $17 million in lobbying fees in 2003, once again the biggest beneficiary. At the same time, other legal loopholes have allowed multinational corporations to increase the sheltering of profits in foreign tax havens by tens of billions of dollars.

Special interests also work through Congress to try to hamstring regulatory agencies or reverse military purchasing decisions they do not like. When the Federal Communications Commission tried to issue licenses for over 1,000 low-power FM stations for schools and community groups, Congress blocked the initiative at the behest of big broadcasting companies, setting standards that will restrict new licenses to a small number of stations in the least populated parts of the country. When the Food and Drug Administration tried to regulate tobacco, Congress refused authorization in 2000 in deference to the tobacco industry. The FDA is now so lax with pharmaceutical companies that one-third of its scientific employees have less than full confidence that it tests new drugs adequately, and two-thirds expressed a lack of complete confidence in its monitoring of the safety of drugs once they are on the market.

The special-interest process often is used to create loopholes in legislation that is accepted by the corporate community in principle. "I spent the last seven years fighting the Clean Air Act," said a corporate lobbyist in charge of PAC donations, who then went on to explain why he gave money to elected officials even though they voted for the strengthening of the Clean Air Act in 1990:

> How a person votes on the final piece of legislation is not representative of what they have done. Somebody will do a lot of things during the process. How many guys voted against the Clean Air Act? But during the process some of them were very sympathetic to some of our concerns.

Translated, this means there are forty pages of exceptions, extensions, and other loopholes in the 1990 version of the act after a thirteen-year standoff between the Business Roundtable's Clean Air Working Group and the liberal-labor coalition's National Clean Air Coalition. For example, the steel industry has thirty years to bring twenty-six large coke ovens into compliance with the new standards. Once the bill passed, lobbyists went to work on the Environmental Protection Agency to win the most lax regulations possible for implementing the legislation. As of 1998, after twenty-eight years of argument and delay, the agency had been able to issue standards for less than ten of the many hazardous chemicals emitted into the air.

The Big Picture

This book began with two seeming paradoxes. How can the owners and managers of highly competitive corporations develop the policy unity to shape government policies? How can large corporations have such great power in a democratic country? The step-by-step argument and evidence presented in previous chapters provide the foundation for a theory that can explain these paradoxes—a *class-domination theory of power* in the United States.

Domination means that the commands of a group or class are carried out with relatively little resistance, which is possible because that group or class has been able to establish the rules and customs through which everyday life is conducted. Domination, in other words, is the institutionalized outcome of great distributive power. The upper class of owners and high-level executives, based in the corporate community, is a dominant class in terms of this definition because the cumulative effect of its various distributive powers leads to a situation where its policies are generally accepted by most Americans. The routinized ways of acting in the United States follow from the rules and regulations needed by the corporate community to continue to grow and make profits.

The overall distributive power of the dominant class is first of all based in its structural economic power, which falls to it by virtue of its members being owners and high-level executives in corporations that sell goods and services for a profit in a market economy. The power to invest or not invest, and to hire and fire employees, leads to a political context where elected officials try to do as much as they can to create a favorable investment climate to avoid being voted out of office in the event of an economic downturn. This structural power is augmented by the ability to create new policies through a complex policy-planning network, which the upper class has been able to institutionalize because common economic interests and social cohesion have given the corporate community enough unity to sustain such an endeavor over many decades.

But even these powers might not have been enough to generate a system of extreme class domination if the bargains and compromises embodied in the Constitution had not led unexpectedly to a two-party system in which one party was controlled by the Northern rich and the other by the Southern rich. This in turn created a personality-oriented candidate-selection process that is heavily dependent on large campaign donations—now and in the past as well. The system of party primaries is the one adaptation to this constrictive two-party system that has provided some openings for insurgent liberals and trade unionists.

Structural economic power and control of the two parties, along with the elaboration of an opinion-shaping network, results in a polity where there is little or no organized public opinion independent of the limits set by debates within the power elite itself. There is no organizational base from which to construct an alternative public opinion, and there have been until recently no openings within the political system that could carry an alternative message to government.

Finally, the fragmented and constrained system of government carefully crafted by the Founding Fathers led to a relatively small federal government that is easily entered and influenced by wealthy and well-organized private citizens, whether through Congress, the separate departments of the executive branch, or a myriad of regulatory agencies. The net result is that the owners and managers of large income-producing properties score very high on all three power indicators: who benefits, who governs, and who wins. They have a greater proportion of wealth and income than their counterparts in any other capitalist democracy, and through the power elite they are vastly overrepresented in key government positions and decision-making groups. They win far more often than they lose on those issues that make it to the government for legislative consideration, although their lack of unity in the face of worker militancy in the 1930s made it possible for organized workers to have far more independence, income, and power than they ever had in the past.

Many Americans feel a sense of empowerment because they have religious freedom, free speech, and a belief that they can strike it rich or rise in the system if they try hard enough. Those with educational credentials and/or secure employment experience a degree of dignity and respect because there is no tradition of public degradation for those of average or low incomes. Liberals and leftists can retain hope because in recent decades they have had success in helping to expand individual rights and freedom—for women, for people of color, and most recently for gays and lesbians. But individual rights and freedoms do not necessarily add up to distributive power. In the same time period, when individual rights and freedoms expanded, corporate power also became greater because unions were decimated and the liberal-labor coalition splintered. This analysis suggests there is class domination in spite of a widening of individual freedoms and an expansion of the right to vote.

G. WILLIAM DOMHOFF is a research professor in psychology and sociology at the University of California, Santa Cruz. His first book, *Who Rules America?,* was a controversial 1960s bestseller arguing that the United States is dominated by an elite ownership class, both politically and economically. It has gone through six editions; the most recent edition was published in 2013.

Sheldon Kamieniecki

 **NO**

Corporate America and Environmental Policy: How Often Does Business Get Its Way?

The findings reported in this study directly challenge prevailing assumptions both in- and outside the scholarly community about the regularity of business involvement in agenda building and policymaking as well as the ability of business to influence government decisions concerning pollution control and natural resource management. This outcome was unexpected. When I first began working on this book more than three years ago, I anticipated finding that American corporations are regularly involved in environmental agenda building and policymaking and that they exert a great deal of influence over government decision making. Like many, I accepted the conventional wisdom that business frequently opposes proposals that will improve environmental quality in order to protect its profits. After all, reports in the media nearly always place the blame for the defeat of environmental initiatives on the undue influence of business. As an environmentalist myself, I have been quite disappointed in the lack of progress the United States has made, especially recently, in the areas of pollution control and natural resource conservation. Most policy analysts attribute this lack of progress to the ability of corporate America to block or dilute critical federal legislation and to the inability of environmental groups to compete in the policymaking process. . . .

I was determined to . . . conduct a fair and balanced assessment of the role of business interests in environmental and natural resource policymaking.

As the data show, business interests do not participate in environmental policy debates at a high rate, and when they do, they have mixed success in influencing policy outcomes. These results generally hold when one examines agenda building in Congress, agency rulemaking, and, to some extent, the courts. Analyses of salient conflicts involving pollution control and natural resources also tend to bear this out. Business interests, instead, appear to select strategically the controversies in which they become involved and how much money they spend on lobbying activities of various kinds. A major conclusion of my work is that agenda building within the environmental policy domain is a highly complex process and cannot be explained by a single theory. This and other surprising related findings are the subject of this book. . . .

The central question of the book is, how often does business get its way on environmental issues? Do corporations, given the immense wealth and resources they command, exert an unequal and unfair influence over American government whereby they are able to compel elected representatives and agency officials to reject or compromise substantially appropriate and necessary environmental rules and regulations? A related concern, often ignored in the interest group literature, is the frequency with which firms are able to prevent environmental and natural resource policy proposals from even reaching the government agenda. Although recent research suggests that firms do not possess the amount of influence necessary to shape or block public policymaking on a consistent basis more generally, few studies have critically analyzed their ability to affect agenda setting specifically within the environmental policy sphere. This investigation addresses this issue by empirically assessing the ability of companies to affect legislative, administrative, and judicial decision making and mold the government's environmental and natural resource policy agenda since the beginning of the environmental movement. . . .

In particular, the size and wealth of business lobbying organizations have grown dramatically since World War Two, prompting some observers to argue that they are now too powerful and are undermining democracy and threatening the well-being of society. The weakening of the political parties, the rising costs of media advertising and election campaigns, and the increasing contributions by Political Action Committees (PACs) to candidates and parties have led to calls for reform in the way American elections are financed. Business interests, among others, are key targets of critics who demand the enactment of meaningful campaign finance reform at the federal level. The campaign finance reform legislation enacted in 2002 bans "soft money," among other things, and is a significant attempt to level the playing field. Loopholes in the act exist, however, and it will be necessary to adopt additional regulations in the future in order to correct inequities in the financing of campaigns. Thus, despite Madison's assurances, the question of how we allow business and other interest groups to form and participate but control their influence remains a dilemma in modern times. . . .

From *Corporate America and Environmental Policy,* by Sheldon Kamieniecki (Stanford Law and Politics, 2006), excerpts from Preface, Chapters 1 and 2, and Conclusion. Copyright © 2006 by the Board of Trustees of Leland Stanford Jr. University. Reprinted by permission of Stanford University Press. www.sup.org

Corporate America and Environmental Policy: Opposing Views

The influence of business over environmental policy is often used as an example of the substantial and unfair leverage certain interest groups have over government actions, especially when compared to the level of influence of average citizens. Many believe that the power business wields in American politics threatens democracy and, among other things, undermines the nation's efforts to control pollution and conserve natural resources. Environmentalists assert that "big business" has continuously been an impediment to the formulation and implementation of clean air and water quality standards. Ranchers and land developers, they argue, have successfully fought endangered species protection; oil, coal, and natural gas companies have opposed strict energy-conservation measures and have lobbied against the adoption of renewable sources of energy; mining companies have thwarted the revision of mining laws and regulations; and chemical companies have fought legislation intended to control pesticides, promote the safe disposal of hazardous waste, and abate old, abandoned toxic waste sites. . . .

Many critics maintain that interest groups subvert democracy, in part by pressing Congress to pass too much "special-interest" legislation that benefits the few at the expense of the majority and in part by blocking legislative initiatives they oppose even when those measures are favored by, or would benefit, the broad public. In addition, critics contend that campaign contributions by interest groups undermine democratic government and degrade the American electoral system. In contrast, Berry rejects these arguments, saying that interest groups help to link citizens to government: "They empower people by organizing those citizens with similar interests and expressing those interests to policymakers. In this regard, the growth of citizen groups reflects an expansion of organizing around interests that have too often received too little attention in Washington." Berry carefully avoids saying that business interests are no longer a force in American politics, but he does argue that their influence has significantly declined. . . .

Interestingly, Berry's findings and conclusions are a throwback to some of the positions of the early pluralists, namely that interest group politics is equitable and fair. For this reason, Berry and his contemporaries, such as Baumgartner and Leech who also share this view, are referred to as *neopluralists* in this volume. Specifically, neopluralists argue that the increasing number and size of citizen groups has furthered democracy and the public good by involving a broad range of interests in policymaking and by substantially countering the influence of business in the political system. The neopluralists, like the early pluralists, point to the positive aspects of group pressures on politics and government. Scholars who believe that public opinion also provides a check on the power of business are considered neopluralists as well. The degree to which environmental groups and public opinion mitigate business influence in environmental policymaking is examined in the present study. . . .

The Business Advantage?

Mark Smith's provocative investigation explores the widely held assumption that business dominates the policymaking process when it is unified on specific policy issues, thereby undermining democracy. Using the policy positions of the U.S. Chamber of Commerce as a guide, he identifies 2,364 unifying issues that were considered by Congress between 1953 and 1996. His list of unifying issues encompasses a wide range of policy areas including employment policy, labor-management relations, and clean air regulation. Agenda building in Congress over time is his dependent variable. Among the independent variables he analyzes are "public mood," public attitudes toward corporations, partisan composition of Congress, "presidential leadership opening" (that is, when partisan turnover in Congress runs in the president's favor), corporate PAC funding, and the state of the economy. Mark Smith finds that

> unity does not increase the direct influence of business and reduce democratic control by the citizenry. Instead, unity coincides with the opposite results. Issues marked by a common business position are precisely those for which government decisions are affected most strongly by election outcomes and the responsiveness of officeholders to their constituents. Policies match the collective desires of business only when citizens, through their policy preferences and voting choices, embrace ideas and candidates supportive of what business wants. To bolster its odds of winning in politics, business needs to seek backing from the broad public.

According to Mark Smith, therefore, only when the public supports the unified positions of business on policy issues does business achieve its legislative goals. When the public opposes the positions of business, however, Congress tends to follow the public will even though business is unified. Since all unifying policy issues are highly ideological, partisan, and salient, Congress nearly always follows the public on these issues. He concludes by stating, "The long-standing debates over unity among pluralists, elite theorists, and ruling class theorists have focused our attention in the wrong place. Widespread scholarly concerns about business unity are misplaced, for unifying issues are marked by the highest, rather than the lowest, degree of democratic control by the citizenry." Smith's interpretation of his findings places him in the neopluralist camp along with Baumgartner and Leech and Berry. . . .

Baumgartner and Jones report significant changes in the environmental interest group sphere and show dramatic growth in the numbers of environmental groups and the resources available to them. Based on their analysis, the number of environmental organizations nearly tripled from 1960 to 1990, and the combined staff reported by those groups increased nearly ten times. This surge in environmental group membership is one of the most important reasons for the enactment of so many major environmental laws during the 1970s and 1980s, often over the protests of powerful business lobbyists. . . .

This book provided a comprehensive investigation of how much corporate America has influenced agenda building and environmental policymaking since 1970. The study began by charting the development of business interests since the founding of the nation and by raising important issues about democratic theory and the role of business in American politics. A review of the literature on interest groups addressed collective-action issues and the emergence of citizen groups in the agenda-setting process. Research by the neopluralists suggests that public opinion and citizen groups have tempered the influence of business interests in social policymaking. Based on their findings, one would expect this to be the case in environmental and natural resource policy. Theories addressing certain political and economic variables, issue definition, framing processes, and agenda building were introduced and applied in the analysis of the role of business in Congress, at the EPA and natural resource agencies, in federal court, and in environmental and natural resource disputes. . . .

Major Findings

This book reports a number of major findings. In sharp contrast to the conventional wisdom that business interests actively oppose environmental and natural resource protection on a continuous basis, the data presented [clearly shows that] corporations do not take a position on proposed legislation in Congress about four-fifths of the time. The widely held belief that business frequently opposes environmental regulation and natural resource conservation is also not true. Regardless of how companies align (that is, unified or particularized), they tend to support environmental legislation more often than not. . . .

The study also reports several important findings concerning the influence of business over federal agencies and the courts. As the data indicate, the number of public comments on proposed environmental and natural resource rules and which segments of the population participate in the rulemaking process varies depending on the saliency and nature of the policy issue involved. As Golden discovers, a large percentage of those who submit comments are located outside Washington DC. The exceptionally large number of comments submitted by citizen groups on the natural resource rules examined in this research supports the position by the neopluralists that the dramatic rise in the number and size of such groups is effectively competing against the lobbying activities of business interests. Comments by corporations were generally hostile toward the EPA's efforts to promulgate new environmental regulations. Overall, public comments on proposed rules by EPA, the Forest Service, and the FWS have no or very little effect on the composition of final rules. Comments that contain new facts and information normally receive the closest attention by agency officials. Thus, as Golden finds, business does not exercise an undue influence over rulemaking involving environmental and natural resource issues. Instead, what kinds of rules are proposed to begin with is most important. This is determined by who occupies the White House and who the president appoints to senior positions in the environmental protection and natural resource agencies. . . .

The findings from the analyses of business influence in government institutions provide compelling reasons for investigating the influence of corporate interests within specific contexts involving disputes over environmental regulation and the use of natural resources. As this study indicated, in the end GE did not get its way in its fight to block the EPA's order that it clean up the PCBs it had dumped in the Hudson River. Likewise, the coal companies and utilities were unable to persuade Congress to exclude controls on sulfur dioxide emissions to reduce acid rain from the clean Air Act Amendments of 1990. In both cases, the scientific evidence concerning the negative impact of PCBs and SO_2 emissions on the environment and public health was overwhelming and undercut opposing political and economic forces in the debate over policy. Public concern was also high, prompting the EPA and Congress, respectively, to take action against the wishes of powerful economic interests.

The battle over controlling GHG emissions and climate change, however, presents a very different story. Extremely influential energy producers and consumers have teamed up to prevent the U.S. government from ratifying the Kyoto agreement and from taking a leadership role at the international level to address the climate change issue. The ratification of the Kyoto treaty by Russia represents a significant step forward to resolving the global climate change problem. Nonetheless, the global effort is considerably weakened without the participation of large CO_2 emitters such as the United States and Australia. It is unlikely that U.S. policy on climate change will reverse course during President Bush's second term.

In addition, the study explored the influence of business in three controversies concerning natural resource issues. Despite calls for reform, mining interests have successfully beaten back attempts to revise the General Mining Law of 1872. Sugarcane growers and development forces were able to thwart efforts to restore the Florida Everglades until scientists and environmentalists banded together and persuaded the federal government, particularly the U.S. Army Corps of Engineers and Congress, to take action. The state government, which has been continuously pressured from all sides, has waffled in its intentions to improve the wetlands ecosystem in South Florida. Environmentalists have been successful in attracting media attention, expanding the scope of conflict beyond the region and the state, and using the courts to protect the northern spotted owl and old-growth forests in the Pacific Northwest. The ESA continues to provide a strong pillar in the debate over logging old-growth trees on public lands. Revision of the ESA by the Republican-controlled White House and Congress in the coming years could place economic interests ahead of habitat protection and eventually spell the demise of the northern spotted owl and other endangered species across the country. . . .

Implications of the Study's Findings

This study's findings have a number of implications for the way analysts view the role of business in environmental and natural resource policymaking. At the aggregate level it is clear that business interests selectively choose which bills to oppose or support in Congress, and they do not, as environmentalists, media commentators, and some scholars assume, continuously and unrelentingly pressure legislators for favorable treatment. They are most likely to become active in critical and salient policy debates. Although their participation in the legislative process is far less than expected, the controversies in which they decide to become involved tend to be ones where there is much at stake for them *and* the environment. In this sense, the lobbying activities of business can have an enormous impact on the nation's effort to protect the environment and natural resources.

When business does choose to lobby Congress on environmental legislation, it more often supports rather than opposes such legislation. This result probably indicates that the views of business interests are often conveyed and considered during the initial writing of bills. The multiple indicators approach used by Mark Smith and employed in this research unfortunately does not include this somewhat hidden but critical facet of the agenda-building process in Congress. Of course, business interests will actively oppose legislation when their views are not reflected in legislative proposals and when there is much at stake. Such legislation is adopted when pressure from environmental groups and public opinion requires congressional representatives to take immediate action to address urgent pollution or natural resource problems. Congress is unable to always act according to the desires of the business community because of the existence of previous, and oftentimes landmark, law. In such cases corporations seldom get their way. . . .

Analysis of the six case studies, however, offers more support for the position of the neopluralists. Generally, when much is at stake, environmental groups tend to mobilize and provide an effective check on the influence of business interests. This is evident in the conflicts involving GE and the dumping of PCBs in the Hudson River, the promulgation of acid rain regulations, the restoration of the Everglades, and protection of the northern spotted owl and old-growth forests. Public opinion was a factor in all these controversies, though to varying degrees. There-

fore, when conflicts are salient, environmental groups and public opinion tend to present an important, countervailing force to business interests. Mancur Olson would not have predicted this finding.

Finally, the overall results of the investigation have important implications for the influence of business in environmental and natural resource policymaking in particular, and democratic theory in general. Corporations strategically select which legislative debates to enter, and they take positions on environmental and natural resource legislation only a small percentage of the time. Furthermore, business interests do not exert an undue influence in the rulemaking process. Yet, they tend to win as many cases as they lose in the federal court of appeals. Overall, however, business does not get what it wants from government institutions a majority of the time, as some argue. This study's findings suggest that the influence of business in environmental and natural resource policymaking is modest at best.

The examination of the case studies presents a similar picture. Although business interests experienced early success in conflicts over the contamination of the Hudson River, SO_2 emissions, the pollution of the Everglades, and the logging of old-growth forests, they eventually were forced to bow to the demands of federal officials. This is not the situation, of course, in disputes over hardrock mining and climate change. In these instances, corporations have thus far been able to defeat efforts to reform the General Mining Act of 1872 and reduce GHG emissions. Based on the overall analysis of the environmental regulatory and the natural resource case studies, however, business interests do not often get their way. As this study shows, they tend to have a mixed rate of success in influencing the outcomes of salient policy controversies.

In addition to environmental groups and public opinion, other factors also mitigate the influence of business in agenda building and policymaking. Competing elites in the media and scientific community, for example, can point out differences between what corporations are claiming and the actual evidence. As this study revealed, the media played a central role in the controversy over the northern spotted owl and old-growth forests. What started out as a regional (Pacific Northwest) issue quickly expanded to the national level as a result of extensive media coverage of the plight of the owl and its habitat. The timber industry was thus forced to reduce logging on public land considerably. Likewise, scientists brought to light the negative impacts of PCB contamination of the Hudson River, SO_2 emissions on aquatic bodies and forests, and agricultural runoff in the Everglades. In each case business groups were forced to moderate significantly their stands. Federal district trial court judges, too, placed controls on pollution of the Everglades and logging in old-growth forests. This was only possible because of the existence of groundbreaking federal laws governing environmental and natural resource protection (for example, the Clean Water Act and the ESA). As James Madison suggested would generally happen in *Federalist Paper Number 10,* the environmental policy arena is characterized by a healthy balance between competing interests and stakeholders. The system of checks and balances between the three branches of government and the protection of individual rights allow business interests to pursue aggressively their aims but at the same time prevent them from completely destroying the environment and severely harming public health.

SHELDON KAMIENIECKI is dean of the Division of Social Sciences and a professor in the Department of Environmental Studies at the University of California, Santa Cruz.

EXPLORING THE ISSUE

Is Government Dominated by Big Business?

Critical Thinking and Reflection

1. Give an example of corporations influencing the federal government to pass or repeal policies they favored or opposed.
2. Can you identify policies that were passed against the opposition of the corporate sector? Can you identify what made that action possible?
3. What regulations or other policies have been used to limit the power of corporations to control or influence the federal government? How effective have they been? What more could be done?
4. What do recent elections reveal about the influence of big business over the government? The Koch brothers' money has been a major support for the Tea Party. What is the difference between the political support by big business and the support by wealthy individuals?
5. How is political influence exercised?
6. Discuss and critique the theory of political power that underlies the "occupy" movement and the conflict between the 99 percent and the 1 percent.

Is There Common Ground?

No one denies that big business has a lot of power and can get their way in many areas including their influence over government. There is agreement that the political system is not a level playing field. The key issue in this debate is the extent of the influence of corporate power over the making and administering of government policies on issues that concern them. The dominant view is that neither the public nor mobilized noncorporate interests can effectively counterpose corporate interests. But EPA was created in 1970 to regulate business and other sources of pollution. NEPA was passed over the objections of business. Wall Street opposed the reforms recently imposed upon them. So everyone agrees that big business has too much power but does not have absolute power. Those are broad boundaries, so there is much room to debate how much power big business has over the federal government.

Create Central

www.mhhe.com/createcentral

Additional Resources

Two political scientists who argue that big business dominates America in a lifetime of publications are G. William Domhoff and Thomas R. Dye. Domhoff's article in this debate contains selections from the fifth edition of his book *Who Rules America?* (McGraw-Hill, 2006). In an earlier book, *Changing the Powers That Be: How the Left Can Stop Losing and Win* (Rowman & Littlefield, 2003), he focused on how to fight this corporate power. Three of Dye's recent books are *Politics in America*, 7th ed. (Pearson Prentice Hall, 2007), *Who's Running America? The Bush*

Restoration (Prentice Hall, 2003), and *Top Down Policymaking* (Chatham House, 2001). Other works supporting this view are Michael Parenti, *Democracy for the Few* (Thomson-Wadsworth, 2008); Melissa L. Rossi, *What Every American Should Know about Who's Really Running America* (Plume Books, 2007); Lou Dobbs, *War on the Middle Class: How Government, Big Business, and Special Interest Groups Are Waging War on the American Dream and How to Fight Back* (Viking, 2006); Charles Perrow, *Organizing America: Wealth, Power, and the Origins of Corporate America* (Princeton University Press, 2002); Peter Kobrak, *Cozy Politics: Political Parties, Campaign Finance, and Compromised Governance* (Lynne Rienner, 2002); Arianna Stassinopoulos Huffington, *Pigs at the Trough: How Corporate Greed and Political Corruption Are Undermining America* (Crown, 2003); Ted Nace, *Gangs of America: The Rise of Corporate Power and the Disabling of Democracy* (Berrett-Koehler, 2003); Dan Clawson et al., *Dollars and Votes: How Business Campaign Contributions Subvert Democracy* (Temple University Press, 1998); John B. Parrott, *Being Like God: How American Elites Abuse Politics and Power* (University Press of America, 2003); Russell Mokhiber and Robert Weissman, *On the Rampage: Corporate Predators and the Destruction of Democracy* (Common Courage Press, 2005); Paul Kivel, *You Call This Democracy? Who Benefits, Who Pays and Who Really Decides?* (Apex Press, 2004); and Charles Derber, *Hidden Power: What You Need to Know to Save Our Democracy* (Berrett-Koehler, 2005).

Several authors advance the thesis that American corporations also seek to some degree to rule the world, including David C. Korten, *When Corporations Rule the World,* 2nd ed. (Kumarian Press, 2001); and Peter Alexis Gourevich and James J. Shinn, *Political Power and Corporate Control: The New Global Politics of Corporate Governance* (Princeton University Press, 2005).

For some pluralist arguments, see Stephen E. Frantzich, *Citizen Democracy: Political Activists in a Cynical*

Age, 3rd ed. (Rowman & Littlefield, 2008); Feliz Kolb, *Protest and Opportunities: The Political Outcomes of Social Movements* (Campus Verlag, 2007); Michael Rabinder James, *Deliberative Democracy and the Plural Polity* (University Press of Kansas, 2004); Kevin Danaher, *Insurrection: Citizen Challenges to Corporate Power* (Routledge, 2003); David S. Meyers et al., eds., *Routing the Opposition: Social Movements, Public Policy, and Democracy* (University of Minnesota Press, 2005); Jeffrey M. Berry, *The New Liberalism: The Rising Power of Citizen Groups* (Brookings Institution, 1999); and *Battling Big Business: Countering Greenwash, Infiltration, and Other Forms of Corporate Bullying* (Common Courage Press, 2002). Recently, the pluralist view is being reworked into political process theory; see Andrew S. McFarland, *Neopluralism: The Evolution of Political Process Theory* (University Press of Kansas, 2004).

Internet References . . .

Sociology—Study Sociology Online

http://edu.learnsoc.org/

Sociology Web Resources

www.mhhe.com/socscience/sociology/resources/index.htm

Sociosite

www.topsite.com/goto/sociosite.net

Socioweb

www.topsite.com/goto/socioweb.com

Selected, Edited, and with Issue Framing Material by:
Kurt Finsterbusch, *University of Maryland, College Park*

ISSUE

Does Capitalism Have Serious Defects?

YES: Jerry Z. Muller, from "Capitalism and Inequality," *Foreign Affairs* (March/April 2013)

NO: Chris Berg, from "Why Capitalism Is Awesome," *Cato Policy Report* (July/August 2013)

Learning Outcomes

After reading this issue, you should be able to:

- Learn how scholars deal with extremely broad and complex phenomena such as "capitalism" and "democracy" and how the actors in these systems impact each other.
- Learn how scholars use historical cases to support very general hypotheses. Understand the resulting imprecision and thus the likelihood of disagreement over the interpretations of the results.
- Understand that a variable or factor can have one set of consequences in one period of time and another set of consequences in another period of time because many conditions have changed.
- Understand that the meaning of concepts can change over time. Democracy when most politics were local is different from democracy in massive federal regimes. Capitalism was small scale in the nineteenth century except for railroads and steel, but is very large scale today. The two forms of capitalism behave very differently.
- Discern differences between the interests of various sectors of corporate America and understand the processes that coordinate their political actions. (Direct collusion is illegal.)

ISSUE SUMMARY

YES: Jerry Z. Muller, professor of history at the Catholic University of America and author of *The Mind and the Market: Capitalism in Western Thought*, reports on how capitalism inevitably increases inequality because competition results in winners and losers. It is productive but it also increases commodification which erodes cultural values. It is a force for both good and bad.

NO: Chris Berg, a research fellow with the Institute of Public Affairs in Melbourne, Australia, and author of *In Defence of Freedom of Speech*, provides an enthusiastic defence of capitalism because it stimulates millions of innovations that improve millions of items that benefit us.

One of the long-standing findings of the social sciences is the connection between capitalism, economic development, and democracy. Capitalism is a major force for economic growth. Then economic growth creates the need for skilled and professional workers and thus the expansion of education and the growth of the middle class. Over time the educated and the middle class pressure for rights, and eventually the right to participate in the selection of leaders and to influence government policies. Economic growth over the long run also tends to create government support for freer markets and individual and organizational initiatives, which can eventually increase opposition to despots. Directly and indirectly, therefore, economic growth is a major cause of democracy.

But is this how economic growth impacts modern developed nations today? Economic growth also has produced powerful multinational corporations with concentrated economic power, and these powerful corporations are a threat to democracy. Corporations finance politicians' campaigns, lobby Congress, arrange to participate in the writing of legislation, and use their resources in many legal and even illegal ways to influence government to serve their interests or to oppose actions that would hurt their interests. The social sciences are united in this view of the alignment of power in America and many other nations. There is a debate, however, about whether this situation is a case of corporate control or only corporate influence. The latter allows other interests, including the public good, to also have influence over the government and thus make it more democratic, that is, rule by the people. The thesis of corporate control versus corporate influence is debated in Issue 10. Issue 11 examines whether capitalism, the driver of economic growth, is mainly good or bad for society. Muller emphasizes the current negative effects of capitalism such as increasing inequality and eroding cultural values by increasing commodification. Berg praises capitalism because it strongly stimulates innovations which greatly benefit our lives.

YES ↵

Jerry Z. Muller

Capitalism and Inequality

What the Right and the Left Get Wrong

Recent political debate in the United States and other advanced capitalist democracies has been dominated by two issues: the rise of economic inequality and the scale of government intervention to address it. As the 2012 U.S. presidential election and the battles over the "fiscal cliff" have demonstrated, the central focus of the left today is on increasing government taxing and spending, primarily to reverse the growing stratification of society, whereas the central focus of the right is on decreasing taxing and spending, primarily to ensure economic dynamism. Each side minimizes the concerns of the other, and each seems to believe that its desired policies are sufficient to ensure prosperity and social stability. Both are wrong.

Inequality is indeed increasing almost everywhere in the postindustrial capitalist world. But despite what many on the left think, this is not the result of politics, nor is politics likely to reverse it, for the problem is more deeply rooted and intractable than generally recognized. Inequality is an inevitable product of capitalist activity, and expanding equality of opportunity only increases it—because some individuals and communities are simply better able than others to exploit the opportunities for development and advancement that capitalism affords. Despite what many on the right think, however, this is a problem for everybody, not just those who are doing poorly or those who are ideologically committed to egalitarianism—because if left unaddressed, rising inequality and economic insecurity can erode social order and generate a populist backlash against the capitalist system at large.

Over the last few centuries, the spread of capitalism has generated a phenomenal leap in human progress, leading to both previously unimaginable increases in material living standards and the unprecedented cultivation of all kinds of human potential. Capitalism's intrinsic dynamism, however, produces insecurity along with benefits, and so its advance has always met resistance. Much of the political and institutional history of capitalist societies, in fact, has been the record of attempts to ease or cushion that insecurity, and it was only the creation of the modern welfare state in the middle of the twentieth century that finally enabled capitalism and democracy to coexist in relative harmony.

In recent decades, developments in technology, finance, and international trade have generated new waves and forms of insecurity for leading capitalist economies, making life increasingly unequal and chancier for not only the lower and working classes but much of the middle class as well. The right has largely ignored the problem, while the left has sought to eliminate it through government action, regardless of the costs. Neither approach is viable in the long run. Contemporary capitalist polities need to accept that inequality and insecurity will continue to be the inevitable result of market operations and find ways to shield citizens from their consequences—while somehow still preserving the dynamism that produces capitalism's vast economic and cultural benefits in the first place.

Commodification and Cultivation

Capitalism is a system of economic and social relations marked by private property, the exchange of goods and services by free individuals, and the use of market mechanisms to control the production and distribution of those goods and services. Some of its elements have existed in human societies for ages, but it was only in the seventeenth and eighteenth centuries, in parts of Europe and its offshoots in North America, that they all came together in force. Throughout history, most households had consumed most of the things that they produced and produced most of what they consumed. Only at this point did a majority of the population in some countries begin to buy most of the things they consumed and do so with the proceeds gained from selling most of what they produced.

The growth of market-oriented households and what came to be called "commercial society" had profound implications for practically every aspect of human activity. Prior to capitalism, life was governed by traditional institutions that subordinated the choices and destinies of individuals to various communal, political, and religious structures. These institutions kept change to a minimum, blocking people from making much progress but also protecting them from many of life's vicissitudes. The advent of capitalism gave individuals more control over and responsibility for their own lives than ever before—which proved both liberating and terrifying, allowing for both progress and regression.

Commodification—the transformation of activities performed for private use into activities performed for sale on the open market—allowed people to use their time more efficiently, specializing in producing what they were relatively good at and buying other things from other people. New forms of commerce and manufacturing used the division of labor to produce common household items cheaply and also made a range of new goods available. The result, as the historian Jan de Vries has noted, was what contemporaries called "an awakening of the appetites of the mind"—an expansion of subjective wants and a new subjective perception of needs. This ongoing expansion of wants has been chastised by critics of capitalism from Rousseau to Marcuse as imprisoning humans in a cage of unnatural desires. But it has also been praised by defenders of the market from Voltaire onward for broadening the range of human possibility. Developing and fulfilling higher wants and needs, in this view, is the essence of civilization.

Because we tend to think of commodities as tangible physical objects, we often overlook the extent to which the creation and increasingly cheap distribution of new cultural commodities have expanded what one might call the means of self-cultivation. For the history of capitalism is also the history of the extension of communication, information, and entertainment—things to think with, and about.

Among the earliest modern commodities were printed books (in the first instance, typically the Bible), and their shrinking price and increased availability were far more historically momentous than, say, the spread of the internal combustion engine. So, too, with the spread of newsprint, which made possible the newspaper and the magazine. Those gave rise, in turn, to new markets for information and to the business of gathering and distributing news. In the eighteenth century, it took months for news from India to reach London; today, it takes moments. Books and news have made possible an expansion of not only our awareness but also our imagination, our ability to empathize with others and imagine living in new ways ourselves. Capitalism and commodification have thus facilitated both humanitarianism and new forms of self-invention.

Over the last century, the means of cultivation were expanded by the invention of recorded sound, film, and television, and with the rise of the Internet and home computing, the costs of acquiring knowledge and culture have fallen dramatically. For those so inclined, the expansion of the means of cultivation makes possible an almost unimaginable enlargement of one's range of knowledge.

Family Matters

If capitalism has opened up ever more opportunities for the development of human potential, however, not everyone has been able to take full advantage of those opportunities or progress. . . . Formal or informal barriers to equality of opportunity, for example, have historically blocked various sectors of the population—such as women, minorities, and the poor—from benefiting fully from all capitalism offers. But over time, in the advanced capitalist world, those barriers have gradually been lowered or removed, so that now opportunity is more equally available than ever before. The inequality that exists today, therefore, derives less from the unequal availability of opportunity than it does from the unequal ability to exploit opportunity. And that unequal ability, in turn, stems from differences in the inherent human potential that individuals begin with and in the ways that families and communities enable and encourage that human potential to flourish.

The role of the family in shaping individuals' ability and inclination to make use of the means of cultivation that capitalism offers is hard to overstate. The household is not only a site of consumption and of biological reproduction. It is also the main setting in which children are socialized, civilized, and educated, in which habits are developed that influence their subsequent fates as people and as market actors. To use the language of contemporary economics, the family is a workshop in which human capital is produced.

Over time, the family has shaped capitalism by creating new demands for new commodities. It has also been repeatedly reshaped by capitalism because new commodities and new means of production have led family members to spend their time in new ways. As new consumer goods became available at ever-cheaper prices during the eighteenth century, families devoted more of their time to market-oriented activities, with positive effects on their ability to consume. . . .

Dynamism and Insecurity

For most of history, the prime source of human insecurity was nature. In such societies, as Marx noted, the economic system was oriented toward stability—and stagnancy. Capitalist societies, by contrast, have been oriented toward innovation and dynamism, to the creation of new knowledge, new products, and new modes of production and distribution. All of this has shifted the locus of insecurity from nature to the economy. . . .

The dynamism and insecurity created by nineteenth-century industrial capitalism led to the creation of new institutions for the reduction of insecurity, including the limited liability corporation, to reduce investor risks; labor unions, to further worker interests; mutual-aid societies, to provide loans and burial insurance; and commercial life insurance. In the middle decades of the twentieth century, in response to the mass unemployment and deprivation produced by the Great Depression (and the political success of communism and fascism, which convinced many democrats that too much insecurity was a threat to capitalist democracy itself), Western democracies embraced the welfare state. Different nations created different combinations of specific programs, but the new welfare states had a good deal in common, including old-age and unemployment insurance and various measures to support families.

The expansion of the welfare state in the decades after World War II took place at a time when the capitalist economies of the West were growing rapidly. The success of the industrial economy made it possible to siphon off profits and wages to government purposes through taxation. The demographics of the postwar era, in which the breadwinner-homemaker model of the family predominated, helped also, as moderately high birthrates created a favorable ratio of active workers to dependents. Educational opportunities expanded, as elite universities increasingly admitted students on the basis of their academic achievements and potential, and more and more people attended institutions of higher education. And barriers to full participation in society for women and minorities began to fall as well. The result of all of this was a temporary equilibrium during which the advanced capitalist countries experienced strong economic growth, high employment, and relative socioeconomic equality.

Life in the Postindustrial Economy

For humanity in general, the late twentieth and early twenty-first centuries have been a period of remarkable progress, due in no small part to the spread of capitalism around the globe. Economic liberalization in China, India, Brazil, Indonesia, and other countries in the developing world has allowed hundreds of millions of people to escape grinding poverty and move into the middle class. Consumers in more advanced capitalist countries, such as the United States, meanwhile, have experienced a radical reduction in the price of many commodities, from clothes to televisions, and the availability of a river of new goods that have transformed their lives.

Most remarkable, perhaps, have been changes to the means of self-cultivation. As the economist Tyler Cowen notes, much of the fruit of recent developments "is in our minds and in our laptops and not so much in the revenue-generating sector of the economy." As a result, "much of the value of the internet is experienced at the personal level and so will never show up in the productivity numbers." Many of the great musical performances of the twentieth century, in every genre, are available on YouTube for free. Many of the great films of the twentieth century, once confined to occasional showings at art houses in a few metropolitan areas, can be viewed by anybody at any time for a small monthly charge. Soon, the great university libraries will be available online to the entire world, and other unprecedented opportunities for personal development will follow.

All this progress, however, has been shadowed by capitalism's perennial features of inequality and insecurity. In 1973, the sociologist Daniel Bell noted that in the advanced capitalist world, knowledge, science, and technology were driving a transformation to what he termed "postindustrial society." Just as manufacturing had previously displaced agriculture as the major source of employment, he argued, so the service sector was now displacing manufacturing. In a postindustrial, knowledge-based economy, the production of manufactured goods depended more on technological inputs than on the skills of the workers who actually built and assembled the products. That meant a relative decline in the need for and economic value of skilled and semiskilled factory workers—just as there had previously been a decline in the need for and value of agricultural laborers. In such an economy, the skills in demand included scientific and technical knowledge and the ability to work with information. The revolution in information technology that has swept through the economy in recent decades, meanwhile, has only exacerbated these trends.

One crucial impact of the rise of the postindustrial economy has been on the status and roles of men and women. Men's relative advantage in the preindustrial and industrial economies rested in large part on their greater physical strength—something now ever less in demand. Women, in contrast, whether by biological disposition or socialization, have had a relative advantage in human skills and emotional intelligence, which have become increasingly more important in an economy more oriented to human services than to the production of material objects. The portion of the economy in which women could participate has expanded, and their labor has become more valuable—meaning that time spent at home now comes at the expense of more lucrative possibilities in the paid work force.

This has led to the growing replacement of male breadwinner-female homemaker households by dual-income households. Both advocates and critics of the move of women into the paid economy have tended to overemphasize the role played in this shift by the ideological struggles of feminism, while underrating the role played by changes in the nature of capitalist production. The redeployment of female labor from the household has been made possible in part by the existence of new commodities that cut down on necessary household labor time (such as washing machines, dryers, dishwashers, water heaters, vacuum cleaners, microwave ovens). The greater time devoted to market activity, in turn, has given rise to new demand for household-oriented consumer goods that require less labor (such as packaged and prepared food) and the expansion of restaurant and fast-food eating. And it has led to the commodification of care, as the young, the elderly, and the infirm are increasingly looked after not by relatives but by paid minders.

The trend for women to receive more education and greater professional attainments has been accompanied by changing social norms in the choice of marriage partners. In the age of the breadwinner-homemaker marriage, women tended to place a premium on earning capacity in their choice of partners. Men, in turn, valued the homemaking capacities of potential spouses more than their vocational attainments. It was not unusual for men and women to marry partners of roughly the same intelligence, but women tended to marry men of higher levels of education and economic achievement. As the economy has passed from an industrial economy to a postindustrial service-and-information economy, women have joined men in attaining recognition through paid work, and the industrious couple today is more likely to be made of peers, with more equal levels of education and more comparable levels of economic achievement—a process termed "assortative mating."

Inequality on the Rise

These postindustrial social trends have had a significant impact on inequality. If family income doubles at each step of the economic ladder, then the total incomes of those families higher up the ladder are bound to increase faster than the total incomes of those further down. But for a substantial portion of households at the lower end of the ladder, there has been no doubling at all—for as the relative pay of women has grown and the relative pay of less-educated, working-class men has declined, the latter have been viewed as less and less marriageable. Often, the limitations of human capital that make such men less employable also make them less desirable as companions, and the character traits of men who are chronically unemployed sometimes deteriorate as well. With less to bring to the table, such men are regarded as less necessary—in part because women can now count on provisions from the welfare state as an additional independent source of income, however meager.

In the United States, among the most striking developments of recent decades has been the stratification of marriage patterns among the various classes and ethnic groups of society. When divorce laws were loosened in the 1960s, there was a rise in divorce rates among all classes. But by the 1980s, a new pattern had emerged: divorce declined among the more educated portions of the populace, while rates among the less-educated portions continued to rise. In addition, the more educated and more well-to-do were more likely to wed, while the less educated were less likely to do so. Given the family's role as an incubator of human capital, such trends have had important spillover effects on inequality. Abundant research shows that children raised by two parents in an ongoing union are more likely to develop the self-discipline and self-confidence that make for success in life, whereas children—and particularly boys—reared in single-parent households (or, worse, households with a mother who has a series of temporary relationships) have a greater risk of adverse outcomes.

All of this has been taking place during a period of growing equality of access to education and increasing stratification of marketplace rewards, both of which have increased the importance of human capital. One element of human capital is cognitive ability: quickness of mind, the ability to infer and apply patterns drawn from experience, and the ability to deal with mental complexity. Another is character and social skills: self-discipline, persistence, responsibility. And a third is actual knowledge. All of these are becoming increasingly crucial for success in the postindustrial marketplace. As the economist Brink Lindsey notes in his recent book *Human Capitalism,* between 1973 and 2001, average annual growth in real income was only 0.3 percent for people in the bottom fifth of the U.S. income distribution, compared with 0.8 percent for people in the middle fifth and 1.8 percent for those in the top fifth. Somewhat similar patterns also prevail in many other advanced economies.

Globalization has not caused this pattern of increasingly unequal returns to human capital but reinforced it. The economist Michael Spence has distinguished between "tradable" goods and services, which can be easily imported and exported, and "untradable" ones, which cannot. Increasingly, tradable goods and services are imported to advanced capitalist societies from less advanced capitalist societies, where labor costs are lower. As manufactured goods and routine services are outsourced, the wages of the relatively unskilled and uneducated in advanced capitalist societies decline further, unless these people are somehow able to find remunerative employment in the untradable sector.

The Impact of Modern Finance

Rising inequality, meanwhile, has been compounded by rising insecurity and anxiety for people higher up on the economic ladder. One trend contributing to this problem has been the financialization of the economy, above all in the United States, creating what was characterized as "money manager capitalism" by the economist Hyman Minsky and has been called "agency capitalism" by the financial expert Alfred Rappaport.

As late as the 1980s, finance was an essential but limited element of the U.S. economy. The trade in equities (the stock market) was made up of individual investors, large or small, putting their own money in stocks of companies they believed to have good long-term prospects. Investment capital was also available from the major Wall Street investment banks and their foreign counterparts, which were private partnerships in which the partners' own money was on the line. All of this began to change as larger pools of capital became available for investment and came to be deployed by professional money managers rather [than] the owners of the capital themselves.

One source of such new capital was pension funds. In the postwar decades, when major American industries emerged from World War II as oligopolies with limited competition and large, expanding markets at home and abroad, their profits and future prospects allowed them to offer employees defined-benefit pension plans, with the risks involved assumed by the companies themselves. From the 1970s on, however, as the U.S. economy became more competitive, corporate profits became more uncertain, and companies (as well as various public-sector organizations) attempted to shift the risk by putting their pension funds into the hands of professional money managers, who were expected to generate significant profits. Retirement income for employees now depended not on the profits of their employers but on the fate of their pension funds.

Another source of new capital was university and other nonprofit organizations' endowments, which grew initially thanks to donations but were increasingly expected to grow further based on their investment performance. And still another source of new capital came from individuals and governments in the developing world, where rapid economic growth, combined with a high propensity to save and a desire for relatively secure investment prospects, led to large flows of money into the U.S. financial system.

Spurred in part by these new opportunities, the traditional Wall Street investment banks transformed themselves into publicly traded corporations—that is to say, they, too, began to invest not just with their own funds but also with other people's money—and tied the bonuses of their partners and employees to annual profits. All of this created a highly competitive financial system dominated by investment managers working with large pools of capital, paid based on their supposed ability to outperform their peers. The structure of incentives in this environment led fund managers to try to maximize short-term returns, and this pressure trickled down to corporate executives. The shrunken time horizon created a temptation to boost immediate profits at the expense of longer-term investments, whether in research and development or in improving the skills of the company's work force. For both managers and employees, the result has been a constant churning that increases the likelihood of job losses and economic insecurity.

An advanced capitalist economy does indeed require an extensive financial sector. Part of this is a simple extension of the division of labor: outsourcing decisions about investing to professionals allows the rest of the population the mental space to pursue things they do better or care more about. The increasing complexity of capitalist economies means that entrepreneurs and corporate executives need help in deciding when and how to raise funds. And private equity firms that have an ownership interest in growing the real value of the firms in which they invest play a key role in fostering economic growth.

These matters, which properly occupy financiers, have important consequences, and handling them requires intelligence, diligence, and drive, so it is neither surprising nor undesirable that specialists in this area are highly paid. But whatever its benefits and continued social value, the financialization of society has nevertheless had some unfortunate consequences, both in increasing inequality by raising the top of the economic ladder (thanks to the extraordinary rewards financial managers receive) and in increasing insecurity among those lower down (thanks to the intense focus on short-term economic performance to the exclusion of other concerns). . . .

What Is to Be Done?

Capitalism today continues to produce remarkable benefits and continually greater opportunities for self-cultivation and personal development. Now as ever, however, those upsides are coming with downsides, particularly increasing inequality and insecurity. As Marx and Engels accurately noted, what distinguishes capitalism from other social and economic systems is its "constant revolutionizing of production, uninterrupted disturbance of all social conditions, [and] everlasting uncertainty and agitation." . . .

The challenge for government policy in the advanced capitalist world is thus how to maintain a rate of economic dynamism that will provide increasing benefits for all while still managing to pay for the social welfare programs required to make citizens' lives bearable under conditions of increasing inequality and insecurity. Different countries will approach this challenge in different ways, since their priorities, traditions, size, and demographic and economic characteristics vary. (It is among the illusions of the age that when it comes to government policy, nations can borrow at will from one another.) But a useful starting point might be the rejection of both the politics of privilege and the politics of resentment and the adoption of a clear-eyed view of what capitalism actually involves, as opposed to the idealization of its worshipers and the demonization of its critics.

JERRY Z. MULLER is professor of history at the Catholic University of America and author of several books including *The Mind and the Market: Capitalism in Western Thought, The Other God That Failed: Hans Freyer and the Deradicalization of German Conservatism,* and *Conservatism: An Anthology of Social and Political Thought from David Hume to the Present.*

Chris Berg

→ **NO**

Why Capitalism Is Awesome

Each year the glossy business magazine *FastCompany* releases a list of what it considers to be the "World's 50 Most Innovative Companies." This list is populated much as you would expect.

In 2012 the leader was Apple, followed by Facebook, Google, and Amazon.com. Spot a theme? In the top 10, there are only two companies that are not primarily digital companies. One, Life Technologies, works in genetic engineering. (The other—try not to laugh—is the Occupy Movement. *FastCompany* describes them as "Transparent. Tech savvy. Design savvy. Local and global. Nimble.") Not only are most of them digital firms, but they're all flashy and unique, and they're almost all household names.

Everybody from *Forbes* to *BusinessWeek* hands out most innovative company awards. They're all pretty similar and predictable. But these lists have a perverse effect. They suggest that the great success of capitalism and the market economy is inventing cutting edge technology and that if we want to observe capitalist progress, we should be looking for sleek design and popular fashion. Innovation, the media tells us, is inventing cures for cancer, solar panels, and social networking.

But the true genius of the market economy isn't that it produces prominent, highly publicized goods to inspire retail queues, or the medical breakthroughs that make the nightly news. No, the genius of capitalism is found in the tiny things—the things that nobody notices.

A market economy is characterized by an infinite succession of imperceptible, iterative changes and adjustments. Free market economists have long talked about the unplanned and uncoordinated nature of capitalist innovation. They've neglected to emphasize just how invisible it is.

One exception is the great Adam Smith. In his *Wealth of Nations*, the example he used to illustrate the division of labor was a pin factory. He described carefully the complex process by which a pin is made. Producing the head of the pin "requires two to three distinct operations." To place the head on the wire is a "peculiar business." Then the pins have to be whitened. The production of a pin, Smith concluded, is an 18-step task.

Smith was making an argument about specialization, but just as important was his choice of example. It would be hard to think of something less impressive, less consequential than a pin. Smith wanted his contemporaries to think about the economy not by observing it from the

lofty heights of the palace or the lecture hall, but by seeing it from the bottom up—to recognise how a market economy is the aggregate of millions of little tasks. It's a lesson many have not yet learned. We should try to recognise the subtleties of the apparently mundane.

Capitalism Means Efficiency

Ikea's Billy bookshelf is a common, almost disposable, piece of household furniture that has been produced continuously since 1979. It looks exactly the same as it did more than three decades ago. But it's much cheaper. The standard model—more than six feet tall—costs $59.99. And from an engineering perspective the Billy bookshelf is hugely different from its ancestors.

In those 30 years the Billy has changed minutely but importantly. The structure of the back wall has changed over and over, as the company has tried to reduce the weight of the back (weight costs money) but increase its strength. Even the studs that hold up the removable book shelves have undergone dramatic changes. The studs were until recently simple metal cylinders. Now they are sophisticated shapes, tapering into a cup at one end on which the shelf rests. The brackets that hold the frame together are also complex pieces of engineering.

Ikea is a massive company. Tiny changes—even to metal studs—are magnified when those products are produced in bulk. There is no doubt somebody, somewhere in the Ikea product design hierarchy whose singular focus has been reducing the weight and increasing the strength of those studs. They went to sleep thinking about studs and metals and the trade-offs between strength and weight. Their seemingly inconsequential work helps keep Ikea's prices down and its profits high. With each minute change to the shape of the Billy's metal studs they earn their salary many times over.

Being massive, however, Ikea has an advantage: it is able to hire specialists whose job is solely to obsess about simple things like studs. Ikea is well-known for its more prominent innovations—for instance, flat-packing, which can reduce to one-sixth the cost of shipping—and the extremely low staffing of its retail stores.

For big-box retailers, innovation is about efficiency, not invention. Extremely resilient supply chains may not win glossy innovation awards but they are the source of much of our modern prosperity. But Ikea is big and famous. So let me suggest another icon of capitalist innovation and dynamism: pizza.

Capitalism Tastes Better, Cheaper

Pizza is one of our most mundane and simple foods. It would be the last place most people would look for innovation and engineering. It is, at its most basic, a thin bread topped by tomatoes and cheese—a food of the poor of Naples exported, which is endlessly interpreted by the rest of the world.

Forty-one percent of Americans eat pizza at least once a week, whether purchased frozen and reheated in home ovens, delivered, taken away, or cooked from scratch at home. All of these choices are more complicated than they seem. Keeping a pizza crisp long out of the oven so that it can be delivered, or making sure it will crisp up in a variable home oven after having been frozen for weeks is anything but simple.

Moisture is the enemy. For frozen pizzas, this means that toppings have to be precooked precisely to avoid some ingredients being burned while others are still heating through. Frozen pizza takes a lot of abuse—it is partially thawed each time it is transferred from manufacturer to supermarket to home freezer. So the dough has to be precisely regulated to manage its water content. Cheese freezes poorly, and consumers expect it to melt evenly across the base, so manufacturers obsess about cheese's pH range and its water and salt content. And of course all these decisions are made with an eye on the customer's budget and the manufacturer's profitability. The consumers of family sized frozen pizzas tend to be extremely price sensitive. The opportunities for innovation in processes, equipment, automation, and chemistry are virtually endless.

It gets even more complicated when we factor in changing consumer tastes. The modern pizza customer doesn't just want cheese, tomato, and pepperoni. As food tastes grow more sophisticated they look for more sophisticated flavors, even in frozen pizza. It's one thing to master how cheddar or mozzarella melts. Dealing with more flavorful brie or smoked Gouda is another thing entirely. Like Ikea's stud specialist, there are hundreds of people across the world obsessed with how frozen cheese melts in a home oven. These sorts of complications are replicated across every ingredient in this simple product. (How does one adapt an automated pepperoni dispenser to dispense feta instead?)

Customers demand aesthetic qualities too. Frozen products have to look authentic. Customers like their pizza crusts to have slight burn marks, even if home ovens won't naturally produce them. So manufacturers experiment with all sorts of heating techniques to replicate the visual result of a wood fired oven.

Takeout pizza seems easier but has almost as many complexities. Some large pizza chains are slowly integrating the sort of sauce and topping applicators used by frozen goods manufacturers. Cheese is costly and hard to spread evenly. The pizza chain Dominos uses a proprietary "auto-cheese," which takes standardized blocks of cheese and, with a push of a button, shreds them evenly across a base.

Moisture problems are even more endemic in takeout pizza. The cooked pizza has to survive, hot and crispy and undamaged, for some time before it is consumed. If the box is closed, the steam from the hot pizza seeps through the bread, making it soft and unappealing. But an open box will lose heat too quickly. Engineers have struck a balance. Vents in the box and plastic tripods in the centre of the pizza encourage airflow. Deliverers carry the pizzas in large insulated sleeves to keep the heat in but reduce risk of steam damage.

We could easily replicate this analysis for almost every processed or manufactured food in the typical supermarket. Then we could reflect on the complexity of serving food, not in a home kitchen, but on an airplane flying more than 600 miles per hour and 37,000 feet in the air, cooked in a tiny galley for hundreds of people at a time.

Some of the most extraordinary logistical accomplishments of the modern world are entirely unnoticed. Some—like airline food—we actively disparage, without recognizing the true effort behind them.

Capitalism Is about Innovation, as Well as Invention

One of the great essays in the free market tradition is Leonard Read's "I, Pencil." Read was the founder of the influential American think tank the Foundation for Economic Education. In his essay, he adopts the perspective of an ordinary wooden lead pencil and purports to write his genealogy. He began as a cedar tree from North California or Oregon, was chopped down and harvested and shipped on a train to a mill in San Leandro, California, and there cut down into "small, pencil-length slats less than one-fourth of an inch in thickness."

Read's point: "Not a single person on the face of this earth" knows how to make a pencil on their own. The construction of a pencil is entirely dispersed among "millions of human beings," from the Italians who mine pumice for the eraser to the coffee manufacturers who supply their drinks to the cedar loggers in Oregon.

Read was vividly illustrating a famous point of Friedrich Hayek's—these separate people manage, through nothing but the price system, to make something extraordinarily complex. None of the pumice miners intend to make a pencil. They simply want to trade their labor for wages. Adam Smith's invisible hand does the rest.

Read published his essay in 1958. The chemical formula for the eraser, known as the "plug," has changed repeatedly over the half century since. The production is highly automated, and the supply lines are tighter. Chemicals are added to keep the eraser from splitting. Synthetic rubber production in 2012 is much different than it was in 1958. These tiny plugs look pretty much the same but have evolved in a dozen different ways.

"I, Pencil" magnificently captures the complexity of markets, but it doesn't quite capture their dynamism. The millions of people involved in pencil production aren't merely performing their market-allocated tasks but are trying to find new ways to make their tiny segment easier, cheaper, and more profitable. The pencil market—as far from a cutting-edge firm like Facebook as you could imagine—is still full of entrepreneurs trying to break apart established business models to shave costs and rationalize supply chains. In 1991 a gross of 144 simple, Chinese-made wood pencils sold on the wholesale market for $6.91. In 2004 that price had dropped to $4.48.

And this is before we consider the variety of pencils available to consumers—not just wooden ones of different shapes, sizes, colors, and densities, but mechanical pencils, jumbo sized children's pencils, rectangular carpenters' pencils (rectangular pencils can't roll away) and on, and on, and on.

It is to capitalism's great disadvantage that there's nothing inherently exciting about pencils. Humans like novelty. We like invention. We like high-technology breakthroughs that will change the world.

I, Pork

The most insightful book about capitalism published in the last decade isn't a treatise on economics or philosophy but an art project. In *Pig 05049*, the Dutch artist Christien Meindertsma starkly shows photographs of the 185 separate products that are made from a single pig.

Every part of a slaughtered pig is sold and repurposed. Obviously, we're familiar with pork and ham but how many people realise that pig bones are converted into a glue that holds sandpaper together? Or that pig fat is a constituent part of paint, helping its spread and giving it a glossy sheen? Pig parts are found in everything from yogurt to train brakes to photography paper to matches—even in bullets.

One response to Meindertsma's book is to see it as simply a modern-day reworking of Leonard Read's pencil. But it's more than that. *Pig 05049* reveals what a market economy tries to obscure: the deep complexities of individual products.

That single pig was stripped down and shipped to factories and markets across the world. It went into matches and copper and crayons and floor wax. These products are as mundane as can be imagined—what consumer spends more than a moment's thought on which crayon to purchase, let alone how those crayons are produced? But as Meindertsma points out, the distinctive smell of many crayons comes from fatty acids, which in turn come from pig bone fat, used as a hardening agent.

Pig 05049 was published in 2007. The oleochemical industry—that is, the industry that derives chemicals from natural oils and fats—is one of the most innovative in the world. Like any industry experiencing rapid technological and scientific change, it is restructuring as well, moving production from Western Europe and the United States to China, Malaysia, and Indonesia.

Six years is a long time in a competitive marketplace. As simple as they seem, those crayons are changing: costs of production have been shaved down, raw materials are being utilized more efficiently, and supply lines are being tightened. Amazon now lists 2,259 separate products in the children's drawing crayon category alone.

Government Doesn't Understand Innovation

If *FastCompany* has a warped view about the nature of innovation in a market economy, it is not alone. Governments do, too.

The Australian federal government has its very own minister for innovation, and his Department of Industry, Innovation, Science, Research and Tertiary Education doles out grants for inventions and startups. Its Commercialisation Australia program sponsors inventors who "have transformed an innovative idea into reality." Innovation Australia funds grant-seekers to turn their "groundbreaking ideas into commercial products." This is the invention fetish—the idea that technological progress occurs when dreamers have great ideas. All society needs to do is subsidize dreams into reality.

But ideas are the easy part. Getting things done is hard. Setting up a business, paring down costs, acquiring and retaining market share: those are the fields in a market economy where firms win or lose. The brilliance of the market economy is found in small innovations made to polish and enhance existing products and services. Invention is a wonderful thing. But we should not pretend that it is invention that has made us rich.

We have higher living standards than our ancestors because of the little things. We ought to be more aware of the continuous, slow, and imperceptible creative destruction of the market economy, the refiners who are always imperceptibly bettering our frozen pizzas, our bookshelves, our pencils, and our crayons.

CHRIS BERG, a research fellow with the Institute of Public Affairs in Melbourne, Australia and author of *In Defence of Freedom of Speech.* He authored *The Growth of Australia's Regulatory State,* and edited *The National Curriculum: A Critique* (2011).

EXPLORING THE ISSUE

Does Capitalism Have Serious Defects?

Critical Thinking and Reflection

1. Provide a definition of capitalism that distinguishes it from socialism, communism, collectivism, and a mixed economy. What aspects of the economy are capitalistic and what aspects are socialistic? (Remember that I teach at the University of Maryland, which is socialism because the public owns the means of production. I would argue that the University of Maryland is good socialism.)
2. How does capitalism supposedly undermine democracy? How does it supposedly help create democracies?
3. Why does capitalism need to be restrained by the government or is it better for capitalism to not be regulated?
4. If the corporations run the country, they have to work together in an organized way to be successful. How are they organized? Many corporations have contrary interests. How and when do they push in unison? Why do we assume that they stand united?
5. How does capitalism cause such great inequality?
6. What would you say are the three greatest positive impacts that capitalism has on society?
7. How does capitalism affect values and culture?
8. Do organizations that oppose corporate interests feel that they succeed sometimes against the corporations? If they do, how do you explain this?

Is There Common Ground?

The foremost issue in understanding our society is the structure of power. Both Issues 10 and 11 address this phenomenon. Issue 10 debates the power elite thesis, and Issue 11 debates the impact of capitalism on society. On both issues, there is common agreement that power is very unevenly distributed in America and this power inequality has been increasing over time. When that inequality gets too large, it can effectively destroy democracy because the votes of most of the people do not really count when they are contrary to the desires of the economic powers. The candidates are selected (funded) by the capitalist class that also controls them when in office. The debate is over whether the inequality in America has reached that point or not. Another issue is whether the economic benefits of capitalism are much greater than the negative impacts of capitalism on values, character, and culture. Everyone agrees that there are both positive and negative effects of capitalism. The debate is over which are greater.

Create Central

www.mhhe.com/createcentral

Additional Resources

In 1962, Milton Friedman convincingly demonstrated that economic freedom is a key precondition for political freedom in his classic book *Capitalism and Freedom* (University of Chicago Press). His thesis became the major argument for the virtues of capitalism. He maintains that capitalism's defects are few and minimal. Other works

that support Friedman's view include Azar Gat, *Victorious and Vulnerable: Why Democracy Won in the 20th Century and How It Is Still Imperiled* (Rowman & Littlefield, 2010); Alasdair Roberts, *The Logic of Discipline: Global Capitalism and the Architecture of Government* (Oxford University Press, 2010); Colin Cremin, *Capitalism's New Clothes: Enterprise, Ethics and Enjoyment in Times of Crisis* (Pluto Press, 2011); Peter L. Berger, *The Capitalist Revolution: Fifty Propositions about Prosperity, Equality, and Liberty* [a classic] (Basic Books, 1986); Andrew Bernstein, *The Capitalist Manifesto: The Historic, Economic and Philosophic Case for Laissez-Faire* (University Press of America, 2005); Dhanjoo N. Ghista, *Socio-Economic Democracy and the World Government: Collective Capitalism, Depovertization, Human Rights, Template for Sustainable Peace* (World Scientific, 2004); Michael G. Heller, *Capitalism, Institutions, and Economic Development* (Routledge, 2009); Dennis C. Mueller, *Capitalism and Democracy: Challenges and Responses in an Increasingly Interdependent World* (Edward Elgar Publishing, 2003); Arthur Seldon, ed., *The Virtues of Capitalism* (Liberty Fund, 2004); and Edward W. Younkins, *Champions of a Free Society: Ideas of Capitalism's Philosophers and Economists* (Lexington Books, 2008). The works that are critical of capitalism's impact on society include Henry A. Giroux, *Zombie Politics and Culture in the Age of Casino Capitalism* (Peter Lang, 2011); Brian C. Anderson, *Democratic Capitalism and Its Discontents* (ISI Books, 2007); Yves Smith, *ECONned: How Unenlightened Self Interest Undermined Democracy and Corrupted Capitalism* (Palgrave Macmillan, 2010); Noreena Hertz, *The Silent Takeover: Global Capitalism and the Death of Democracy* (Heinemann, 2001); Michael Parenti, *Democracy for the Few* (Thompson-Wadsworth, 2008); Alex Callinicos, *An Anti-Capitalist Manifesto* (Polity Press, 2003); Mark A.

Martinez, *The Myth of the Free Market: The Role of the State in a Capitalist Economy* (Kumarian Press, 2009); and Robert Reich's *Super-Capitalism: The Transformation of Business, Democracy, and Everyday Life* (Alfred A. Knopf, 2007). Jacob S. Hacker examines a prosperous United States where citizens increasingly feel politically powerless in *Great Risk Shift: The Assault on American Jobs, Families, Health Care and Retirement—And How You Can Fight Back* (Oxford University Press, 2006). A major response to the above critics of capitalism is Martin Wolf's "The Morality of the Market," *Foreign Policy* (September/October 2003), in which he tries to refute the allegation that the global economy undermines democracy. Three works that study the connection of capitalism and democracy more neutrally are Tony Porter and Karsten Ronit, eds., *The Challenges of Global Business Authority: Democratic Renewal, Stalemate, or Decay?* (State University of New York Press, 2010); Amiya Kumar Bagchi, *Perilous Passage: Mankind and the Global Ascendancy of Capital* (Rowman & Littlefield, 2005), and Peter Nolan,

Capitalism and Freedom: The Contradictory Character of Globalisation (Anthem Press, 2007). Two works that see very positive effects of capitalism if it were modified in certain ways are Sandra A. Waddock, *See Change: Making the Transition to a Sustainable Enterprise Economy* (Greenleaf Publishing, 2011) and R. P. Bootle, *The Trouble with Markets: Saving Capitalism from Itself* (Nicholas B Realey Publishing, 2011). Several authors propose alternative economic systems to capitalism which will better support democracy, including Allen Engler, *Economic Democracy: The Working-Class Alternative to Capitalism* (Fernwood Publishing, 2010); Chris Wyatt, *The Defetishized Society: New Economic Democracy as a Libertarian Alternative to Capitalism* (Continuum, 2011); Peer Hull Kristensen and Kari Lilja, eds., *Nordic Capitalisms and Globalization: New Forms of Economic Organization and Welfare Institutions* (Oxford University Press, 2011); and Costas Panayotakis, *Remaking Scarcity: From Capitalist Inefficiency to Economic Democracy* (Pluto, 2011).

Internet References . . .

Sociology—Study Sociology Online

http://edu.learnsoc.org/

Sociology Web Resources

**www.mhhe.com/socscience/sociology/resources
/index.htm**

Sociosite

www.topsite.com/goto/sociosite.net

Socioweb

www.topsite.com/goto/socioweb.com

Selected, Edited, and with Issue Framing Material by:
Kurt Finsterbusch, *University of Maryland, College Park*

ISSUE

Is Stimulus the Best Way to Get the American Economy Back on Its Feet?

YES: Joshua Holland, from "Paul Krugman: We Could End This Depression Right Now," *Alternet* (May 24, 2012)

NO: Dwight R. Lee, from "The Keynesian Path to Fiscal Irresponsibility," *Cato Journal* (vol. 32, no. 3, Fall 2012)

Learning Outcomes

After reading this issue, you should be able to:

- Understand the advantages and disadvantages of additional government spending (stimulus) in times of recession.
- Understand the theory behind the stimulus approach to recovering a nation's economy.
- Understand the theory behind the debt reduction (austerity) approach to recovering a nation's economy.
- Explain *Wall Street*'s degree of support for various policies for making the national economy strong again.
- Understand various public preferences for government policies for growing the economy.

ISSUE SUMMARY

YES: Freelance writer Joshua Holland and Paul Krugman, Nobel laureate economist and professor of economics and international affairs at the Woodrow Wilson School of Public and International Affairs at Princeton University, argue that while unemployment is high, the government must stimulate the economy to produce many more jobs and thus more earnings, which will increase spending, which will stimulate more business and jobs and more spending, and so on. When the economy has recovered, the government should institute policies to reduce the debt.

NO: Dwight R. Lee, the O'Neil Professor of Global Markets and Freedom in the Cox School of Business at Southern Methodist University, argues that the Keynesian approach of Paul Krugman and others will have disastrous results for America. The Keynesian prescriptions are reasonable in the abstract, but when filtered through the political system controlled by special interests, the results are some short-run benefits but long-run costs including relative economic stagnation.

Currently a debate that is tearing this country apart is whether to shrink government and the debt or to stimulate the economy. The current situation provides support and opposition for both theories. The current high unemployment and slow economic growth suggest the need for government spending to stimulate the economy. On the other hand, the high debt opposes the stimulus because it would increase the debt. The other side advocates cutting government spending to keep government debt small and allow the private sector to invest and innovate to grow the economy. The stimulus, or Keynesian, side thinks that cutting government spending would increase unemployment, decrease earnings, reduce consumption,

reduce production, and stymie economic growth, which could put America back into a deeper recession. The austerity side, the opponents of Keynesian theory, admits that cutting government spending could cause a short-term economic decline but would greatly increase long-term growth.

Evidence for this debate is hard to come by. A $700 billion stimulus was enacted in 2009, though some experts argued it should have been $1.2 trillion. Did it work? Steve Benen wrote in *Washington Monthly* in 2011: "Was the effort successful? Insofar as it prevented a calamity, of course it was—the stimulus took an economy that was shrinking and made it grow; it took an economy that was hemorrhaging jobs and created conditions in which it created jobs. There are millions of Americans working today who'd be unemployed were it not for the Recovery Act. . . . And yet, it was terribly unsuccessful insofar as the economy still stinks and the jobs crisis hasn't gone away." So the Keynesians can say that it created millions of jobs and prevented a deeper recession, but the austerity side can say that the stimulus did not do what it was supposed to do and then deny the job creation estimates because no one knows the job situation if the stimulus were not passed. The Keynesians can say the austerity policies in Europe have had much worse results than the considerably less austere American policies, but the anti-Keynesians can say the future may tell a different story and the two situations are not the same anyway. Joshua Holland and Paul Krugman strongly advocates Keynesian policies under the current slow growth and high unemployment conditions. When unemployment and economic growth substantially improve (approaching full utilization of labor, assets, and resources), government policy should shift to address debt reduction. Krugman criticizes President Obama for showing a willingness to consider more spending cuts than are advisable in a slow growth economy. Dwight R. Lee hopes Obama does not listen to Krugman and greatly harm the American economy with stimulus policies that expand government and deficits. He fears that the political system will not produce much true stimulus but will instead produce "pork," which achieves little and creates heavy debts that will be a drag on the economy for decades.

YES ↩

Joshua Holland

Paul Krugman: We Could End This Depression Right Now

The central message of Paul Krugman's new book, *End This Depression Now!* is simple: It doesn't have to be like this. No external dynamic is keeping unemployment at more than 8 percent and consigning a generation of young workers to an economy in which risk is plentiful and opportunities scarce. It is only a failure of political will—and an almost universal embrace of conservative voodoo economics—that is keeping us mired in this dark economic moment.

Of the 2009 stimulus, Krugman writes, "Those who had more or less the right ideas about what the economy needed, including President Obama, were timid, never willing either to acknowledge just how much action was required or to admit later on that what they did in the first round was inadequate." Instead of treating the dismal jobs picture as a crisis requiring their full attention, Washington "pivoted" to talking about the deficit—a phantom menace—at precisely the wrong time. "People with the wrong ideas," Krugman writes, "were vehement and untroubled by self-doubt."

This week, Paul Krugman appeared on the AlterNet Radio Hour to discuss his book. Below is a lightly edited transcript of the conversation.

Joshua Holland: Let me ask you first about a somewhat provocative word in your title, the D-word. What makes this a depression rather than a so-called "Great Recession" that we've heard so much about?

Paul Krugman: A recession is when things are going down, when the economy is heading down. A depression is when the economy is down, and stays down for a long time. We have the Great Depression, which was more than a decade. There were two recessions in there and there were two periods that were recoveries in the sense that things were getting better, but not much better. The whole period was a period that was really terrible for America and for the world. We're in a period like that right now. Not as bad as the Great Depression, but that's not much to recommend it. It's a sustained thing. We're now in year five of very high unemployment with terrible prospects for young people. It's a depression.

JH: I wonder if it's similar to the so-called Long Depression in the late 19th century. It was kind of two recessions sandwiched around a period of growth. The reason I ask that is because median wages really did not recover after the so-called tech bubble burst in 2000 before we hit this crash. Isn't that right?

PK: There is an argument that even the so-called "Bush boom"—that period of the middle years of the last decade—was still not very good for most Americans. There is that, but clearly things got an order of magnitude worse after 2007. That's mostly what I'm focusing on in *End This Depression Now*.

JH: I want to encourage people to read the book, but can you just give readers a sense of what you think is the most important thing policy makers should be thinking about doing right now?

PK: The moral of the book is: this doesn't have to be happening. This is essentially a technical process; it's a small thing. It's like having a dead battery in a car, and while there may be a lot wrong with the car, you can get the car going remarkably easily, if you're willing to accept that's what the problem really is.

First and foremost, what we have is an economy that just doesn't have enough spending. Consumers are hobbled by debt, corporations don't want to spend if they don't see consumer demand. Somebody has to step in and spend, and that somebody is the government. The government could—and by all means let's talk about forward-looking, big projects—right away get a big boost in the economy just by reversing the big cutbacks that have taken place in state and local governments these past three years. Get the schoolteachers rehired and get the policemen and firefighters back on the beat. Fill those potholes that have been developing in New Jersey and I believe all over America. We'd then be most of the way back to a decent economy again.

JH: It seems like we take two steps forward with private sector hiring, and then one step back as we're laying off public sector employees at the state and local levels. Do you have a sense of where the unemployment rate would be had we not been beset by this austerity madness?

PK: If we had had state and local governments expanding at the rate they normally do, which is by population—which is also by the way the rate in which it expanded in Bush's first term—then right there we'd have 1.3 million jobs more than we do right now. That's just the public sector jobs. There'd be indirect effects. People would have more spending power and there would be private sector jobs as well. That's something like 2 million jobs right there. When you put it all together my back of the envelope says if we weren't doing this austerity, GDP would be around 3 percentage points higher right now, the unemployment rate would be at least 1.5 points lower, which means we'd be at 6.5 percent unemployment. That's not great, but it's not a depression. We'd be in vastly better shape than we are right now.

JH: I have to ask if you're constantly banging your head against the table. Everything you write in the book strikes me as so much common sense, and yet even Democrats say the government has to pull in spending when families do. Isn't that the reverse of the truth? Isn't it the fact that when families are tightening their belts the government needs to loosen its belt to make up for that loss of demand?

PK: That's right. The whole mistake that people make is that we're all like a family. We're not because we're interdependent. Your spending is my income and my spending is your income. If we both tighten our belts at the same time thinking that's going to make us better off, it actually makes us worse off. This is a fundamental fallacy.

I'm not going to complain about being me. I've got a good job. I've got a solid income. It is frustrating, but it's frustrating because there are 4 million Americans who have been out of work for more than a year. There's a whole generation of students who are graduating who can't find jobs, or can't find jobs that are making use of the education that they've acquired at great expense. Those are the people to be concerned about.

JH: I find it frustrating that there is such a concerted effort to create this alternative reality where Keynesian economics has failed and giving tax cuts to the wealthy will create jobs. It's a parallel universe. Let me ask you for responses to a couple of common talking points. We hear these again and again. Speaking of wealthy people, are they job creators?

PK: No more than anyone else. In general, anyone who spends money is going to be helping to create jobs, but no more so if it's coming from

a rich person. This notion that we have to have extreme income inequality in order to have a successful, growing economy requires that you forget history that's live in the minds of everybody over the age of 50. The best generation of economic growth we've ever had in America was the generation right after World War II. That was a society in which the rich were not even remotely as rich as they are now. How come we created all those jobs—all those good jobs—at a time when the top tax rate was as high sometimes as 90 percent? So no, this just flies in the face of all the experience we've had in the last half-century.

JH: It seems like humans are supposed to accumulate knowledge, but we haven't done a very good job in this respect. Is there any chance that we might come to look like Greece?

PK: It's pretty hard for us to look like Greece. The thing about Greece is that they don't have their own currency. That makes you vulnerable to a lot of stuff in a way that having your own currency insulates you. Now what we could have is political dysfunction, and we're working on that, but the people who are working on that are the ones who say because of Greece we must not only slash spending and cut social programs, but also for some reason we must slash taxes on rich and the corporations.

We are nowhere near having a Greek scenario. It's much more likely that we're going to find ourselves looking like ourselves in the 1930s or Japan. We're actually well on our way to a Japan-type long-term stagnation. Greece is the wrong country to be afraid of. They are not a model for us.

JH: It's the politics. Last year when our credit was downgraded it wasn't downgraded because of any economic reality, but because Congress couldn't get it together to lift the debt ceiling.

What about the bond markets? We're hearing again and again that they'll punish us if we don't cut Social Security or if we don't transfer healthcare costs onto elderly retirees. Have we seen any evidence for this? Is there anything behind this assertion?

PK: Gosh, if you believe the people saying that you would have lost a lot of money. I know people have lost a lot of money doing that. The bond markets are willing to lend America—the US government—long-term money at about 1.7 percent as of right now. That's ridiculously low. The index bonds that are protected from inflation actually have a negative interest rate. The bond markets are saying they're worried about economic stagnation. They're worried there aren't going to be investment opportunities because the demand is so weak. So they're going to park their money in

US government debt, which is considered safe. The last thing you should be worrying about, at least according to the bond market, is those deficits. Those are not the problem right now.

JH: We're not the only ones who have been afflicted by this scourge of irrational deficit hysteria—the idea that we should cut spending when private sector demand is deep in a hole. Let's talk about Europe. Are we headed toward the end of the European economic union? Basically, as I understand it when you look at the very heavily indebted countries, they've essentially created a gold standard. They can't devalue their currencies and can't do any of the monetary tricks that one would logically pursue in these circumstances.

PK: They created something that's actually worse than the gold standard. If you're serious about economic history then you know the gold standard was a major reason that the Great Depression got as bad as it did. But at least countries had their own currencies. All they had to do was say all right, enough of this gold standard business, and they could escape. Now it's much harder.

I don't see how Greece stays in the euro. Leaving will be terrible, but staying is a no-hope situation. They will leave. Once people see that can happen, there will be in effect bank runs in Spain and Italy, which are much bigger players. That can only be contained if European elites start to behave very differently. They have to say, wait a second—punishing people for their alleged fiscal sins is not the priority now—saving the euro is. That means open-ended lending to the banks and the governments of those countries. It means having a much more expansionary and somewhat inflationary monetary policy. Maybe that will offer enough hope to save the system. It's moved pretty fast now. I think you can see that there's quite a large chance that there will be no euro a year from now.

JH: Let me turn you to another topic. We've seen stagnant middle-class wage growth for basically a generation. There are all sorts of theories popular in conservative think tanks about why this is either a myth or a really good thing. You wrote a piece recently about how income inequality is driving what one might call "political inequality"—one follows the other. Can you unpack that idea for us?

PK: First it starts with an observation. Inequality has had its ups and downs. We were a very unequal society before the Great Depression. We became a much more equal society during the 1930s and especially during the 1940s. We stayed middle-class for a while, then became unequal again. Political polarization, which you can actually measure using various statistical things on congressional voting, also has had its ups and downs. They track each other perfectly. Political polarization and income inequality march hand in hand. There's every reason to believe that relationship is not an accident.

What happens is when the wealthy are very wealthy they can in effect buy political support. The way that's worked in practice in the United States is that the Republican party moves with the interests of the super elite. Not the 1 percent, but the .01 percent. So the extraordinary explosion in incomes of the .01 percent relative to everybody else has pulled the Republican party far to the right to the point where there is no center. The center did not hold, it dissolved and turned into a chasm. That's not because Democrats moved to the left, because they didn't; they moved right. It's because the Republicans moved off into the Gamma quadrant. That is at the root of our political paralysis right now.

JH: They not only spend money directly on campaigns, but they also fund these networks of what I call alternative information infrastructure. If you look at for example billionaire Pete Peterson he's put $1 billion of his own money into a network of think tanks and media projects to help us understand that the greatest threat that we face are deficits, far-off deficits projected 30 or 40 years out.

I just want to turn quickly to trade. You won your Nobel Prize for your new trade theory. You were a vocal free trader in the 1990s. You got the *New York Times* column and I think you started to think more about politics. It's my long-held belief that the purely economic arguments about the benefits of trade are somewhat irrelevant in the real world, because when they go to negotiate these trade deals the US trade representative—like its counterparts in Europe and Japan—is heavily influenced by corporate lobbying. So while we may have a theoretical idea of the benefits of trade, when we're talking about the actual treaties being negotiated behind closed doors under a barrage of lobbying, can they actually yield those theoretical benefits?

PK: I would say that the first 50 years of post-war trade negotiations were a good thing because they produced a world with relatively low barriers, especially to exports of manufactured goods from poor countries. That's really important because you have success stories, countries that have moved their way up into becoming decent places to live through those exports, and countries that keep their heads above water through exports. If Bangladesh couldn't sell their exports of cheap clothing through the world market they would be a disaster area.

A lot of trade agreements in the last couple of decades haven't really been trade agreements. They've been agreements about protecting various kinds of interests. I teach a course on and off about this stuff. You look at something like the Central America Free Trade Agreement and that wasn't really a trade agreement. That was actually an intellectual property agreement largely about making sure our pharmaceutical companies had their monopoly power. So that's the sense in which you're right. A lot of what passes under the banner of free trade is actually something else and is often detrimental to the interests of workers both here and abroad.

JH: That was actually a trade protectionism agreement then?

PK: It was in effect. If you really look through it you found out that basically workers in those countries were gaining only a little bit more market access, but pharma companies here and in Europe were gaining a lot more in the ability to basically enforce their monopoly position.

JH: Now you have this elite discourse about the deficit and that elides the success that we've seen over generations in terms of Keynesian economics. Do you think the fact that we have a half-dozen countries in Europe have gone back into recession—and a couple more are teetering on the brink of going back in recession as a result of this austerity madness—is that changing people's minds in terms of policy makers?

PK: Well, some. Not enough, but I think we're making progress. I've been writing columns for a dozen years and my first principle is that to a first approximation nobody ever admits that they were wrong about anything. But you can see that, clearly, the tone of the discussion has changed quite a lot over the last six months—that we are moving back towards sanity. Whether it'll be time enough to avoid catastrophe I don't know. I think hammering on these points and pointing to the evidence does seem to work, which is why I published the book. It's in the hope we can get the debate to move a little bit further in the direction of doing the right thing.

JH: It's been interesting to watch your progression as a blogger. You're obviously a leading public intellectual, but you're not above posting silly cat videos, are you?

PK: Well, that's what you've got to do. That's a great medium for somebody who thinks the way I do. It's kind of a scratch pad for things that end being in columns and books. I find it an all-around fulfilling exercise, although it's taking up too much time everyday.

JOSHUA HOLLAND is a freelance writer and editor-at-large at AlterNet. He is also the author of "The 15 Biggest Lies About the Economy."

Dwight R. Lee

NO

The Keynesian Path to Fiscal Irresponsibility

The basic idea behind Keynesian policy for achieving stable economic growth is straightforward, and superficially plausible. When the economy is in a downturn with underutilized resources, Keynesians believe the federal government should increase aggregate demand by increasing deficit spending through some combination of more spending and lower taxes. With the aid of a multiplier effect augmenting the government's increase in aggregate demand, the economy will move back toward full employment. In contrast, they believe that when aggregate demand exceeds the productive capacity of the economy, the federal government can prevent inflationary overheating by reducing demand with a budget surplus generated by some combination of less spending and higher taxes. The resulting decrease in government demand will be augmented by a reverse multiplier effect, which will reduce inflationary pressures by bringing aggregate demand back in line with the economy's productive capacity. As discussed by Keynes and his early followers, there was nothing fiscally irresponsible about such a policy. While the budget would not be balanced on a yearly basis, it would be balanced over time as budget deficits intended to moderate recessions would be offset by budget surpluses used to restrain economic exuberance.

Of course there are problems with Keynesian policy that have to do with the difficulty of forecasting economic trends and making timely fiscal adjustments. These are problems that are widely recognized as troublesome. They are not my concern, however, since I shall argue that even if Keynesian remedies could be implemented in a timely manner, there are other serious problems undermining Keynesian hopes for moderating the decline, duration, and frequency of economic downturns. The first problem is that Keynesian prescriptions are filtered through a political process being driven by many competing agendas, of which balanced economic growth is only one. The second problem is that both Keynesian economics and the political process are almost entirely focused on short-run demand-side concerns while largely ignoring the long-run importance of economic productivity. The result is a political dynamic that has increasingly turned Keynesian economics into a prescription for fiscal irresponsibility that undermines economic growth without promoting economic stability.

Fiscal History before the Great Depression

From 1792 until 1930 the federal budget averaged 3.2 percent of gross domestic product. Peacetime spending (excluding the Civil War and World War I) averaged 2.7 percent of GDP. Over that 139-year period, the federal budget was roughly in balance, with federal deficits occurring in only 38 years. Those deficits occurred almost entirely because of spending increases during wartime or reduced revenues during economic downturns. The prevailing view was that such downturns would correct themselves through market adjustments, with increased government spending being neither necessary nor desirable. . . .

An important lesson from this experience, indeed from the entire U.S. experience until the early 1930s, is that while market economies suffer from occasional recessions, they recover and continue growing without the need of increased government spending and budget deficits called for by Keynesian prescriptions.

The fact that market economies self-correct from economic downturns without fiscal stimulus does not imply that federal spending was unimportant to U.S. economic success during the nation's first 140-plus years. The federal budget was spent primarily on such activities as providing national defense, infrastructure, law enforcement, and establishing standards on weights and measures. These activities create an environment that unleashes the power of private enterprise and entrepreneurship to create wealth. But as important as what the federal government did to promote economic success, what it did not do was just as important. It did little to override the decisions of consumers and producers with regulations and spending programs as they pursued their interests in response to market incentives. Government action was limited by the prevailing view that prosperity resulted from people keeping most of their earnings because it is their investments and spending choices that do the most to create productive jobs and general prosperity. The idea that the federal government could promote prosperity by spending more of the nation's wealth would have been widely dismissed as foolish.

Fiscal History in the Modern Era

A clear divide in U.S. fiscal history took place in the early 1930s. The proximate cause of this divide was the Great Depression, but it can be traced to a shift in the prevailing political ideology that began in the late 1800s with the populist and progressive movements. Those movements were rooted in a growing belief that market economies required the detailed guidance of the federal government. Beginning as a minority view, it became increasingly accepted that only through government regulation of economic decisions and the stimulus of more federal spending and transfers could economic growth be maintained and economic output be distributed fairly. By the 1930s this belief was sufficiently widespread to give political traction to the idea that more government spending (particularly deficit spending) and control over the economy could reverse the economic downturn that became the Great Depression. This view was given intellectual impetus with the 1936 publication of *The General Theory of Employment, Interest and Money* by John Maynard Keynes, which provided an argument for the use of fiscal policy by central governments to smooth out business cycles. The result was that federal spending expanded and its composition changed.

With the ideological shift, supported by the intellectual acceptance of Keynes's *General Theory*, politicians found themselves with an excuse to do what most had always wanted to do—take more money from the general public and transfer it to favored groups (or voting blocs). The benefits are invariably less than the costs, but they are visible, readily appreciated, and easily credited to politicians. Predictably, beginning in the 1930s federal spending began increasing as a share of GDP. It was about 4 percent of GDP in 1930, increased during the Great Depression and spiked to a historical high of about 47 percent during World War II. The federal government share of GDP then dropped to about 13 percent in 1948, reached a bumpy plateau in the early 1960s at slightly below to slightly above 20 percent that lasted for over 40 years, and then escalated rapidly in late 2008 to an estimated 25 percent in 2011.

It is not just the growth of total federal spending, however, that deserves attention. As the federal spending has grown, its composition experienced a fundamental change. Except for World War II, the bulk of the growth in federal spending has gone to funding transfers from those who earn it to those with the political influence to take it. Currently almost 45 percent of federal spending consists of transfer payments paid out by the big three transfer program—Social Security, Medicare, and Medicaid.

The growth in transfers seen in the post-WWII era would have been unimaginable in earlier times. It was obviously facilitated by the ideological shift begun in the Progressive Era and found expression in Keynesianism—namely, the idea that a government wise enough to manage the macroeconomy could also be trusted to promote both economic fairness and efficiency by taking from some and giving to "deserving" others. Once such transfers began growing, a reinforcing dynamic kicked in. As more groups were favored with transfers, the more other groups felt they deserved their share of the booty, and the less fair it seemed to deny them.

Chronic Peacetime Deficits

Keynes, and his early disciples, almost certainly did not imagine the chronic peacetime deficits experienced since 1960. The original Keynesian prescription called for offsetting the budget deficits during recessions with budget surpluses during economic booms, with the budget remaining at least roughly in balance over time. But given the political incentives, chronic and increasing budget deficits are inherent in the interaction between Keynesian economics and political incentives.

Political incentives, along with greater public acceptance of activist government, can explain the move to chronic deficits. But chronic deficits mean that when an economic contraction occurs it is highly likely to occur when the federal budget is already in deficit. Couple this with the Keynesian view that it is an increase in deficit spending—not the level—that is needed to stimulate economic activity. As expressed by Jared Bernstein, former economic advisor to Vice President Joe Biden, "To keep your foot where it is on the accelerator—even if it is pretty far down—doesn't add speed (or growth). To go (grow) faster, you've got to press down harder." This creates a dynamic that almost guarantees increasing deficits.

So without resistance to Keynes's orthodoxy (and there has always been scholarly resistance and some political resistance as well), the tendency is for budget deficits to become both chronic and to increase as a percentage of national income. Ultimately this does little, if anything, to reduce the likelihood of the next downturn. And, as shall be seen, when government spending and deficits increase, given their current levels, they destroy wealth by reducing the productive capacity of the economy below what it would otherwise be. So even if increasing deficit spending did impart a short-run stimulus effect, its long-run effect would still be negative since it is impossible to increase economic production beyond an economy's productive capacity. Unfortunately, this long-run cost has little effect when fiscal decisions are made in response to short-run political considerations.

Even the most enthusiastic Keynesians, if they value their reputations as economists, acknowledge that government spending and deficits can become large enough to reduce economic growth and the long-run prosperity of a nation. But even when they see the importance of restoring some semblance of fiscal responsibility, they argue that we should wait until larger deficits stimulate economic growth. For example, according to Krugman,

"It's politically fashionable to rant against government spending and demand fiscal responsibility. But right now, increased government spending is just what the doctor ordered, and concerns about the budget deficit should be put on hold." This short-run view is not new.

Short-Run Politics vs. Long-Run Productivity

... The decline in fiscal discipline encouraged by Keynesian policy has led to expansions in federal spending that undermines the ability of Keynesian spending to stimulate even short-run economic growth. When the economy is in a recession, government spending motivated and directed primarily by short-run political concerns invariably slows up the adjustments necessary for economic recovery. Simple political calculus motivates undermining the self-correcting adjustments inherent in free markets by protecting favored groups against market discipline and distorting the information provided by market prices. For example, the recent Great Recession was largely precipitated by the government policies that motivated the excessive building of houses. Given this malinvestment, one important adjustment needed to make the best use of the existing stock of housing and redirect resources into employments more productive than adding to the housing stock is for housing prices to drop. This, of course, is a market adjustment that needed no help from government attempts to influence housing prices. And, of course, housing prices did fall. But they would have fallen faster except for the fact that the federal government spent a great deal of taxpayer money to prop them up.

The expansion in federal spending since 1930 has been accompanied by an increase in transfers as a percentage of the federal budget and of national income. Unfortunately, government transfers and spending in general damage long-run growth in several ways. First, it has been estimated by Payne that raising another dollar in taxes costs $0.65 in lost output. Second, transfers are commonly used to finance wasteful activities such as growing cotton in the desert, turning corn into ethanol, and producing so-called green energy in politically favored companies that manage to fail despite massive subsidies. Third, government transfers create opportunities for some to capture the wealth of others, which motivates political rent-seeking that replaces otherwise productive activities, not to mention the costly efforts people make to protect their wealth from political capture. Fourth, federal transfers, and the myriad regulations that invariably accompany them, commonly provide protection against market competition, and by doing so deflect, delay, or distort the investments needed to maintain, much less increase, economic productivity. In the final analysis, when a dollar is taken from Peter so it can be transferred to Paul, Peter ends up losing more than a dollar, Paul receives less than a dollar, and the economy's capacity to create more wealth is diminished. . . .

What about the Multiplier Effect?

The demand-side perspective of Keynesian economies makes it easy to overlook the importance of productivity to economic growth. This is vividly seen in the Keynesian belief that deficit spending by government to hire the unemployed is good for the economy even when they are hired to do unproductive tasks. This belief is based on the argument that the money paid to those being hired is all additional income for the economy since it didn't require reducing the income of others with a tax. Some portion of this additional income is then spent to provide a secondary increase in income to others, which continues to produce a sequence of additional income and spending which supposedly expands the economy by some multiple of the original government expenditure. This multiplier effect was famously used by Keynes to argue that using savings to hire the unemployed "to dig holes in the ground" is better than not increasing spending.

While the idea of a multiplier effect seems superficially plausible to many, it does not receive support from the historical record. If the multiplier effect were operative, the United States economy since the end of the Great Recession in 2009 would have been growing far faster than it did for over the quarter of a century after 1865 when the federal government was spending only around 3 percent of the GDP, and running budget surpluses every year except for three years when the budget was balanced. . . .

Conclusion

Keynesians commonly talk as if they seriously believe that a depressed economy can be trapped in a high-unemployment equilibrium and that stimulus from government spending—preferably deficit spending—is the only hope for returning to full employment. A casual look at the historical record is enough to dismiss that view. The self-correcting adjustments motivated by the combination of harsh realities imposed by market discipline and profitable opportunities revealed by market prices are not only enough to restore growth to a depressed economy, but the most effective way to do so. Keynesians have persistently ignored self-correcting market forces and the depressing effect on long-run economic productivity of escalating government spending and budget deficits caused by the interaction between Keynesian policies and political incentives. The result is that Keynesian attempts to increase economic growth by moderating economic downturns are counterproductive—they do little to stimulate economic activity in the short run while they reduce the growth of economic productivity in the long run.

Some will see the argument that Keynesian spending fails to stimulate economic recovery and harms long-run growth as pessimistic. I disagree. There is nothing pessimistic in recognizing that doing the most to promote long-run economic growth while moderating economic fluctuations is hardly likely to be achieved by unleashing politicians from the constraints required for fiscal responsibility. The political implications of my argument can be seen as pessimistic, however, since it implies that the failure of Keynesian attempts to stimulate the economy generate a temporal pattern of concentrated benefits and diffused costs that yield social benefit-cost ratios of less than one but political benefit-cost ratios of greater than one. Keynesian economics is another example of bad economics making for good politics.

Indeed, my argument is more pessimistic than indicated by the political popularity of Keynesian economics as an excuse for fiscal irresponsibility. Keynesian policies can trap politicians into continuing excessive spending and chronic budget deficits even though they realize that doing so does little to stimulate the economy in the short run and harms economic growth in the long run. The problem is that reducing government spending and deficits may cause decreased economic activity and increased unemployment in the short run. People will have made decisions in response to existing levels of government spending rendering them and their investments dependent on that spending. These workers and resources will be redeployed in response to market incentives into more productive employments if government budgets were reduced, but the transition would take a length of time that is politically unacceptable, even though the temporary loss would be small compared to the long-run gain.

Keynesian policies can also trap politicians into continuing those policies by creating support for the Keynesian claim that a depressed market economy cannot return to full employment on its own. As argued above, our market economy still maintains a great deal of self-correcting resiliency in recovering from downturns despite Keynesian views to the contrary. But the spending and budget deficits that are inherent in Keynesian efforts to direct economic growth are inevitably accompanied by a host of government rules, regulations, mandates, and subsidies that are undermining self-correcting market forces. The weaker these forces become, the less politically attractive relying on them will become relative to another round of spending increases funded by yet larger budget deficits as the best response to the next recession. The unfortunate dynamic here is obvious.

But the situation is not hopeless. Even politicians can learn from experience and, more critically, the prevailing political philosophy can shift back toward the healthy skepticism toward government activism that existed for the first 140-plus years of U.S. history, which will significantly alter political incentives. In the meantime, examining the implications for long-run productivity of implementing Keynesian policies in response to short-run political incentives can hardly do any harm.

DWIGHT R. LEE is a research fellow at The Independent Institute and the William J. O'Neil Endowed Chair in Global Markets and Freedom and Scholar in Residence at Southern Methodist University. He is former president of the Association of Private Enterprise Education and president of the Southern Economic Association.

EXPLORING THE ISSUE

Is Stimulus the Best Way to Get the American Economy Back on Its Feet?

Critical Thinking and Reflection

1. What are the causes of the recent recession and the current slow economic growth?
2. Evaluate the effectiveness or potential effectiveness of the policies that have been implemented or that have been proposed but not implemented.
3. What lessons do you draw from previous recessions, and how were they addressed?
4. How are Greek, European, and Asian economies affecting the American economy?
5. When is the best time to focus on debt reduction?

Is There Common Ground?

Holland, Krugman and Lee agree that a stimulus involving more spending and lower taxes is appropriate in times of economic decline and underutilized resources. Lee admits that "there was nothing fiscally irresponsible about such a policy." It should help the economy move back toward full employment. Their disagreement is about how the stimulus will actually work. Lee argues that perversions in the political system and inadequate knowledge will screw things up and produce "fiscal irresponsibility that undermines economic growth without promoting economic stability." Holland and Lee also agree that deficits must not be allowed to get too large. They disagree on when is the best time to reduce government spending and produce surpluses that reduce the debt. They both use history to support their arguments but use different portions of history.

Create Central

www.mhhe.com/createcentral

Additional Resources

This issue of how to get the economy growing again traces back to the debate between John Maynard Keynes and Friedrich von Hayek. Keynes believed that government could stimulate growth, and Hayek believed the government probably would do more harm than good. Their debate is the subject of Nicholas Wapshott's book *Keynes Hayek: The Clash that Defined Modern Economics* (W. W. Norton, 2012). Keynes' major work is *The General Theory of Employment, Interest and Money* (Cambridge University Press, 1936). The two views today tend to be labeled stimulus versus austerity, and Paul Krugman is the leading public exponent of the stimulus side. His major work is *End This Depression Now!* (W. W. Norton, 2013). He is a frequent contributor of op-ed articles for *The New York*

Times, often promoting the stimulus view and blasting the failure of the austerity, policies, as in the following: "Austerity, Italian Style" (*The New York Times*, February 25, 2013); "Kick that Can" (*The New York Times*, February 5, 2013); "Looking for Mr. Goodpain" (*The New York Times*, February 1, 2013); "The Dwindling Deficit" (*The New York Times*, January 18, 2013); "The Terrible Trillions" (*The New York Times*, December 17, 2012). Another stimulus advocate is Ezra Klein, who provides an excellent account of the recession and the government response to it in "Financial Crisis and Stimulus: Could This Time Be Different?" (*Washington Post*, October 8, 2011). He argues against the austerity policy in "It's Not a Fiscal Cliff, It's an Austerity Crisis" (*Bloomberg View Newsletter*, November 28, 2012). Finally, Daniel W. Drezner documents how austerity policies have largely failed and fallen out of favor in "Have we reached consensus on austerity #fail?" (posted online at *Foreign Policy*, Wednesday, February 27, 2013).

The small-government spending proponents in America are in the austerity camp and against the Keynesians. Austerity is the policy in Europe and promoted by the World Bank. It currently is not doing well, and publics are increasingly protesting its policies. A major defender of the austerity approach is Britain's Chancellor of the Exchequer, George Osborne, who defended his government's austerity program against the protesters. Now the World Bank is saying that perhaps some of the countries pushing austerity should ease up. This shows that at times the austerity approach may hurt too much to be politically practical. Nevertheless, many hang on to the theory and push austerity to limit deficits. Reduced government spending has support from the Tea Party and conservatives who want government limited as much as possible so as not to encroach on personal liberties. We do not pursue this aspect of the austerity debate. A well-reasoned argument against the stimulus view is presented by Andrew T. Young in "Why in the World Are We All Keynesians Again? The Flimsy Case for Stimulus Spending" (*Policy Analysis*, February 14, 2013).

Two other anti-stimulus articles are by David Malpass, "The U.S. Needs to Win the Battle to Limit Government Now" (*Forbes*, February 11, 2013), and Jeffrey Miron, "Should U.S. Fiscal Policy Address Slow Growth or the Debt? A Nondilemma" (*Cato Institute Policy Analysis*, no. 718, January 8, 2013). *The Cambridge Journal of Economics* is preparing a special issue on austerity, which will include both advocates and opponents.

Internet References . . .

Sociology—Study Sociology Online

http://edu.learnsoc.org/

Sociology Web Resources

www.mhhe.com/socscience/sociology/resources/index.htm

Sociosite

www.topsite.com/goto/sociosite.net

Socioweb

www.topsite.com/goto/socioweb.com

Selected, Edited, and with Issue Framing Material by:
Kurt Finsterbusch, *University of Maryland, College Park*

ISSUE

Was the Welfare Reform the Right Approach to Poverty?

YES: David Coates, from "Cutting 'Welfare' to Help the Poor," in *A Liberal Toolkit: Progressive Responses to Conservative Arguments* (Praeger, 2007)

NO: Stephanie Mencimer, from "Brave New Welfare," *Mother Jones* (January/February 2009)

Learning Outcomes
After reading this issue, you will be able to:
• Understand labor force changes since the 1950s and the changing role of welfare (Aid to Families with Dependent Children (AFDC)) up to the Welfare Reform Act in 1996.
• Understand the basic changes that the new welfare law made. Know the main differences between AFDC and TANF (Temporary Assistance for Needy Families).
• Understand what was wrong with AFDC which made both Republicans and Democrats want to abolish it and replace it with a very different welfare system.
• Evaluate how successful the new welfare bill was in creating widespread welfare-to-work transitions.
• Understand the problems that are occurring in administering the new welfare law and assess how it needs to be improved.

ISSUE SUMMARY

YES: David Coates, the Worrell Professor of Anglo-American Studies at Wake Forest University, argues that the 1996 welfare reform was badly needed to reduce dependency and encourage working and thus improve the lives of the poor. Thus it is a very successful policy.

NO: Stephanie Mencimer, staff reporter for *Mother Jones,* does not denigrate the current welfare law but documents the horrible way welfare is administered in many states. Many welfare workers deny many benefits to many people who qualify for welfare. Thus, many welfare benefits do not reach the poor.

In his 1984 book *Losing Ground: American Social Policy, 1950–1980* (Basic Books), policy analyst Charles Murray recommended abolishing Aid to Families with Dependent Children (AFDC), the program at the heart of the welfare debate. At the time of the book's publication, this suggestion struck many as simply a dramatic way for Murray to make some of his anti-welfare points. However, 14 years later this idea became the dominant idea in Congress. In 1996, President Bill Clinton signed into law the Work Opportunity Reconciliation Act and fulfilled his 1992 campaign pledge to "end welfare as we know it." Murray's thesis that welfare hurt the poor had become widely accepted.

In "What to Do about Welfare," *Commentary* (December 1994), Murray argues that welfare contributes to dependency, illegitimacy, and the number of absent fathers, which in turn can have terrible effects on the children involved. He states that workfare, enforced child

support, and the abolition of welfare would greatly reduce these problems. One reason why Congress ended AFDC was the emergence of a widespread backlash against welfare recipients. Much of the backlash, however, was misguided. It often rested on the assumptions that welfare is generous and that most people on welfare are professional loafers. In fact, over the previous two decades, payments to families with dependent children eroded considerably relative to the cost of living. Average monthly benefits went from $238 in 1978 to $154 in 2006. Furthermore, most women with dependent children on welfare had intermittent periods of work, were elderly, or were disabled. Petty fraud may be common because welfare payments are insufficient to live on in many cities, but "welfare queens" who cheat the system for spectacular sums are so rare that they should not be part of any serious debate on welfare issues. The majority of people on welfare are those whose condition would become desperate if payments were cut off. Although many believe that women on welfare commonly bear children in order to increase their benefits, there is no conclusive evidence to support this idea.

Not all objections to AFDC can be easily dismissed, however. There does seem to be evidence that in some cases AFDC reduces work incentives and increases the likelihood of family breakups. But there is also a positive side to AFDC: it helped many needy people get back on their feet. When all things are considered together, therefore, it is not clear that welfare, meaning AFDC, was bad enough to be abolished. But it was abolished on July 1, 1997, when the Work Opportunity Reconciliation Act went into effect. Now the question is whether the new policy is better than the old policy.

It is too soon to obtain an accurate assessment of the long-term impacts of the Act. Nevertheless, AFDC rolls have declined since the Act was passed, so many conclude that it is a success rather than a failure. Of course, the early leavers are the ones with the best prospects of succeeding in the work world; the welfare-to-work transition gets harder as the program works with the more difficult cases. The crucial question is whether the reform will benefit those it affects. Already, many working former welfare recipients are better off. But what about the average or more vulnerable recipient.

In the readings that follow, David Coates presents a fair summary of the case for the benefits of welfare reform. Stephanie Mencimer tells the unseemly story of how many states seek to keep welfare payment to a minimum, and therefore cheat many people who need and deserve welfare.

YES ◀

David Coates

Cutting "Welfare" to Help the Poor

Welfare states in the modern world aren't very old—60 or 70 years at most. Some parts are older—the German social insurance system started with Bismarck—but in general the provision of government help to the poor, the sick, the disabled, and the elderly is a recent phenomenon. Not all governments make that provision even now, but most do. Certainly in recent times, all governments in the advanced democracies have taken on a major welfare role, and that includes federal and state authorities here in the United States.

Yet in this, as in so much else, the United States has proved to be unique. Unique in coverage: No universal system of health care, free at the point of use, emerged here in the late 1940s as it did in much of Western Europe. Unique in delivery system: From the early 1950s, pensions and health care were tied directly to wage settlements here, in wage-and-benefit packages with few foreign parallels. Unique in timing: The United States set the pace in the 1930s with the New Deal, and again in the late 1960s with its own War on Poverty. Unique in vocabulary: The U.S. state pension system is known as *social security* and the term *welfare* is restricted to payments to the poor, giving it a stigma it lacks in much of Western Europe. And unique in fragility: The United States is the only major industrial democracy formally committed to the "ending of welfare as we know it," through the 1996 Personal Responsibility and Work Opportunity Reconciliation Act.

The result has been the consolidation in the United States of a publicly financed welfare system, which, in comparative terms, is now both residual and modest. It's residual in that it leaves the bulk of provision for the sick and the old to the private sector. It's modest in that the public provision made available (pensions apart) is less generous than that now commonplace in Western Europe and Japan. For many American liberals, there's something profoundly embarrassing about the richest country on earth getting by with the most limited welfare system in the advanced industrial world. But that's not how the Conservative Right sees it. On the contrary, having a residual and modest welfare state is, for them, one of the key reasons why the United States is the richest country on earth. Protecting that economic success then requires U.S. welfare provision to be made ever more residual and modest over time. In a manner and scale without precedence

elsewhere, *cutting welfare*—either to the bone, or away completely—is regularly and seriously canvassed by conservative forces in the United States as the best way to help the poor. . . .

⸙

A Liberal Response

Oh, if it was only that simple. But, for the following reasons at least, it's not. . . .

There's More Poverty Out There Than You Might Think

12.7 percent of all Americans now live on incomes that fall at or below the official poverty lines. Even worse, of the 37 million people living in officially defined poverty in 2004, 13 million were children. That's equivalent to the entire populations of Sweden and Norway. The poverty rate for very young children in the United States in the first half-decade of the twenty-first century was slightly over 20 percent: That's one preschool child in every five. And around them are what the Economic Policy Institute (EPI) calls "the twice-poor," that is, Americans living on or below incomes that are only twice the officially defined level for their family size. Amazingly, more than 89 million Americans fell into that broader category in 2003—all close to poverty and all accordingly obliged to watch every penny. Collectively, the poor and the twice-poor now constitute 31 percent of the population—that's 3 in every 10 Americans. That's a lot of people in or near the poverty margin, no matter what Congress is or isn't being told by the people in suits.

What they experience is real poverty, in both the absolute and relative senses of the term. Currently, 39 million Americans are classified as "food insecure" and 40 percent of all those using food banks live in families in which at least one adult is working. . . . It doesn't help them—or indeed us—to be told that most of them have cars. Of course they do. Given the absence of adequate systems of public transport in vast swathes of the United States, how

---

else are they meant to get to shops or to the food bank? A car in the United States isn't a luxury. It's a necessity; an extra financial burden that can't be avoided if doing the ordinary things of life is not to become nearly impossible. The Western European poor don't need cars to anything like the same degree, because the scale of public provision—the size of the social wage that everyone enjoys regardless of income—is so much larger in those countries.

That's one reason why it's simply untrue to claim that the American poor are better off than most ordinary Europeans and better off than the entirety of the Western European poor. Sadly, they're not. On the contrary, the child poverty rate in the United States is currently *four* times that of northern Europe. There are *only three* Western European countries whose poor children have a lower living standard than do poor children in the United States. . . .

If All This Poverty Is Self-Inflicted, Then Masochism in the United States Is Amazingly Rife

This is why there's something particularly offensive about the speed and ease with which so many commentators on the American Right, instead of probing beneath the surface for the underlying causes of the "pathologies" of poverty they so dislike, move instead to demonize the poor, endlessly blaming them for making "bad choices" as though good ones were plentiful and immediately at hand. Telling young black women to marry the fathers of their children, for example, carries with it the premise that the men are there to be married. Yet "twelve percent of all black men between eighteen and thirty-four are [currently] in jail," a bigger proportion of "men away" than the United States as a whole experienced during the entirety of World War II. Unemployment rates among young black men are double those among their white contemporaries. "The problem is not that the nation's poorest women have systematically passed up good jobs and good marriage partners. The problem is that there are significant economic and cultural inadequacies in the choices available to them. They, like the rest of America, value children; but unlike the rest of America, they cannot easily support them." . . .

Given a Chance, Welfare Works Better Than Is Claimed

The payment of welfare stands accused by many on the American Right of creating poverty and damaging those to whom it is given. With one important caveat—welfare traps—to which we will come later, the claim is literally ludicrous. Welfare did not create poverty in America. Poverty was here long before the New Deal and long before Johnson's "war." Neither set of welfare initiatives created their clienteles. They simply responded to their prior existence. The poverty of the 1930s was of a mass kind, the product of a general economic collapse that was rectified

not by welfare programs but by the United States' mobilization for war. Within it, however, were categories of the poor that had existed before 1929 and that continued to exist after 1941—the temporarily unemployed, the genetically infirm, widows, and the elderly. By the 1960s, those categories of the poor had been joined by another, one explicitly excluded from the coverage of the original New Deal. To get any sort of legislative package through a Congress whose committees were dominated by southern Democrats, Roosevelt had excluded black workers in the south. Servants and agricultural workers gained no benefits from the core programs of the New Deal. They survived instead in the invisible southern poverty, poverty which—as prosperity returned with the war—then drew them out of the south into the cities and industries of the northeast and the midwest. In the first half of the postwar period, African Americans increasingly exchanged *invisible* southern rural poverty for its *visible* urban northern equivalent. It was an exchange to which the welfare programs of the 1960s were a belated response.

So it was a case of poverty first, and welfare second, and not the other way around. It was also a case of a welfare response that, when properly funded, took the rate of poverty *down* not up: a response that over time definitely improved the lives of many categories of the American poor. The official poverty rate in 1959—the first year in the United States that it was taken—was 22.4 percent: By 1973, with the War on Poverty at its height, that rate had halved. Then, as programs were cut back in the 1970s and 1980s, the rate grew again. It was back to 14.5 percent by 1992, although it's slightly lower now, as we've seen. . . .

The Charity Illusion

Unless, of course, as the Cato people would have it, private charity would have stepped into the breach and done a better job. But there's just no evidence to sustain that claim. There's certainly no evidence that private charity could, or did, scratch more than the surface of the poverty experienced by the old, the infirm, and the widowed before the New Deal. And of the nature of things, no evidence can sustain the claim that if welfare were entirely removed (and tax levels cut accordingly), those benefiting from the tax cuts would then redirect all or most of their extra income into charitable endeavors. American altruism—although impressive by international standards—is not without limit, and because it isn't, the private sector can't be treated as a reliable and problem-free alternative to existing welfare programs. Charity-based welfare contains no mechanisms to guard against unevenness of provision, moralizing in the terms set for aid given, or the onset of "gift exhaustion" over time. The gathering of funds by private charities is in any case always time-consuming, intrusive, and administratively inefficient; and the distribution of funds as private handouts only serves to reinforce—for those who receive them—the very sense of dependency and impotence that conservatives are apparently so keen to avoid. . . .

The Fallacy of the Incompetent State

In any event, in making the pitch for the full privatization of welfare, the Charles Murrays and Michael Tanners of this world are not comparing like with like. They're also generalizing from an extraordinarily parochial base. They advocate the replacement of the American welfare system by an idealized and untested network of private charities, using as their evidence inadequacies in American public welfare policy since the 1970s. With few exceptions, they don't appear to have looked in any systematic way at Western Europe, where states have run welfare systems successfully for years. Nor have they engaged with—indeed have they even read—the fabulous and extensive scholarly literature on comparative welfare systems. If they had, they'd quickly have come to see that the great tragedy of Lyndon Johnson's War on Poverty was not that poverty won, but that the war itself was not pursued with sufficient consistency and zeal.

All governments—European and American alike—distribute income and dispense welfare. They're all, in James Galbraith's telling term, "transfer states," and inequality always shows what he called "the fingerprints of state policy." The War on Poverty required those fingerprints to distribute income downward, and initially it did. General poverty levels fell. But command of the war then shifted. Under Reagan and the two Bush administrations, the fingerprints were deployed differently. Income was consciously moved upward. Welfare systems can always be made to fail, if inadequately financed and led. An agency such as Federal Emergency Management Agency (FEMA) will always fail if it's led by cronies and managed by fools. But by the same token, welfare systems can always be made to work well if supplied with sufficient funds and commitment. Indeed, take a welfare system up to about 40 percent of gross domestic product (GDP)—when it's servicing the entire community and not just the poor—and popular support for it will rise, not fall. That's been the universal Western European experience. . . .

The Limits of Welfare-to-Work Programs in a World of Low Pay

The 1996 Act is the Republicans' ace card in their attempt to roll back the American welfare state, and they have one huge piece of evidence going in their favor: the dramatic fall in the number of people—especially young single mothers—in receipt of welfare since its passing. But the figures on caseload reduction, although real, are also deceptive, and we need to say so. They're deceptive in a *causal* sense: in that the full implementation of the Act coincided with a significant period of job growth in the American economy. When that growth stalled, so too did the rate of job take-up by single mothers. The figures on caseload reduction are deceptive, too, in a *social* sense. People came off welfare, but then ran into a whole series of new problems that the figures don't catch. Women fleeing domestic violence lost a vital source of autonomy from the men who had violated them. Young women with small children lost a significant percentage of their new wages on child care and transport costs; and the children themselves—whose enhanced well-being was, after all, a key aim of the new legislation—often found themselves in inadequate child care, looked after by undertrained and underpaid female staff. Women didn't stop providing child care. They simply stopped providing their own. And, overwhelmingly, the figures on caseload reduction are deceptive in an *economic* sense. Going off welfare, although it reduced the numbers, did not reduce the scale and rate of poverty among those who previously had been in receipt of aid. The Cato Institute's Michael Tanner has conceded as much, noting that "self-sufficiency appears to be eluding the grasp of many, if not most, former recipients." And of course it is, because (quite predictably) the vast majority of the jobs into which former welfare recipients were moved turned out to be *low-paid* jobs. Welfare-to-work moved people from government-sponsored poverty to private sector-based poverty, adding to their transport and child care costs as it did so. Workfare changed the source of poverty; but not the poverty itself. . . .

The "Welfare Poor" and the "Working Poor" Are on the Same Side

Republicans like to present themselves as champions of the working poor against the welfare poor, implying that the interests of the two groups are in tension and painting the Democratic Party into a "tax-and-spend" corner as they do so. But the argument is false in both of its premises: The interests of the two are not in tension and the Republicans are not the defenders of the real interests of the working poor.

The existence of a large group of full-time workers—paid so little that they themselves are on the margin of poverty—actually traps the welfare poor a second time. If you're on welfare, you're poor. If you get out of welfare and into work, you'll still be poor, because the move will only take you into the bottom tier of the poorly paid. If the people in that low-pay group are then financially pressed—and they definitely are—it's not because of the weight of any welfare taxation that they carry. It's because their wages are low. It's not taxes that make them poor, but the lack of income growth. What really hurts the low paid is not the poverty of the people below them but the greed of the people above. As we read in Chapter 3, the truly unique feature of the recent American income story is the proportion of total income growth taken by the ultrarich. You remember, 24 percent of all income growth in the U.S. economy between 1997 and 2001 was taken by just 1 percent of the population, and it was taken at the end of a quarter-century in which wages remained flat for the majority of working Americans. What the working poor need is not welfare retrenchment but higher wages. They *and* the welfare poor need the creation of a high-wage, high-growth economy to ease the burden of poverty on them both. They both need full employment and rising wages in an economy in which there is a fair distribution of rewards. That's the kind of economy that the Republicans always promise in the run-up to elections, but it's also the kind of economy that after the elections, for 80 million Americans at least, the party regularly fails to deliver. . . .

Welfare Doesn't Trap the Poor in an Underclass—We Do

Welfare critics are right on at least this: There is a welfare trap, work disincentive issue in any welfare system. As people come off welfare and lose benefits, the effective tax rate on their own earnings can be extraordinarily high. Depending on the rules, in the move from welfare to work you might lose 60 cents of welfare provision for every dollar you earn, and effectively be only 40 cents better off—a rate of taxation against which the rich regularly howl when experiencing it themselves. So there is a problem of "disincentives to work" associated with welfare, one on which the Right regularly latch. But it's not the only, or indeed the main, problem currently facing young mothers in search of good jobs in America's inner cities. Good jobs are scarce because the middle-class workers have left those cities, taking the jobs with them. Available child care is poor because the programs have been cut. Young men are scarce because incarceration rates have been systematically ratcheted up. Suburban flight, welfare retrenchment, drugs, and the rise of a prison economy are the real villains here. As Barack Obama said, "the people of New Orleans weren't just abandoned during the hurricane. They were abandoned long ago—to murder and mayhem in the streets, to sub-standard schools, to dilapidated housing, to inadequate health care, to a pervasive sense of hopelessness." Underclasses don't create themselves. They're created. You can't be trapped unless somebody does the trapping.

The great thing about traps, however, is that they can be sprung. The solution to the disincentive effect of welfare payments is to phase in benefit reductions slowly—allowing people to earn and receive benefits in parallel until their incomes reach a tolerable level. . . .

Poverty Is a Matter of Choice—It's Just Not a Choice Made by the Poor

The ultimate irony here is that poverty, as the Republican Right regularly claims, is indeed a matter of choice. It's just not a choice that the poor themselves are called on to make. It's a choice made by the rest of us. In the main, for most of us, by how we vote, and for those who govern us, by how they legislate. They and us, not the poor, have the power to choose. We can choose, as an economy and a society, to meet the arrival of intensified global competition by outsourcing production, lowering American wages, and increasing income inequality. Or we can choose to reset the way we organize the economy and regulate trade to pull jobs back to the United States and to improve the quality of work and levels of remuneration attached to them. There is a choice to be made. If we take the first route, we'll create new sources of poverty for those low-skilled American workers currently in employment and extra barriers for those trying to move into work from welfare dependency. If we take the second, we'll have to dismantle much of the hidden welfare state now going to the rich, and perhaps not just to them. A proper system of rent subsidy for people on low incomes, for example, may have to be financed by phasing out the enormous tax subsidy currently provided to those of us fortunate enough to be buying rather than renting our houses. But at least the more affluent among us have a choice. The poor do not. Or perhaps more accurately, the affluent have the choice of making a big difference by making a small sacrifice. The poor, by contrast, have to labor mightily just to change their individual circumstances by merely an inch.

"Poor people and investment bankers have one thing in common. They both spend considerable energy thinking about money." Which is why, on this topic at least, the Republicans are both right and wrong. They're right: When discussing poverty, policy is ultimately a matter of making right choices. But they're also wrong. Over and over again, the choices they make are the wrong ones—and we need to say so.

DAVID COATES is the Worrel Professor of Anglo-American Studies in the Political Science Department at Wake Forest University. He has published *The Liberal Toolkit: Progressive Answers to Conservative Arguments,* from which the reprinted articles were taken.

Stephanie Mencimer   ➜ **NO**

Brave New Welfare

Georgia officials lied to Gabby's mom to keep her from getting a $100 monthly check. From red tape to dirty tricks and outright abuse, here's what awaits if your luck runs out.

In 2006, Letorrea Clark was 22 years old, unemployed, and living with her boyfriend in Homerville, a tiny town near the Okefenokee Swamp in southern Georgia, when she discovered she was pregnant. The timing wasn't ideal. Her boyfriend's job at the local can-manufacturing plant supported them both, but his largesse came at a price. The man was controlling, unfaithful, and jealous, a problem only enhanced by the wide array of drugs that filled his freezer. Clark had hit the stash, too, but the pregnancy pushed her to get clean and get out. She slept on a park bench until a friend helped her secure a place to stay.

Two-year-old Gabby and her mother are among thousands eligible for welfare who have been denied benefits as states push to trim the rolls.

Desperate, with her due date fast approaching, Clark decided to apply for Temporary Assistance for Needy Families (TANF), better known as welfare. But when she went to the local Division of Family and Children Services office, a caseworker told her—wrongly—that she couldn't apply until after the baby was born. "They basically said, 'Go get a job,'" says Clark. "I was eight months pregnant."

Gabby arrived by C-section a month later, and Clark brought the chubby newborn home to a sweltering trailer with a busted fridge, no air conditioning, and no running water. (Her ex had reneged on promises to get the water turned on.) Clark got by with help from her church and her landlord, who let her stay for free until she was able to move. Later, she found a job in a day care. But the center docked her paycheck for Gabby's care, an expense the state would have picked up had she been able to get on TANF. Sometimes she'd go home with just $20 at the end of the week.

Clark patched things together with food stamps and $256 a month in child support. But after nine months, Gabby's father stopped paying just long enough for Clark to get evicted. She went back to the welfare office, where caseworkers turned her away, saying—falsely again—that because she'd been getting child support she was ineligible for TANF.

What Clark didn't know was that Georgia, like many other states, was in the midst of an aggressive push to get thousands of eligible mothers like her off TANF, often by duplicitous means, to use the savings elsewhere in the state budget. Fewer than 2,500 Georgia adults now receive benefits, down from 28,000 in 2004—a 90 percent decline. Louisiana, Texas, and Illinois have each dropped 80 percent of adult recipients since January 2001. Nationally, the number of TANF recipients fell more than 40 percent between then and June 2008, the most recent month for which data are available. In Georgia last year, only 18 percent of children living below 50 percent of the poverty line—that is, on less than $733 a month for a family of three—were receiving TANF.

Plunging welfare rolls were big news in the wake of Bill Clinton's 1996 welfare reform, which limited benefits and required recipients to engage in "work related" activities. Those declines coincided with record numbers of poor single mothers heading into the workplace and a significant drop in child poverty—proof, supporters said, that the new policy was a success. But the reform took effect at a time when unemployment was at a historic low—there were actually jobs for welfare moms to go to. In recent years, by contrast, TANF caseloads have been falling even as unemployment has soared and other poverty programs have experienced explosive growth. (Nearly 11 million more people received food stamps last year than did in 2000.) With the economy settling into a prolonged slump, this trend could be devastating.

Welfare is the only cash safety-net program for single moms and their kids, notes Rebecca Blank, an economist at the Brookings Institution and one of the nation's leading experts on poverty. "One has to worry, with a recession, about the number of women who, if they get unemployed, are not going to have anywhere to turn."

No longer the polarizing, racially tinged political issue it was when Ronald Reagan attacked "welfare queens," the welfare system today is dying a quiet death, neatly chronicled in the pages of academic and policy journals, largely unnoticed by the rest of us. Yet its demise carries significant implications. Among the most serious: the rise of what academics call the "disconnected," people who live well below the poverty line and are neither working nor receiving cash benefits like Social Security disability or TANF. Estimates put this group at roughly 2 million women caring for 4 million children, many dealing with a host of challenges from mental illness to domestic violence. "We don't really know how they survive," says Blank.

Women turned away from TANF lose more than a check. TANF is a gateway to education, drug rehab or mental health care, child care, even transportation and disability benefits—tools for upward mobility. Without those options, some women are driven to more desperate measures. In one of the towns in Georgia where I traveled to research this story, arrests of women for prostitution and petty crime went up as more and more families were pushed off welfare. And women are increasingly vulnerable to sexual assault and exploitation—sometimes, as I discovered, from the very officials or caseworkers who are supposed to help them. In the worst cases, they are losing custody of their children, precisely what TANF was designed to prevent. "I worry a lot about the kids in these families," Blank says. "We don't know where the kids are going."

One good thing did come from Letorrea Clark's final attempt to get on TANF. Federal law requires caseworkers to ask applicants about domestic violence, and when Clark mentioned that Gabby's father was stalking her, a concerned caseworker sent her to a shelter in another city. When the ex found Clark there, she was transferred to a shelter an hour away in Albany, a midsize town nestled among some of the nation's most impoverished rural counties.

The shelter staff did for Clark what the TANF office would not: extended her a lifeline. With their help, Clark and Gabby moved to a dingy one-room apartment in a low-slung brick complex filled with ex-cons and drug addicts, clients of the nonprofit group that runs the building. This is where I found them during several visits over the summer. Mother and daughter slept on a donated mattress; crates set inside an oversize, listing four-poster frame served as the box spring. Free rent made the roaches tolerable, but there were other liabilities. Upon Clark's arrival, the nonprofit group's caseworker asked her for sex. "He said, 'You ain't got nothing; you might as well,'" she said.

As we spoke in July, Clark sat in an overstuffed chair holding Gabby, a vivacious toddler whose head sprouted with braids. Clark was worried. She needed to get a job so she could keep food in the house; she was haunted by the possibility of losing Gabby if she didn't. But there were serious obstacles. She's been diagnosed with bipolar disorder and ADHD; "I don't like to be around a lot of people," she said. She can't drive and fears the bus because "I suffer from paranoia. I always think I'm going to fall off those seats."

Born in Hattiesburg, Mississippi, one of six children, Clark barely knows her father. She suspects both her mother and grandmother suffer from mental illness. One day when she was five, she told me, her mother whipped her back with an extension cord and then made her stand in a corner all night long. In kindergarten the next day, a concerned teacher lifted up her shirt and fell to her knees at the sight of so much blood. Social workers investigated but didn't take Clark away from her mother for another six years of crushing abuse.

In school, she languished in special education classes; her behavior turned violent. At 11, the state finally put her into foster care, and later, when foster families wouldn't have her, a mental hospital. Eventually she was returned to her mother, who coveted her monthly disability check. "When I turned 18, my mom wanted me to stay home to live off my tit," she says. Instead, "I saw an ad on TV for Job Corps and thought that was my ticket out." After she got her GED and became certified as a nursing assistant, Job Corps helped her find work in a nursing home, but the death of a woman she cared for left her rattled. She quit and was soon homeless. Somewhere along the way, she lost the disability benefits she'd received since she was a child. After she was raped in a crack house, Clark sought refuge in the only safe place she could think of: jail. "I hadn't ate in like two weeks," she says, so she went to Wal-Mart and started taking things off the shelves—a sandwich, soda, candy. "I knew I was going to get caught, but I just kept eating. I kept thinking that if I went to jail I could sleep."

After her sojourn in lockup, she met Gabby's father and moved in with him. While her pregnancy was unplanned, Clark believes that Gabby saved her life. "If I didn't have her, I'd have probably lost my mind," says Clark. "She's my pride and joy."

In his 1903 book *The Souls of Black Folk,* W.E.B. Du Bois described Albany as the capital of Georgia's "Black Belt." At the time, the area was home to 2,000 white people and 10,000 blacks; the cotton trade had collapsed, and Albany was a landscape of decaying one-room slave cabins occupied by tenant farmers eking out a meager existence from the depleted soil.

Things have improved since then, but only slightly. Despite the addition of an aquarium and civic center, the downtown looks much as it must have when Martin Luther King Jr. was jailed here after a civil rights protest in 1961. The main drags offer gas stations, dollar stores, and an outfit advertising $99 headstones. More than one-fifth of Albany families live below the poverty line—nearly twice the national average. About one in three adults is illiterate. Nearly 16 percent are unemployed. Eighty percent of children born here in 2007 had single mothers, many of them teenagers.

Despite those dismal demographics, in July 2006, only 143 adults in the 14 surrounding counties—some of whose demographics make Albany look downright prosperous—were receiving TANF benefits. The number had fallen 96 percent from 2002, according to the Georgia Budget and Policy Institute, though not because poverty was on the retreat: During the same period, unemployment in the area shot up 15 percent and food stamp use increased 24 percent.

After interviewing dozens of clients of Liberty House, the Albany domestic violence shelter where Clark sought refuge, I discovered that getting TANF in Albany is virtually impossible. While most of the women were eligible for benefits under state rules, many had been turned away for some reason or another. A caseworker incorrectly told one woman that she didn't qualify because her three kids—all under 15—were too old. Another, a 30-year-old with six kids between the ages of 2 and 12, had been in the shelter for a month after the district attorney from her hometown drove her there from the hospital. ("The guy that I was dating tried to kill me," she explained matter-of-factly.) She'd applied for TANF to get subsidized child care and go back to work. But a four-hour visit to the welfare office produced nothing but a promise that she'd receive a letter with an appointment date. A month later, she still hadn't gotten the letter. She says the county offered her three weeks of child care with the warning—false—that if she didn't find a job during that time, she wouldn't be eligible for TANF. "But if I find a job, I don't need TANF," she said with a laugh.

In 2006, the Georgia Coalition Against Domestic Violence conducted a survey to figure out why so many women were suddenly failing to get TANF benefits. They discovered that caseworkers were actively talking women out of applying, often using inaccurate information. (Lying to applicants to deny them benefits is a violation of federal law, but the 1996 welfare reform legislation largely stripped the Department of Health and Human Services of its power to punish states for doing it. Meanwhile, county officials have tried to head off lawyers who might take up the issue by pressing applicants to sign waivers saying they voluntarily turned down benefits.) Allison Smith, the economic justice coordinator at the coalition, says the group has gotten reports of caseworkers telling TANF applicants they have to be surgically sterilized before they can apply. Disabled women have been told they can't apply because they can't meet the work requirement. Others have been warned that the state could take their children if they get benefits. Makita Perry, a 23-year-old mother of four who did manage to get on TANF for a year, told me caseworkers "ask you all sorts of personal questions, like when the last time you had sex was and with who." Elsewhere, women are being told to get a letter proving they've visited a family-planning doctor.

Simply landing an appointment with a caseworker is an ordeal that can take 45 days, according to some of the women I interviewed—and applicants must clear numerous other hurdles, including conducting a job search, before being approved. Few complete the process. One study found that in April 2006, caseworkers in Georgia green-lighted only 20 percent of TANF applications, down from 40 percent in 2004. The lucky few who are accepted must often work full time in "volunteer" jobs in exchange for their benefits, which max out at $280 a month for a family of three.

Even as it blocks potential applicants, Georgia is also pushing current TANF recipients off the rolls at a rapid clip. Sandy Bamford runs a federally funded family literacy program in Albany where single mothers can get their GEDs. TANF allows recipients to attend school, but Bamford says officials routinely tell her clients otherwise: In a single month, one caseworker informed three of her students (incorrectly) that because they had turned 20, they could no longer receive benefits while completing their degrees. One was about to become the first in her family to graduate from high school. She quit and took a job as a dishwasher. Students as young as 16 have been told they must go to work full time or lose benefits. The employee who threatened to drop the students, says Bamford, became "caseworker of the month" for getting so many people off TANF.

As welfare officials go, B.J. Walker is something of a rock star. Appointed commissioner of Georgia's Department of Human Resources in 2004, Walker quickly became famous for her push to get virtually every adult off the state's public assistance rolls. By 2006, the state claimed Walker's agency had produced an astounding increase in the work participation rate of its TANF recipients, which in four years had jumped from 8 percent to nearly 70 percent.

Those numbers caught the attention of the Bush administration, which was in the midst of writing strict new regulations to require states to put 50 percent of their TANF caseloads into work activities, a target that only a handful of states had ever met. To unveil the new regs, administration officials brought Walker to Washington for a photo op and declared Georgia a model for other states.

To researchers, though, Georgia's rosy statistics looked too good to be true—especially given that Walker's own agency had found that the collapse of Georgia's textile industry and other manufacturing sectors left former TANF clients with far fewer job opportunities. In fact, even as the number of TANF recipients fell nearly 90 percent between January 2002 and November 2007, unemployment jumped 30 percent.

So how did Georgia put all those welfare moms to work? It didn't. As the Center on Budget and Policy Priorities' Liz Schott explained in a 2007 paper, "the increased work participation rate is primarily a factor of fewer families receiving assistance."

As for that "work participation," Stacy Haire, an outreach worker at Liberty House, says it's unlikely to help recipients find actual jobs. "They will put you at a police department. You'll be cleaning up behind toilets, picking up trash," she says. The TANF office once sent a client of hers to see a local government official about a job. The official told her he'd be glad to help out if she'd have sex with him. The woman filed a police report, but the man was never prosecuted. "That's what they can do in these towns," Haire says. "I see some sickening stuff."

Georgia isn't the only state that's found that dropping people from TANF is the easiest and cheapest way to meet federal work requirements. Texas reduced its caseloads by outsourcing applications to a call center, which wrongfully denied some families and lost others' applications altogether. In Florida, one innovative region started requiring TANF applicants to attend 40 hours of classes before they could even apply. Clients trying to restore lost benefits had once been able to straighten out paperwork with the help of caseworkers. In 2005, officials assigned all such work to a single employee, available two hours a week. The area's TANF caseload fell by half in a year.

Walker admits that Georgia has actively discouraged people from getting on TANF, primarily by emphasizing how meager the benefits are. "Two hundred eighty dollars a month does not make for a very good life," she told me. "This is really in the best interest of the children."

Walker acknowledges that some people struggle. "A lot of the people we see on TANF have made a mistake in choosing to have children," she offers. "We meet them at the front door and try to make sure that from day one they're engaged in some sort of productive activity." As for people like Clark who can't seem to get and keep a full-time job, Walker responds simply, "Can't? Won't."

Whatever their philosophical convictions, officials have another incentive for paring the TANF rolls: money. That's because the Clinton-era welfare reform turned what had been an entitlement program like Social Security—the more people needed help, the more money was spent—into a block grant, a fixed amount of money given to the states, regardless of need. The money, $16.5 billion a year, came mostly unencumbered by regulation. States could divert the funds to any program vaguely related to serving the needy.

Not only did the block grant doom the program to a slow death by inflation (by 2010, it will have lost 27 percent of its value), it also encouraged states to deny benefits to families, since they'd get the same amount of federal funds regardless of how many people received assistance. Georgia's share of the federal grant is nearly $370 million a year. "Even if caseloads go to zero, they get the same amount of money," notes Robert Welsh of the Georgia Budget and Policy Institute.

Some states have used surplus TANF money to expand child care, job training, and transportation to help recipients find jobs. But Georgia didn't use the bulk of its money for those programs—instead, it cut spending on child care and put the money into child protective services in the wake of a lawsuit against the state over the mistreatment of children in foster care. "The Feds are just fine with that," Walker insists. "We use our block grant to support other vulnerable families. That was the intent of the block grant."

Georgia is not alone in shifting its TANF money to other areas. The Government Accountability Office found in 2006 that many states were moving federal welfare funds away from cash assistance to the poor, or even "work supports" like child care, to plug holes in state budgets. Yet over the past 12 years, federal regulators have cited states only 11 times for misusing their TANF block grant, and only two suffered any financial penalty, according to Ken Wolfe, a spokesman for the Administration for Children and Families, which oversees the program. "As far as the federal government's concerned, it's not a big problem," he says.

On the run from an abusive boyfriend, Letorrea Clark struggles to keep food in the house for her daughter.

Terrell County, population 10,260, covers a rural corner of southwest Georgia not far from Jimmy Carter's boyhood peanut farm. Forty percent of the children here live below the poverty line; since the civil rights era the place has been known as "Terrible Terrell" because of the racial violence that erupted in the area. When I visited the Martin Luther King Jr. public housing project in the town of Dawson, a cluster of postwar-era brick buildings in the shadow of the Golden Peanut factory, three women sat in folding chairs, drinking Miller Lites under a big oak tree, bird-dogging the gaggle of children darting through the shirts flapping on laundry lines. One of them was a sturdy 30-year-old in a yellow T-shirt with three children, 13, 11, and 10, no husband, and no job.

The woman, who did not want her name used, had her first baby at 17, dropped out, and moved into the three-bedroom apartment where she's been ever since. For a decade, she had help from her children's father, who worked at the peanut factory. But three years ago they broke up, and he hasn't been heard from since. Not long ago, she got a letter from the state saying it had seized $900 from his tax refund for child support, but rather than sending it to his kids, the state would keep it as "back pay" for TANF checks she received years ago. She long ago exhausted her TANF benefits, which Georgia limits to 48 months over the course of a lifetime. She and the kids get $542 a month in food stamps; her electric bill alone runs $265 a month when the air conditioning's on.

So, as some women have always done in desperate times, she gets help from men. "Shit like that happens," she says. "If it was me, I probably wouldn't do stuff like that, but I got three babies to care for." She has held down jobs in the past, at Dawson Manufacturing, which made auto parts, and the Tyson chicken plant. But Dawson closed in 2007. Tyson won't rehire her because she had too many write-ups on the job. The only other major employer in town is Golden Peanut, right next door, but applying requires a trip to a temp agency in Sylvester, 45 miles away with no bus connection, which might as well be outer Mongolia for someone with no car and no money for gas. "I get on my knees and pray to that man above to make things change," she says.

In the meantime, she's getting by with help from her mom, and the man who slips in and out of her house when the kids aren't home. "I keep it on the down low from them," she explains. When she has bills due, her friend will give her $200 or $250, just about what she used to get in TANF benefits. "If he wants some and I need some money to keep the lights on, he hands out a pretty good penny," she says with a laugh.

Her experience isn't especially unusual. Toni Grebel, a relief worker at the Lord's Pantry, an Albany food bank, says she's heard many similar stories from her clients, who, at one time, were virtually all receiving TANF. Stacy Haire, the domestic violence outreach worker, says, "A lot of my clients, they're resorting to favors from men to get money." Albany police data show a sharp jump in arrests for prostitution and other crimes committed by women in 2005—shortly after the state began dumping its TANF caseloads.

Other women are turning to various illicit schemes: trading food stamps for cash to buy diapers; selling their kids' Social Security numbers to people with jobs, who use them to collect the Earned Income Tax Credit. One woman told me she got $800 each for her children's Social Security numbers, which she used to buy her kids summer clothes and new beds. "That money comes in handy. If you're not using it, why not help someone else?" she said.

One afternoon last fall, Letorrea Clark's caseworker from Liberty House, Ellen Folmar, stopped in to give her a ride to the post office. For a while, Clark had landed a job as a nanny, but that ended when school started. A Legal Aid lawyer helped her try to regain her lost disability benefits, but the appeal had recently been denied. Now, she'd lost her food stamp card. For the past few weeks, Gabby had subsisted on little but eggs and rice, and Clark was frantic.

Clark's life is a string of these sorts of crises. Mental illness wreaks havoc with her organizational skills. Medicaid doesn't pay for all her drugs, so when her child support money runs out, she doesn't always take the medication that keeps her stable. Finding no food stamp card at the post office, Clark fell apart. She was such a pathetic sight that a woman handed her $40. A weepy Clark got back in the van, consoled only after Folmar rounded up some emergency food from the shelter to tide the family over. "I got gravy!" Clark exclaimed with delight as she examined her bounty.

Back home later that week, Clark was happily entertaining a fellow Jehovah's Witness, who had a daughter Gabby's age. Gabby danced around the tiny space in her princess nightgown while Clark made the girls a brunch of eggs, bologna slices, tortilla chips, and apple juice cut with water to make it last longer. She put the paper plates on a plastic crate serving as a table. Clark was hoping her friend would get a job so that she could babysit her daughter. "Even in high school I worked with kids. That's my niche," she said. "That's the only thing that makes me happy. If it paid better, I'd be real happy."

As she talked, Clark stuck some donated chicken nuggets into the oven. She joked that her ADD was showing as she burned the first batch. As she started over, the two women swapped stories about ringing doorbells for the Lord. "I get a better response rate with Gabby," Clark said with a laugh. The Witnesses' generosity was on display in her apartment—a donated microwave, the TV, curtains, toys. Clark had piles of religious tracts in the apartment, some in Spanish, a language she was trying to learn from CDs, "so I can find me a Spanish husband," she joked.

The happy scene was but a temporary respite. Gabby's father had found Clark again. Two weeks later, her nonprofit landlord would tell her she had to move, citing budget woes. Shelter workers would search frantically to find her somewhere else to go. (They eventually found a place in yet another town.) Right now, though, Clark was focused on the chicken nuggets, and on Gabby, who climbed up, kissed her mother, and erupted into giggles. "I'm doing a good job with her," Clark said.

Stephanie Mencimer is a contributing editor of *The Washington Monthly*. She was previously an investigative reporter for *The Washington Post* and a staff writer for *Legal Times*. A native of Ogden, Utah, and a graduate of the University of Oregon, Mencimer won the 2000 Harry Chapin Media Award for reporting on hunger and poverty.

EXPLORING THE ISSUE

Was the Welfare Reform the Right Approach to Poverty?

Critical Thinking and Reflection

1. How can welfare actually hurt the people than it helps?
2. How has the bill that abolished AFDC created a program that avoids the problems and failures of its predecessor?
3. Is there a legitimate place for the old style of welfare?
4. A welfare hand up can make the recipient dependent but can also help him or her to become independent. What factors make the difference?
5. To what extent is the welfare problem a cultural or values problem?
6. Does our country provide the opportunities that encourage and enable the poor to get out of their poverty?
7. Are the welfare aspects of the United States harmful or helpful?

Is There Common Ground?

There was considerable national agreement that the old welfare system had to be changed so that it would encourage people to find jobs and achieve self-sufficiency. Much success has been gained regarding this goal so far, but some analysts point out that numerous problems still remain. Coates focuses on the positive results of the new system and Mencimer focuses on shortcomings of the administration of the welfare. One of the reforms under this act was the welfare-to-work initiative, which required work of at least 20 hours per week in exchange for time-limited financial assistance. It also listed 12 authorized activities that could meet this requirement. According to reports, within 3 years millions of Americans had moved from being dependent on welfare to being self-sufficient. At the same time welfare rolls declined significantly. In 2003, welfare was reformed again with the goal of protecting children and strengthening families as well as providing assistance to individuals and families in achieving financial independence from the government.

Create Central

www.mhhe.com/createcentral

Additional Resources

Michael B. Katz, in *The Undeserving Poor: From the War on Poverty to the War on Welfare* (Pantheon Books, 1989), traces the evolution of welfare policies in the United States from the 1960s through the 1980s. Charles Noble, in *Welfare as We Knew It: A Political History of the American Welfare State* (Oxford University Press, 1997), traces the evolution of welfare policies into the late 1990s and argues that the structure of the political economy has greatly limited the welfare state. Joel F. Handler, in *Blame*

Welfare, Ignore Poverty and Inequality (Cambridge University Press, 2007), carries the historical analysis of welfare in the United States close to the present. Bruce S. Johnson, in *The Sixteen-Trillion-Dollar Mistake: How the U.S. Bungled Its National Priorities from the New Deal to the Present* (Columbia University Press, 2001), criticizes welfare policies in the United States since the 1930s. For discussions of welfare reform, see Jeff Grogger and Lynn A. Karoly, *Welfare Reform: Effects of a Decade of Change* (Harvard University Press, 2005); Ron Haskins, *Work Over Welfare: The Inside Story of the 1996 Welfare Reform Law* (Brookings Institution Press, 2006); Mary Reintsma, *The Political Economy of Welfare Reform in the United States* (Edward Elgar, 2007); Harrell R. Rodgers Jr., *American Poverty in a New Era of Reform* (M. E. Sharpe, 2006); Sharon Hayes, *Flat Broke with Children: Women in the Age of Welfare Reform* (Oxford University Press, 2003); Scott W. Allard, *Out of Reach: Place, Poverty, and the New American Welfare State* (Yale University Press, 2009); Frank Ridzi, *Selling Welfare Reform: Work-First and the New Common Sense of Employment* (New York University Press, 2009); and Frances Fox Piven et al., eds., *Work, Welfare and Politics: Confronting Poverty in the Wake of Welfare* (University of Oregon Press, 2002). Four works that suggest how welfare should be handled under current conditions are David Snow, *What's Wrong with Benevolence: Happiness, Private Property, and the Limits of Enlightenment* (Encounter Books, 2011); Lawrence M. Mead, *From Prophecy to Charity: How to Help the Poor* (AEI Press, 2011); Andrew R. Feldman, *What Works in Work-First Welfare: Designing and Managing Employment Programs in New York City* (W. E. Upjohn Institute for Employment Research, 2011); and Matthew D. Adler, *Well-Being and Fair Distribution: Beyond Cost-Benefit Analysis* (Oxford University Press, 2011). A great deal of information can be obtained from the reauthorization hearings in the House Committee on Education and the Workforce, *Welfare Reform: Reauthorization of Work and Child Care* (March 15, 2005). A new emphasis in current welfare policy involves faith-based programs, which are discussed in Mary Jo Bane and Lawrence M. Mead, *Lifting Up the Poor: A Dialogue on Religion, Poverty, and Welfare Reform* (Brookings Institution Press, 2003), and John P. Bartkowski, *Charitable Choices: Religion, Race, and Poverty in the Post-Welfare Era* (New York University Press, 2003).

Most assessments of the 1996 welfare reform are positive. Two works that explore the negative consequences of this bill are Jane Henrici, ed., *Doing Without: Women and Work after Welfare Reform* (University of Arizona Press, 2006), and Kathleen M. Shaw et al., *Putting Poor People to Work: How the Work-First Idea Eroded College Access for the Poor* (Russell Sage Foundation, 2006). Many recognize that the key to reducing welfare rolls is to make work profitable. To understand welfare from this perspective, see Robert Kuttner, ed., *Making Work Pay: America after Welfare: A Reader* (New York Press, 2002), and Dave Hage, *Reforming Welfare by Rewarding Work: One State's Successful Experiment* (University of Minnesota Press, 2004). Two books that offer explanations as to why welfare provision is so minimal in the United States are Frank Stricker, *Why America Lost the War on Poverty—And How to Win It* (University of North Carolina Press, 2007), and Linda Gordon, *Pitied but Not Entitled: Single Mothers and the History of Welfare* (Free Press, 1994).

Internet References . . .

Sociology—Study Sociology Online

http://edu.learnsoc.org/

Sociology Web Resources

www.mhhe.com/socscience/sociology/resources
/index.htm

Sociosite

www.topsite.com/goto/sociosite.net

Socioweb

www.topsite.com/goto/socioweb.com

Selected, Edited, and with Issue Framing Material by:
Kurt Finsterbusch, *University of Maryland, College Park*

ISSUE

Are Teachers the Key to Greatly Improving American Education?

YES: **Jal Mehta**, from "Why American Education Fails," *Foreign Affairs* (May/June 2013)

NO: **Jen Scott Curwood**, from "10 Big Ideas to Improve Your Schools," *Scholastic Administrator* (2013)

Learning Outcomes

After reading this issue, you will be able to:

- Identify many weaknesses in the current K–12 school system.
- Criticize the current emphasis on the rewarding and sanctioning of schools on the basis of testing as in No Child Left Behind.
- Discuss the types of teachers and teaching styles that can produce students who are ready for the new world of the twenty-first century.
- Describe the type of student culture needed for school success.
- Discuss some excellent examples of really good schools.

ISSUE SUMMARY

YES: Jal Mehta, an assistant professor at the Harvard Graduate School of Education, advocates radical changes to American 1–12 education, which is currently a complete failure. It is designed for the needs of a half century ago and does not prepare students for dealing with the kind of complex learning and critical thinking that the twenty-first-century U.S. economy demands. This will require that teaching must be made into a true modern profession.

NO: Jen Scott Curwood, senior lecturer in English education and media studies at the University of Sydney, agrees that K to 12 education must be improved but not in the radical way that Mehta proposes. She proposes 10 improvements including establishing professional learning communities, encouraging social networking, making collaboration a priority, reexamining staffing, and using free digital tools to enhance teaching and learning. Her approach is continuous improvement rather than radical change.

The quality of American public schooling has been criticized for several decades. Secretary of Education Richard Riley said in 1994 that some American schools are so bad that they "should never be called schools at all." The average school year in the United States is 180 days, whereas Japanese children attend school 240 days of the year. American schoolchildren score lower than the children of many other Western countries on certain standardized achievement tests. In 1983, the National Commission on Excellence in Education published *A Nation at Risk*, which argued that American education was a failure.

Critics of *A Nation at Risk* maintain that the report produced very little evidence to support its thesis, but the public accepted it anyway. Currently, much of the public still thinks that the American school system is failing and needs to be fixed. The solution that the Bush administration instituted in 2002 with overwhelming bipartisan support in Congress was the No Child Left Behind Act (NCLB).

The main feature of NCLB is standards-based education. High standards and measurable goals are set and monitored by the states. All government run schools receiving federal funding to administer a state-wide standardized test. The students' scores determine the performance score of the schools and progress is expected annually. If schools fall below their goals then increasingly radical steps are taken to fix the problems. Five failing years results in plans to restructure the entire school. Common options include closing the school, turning the school into a charter school, hiring a private company to run the school, or asking the state office of education to run the school directly. This is a tough standard and drew much criticism for being unreasonable. The main criticism, however, is its focus on testing. Test results lead to rewards or sanctions so teachers teach to the tests with poor educational results.

The two readings in this issue want to put NCLB behind us and follow the guidance of recent research and the experience of other countries and really change K–12 education to suit the twenty-first century. Jal Mehta blasts American K–12 education for making schools into education factories that do not prepare students for the complex competitive world of today. (This critique also applies to NCLB.) The system is too hierarchical and is based on teachers with too little training because their job was seen as fairly simple. The research on countries on top of the educational rankings find them to have educational systems that are almost the inverse of the American system. Their students do well on measures of higher-order problem solving in math, reading, and science. "They choose their teachers from among their most talented graduates, train them extensively, create opportunities for them to collaborate with their peers within and across schools to improve their practice, provide them the external supports that they need to do their work well, and underwrite all these efforts with a strong welfare state." In this system external monitoring is unimportant. Their system is very professional and America's is amateurish.

Jen Scott Curwood agrees that American schools are bad but proposes different less radical solutions. She proposes ten research based improvements which utilize new technologies and social networking patterns while incorporating business practices for continuous improvements and cost controls.

YES ↵

Jal Mehta

Why American Education Fails

And How Lessons from Abroad Could Improve It

In his landmark 1973 book, *The Coming of Post-industrial Society*, the sociologist Daniel Bell heralded the United States' transition from a labor-intensive economy that produced goods to a knowledge-based one geared toward providing services. No longer could success be achieved through manual, assembly-line work; it would require advanced skills and creativity. At least since then, American politicians and pundits have regularly stressed that education holds the key to the country's future. Everyone seems to agree that good schools are prerequisites for broad economic prosperity, individual social mobility, and a healthy civil society in which informed voters engage in the public issues of the day.

Although no one disputes the value of education, how the country should improve it is fiercely contested. Every few years, along comes a new idea to save American schools, be it enforcing standards, opening charter schools, providing vouchers for private education, or paying teachers based on their performance. Most recently, two federal programs have sought to remake the U.S. education system: No Child Left Behind, a 2001 law that sought to use standards and accountability to push all students to proficiency by 2014, and Race to the Top, an Obama administration initiative that has tried to incentivize change by offering competitive grants to states pursuing reform agendas. All this activity has generated progress in some areas, but it has not led to widespread improvement. U.S. schools still languish in the middle of international rankings, behind the schools of such countries as Estonia and Slovenia. And half a century after the end of official segregation, huge gaps continue to divide students by race and class, with the average black 12th grader scoring in reading at a level equivalent to the average white eighth grader on the National Assessment of Educational Progress, the most trusted long-term yardstick of U.S. school performance.

The United States needs a more thoroughgoing and systematic approach to educational improvement. To see what such an effort might look like, consider that any professional field consists of the following four components: human capital, which involves attracting, selecting, training, and retaining the people who work in the field; a core of knowledge that guides the field; effective organizational structures; and overall performance management and accountability. Every profession needs to set its priorities within and among these four elements; ideally, they work together in harmony.

In recent years, the U.S. education system has become overly focused on the last element—accountability—at the expense of progress on the others. The most ambitious federal education reform in recent years, No Child Left Behind, increased accountability by measuring schools annually on student tests in reading and math, with escalating consequences for those that did not improve. But it largely failed to address the other elements of the field, an imbalance that partially explains why the initiative has not achieved its aims. By contrast, stronger professions in the United States, such as medicine, law, and engineering, focus more on building their foundations than on holding their practitioners accountable. Doctors, for example, must clear a series of high bars before entering the field; develop a broad knowledge base, through course work and then extensive clinical training; and continually revisit their training, with practices such as hospital rounds. The medical profession places less emphasis on setting targets and making sure physicians meet them—there is no such thing as No Patient Left Behind.

Other countries, meanwhile, have figured out a better way to educate their children, one that looks less like the United States' education system and more like its stronger professions. Recent international research suggests that the countries that top international education rankings owe their success to approaches that are in many ways the inverse of the American one. Such countries—which include Canada, Finland, Japan, Singapore, and South Korea, top scorers on the Program for International Student Assessment, an internationally recognized test for 15-year-olds that measures higher-order problem solving in math, reading, and science—all do certain things similarly. They choose their teachers from among their most talented graduates, train them extensively, create opportunities for them to collaborate with their peers within and across schools to improve their practice, provide them the external supports that they need to do their work well, and underwrite all these efforts with a strong welfare state. Because these countries do a good job of honing the expertise of their educators to begin with, they have less of a need for external monitoring of school performance.

If the United States wants to lead the world in student achievement, it will need to borrow some ideas from the countries that currently top international rankings. Rather than simply holding accountable the teachers and schools that have failed to live up to expectations, the country will need to build a new system from the ground up—an expert profession that can consistently deliver high levels of performance.

Schoolhouse as Factory

The U.S. school system assumed its contemporary form a little more than a century ago, during the Progressive Era. In one generation, between 1890 and 1920, a group of civic elites transformed a country of one-room schoolhouses into a set of district school systems. Influenced by prevailing models of business organization, which prioritized efficiency, this system empowered mostly male superintendents to act as the CEOS of school districts, where mostly female teachers would follow the rules and programs that their superiors chose.

In this hierarchical model, teachers had little formal power to resist dictates from above, although the system's "loose coupling"—the lack of close monitoring of practitioners by supervisors—gave teachers considerable control over what happened inside their classroom walls. Teachers received minimal training, the assumption being that they did not have a complicated job. The top education schools mostly avoided training teachers, seeing teaching as carrying the stigma of low-status, feminine work; they instead focused on cultivating the male administrators who would govern the system.

For half a century, this model worked relatively well, largely because the expectations for what schools needed to produce were fairly limited. Loose coupling left the teachers with enough autonomy to make them feel as if they were in charge. School boards and superintendents had enough formal power to preserve the sense that their school systems were supervised and, since these leaders were elected or appointed by elected officials, that the schools were subject to democratic control. Teachers were mostly women, who had few other employment options and were generally not the breadwinners in their families, so their low pay did not provoke significant resistance.

More broadly, Americans tolerated the system because by 1960, most white students graduated with a high school degree, which qualified them for middle-class occupations in manufacturing and other similar sectors, regardless of how much they had actually learned in school. A small number of privileged youth went to better public schools or to private schools and then on to college. The result was that people throughout the system got what they needed, even though the country was not doing much to maximize the learning of all its students.

Over the past 50 years, the limits of this model have become more apparent as the expectations for schooling have increased. Driven both by civil rights imperatives and the shift from an industrial to a post-industrial economy, policymakers now expect all students to achieve at fairly high levels. But the means to realize these ambitions are not there. American poverty rates, always high by international standards because of the country's weak welfare state, have been exacerbated by the collapse of manufacturing and increasing segregation and joblessness in many of the nation's largest cities—and schools in high-poverty neighborhoods have been largely impervious to reform. Educated women, who had always turned to teaching in large numbers, have seen their options proliferate, shrinking the talent pool for the profession. The highly decentralized nature of U.S. education has become a weakness rather than a strength, because, as the scholars David Cohen and Susan Moffitt have pointed out, it has limited the ability of the federal government to foster good teaching throughout the nation. Now, the country wants consistent, high-level performance across the school system, but it has not built the system to achieve that.

The result has been a vicious cycle in the interaction between policymakers and practitioners, one that leaves little hope for the much-needed improvements in American education. Policymakers understandably want to intervene in the failing system, given the highly uneven performance among schools, with dropout rates as high as 40–50 percent in some urban districts. They have done so through a variety of mechanisms, but most notably through an effort to set higher standards for student performance and to create consequences for schools that fail to improve. Teachers, for their part, resent the external mandates developed by people who know little of their daily work and who are unwilling to provide the social support that their students need. Teachers' unions worry that their members are being scapegoated for their schools' failure, and so they frequently harden their positions and seek to resist what they see as unfair and unwise external accountability measures. Many policymakers, in turn, see schools as units that need tighter coupling to overcome the teachers' opposition and think of unions as an obstruction to necessary reforms. The cycle continues, with each group playing its appointed role, but with no improvement in sight.

American Unexceptionalism

The country needs to stop this downward spiral and build a better system from the ground up. A good place to start would be to address the technical requirements for teaching. Education scholars identify three kinds of knowledge that good teachers have: "substantive knowledge," that is, knowledge about the subjects they teach; "pedagogical knowledge," about how to teach; and "pedagogical content knowledge," about how students are likely to understand the subject, what errors or preconceptions they may harbor, and how to respond to these misunderstandings. Good teachers know how to draw on and apply these different forms of knowledge in real and fast-changing situations; research by the University of Chicago's Philip Jackson suggests that teachers make more than a thousand decisions over the course of a single day.

The problem in American education is that developing these skills is not systematized in any way. Teachers learn mostly through experience, and U.S. teachers generally report that the training they do receive is of limited utility in practice. Licensing exams for teachers lack the rigor of the bar and board exams that exist in law, medicine, engineering, accounting, and many other professions. Some teachers master their craft over time, but others merely learn to control a classroom. A recent study by the Bill and Melinda Gates Foundation of more than 3,000 classrooms in the United States found that over 60 percent were competently managed, meaning that the students were not unruly and did the work assigned by the teacher, but only 20 percent were engaged in ambitious learning that challenged students to think, reason, and analyze texts or problems.

Not surprisingly, these patterns in how teachers teach are mirrored in what students can do. Results from the National Assessment of Educational Progress regularly show that two-thirds or more of American students of all ages have mastered basic skills, such as reading and recalling information, but only one-third can do more advanced work that involves the application of information or analysis. American students fall in the middle of the pack on international assessments that measure higher-order thinking, scoring 14th in reading, 17th in science, and 25th in math on the 2009 Program for International Student Assessment. Building a twenty-first-century school system will require teachers who can help students do this kind of advanced work.

What would such a system look like? Examining the countries that lead international educational rankings, several patterns emerge. Very broadly, they do a better job at nurturing human capital, developing knowledge, and helping teachers grow. Unlike the United States, whose strategy emphasizes using tests to hold teachers and schools accountable, more successful countries rely on investments on the front end to achieve quality control. The success of schools in these countries creates a virtuous cycle, boosting public support for investing in education and making teaching a more attractive profession. Although correlation is not causation and more research remains to be done, these countries share certain approaches to reform that look quite different from the ones pursued by the United States.

To be sure, the countries that lead the international assessments differ from the United States in many ways, making it difficult to directly import their lessons. Most notably, they are generally smaller and more racially homogeneous than the United States. That said, it would be wrong to conclude that the United States can learn nothing from foreign countries, particularly given how much successful educational systems have in common across otherwise very different cultures. The characteristics they share can also be seen in other, stronger professions in the United States, as well as in leading American charter-school networks, suggesting that they are central elements to improved performance.

Raising the Bar

Any attempt to reform American education would have to start with attracting better teachers, retaining them, and helping them develop their practice. The most striking finding of comparative international research is that the best-performing school systems draw their teachers from the top third of college graduates, whereas lower-ranking school systems do not. A recent McKinsey report found that most U.S. teachers come "from the bottom two-thirds of college classes, and, for many schools in poor neighborhoods, from the bottom third." In Finland, teaching is the single most preferred career for 15-year-olds, a priority that allows the country to accept only one in ten applicants to its teacher-training programs. Similarly, in Singapore, only one in eight is accepted to such programs. By contrast, in the United States, even the most prestigious education schools commonly accept 50 percent or more of the applicants to their teacher-training programs.

How might the United States make teaching a more attractive and selective occupation? In the past year, the country's two largest teachers' unions (the American Federation of Teachers and the National Education Association) and the Council of Chief State School Officers, which is the main organization representing state-level education officials, have released reports advocating raising the bar for entry into teaching. Under their proposals, prospective teachers would start out with provisional status for their first several years. Before becoming fully licensed, they would need to demonstrate their knowledge of their subjects and their skill in the classroom. Tenure would no longer be an expected and near-immediate step but would become an accomplishment similar to getting tenure at a university or making partner at a law firm. These changes have the potential to remake the whole field: if it became harder to become a teacher, respect for the profession would grow, and schools might start to show better results. This process could boost public confidence in schools, potentially leading to higher teachers' pay and, in the long run, a greater desire by talented people to join the profession.

A higher bar for teaching should go hand in hand with a revamped approach to teacher education. The United States has more than 1,300 traditional institutions for teacher preparation, a growing number of alternative certification providers, a smaller number of city-sponsored "teacher residencies," and a few primary and secondary schools that run their own training programs. The most successful of these programs share several common features. They attract people who majored as undergraduates in the subjects that they wish to teach, they focus more on clinical practice than on classroom theory, they choose their applicants carefully (rather than simply treating students as a revenue stream), and they use data about how their students ultimately fare as teachers to assess and revise their approaches. Ideally, many lower-quality providers would be closed, but shutting down existing programs would prove difficult politically. Instead, the equivalent of a bar exam for teachers, which could measure demonstrated teaching skills, as well as substantive and pedagogical knowledge, might achieve the same outcome. The training programs whose graduates passed this comprehensive exam would attract more applicants, whereas those whose students did not would become irrelevant.

What Teachers Know

Improving teacher training will also require educators to better develop granular, usable knowledge to guide the field. Professions are fundamentally grounded in their claims to specialized information. Pilots are permitted to fly planes, lawyers to draw up contracts, and doctors to prescribe drugs because they possess an exclusive understanding of how to do these things. Teaching, however, lacks the type of codified, shared knowledge that ensures quality control in other professions—hence the huge inconsistencies from classroom to classroom. In some regards, American education today is where medicine was a little more than a century ago: instead of relying on a shared knowledge base, teachers draw on a mix of hunches, occasional research, and some outright quackery.

A major obstacle to progress in education is that nobody is specifically tasked with developing such a shared knowledge base. Education researchers write mainly for other researchers; teachers generate new ideas daily but don't necessarily share them or put them to a test; an entire industry creates classroom materials, but it focuses more on what will be bought by districts and states than on what would improve learning for teachers or students. Anthony Bryk, the president of the Carnegie Foundation for the Advancement of Teaching, has estimated that whereas fields such as medicine and engineering spend 5–15 percent of their budgets on research and development, the U.S. education system invests less than one-quarter of one percent for those purposes. Not only does the field lack knowledge; it lacks the resources and infrastructure needed to produce it.

The good news is that there are a number of independent pockets of knowledge that the profession can expand on. Education scholars have conducted serious academic research on several practical topics, including how to teach early reading, the guidelines of which are developed and specific enough to be used in the classroom. Charter-school operators and independent researchers have also studied what the best teachers and principals are doing and, through books and videos, have shared these insights. Teacher-to-teacher websites help break down the isolation of teaching and allow educators to draw on the work of their peers in developing lessons and units. Schools and teachers can turn to many commercial and nonprofit institutions that offer advice and programs, although they vary widely in quality and few mechanisms exist to separate the wheat from the chaff. What is needed is a substantial push, either from the government or from private philanthropy, to integrate these different sources of information, develop shared standards by which they can be vetted, and build new knowledge where it is lacking.

Isolation Is the Enemy of Improvement

Knowledge and training will be of little use without organizational processes to ensure that educators apply what they learn. K-12 education largely lacks the common standards that govern day-to-day work in other professions, such as peer review in the academy. (These are standards internal to the profession that guide everyday work, not external accountability measures, which offer punishment but little guidance.) What happens in one classroom generally has little bearing on what happens in another. This kind of isolation is the enemy of consistent improvement; if teachers are going to get better, they need time to work together, discuss lessons, reflect on their students' performance, and develop new and better approaches.

In this regard as well, the countries whose schools top international education rankings have it right. In Japanese schools, for example, teachers regularly come together to study one another's lessons and refine them. Doing this sort of work well depends on both structure and culture. Structurally, U.S. teachers spend more time in the classroom and less time planning and working with one another than do teachers in countries with higher-performing schools. Secondary school teachers in the United States teach an average of nearly 1,100 hours a year, compared with an average of 660 hours across the countries of the Organization for Economic Cooperation and Development and fewer than 600 hours in Japan and South Korea. Culturally, for growth through professional collaboration to be effective, U.S. teachers need to feel as though they are members of a shared profession with a common knowledge base, rather than freelancers accountable only to what they think is right.

Here, too, there have been a number of recent developments that the U.S. education system should build on. Principals in the United States have historically acted mostly as building managers and have thus relied largely on administrative skills. The recent push for greater academic performance, however, has led to an increasing recognition that successful schools require pedagogical leadership, and preparation programs for administrators have started training principals on how to work with teachers to improve instruction. The field has also seen the proliferation of "professional learning communities"—teams of teachers who work together on problems that they encounter in the classroom. The challenge for the next generation will be to combine and accelerate these efforts, in particular to link the largely local initiatives to improve particular schools or districts to a broader effort to build a shared knowledge base.

Schools also need ways to more formally recognize and incorporate different levels of expertise. The

U.S. education system has long operated on the principle of teacher equality—the idea that each teacher possesses equivalent levels of knowledge and skill. But this is clearly not true, and the country should not organize its schools as if it were. Singapore, for example, offers advanced teachers the same type of salary increases that in the United States are generally available only to those who move out of teaching and into administration. The United States could implement a similar system in order to create career ladders in teaching, which would formally reward teachers who have more expertise and are willing to take on more responsibility by upping their pay and status. In the long run, career ladders could better integrate teacher training into the profession. New teachers, carefully trained in effective methods by experienced mentors, would enter schools where what they had learned would be reinforced and strengthened over time; then, as they gained expertise, they would develop and share their knowledge to train the next generation.

A Different Role for the State

If the country succeeded in building a skilled and knowledgeable teaching force, the role of the state—including federal, state, and local government bodies—would change. Currently, a central part of the problem in American education is that government officials are trying to remake teaching from afar. But teaching is hard work and has proved difficult to change from above; efforts to do so have set teachers against policymakers. If the country implemented the needed processes to ensure skilled teaching—better recruitment, training, knowledge development, and school organization—teachers would come to be seen as experts, like those in other professions. The state could then shift its function from holding teachers accountable to taking on roles in which it has more of a comparative advantage and is more likely to be effective.

In particular, the state could assist in the creation of curricula, invest in research and development, screen teacher resumes, and provide expert technical assistance. It also could perform administrative functions, dealing with payroll, real estate, and food services. It could do a better job supporting students outside of school, in ways that would mitigate some of the worst consequences of the weak American welfare state. And it could retain some accountability functions: presumably, many more schools would be performing well given how much the field would be investing in training, knowledge, and organization, but if some consistently were not, they could still be closed by districts or states.

But the government should not try to micromanage education from above, putting forward an endless array of requirements, regulations, and accountability targets, in the hopes that doing so will somehow force schools to improve. This approach has been tried before, again and again, and it has yielded what the sociologist Charles Payne has called "so much reform, so little change."

The U.S. school system still bears the imprint of its origins. Created in the era of the assembly line, it was never intended to push all its students to engage in the kind of complex learning and critical thinking that the twenty-first-century U.S. economy demands. In the intervening years, the country has layered more rules and higher expectations on top of that initial structure, but it has not fundamentally remade teaching into a modern profession. To do so will not be easy; it will require political will and significant changes to long-standing institutions. But it is time to start anew and to build the school system that might actually yield the results that the country seeks and that its students deserve.

JAL MEHTA is an assistant professor at the Harvard Graduate School of Education and teaches the Education School's Introduction to Education Policy class.

Jen Scott Curwood → **NO**

10 Big Ideas to Improve Your Schools

Establish professional learning communities, encourage social networking, reexamine staffing, and use free digital tools to enhance teaching and learning.

Two goals every school leader can embrace are continuous improvement and wringing as much value as possible from every dollar in the budget. These two tasks do not have to be mutually exclusive.

Here are 10 ways—from finding partners in higher ed to exploring free tools to reexamining staffing—that you can use to improve teaching and learning while keeping an eye on your bottom line.

1. Establish Professional Learning Communities.

There's no doubt about it: Traditional professional development can be very pricey. By the time you consider speaker fees, the cost of texts, and hiring substitutes to cover classes, districts can easily spend tens (or hundreds) of thousands of dollars on PD initiatives. "But this model of professional development—with a workshop here and a day-long meeting there—doesn't produce lasting results," says Mike Mattos, principal of Pioneer Middle School in Tustin, California, and co-author of Pyramid *Response to Intervention: RTI, Professional Learning Communities, and How to Respond When Kids Don't Learn.* That's where professional learning communities come in. By emphasizing the establishment of a shared vision, collective learning, instructional collaboration, peer observation, and action research, PLCs create the opportunity for continuous, teacher-directed staff development. "And it's free," adds Mattos. At his school, teachers have successfully engaged in PLCs to address key issues, such as establishing effective grading practices, meeting Hispanic students' needs, and working with at-risk students.

2. Partner with Researchers.

Around the country, university faculty are working to develop innovative classroom lessons, test new educational technologies, and uncover effective instructional practices. Dr. Dawnene Hassett, assistant professor of curriculum and instruction at the University of Wisconsin–Madison, says, "In a study I am conducting with K–3 teachers, we are looking at how highly visual and interactive children's literature can help teach reading and writing skills. As a result, the classroom teachers [get] les-

son plans, materials, and ideas they can use for years." Researchers are often developing new resources and tools. By partnering with local university faculty and other researchers, teachers may get to pilot a new math curriculum that emphasizes social justice, try out a revolutionary iPhone application, or experiment with using videogames to enhance content area learning.

3. Encourage Teachers to Use Social-Networking Sites.

In schools, a lot of the discussion about social networking focuses on how students are using (or misusing) popular sites like Facebook or MySpace. But social-networking sites can be incredibly useful for teachers, too. Need an idea for how to teach the popular young adult novel *The Book Thief?* Curious about how Second Life can enhance classroom learning? The answers to all these questions can be found online. But social-networking sites aren't just about linking people to resources. They're about linking people to people—and fostering critical discussion.

In the U.S., one in four classrooms now has an interactive whiteboard. As teachers work to use whiteboards to enhance learning, they are finding Promethean Planet and SMART Exchange invaluable. Teachers can also join the discussions on the Classroom 2.0 website to learn more about Web 2.0 tools and collaborative technologies, visit RezEd.org to discover how virtual worlds can facilitate classroom instruction, or take part in the community at Ning in Education (education.ning.com).

4. Make Collaboration a Priority.

In theory, most schools want teachers to collaborate with one another to develop lessons, address individual students' learning needs, and share ideas and resources. In reality, most teachers have little time within the school day to do so. In elementary schools with 20-minute lunch periods or high schools with five minutes between classes, there simply isn't enough time to have meaningful (let alone ongoing) discussions. To address that, administrators are rethinking how to structure the school day to value teachers' collaborative work and professional dialogue.

In some elementary and middle schools, for instance, all same-grade-level teachers have a common preparation time each day. At high schools, all teachers within a single department could share the same prep time. This would allow teachers to work closely with colleagues and encourage them to engage in ongoing discussions about their curriculum and how to meet the needs of each learner. In other districts, an entire half day is set aside each week for staff development, in part to help align curricula among grade levels.

5. Manage and Share Data.

This year, Atlanta Public Schools began piloting its Teacher Quality Dashboard Initiative. Partially funded by a $390,000 grant from the Bill & Melinda Gates Foundation, the district is gathering and storing information about the performance of its estimated 4,000 teachers, primarily their students' grades, test scores, and attendance, in an online data warehouse, says Chuck Burbridge, the district's chief financial officer. The dashboard will enable school administrators to quickly review teacher performance, identify those who may need coaching, and build teacher teams more effectively.

This all-in-one system for school performance management will allow administrators to better evaluate the impact and effectiveness of its plans to improve curriculum and professional development programs.

The district plans to finish the prototype this year, though it will take another year to get the online dashboard running. Since many teachers are data-driven and track student performance throughout the year, the pilot has drawn much interest. Although the district recently trimmed millions of dollars from its budget—even eliminating cost-of-living allowances this year—Burbridge calls the project a top priority. Why? Teacher quality is the top predictor of student outcomes.

6. Use Free Digital Tools.

Want to get teachers excited about using media and technology in the classroom? Show them what's available—free and online. Take Wordle, for instance, which could be used by elementary teachers to create a highly visual word wall. Or there's audio-editing software like Audacity and Jamglue. Students can use these to create their own podcasts and public service announcements. New media presentation software makes it easy to combine photos, video, music, and text—check out Empressr, Animoto, and JayCut.

Joe Geocaris, an English teacher at Stevenson High School in Lincolnshire, Illinois, has successfully used nings, user-created social networks, with his students. At Ning.com, anyone can create a network, which can be public or private; members can keep blogs, post to the forum, link to other resources, upload videos, and form interest groups. "When I first set up the ning with my students, we talked about security and online credibility. But we also covered how they could create a valid identity and what would make them credible to others in the network," Geocaris says. Students used the online space

to post resources and ask questions of their teacher and peers. He adds, "Students had a better understanding of their audience, they were authorities on their research topic, and they engaged each other in critical discussion."

7. Reduce Fixed Costs.

Five years ago, Bowling Green Independent Schools in Kentucky introduced a music program featuring string instruments donated by a local music foundation, says Superintendent Joe Tinius. But the program's expansion from 60 students to 300 forced the district to spend $10,000 to hire a part-time teacher.

Tinius found the money. The district saved $5,000 a year by canceling a biweekly sweeping service for its parking lots, which are now cleaned as needed. Emptying large garbage Dumpsters less frequently saved another $5,000. The district also purchased equipment to clean school doormats instead of having them replaced weekly. By fall, Tinius says, the equipment will have paid for itself—while the music program continues to grow.

8. Share Work.

As an instructional technology resource teacher with the San José (CA) Unified School District, Felicia Webb learned about www.curriki.org, a free website for teachers that offers more than 25,000 classroom lessons. Teachers upload their lessons for other educators to use, and they collaborate with one another to modify, improve, or update existing lessons. The district used the website as part of a pilot program. Earlier this year, 45 teachers in its technology integration leadership program created more than 50 new lessons, uploaded them, then downloaded other lessons from the site that involved technology. It has been a great success, says Webb. Now the district is developing creative ways to expand its use of the website, focusing on specific areas that need improvement. The plan is to roll it out to teachers across the district and explore collaboration opportunities with teachers worldwide.

9. Turn Energy Savings into New Equipment.

Clark County School District in Las Vegas supports an energy conservation program that is managed by a team of 22 energy inspectors, says Paul Gerner, associate superintendent for facilities at CCSD.

Each inspector rotates working the midnight shift to ensure schools are properly shut down. Last year, he says, the district won the 2008 Cashman Good Government Award from the Nevada Taxpayers Association for saving more than $10 million on utility costs. The district expects to save the same amount this year. The self-funded program has significantly changed how the district schools operate, he says, adding that 90 percent of the district's schools earn energy rebates by saving at least 10 percent in energy costs over the previous year.

Several years ago, the district began using a portion of these savings to equip classrooms with PCs, printers, and whiteboards to help prepare students for 21st-century work and learning.

10. Reexamine Staffing Needs.

Back in 2006, money was tight at Fridley Public Schools, a K–12 district just north of Minneapolis that supports 2,800 students. One or two teachers were facing layoffs. So Superintendent Mark Robertson tried something new. He realized employing a full-time business manager and an accountant was overkill: Their combined salaries and benefits packages totaled almost $200,000. To make matters worse, roughly five accountants had quit in six years, accepting higher-paying jobs with other districts.

Robertson outsourced the positions. After one year, the company he hired had taken on too many clients, which negatively affected the quality of its work. So the two parted ways. Robertson then hired a subcontractor for each position and reduced their hours to 80 percent. Total savings: roughly $75,000. The district avoided cutting 1.5 teachers in the classroom with these savings and was able to maintain small class sizes.

JEN SCOTT CURWOOD is a freelance writer for *Scholastic Administrator*.

EXPLORING THE ISSUE

Are Teachers the Key to Greatly Improving American Education?

Critical Thinking and Reflection

1. Why are there constant, frequent, and fervent cries for school reforms and yet it always seems to need to be reformed again? Why do the reforms not work most of the time?
2. Do you see a way to improve NCLB or should it be abandoned?
3. What are the impacts of attaching rewards and sanctions to the type of testing promoted in NCLB?
4. Why do American students score lower on standard tests than most European students?
5. Explain why American teachers and teaching methods are inferior to European teachers.
6. How can students be made more creative and capable of complex thinking?
7. Is there a school model which you think is the best?

Is There Common Ground?

As I read the provisions of the NCLB, I noted how much hard work and intelligence went into this bill. The authors strongly sought to push school systems to improve and do it with a complex set of rewards and sanctions. The problem is that new policies have multiple consequences and some of the unintended consequences are quite negative. NCLB has improved many schools, as demonstrated by improving test scores. But critics such as the two authors presented here point to resulting problem of teaching to the test and focusing on the poorer students to the neglect of the better students. No one wants these and other negative impacts but they seem to be unavoidable. Experts at least agree that something needs to be done.

Both Mehta and Curwood agree that this latest school reform is a failure. It does not inspire learning nor teach creativity and complex thinking. Mehta argues that a much higher grade of teachers are needed to work in a less structured and restricting framework. Europe supplies some useful models. Curwood advocates better utilizing new technologies and social practices and incorporating the lessons of recent research on effective educational techniques and practices.

Create Central

www.mhhe.com/createcentral

Additional Resources

NCLB is the current major education policy but its critics are numerous. Richard Rothstein, in "The Corruption of School Accountability," *The School Administrator* (June 2008), critiques NCLB as relying on flawed numerical measures to evaluate performance but this causes an emphasis on drill, teaching to the test, and manipulating data. Similarly, W. James Popham, in *America's Failing*

Schools: How Parents and Teachers Can Cope with "No Child Left Behind" (Routledge, 2004), argues that the prescribed achievement goals are altogether unrealistic, that "the establishment of expectations that are unattainable will rarely spur people to perform at new levels of excellence." Other critiques include Mark F. Goldberg, "The Test Mess," *Phi Delta Kappan* (January 2004) and "Test Mess 2: Are We Doing Better a Year Later?" *Phi Delta Kappan* (January 2005); Thomas Toch, "Turmoil in the Testing Industry," *Educational Leadership* (November 2006); and Lawrence A. Uzzell, "Cheat Sheets: No Child Left Behind Has Taught Our Nation's Schools One Thing—How to Lie," *The American Spectator* (September 2005). Important books on NCLB include Joanne M. Carris, *Ghosts of No Child Left Behind* (P. Lang, 2011); John E. Chubb, *Learning from No Child Left Behind: How and Why the Nation's Most Important but Controversial Education Law Should Be Renewed* (Hoover Institution Press, 2009); Todd Alan Price and Elizabeth Peterson, eds., *The Myth and Reality of No Child Left Behind: Public Education and High Stakes Assessment* (University Press of America, 2009); and Michael A. Rebell and Jessica R. Wolff, eds., *NCLB at the Crossroads: Reexamining the Federal Effort to Close the Achievement Gap* (Teachers College, Columbia University, 2009). For the history of education reform, see William J. Reese, *America's Public Schools: From the Common School to "No Child Left Behind"* (Johns Hopkins University Press, 2011). For more general treatments of accountability in education, see Kathryn A. McDermott, *High-Stakes Reform: The Politics of Educational Accountability* (Georgetown University Press, 2011); Keven Carey and Mark Schneider, eds., *Accountability in American Higher Education* (Palgrave Macmillan, 2010); Theodore Hershberg and Claire Robertson-Kraft, eds., *A Grand Bargain for Education Reform: New Rewards and Supports for New Accountability* (Harvard University Press, 2009); and Sherman Dorn, *Accountability Frankenstein: Understanding and Taming the Monster* (Information Age Publishing, 2007). Covering some other crucial related issues are these recommended articles: David Mathews, "The Public and the Public Schools: The Coproduction of Education," *Phi Delta Kappan* (April 2008); Paul D. Houston, "The Seven Deadly Sins of No Child Left Behind," *Phi Delta Kappan* (June 2007); and John Chubb and Diane Ravitch, "The Future of No Child Left Behind: End It? Or Mend It?" *Education Next* (Summer 2009).

Though most works on education focus on NCLB, the following agree with the thinking of the issue authors: Jal Mehta, Robert B. Schwartz, and Frederick M. Hess, eds., *The Futures of School Reform* (Harvard Education Press, 2012); Jal Mehta, *The Allure of Order: High Hopes, Dashed Expectations and the Troubled Quest to Remake American Schooling* (Oxford University Press, 2013).

Internet References . . .

Sociology—Study Sociology Online

http://edu.learnsoc.org/

Sociology Web Resources

www.mhhe.com/socscience/sociology/resources/index.htm

Sociosite

www.topsite.com/goto/sociosite.net

Socioweb

www.topsite.com/goto/socioweb.com

Selected, Edited, and with Issue Framing Material by:
Kurt Finsterbusch, *University of Maryland, College Park*

ISSUE

Will Biotechnology Have the Greatest Impact on the Next Half Century?

YES: **President's Council on Bioethics,** from *Beyond Therapy: Biotechnology and the Pursuit of Happiness* (October 2003)

NO: **Neil Gershenfeld,** from "How to Make Almost Anything," *Foreign Affairs* (November/December 2012)

Learning Outcomes

After reading this issue, you will be able to:

- Have a general understanding of where genetic research stands today and what it has accomplished up to now.
- Have a general understanding of what promising technological research might achieve in the future and how these might affect societies.
- Know what choices individuals are making that involve genetic modification.
- Know the potential dangers of genetic engineering and, where possible, evaluate their likelihood.
- Know the potential achievements that 3D printing and other innovations in production could make possible.
- Understand the moral debates about genetic engineering. Know especially the moral issues concerning genetically engineered babies.

ISSUE SUMMARY

YES: The President's Council on Bioethics was commissioned by George Bush to report to him their findings about the ethical issues involved in the uses of biotechnology. Included in this selection are the expected positive benefits from the biotechnologies that are on the horizon. They could change society in major ways.

NO: Neil Gershenfeld, professor at the Massachusetts Institute of Technology and director of MIT's Center for Bits and Atoms, argues that the coming digital revolution in fabrication will allow individuals to design and produce tangible objects on demand, wherever and whenever they need them. Widespread access to these technologies will challenge traditional models of business, aid, and education. In fact, it will transform how we learn, work, and live and produce great worldwide prosperity.

As a sociologist I feel that I am on relatively firm ground discussing the 21 other issues in this book. I am not on firm ground discussing the issue of how biotechnology should or should not be used. And I am not alone. The nation does not know what to think about this issue, at least not in a coherent way. But the discussion must begin because the issue is coming at us like a tornado. Already America is debating the use of drugs to enhance athletic performance. Athletes and body builders want to use them to build muscle, strength, and/or endurance, but much of the public do not approve. They have been outlawed from competitive sports, and users have been publicly discredited. Soon, however, parents will be able to pay for genetic engineering to make their children good athletes and perhaps even great athletes. Will that also be illegal? This is only the tip of the iceberg. Thousands of difficult questions will arise as the technology for designing babies will become more and more powerful. Stem cell research is currently a divisive issue. Are we blocking the development of technologies that can save thousands of lives by severely limiting stem cell research?

The classic expression of this issue is in the stories and legends of a very learned sixteenth-century German doctor named Faust. According to legend, he sold his soul to the devil in exchange for knowledge and magical power. The first printed version of the legend was by Johann Spiess, which was later used by Christopher Marlow as the basis for his famous play, *Dr. Faustus* (1593). Spiess and Marlow presented Faust as a scoundrel who deserved damnation. Some of the other representations of Faust made him a heroic figure who strived for knowledge and power for good. This theme was continued by the most famous Faust legend of all, written by Johann Wolfgang von Goethe in both a poem and a play. In the beginning, Faust's bargain with the devil was for a moment of perfect happiness or contentment. The devil, however, could not deliver this to Faust. More elements are added to the story, including women's love. In the end, Faust finds a moment of perfect contentment and happiness in helping others and dies because of the wager. But Goethe gives the story a Hollywood ending and Faust, the hero, goes to heaven.

Many of the issues in the biotechnology debate are found in the Faust legends. Both are focused on the search for knowledge and its use. Is the knowledge-seeking Faust a scoundrel or a saint? Will his knowledge be used for selfish or altruistic purposes? Is mankind better off with it or without it? If powerful new biotechnologies are able to make our babies safe from diseases and defects, certainly we should use them. By the same logic, we should also use them when they can enhance our children's physical and mental powers. Continuing this line of reasoning, we should also use them to enhance our physical and mental powers as adults. Sooner or later, however, we must face the Faustian myth, which suggests that at some point mankind's reach for knowledge may transcend man's proper role in the universe and be devilish. But this question takes us into realms where I get quickly lost. How do I discuss mankind's proper role in the universe? The wise thing for me to do is not to try, but to leave it to you and the readings.

The other candidate for most promising technology does not involve moral dilemmas. Everyone hopes that the promise of super abundance by new production technologies comes true. All the strife in America today would be muted if these technological innovations created worldwide affluence. Let's hope.

YES ↵

President's Council on Bioethics

Beyond Therapy: Biotechnology and the Pursuit of Happiness

Chapter Five

Who has not wanted to escape the clutches of oppressive and punishing memories? Or to calm the burdensome feelings of anxiety, disappointment, and regret? Or to achieve a psychic state of pure and undivided pleasure and joy? The satisfaction of such desires seems inseparable from our happiness, which we pursue by right and with passion.

. . .

In these efforts at peace of mind, human beings have from time immemorial sought help from doctors and drugs. In a famous literary instance, Shakespeare's Macbeth entreats his doctor to free Lady Macbeth from the haunting memory of her own guilty acts:

> Macbeth. Canst thou not minister to a mind diseas'd,
> Pluck from the memory a rooted sorrow,
> Raze out the written troubles of the brain,
> And with some sweet oblivious antidote
> Cleanse the stuff'd bosom of that perilous stuff
> Which weighs upon the heart?
>
> Doctor. Therein the patient
> Must minister to himself.

Ministering to oneself, however, is easier said than done, and many people have found themselves unequal to the task without some outside assistance. For centuries, they have made use of external agents to drown their sorrows or lift their spirits.

. . .

The burgeoning field of neuroscience is providing new, more specific, and safer agents to help us combat all sorts of psychic distress. Soon, doctors may have just the "sweet oblivious antidote" that Macbeth so desired: drugs (such as beta-adrenergic blockers) that numb the emotional sting typically associated with our intensely bad memories.

. . .

To be sure, these agents—and their better versions, yet to come—are, for now at least, being developed not as means for drug-induced happiness but rather as agents for combating major depression or preventing post-traumatic stress disorder (PTSD). Yet once available for those purposes, they could also be used to ease the soul and enhance the mood of nearly anyone.

. . .

By using drugs to satisfy more easily the enduring aspirations to forget what torments us and approach the world with greater peace of mind, what deeper human aspirations might we occlude or frustrate? What qualities of character may become less necessary and, with diminished use, atrophy or become extinct, as we increasingly depend on drugs to cope with misfortune? How will we experience our incompleteness or understand our mortality as our ability grows to medically dissolve all sorts of anxiety? Will the availability of drug-induced conditions of ecstatic pleasure estrange us from the forms of pleasure that depend upon discipline and devotion? And, going beyond the implications for individuals, what kind of a society are we likely to have when the powers to control memory, mood, and mental life through drugs reach their full maturity and are widely used?

. . .

I. What Are "Happy Souls"?

. . .

Because the happiness we seek we seek for *ourselves*—for *our* self, not for someone else's, and for our *self* or embodied soul, not for our bodies as material stuff—our happiness is bound up with our personhood and our identity. We would not want to attain happiness (or any other object of our desires) if the condition for attaining it required that we become someone else, that we lose our identity in the process.

The importance of identity for happiness implies necessarily the importance of memory. If experiencing our happiness depends upon experiencing a stable identity, then our happiness depends also on our memory, on knowing who we are in relation to who we have been.

. . .

But if enfeebled memory can cripple identity, selectively altered memory can distort it. Changing the content

From the President's Council on Bioethics, October 2003.

of our memories or altering their emotional tonalities, however desirable to alleviate guilty or painful consciousness, could subtly reshape who we are, at least to ourselves. With altered memories we might feel better about ourselves, but it is not clear that the better-feeling "we" remains the same as before. Lady Macbeth, cured of her guilty torment, would remain the murderess she was, but not the conscience-stricken being even she could not help but be.

. . .

[A]n unchecked power to erase memories, brighten moods, and alter our emotional dispositions could imperil our capacity to form a strong and coherent personal identity. To the extent that our inner life ceases to reflect the ups and downs of daily existence and instead operates independently of them, we dissipate our identity, which is formed through engagement with others and through immersion in the mix of routine and unpredictable events that constitute our lives.

. . .

II. Memory and Happiness

. . .

Our identity or sense of self emerges, grows, and changes. Yet, despite all the changes, thanks to the integrating powers of memory, our identity also, remarkably, persists *as ours*.

. . .

We especially want our memories to be not simply a sequence of disconnected experiences, but a narrative that seems to contain some unfolding purpose, some larger point from beginning to end, some aspiration discovered, pursued, and at least partially fulfilled.

Memory is central to human flourishing, in other words, precisely because we pursue happiness in time, as time-bound beings. We have a past and a future as well as a present, and being happy through time requires that these be connected in a meaningful way. If we are to flourish as ourselves, we must do so without abandoning or forgetting who we are or once were. Yet because our lives are time-bound, our happiness is always incomplete—always not-yet and on-the-way, always here but slipping away, but also always possible again and in the future. Our happiest experiences can be revivified. And, as we reminisce from greater distance and with more experience, even our painful experiences can often acquire for us a meaning not in evidence when they occurred.

The place of memory in the pursuit of happiness also suggests something essential about human identity, a theme raised in various places and in different ways throughout this report: namely, our identities are formed both by what we do and by what we undergo or suffer. We actively choose paths and do deeds fit to be remembered.

But we also live through memorable experiences that we would never have chosen—experiences we often wish never happened at all. To some extent, these unchosen memories constrain us; though we may regret the shadows they cast over our pursuit of happiness, we cannot simply escape them while remaining who we really are. And yet, through the act of remembering—the act of discerning and giving meaning to the past as it really was—we can shape, to some degree, the meaning of our memories, both good and bad.

. . .

The capacity to alter or numb our remembrance of things past cuts to the heart of what it means to remember in a human way, and it is this biotechnical possibility that we focus on here. Deciding when or whether to use such biotechnical power will require that we think long and hard about what it means to remember truthfully, to live in time, and to seek happiness without losing or abandoning our identity. The rest of this discussion of "memory and happiness" is an invitation to such reflection.

A. Good Memories and Bad

. . .

[T]he significance of past events often becomes clear to us only after much rumination in light of later experience, and what seems trivial at one time may appear crucial at another. Neither can an excellent memory be one that remembers only what we *want* to remember: sometimes our most valuable memories are of events that were painful when they occurred, but that on reflection teach us vital lessons.

. . .

B. Biotechnology and Memory Alteration

It is a commonplace observation that, while some events fade quickly from the mind, emotionally intense experiences form memories that are peculiarly vivid and long-lasting. Not only do we recall such events long after they happened, but the recollection is often accompanied, in some measure, by a recurrence of the emotions aroused during the original experience.

. . .

When a person experiences especially shocking or violent events (such as a plane crash or bloody combat), the release of stress hormones may be so intense that the memory-encoding system is over-activated. The result is a consolidation of memories both far stronger and more persistent than normal and also more apt, upon recollection, to call forth the intense emotional response of the original experience. In such cases, each time the person relives the traumatic memory, a new flood of stress hormones is released, and the experience may be so emotionally intense as to be encoded as a new experience. With time, the memories grow more recurrent and intrusive, and the response—fear, helplessness, horror—more incapacitating. As we shall see, drugs that might prevent or alleviate the symptoms of PTSD are among the chief medical benefits that scientists expect from recent research in the neurochemistry of memory formation.

In fact, the discovery of hormonal regulation of memory formation was quickly followed up by clinical studies on human subjects demonstrating that memory of emotional experiences can be altered pharmacologically. In one particularly interesting series of experiments, Larry Cahill and his colleagues showed that injections of beta-blockers can, by inhibiting the action of stress hormones, suppress the memory-enhancing effects of strong emotional arousal.

. . .

[T]aking propranolol appears to have little or no effect on how we remember everyday or emotionally neutral information. But when taken at the time of highly emotional experiences, propranolol appears to suppress the normal memory-enhancing effects of emotional arousal—while leaving the immediate emotional response unaffected. These results suggested the possibility of using beta-blockers to help survivors of traumatic events to reduce their intrusive—and in some cases crippling—memories of those events.

. . .

"[A]lthough the pharmacology of memory alteration is a science still in its infancy, the significance of this potential new power—to separate the subjective experience of memory from the truth of the experience that is remembered—should not be underestimated. It surely returns us to the large ethical and anthropological questions with which we began—about memory's role in shaping personal identity and the character of human life, and about the meaning of remembering things that we would rather forget and of forgetting things that we perhaps ought to remember.

C. Memory-Blunting: Ethical Analysis

If we had the power, by promptly taking a memory-altering drug, to dull the emotional impact of what could become very painful memories, when might we be tempted to use it? And for what reasons should we yield to or resist the temptation?

At first glance, such a drug would seem ideally suited for the prevention of PTSD, the complex of debilitating symptoms that sometimes afflict those who have experienced severe trauma. These symptoms—which include persistent re-experiencing of the traumatic event and avoidance of every person, place, or thing that might stimulate the horrid memory's return[1]—can so burden mental life as to make normal everyday living extremely difficult, if not impossible.[2] For those suffering these disturbing symptoms, a drug that could separate a painful

memory from its powerful emotional component would appear very welcome indeed.

Yet the prospect of preventing (even) PTSD with beta-blockers or other memory-blunting agents seems to be, for several reasons, problematic. First of all, the drugs in question appear to be effective only when administered during or shortly after a traumatic event—and thus well before any symptoms of PTSD would be manifested. How then could we make, and make on the spot, the *prospective* judgment that a particular event is sufficiently terrible to warrant preemptive memory-blunting? Second, how shall we judge *which* participants in the event merit such treatment? After all, not everyone who suffers through painful experiences is destined to have pathological memory effects. Should the drugs in question be given to everyone or only to those with an observed susceptibility to PTSD, and, if the latter, how will we know who these are? Finally, in some cases merely witnessing a disturbing event (for example, a murder, rape, or terrorist attack) is sufficient to cause PTSD-like symptoms long afterwards. Should we then, as soon as disaster strikes, consider giving memory-altering drugs to all the witnesses, in addition to those directly involved?

. . .

If the apparent powers of memory-blunting drugs are confirmed, some might be inclined to prescribe them liberally to all who are involved in a sufficiently terrible event. After all, even those not destined to come down with full-blown PTSD are likely to suffer painful recurrent memories of an airplane crash, an incident of terrorism, or a violent combat operation. In the aftermath of such shocking incidents, why not give everyone the chance to remember these events without the added burden of painful emotions? This line of reasoning might, in fact, tempt us to give beta-blockers liberally to soldiers on the eve of combat, to emergency workers en route to a disaster site, or even to individuals requesting prophylaxis against the shame or guilt they might incur from future misdeeds—in general, to anyone facing an experience that is likely to leave lasting intrusive memories.

Yet on further reflection it seems clear that not every intrusive memory is a suitable candidate for prospective pharmacological blunting. As Daniel Schacter has observed, "attempts to avoid traumatic memories often backfire."

Intrusive memories need to be acknowledged, confronted, and worked through, in order to set them to rest for the long term. Unwelcome memories of trauma are symptoms of a disrupted psyche that requires attention before it can resume healthy functioning. Beta-blockers might make it easier for trauma survivors to face and incorporate traumatic recollections, and in that sense could facilitate long-term adaptation. Yet it is also possible that beta-blockers would work against the normal process of recovery: traumatic memories would not spring to mind with the kind of psychological force that demands attention and perhaps intervention. Prescription of beta-blockers could bring about an effective trade-off between short-term reductions in the sting of traumatic memories and long-term increases in persistence of related symptoms of a trauma that has not been adequately confronted.[3]

The point can be generalized: in the immediate aftermath of a painful experience, we simply cannot know either the full meaning of the experience in question or the ultimate character and future prospects of the individual who experiences it. We cannot know how this experience will change this person at this time and over time. Will he be cursed forever by unbearable memories that, in retrospect, clearly should have been blunted medically? Or will he succeed, over time, in "redeeming" those painful memories by actively integrating them into the narrative of his life? By "rewriting" memories pharmacologically we might succeed in easing real suffering at the risk of falsifying our perception of the world and undermining our true identity.

Finally, the decision whether or not to use memory-blunting drugs must be made in the absence of clearly diagnosable disease. The drug must be taken right after a traumatic experience has occurred, and thus before the different ways that different individuals handle the same experience has become clear. In some cases, these interventions will turn out to have been preventive medicine, intervening to ward off the onset of PTSD before it arrives—though it is worth noting that we would lack even post hoc knowledge of whether any particular now-unaffected individual, in the absence of using the drug, would have become symptomatic.[4] In other cases, the interventions would not be medicine at all: altering the memory of individuals who could have lived well, even with severely painful memories, without pharmacologically dulling the pain. Worse, in still other cases, the use of such drugs would inoculate individuals in advance against the psychic pain that *should* accompany their commission of cruel, brutal, or shameful deeds. But in all cases, from the defensible to the dubious, the use of such powers changes the character of human memory, by intervening directly in the way individuals "encode," and thus the way they understand, the happenings of their own lives and the realities of the world around them.

. . .

1. Remembering Fitly and Truly.

Altering the formation of emotionally powerful memories risks severing what we remember from how we remember it and distorting the link between our perception of significant human events and the significance of the events themselves. It risks, in a word, falsifying our perception and understanding of the world. It risks making shameful acts seem less shameful, or terrible acts less terrible, than they really are.

Imagine the experience of a person who witnesses a shocking murder. Fearing that he will be haunted by images of this event, he immediately takes propranolol (or its more potent successor) to render his memory of the murder less painful and intrusive. Thanks to the drug, his memory of the murder gets encoded as a garden-variety, emotionally neutral experience. But in manipulating his memory in this way, he risks coming to think about the murder as more tolerable than it really is, as an event that should not sting those who witness it. For our opinions about the meaning of our experiences are shaped partly by the feelings evoked when we remember them. If, psychologically, the murder is transformed into an event our witness can recall without pain—or without *any* particular emotion—perhaps its moral significance will also fade from consciousness. If so, he would in a sense have ceased to be a genuine witness of the murder. When asked about it, he might say, "Yes, I was there. But it wasn't so terrible."

This points us to a deeper set of questions about bad memories: Would dulling our memory of terrible things make us too comfortable with the world, unmoved by suffering, wrongdoing, or cruelty? Does not the experience of hard truths—of the unchosen, the inexplicable, the tragic—remind us that we can never be fully at home in the world, especially if we are to take seriously the reality of human evil? Further, by blunting our experience and awareness of shameful, fearful, and hateful things, might we not also risk deadening our response to what is admirable, inspiring, and lovable? Can we become numb to life's sharpest sorrows without also becoming numb to its greatest joys?

. . .

There seems to be little doubt that some bitter memories are so painful and intrusive as to ruin the possibility for normal experience of much of life and the world. In such cases the impulse to relieve a crushing burden and restore lost innocence is fully understandable: If there are some things that it is better never to have experienced at all—things we would avoid if we possibly could—why not erase them from the memory of those unfortunate enough to have suffered them? If there are some things it is better never to have known or seen, why not use our power over memory to restore a witness's shattered peace of mind? There is great force in this argument, perhaps especially in cases where children lose prematurely that innocence that is rightfully theirs.

And yet, there may be a great cost to acting compassionately for those who suffer bad memories, if we do so by compromising the truthfulness of how they remember. We risk having them live falsely in order simply to cope, to survive by whatever means possible.

. . .

2. The Obligation to Remember.

Having truthful memories is not simply a personal matter. Strange to say, our own memory is not merely our own; it is part of the fabric of the society in which we live. Consider the case of a person who has suffered or witnessed atrocities that occasion unbearable memories: for example, those with first-hand experience of the Holocaust. The life of that individual might well be served by dulling such bitter memories,[5] but such a humanitarian intervention, if widely practiced, would seem deeply troubling: Would the community as a whole—

would the human race—be served by such a mass numbing of this terrible but indispensable memory? Do those who suffer evil have a duty to remember and bear witness, lest we all forget the very horrors that haunt them?

. . .

Surely, we cannot and should not force those who live through great trauma to endure its painful memory *for the benefit of the rest of us.* But as a community, there are certain events that we have an obligation to remember—an obligation that falls disproportionately, one might even say unfairly, on those who experience such events most directly.[6] What kind of people would we be if we did not "want" to remember the Holocaust, if we sought to make the anguish it caused simply go away? And yet, what kind of people are we, especially those who face such horrors firsthand, that we can endure such awful memories?

The answer, in part, is that those who suffer terrible things cannot or should not have to endure their own bad memories alone. If, as a people, we have an obligation to remember certain terrible events truthfully, surely we ought to help those who suffered through those events to come to terms with their worst memories. Of course, one might see the new biotechnical powers, developed precisely to ease the psychic pain of bad memories, as the mark of such solidarity: perhaps it is our new way of meeting the obligation to aid those who remember the hardest things, those who bear witness to us and for us. But such solidarity may, in the end, prove false: for it exempts us from the duty to suffer-with (literally, to feel *com*-passion for) those who remember; it does not demand that we preserve the truth of their memories; it attempts instead to make the problem go away, and with it the truth of the experience in question.

4. The Soul of Memory, The Remembering Soul.

. . .

[W]e might often be tempted to sacrifice the accuracy of our memories for the sake of easing our pain or expanding our control over our own psychic lives. But doing so means, ultimately, severing ourselves from reality and leaving our own identity behind; it risks making us false, small, or capable of great illusions, and thus capable of great decadence or great evil, or perhaps simply willing to accept a phony contentment. We might be tempted to alter our memories to preserve an open future—to live the life we wanted to live before a particular experience happened to us. But in another sense, such interventions assume that our own future is not open—that we cannot and could never redeem the unwanted memory over time, that we cannot and could never integrate the remembered experience with our own truthful pursuit of happiness.

. . .

To have only happy memories would be a blessing—and a curse. Nothing would trouble us, but we would probably be shallow people, never falling to the depths of despair

because we have little interest in the heights of human happiness or in the complicated lives of those around us. In the end, to have only happy memories is not to be happy in a truly human way. It is simply to be free of misery—an understandable desire given the many troubles of life, but a low aspiration for those who seek a truly human happiness.

Footnotes

1. There is no definitive diagnostic criterion for PTSD, but the core symptoms are thought to include persistent re-experiencing of the traumatic event, avoidance of associated stimuli, and hyperarousal. See *Diagnostic and Statistical Manual of Mental Disorders, Fourth Edition,* text revision, Washington, D.C.: American Psychiatric Association, 2000, pp. 463–486.

2. These symptoms are observed especially among combat veterans; indeed, PTSD is the modern name for what used to be called "shell shock" or "combat neurosis." Among veterans, PTSD is frequently associated with recurrent nightmares, substance abuse, and delusional outbursts of violence. There is controversy about the prevalence of PTSD, with some studies finding that up to 8 percent of adult Americans have suffered the disorder, as well as a third of all veterans of the Vietnam War. See Kessler, R. C., et al., "Post-Traumatic Stress Disorder in the National Comorbidity Survey," *Archives of General Psychiatry* 52(12): 1048–1060, 1995; Kulka, R. A., et al., *Trauma and the Vietnam War Generation: Report of Findings from the National Vietnam Veterans Readjustment Study,* New York: Brunner/Mazel, 1990.

3. Schacter, D., *The Seven Sins of Memory: How the Mind Forgets and Remembers,* New York: Houghton Mifflin, 2001, p. 183.

4. There is already ongoing controversy about excessive diagnosis of PTSD. Many psychotherapists believe that a patient's psychic troubles are generally based on some earlier (now repressed) traumatic experience which must be unearthed and dealt with if relief is to be found. True PTSD is, however, generally transient, and the search for treatment is directed against the symptoms of its initial (worst) phase—the sleeplessness, the nightmares, the excessive jitteriness.

5. Of course, many Holocaust survivors managed, without pharmacological assistance, to live fulfilling lives while never forgetting what they lived through. At the same time, many survivors would almost certainly have benefited from pharmacological treatment.

6. For a discussion of memory-altering drugs and the meaning of "bearing witness," see the essay by Cohen, E., "Our Psychotropic Memory," *SEED,* no. 8, Fall 2003, p. 42.

President's Council on Bioethics (PCBE) was created in 2001 to advise the Bush administration on bioethics.

Neil Gershenfeld

→ **NO**

How to Make Almost Anything

The Digital Fabrication Revolution

A new digital revolution is coming, this time in fabrication. It draws on the same insights that led to the earlier digitizations of communication and computation, but now what is being programmed is the physical world rather than the virtual one. Digital fabrication will allow individuals to design and produce tangible objects on demand, wherever and whenever they need them. Widespread access to these technologies will challenge traditional models of business, aid, and education.

. . .

Today, numerically controlled machines touch almost every commercial product, whether directly (producing everything from laptop cases to jet engines) or indirectly (producing the tools that mold and stamp mass-produced goods). And yet all these modern descendants of the first numerically controlled machine tool share its original limitation: they can cut, but they cannot reach internal structures. This means, for example, that the axle of a wheel must be manufactured separately from the bearing it passes through.

In the 1980s, however, computer-controlled fabrication processes that added rather than removed material (called additive manufacturing) came on the market. Thanks to 3-D printing, a bearing and an axle could be built by the same machine at the same time. A range of 3-D printing processes are now available, including thermally fusing plastic filaments, using ultraviolet light to cross-link polymer resins, depositing adhesive droplets to bind a powder, cutting and laminating sheets of paper, and shining a laser beam to fuse metal particles. Businesses already use 3-D printers to model products before producing them, a process referred to as rapid prototyping. Companies also rely on the technology to make objects with complex shapes, such as jewelry and medical implants. Research groups have even used 3-D printers to build structures out of cells with the goal of printing living organs.

. . .

Think Globally, Fabricate Locally

I first appreciated the parallel between personal computing and personal fabrication when I taught a class called "How to Make (almost) Anything" at MIT's Center for Bits and Atoms, which I direct. CBA, which opened in 2001 with funding from the National Science Foundation, was developed to study the boundary between computer science and physical science. It runs a facility that is equipped to make and measure things that are as small as atoms or as large as buildings.

We designed the class to teach a small group of research students how to use CBA's tools but were overwhelmed by the demand from students who just wanted to make things. Each student later completed a semester-long project to integrate the skills they had learned. One made an alarm clock that the groggy owner would have to wrestle with to prove that he or she was awake. Another made a dress fitted with sensors and motorized spine-like structures that could defend the wearer's personal space. The students were answering a question that I had not asked: What is digital fabrication good for? As it turns out, the "killer app" in digital fabrication, as in computing, is personalization, producing products for a market of one person.

Inspired by the success of that first class, in 2003, CBA began an outreach project with support from the National Science Foundation. Rather than just describe our work, we thought it would be more interesting to provide the tools. We assembled a kit of about $50,000 worth of equipment (including a computer-controlled laser, a 3-D printer, and large and small computer-controlled milling machines) and about $20,000 worth of materials (including components for molding and casting parts and producing electronics). All the tools were connected by custom software. These became known as "fab labs" (for "fabrication labs" or "fabulous labs"). Their cost is comparable to that of a minicomputer, and we have found that they are used in the same way: to develop new uses and new users for the machines.

Starting in December of 2003, a CBA team led by Sherry Lassiter, a colleague of mine, set up the first fab lab at the South End Technology Center, in inner-city Boston. SETC is run by Mel King, an activist who has pioneered the introduction of new technologies to urban communities, from video production to Internet access. For him, digital fabrication machines were a natural next step. For all the differences between the MIT campus and the South End, the responses at both places were equally enthusiastic. A group of girls from the area used the tools in the lab to put on a high-tech street-corner craft sale, simultaneously having fun, expressing themselves, learning technical skills, and earning income. Some of the home-schooled children in the neighborhood who have used the fab lab for hands-on training have since gone on to careers in technology.

The SETC fab lab was all we had planned for the outreach project. But thanks to interest from a Ghanaian community around SETC, in 2004, CBA, with National Science Foundation support and help from a local team, set up a second fab lab in the town of Sekondi-Takoradi, on Ghana's coast. Since then, fab labs have been installed everywhere from South Africa to Norway, from downtown Detroit to rural India. In the past few years, the total number has doubled about every 18 months, with over 100 in operation today and that many more being planned. These labs form part of a larger "maker movement" of high-tech do-it-yourselfers, who are democratizing access to the modern means to make things.

Local demand has pulled fab labs worldwide. Although there is a wide range of sites and funding models, all the labs share the same core capabilities. That allows projects to be shared and people to travel among the labs. Providing Internet access has been a goal of many fab labs. From the Boston lab, a project was started to make antennas, radios, and terminals for wireless networks. The design was refined at a fab lab in Norway, was tested at one in South Africa, was deployed from one in Afghanistan, and is now running on a self-sustaining commercial basis in Kenya. None of these sites had the critical mass of knowledge to design and produce the networks on its own. But by sharing design files and producing the components locally, they could all do so together. The ability to send data across the world and then locally produce products on demand has revolutionary implications for industry.

. . .

Why might one want to own a digital fabrication machine? Personal fabrication tools have been considered toys, because the incremental cost of mass production will always be lower than for one-off goods. A similar charge was leveled against personal computers. Ken Olsen, founder and CEO of the minicomputer-maker Digital Equipment Corporation, famously said in 1977 that "there is no reason for any individual to have a computer in his home." His company is now defunct. You most likely own a personal computer. It isn't there for inventory and payroll; it is for doing what makes you yourself: listening to music, talking to friends, shopping. Likewise, the goal of personal fabrication is not to make what you can buy in stores but to make what you cannot buy. Consider shopping at IKEA. The furniture giant divines global demand for furniture and then produces and ships items to its big-box stores. For just thousands of dollars, individuals can already purchase the kit for a large-format computer-controlled milling machine that can make all the parts in

an IKEA flat-pack box. If having the machine saved just ten IKEA purchases, its expense could be recouped. Even better, each item produced by the machine would be customized to fit the customer's preference. And rather than employing people in remote factories, making furniture this way is a local affair.

This last observation inspired the Fab City project, which is led by Barcelona's chief architect, Vicente Guallart. Barcelona, like the rest of Spain, has a youth unemployment rate of over 50 percent. An entire generation there has few prospects for getting jobs and leaving home. Rather than purchasing products produced far away, the city, with Guallart, is deploying fab labs in every district as part of the civic infrastructure. The goal is for the city to be globally connected for knowledge but self-sufficient for what it consumes.

The digital fabrication tools available today are not in their final form. But rather than wait, programs like Barcelona's are building the capacity to use them as they are being developed.

Bits and Atoms

. . .

The digitization of material is not a new idea. It is four billion years old, going back to the evolutionary age of the ribosome, the protein that makes proteins. Humans are full of molecular machinery, from the motors that move our muscles to the sensors in our eyes. The ribosome builds all that machinery out of a microscopic version of LEGO pieces, amino acids, of which there are 22 different kinds. The sequence for assembling the amino acids is stored in DNA and is sent to the ribosome in another protein called messenger RNA. The code does not just describe the protein to be manufactured; it becomes the new protein.

Labs like mine are now developing 3-D assemblers (rather than printers) that can build structures in the same way as the ribosome. The assemblers will be able to both add and remove parts from a discrete set. One of the assemblers we are developing works with components that are a bit bigger than amino acids, cluster of atoms about ten nanometers long (an amino acid is around one nanometer long). These can have properties that amino acids cannot, such as being good electrical conductors or magnets. The goal is to use the nanoassembler to build nanostructures, such as 3-D integrated circuits. Another assembler we are developing uses parts on the scale of microns to millimeters. We would like this machine to make the electronic circuit boards that the 3-D integrated circuits go on. Yet another assembler we are developing uses parts on the scale of centimeters, to make larger structures, such as aircraft components and even whole aircraft that will be lighter, stronger, and more capable than today's planes—think a jumbo jet that can flap its wings.

A key difference between existing 3-D printers and these assemblers is that the assemblers will be able to create complete functional systems in a single process. They will be able to integrate fixed and moving mechanical structures, sensors and actuators, and electronics. Even more important is what the assemblers don't create: trash. Trash is a concept that applies only to materials that don't contain enough information to be reusable. All the matter on the forest floor is recycled again and again. Likewise, a product assembled from digital materials need not be thrown out when it becomes obsolete. It can simply be disassembled and the parts reconstructed into something new.

The most interesting thing that an assembler can assemble is itself. For now, they are being made out of the same kinds of components as are used in rapid prototyping machines. Eventually, however, the goal is for them to be able to make all their own parts. The motivation is practical. The biggest challenge to building new fab labs around the world has not been generating interest, or teaching people how to use them, or even cost; it has been the logistics. Bureaucracy, incompetent or corrupt border controls, and the inability of supply chains to meet demand have hampered our efforts to ship the machines around the world. When we are ready to ship assemblers, it will be much easier to mail digital material components in bulk and then e-mail the design codes to a fab lab so that one assembler can make another.

. . .

Planning Innovation

Communities should not fear or ignore digital fabrication. Better ways to build things can help build better communities. A fab lab in Detroit, for example, which is run by the entrepreneur Blair Evans, offers programs for at-risk youth as a social service. It empowers them to design and build things based on their own ideas.

It is possible to tap into the benefits of digital fabrication in several ways. One is top down. In 2005, South Africa launched a national network of fab labs to encourage innovation through its National Advanced Manufacturing Technology Strategy. In the United States, Representative Bill Foster (D-Ill.) proposed legislation, the National Fab Lab Network Act of 2010, to create a national lab linking local fab labs. The existing national laboratory system houses billion-dollar facilities but struggles to directly impact the communities around them. Foster's bill proposes a system that would instead bring the labs to the communities.

Another approach is bottom up. Many of the existing fab lab sites, such as the one in Detroit, began as informal organizations to address unmet local needs. These have joined regional programs. These regional programs, such as the United States Fab Lab Network and FabLab.nl, in Belgium, Luxembourg, and the Netherlands, take on tasks that are too big for an individual lab, such as supporting the launch of new ones. The regional programs, in turn, are linking together through the international Fab Foundation, which will provide support for global challenges, such as sourcing specialized materials around the world.

To keep up with what people are learning in the labs, the fab lab network has launched the Fab Academy. Children working in remote fab labs have progressed so far beyond any local educational opportunities that they would have to travel far away to an advanced institution to continue their studies. To prevent such brain drains, the Fab Academy has linked local labs together into a global campus. Along with access to tools, students who go to these labs are surrounded by peers to learn from and have local mentors to guide them. They participate in interactive global video lectures and share projects and instructional materials online.

. . .

Digital fabrication consists of much more than 3-D printing. It is an evolving suite of capabilities to turn data into things and things into data. Many years of research remain to complete this vision, but the revolution is already well under way. The collective challenge is to answer the central question it poses: How will we live, learn, work, and play when anyone can make anything, anywhere?

Neil Gershenfeld is a professor at the Massachusetts Institute of Technology and director of MIT's Center for Bits and Atoms and has authored several books including *Fab, The Coming Revolution on Your Desktop—From Personal Computers to Personal Fabrication* (2005).

EXPLORING THE ISSUE

Will Biotechnology Have the Greatest Impact on the Next Half Century?

Critical Thinking and Reflection

1. What are the potential benefits of biotechnologies for enhancing humans?
2. If babies can be genetically engineered to be relatively disease-free or resistant and also intellectually and physically improved, why not do it?
3. What moral values would oppose gains from safe genetic engineering?
4. Who would make the decisions about bioengineering? Should it be left to the parents for bioengineering babies? What role should society via government have in these decisions? Should religions have a say or even a final say?
5. Enhancement drugs are regulated in sports. Should they be regulated outside of sports if they are not harmful?
6. Do you have high hopes about the potential of new digital technologies to produce abundantly and generate worldwide affluence?
7. Will digital production require special regulations?

Is There Common Ground?

The most often cited arguments in favor of using biotechnologies for altering and enhancing humans are the benefits of protecting children from diseases, preventing handicaps and deficiencies, and enhancing physical and mental abilities. The main arguments against using biotechnology include the moral arguments against playing God and too mightily interfering in nature. But what about the possibility of making people more moral in the sense of more caring, compassionate, cooperative, trusting, and helpful and less uncooperative, unsympathetic, and easily irritated? A number of scientists believe that these characteristics are fairly closely related to genes, so the moral improvement of the human race could be assisted by bioengineering. Furthermore, chemical treatments could help adults become less selfish and aggressive and become more altruistic and cooperative. In sum, bioengineering could produce many benefits, but society should proceed cautiously because risks and unintended consequences are associated with these life-changing technologies.

There is more agreement on the moral value of digital production. Everyone is for it. The only debate is on how successful it will be. Some are quite skeptical that it will accomplish much. It has been around for three decades without much impact. Its supporters point out how rapidly new innovations are overcoming past problems and think that the future is very bright.

Create Central

www.mhhe.com/createcentral

Additional Resources

The moral argument can be used both for or against biotechnologies. In some sense, this is an old debate, as the Faust legend indicates. Nevertheless, it is only recently that science has brought us to the doorstep of the bioengineering of humans so it is time to revive the Faustian debate. Two books from the mid-1980s serve as classics in this field: Jeremy Rivkin and Nicanor Perlas warn against bioengineering in *Algeny* (Penguin Books, 1984). They argue that biotechnology's destructive power far exceeds its potential benefits. Jonathan Glover reverses the weights for benefits and costs and champions bioengineering in *What Sort of People Should There Be?* (Penguin Books, 1984).

Other works that are opposed to bioengineering include: Marcus Wohlsen, *Biopunk: DIY Scientists Hack the Software of Life* (Current, 2011); Craig Holdrege, *Beyond Biotechnology: The Barren Promise of Genetic Engineering* (University of Kentucky Press, 2010); Jeremy Rivkin, *The Biotech Century* (Tarcher/Putnam, 1998); Francis Fukuyama, *Our Posthuman Future* (Farrar, Strauss, and Giroux, 2002); and Bill McKibben, *Enough* (Henry Holt, 2003).

More positive views of genetic engineering are found in the following: Eric S. Grace, *Biotechnology Unzipped: Promises and Realities* (Joseph Henry Press, 2006); Ramex Naam, *More Than Human: Embracing the Promise of Biological Enhancement* (Broadway Books, 2005); Gregory Stock, *Redesigning Humans: Our Inevitable Genetic Future* (Houghton Mifflin Harcourt, 2002); Allan Buchanan et al., *From Chance to Choice: Genetics and Justice* (Cambridge University Press, 2000); and Emirates Center for Strategic Studies and Research, *Biotechnology and the Future of Society:*

Challenges and Opportunities (Emirates Center for Strategic Studies and Research, 2004).

For works that present multiple views, see: Allen E. Buchanan, *Better Than Human: The Promise and Perils of Enhancing Ourselves* (Oxford University Press, 2011); Robert H. Carlson, *Biology Is Technology: The Promise, Peril, and New Business of Engineering Life* (Harvard University Press, 2010); Linda L. McCabe, *DNA: Promise and Peril* (University of California Press, 2008); Bernard E. Rollin, *Science and Ethics* (Cambridge University Press, 2006); Lori P. Knowles and Gregory E. Kaebnick, eds., *Reprogenetics: Law, Policy, and Ethical Issues* (Johns Hopkins University Press, 2007); Rose M. Morgan, *The Genetics Revolution: History, Fears, and Future of a Life-Altering Science* (Greenwood Press, 2006); Pete Shanks, *Human Genetic Engineering: A Guide for Activists, Skeptics, and the Very Perplexed* (Nation Books, 2005); Gerald Magill, ed., *Genetics and Ethics: An Interdisciplinary Study* (Saint Louis University Press, 2004); Audrey R. Chapman and Mark S. Frankel, eds., *Designing Our Descendants: The Promises and Perils of Genetic Modifications* (Johns Hopkins University Press, 2003); Scott Gilbert et al., *Bioethics and the New Embryology: Springboards for Debate* (W. H. Freeman, 2005); Howard W. Baillie and Timothy K. Casey, eds., *Is Human Nature Obsolete? Genetics, Bioengineering, and the Future of the Human Condition* (MIT Press, 2005); and Rose M. Morgan, *The Genetic Revolution: History, Fears, and Future of a Life-Altering Science* (Greenwood Press, 2006).

For discussions of human cloning, see: Martha C. Nussbaum and Cass R. Sunstein, eds., *Clones and Clones: Facts and Fantasies about Human Cloning* (W. W. Norton, 1998); and President's Council on Bioethics, *Human Cloning and Human Dignity: An Ethical Inquiry* (Government Printing Office, 2002).

Obviously, this issue is at rock bottom an ethical issue and a confusing one at that. Representatives of different ethical positions might be on either side. Theological viewpoints, however, tend to advise against tinkering with human nature.

The following books discuss the ethical issues from a variety of points of views: Sheila Jasanoff, ed., *Reframing Rights: Bioconstitutionalism in the Genetic Age* (MIT Press, 2011); Lawrence E. Johnson, *A Life-Centered Approach to Biocentric Ethics* (Cambridge University Press, 2011); Neil Messer, *Respecting Life: Theology and Bioethics* (SCM Press, 2011); Richard Scherlock, *Nature's End: The Theological Meaning of the New Genetics* (ISI Books, 2010); Alexandra Plows, *Debating Human Genetics: Contemporary Issues in Public Policy and Ethics* (Routledge, 2011); and Ronald Michael Green, *Babies by Design: The Ethics of Genetic Choice* (Yale University Press, 2007).

The digital production side of the discussion has a minuscule literature that gives serious attention to its prospects. Most articles on 3D printing are journalistic or online articles. Three major works are: Neil A. Gershenfeld, *Fab: The Coming Revolution on your Desktop—From Personal Computers to Personal Fabrication* (Basic Books, 2005); William E. Halal, *Technology's Promise: Expert Knowledge on the Transformation of Business and Society* (Palgrave Macmillan, 2008); and Rutger van Santen, Djan Khoe, and Bram Vermeer, *2030: Technology That Will Change the World* (Oxford University Press, 2010).

Internet References . . .

Sociology—Study Sociology Online

http://edu.learnsoc.org/

Sociology Web Resources

www.mhhe.com/socscience/sociology/resources/index.htm

Sociosite

www.topsite.com/goto/sociosite.net

Socioweb

www.topsite.com/goto/socioweb.com

Unit 5

UNIT

Crime and Social Control

*A*ll societies label certain hurtful actions as crimes and punish those who commit them. Other harmful actions, however, are not defined as crimes, and the perpetrators are not punished. Today the definition of crime and the appropriate treatment of criminals is widely debated.

Selected, Edited, and with Issue Framing Material by:
Kurt Finsterbusch, *University of Maryland, College Park*

ISSUE

Is the Crime Rate the Best Measure for Understanding and Treating Crime?

YES: **The Economist**, from "The Curious Case of the Fall in Crime," *The Economist* (July 20, 2013)

NO: **Jacek Czabański**, from *Estimates of Cost of Crime: History, Methodologies, and Implications* (Springer, 2008)

Learning Outcomes

After reading this issue, you will be able to:

- Know that the crime rate has noticeably declined in America and the rest of the developed world since the 1970s and the recession has not interrupted the decline.
- Identify some of the common theories about what contributes to crime which are contradicted by these data.
- Identify some of the reasons for this decline.
- Relate crime rate data to recommendations for changes in criminal justice policies such as rehabilitation and new policing policies.
- Understand the many costs of various crimes including law enforcement, security costs, health and death costs, fear and deprivation, lost work time, and the value of stolen goods.
- Know that the costs of crime exceed $1 trillion a year and that most of the public is largely unaware of many of these costs.
- Know the relative costs in all of its dimensions of street crime versus white-collar crime and make a judgment of which set of crimes is worse according to your values.
- Analyze where guilt lies when decisions made in board rooms end up causing deaths through a long causal chain.

ISSUE SUMMARY

YES: *The Economist* provides considerable data showing that the crime rate has fallen significantly in America and the rest of the developed world since the 1970s, contrary to public opinion. These data refute a number of cherished social theories such as the decline of marriage is a major cause of crime. They are useful in the treatment of crime and criminals. They also should be used to change the way criminals are treated and how the police operate.

NO: Jacek Czabański documents the enormous burden that crime imposes on societies. His calculations include pain, suffering, lost property, health consequences, the criminal justice system, and the costs of avoiding crime. Cost figures should guide the treatment and responses to crime.

The word *crime* entered the English language (from the Old French) around AD 1250, when it was identified with "sinfulness." Later, the meaning of the word was modified: Crime became the kind of sinfulness that was rightly punishable by law. Even medieval writers, who did not distinguish very sharply between church and state, recognized that there were some sins for which punishment was best left to God; the laws should punish only those that cause harm to the community. Of course, their concept of harm was a very broad one, embracing such offenses as witchcraft and blasphemy. Modern jurists, even those who deplore such practices, would say that the state has no business punishing the perpetrators of these types of offenses.

What, then, should the laws punish? The answer depends in part on our notion of harm. We usually limit the term to the kind of harm that is tangible and obvious: taking a life, causing bodily injury or psychological trauma, and destroying or taking property. For most

Americans today, particularly those who live in cities, the word *crime* is practically synonymous with street crime. Anyone who has ever been robbed or beaten by street criminals will never forget the experience. The harm that these criminals cause is tangible, and the connection between the harm and the perpetrator is very direct.

But suppose the connection is not so direct. Suppose, for example, that A hires B to shoot C. Is that any less a crime? B is the actual shooter, but is A any less guilty? Of course not, we say; he may even be more guilty because he is the ultimate mover behind the crime. A would be guilty even if the chain of command were much longer, involving A's orders to B, and B's to C, then on to D, E, and F to kill G. Organized crime kingpins go to jail even when they are far removed from the people who carry out their orders. High officials of the Nixon administration, even though they were not directly involved in the burglary attempt at the Democratic National Committee headquarters at the Watergate Hotel complex in 1972, were imprisoned.

This brings us to the topic of white-collar crime. The burglars at the Watergate Hotel were acting on orders that trickled down from the highest reaches of political power in the United States. Other white-collar criminals are as varied as the occupations from which they come. They include stock brokers who make millions through insider trading, as Ivan Boesky did; members of Congress who take payoffs; and people who cheat on their income taxes, like hotel owner and billionaire Leona Helmsley. Some, like Helmsley, get stiff prison sentences when convicted, although many others (like most of the officials in the Watergate scandal) do little or no time in prison. Do they deserve stiffer punishment, or are their crimes less harmful than the crimes of street criminals?

Although white-collar criminals do not directly cause physical harm or relieve people of their wallets, they can still end up doing considerable harm. The harm done by Nixon's aides threatened the integrity of the U.S. electoral system. Every embezzler, corrupt politician, and tax cheat exacts a toll on our society. Individuals can be hurt in more tangible ways by decisions made in corporate boardrooms: Auto executives, for example, have approved design features that have caused fatalities. Managers of chemical companies have allowed practices that have polluted the environment with cancer-causing agents. And heads of corporations have presided over industries wherein workers have been needlessly killed or maimed.

Whether these decisions should be considered crimes is debatable. A crime must always involve "malicious intent," or what the legal system calls *mens rea*. This certainly applies to street crime—the mugger obviously has sinister designs—but does it apply to every decision made in a boardroom that ends up causing harm? And does that harm match or exceed the harm caused by street criminals?

The above deals with the conceptualization of crime. The readings below deal mainly with the facts of crime. *The Economist* reports the facts about the significant decline of crime since the 1970s throughout the developed world and uses them to discredit common notions about the causes of crime. Then he uses them to recommend many changes in the treatment of criminals and in police practices. Jacek Czabański presents a lot of data on the costs of crime which show how very expensive it is when all costs are taken into account.

YES ←   The Economist

The Curious Case of the Fall in Crime

In the 1990s John Dilulio, a conservative American academic, argued that a new breed of "superpredators", "kids that have absolutely no respect for human life and no sense of the future", would terrorise Americans almost indefinitely. He was not alone. Experts were convinced that crime would keep rising. Law-abiding citizens would retreat to gated communities, patrolled by security guards. Politicians and police chiefs could do little except bluster and try to fiddle the statistics.

Mr Dilulio later recanted and it is clear that the pessimists were wrong. Even as he wrote, America's crime wave was breaking. Its cities have become vastly safer, and the rest of the developed world has followed. From Japan to Estonia, property and people are now safer than at almost any time since the 1970s. Confounding expectations, the recession has not interrupted the downward trend. Even as America furiously debates the shooting of Trayvon Martin, new data show that the homicide rate for young Americans is at a 30-year low.

Some crimes have all but died out. Last year there were just 69 armed robberies of banks, building societies and post offices in England and Wales, compared with 500 a year in the 1990s. In 1990 some 147,000 cars were stolen in New York. Last year fewer than 10,000 were. In the Netherlands and Switzerland street dealers and hustlers have been driven out of city centres; addicts there are now elderly men, often alcoholics, living in state hostels. In countries such as Lithuania and Poland the gangsters who trafficked people and drugs in the 1990s have moved into less violent activities such as fraud.

The Receding Tide

Cherished social theories have been discarded. Conservatives who insisted that the decline of the traditional nuclear family and growing ethnic diversity would unleash an unstoppable crime wave have been proved wrong. Young people are increasingly likely to have been brought up by one parent and to have played a lot of computer games. Yet they are far better behaved than previous generations. Left-wingers who argued that crime could never be curbed unless inequality was reduced look just as silly.

There is no single cause of the decline; rather, several have coincided. Western societies are growing older, and most crimes are committed by young men. Policing has improved greatly in recent decades, especially in big cities such as New York and London, with forces using computers to analyse the incidence of crime; in some parts of Manhattan this helped to reduce the robbery rate by over 95%. The epidemics of crack cocaine and heroin appear to have burnt out.

The biggest factor may be simply that security measures have improved. Car immobilisers have killed joyriding; bulletproof screens, security guards and marked money have all but done for bank robbery. Alarms and DNA databases have increased the chance a burglar will be caught. At the same time, the rewards for burglary have fallen because electronic gizmos are so cheap. Even small shops now invest in CCTV cameras and security tags. Some crimes now look very risky—and that matters because, as every survey of criminals shows, the main deterrent to crime is the fear of being caught.

Loosen the Cuffs

Many conservatives will think this list omits the main reason crime has declined: the far harsher prison sentences introduced on both sides of the Atlantic over the past two decades. One in every hundred American adults is now in prison. This has obviously had some effect—a young man in prison cannot steal your car—but if tough prison sentences were the cause, crime would not be falling in the Netherlands and Germany, which have reduced their prison populations. New York's prison population has fallen by a quarter since 1999, yet its crime rate has dropped faster than that of many other cities.

Harsh punishments, and in particular long mandatory sentences for certain crimes, increasingly look counterproductive. American prisons are full of old men, many of whom are well past their criminal years, and non-violent drug users, who would be better off in treatment. In California, the pioneer of mandatory sentencing, more than a fifth of prisoners are over 50. To keep each one inside costs taxpayers $47,000 a year (about the same as a place at Stanford University). And because prison stresses punishment rather than rehabilitation, most of what remains of the crime problem is really a recidivism issue. In England and Wales, for example, the number of first-time offenders has fallen by 44% since 2007. The number with more than 15 convictions has risen.

Politicians seem to have grasped this. In America the number of new mandatory sentences enacted by Congress has fallen. Even in the Republican South, governors such as Rick Perry and Bobby Jindal have adopted policies favouring treatment over imprisonment for drug users. Britain has stopped adding to its prison population. But more could be done to support people when they come out of prison (at the moment, in Britain, they get £46) and to help addicts. In the Netherlands and Switzerland hard-drug addiction is being reduced by treatment rather than by punishment. American addicts, by contrast, often get little more than counselling.

Policing can be sharpened, too—and, in an era of austerity, will have to be. Now that officers are not rushed off their feet responding to car thefts and burglaries, they can focus on prevention. Predictive policing, which employs data to try to anticipate crime, is particularly promising. More countries could use civilian "community support officers" of the sort employed in Britain and the Netherlands, who patrol the streets, freeing up better-paid police officers to solve crimes.

Better-trained police officers could focus on new crimes. Traditional measures tend not to include financial crimes such as credit-card fraud or tax evasion. Since these are seldom properly recorded, they have not contributed to the great fall in crime. Unlike rapes and murders, they do not excite public fear. But as policing adapts to the technological age, it is as well to remember that criminals are doing so, too.

THE ECONOMIST is a world renowned weekly journal in England.

Jacek Czabański

 **NO**

Estimates of Cost of Crime: History, Methodologies, and Implications

. . . There are some crimes that have been recognized everywhere and in any time. These crimes include traditional ones like murder, rape, assault, robbery, larceny, that is to say: inflicting harm to others.

Focusing my attention on traditional crimes only, I will avoid discussion about the proper limits of criminal law. It is worth noting, however, that costs of crime estimates are connected with the economic theory of law. According to the economic theory of law, the ultimate goal of law is to maximize social welfare, and criminal law is preferred to other means (like contract or tort law) under certain circumstances (see, for example, Posner). Following Benthamic concept, the economic theory of law postulates that only harmful behavior should be made criminal. Harm is considered as a decrease in the individual's well-being.

Therefore, there is a class of behavior, namely victimless crimes, that poses particular problems for the economic analysis. Examples of this class include drug trade, prostitution, gambling, et cetera. The most basic economic assumption is that by exchange people can enhance their utility, but in the above mentioned examples that very process of exchange is forbidden by law. The fact that the exchange, potentially beneficial for both parties, is forbidden by society for whatever reason, suggests that there are some external effects that make society so attentive to this transaction. The conflict between private and public interest is clear in such circumstances and any relevant analysis of cost of these crimes has to weight these factors as well. . . .

There is no one way that the costs of crime may be categorized. Generally, the costs of crime can be divided into three broad categories:

1. Costs of crime itself (pain and suffering, stolen/damaged property, health consequences for victims);
2. Costs of society's response to crime (costs of criminal justice system: police, prosecutors, judges, prisons, and other correctional facilities); and
3. Costs in anticipation of crime (costs of avoidance behavior and precautionary expenditures). . . .

Total Cost of Crime

As was previously described, from the historic perspective the direct costs of crime estimates were the first methodology employed. Costs of law enforcement were easily to calculate so costs of police, prosecution, judges, and prisons and other institutions were included in all estimates. But it was also very clear that these costs formed only one side of the equation. The very reason why society spends money on crime prevention is to lower crime and the burden associated with it. The economic consequences of crime were then estimated: Smith used an approximation of criminal gains as an equivalent of public losses due to crime; National Commission on Law Observance and Enforcement used available data on some crime prevention costs and used labor wages to calculate the value of time lost by criminals behind bars and law officers; President's Commission on Law Enforcement and Administration of Justice provided only loss of earnings due to homicide, but excluded all costs of pain and suffering. Moreover, the Report included costs of illegal activities measured as a total income for illegal goods and services—this shifted an accent from street crimes into organized and white-collars crimes.

What was certainly lacking in all these calculations was the comprehensive list of all (or at least the main) consequences of crime, particularly those that affect victims. Although some methods of valuation (e.g. property prices, happiness loss) also have tried to capture the total cost of crime, they have been unsuccessful in this attempt.

A total cost of crime calculation should include as many consequences of crime as possible, even if they were assessed with different methodologies. The point of reference is a hypothetical state of no crime. Therefore, these kinds of assessments do not answer the question of how much people would like to pay for crime reduction, but rather a question of what is the total burden of crime, compared to the ideal world without it.

While historically the first studies of crime were of this kind, they lacked too many important costs. Modern estimates of the total cost have tried to capture the whole picture.

Anderson included in his analyses a wide spectrum of costs:

Crime-induced production covers personal protection devices (guns, locks, safes, etc.), operation of correctional facilities, and drug trafficking. In the absence of crime, time, money and other resources would be used for other purposes.

Opportunity costs—the value of time of criminals which could have been devoted to legal activities instead. Similarly, the value of victims' time lost due to having been victimized.

Value of risk to life and health—this is the value people place on the risk that they will suffer injury or die due to crime.

Transfers—some crimes involve transfers of property, for example theft. However, according to standard economic reasoning, transfers are not considered to be a net loss to society.

Main Anderson's numerical estimates are reported below (Table 1).

The total burden of crime (net of transfers) was estimated at 1.1 trillion. But as high as it may appear, these estimates did not include all costs, for lack of data. Nevertheless, this collection of costs, limited by data availability, provokes one to asking many questions. For example, the biggest position in crime-induced production is drug trafficking. This amount was taken from the report of the President's Commission on Organized Crime and is simply an amount of money spent on the yearly consumption of drugs. But as was argued before, this can be hardly viewed as a cost of crime. The very fact that people willingly buy drugs stands as an argument for classifying it rather as social benefit than cost.[1] While it is true that there are negative externalities connected with drug consumption (higher mortality rate, lower productivity, and so on), the same is true with many other human activities like alcohol and tobacco consumption, junk food consumption or extreme sports practicing.[2] Moreover, it seems to be a pure transfer from a buyer to a seller, so it should instead be classified under that heading. In Anderson's study there are more inconsistencies like this: in the cost of driving under the influence, penalties and fees were included (another transfer), costs of exposure to cocaine and heroine were exaggerated and for no reason the costs of exposure to alcohol or tobacco were not included.

One of the most surprising components was the value of time lost on securing assets. This is mainly the value of time spend on locking, and unlocking doors. Anderson estimated that each adult spends 2 min a day locking and unlocking doors, and more than 2 min looking for keys.

Anderson also included such minor items, as antitheft devices in libraries, but did not include such costs as pain and suffering of victims (only lost working days were included). He also did not include any estimates of fear of crime, which has an impact not only on an individual's well-being, but also on his behavior. His estimates then are likely to understate the true impact of crime, even if his selection was highly arbitrary. The report also did not allow for differentiating between different categories of crimes, and he only estimated the total cost for all crimes. . . .

Nevertheless, calculations of the total cost of crime show that the burden of crime is enormous. Victimization studies confirm that a substantial part of society is victimized every year. The society's fear of crime is then understandable. . . .

Conclusions

. . . I have argued that the development of costs of crime estimates makes them a valuable, and indeed irreplaceable, tool in criminal law and crime policy. While the concept of monetizing pain and suffering, which are necessarily connected with crime, for many people seem unfeasible, and maybe even unreasonable, such calculations have many advantages over more intuitive approach that has been in use so far.

Averting crimes has always been the aim of crime policy. The lack of reliable estimates as to the real benefits of averting crimes led to the biased perspective of the criminal justice system. Costs of the system were easily seen, as they were borne mainly by state budgets. At the same time, the benefits eluded quantification.

Table 1

Total Cost of Crime in the U.S. 1999

Category	Cost (billion dollars)
Crime-induced production, including	397
Drug trafficking	161
Police protection	47
Corrections	36
Prenatal exposure to cocaine and heroin	28
Federal agencies	23
Judicial and legal services	19
Guards	18
Drug control	11
DUI costs to driver	10
Opportunity costs, including	130
Time spent securing assets	90
Criminals, lost work days	39
The value of risk to life and health	574
Value of lost life	440
Value of injuries	134
Transfers	603
Occupational fraud	204
Unpaid taxes	123
Health insurance fraud	109
Total burden	1,705
Net of transfers	1,102
Per capita (in dollars)	4,118

Source: Anderson (1999), Table 1–7, combined and shortened.

Table 2

Total Cost of Crime in Different Countries

Country	Year	Total cost of crime (local currency)	Cost of crime as % of GDP	Source
US	1900	USD 600m	2.9%	Smith (1901)
US	1930	USD 1 bn	1.1%	Report on the Cost of Crime and Cirminal Justice in the United States (1931)
US	1965	USD 107 bn	14.9%	President's Commission on Law Enforcement and Administration of Justice (1967)
US	1993	USD 451 bn	6.8%	Miller et al. (1996)
England and Wales	1999	GBP 59 bn	6.5%	Brand and Price (2000)
US	1999	USD 1,102 bn	11.9%	Anderson (1999)
Australia	2002	AUD 31.8 bn	4.2%	Mayhew (2003)
England and Wales	2003	GBP 36.2 bn	3.5%	Dubourg et al. (2005) [only for households and individuals]
New Zealand	2003	NZD 9.1 bn	6.5%	Roper and Thompson (2006)

Note: GDP in current prices taken from the tatabase of the International Monetary Fund: http://www.imf.org/external/bubs/ft/weo/2006/02/data/index.aspx. Last accessed 30 November 2006.

Lives lost, pain and suffering, costs of healthcare, property damaged and stolen—all these constitute direct costs of crime. Yet, this list is far from being comprehensive—behavioral responses, changing patterns of life, counter-crime measures, and reduced quality of living all comprise another part of the costs of crime. And the emergence of the criminal justice system with its own costs of police, courts, and prisons make the final part of the total costs. The enormous burden that crime imposes on societies for long was as obvious as vaguely quantified.

Notes

1. Phillips and Votey. Anderson tried to catch the point when he wrote "if there were no laws but what is currently deemed criminal behavior continued, the cost of law enforcement might be zero, but the damage and deterrence cost of said behavior would not cease," but then contradicted himself with the mentioned costs of drug trafficking: if drug trafficking was legal, what would be the damage then?

2. It could be true that a world without such "social bads" would be a better one, but it also means that we would simply like to change people's preferences. Whether the society is legitimate to punish non-victim behaviors is highly debatable.

JACEK CZABAŃSKI is the Deputy Secretary General of Europe of Freedom and Democracy Group in the European Parliament and heads Legal Affairs, and Civil Liberties, and Justice and Home Affairs.

EXPLORING THE ISSUE

Is the Crime Rate the Best Measure for Understanding and Treating Crime?

Critical Thinking and Reflection

1. Why has the crime rate declined throughout the developed world since the 1970s?
2. What common ideas about crime are contradicted by the crime rate data?
3. What changes in the treatment of criminals are suggested by the data on the decline of crime? What changes in police practices are suggested?
4. How would a greater emphasis on rehabilitation of criminals effect future crime rates?
5. People fear street crime more than white-collar crime, but which causes more harm to the public and which costs more money when all costs are counted?
6. Why are the punishments for street crimes so much greater than for white-collar crime?
7. Many white-collar criminals are highly respected persons. Often they continue to be respected even when sentenced to prison as in the case of Martha Stewart. Can you explain this?
8. The most famous statement about crime is "Crime does not pay." Is this a defensible statement today?

Is There Common Ground?

Both authors are deeply concerned with the harm that crime causes and want to make the criminal justice system as effective as possible. *The Economist* uses data on crime rates to correct misperceptions of crime rates which are responsible for several costly and largely ineffective approaches to crime, criminals, and punishments. It recommends more emphasis on rehabilitation because most crime is done by repeat offenders. It also recommends shifting the focus of the police system from apprehending and punishing to crime prevention, because there is less need for the former since crimes are declining.

Czabański researches the costs of crime to use the costs as tools in criminal law and crime policy. His calculations of the total costs of crime show the enormous burden of crime. Thus these calculations show the enormous benefits of averting crime. He also shows that the costs of white-collar crime is far greater than the costs of street crime. We may fear street crime more than white-collar crime but the latter costs us more.

Create Central

www.mhhe.com/createcentral

Additional Resources

Readings that show the costliness of white collar crime include: Roger J. Berger, *White-Collar Crime: The Abuse of Corporate and Government Power* (Lynne Rienner Publishers, 2011); Nicholas Ryder, *Financial Crime in the 21st Century: Law and Polity* (Edward Elgar, 2011); Loretta Napoleoni, *Rogue Economics: Capitalism's New Reality* (Seven Stories Press, 2009); Michael L. Benson and Sally S. Simpson, *White-Collar Crime: An Opportunity Perspective* (Routledge,

2009); Matthew Robinson, *Greed Is Good: Maximization and Elite Deviance in America* (Rowman & Littlefield, 2009); Peter Gottschalk, *White-Collar Criminals: Theoretical and Managerial Perspectives of Financial Crime* (Nova Science, 2010); Peter Fleming, *Charting Corporate Corruption: Agency, Structure, and Escalation* (Edward Elgar, 2009); Scott B. MacDonald, *Separating Fools from Their Money: A History of American Financial Scandals* (Transaction Publishers, 2007); David O. Friedrichs, *Trusted Criminals: White Collar Crime in Contemporary Society* (Thomson Higher Education, 2007); Stuart L. Hills, ed., *Corporate Violence: Injury and Death for Profit* (Rowman & Littlefield, 1987); Steve Tombs and Dave Whyte, eds., *Unmasking the Crimes of the Powerful: Scrutinizing States and Corporations* (P. Lang, 2003); Joel Bakan, *The Corporation: The Pathological Pursuit of Profit and Power* (Free Press, 2004); Stephen M. Rosoff, et al., *Looting America: Greed, Corruption, Villains, and Victims* (Prentice Hall, 2003).

Most works on crime deal mainly with theft, drugs, and violence, and the injury and fear that they cause, including: Danielle Lively Neal, *Social Capital and Urban Crime* (LFB Scholarly Publishing, 2011); Marcus Felson and Rachel L. Boba, *Crime and Everyday Life* (Sage, 2010); Elizabeth Kandel Englander, *Understanding Violence* (Lawrence Erlbaum Associates, 2007); Leslie Williams Reid, *Crime in the City: A Political and Economic Analysis of Urban Crime* (LFB Scholarly Publishing, 2003); Walter S. DeKeseredy, *Under Siege: Poverty and Crime in a Public Housing Community* (Lexington Books, 2003); Alex Alverez and Ronet Bachman, *Murder American Style* (Wadsworth, 2003); Claire Valier, *Crime and Punishment in Contemporary Culture* (Routledge, 2004); Matthew B. Robinson, *Why Crime? An Integrated Systems Theory of Antisocial Behavior* (Pearson, 2004); Ronald B. Flowers, *Male Crime and Deviance: Exploring Its Causes, Dynamics, and Nature* (C. C. Thomas, 2003); and Meda Chesney-Lind and Lisa Pasko, *The Female Offender: Girls, Women, and Crime*, 2nd ed. (Sage, 2004).

Five works on gangs, which are often connected with violent street crime, are: William J. Mitchell, ed., *Code of the Street: Violent Youths and Gangs* (Nova Science, 2011); Robert J. Franzese, Herbert C. Covey, and Scott Menard, *Youth Gangs* (Charles C. Thomas, 2006); Jay T. Soordhas, ed., *Gangs: Violence, Crime and Antigang Initiatives* (Nova Science, 2009); Martin Sanchez Jankowski, *Islands in the Street: Gangs and American Urban Society* (University of California Press, 1991); and Felix M. Padilla, *The Gang as an American Enterprise* (Rutgers University Press, 1992).

William J. Bennett, John J. DiIulio, and John P. Walters, in *Body Count: Moral Poverty And How to Win America's War Against Crime and Drugs* (Simon & Schuster, 1996), argue that moral poverty is the root cause of crime (meaning street crime). How applicable is this thesis to white-collar crime?

One interesting aspect of many corporate, or white-collar, crimes is that they involve crimes of obedience, as discussed in Herman C. Kelman and V. Lee Hamilton, *Crimes of Obedience: Toward a Social Psychology of Authority and Responsibility* (Yale University Press, 1989).

For recent effort to calculate the costs of crime and law enforcement, see: Jacek Czabański, *Estimates of Cost of Crime: History, Methodologies, and Implications* (Springer, 2008) and Mark A. Cohen, *The Costs of Crime and Justice* (Routledge, 2005).

Finally, there is a new type of crime that is increasingly troublesome: digital crime and terrorism. This is thoroughly examined by Robert W. Taylor, et al., in *Digital Crime and Digital Terrorism* (Pearson/Prentice Hall, 2006).

Internet References . . .

Sociology—Study Sociology Online

http://edu.learnsoc.org/

Sociology Web Resources

www.mhhe.com/socscience/sociology/resources/index.htm

Sociosite

www.topsite.com/goto/sociosite.net

Socioweb

www.topsite.com/goto/socioweb.com

Selected, Edited, and with Issue Framing Material by:
Kurt Finsterbusch, *University of Maryland, College Park*

ISSUE

Should Laws Against Drug Use Remain Restrictive?

YES: Herbert Kleber and Joseph A. Califano Jr., from "Legalization: Panacea or Pandora's Box?" *The National Center on Addiction and Substance Abuse at Columbia University* (January 2006)

NO: Jacob Sullum, from "The War Over Weed," *Reason* (January 2013)

Learning Outcomes

After reading this issue, you will be able to:

- Understand that government laws that outlaw behavior that citizens do not think are wrong have a legitimacy problem. Laws against prostitution, alcohol, smoking, business on Sundays, pornography, kissing in public, etc. will lack moral authority for many and perhaps for the majority and will be ignored by many if they can get away with it. In the long run, these laws are likely to be repealed or ignored.
- Understand how moralists can get public support for these types of laws including drug laws and put people who oppose such laws in a bad light. They do it to protect drug users from themselves. Seldom are these laws the result of scientific studies. They generally result from emotional responses to stories about the evil that happens to the "victims."
- Sort out how much factual support there is for the main arguments on both sides of this debate.
- Estimate the extent of corruption of the police force which results from the drug laws.
- Know that the proportion of arrests, convictions, prison time, and prisoners are due to drug enforcement.
- Identify the options for policies dealing with recreational drugs.

ISSUE SUMMARY

YES: Herbert Kleber, the executive vice president of the Center on Addiction and Substance Abuse (CASA), and Joseph Califano, founder of CASA, maintain that drug laws should remain restrictive because legalization would result in increased use, especially by children. Kleber and Califano contend that drug legalization would not eliminate drug-related violence nor the harm caused by drugs.

NO: Jacob Sullum, Senior Editor of *Reason*, uses a review of two books to establish that the legalization of marijuana clearly has more benefits than costs. The books are: *Marijuana Legalization: What Everyone Needs to Know*, by Jonathan P. Caulkins, Angela Hawken, Beau Kilmer, and Mark A. R. Kleiman (Oxford University Press, 2012) and *Smoke Signals: A Social History of Marijuana—Medical, Recreational, and Scientific*, by Martin A. Lee (Scribner, 2012).

In 2008, the federal government allocated nearly $13 billion to control drug use and to enforce laws that are designed to protect society from the perils created by drug use. Some people believe that the government's war on drugs could be more effective but that governmental agencies and communities are not fighting hard enough to stop drug use. They also hold that laws to halt drug use are too few and too lenient. Others contend that the war against drugs is unnecessary, that, in fact, society has already lost the war on drugs. These individuals feel that the best way to remedy drug problems is to end the fight altogether by ending the current restrictive policies regarding drug use. There are conflicting views among both liberals and conservatives on whether legislation has had the intended result of curtailing the problems of drug use. Many argue that legislation and the criminalization of drugs have been counterproductive in controlling drug problems. Some suggest that the criminalization of drugs has actually contributed to and worsened the social ills associated with drugs. Proponents of drug legalization maintain that the war on drugs, not drugs themselves, is damaging to American society. They do not advocate drug use; they argue only that laws against drugs exacerbate problems related to drugs.

Proponents of drug decriminalization argue that the strict enforcement of drug laws damages American society because it drives people to violence and crime and that the drug laws have a racist element associated with them.

People arrested for drug offenses overburden the court system, thus rendering it ineffective. Moreover, proponents contend that the criminalization of drugs fuels organized crime, allows children to be pulled into the drug business, and makes illegal drugs more dangerous because they are manufactured without government standards or regulations. Hence, drugs may be adulterated or of unidentified potency. Decriminalization advocates also argue that decriminalization would take the profits out of drug sales, thereby decreasing the value of and demand for drugs. In addition, the costs resulting from law enforcement are far greater than the benefits of criminalization.

Some decriminalization advocates argue that the federal government's prohibition stance on drugs is an immoral and impossible objective. To achieve a "drug-free society" is self-defeating and a misnomer because drugs have always been a part of human culture. Furthermore, prohibition efforts indicate a disregard for the private freedom of individuals because they assume that individuals are incapable of making their own choices. Drug proponents assert that their personal sovereignty should be respected over any government agenda, including the war on drugs. Less restrictive laws, they argue, would take the

emphasis off of law enforcement policies and allow more effort to be put toward education, prevention, and treatment. Also, it is felt that most of the negative implications of drug prohibition would disappear.

Opponents of this view maintain that less restrictive drug laws are not the solution to drug problems and that it is a very dangerous idea. Less restrictive laws, they assert, will drastically increase drug use. This upsurge in drug use will come at an incredibly high price: American society will be overrun with drug-related accidents, lost worker productivity, and hospital emergency rooms filled with drug-related emergencies. Drug treatment efforts would be futile because users would have no legal incentive to stop taking drugs. Also, users may prefer drugs rather than rehabilitation, and education programs may be ineffective in dissuading children from using drugs.

Advocates of less restrictive laws maintain that drug abuse is a "victimless crime" in which the only person being hurt is the drug user. Opponents argue that this notion is ludicrous and dangerous because drug use has dire repercussions for all of society. Drugs can destroy the minds and bodies of many people.

Also, regulations to control drug use have a legitimate social aim to protect society and its citizens from the harm of drugs.

In the following selections, Herbert Kleber and Joseph Califano Jr. explain why they feel drugs should remain illegal, whereas Jacob Sullum describes the detrimental effects that he believes occur as a result of the restrictive laws associated with drugs.

YES ↵

**Herbert Kleber and
Joseph A. Califano Jr.**

Legalization: Panacea or Pandora's Box?

Introduction

Legalization of drugs has recently received some attention as a policy option for the United States. Proponents of such a radical change in policy argue that the "war on drugs" has been lost; drug prohibition, as opposed to illegal drugs themselves, spawns increasing violence and crime; drugs are available to anyone who wants them, even under present restrictions; drug abuse and addiction would not increase after legalization; individuals have a right to use whatever drugs they wish; and foreign experiments with legalization work and should be adopted in the United States.

In this, its first White Paper, the Center on Addiction and Substance Abuse at Columbia University (CASA) examines these propositions; recent trends in drug use; the probable consequences of legalization for children and drug-related violence; lessons to be learned from America's legal drugs, alcohol and tobacco; the question of civil liberties; and the experiences of foreign countries. On the basis of its review, CASA concludes that while legalization might temporarily take some burden off the criminal justice system, such a policy would impose heavy additional costs on the health care system, schools, and workplace, severely impair the ability of millions of young Americans to develop their talents, and in the long term overburden the criminal justice system.

Drugs like heroin and cocaine are not dangerous because they are illegal; they are illegal because they are dangerous. Such drugs are not a threat to American society because they are illegal; they are illegal because they are a threat to American society.

Any relaxation in standards of illegality poses a clear and present danger to the nation's children and their ability to learn and grow into productive citizens. Individuals who reach age 21 without using illegal drugs are virtually certain never to do so. Viewed from this perspective, substance abuse and addiction is a disease acquired during childhood and adolescence. Thus, legalization of drugs such as heroin, cocaine, and marijuana would threaten a pediatric pandemic in the United States.

While current prohibitions on the import, manufacture, distribution, and possession of marijuana, cocaine, heroin, and other drugs should remain, America's drug policies do need a fix. More resources and energy should be devoted to prevention and treatment, and each citizen and institution should take responsibility to combat drug abuse and addiction in America. . . .

Legalization, Decriminalization, Medicalization, Harm Reduction: What's the Difference?

The term "legalization" encompasses a wide variety of policy options from the legal use of marijuana in private to free markets for all drugs. Four terms are commonly used: legalization, decriminalization, medicalization, and harm reduction—with much variation in each.

Legalization usually implies the most radical departure from current policy. Legalization proposals vary from making marijuana cigarettes as available as tobacco cigarettes to establishing an open and free market for drugs. Variations on legalization include: making drugs legal for the adult population, but illegal for minors; having only the government produce and sell drugs; and/or allowing a private market in drugs, but with restrictions on advertising, dosage, and place of consumption. Few proponents put forth detailed visions of a legalized market.

Decriminalization proposals retain most drug laws that forbid manufacture, importation, and sale of illegal drugs, but remove criminal sanctions for possession of small amounts of drugs for personal use. Such proposals suggest that possession of drugs for personal use be legal or subject only to civil penalties such as fines. Decriminalization is most commonly advocated for marijuana.

Medicalization refers to the prescription of currently illegal drugs by physicians to addicts already dependent on such drugs. The most frequently mentioned variation is heroin maintenance. Proponents argue that providing addicts with drugs prevents them from having to commit crimes to finance their habit and insures that drugs they ingest are pure.

Harm reduction generally implies that government policies should concentrate on lowering the harm associated with drugs both for users and society, rather than on eradicating drug use and imprisoning users. Beginning with the proposition that drug use is inevitable, harm reduction proposals can include the prescription of heroin and other drugs to addicts; removal of penalties for personal use of marijuana; needle-exchange programs for injection drug users to prevent the spread of AIDS and other diseases that result from needle sharing among addicts; and making drugs available at low or no cost to eliminate the harm caused by users who commit crimes to support a drug habit.

Variations on these options are infinite. Some do not require any change in the illegal status of drugs. The government could, for instance, allow needle exchanges while maintaining current laws banning heroin, the most commonly injected drug. Others, however, represent a major shift from the current role of government and the goal of its policies with regard to drug use and availability. Some advocates use the term "harm reduction" as a politically attractive cover for legalization.

Where We Are

Most arguments for legalization in all its different forms start with the contention that the "war on drugs" has been lost and that prevailing criminal justice and social policies with respect to drug use have been a failure. To support the claim that current drug policies have failed, legalization advocates point to the 80 million Americans who have tried drugs during their lifetime. Since so many individuals have broken drug laws, these advocates argue, the laws are futile and lead to widespread disrespect for the law. A liberal democracy, they contend, should not ban what so many people do.[1]

The 80 million Americans include everyone who has ever smoked even a single joint. The majority of these individuals have used only marijuana, and for many their use was brief experimentation. In fact, the size of this number reflects the large number of young people who tried marijuana and hallucinogenic drugs during the late 1960s and the 1970s when drug use was widely tolerated. During this time, drug use was so commonly accepted that the 1972 Shafer Commission, established during the Nixon Administration, and later, President Jimmy Carter called for decriminalization of marijuana.[2]

Since then, concerned public health and government leaders have mounted energetic efforts to denormalize drug use, including First Lady Nancy Reagan's "Just Say No" campaign. As a result, current* users of any illicit drugs, as measured by the National Household Survey on Drug Abuse, decreased from 24.8 million in 1979 to 13 million in 1994, a nearly 50 percent drop. Over the same time period, current marijuana users dropped from 23 million to 10 million and cocaine users from 4.4 million to 1.4 million.[3] The drug-using segment of the population is also aging. In 1979, 10 percent of current drug users were older than 34; today almost 30 percent are.[4]

With these results and only 6 percent of the population over age 12 currently using drugs,[5] it is difficult to say

that drug reduction efforts have failed. This sharp decline in drug use occurred during a period of strict drug laws, societal disapproval, and increasing knowledge and awareness of the dangers and costs of illegal drug use.

Several factors, however, lead many to conclude that we have not made progress against drugs. This feeling of despair stems from the uneven nature of the success. While casual drug use and experimentation have declined substantially, certain neighborhoods and areas of the country remain infested with drugs and drug-related crime, and these continuing trouble spots draw media attention. At the same time, the number of drug addicts has not dropped significantly and the spread of HIV among addicts has added a deadly new dimension to the problem. The number of hardcore** cocaine users (as estimated by the Office of National Drug Control Policy based on a number of surveys including the Household Survey, Drug Use Forecasting, and Drug Abuse Warning Network) has remained steady at roughly 2 million.[6] The overall number of illicit drug addicts has hovered around 6 million, a situation that many experts attribute both to a lack of treatment facilities[7] and the large numbers of drug-using individuals already in the pipeline to addiction, even though overall casual use has dropped.

Teenage drug use has been creeping up in the past three years. In the face of the enormous decline in the number of users, however, it is difficult to conclude that current policies have so failed that a change as radical as legalization is warranted. While strict drug laws and criminal sanctions are not likely to deter hardcore addicts, increased resources can be dedicated to treatment without legalizing drugs. Indeed, the criminal justice system can be used to place addicted offenders into treatment. In short, though substantial problems remain, we have made significant progress in our struggle against drug abuse.

Will Legalization Increase Drug Use?

Proponents of drug legalization claim that making drugs legally available would not increase the number of addicts. They argue that drugs are already available to those who want them and that a policy of legalization could be combined with education and prevention programs to discourage drug use.[8] Some contend that legalization might even reduce the number of users, arguing that there would be no pushers to lure new users and drugs would lose the "forbidden fruit" allure of illegality, which can be seductive to children.[9] Proponents of legalization also play down the consequences of drug use, saying that most drug users can function normally.[10] Some legalization advocates assert that a certain level of drug addiction is inevitable and will not vary, regardless of government policies; thus, they

---

*Throughout this paper, "current" drug users refers to individuals who have used drugs within the past month, the definition used in most drug use surveys.

**Throughout this paper, "hardcore" users refers to individuals who use drugs at least weekly.

claim, even if legalization increased the number of users, it would have little effect on the numbers of users who become addicts.[11]

The effects of legalization on the numbers of users and addicts is an important question because the answer in large part determines whether legalization will reduce crime, improve public health, and lower economic, social, and health care costs. The presumed benefits of legalization evaporate if the number of users and addicts, particularly among children, increases significantly.

Availability

An examination of this question begins with the issue of availability, which has three components:

- **Physical**, how convenient is access to drugs.
- **Psychological**, the moral and social acceptability and perceived consequences of drug use.
- **Economic**, the affordability of drugs.

Physical

Despite assertions to the contrary, the evidence indicates that presently drugs are not accessible to all. Fewer than 50 percent of high school seniors and young adults under 22 believed they could obtain cocaine "fairly easily" or "very easily."[12] Only 39 percent of the adult population reported they could get cocaine; and only 25 percent reported that they could obtain heroin, PCP, and LSD.[13] Thus, only one-quarter to one-half of people can easily get illegal drugs (other than marijuana). After legalization, drugs would be more widely and easily available. Currently, only 11 percent of individuals reported seeing drugs available in the area where they lived;[14] after legalization, there could be a place to purchase drugs in every neighborhood. Under such circumstances, it is logical to conclude that more individuals would use drugs.

Psychological

In arguing that legalization would not result in increased use, proponents of legalization often cite public opinion polls, which indicate that the vast majority of Americans would not try drugs even if they were legally available.[15] They fail to take into account, however, that this strong public antagonism towards drugs has been formed during a period of strict prohibition when government and institutions at every level have made clear the health and criminal justice consequences of drug use. Furthermore, even if only 15 percent of population would use drugs after legalization, this would be triple the current level of 5.6 percent.

Laws define what is acceptable conduct in a society, express the will of its citizens, and represent a commitment on the part of the Congress, the President, state legislatures, and governors. Drug laws not only create a criminal sanction, they also serve as educational and normative statements that shape public attitudes.[16] Criminal laws constitute a far stronger statement than civil laws,

but even the latter can discourage individual consumption. Laws regulating smoking in public and workplaces, prohibiting certain types of tobacco advertising, and mandating warning labels are in part responsible for the decline in smoking prevalence among adults.

The challenge of reducing drug abuse and addiction would be decidedly more difficult if society passed laws indicating that these substances are not sufficiently harmful to prohibit their use. Any move toward legalization would decrease the perception of risks and costs of drug use, which would lead to wider use.[17] During the late 1960s and the 1970s, as society, laws, and law enforcement became more permissive about drug use, the number of individuals smoking marijuana and using heroin, hallucinogens, and other drugs rose sharply. During the 1980s, as society's attitude became more restrictive and anti-drug laws stricter and more vigorously enforced, the perceived harmfulness of marijuana and other illicit drugs increased and use decreased.

Some legalization advocates point to the campaign against smoking as proof that reducing use is possible while substances are legally available.[18] But it has taken smoking more than 30 years to decline as much as illegal drug use did in 10.[19] Moreover, reducing use of legal drugs among the young has proven especially difficult. While use of illegal drugs by high school seniors dropped 50 percent from 1979 to 1993, tobacco use remained virtually constant.[20]

Economic

By all of the laws of economics, reducing the price of drugs will increase consumption.[21] Though interdiction and law enforcement have had limited success in reducing supply (seizing only 25 percent to 30 percent of cocaine imports, for example)[22] the illegality of drugs has increased their price.[23] Prices of illegal drugs are roughly 10 times what they would cost to produce legally. Cocaine, for example, sells at $80 a gram today, but would cost only $10 a gram legally to produce and distribute. That would set the price of a dose at 50 cents, well within the reach of a school child's lunch money.[24]

Until the mid-1980s, cocaine was the drug of the middle and upper classes. Regular use was limited to those who had the money to purchase it or got the money through white collar crime or selling such assets as their car, house, or children's college funds. In the mid-1980s, the $5 crack cocaine vial made the drug inexpensive and available to all regardless of income. Use spread. Cocaine-exposed babies began to fill hospital neonatal wards, cocaine-related emergency room visits increased sharply, and cocaine-related crime and violence jumped.[25]

Efforts to increase the price of legal drugs by taxing them heavily in order to discourage consumption, if successful, would encourage the black market, crime, violence, and corruption associated with the illegal drug trade. Heroin addicts, who gradually build a tolerance to the drug, and cocaine addicts, who crave more of the drug as soon as its effects subside, would turn to a black market if an affordable and rising level of drugs were not made available to them legally.

Children

Drug use among children is of particular concern since almost all individuals who use drugs begin before they are 21. Furthermore, adolescents rate drugs as the number one problem they face.[26] Since we have been unable to keep legal drugs, like tobacco and alcohol, out of the hands of children, legalization of illegal drugs could cause a pediatric pandemic of drug abuse and addiction.

Most advocates of legalization support a regulated system in which access to presently illicit drugs would be illegal for minors.[27] Such regulations would retain for children the "forbidden fruit" allure that many argue legalization would eliminate. Furthermore any such distinction between adults and minors could make drugs, like beer and cigarettes today, an attractive badge of adulthood.

The American experience with laws restricting access by children and adolescents to tobacco and alcohol makes it clear that keeping legal drugs away from minors would be a formidable, probably impossible, task. Today, 62 percent of high school seniors have smoked, 30 percent in the past month.[28] Three million adolescents smoke cigarettes, an average of one-half a pack per day, a $1 billion a year market.[29] Twelve million underage Americans drink beer and other alcohol, a market approaching $10 billion a year. Although alcohol use is illegal for all those under the age of 21, 87 percent of high school seniors report using alcohol, more than half in the past month.[30] These rates of use persist despite school, community, and media activities that inform youths about the dangers of smoking and drinking and despite increasing public awareness of these risks. This record indicates that efforts to ban drug use among minors while allowing it for adults would face enormous difficulty.

Moreover, in contrast to these high rates of alcohol and tobacco use, only 18 percent of seniors use illicit drugs, which are illegal for the entire society.[31] It is no accident that those substances which are mostly easily obtainable—alcohol, tobacco, and inhalants such as those found in household cleaning fluids—are those most widely used by the youngest students.[32]

Supporters and opponents of legalization generally agree that education and prevention programs are an integral part of efforts to reduce drug use by children and adolescents. School programs, media campaigns such as those of the Partnership for a Drug-Free America (PDFA), and news reports on the dangers of illegal drugs have helped reduce use by changing attitudes towards drugs. In 1992, New York City school children were surveyed on their perceptions of illegal drugs before and after a PDFA campaign of anti-drug messages on television, in newspapers, and on billboards. The second survey showed that the percentage of children who said they might want to try drugs fell 29 points and those who said drugs would

make them "cool" fell 17 points.[33] Another study found that 75 percent of students who saw anti-drug advertisements reported that the ads had a deterrent effect on their own actual or intended use.[34]

Along with such educational programs, however, the stigma of illegality is especially important in preventing use among adolescents. From 1978 to 1993, current marijuana use among high school seniors dropped twice as fast as alcohol use.[35] California started a $600 million anti-smoking campaign in 1989, and by 1995, the overall smoking rate had dropped 30 percent. But among teenagers, the smoking rate remained constant—even though almost one-quarter of the campaign targeted them.[36]

In separate studies, 60 to 70 percent of New Jersey and California students reported that fear of getting in trouble with the authorities was a major reason why they did not use drugs.[37] Another study found that the greater the perceived likelihood of apprehension and swift punishment for using marijuana, the less likely adolescents are to smoke it.[38] Because a legalized system would remove much, if not all of this deterrent, drug use among teenagers could be expected to rise. Since most teens begin using drugs because their peers do[39]—not because of pressure from pushers[40]—and most drugs users initially exhibit few ill effects, more teenagers would be likely to try drugs.[41]

As a result, legalization of marijuana, cocaine, and heroin for adults would mean that increased numbers of teenagers would smoke, snort, and inject these substances at a time when habits are formed and the social, academic, and physical skills needed for a satisfying and independent life are acquired.

Hardcore Addiction

A review of addiction in the past shows that the number of alcohol, heroin, and cocaine addicts, even when adjusted for changes in population, fluctuates widely over time, in response to changes in access, price, societal attitudes, and legal consequences. The fact that alcohol and tobacco, the most accepted and available legal drugs, are the most widely abused, demonstrates that behavior is influenced by opportunity, stigma, and price. Many soldiers who were regular heroin users in Vietnam stopped once they returned to the United States where heroin was much more difficult and dangerous to get.[42] Studies have shown that even among chronic alcoholics, alcohol taxes lower consumption.[43]

Dr. Jack Homer of the University of Southern California and a founding member of the International System Dynamics Society estimates that without retail-level drug arrests and seizures—which reduce availability, increase the danger of arrest for the drug user, and stigmatize use—the number of compulsive cocaine users would rise to between 10 and 32 million, a level 5 to 16 times the present one.[44]

Not all new users become addicts. But few individuals foresee their addiction when they start using; most think they can control their consumption.[45] Among the new users created by legalization, many, including children, would find themselves unable to live without the drug, no longer able to work, go to school, or maintain personal relationships. In fact, as University of California at Los Angeles criminologist James Q. Wilson points out with regard to cocaine,[46] the percentage of drug triers who become abusers when the drugs are illegal, socially unacceptable, and generally hard to get, may be only a fraction of the users who become addicts when drugs are legal and easily available—physically, psychologically, and economically.

Harming Thy Neighbor and Thyself: Addiction and Casual Drug Use

To offset any increased use as a result of legalization, many proponents contend that money presently spent on criminal justice and law enforcement could be used for treatment of addicts and prevention.[47] In 1995, the federal government is spending $13.2 billion to fight drug abuse, nearly two-thirds of that amount on law enforcement; state and local governments are spending at least another $16 billion on drug control efforts, largely on law enforcement.[48] Legalization proponents argue that most of this money could be used to fund treatment on demand for all addicts who want it and extensive public health campaigns to discourage new use.

With legalization, the number of prisoners would initially decrease because many are currently there for drug law violations. But to the extent that legalization increases drug use, we can expect to see more of its familiar consequences. Costs would quickly rise in health care, schools, and businesses. In the long term, wider use and addiction would increase criminal activity related to the psychological and physical effects of drug use and criminal justice costs would rise again. The higher number of casual users and addicts would reduce worker productivity and students' ability and motivation to learn, cause more highway accidents and fatalities, and fill hospital beds with individuals suffering from ailments and injuries caused or aggravated by drug abuse.

Costs

It is doubtful whether legalization would produce any cost savings, over time even in the area of law enforcement. Indeed, the legal availability of alcohol has not eliminated law enforcement costs due to alcohol-related violence. A third of state prison inmates committed their crimes while under the influence of alcohol.[49] Despite intense educational campaigns, the highest number of arrests in 1993—1.5 million—was for driving while intoxicated.[50] Even if, as some legalization proponents propose, drug sales were taxed, revenues raised would be more than offset by erosion of the general tax base as abuse and addiction limited the ability of individuals to work.

Like advocates of legalization today, opponents of alcohol prohibition claimed that taxes on the legal sale of alcohol would dramatically increase revenues and even help erase the federal deficit.[51] The real-world result has been quite different. The approximately $20 billion in state and federal revenues from alcohol taxes in 1995[52] pay for only half the $40 billion that alcohol abuse imposes in direct health care costs,[53] much less the costs laid on federal entitlement programs and the legal and criminal justice systems, to say nothing of lost economic productivity. The nearly $13 billion in federal and state cigarette tax revenue[54] is one-sixth of the $75 billion in direct health care costs attributable to tobacco,[55] to say nothing of the other costs such as the $4.6 billion in social security disability payments to individuals disabled by cancer, heart disease, and respiratory ailments caused by smoking.[56]

Health care costs directly attributable to illegal drugs exceed $30 billion,[57] an amount that would increase significantly if use spread after legalization. Experience renders it unrealistic to expect that taxes could be imposed on newly legalized drugs sufficient to cover the costs of increased use and abuse.

Public Health

Legalization proponents contend that prohibition has negative public health consequences such as the spread of HIV from addicts who share dirty needles, accidental poisoning, and overdoses from impure drugs of variable potency. In 1994, more than one-third of new AIDS cases were among injection drug users who shared needles, cookers, cottons, rinse water, and other paraphernalia; many other individuals contracted AIDS by having sex, often while high, with infected injection drug users.[58]

Advocates of medicalization argue that while illicit drugs should not be freely available to all, doctors should be allowed to prescribe them (particularly heroin, but also cocaine) to addicts. They contend that giving addicts drugs assures purity and eliminates the need for addicts to steal in order to buy them.[59]

Giving addicts drugs like heroin, however, poses many problems. Providing them by prescription raises the danger of diversion for sale on the black market. The alternative—insisting that addicts take drugs on the prescriber's premises—entails at least two visits a day, thus interfering with the stated goal of many maintenance programs to enable addicts to hold jobs.

Heroin addicts require two to four shots each day in increasing doses as they build tolerance to its euphoric effect. On the other hand, methadone can be given at a constant dose since euphoria is not the objective. Addicts maintained on methadone need only a single dose each day and take it orally, eliminating the need for injection.[60] Because cocaine produces an intense, but short euphoria and an immediate desire for more,[61] addicts would have to be given the drug even more often than heroin in order to satisfy their craving sufficiently to prevent them from seeking additional cocaine on the street.

Other less radical harm reduction proposals also have serious flaws. Distributing free needles, for example, does not guarantee that addicts desperate for a high would refuse to share them. But to the extent that needle exchange programs are effective in reducing the spread of the AIDS virus and other diseases without increasing drug use, they can be adopted without legalizing drugs. Studies of whether needle exchange programs increase drug use have generally focused on periods of no longer than 12 months.[62] While use does not seem to increase in this period, data is lacking on the long-term effects of such programs and whether they prompt attitude shifts that in turn lead to increased drug use.

Some individuals do die as a result of drug impurities. But while drug purity could be assured in a government-regulated system (though not for those drugs sold on the black market), careful use could not. The increased numbers of users would probably produce a rising number of overdose deaths, similar to those caused by alcohol poisoning today.

The deaths and costs due to unregulated drug quality pale in comparison to the negative impact that legalization would have on drug users, their families, and society. Casual drug use is dangerous, not simply because it can lead to addiction or accidental overdoses, but because it is harmful per se, producing worker accidents, highway fatalities, and children born with physical and mental handicaps. Each year, roughly 500,000 newborns are exposed to illegal drugs in the womb; many others are never born because of drug-induced spontaneous abortions.[63] Newborns already exposed to drugs are far more likely to need intensive care and suffer the physical and mental consequences of low birth weight and premature birth, including early death.[64] The additional costs just to raise drug-exposed babies would outweigh any potential savings of legalization in criminal justice expenditures.[65]

Substance abuse aggravates medical conditions. Medicaid patients with a secondary diagnosis of substance abuse remain in hospitals twice as long as patients with the same primary diagnosis but with no substance abuse problems. Girls and boys under age 15 remain in the hospital three and four times as long, respectively, when they have a secondary diagnosis of substance abuse.[66] One-third to one-half of individuals with psychiatric problems are also substance abusers.[67] Young people who use drugs are at higher risk of mental health problems, including depression, suicide, and personality disorders.[68] Teenagers who use illegal drugs are more likely to have sex[69] and are less likely to use a condom than those who do not use drugs.[70] Such sexual behavior exposes these teens to increased risk of pregnancy as well as AIDS and other sexually transmitted diseases.

In schools and families, drug abuse is devastating. Students who use drugs not only limit their own ability to learn, they also disrupt classrooms, interfering with the education of other students. Drug users tear apart families by failing to provide economic support, spending money on drugs, neglecting the emotional support of the spouse and guidance of children, and putting their children at greater risk of becoming substance abusers themselves.[71] With the advent of crack cocaine in the mid-1980s, foster care cases soared over 50 percent nationwide in five years; more than 70 percent of these cases involved families in which at least one parent abused drugs.[72]

Decreased coordination and impaired motor skills that result from drug use are dangerous. A recent study in Tennessee found that 59 percent of reckless drivers who, having been stopped by the police, test negative for alcohol on the breathalyzer, test positive for marijuana and/or cocaine.[73] Twenty percent of New York City drivers who die in automobile accidents test positive for cocaine use.[74] The extent of driving while high on marijuana and other illegal drugs is still not well-known because usually the police do not have the same capability for roadside drug testing as they do for alcohol testing. . . .

Crime and Violence

Legalization advocates contend that *drug-related* violence is really *drug-trade-related* violence. They argue that what we have today is not a drug problem but a drug prohibition problem, that anti-drug laws spawn more violence and crime than the drugs themselves. Because illegality creates high prices for drugs and huge profits for dealers, advocates of legalization point out that users commit crimes to support their habit; drug pushers fight over turf; gangs and organized crime thrive; and users become criminals by coming into contact with the underworld.[75]

Legalization proponents argue that repeal of current laws, which criminalize drug use and sales, and wider availability of drugs at lower prices will end this black market and thus reduce the violence, crime, and incarceration associated with drugs.

Researchers divide drug-related violence into three types: systemic, economically compulsive, and psychopharmacological:[76]

- **Systemic violence** is that intrinsic to involvement with illegal drugs, including murders over drug turf, retribution for selling "bad" drugs, and fighting among users over drugs or drug paraphernalia.
- **Economically compulsive violence** results from addicts who engage in violent crime in order to support their addiction.
- **Psychopharmacological violence** is caused by the short or long-term use of certain drugs which lead to excitability, irrationality and violence, such as a brutal murder committed under the influence of cocaine.

Legalization of the drug trade and lower prices might decrease the first two types of violence, but higher use and abuse would increase the third. Dr. Mitchell Rosenthal, President of the Phoenix House treatment centers, warns, "What I and many other treatment professionals would expect to see in a drug-legalized America is a sharp rise in the amount of drug-related crime that is *not* committed for gain—homicide, assault, rape, and child abuse. Along with this, an increase in social disorder, due to rising levels of drug consumption and a growing number of drug abusers."[77]

In a study of 130 drug-related homicides, 60 percent resulted from the psychopharmacological effects of the drug; only 20 percent were found to be related to the drug trade; 3.1 percent were committed for economic reasons. (The remaining 17 percent either fell into more than one of these categories or were categorized as "other.")[78] U.S. Department of Justice statistics reveal that six times as many homicides, four times as many assaults, and almost one and a half times as many robberies are committed under the influence of drugs as are committed in order to get money to buy drugs.[79] Given these facts, any decreases in violent acts committed because of the current high cost of drugs would be more than offset by increases in psychopharmacological violence, such as that caused by cocaine psychosis.

The threat of rising violence is particularly serious in the case of cocaine, crack, methamphetamine, and PCP—drugs closely associated with violent behavior. Unlike marijuana or heroin, which depress activity, these drugs cause irritability and physical aggression. For instance, past increases in the New York City homicide rate have been tied to increases in cocaine use.[80]

Repeal of drug laws would not affect all addicts in the same way. Addicts engage in criminal behavior for different reasons. A small proportion of addicts is responsible for a disproportionately high number of drug-related crimes and arrests. Virtually all of these addicts committed crimes before abusing drugs and use crime to support themselves as well as their habits. Their criminal activity and drug use are symptomatic of chronic antisocial behavior and attitudes. Legally available drugs at lower prices would do little to discourage crime by this group. For a second group, criminal activity is associated with the high cost of illegal drugs. For these addicts, lower prices would decrease drug-related crimes. For a third group, legally available drugs would mean an opportunity to create illegal diversion markets, as some addicts currently do with methadone.[81]

Legalization advocates point to the exploding prison population and the failure of strict drug laws to lower crime rates.[82] Arrests for drug offenses doubled from 470,000 in 1980 to 1 million in 1993.[83] Some 60 percent of the 95,000 federal inmates are incarcerated for drug-law violations.[84]

Rising prison populations are generated in large part by stricter laws, tough enforcement, and mandatory minimum sentencing laws—policy choices of the public and Congress. But the growing number of prisoners is also a product of the high rate of recidivism—a phenomenon tied in good measure to the lack of treatment facilities, particularly in prison. Eighty percent of prisoners have prior convictions and 60 percent have served time before.[85] Despite the fact that more than 60 percent of all state inmates have used illegal drugs regularly and 30 percent were under the influence of drugs at the time they committed the crime for which they were incarcerated,[86] fewer than 20 percent of inmates with drug problems receive any treatment.[87] Many of these inmates also abuse alcohol, but there is little alcoholism treatment either for them or for those prisoners dependent only on alcohol.[88]

While strict laws and enforcement do not deter addicts from using drugs, the criminal justice system can be used to get them in treatment. Because of the nature of addiction, most drug abusers do not seek treatment voluntarily, but many respond to outside pressures including the threat of incarceration.[89] Where the criminal justice system is used to encourage participation in treatment, addicts are more likely to complete treatment and stay off drugs. . . .[90]

Notes

1. Kurt Schmoke, "Decriminalizing Drugs: It Just Might Work—And Nothing Else Does," in *Drug Legalization: For and Against,* ed. Rod Evans and Irwin Berent (Lasalle: Open Court Press, 1992), p. 216; Merrill Smith, "The Drug Problem: Is There an Answer?" in Evans and Berent, eds., p. 84; Steven Wisotsky, "Statement Before the Select Committee on Narcotics Abuse and Control," in Evans and Berent, eds., p. 189.
2. National Commission on Marijuana and Drug Abuse, *Marijuana: Signal of Misunderstanding* (Washington, DC: GPO, 1972); Musto, p. 267.
3. U.S. Department of Health and Human Services, *Preliminary Estimates from the 1994 National Household Survey on Drug Abuse* (September 1995), pp. 2, 58.
4. Dept. of Health and Human Services (1995), p. 11.
5. Dept. of Health and Human Services (1995), p. 2.
6. Office of National Drug Control Policy (ONDCP), *National Drug Control Strategy: Strengthening Communities' Response to Drugs and Crime* (February 1995), p. 139.
7. ONDCP, *Breaking the Cycle of Drug Abuse* (September 1993), pp. 6–9.
8. Todd Austin Brenner, "The Legalization of Drugs: Why Prolong the Inevitable," in Evans and Berent, eds., p. 173; Schmoke, in Evans and Berent, eds., p. 218; Smith, in Evans and Berent, eds., p. 85.
9. Smith, in Evans and Berent, eds., pp. 83–86; Kevin Zeese, "Drug War Forever?" in *Searching*

for Alternatives: Drug-Control Policy in the United States, eds. Melvyn Krauss and Edward Lazear (Stanford: Hoover Institute Press, 1992), p. 265.

10. Ethan Nadelmann, "The Case for Legalization," in *The Drug Legalization Debate, ed. James Inciardi* (Newbury Park: Sage Publications, 1991), pp. 39–40.

11. Michael Gazzaniga, "The Opium of the People: Crack in Perspective," in Evans and Berent, eds., p. 236.

12. Lloyd Johnston, Patrick O'Malley, and Jerald Bachman, *National Survey Results on Drug Use from the Monitoring the Future Study, 1975–1993* (Rockville: 1994), Vol. 1, p. 191 and Vol. 2, p. 144; Center on Addiction and Substance Abuse at Columbia University, *National Survey of American Attitudes on Substance Abuse* (July 1995).

13. Dept. of Health and Human Services *Preliminary Estimates from the 1993 National Household Survey: Press Release* (July 1994), p. 4.

14. Dept. of Health and Human Services (July 1994), p. 4.

15. See for example, Lester Grinspoon and James Bakalar, "The War on Drugs—A Peace Proposal," *The New England Journal of Medicine, 330*(5) 1994, pp. 357–60; Arnold Trebach, "For Legalization of Drugs" in *Legalize It? Debating American Drug Policy,* Arnold Trebach and James Inciardi, eds., (Washington: American University Press, 1993), p. 108.

16. Mark Moore, "Drugs: Getting a Fix on the Problem and the Solution," in Evans and Berent, eds., p. 152.

17. Johnston, O'Malley and Bachman, Vol. 1, p. 206.

18. Schmoke, in Evans and Berent, eds., p. 218; Brenner, in Evans and Berent, eds., p. 171; Wisotsky in Evans and Berent, eds., p. 210.

19. ONDCP (1995), p. 139; Centers for Disease Control, *Morbidity and Mortality Weekly Report, 34*(SS-3) 1994, p. 8.

20. Johnston, O'Malley and Bachman, Vol. 1, p. 79.

21. Moore in Evans and Berent, eds., p. 148; and Mark Moore, "Supply Reduction and Law Enforcement" in *Drugs and Crime,* Michael Tonry and James Wilson, eds., *Crime and Justice: A Review of Research,* Volume 13 (Chicago: University of Chicago Press, 1990), pp. 109–158; Michael Grossman, Gary Becker and Kevin Murphy, "Rational Addiction and the Effect of Price on Consumption," in Krauss and Lazear, eds., p. 83.

22. ONDCP (1995), p. 146.

23. Michael Farrell, John Strang and Peter Reuter, "The Non-Case for Legalization" in *Winning the War on Drugs: To Legalize or Not* (Institute of Economic Affairs: London, 1994).

24. Herbert Kleber, "Our Current Approach to Drug Abuse—Progress, Problems, Proposals," *The New England Journal of Medicine 330*(5), 1994, pp. 362–363; for higher estimates of the differences between illegal and legal costs see Moore,

25. in Evans and Berent, eds., p. 148 and Wisotsky, in Evans and Berent, eds., p. 190.

26. Moore, in Evans and Berent, eds., pp. 129–130.

27. Center on Addiction and Substance Abuse at Columbia University, *National Survey of American Attitudes on Substance Abuse* (July 1995).

28. See for example, Wisotsky, in Evans and Berent, eds., p. 204.

29. Johnston, O'Malley and Bachman, Vol. 1, pp. 76–79.

30. K. Michael Cummings, Terry Pechacek and Donald Shopland, "The Illegal Sale of Cigarettes to US Minors: Estimates by State," *American Journal of Public Health,* 84(2) 1994, pp. 300–302.

31. Johnston, O'Malley and Bachman, Vol. 1, pp. 76–79.

32. Johnston, O'Malley and Bachman, Vol. 1, p. 79.

33. Lloyd Johnston, "A Synopsis of the Key Points in the 1994 Monitoring the Future Results" (December 1994), Table 1; Johnston, O'Malley and Bachman, Vol. 1, pp. 136–137.

34. Drug Strategies, *Keeping Score* (Washington, DC: 1995), p. 11.

35. Evelyn Cohen Reis et al., "The Impact of Anti-Drug Advertising: Perceptions of Middle and High School Students," *Archives of Pediatric and Adolescent Medicine,* 148, December 1994, pp. 1262–1268.

36. Johnston, O'Malley and Bachman, Vol. 1, p. 79.

37. "Hooked on Tobacco: The Teen Epidemic," *Consumer Reports,* March 1995, pp. 142–148.

38. Rodney Skager and Gregory Austin, *Fourth Biennial Statewide Survey of Drug and Alcohol Use Among California Students in Grades 7, 9, and 11,* Office of the Attorney General, June 1993; Wayne Fisher, *Drug and Alcohol Use Among New Jersey High School Students,* New Jersey Department of Law and Public Safety, 1993.

39. David Peck, "Legal and Social Factors in the Deterrence of Adolescent Marijuana Use," *Journal of Alcohol and Drug Education,* 28(3) 1983, pp. 58–74.

40. Diedre Dupre, "Initiation and Progression of Alcohol, Marijuana and Cocaine Use Among Adolescent Abusers," *The American Journal on Addiction,* 4, 1995, pp. 43–48.

41. Ronald Simmons, Rand Conger and Leslie Whitbeck, "A Multistage Learning Model of the Influences of Family and Peers Upon Adolescent Substance Abuse," *Journal of Drug Issues* 18(3) 1988, pp. 293–315.

42. Simmons, Conger and Whitbeck, p. 304; Mark Moore, "Drugs: Getting a Fix on the Problem and the Solution," in Evans and Berent, eds., p. 143.

43. Musto, pp. 258–259.

44. Philip Cook, "The Effect of Liquor Taxes on Drinking, Cirrhosis, and Auto Accidents" in *Alcohol and Public Policy: Beyond the Shadow of Prohibition,* Mark Moore and Dean Gerstein, eds. (Washington, DC: National Academy Press, 1981), p. 256.

44. Jack Homer, "Projecting the Impact of Law Enforcement on Cocaine Prevalence: A System Dynamics Approach," *Journal of Drug Issues* 23(2) 1993, pp. 281–295.

45. Kleber, p. 361.

46. James Q. Wilson, "Against the Legalization of Drugs," *Commentary* (February 1990), pp. 21–28.

47. See for example, Schmoke in Evans and Berent, eds., p. 218.

48. ONDCP (1995), p. 138.

49. Bureau of Justice Statistics, *Survey of State Prison Inmates, 1991* (Washington, DC: 1993), p. 26.

50. Bureau of Justice Statistics, *Prisoners in 1994* (Washington, DC: 1995), p. 13.

51. Paul Aaron and David Musto, "Temperance and Prohibition in America: A Historical Overview," in Moore and Gerstein, eds., p. 172.

52. Drug Enforcement Administration (DEA), *How to Hold Your Own in a Drug Legalization Debate* (Washington, DC, 1994), p. 26, adjusted to 1995.

53. Center on Addiction and Substance Abuse at Columbia University (CASA), *The Cost of Substance Abuse to America's Health Care System, Final Report* (To be issued, 1995).

54. The Tobacco Institute (1994), adjusted to 1995.

55. CASA (To be issued, 1995).

56. Center on Addiction and Substance Abuse at Columbia University, *Substance Abuse and Federal Entitlement Programs* (February 1995).

57. CASA (To be issued, 1995).

58. Centers for Disease Control, National AIDS Clearinghouse (1994).

59. See for example, "Prescribing to Addicts Appears to Work in Britain: Interview with Dr. John Marks," *Psychiatric News,* December 17, 1993, pp. 8, 14.

60. Joyce Lowinson et al., "Methadone Maintenance," pp. 550–561; Jerome Jaffe, "Opiates: Clinical Aspects," pp. 186–194; and Eric Simon, "Opiates: Neurobiology," pp. 195–204 in *Substance Abuse: A Comprehensive Textbook,* 2nd ed., Joyce Lowinson, Pedro Ruiz and Robert Millman, eds. (Baltimore: Williams and Wilkins, 1992).

61. Mark Gold, "Cocaine (and Crack): Clinical Aspects," in Lowinson, Ruiz and Millman, eds., pp. 205–221.

62. Peter Lurie, Arthur Reingold et al., *The Public Health Impact of Needle Exchange Programs in the United States and Abroad,* 2 vols. (University of California, 1993).

63. Dept. of Justice (1992), p. 12; Paul Taubman, "Externalities and Decriminalization of Drugs," in Krauss and Lazear, eds., p. 99.

64. Dept. of Justice (1992), p. 12; Joel Hay, "The Harm They Do to Others," in Krauss and Lazear, eds., pp. 204–213.

65. Hay, in Krauss and Lazear, eds., p. 208.

66. Center on Addiction and Substance Abuse at Columbia University (CASA), *The Cost of Substance Abuse to America's Health Care System,* *Report 1: Medicaid Hospital Costs* (July 1993), pp. 38–46.

67. Ronald Kessler et al., "Lifetime and 12-month prevalence of DSM-III-R psychiatric disorders in the United States: Results from the National Comorbidity Study," *Archives of General Psychiatry,* 51(1) 1994, pp. 8–19.

68. Dept. of Justice (1992), p. 11.

69. Centers for Disease Control, "Youth Risk Behavior Survey, 1991."

70. M. Lynne Cooper, Robert Pierce, and Rebecca Farmer Huselid, "Substance Abuse and Sexual Risk Taking Among Black Adolescents and White Adolescents," *Health Psychology* 13(3) 1994, pp. 251–262.

71. Dept. of Justice (1992), p. 9.

72. General Accounting Office, *Foster Care: Parental Drug Abuse Has Alarming Impact on Young Children* (Washington, DC: 1994).

73. Daniel Brookoff et al., "Testing Reckless Drivers for Cocaine and Marijuana," *The New England Journal of Medicine* 331(8) 1994, pp. 518–522.

74. Peter Marzuk, Kenneth Tardiff, et al., "Prevalence of Recent Cocaine Use among Motor Vehicle Fatalities in New York City," *Journal of the American Medical Association* 1990; 263, pp. 250–256.

75. See for example, Nadelmann, in Inciardi (1991), ed., pp. 31–32; Brenner, in Evans and Berent, eds., p. 174; Ira Glasser, "Drug Prohibition: An Engine for Crime," in Krauss and Lazear, eds., pp. 271–283; Milton Friedman, "The War We Are Losing," in Krauss and Lazear, eds., pp. 53–57.

76. Paul J. Goldstein, "The Drugs/Violence Nexus: A Tripartite Conceptual Framework," *Journal of Drug Issues* (Fall 1985), pp. 493–516.

77. Mitchell Rosenthal, "Panacea or Chaos: The Legalization of Drugs in America," *Journal of Substance Abuse Treatment* 11(1) 1994, pp. 3–7.

78. Henry Brownstein and Paul J. Goldstein, "A Typology of Drug-Related Homicides" in *Drugs, Crime and the Criminal Justice System, Ralph Weisheit,* ed. (Cincinnati, OH: Anderson Publishing Co., 1990), pp. 171–191.

79. Bureau of Justice Statistics (1993), p. 22.

80. Kenneth Tardiff et al., "Homicide in New York City: Cocaine Use and Firearms," *Journal of the American Medical Association* 272(1) 1994, pp. 43–46.

81. Jon Chaiken and Marcia Chaiken, "Varieties of Criminal Behavior" (Santa Monica: Rand, 1982); HK Wexler and George De Leon, "Criminals as Drug Abusers and Drug Abusers Who Are Criminals," Paper presented to the Annual Convention of the American Psychological Association, Washington, DC, 1980; cited in George De Leon, "Some Problems with the Anti-Prohibitionist Position on Legalization of Drugs," *Journal of Addictive Diseases* 13(2) 1994, p. 38.

82. See for example, New York City Bar Association, "A Wiser Course: Ending Drug Prohibition," *The Record* 49(5) 1994, pp. 525–534.

83. Bureau of Justice Statistics (1995), p. 13.
84. Bureau of Justice Statistics (1995), pp. 1, 10.
85. Bureau of Justice Statistics (1993), p. 11.
86. Bureau of Justice Statistics (1993), p. 21.
87. General Accounting Office, *Drug Treatment: State Prisons Face Challenges in Providing Services* (Washington, DC: 1991).
88. Bureau of Justice Statistics (1993), p. 26.
89. De Leon, p. 38.
90. M. Douglas Anglin. "The Efficacy of Civil Commitment in Treating Narcotic Addiction" in *Compulsory Treatment of Drug Abuse: Research and Clinical Practice*, NIDA Research Monograph 86, 1988, pp. 8–34; Robert Hubbard et al., *Drug Abuse Treatment: A National Study of Effectiveness* (Chapel Hill: University of North Carolina Press, 1989).

HERBERT KLEBER has been a pioneer in research and treatment of substance abuse for over 35 years. From 1968 to 1989, he founded and headed the Drug Dependence Unit at Yale University. Kleber is the author of more than 200 papers and the co-editor of the *American Psychiatric Press Textbook of Substance Abuse Treatment*. He has received numerous prestigious awards and two honorary degrees, is listed as one of the "Best Doctors in America" and "Best Doctors in New York," and was elected in 1996 to be a member of the Institute of Medicine of the National Academy of Science.

JOSEPH A. CALIFANO JR. is founder and chairman of the National Center on Addiction and Substance Abuse (CASA) at Columbia University.

Jacob Sullum

→ NO

The War Over Weed

In November, voters in Colorado and Washington approved groundbreaking ballot initiatives legalizing marijuana for recreational use. The measures immediately eliminated penalties for possessing up to an ounce and required state regulators to adopt rules for commercial production and sale by next July in Colorado and next December in Washington. Meanwhile, recent national surveys put support for legalization at 50 percent or more—the highest numbers ever recorded.

In this context of unprecedented public receptiveness to repealing cannabis prohibition, four centrist drug policy specialists—Jonathan Caulkins of Carnegie Mellon, Angela Hawken of Pepperdine, Beau Kilmer of the RAND Corporation, and Mark Kleiman of UCLA—have published *Marijuana Legalization*, a handy little paperback that aims to tell us "What Everyone Needs to Know" about the subject. Assiduously dedicated to a utilitarian, just-the-facts approach, Caulkins and his co-authors consider marijuana's benefits as well as its hazards, the harm caused by prohibition as well as the harm it prevents, the impact that legalization is apt to have not only on pot smoking but also on drinking, and the fiscal advantages, in terms of new tax revenue and lower law enforcement costs, of treating marijuana more like alcohol.

Along the way, they offer calm and generally fair-minded excursions into controversies such as the perils of increasing pot potency, the alleged link between cannabis and schizophrenia, and the extent to which marijuana prohibition enriches Mexican drug cartels. But after all this judicious weighing of costs and benefits, the authors conclude that the question of whether to legalize marijuana hinges on how you feel about getting high.

"In the end," Caulkins et al. write, "all the fancy benefit-cost analysis boils down to a rather simple proposition. . . . If you think marijuana intoxication is, on average, a good thing—counting both the happy controlled users and the unhappy dependent users—then a benefit-cost analysis done in a way that reflects your values will probably conclude that legalization improves social welfare. If you think marijuana intoxication is, on average, a bad thing, then an analysis that reflects your values will probably conclude that legalization harms social welfare—because the dominant outcome of legalization will be more marijuana use."

Although Caulkins and his colleagues do not put it this way, the implication is that the war on marijuana,

ostensibly aimed at promoting public health and safety, is fundamentally a matter of taste. It is not even a moral crusade, strictly speaking, since there is no moral principle underlying the arbitrary legal distinction between marijuana and alcohol, which Hawken, in a separate essay toward the end of the book, concedes "makes no sense." As Martin Lee shows in *Smoke Signals*, his engaging and illuminating new history, marijuana's contraband status is a result of historical accident, racial prejudice, xenophobia, loads of cultural baggage, and an astonishing amount of ignorance. In this light, the coolheaded analysis offered by Caulkins et al. seems almost comical, since it presupposes that marijuana was banned for rational reasons.

While there is no shortage of books about marijuana, Lee, co-author of the fine LSD history *Acid Dreams*, brings new breadth and depth to the subject. His rich, wide-ranging account is a little skimpy in its coverage of recent developments but full of fascinating details from further back, including ancient medical uses of cannabis, the West's belated discovery of the plant's benefits, and its popularity within pre-hippie bohemian circles such as the 19th-century Club des Haschischins, jazz musicians of the 1920s and '30s, and Beat writers in the '40s and '50s.

Although cannabis has been consumed for thousands of years in India and China, Americans associated it with Mexico when they first became aware of it as a smoked intoxicant (as opposed to an ingredient in orally consumed patent medicines). Lee explains that Mexican peasants began smoking cannabis, possibly descended from hemp cultivated for fiber by Spanish colonists, in the early 1800s. Its use by Pancho Villa's revolutionary soldiers is memorialized in the folk song "La Cucaracha"—hence the term roach, "modern-day slang for the butt of a marijuana cigarette."

Marijuana's association with blacks and Mexicans, which marked it as an exotic drug used by inferior but scary outsiders, proved crucial to its prohibition. The bans began at the state level in 1915, when California outlawed the plant, and culminated in the federal Marihuana Tax Act of 1937. With marijuana as with opium, Lee observes, "the target of the prohibition was not the drug so much as those associated with its use."

Federal Bureau of Narcotics Commissioner Harry Anslinger warned that "marihuana causes white women to seek sexual relations with Negroes" and claimed that half the violent crimes in areas occupied by "Mexicans, Greeks, Turks, Filipinos, Spaniards, Latin Americans, and

Negroes may be traced to the use of marihuana." Anslinger, who collected and circulated accounts of bloody crimes allegedly caused by marijuana, portrayed it as "the most violence-causing drug in the history of mankind" (a title that has since been seized by a succession of other drugs, often based on equally dubious evidence).

The notion that marijuana turns people into homicidal maniacs—which, Lee notes, was later replaced by the contradictory claim that marijuana turns people into passive, unmotivated layabouts—would have struck people familiar with the drug as patently absurd. But those people were not writing drug legislation. "Few members of Congress knew anything about cannabis when they voted to outlaw the herb," Lee notes. "'What is this bill about?' a congressman asked House Majority Leader Sam Rayburn from Texas, who replied, 'It has something to do with a thing called marihuana. I think it is a narcotic of some kind.'"

Marijuana's beyond-the-pale status was cemented when self-conscious dissidents (the Beats and then the hippies) embraced it, attracted largely by its illegality. Marijuana prohibition became self-perpetuating: The sort of people who were eager to use it as a signal of rebellion disgusted the sort of people who were determined to keep it illegal, and the plant's countercultural connotations have helped keep it illegal ever since.

"The serrated marijuana leaf had become a totem of rebellion, a multivalent symbol of societal conflict," Lee writes. "Condemning cannabis was a way to denounce the social and political movements that were in open revolt against 'the American way of life.'" While Lee gives a respectful hearing to Allen Ginsberg's view that "marijuana consciousness" is inherently subversive, he is appropriately skeptical of the notion that cannabis itself promotes a particular worldview, citing the old hippie saw that the drug might stop working if it were legalized.

Lee is much more excited about marijuana's medical potential. Perhaps a little too excited: His excursions into cannabinoid pharmacology and biology may tax the general reader's patience. Still, Lee is right to emphasize the importance of the medical marijuana movement, which is where most of the action in cannabis-related legal reform has been in recent years, especially when it comes to testing the boundaries between state and federal power.

One of the few disappointments in Lee's book is his discussion of *Gonzales v. Raich,* the 2005 case in which the Supreme Court ruled that the federal government's power to regulate interstate commerce extends even to home-grown marijuana used by patients in states that recognize the plant as a medicine. "Federal drug laws are rooted in the Commerce Clause, which empowers Congress to regulate interstate commerce," he writes. "This provision once served as an important tool for promoting progressive federal policies from the New Deal to Civil Rights, but over the years it became an all-purpose excuse for Congress to meddle in virtually every aspect of human behavior."

Contrary to what Lee seems to think, he is not describing two different legal trends. The Commerce Clause "became an all-purpose excuse for Congress to meddle in virtually every aspect of human behavior" *because* it "served as an important tool for promoting progressive federal policies from the New Deal to Civil Rights." If the Commerce Clause authorizes the federal government to punish a farmer for growing too much wheat, even when the extra grain never leaves his farm (as the Supreme Court held in the New Deal case *Wickard v. Filburn*), it is not much of a stretch to argue that the Commerce Clause also authorizes the federal government to punish patients for growing marijuana, even when the crop never leaves the state. If, as the Civil Rights Act of 1964 asserted, Congress can regulate any restaurant, cafeteria, lunchroom, lunch counter, or soda fountain when "its operations affect commerce" (e.g., when an Alabama diner uses Idaho potatoes to make French fries), surely the feds can shut down medical marijuana dispensaries, even when their activities are purely local and authorized by state law.

Notwithstanding the Supreme Court's absurdly broad reading of the Commerce Clause, states have room to experiment with new approaches to cannabis (and other drugs). As Caulkins et al. note, "The Constitution does not allow the federal government either to order state governments to create any particular criminal law or to require state and local police to enforce federal criminal laws." That's why opponents of Proposition 19, the California legalization initiative that lost by five percentage points in 2010, were wrong when they argued that the Supremacy Clause, which declares legitimate acts of Congress "the supreme law of the land," made the measure unconstitutional.

Even under national alcohol prohibition, which unlike the federal ban on marijuana was authorized by a constitutional amendment, states were free to go their own way. They could decline to pass their own versions of the Volstead Act (as Maryland did), repeal them (as a dozen states, including Colorado and Washington, did while the 18th Amendment was still in force), or simply refrain from prosecuting people under them (which was common in the wetter districts of the country). "The question is not whether a state could change its own laws," Caulkins et al. write. "Rather, the question is how the conflict with the continued federal prohibition would play out."

While the feds certainly can make trouble for any state that dares to legalize pot, there is a practical limit to what they can accomplish on their own. According to the FBI, there were 758,000 marijuana arrests nationwide in 2011, the vast majority for possession. State and local police departments were responsible for 99 percent of those arrests. It simply is not feasible for the Drug Enforcement Administration (DEA)—which has about 5,500 special agents nationwide, compared to about 765,000 sworn personnel employed by state and local law enforcement agencies—to bust a significant percentage of people who grow pot for themselves and their friends (as Colorado's law allows), let alone people who possess it for recreational use.

The DEA can raid state-legal pot shops, as it has done with medical marijuana dispensaries, but the number of potential targets will be considerably larger once the market officially expands to include recreational users. The Justice Department can use asset forfeiture as an intimidation tactic against landlords and threaten banks that accept deposits from pot businesses with money laundering charges. The Internal Revenue Service can make life difficult for pot sellers by disallowing their business expenses (but not, thanks to a tax law wrinkle, their "cost of goods sold," which includes the cost of buying marijuana). The feds could even threaten state regulators with prosecution for facilitating the trade, although that seems less likely, since it would provoke a direct confrontation with state officials. The one thing federal drug warriors cannot do, judging from their track record even when they have the full cooperation of state and local law enforcement agencies, is suppress the business entirely.

The ineffectiveness of prohibition is only part of the story, however, and it is not the most morally salient part. Lee highlights the basic injustice of using force to prevent people from smoking a politically incorrect plant, telling the stories of jazzmen hounded by Anslinger because of their deviant recreational preferences, activists targeted because of their conspicuous advocacy, medical users given outrageously long prison sentences, and people treated like drug kingpins because they grew pot for patients. "There is no moral justification for a policy that criminalizes people for trying to relieve their suffering," Lee writes. "Reefer madness has nothing to do with smoking marijuana—for therapy or fun or any other reason—and everything to do with how the U.S. government has stigmatized, prosecuted, and jailed users of this much maligned and much venerated plant."

Caulkins and his co-authors, by contrast, explicitly defend the proposition that forcibly protecting you from your own mistakes is a legitimate function of government, that it is not only possible to "make someone better off by coercing behavioral change" but desirable to do so, provided it can be done at an acceptable cost. Even if you buy that premise, shouldn't the distribution of these costs and benefits matter? For the most part, the people who are better off because prohibition stopped them from developing a life-disrupting addiction to pot are not the people who bear the burdens of this policy. Under prohibition, some are punished so that others may benefit.

"Tens of thousands of marijuana distributors are in prison," Caulkins et al. write, and "hundreds of thousands of people are arrested and convicted of marijuana violations each year. Quite apart from the budgetary costs to enforcement agencies, there is a real, though hard-to-quantify, cost to those individuals' welfare, in terms of direct suffering, reduced job prospects, and other effects." No kidding. But where Caulkins et al. see a cost that must be weighed (even though it can't really be measured), Lee sees a moral scandal built on a mountain of lies.

The two books nevertheless converge on something like a practical consensus. In four separate essays at the end of their book, Caulkins and his colleagues suggest a range of more tolerant approaches to cannabis, including "decriminalization plus home growing and sharing" (Caulkins), "permission for production and use through small not-for-profit cooperatives" (Kleiman), and experimenting with various forms of legalization (Hawken and Kilmer). "As a first step," Hawken says, "the federal government should step aside and let the states determine their own fate." We will soon discover how realistic that expectation is.

JACOB SULLUM, Senior Editor of *Reason*, focuses most of his writings on shrinking the realm of politics and expanding individual choice.

EXPLORING THE ISSUE

Should Laws Against Drug Use Remain Restrictive?

Critical Thinking and Reflection

1. Should individuals (adults) or governments decide what drugs they can take?
2. What would happen if drugs were legalized?
3. What are all the consequences of America's drug laws?
4. In your estimate, do the benefits of America's drug laws outweigh the costs?
5. How could drug laws banning drugs be modified to greatly reduce their costs?
6. Would legalizing only marijuana use be a good policy? Why?
7. Can a society maintain its moral integrity and authority when it is lax on these types of laws?

Is There Common Ground?

Everyone agrees that America has a drug problem. Drugs have ruined many lives. Everyone agrees that something should be done about it. But what? The answer is easy, outlaw drug use. So we did that. Everyone agrees the result was not what we were hoping for. Now we are not sure whether outlawing drugs was the right action to take, but other options also have bad consequences. Kleber and Califano assert that utilizing the criminal justice system to maintain the illegal nature of drugs is necessary to keep society free of the detrimental effects of drugs. Loosening drug laws is unwise and dangerous. They argue that international control efforts, interdiction, and domestic law enforcement are effective and that many problems associated with drug use are mitigated by drug regulation policies. They maintain that restrictive drug laws are a feasible and desirable means of dealing with the drug crisis.

Sullum presents a review of all sides regarding the legalization of marijuana but largely undermines the reasons for criminalizing it. He points out that restrictive drug laws are highly destructive and discriminatory. He professes that if drug laws remain stringent, the result would be more drug users in prison and that drug abusers and addicts would engage in more criminal activity. Also, there is the possibility that more drug-related social problems would occur. He concludes that society cannot afford to continue its tragic criminalization of drugs. The potential risks of the current federal policies on drug criminalization outweigh any potential benefits. One risk is the loss of many of our civil liberties.

Proponents of less restrictive drug laws argue that such laws have not worked and that the drug battle has been lost. They believe that drug-related problems would diminish if more tolerant policies were implemented.

Legalization opponents, however, point out that the legalization of alcohol and tobacco does not make problems associated with them disappear (alcohol and tobacco have extremely high addiction rates as well as a myriad of other problems associated with their use). The counter argument is that many European countries, such as the Netherlands and Switzerland, have a system of legalized drugs, and most have far lower addiction rates and lower incidences of drug-related violence and crime than the United States.

These countries make a distinction between soft drugs (those identified as less harmful) and hard drugs (those with serious consequences). However, would the outcomes of less restrictive laws in the United States be the same as in Europe? Relaxed drug laws in the United States could still be a tremendous risk because its drug problems could escalate and reimposing strict drug laws would be difficult. This was the case with Prohibition in the 1920s, which, in changing the status of alcohol from legal to illegal, produced numerous crime and alcohol-related problems.

Create Central

www.mhhe.com/createcentral

Additional Resources

Many good articles debate the pros and cons of this issue. These include "Who's Using and Who's Doing Time: Incarceration, the War on Drugs, and Public Health," by Lisa Moore and Amy Elkavich (*American Journal of Public Health*, September 2008); "Too Dangerous Not to Regulate," by Peter Moskos (*U.S. News & World Report*, August 4, 2008); "Reorienting U.S. Drug Policy," by Jonathan Caulkins and Peter Reuter (*Issues in Science and Technology*, Fall 2006); "No Surrender: The Drug War Saves Lives," by John Walters (*National Review*, September 27, 2004), the current director of the Office of National Drug Control Policy; "Lighting Up in Amsterdam," by John Tierney (*The New York Times*, August 26, 2006); "What Drug Policies

Cost: Estimating Government Drug Policy Expenditures," by Peter Reuter (*Addiction*, March 2006); "An Effective Drug Policy to Protect America's Youth and Communities," by Asa Hutchinson (*Fordham Urban Law Journal*, January 2003); and "The War at Home: Our Jails Overflow with Nonviolent Drug Offenders. Have We Reached the Point Where the Drug War Causes More Harm Than the Drugs Themselves?" by Sanho Tree (*Sojourners*, May–June 2003).

Recent books that deal with drugs, drug policies and laws, and the consequences of drugs include Richard F. Isralowitz and Peter L. Myers, *Illicit Drugs* (Greenwood, 2011); J. Bryan Page and Merrill Singer, *Comprehending Drug Use: Ethnographic Research at the Social Margins* (Rutgers University Press, 2010); Alex Stevens, *Drugs, Crime and Public Health: The Political Economy of Drug Policy* (Routledge, 2011); Thomas Babor et al., *Drug Policy and the Public Good* (Oxford University Press, 2010); Damon

Barrett, ed., *Children of the Drug War: Perspectives on the Impact of Drug Policies on Young People* (International Debate Education Association, 2011); Paul Manning, ed., *Drugs and Popular Culture: Drugs, Media and Identity in Contemporary Society* (Willan Publishing, 2007); William L. Marcy, *the Politics of Cocaine: How U.S. Policy Has Created a Thriving Drug Industry in Central and South America* (Lawrence Hill Books, 2010); and World Health Organization, *Ensuring Balance in National Policies on Controlled Substances* (World Health Organization, 2011). Marina Barnard covers the effects of drugs on families in *Drug Addiction and Families* (Jessica Kingsley Publishers, 2007). Some excellent works on drugs and drug policies examine the drug situation in Great Britain, including Martin Plant et al., *Drug Nation: Patterns, Problems, Panics, and Policies* (Oxford University Press, 2011); Philip Bean, *Legalizing Drugs: Debates and Dilemmas* (Policy, 2010); and Trevor Bennett, *Drug-Crime Connections* (Cambridge University Press, 2007).

Internet References . . .

ACLU Criminal Justice Home Page

www.aclu.org/crimjustice/index.html

Sociology—Study Sociology Online

http://edu.learnsoc.org/

Sociology Web Resources

www.mhhe.com/socscience/sociology
/resources/index.htm

Sociosite

www.topsite.com/goto/sociosite.net

Socioweb

www.topsite.com/goto/socioweb.com

Selected, Edited, and with Issue Framing Material by:
Kurt Finsterbusch, *University of Maryland, College Park*

ISSUE

Are We Headed Toward a Nuclear 9/11?

YES: Brian Michael Jenkins, from "Terrorists Can Think Strategically: Lessons Learned from the Mumbai Attacks," *Testimony Series* (Rand Corporation, January 2009)

NO: Graham Allison, from "Time to Bury a Dangerous Legacy—Part I," *YaleGlobal Online* (March 14, 2008)

Learning Outcomes
After reading this issue, you will be able to:
• Understand the reasons why a nuclear terrorist act in the United States is a likely event.
• Understand the reasons why others believe that a nuclear terrorist event in the United States is unlikely.
• Identify important factors that you should examine more closely to gain more confidence in your judgment about the likelihood of a nuclear terrorist event. For example, you might examine further how easy it is for terrorists to obtain nuclear materials.
• Identify the actions that America can take to reduce the likelihood of a nuclear terrorist event.
• Attempt to figure out how what you learned should affect your life.

ISSUE SUMMARY

YES: Brian Michael Jenkins, senior advisor to the president of the Rand Corporation, in testimony before the U.S. Senate Committee on Homeland Security and Governmental Affairs, posited that a team of terrorists could be inserted into the United States and carry out a Mumbai-style attack, as terrorism has "increasingly become an effective strategic weapon."

NO: Graham Allison, Harvard professor and director of the Belfer Center for Science and International Affairs, affirms that we are not likely to experience a nuclear 9/11 because "nuclear terrorism is preventable by a feasible, affordable agenda of actions that . . . would shrink the risk of nuclear terrorism to nearly zero."

Since the terrorist attacks of September 11, 2001, much has been written about the specter of nuclear terrorism and the releasing of a dirty bomb (one loaded with radioactive material) in an urban/civilian setting. The events of September 11 have all but ensured the world's preoccupation with such an event for the foreseeable future. Indeed, the arrest of a U.S. man that was suspected of having dirty bomb materials indicates that such plans may indeed be in the works between Al-Qaeda and other terrorist cells. When this horror is combined with the availability of elements of nuclear-related material in places like the states of the former Soviet Union, Pakistan, India, Iraq, Iran, North Korea, and many other states, one can envision a variety of sobering scenarios.

Hollywood feeds these views with such films as *The Sum of All Fears* and *The Peacemaker*, in which nuclear terrorism is portrayed as all too easy to carry out and likely to occur. It is difficult in such environments to separate fact from fiction and to ascertain objectively the prob-abilities of such events. So many factors go into a successful initiative in this area. One must find a committed cadre of terrorists, sufficient financial backing, technological know-how, intense security and secrecy, the means of delivery, and many other variables, including luck. In truth, such acts may have already been advanced and thwarted by governments, security services, or terrorist mistakes and incompetence. We do not know, and we may never know.

Regional and ethnic conflicts of a particularly savage nature in places like Chechnya, Kashmir, Colombia, and Afghanistan help to fuel fears that adequately financed zealots will see in nuclear weapons a swift and catastrophic answer to their demands and angers. Osama bin Laden's contribution to worldwide terrorism has been the success of money over security and the realization that particularly destructive acts with high levels of coordination can be "successful." This will undoubtedly encourage others with similar ambitions against real or perceived enemies.

Conversely, many argue that fear of the terrorist threat has left us imagining that which is not likely. They point to a myriad of roadblocks to terrorist groups' obtaining all of the elements necessary for a nuclear or dirty bomb. They cite technological impediments, monetary issues, lack of sophistication, and inability to deliver. They also cite governments' universal desire to prevent such actions. Even critics of former Iraqi leader Saddam Hussein have argued that were he to develop such weapons, he would not deliver them to terrorist groups, nor would he use them except in the most dire of circumstances, such as his own regime's survival. They argue that the threat is overblown and, in some cases, merely used to justify increased security and the restriction of civil liberties.

The following selections reflect the debate about a nuclear 9/11. Jenkins focuses on the ability and resourcefulness of the terrorists and argues that recent events indicate a real ability to carry out such an attack. Allison focuses on the targets, the United States and the West, and insists that a coordinated strategy can stop such an event.

YES ↵   **Brian Michael Jenkins**

Terrorists Can Think Strategically:
Lessons Learned from the Mumbai Attacks

Mr. Chairman and Members of the Committee, it is an honor to appear before you today. The Mumbai attack was still ongoing when RAND initiated an analysis to determine what lessons might be learned from it. This analysis, part of RAND's continuing research on terrorism and homeland security, was documented in a report I co-authored along with other RAND analysts. Specifically, I contributed the sections on the terrorists' strategic motives and the execution of the attack.

We relied on both informed official sources and media reporting. My analysis benefited greatly from the detailed descriptions of the attack provided by officers from the New York Police Department, who were on the scene and whose reports were shared with law enforcement and others in the United States.

Copies of our report have been made available to members of the Committee. Additional copies are available here, and the report is also on RAND's website. For convenience, I have appended the key findings to my testimony. The following observations derive from this report and other relevant research.

Terrorism has increasingly become an effective strategic weapon. Earlier generations of terrorists seldom thought beyond the barrels of their guns. In contrast, the masterminds of the Mumbai terrorist attacks displayed sophisticated strategic thinking in their choice of targets and their efforts to achieve multiple objectives. They were able to capture and hold international attention. They sought to exacerbate communal tensions in India and provoke a crisis between India and Pakistan, thereby persuading Pakistan to redeploy troops to its frontier with India, which in turn would take pressure off of the Taliban, al Qaeda, and other groups operating along the Afghan frontier. All terrorist attacks are recruiting posters. The Mumbai attackers established their terrorist credentials and now rival al Qaeda in reputation.

Al Qaeda is not the only galaxy in the jihadist universe—new contenders have signed on to al Qaeda's ideology of global terror. Even as we have degraded al Qaeda's operational capabilities, the idea of a violent global jihad has spread from North Africa to South Asia. The Mumbai attack foreshadows a continuing terror-ist campaign in India. More broadly, it suggests that the global struggle against the jihadists is far from over.

Terrorists can innovate tactically to obviate existing security measures and confuse authorities. Authorities are obliged to prevent the recurrence of the most recent attack, while knowing that other terrorists will analyze the security in place, devise new tactics, and do the unexpected. The Mumbai attackers did not plant bombs in crowded train coaches, as in the 2006 Mumbai terrorist attack. Instead, gunmen attacked the train station. They did not detonate car bombs as in the 1993 Mumbai attacks or the more recent terrorist attacks on hotels in Indonesia, Egypt, Jordan and Pakistan. They seized control of hotels where they started fires. Multiple attacks at different locations prevented authorities from developing an overall assessment of the situation.

Once again, terrorists have demonstrated that with simple tactics and low-tech weapons, they can produce vastly disproportionate results. The Mumbai attack was sequential, highly mobile, and a departure from the now common suicide bombings, but the tactics were simple—armed assaults, carjackings, drive-by shootings, building takeovers, barricade and hostage situations. The attack was carried out by ten men armed with easily obtained assault weapons, semi-automatic pistols, hand grenades, and simple improvised explosive devices—little more than the arsenal of an infantryman in the 1940s—along with 21st century cell phones, BlackBerries, and GPS locators.

Terrorists will continue to focus on soft targets that offer high body counts and that have iconic value. Nationally and internationally recognized venues that offer ease of access, certainty of tactical success, and the opportunity to kill in quantity will guide target selection. Public spaces are inherently difficult to protect. Major investments in target hardening make sense for government only when these provide a net security benefit, that is, when they do not merely displace the risk to another equally lucrative and accessible target.

Terrorists view public surface transportation as a killing field. One of the two-man terrorist teams went to Mumbai's main train station and opened fire on commuters.

While the attacks on the other targets were theoretically aimed at killing foreigners, the attack at the train station was aimed solely at slaughter. It accounted for more than a third of the total deaths.

This underscores a trend that should be a priority issue in the United States. Public surface transportation offers terrorists easily accessible, dense populations in confined environments—ideal killing zones for gunmen or improvised explosive devices, which remain the most common form of attack. According to analysis by the Mineta Transportation Institute's National Transportation Security Center, two-thirds of all terrorist attacks on surface transportation were intended to kill; 37 percent resulted in fatalities (compared with between 20 and 25 percent of terrorist attacks overall); 75 percent of the fatal attacks involved multiple fatalities; and 28 percent of those involved 10 or more fatalities.

Terrorist attacks on flagship hotels are increasing in number, in total casualties, and in casualties per incident. This trend places increasing demands on hotel security. However, while terrorist attacks are spectacular, they are statistically rare in comparison to ordinary violent crime. In the past forty years, fewer than five hundred hotel guests in the entire world have been killed by terrorists, out of a total global hotel guest population at any time of nearly ten million.

Pakistan's principal defense against external pressure is not its nuclear arsenal, but its own political fragility—its government's less-than-full cooperation is preferable to the country's collapse and descent into chaos. Pakistan continues to play a prominent and problematic role in the overlapping armed conflicts and terrorist campaigns in India, Afghanistan, and Pakistan itself. Al Qaeda, the Taliban, Lashkar-e-Taiba and other insurgent and terrorist groups find sanctuary in Pakistan's turbulent tribal areas. Historically, some of them have drawn on support from the Pakistan government itself. While the Government of Pakistan has been helpful in capturing some key terrorist operatives, Pakistan is accused of protecting others. And it has been understandably reluctant to use military force against its own citizens in the remote tribal areas where these groups reside. When it has used military force, government forces have not fared well. Public sentiment imposes further constraints. Many Pakistanis regard India and the United States, not al Qaeda or the Taliban, as greater threats

to Pakistan's national security. This was perceived as an obstacle to U.S. counterterrorist efforts even before 9/11.

The success of the Mumbai attackers in paralyzing a large city and commanding the attention of the world's news media for nearly three days will encourage similar operations in the future. Terrorists will continue to effectively embed themselves among civilians, taking hostages and using them as human shields to impede responders and maximize collateral casualties. We should expect to see more of this tactic.

Could a Mumbai-style attack happen in the United States? It could. The difference lies in planning and scale. Assembling and training a ten-man team of suicidal attackers seems far beyond the capabilities of the conspirators identified in any of the local terrorist plots discovered in this country since 9/11. We have no evidence of that level of dedication or planning skills.

However, we have seen lone gunmen and pairs of shooters, motivated by mental illness or political cause, run amok, determined to kill in quantity. The Long Island Railroad, Empire State Building, LAX, Virginia Tech, and Columbine cases come to mind. In 1955, four Puerto Rican separatists opened fire in a then unguarded Capitol Building, wounding five members of Congress. Firearms are readily available in the United States. And some of the perpetrators of the attacks mentioned above planned for their attacks for months, while building their arsenals. Therefore, an attack on the ground, carried out by a small number of self-radicalized, homegrown terrorists armed with readily available weapons, perhaps causing scores of casualties, while still far beyond what we have seen in the terrorist plots uncovered thus far, is not inconceivable.

Could a team of terrorists, recruited and trained abroad as the Mumbai attackers were, be inserted into the United States, perhaps on a U.S.-registered fishing vessel or pleasure boat, to carry out a Mumbai-style attack? Although our intelligence has greatly improved, the answer again must be a qualified yes. It could conceivably happen here, although I would expect our police response to be much swifter and more effective than we saw in Mumbai.

BRIAN MICHAEL JENKINS, a senior advisor to the president of the Rand Corporation and director of the Transportation Security Center, is an expert on terrorism and transportation security.

Graham Allison

→ **NO**

Time to Bury a Dangerous Legacy—Part I

One month after the terrorist assault on the World Trade Center and the Pentagon, on October 11, 2001, President George W. Bush faced a more terrifying prospect. At that morning's presidential daily intelligence briefing, George Tenet, the director of central intelligence, informed the president that a CIA agent codenamed "Dragonfire" had reported that Al Qaeda terrorists possessed a 10-kiloton nuclear bomb, evidently stolen from the Russian arsenal. According to Dragonfire, this nuclear weapon was in New York City.

The government dispatched a top-secret nuclear emergency support team to the city. Under a cloak of secrecy that excluded even Mayor Rudolph Giuliani, these nuclear ninjas searched for the bomb. On a normal workday, half a million people crowd the area within a half-mile radius of Times Square. A noon detonation in Midtown Manhattan would kill them all instantly. Hundreds of thousands of others would die from collapsing buildings, fire and fallout in the hours thereafter. The electromagnetic pulse generated by the blast would fry cell phones and other electronic communication. The wounded would overwhelm hospitals and emergency services. Firemen would fight an uncontrolled ring of fires for days afterward.

In the hours that followed, Condoleezza Rice, then national security adviser, analyzed what strategists call the "problem from hell." Unlike the Cold War, when the US and the Soviet Union knew that an attack against the other would elicit a retaliatory strike or greater measure, Al Qaeda—with no return address—had no such fear of reprisal. Even if the president were prepared to negotiate, Al Qaeda has no phone number to call.

Concerned that Al Qaeda could have smuggled a nuclear weapon into Washington as well, the president ordered Vice President Dick Cheney to leave the capital for an "undisclosed location," where he would remain for weeks to follow—standard procedure to ensure "continuity of government" in case of a decapitation strike against US political leadership. Several hundred federal employees from more than a dozen government agencies joined the vice president at this secret site, the core of an alternative government that would seek to cope in the aftermath of a nuclear explosion that destroyed Washington.

Six months earlier the CIA's Counterterrorism Center had picked up chatter in Al Qaeda channels about an "American Hiroshima." The CIA knew that Osama bin Laden's fascination with nuclear weapons went back at least to 1992, when he attempted to buy highly enriched uranium from South Africa. Al Qaeda operatives were alleged to have negotiated with Chechen separatists in Russia to buy a nuclear warhead, which the Chechen warlord Shamil Basayev claimed to have acquired from Russian arsenals. The CIA's special task force on Al Qaeda had noted the terrorist group's emphasis on thorough planning, intensive training and repetition of successful tactics. The task force highlighted Al Qaeda's preference for symbolic targets and spectacular attacks.

As CIA analysts examined Dragonfire's report and compared it with other bits of information, they noted that the September attack on the World Trade Center had set the bar higher for future terrorist attacks. Psychologically, a nuclear attack would stagger the world's imagination. New York was, in the jargon of national-security experts, "target rich."

As it turned out, Dragonfire's report proved to be a false alarm. But the central takeaway from the case is this: The US government had no grounds in science or logic to dismiss this possibility, nor could it do so today.

There's no established methodology for assessing the probability of an unprecedented event that could have such catastrophic consequences. Nonetheless, in "Nuclear Terrorism" I state my considered judgment that if the US and other governments just keep doing what they are doing today, a nuclear terrorist attack in a major city is more likely than not by 2014.

Richard Garwin, a designer of the hydrogen bomb, whom Enrico Fermi once called, "the only true genius I had ever met," told Congress in March 2007 that he estimated a "20 percent per year probability of a nuclear explosion with American cities and European cities included." My Harvard colleague Matthew Bunn has created a model that estimates the probability of a nuclear terrorist attack over a 10-year period to be 29 percent—identical to the average estimate from a poll of security experts commissioned by Senator Richard Lugar in 2005.

Former Secretary of Defense William Perry has expressed his own view that my work may underestimate the risk. Warren Buffett, the world's most successful investor and legendary odds-maker in pricing insurance policies for unlikely but catastrophic events, concluded that nuclear terrorism is "inevitable." As he has stated: "I don't see any way that it won't happen."

The good news is that nuclear terrorism is preventable by a feasible, affordable agenda of actions that, if taken, would shrink the risk of nuclear terrorism to nearly zero. A global strategy to prevent this ultimate catastrophe can be organized under a Doctrine of Three No's: No loose nukes, no new nascent nukes, no new nuclear weapons. The first requires securing all nuclear weapons and weapons-usable material, on the fastest possible timetable, to a new "gold standard." The second does not allow for any new national capabilities to enrich uranium or reprocess plutonium. The third draws a line under the current eight and a half nuclear powers—the five members of the Security Council and India, Israel, Pakistan and North Korea—and says unambiguously: "Stop. No More."

The US cannot unilaterally sustain a successful strategy to prevent nuclear terrorism. Nor can the necessary actions simply be commanded, compelled or coerced. Instead, they require deep and steady international cooperation rooted in the recognition that nations share a common threat that requires a common strategy. A Global Alliance Against Nuclear Terrorism is therefore in order. The mission of this alliance should be to minimize the risk of nuclear terrorism by taking every action physically, technically and diplomatically possible to prevent nuclear weapons or materials from falling into the hands of terrorists.

Constructing such an alliance will require the US and other nuclear-weapons states to confront the question of a "fourth no": no nuclear weapons. While US or Russian possession of nuclear arsenals is not a major driver of Iran's nuclear ambitions, and while Osama bin Laden would not be less interested in acquiring a nuclear weapon if the US eliminated its current arsenals, the proposition that nuclear weapons are necessary for the security of US

and Russia but intolerably dangerous if acquired by Iran or South Africa is difficult to sell to nuclear have-nots.

The question of a categorical "fourth no" has come to the fore with the January 2007 opinion piece in the *Wall Street Journal* by George P. Shultz, William J. Perry, Henry A. Kissinger and Sam Nunn, calling upon the US and other states to act to realize their Non-Proliferation Treaty commitment and President Reagan's vision of "a world free of nuclear weapons." Towards that goal, the immediate agenda should be to devalue nuclear weapons and minimize their role in international affairs. This should begin with nuclear-weapons states pledging to the following principles: no new national enrichment, no nuclear tests, no first use of a nuclear bomb and no new nuclear weapons.

Faced with the possibility of an American Hiroshima, many are paralyzed by a combination of denial and fatalism. This is unwarranted. Through a combination of imagination, a clear agenda for action and fierce determination to pursue it, the countdown to a nuclear 9/11 can be stopped.

GRAHAM ALLISON is an American political scientist and professor at the John F. Kennedy School of Government at Harvard. He is renowned for his book *Remaking Foreign Policy: The Organizational Connection*, co-written with Peter Szanton, which was published in 1976 and had some influence on the foreign policy of the administration of President Jimmy Carter. Since the 1970s, Allison has also been a leading analyst of U.S. national security and defense policy.

EXPLORING THE ISSUE

Are We Headed Toward a Nuclear 9/11?

Critical Thinking and Reflection

1. Why would anyone want to nuclear bomb America?
2. What can be done to minimize the desire of people to terrorize us?
3. How much expansion of police powers should we accept to increase our security? How much more should we bar people from entering the United States to increase our security?
4. What more can we do to protect ourselves?

Is There Common Ground?

There are many arguments to support the contention that nuclear and dirty bombs are hard to obtain, difficult to move and assemble, and even harder to deliver. There is also ample evidence to suggest that most, if not all, of the U.S. government's work is in one way or another designed to thwart such actions because of the enormous consequences were such acts to be carried out. These facts should make Americans rest easier and allay fears if only for reasons of probability.

However, Allison's contention that failure to assume the worst may prevent the thwarting of such terrorist designs is persuasive. Since September 11, it is clear that the world has entered a new phase of terrorist action and a new level of funding, sophistication, and motivation. It is dangerous for a nation to believe that because something is difficult it is unlikely to take place. The collapse of the USSR has unleashed a variety of forces, some positive and some more sinister and secretive. The enormous prices that radioactive material and nuclear devices can command on the black market make the likelihood of temptation strong and possibly irresistible.

What everyone agrees on is that terrorism and especially nuclear terrorism is a major concern for this country, and that almost everything possible should be done to prevent such an attack. Also, most people agree that if states are to err, perhaps they should err on the side of caution and preventive action rather than on reliance on the statistical probability that nuclear terrorism is unlikely. We may never see a nuclear terrorist act in this century, but it is statistically likely that the reason for this will not be lack of effort on the part of motivated terrorist groups. Most people also agree that we must not panic. However, when the time comes we probably will panic. Extraordinary leadership may lead us to a different response, but I would not bet on it.

Create Central

www.mhhe.com/createcentral

Additional Resources

Some important research and commentary on nuclear terrorism can be found in Benjamin Cole, *The Changing Face of Terrorism: How Real Is the Threat from Biological, Chemical and Nuclear Weapons?* (I. B. Tauris, 2011); Brian Michael Jenkins, *Will Terrorists Go Nuclear?* (Prometheus Books, 2008); Todd Masse, *Nuclear Jihad: A Clear and Present Danger?* (Potomac Books, 2011); Jack Caravelli, *Nuclear Insecurity: Understanding the Threat from Rogue Nations and Terrorists* (Praeger Security International, 2008); John E. Mueller, *Atomic Obsession: Nuclear Alarmism from Hiroshima to al-Qaeda* (Oxford University Press, 2010); Michael A. Levi, *On Nuclear Terrorism* (Harvard University Press, 2007); Elaine Landau, *Osama bin Laden: A War Against the West* (Twenty-First Century Books, 2002); Jan Lodal, *The Price of Dominance: The New Weapons of Mass Destruction and Their Challenge to American Leadership* (Council on Foreign Relations Press, 2001); Jessica Stern, *The Ultimate Terrorists* (Harvard University Press, 1999); Graham Allison, *Nuclear Terrorism: The Ultimate Preventable Catastrophe* (Times Books, 2004); Gavin Cameron, *Nuclear Terrorism: A Threat Assessment for the 21st Century* (St. Martin's Press, 1999); Charles D. Ferguson and William C. Potter, with Amy Sands et al., *The Four Faces of Nuclear Terrorism* (Routledge, 2005); Robin M. Frost, *Nuclear Terrorism After 9/11* (Routledge (for the International Institute for Strategic Studies), 2005); and Zbigniew Brzezinski, *The Choice: Global Domination or Global Leadership* (Basic Books, 2005).

Some recent general works on terrorism include Jonathan Barker, *The No-Nonsense Guide to Global Terrorism,* 2nd ed. (New Internationalist, 2008); Cornelia Beyer, *Violent Globalisms: Conflict in Response to Empire* (Ashgate, 2008); Michael Chandler and Rohan Gunaratna, *Countering Terrorism: Can We Meet the Threat of Global Violence?* (Reaktion, 2007); Peter R. Neumann, *Old and New Terrorism: Late Modernity, Globalization and the Transformation of Political Violence* (Polity, 2009); John Robb, *Brave New War: The Next Stage of Terrorism and the End of Globalization* (John Wiley & Sons, 2007); Paul J. Smith, *The Terrorism Ahead: Confronting Transnational Violence in the Twenty-First Century* (M. E. Sharpe, 2008); and Ian Bellany,

Terrorism and Weapons of Mass Destruction: Responding to the Challenge (Routledge, 2007). For information on how to respond to a nuclear terrorist event, see *Responding to a* *Radiological or Nuclear Terrorism Incident: A Guide for Decision Makers* (National Council on Radiation Protection and Measurements, 2010).

Internet References . . .

Sociology—Study Sociology Online

http://edu.learnsoc.org/

Sociology Web Resources

www.mhhe.com/socscience/sociology/resources/index.htm

Sociosite

www.topsite.com/goto/sociosite.net

Socioweb

www.topsite.com/goto/socioweb.com

Unit 6

UNIT

The Future: Population/Environment/Society

*T*he leading issues for the beginning of the twenty-first century include global warming, environmental decline, and globalization. The state of the environment and the effects of globalization produce strong arguments concerning what can be harmful or beneficial. Technology has increased enormously in the last 100 years, as have world-wide population growth, consumption, and new forms of pollution that threaten to undermine the world's fragile ecological support system. Although all nations have a stake in the health of the planet, many believe that none are doing enough to protect its health. Will technology itself be the key to controlling or accommodating the increase in population and consumption, along with the resulting increase in waste production? Perhaps so, but new policies will also be needed. Technology is driving the process of globalization, which can be seen as both good and bad. Those who support globalization theory state that globalization increases competition, production, wealth, and the peaceful integration of nations. However, not everyone agrees. This unit explores what is occurring in our environment and in our current global economy.

Selected, Edited, and with Issue Framing Material by:
Kurt Finsterbusch, *University of Maryland, College Park*

ISSUE

Does Immigration Benefit the Economy?

YES: Robert Lynch and Patrick Oakford, from "The Economic Effects of Granting Legal Status and Citizenship to Undocumented Immigrants," Center for American Progress (March 20, 2013)

NO: Steven A. Camarota, from "Testimony Before the U.S. House of Representatives Committee on the Judiciary, Subcommittee on Immigration, Citizenship, Refugees, Border Security and International Law" (U.S. House of Representatives, September 30, 2010)

Learning Outcomes
After reading this issue, you will be able to:
• With effort understand the economic arguments on which the different sides are based.
• Sort out where the two articles agree and where they disagree.
• Understand how terrorism has radically changed the debate on immigration.
• Understand how the country could benefit from immigration but certain groups could lose benefits due to the immigration.
• Understand that most immigrants have mostly positive values like the importance of strong family ties, hard work, ambition to better themselves, etc.
• Know that illegal immigration raises other issues and greater public resentment.

ISSUE SUMMARY

YES: Robert Lynch, Everett E. Nuttle Professor and chair of the Department of Economics at Washington College, and Patrick Oakford, research assistant at the Center for American Progress, show that legal status and a road to citizenship for the unauthorized will bring about significant economic gains in terms of economic growth, earnings, tax revenues, and jobs and the sooner we provide legal status and citizenship, the greater the economic benefits will be for the nation. The main reason is that the immigrants will produce and earn significantly more than they cost and the results will ripple throughout the economy.

NO: Steven A. Camarota, director of research at the Center for Immigration Studies, argues that immigration's benefit to the economy is so tiny that it should be ignored. On the other hand, immigration reduces the income of the poor with whom many immigrants compete for jobs.

Immigrants move to the United States for various reasons: to flee tyranny and terrorism, to escape war, or to join relatives who have already settled. Above all, they immigrate because in their eyes America is an island of affluence in a global sea of poverty; here they will earn many times what they could only hope to earn in their native countries. One hotly debated question is, What will these new immigrants do to the United States or for it?

Opposition to immigration comes from several sources. One is prejudice based on race, ethnicity, religion, or some other characteristic. Second, more legitimate in the view of many, is worry that immigrants are diluting the host country's language and other aspects of its national culture.

Security concerns are a third source of opposition to immigration.

Some critics of immigration argue that crime is higher among immigrant populations, and in recent years the possibility of immigrants being terrorists has increased this worry for some. Economic concerns are a fourth source of opposition to immigrants and are the focus of this debate. One economic argument is that immigrants work for low wages, thereby undercutting the wages of native-born workers. Also, they are seen as taking jobs away from American workers. Another charge is that immigrants are an economic burden, requiring far more in terms of welfare, medical care, education, and other services than the migrants return to their host country in terms of productivity and taxes.

These charges are met by counter-arguments that depict immigrants as providing needed workers and filling jobs that American workers do not want anyway. Finally, it can be argued that they give a boost to their new country's economy. In fact, several countries including the United States were largely developed by immigrants. Sometimes such influxes have gone fairly smoothly.

At other times, they have met significant opposition within the country of destination. Such is the case currently, with the global tide of refugees and immigrants, both legal and illegal, facing increasing resistance. Certainly, the fact that immigrants attacked the World Trade Center and the Pentagon on September 11, 2001, made many Americans favor the reduction of immigration.

But if we would have a better economy if we continued to allow immigration on a generous scale, they would be worth the risk.

Since 1965, the number of immigrants has changed markedly. Legal immigration has grown almost 300 percent from a yearly average of 330,000 in the 1960s to an annual average of 978,000 in the 1990s and just over 1 million during 2000–2007. Illegal (undocumented, unauthorized) immigrants probably add over 1 million to this total. Perhaps 11 million such immigrants are currently in the United States, with approximately 80 percent of them from Central America, especially Mexico. The presence of so many undocumented immigrants has become a major political issue in the United States.

American attitudes are strongest against illegal immigration, but are also hostile to legal immigration. Polls find that most Americans favor decreasing all immigration. When Americans are asked what bothers them about illegal immigration, they talk about its impacts on wages, job availability, and the cost of social and educational services. In other words, they are concerned about economic issues. Taking up this concern, Lynch and Oakford examine the economic impact of immigrants on the United States in the first reading and find that the country benefits. Steven A. Camarota disagrees in the second reading, finding that immigration has negative economic effects.

YES ↙   **Robert Lynch and Patrick Oakford**

The Economic Effects of Granting Legal Status and Citizenship to Undocumented Immigrants

[T]he debate over immigration reform has important legal, moral, social, and political dimensions. Providing or denying legal status or citizenship to the undocumented has implications for getting immigrants in compliance with the law, affects whether or not immigrant families can stay in their country of choice, and determines whether they have the opportunity to become full and equal members of American society.

But legal status and citizenship are also about the economic health of the nation as a whole. As our study demonstrates, legal status and a road map to citizenship for the unauthorized will bring about significant economic gains in terms of growth, earnings, tax revenues, and jobs—all of which will not occur in the absence of immigration reform or with reform that creates a permanent sub-citizen class of residents. We also show that the timing of reform matters: The sooner we provide legal status and citizenship, the greater the economic benefits are for the nation.

The logic behind these economic gains is straightforward. As discussed below, legal status and citizenship enable undocumented immigrants to produce and earn significantly more than they do when they are on the economic sidelines. The resulting productivity and wage gains ripple through the economy because immigrants are not just workers—they are also consumers and taxpayers. They will spend their increased earnings on the purchase of food, clothing, housing, cars, and computers. That spending, in turn, will stimulate demand in the economy for more products and services, which creates jobs and expands the economy.

This paper analyzes the 10-year economic impact of immigration reform under three scenarios. The first scenario assumes that legal status and citizenship are both accorded to the undocumented in 2013. The second scenario assumes that the unauthorized are provided legal status in 2013 and are able to earn citizenship five years thereafter. The third scenario assumes that the unauthorized are granted legal status starting in 2013 but that they are not provided a means to earn citizenship—at least within the 10-year timeframe of our analysis.

Under the first scenario—in which undocumented immigrants are granted legal status and citizenship in 2013—U.S. gross domestic product, or GDP, would grow by an additional $1.4 trillion cumulatively over the 10 years between 2013 and 2022. What's more, Americans would earn an additional $791 billion in personal income over the same time period—and the economy would create, on average, an additional 203,000 jobs per year. Within five years of the reform, unauthorized immigrants would be earning 25.1 percent more than they currently do and $659 billion more from 2013 to 2022. This means that they would also be contributing significantly more in federal, state, and local taxes. Over 10 years, that additional tax revenue would sum to $184 billion—$116 billion to the federal government and $68 billion to state and local governments.

Under the second scenario—in which undocumented immigrants are granted legal status in 2013 and citizenship five years thereafter—the 10-year cumulative increase in U.S. GDP would be $1.1 trillion, and the annual increases in the incomes of Americans would sum to $618 billion. On average over the 10 years, this immigration reform would create 159,000 jobs per year. Given the delay in acquiring citizenship relative to the first scenario, it would take 10 years instead of five for the incomes of the unauthorized to increase 25.1 percent. Over the 10-year period, they would earn $515 billion more and pay an additional $144 billion in taxes—$91 billion to the federal government and $53 billion to state and local governments.

Finally, under the third scenario—in which undocumented immigrants are granted legal status starting in 2013 but are not eligible for citizenship within 10 years—the cumulative gain in U.S. GDP between 2013 and 2022 would still be a significant—but comparatively more modest—$832 billion. The annual increases in the incomes of Americans would sum to $470 billion over the 10-year period, and the economy would add an average of 121,000 more jobs per year. The income of the unauthorized would be 15.1 percent higher within five years. Because of their increased earnings, undocumented immigrants would pay an additional $109 billion in taxes over the 10-year period—$69 billion to the federal government and $40 billion to state and local governments.

These immigration reform scenarios illustrate that unauthorized immigrants are currently earning far less than their potential, paying much less in taxes, and contributing significantly less to the U.S. economy than they potentially could. They also make clear that Americans stand to gain more from an immigration reform policy of legalization and citizenship than they do from one of legalization alone—or from no reform at all. Finally, the magnitude of potential economic gains depends significantly on how quickly reforms are implemented. The sooner that legal status and citizenship are granted to the unauthorized, the greater the gains will be for the U.S. economy.

Analyzing the Economic Effects of Legal Status and Citizenship

Numerous studies and government data sets have shown that positive economic outcomes are highly correlated with legal status and citizenship. Large and detailed government datasets—such as the U.S. Census Bureau's American Community Survey and Current Population Survey—have documented, for example, that U.S. citizens have average incomes that are 40 percent greater or more than the average incomes of noncitizen immigrants, both those here legally and the unauthorized.

Within the immigrant community, economic outcomes also vary by legal status. A study done by George Borjas and Marta Tienda found that prior to 1986 Mexican immigrant men legally in the United States earned 6 percent more than unauthorized Mexican male immigrants. Research suggests that undocumented immigrants are further "underground" today than they were in 1986—and that they experience an even wider wage gap. Katherine Donato and Blake Sisk, for example, found that between 2003 and 2009, the average hourly wage of Mexican immigrants legally in the United States was 28.3 percent greater than it was for undocumented Mexican immigrants.

In addition, a U.S. Department of Labor study—based on a carefully constructed and large longitudinal survey of the nearly 3 million unauthorized immigrants who were granted legal status and given a road map to citizenship under the Immigration Reform and Control Act of 1986—found that these previously undocumented immigrants experienced a 15.1 percent increase in their average inflation-adjusted wages within five years of gaining legal status. Studies have also reported that citizenship provides an added economic boost above and beyond the gains from legalization. Manuel Pastor and Justin Scoggins, for instance, found that even when controlling for a range of factors such as educational attainment and national origin, naturalized immigrants earned 11 percent more than legal noncitizens.

There are several reasons why legalization and citizenship both raise the incomes of immigrants and improve economic outcomes. Providing a road map to citizenship to undocumented immigrants gives them legal protections that raise their wages. It also promotes investment in the education and training of immigrants that eventually pays off in the form of higher wages and output; grants access to a broader range of higher-paying jobs; encourages labor mobility which increases the returns on the labor skills of immigrants by improving the efficiency of the labor market such that the skillsets of immigrants more closely match the jobs that they perform; and makes it more possible for immigrants to start businesses and create jobs. . . .

We estimate that the income premium of citizenship for all immigrants—both documented and undocumented—by comparing the earnings of naturalized and noncitizen immigrant populations while statistically controlling for observable differences other than citizenship that may affect income-level differences between the two groups. We find that citizenship is associated with a statistically significant boost in the incomes of immigrants.

To estimate the effect of citizenship on the earnings of unauthorized immigrants alone, we then decompose the income effect of citizenship that we estimated for all noncitizens into two components: one to estimate the percentage gain in income that the unauthorized experience as a consequence of attaining legal status and the other to estimate the percentage gain in income that they obtain from becoming naturalized citizens.

For the first component, we estimated that the unauthorized would gain a 15.1 percent increase in income from obtaining legal status. For the second component, we estimate that previously unauthorized and newly legalized immigrants would experience an additional 10 percent gain in income if they acquired citizenship.

Taking into account both components, our most likely estimate of the full effect of granting legal status and citizenship to unauthorized immigrants is an income gain of 25.1 percent. Of this boost in income, about three-fifths comes from legalization and about two-fifths is attributable to transitioning from legal status to citizenship.

10-Year Projections of the Economic Gains from Immigration Reform

Applying our 25.1 percent citizenship effect on the income of the undocumented, we project the economic gains from immigration reform under three scenarios. The first and most politically unlikely scenario—but one that is nonetheless useful for comparison purposes—assumes that legal status and citizenship are both conferred on the undocumented in 2013. The second scenario assumes that the unauthorized are provided legal status in 2013 and citizenship five years thereafter. The third scenario assumes that the unauthorized are granted legal status starting in 2013 but that they are not given a road map to citizenship.

Under the first scenario—both legal status and citizenship in 2013—U.S. GDP would grow by an additional $1.4 trillion cumulatively, and the personal income of Americans would grow an additional $791 billion over the 10 years between 2013 and 2022. Over the same time period, there would be an average of 203,000 more jobs per year.

Unauthorized immigrants would also be better off. Within five years they would be earning 25.1 percent more annually. As a consequence, over the full 10-year period, the formerly unauthorized would earn an additional $659 billion and pay at least $184 billion more in federal, state, and local taxes—$116 billion more to the federal government and $68 billion more to state and local governments.

Under the second scenario—legal status in 2013 followed by citizenship five years thereafter—the 10-year cumulative increase in the economy of the United States would be $1.1 trillion, and the annual increases in the incomes of Americans would sum to $618 billion. Over the 10 years, this immigration reform would create an average of 159,000 jobs per year. Given the delay in acquiring citizenship relative to the first scenario, it would take 10 years instead of five years for the incomes of the unauthorized to increase 25.1 percent. Over the 10-year period, they would earn $515 billion more and pay an additional $144 billion in taxes—$91 billion to the federal government and $53 billion to state and local governments.

Finally, under the third scenario—legal status only starting in 2013—the cumulative gain in U.S. GDP between 2013 and 2022 would be a more modest $832 billion. The annual increases in the incomes of residents of the United States would sum to $470 billion over the 10 years, and the economy would have an average of 121,000 more jobs per year. The income of the unauthorized would be 15.1 percent higher within five years. Over the 10-year period, they would earn $392 billion more and pay an additional $109 billion in taxes—$69 billion to the federal government and $40 billion to state and local governments.

In each of the three scenarios we have almost certainly understated the amount of additional taxes that will be paid by undocumented immigrant workers because the tax estimates include only taxes from the increased earnings of the previously undocumented. While it has been widely documented that unauthorized workers are contributing billions of dollars in federal, state, and local taxes each year, the Congressional Budget Office estimates that between 30 percent and 50 percent of the undocumented population fails to declare their income. To the extent that some of these immigrants—who are working in the underground economy—are not reporting their incomes

for fear of being discovered and deported, however, legal status and citizenship is likely to push them into the legal economy, where they will be declaring their income and paying billions of dollars in taxes in addition to the amounts that we have calculated above. The reporting of this income, however, may increase business deductions for labor compensation, offsetting part of the tax gain. In addition, some currently unauthorized immigrants who have income taxes withheld may—upon attaining legal status—file returns and claim refunds or deductions and exemptions that will offset some of the tax revenue gained from the higher reporting of income.

Conclusion

The positive economic impacts on the nation and on undocumented immigrants of granting them legal status and a road map to citizenship are likely to be very large. The nation as a whole would benefit from a sizable increase in GDP and income and a modest increase in jobs. The earnings of unauthorized immigrants would rise significantly, and the taxes they would pay would increase dramatically. Given that the full benefits would phase in over a number of years, the sooner we grant legal status and provide a road map to citizenship to unauthorized immigrants, the sooner Americans will be able to reap these benefits. It is also clear that legalization and a road map to citizenship bestow greater gains on the American people and the U.S. economy than legalization alone.

Robert Lynch is Everett E. Nuttle Professor and chair of the Department of Economics at Washington College. He is the author of numerous works. One of his research interests is in assessing the impact of public investment in early childhood education on government budgets, the economy, and crime. One of his publications in this area is *Exceptional Returns: Economic, Fiscal, and Social Benefits of Investment in Early Childhood Development* (2004).

Patrick Oakford is a research assistant at the Center for American Progress. His research focuses on issues relating to U.S. immigration policy and the labor force.

Steven A. Camarota   **NO**

Testimony Before the U.S. House of Representatives Committee on the Judiciary, Subcommittee on Immigration, Citizenship, Refugees, Border Security and International Law

Introduction

In my very brief comments I will touch on several key issues surrounding immigration and the economy. My goal will be to clear up some of the confusion that often clouds the immigration debate. In particular, I will explain the difference between increasing the overall size of the U.S. economy and increasing the per-capita income of Americans. Finally, I will touch on the issue of immigration's impact on public coffers.

Immigration and the Size of the U.S. Economy

Immigration increases the overall size of the U.S. economy. Of this there is no question. In 2009 immigrants accounted for 15 percent of all workers. More workers and more people mean a bigger GDP. Immigrants are 15 percent of U.S. workers. They likely account for about 10 percent of GDP or more than a trillion dollars annually. However, this does not mean that the native-born population benefits from immigration. Basic economic theory shows that the overwhelming majority of this increase in economic activity goes to the immigrants themselves in the form of wages and other compensation. It is important to understand that the increase in the size of the economy is not, by itself, a benefit to the existing population. Moreover, immigrants who arrived in the last 10, 20, or 50 years are without question earning and living better on average than they would be had they remained in their home countries.

If the question is how much does the existing population benefit, then the key measure is the impact of immigration on per-capita GDP in the United States, particularly the per-capita GDP of the existing population. We can see the importance of per-capita GDP versus aggregate GDP by simply remembering that the economy of Mexico and Canada are similar in size. But this does not mean the two countries are equally rich because Mexico's population is roughly three times that of Canada's.

Benefits to Natives

There is a standard way of calculating the benefit from immigration, also referred to as the immigrant surplus, that goes to the existing population. A 1997 study by National Academy of Sciences (NAS),[1] authored by many of the top economists in the field, summarizes the formula for calculating the benefit (see pages 151–152). The NAS study updates an earlier study by the nation's top immigration economist, George Borjas of Harvard (see page 7).[2] In 2007 the President's Council of Economic Advisers (CEA) again used the same formula to estimate the benefit of immigration to Americans.[3] A blog by professor Borjas has a clear non-technical explanation of the calculation, from which I borrow heavily in this paper.[4]

The next gain from immigration can be estimated using the following formula:

Net gain from immigration as a share of GDP
$= -.5 \times$ labor's share of income $\times$ wage elasticity
$\times$ immigrant share of labor force squared.

"Labor share" refers to the percentage of GDP that goes to workers, which is usually thought to be 70 percent, the rest being capital. The immigrant share of the labor force is well known, and is currently 15 percent. "Wage elasticity" refers to the percentage change in wages from immigration increasing the size of the labor force by 1 percent. The size of the elasticity is a contentious issue. The NAS study assumed an elasticity of .3, and so will I in the calculation below. This means that each 1 percent increase in supply of labor caused by immigration reduces wages by 0.3 percent. Put a different way, if immigration increased the supply of workers by 10 percent, it would reduce the wages of American workers by 3 percent. Putting the values into the formula produces the following estimate:

$$0.24\% = -.50 \times .70 \times -0.3 \times (.15 \times .15)$$

Thus the net gain from immigration is 0.24 percent of GDP. (Expressed as decimal it is .0024.) If GDP is

U.S. House of Representatives, September 2010.

$14 trillion, then the net benefit would be $33 billion. Three important points emerge from this analysis. First, the net effect of immigration on the existing population is positive overall, though not for all workers. Second, the benefits are trivial relative to the size of the economy, less than one-quarter of 1 percent. Third, the benefit is dependent on the size of the wage losses suffered by the existing population of workers. Or put a different way, the bigger the wage loss, the bigger the net benefit. Those who contend that immigration has no impact on the wages of immigrants are also arguing, sometimes without realizing it, that there is no economic benefit from immigration.

The same model can be used to estimate the wage losses suffered [by] American workers.

Wage loss as a fraction of GDP
= −"labor's share of income" × "wage elasticity"
   × "immigrant share of labor force"
   × "native-born share of labor force."

Putting the numbers into the equation you get the following:

$$2.7\% = -0.7 \times -0.3 \times 0.15 \times 0.85$$

This is 2.7 percent of GDP, or $375 billion in wage losses suffered by American workers because of immigration. This is not trivial. There is nothing particularly controversial about this estimate and it stems from the same basic economic formula as the one above. Think of it this way: Labor is 70 percent of the economy, which is $14 trillion in total. If the elasticity is .3 and immigrants are 15 percent of the labor force, then wages will decline several percentage points (15 × .3). Thus the total wage loss must run into the hundreds of billions of dollars. If we are to accept the benefit that the model implies from immigration, then we must also accept the wage losses that the model implies.

The money that would have gone to workers as wages if there had been no immigration does not vanish into thin air. It is retained by owners of capital as higher profits or passed on to consumers in the form of lower prices. The fact that business owners lobby so hard to keep immigration levels high is an indication that much of the lost wages are likely retained by them. Also, workers who face little or no competition from immigrants will not suffer a wage loss. In fact, demand for their labor may increase and their incomes rise as a result. For example, if you are an attorney or a journalist at an English-language news outlet in the United States you face very little competition from immigrants.[5] In fact, immigration may increase your wages as demand for your occupation rises. In contrast, if you are a nanny, maid, bus boy, cook, meat packer, or construction laborer, the negative wage impact is likely to be large because immigration has increased the supply of workers in these sectors quite a bit. But overall the gain to some workers, businesses, and consumers is still slightly larger than the loss suffered by the losers; hence the tiny net benefit reported above.

Immigrant and Native Job Competition

Some may feel that there is no job competition between immigrants and native-born workers. The argument is often made, mostly by non-economists, that immigrants only do jobs Americans don't want. But analysis of all 465 occupations defined by the Department of Commerce shows that even before the current recession only four are majority immigrant. These four occupations account for less than 1 percent of the total U.S. workforce. Many jobs often thought to be overwhelmingly immigrant are, in fact, majority native-born. For example, 55 percent of maids and housekeepers are native-born, as are 58 percent of taxi drivers and chauffeurs, 63 percent of butchers and meat processors, 65 percent of construction laborers, and 75 percent of janitors. There are 93 occupations in which at least 20 percent of workers are immigrants. There are about 24 million native-born Americans in these high-immigrant occupations.[6] Thus, the argument that immigrants and natives never compete for jobs is simply incorrect. The real question is how have the poorest and the least educated American workers fared in recent decades as immigration has increased.

Deterioration at the Bottom of the Labor Market

There has been a long-term decline in wages, even before the current recession, among the less educated. Hourly wages for those who have not completed high school declined 22 percent in real terms (adjusted for inflation) from 1979 to 2007. Hourly wages for those with only a high school education declined 10 percent in real terms from 1979 to 2007.[7]

The share of less educated adults holding a job has been deteriorating for some time. This is true even before the current recession. From 2000 to 2007 the share of adult natives (ages 18 to 65) without a high school diploma holding a job fell from 54 percent to 48 percent. For those with only a high school education, the share [of] employed fell from 73 percent to 70 percent. By 2009 it was down to 43 percent for those without a high school diploma and 65 percent for those with only a high school education. There is a huge supply of less-educated people available as potential workers. In 2007, before the recession, there were more than 22 million native-born Americans (18 to 65) with no more than high school education who were not working. By 2009 that number was 26 million.[8]

If there was a tight labor market and unskilled workers really were in short supply, then we would expect that wages to rise for the less educated. We would also expect that the share of these workers holding a job would be climbing. But even before the current recession, this was not what has happening. The deterioration in wages and employment for the less educated is the kind of pattern we would expect to see as a result of immigrant competition.

Fiscal Impact of Immigration

The impact of immigration on public coffers is not directly part of a discussion on immigration and the economy. But when thinking about the overall effect of immigration on our pocketbooks, the taxes paid and services used by immigrants are important issues. It may be the most important issue. The previously mentioned National Academy of Sciences study estimated that the net fiscal drain (taxes paid minus services used) from immigrant households in 1997 was $11 to $20 billion a year. At the same time, using the same formula discussed above, the NAS study estimated a net economic benefit of $1 billion to $10 billion a year from immigration. Thus, the estimated fiscal drain was larger than the economic benefit. (Today the economic benefit and fiscal drain are larger reflecting our larger economy and government.)

It also must be remembered that there are still wage losses for less-skilled workers. The NAS study indicated that the wages of the poorest 10 percent of American workers were reduced by 5 percent as a result of immigrant-induced increases in the supply of labor.

More recent analysis indicates that the fiscal costs of immigration remain large. Census Bureau data indicate that one-third of those without health insurance in the United States are either immigrants (legal or illegal) or U.S.-born children (under 18) of immigrants. One-fourth of children living in poverty in the United States have immigrant fathers. In 2008, 53 percent of immigrant households with children used at least one major welfare program, primarily food assistance and Medicaid.[9] These fiscal costs are incurred despite immigrants' high rates of labor force participation. Their high welfare use rates and the resulting fiscal drain they create stem from the fact that a large share have relatively little education. About one-third of immigrants who arrive as adults have not graduated from high school. The modern American economy offers limited opportunities to such workers. This fact, coupled with a welfare state designed to help low-income workers with children, is the reason for the above statistics.

Conclusion

When thinking about immigration it is important to recognize that its impact on the size of the economy is not a measure of the benefit to natives. There is no question that U.S. GDP is significantly larger because of immigrant workers. However, a larger economy is entirely irrelevant to the key question of whether the per-capita GDP of natives is higher because of immigration. Efforts to measure the impact of immigration on the per-capita GDP of Americans using the standard economic model show that the benefit is trivial relative to the size of the economy. Perhaps most important, these trivial gains are the result of reduced wages for American workers in competition with immigrants. These workers tend to be the least educated and poorest already. If there is no wage reduction, then there is no economic gain. Finally, the tiny economic gain is probably entirely offset by the fiscal drain immigrants create on taxpayers.

In the end, arguments for or against immigration are as much political and moral as they are economic. The latest research indicates that we can reduce immigration without harming the economy. Doing so makes sense if we are very concerned about low-wage and less-educated workers in the United States. On the other hand, if one places a high priority on helping unskilled workers in other countries, then we should continue to allow in a large number of such workers. Of course, only an infinitesimal proportion of the world's poor could ever come to this country even under the most open immigration policy one might imagine. Those who support the current high level of immigration should at least understand that the American workers harmed by the policies they favor are already the poorest and most vulnerable.

Notes

1. Edmonston, Barry, and James Smith, Eds., *The New Americans: Economic, Demographic, and Fiscal Effects of Immigration,* Washington D.C., National Academy Press, 1997, http://books.nap.edu/openbook.php?isbn=0309063566.
2. George Borjas, "The Economic Benefits of Immigration," *Journal of Economic Perspectives* Vol. 9, No. 2, Spring 1995, www.hks.harvard.edu/fs/gborjas/Papers/Economic_Benefits.pdf.
3. "Immigration's Economic Impact," white paper, June 20, 2007, http://georgewbush-whitehouse.archives.gov/cea/cea_immigration_062007.html.
4. "No Pain No Gain," June 8, 1997, http://borjas.typepad.com/the_borjas_blog/ 2007/06/index.html.
5. Steven Camarota and Karen Jensenius, "Jobs Americans Won't Do? A Detailed Look at Immigrant Employment by Occupation," Center for Immigration Studies *Memorandum,* August 2009, www.cis.org/illegalimmigration-employment.
6. *Ibid.*
7. Lawrence Mishel, Jared Bernstein and Heidi Shierholz, "The State of Working America 2008/2009," Economic Policy Institute, Table 3.16, p. 166.
8. All figures for employment are based on the author's calculation of employment and labor force participation from the public-use files of the Current Population Survey in the third quarters of 2000, 2007, and 2009.
9. Figures come from the March 2009 Current Population Survey, which asks about health insurance coverage and welfare use in the prior calendar year. It also asks where respondents' parents were born. Thus, indentifying the children of immigrant parents is a simple calculation.

STEVEN A. CAMAROTA is Director of Research at the Center for Immigration Studies and an expert in economics and demographics.

EXPLORING THE ISSUE

Does Immigration Benefit the Economy?

Critical Thinking and Reflection

1. The simple rule of morality is the greatest good for the greatest number (utilitarianism). Apply this rule to the issue of immigration. Do you accept the outcome or would you amend the rule?
2. Who benefits from heavy immigration and who benefits from very light immigration?
3. Why is America at an impasse on immigration legislation?
4. What are the various economic impacts of immigration and on sum does it help or harm the economy?
5. When did you or your ancestors come to America? Was that immigration good for America?
6. What should be done about "illegal" immigrants living in America? What should be done about children of illegal immigrants who were born here and are U.S. citizens?

Is There Common Ground?

This nation was built by immigration. Now most Americans want to keep what we have largely to ourselves and greatly limit immigration. Now pro-immigration commentators have to justify immigration by demonstrating the benefits of immigration for America. Lynch and Oakford claim that immigration is making America stronger. Many people like Camarota disagree because they fear the consequences of today's immigration.

This issue has deeply divided the country. It seems that Congress cannot agree on immigration policy and pass meaningful immigration legislation.

At the moment, there is no common ground except all sides are committed to trying to keep illegal immigrants out. Beyond that there are options but not agreement. Some want to deport the illegal immigrants in the United States. Others favor a guest-worker program that permits undocumented immigrants currently in the country to remain for several years as temporary workers but that also requires them to leave the country. Yet others support allowing unauthorized immigrants already in the country to get a work permit and eventually to apply for citizenship. A 2007 poll found 30 percent of Americans favoring the first option, 28 percent supporting the second, and 37 percent preferring the third option, with 5 percent unsure. Opinions were similarly split in the halls of Congress, so it has failed to enact a comprehensive plan. As of this writing it is on the agenda of Congress but no one seems to believe anything will pass this Congress.

Create Central

www.mhhe.com/createcentral

Additional Resources

Several major works debate whether or not immigrants, on average, economically benefit America and can assimilate. Sources that argue that immigrants largely benefit America include Jason L. Riley, *Let Them In: The Case for Open Borders* (Gotham, 2008); Darrell M. West, *Brain Gain: Rethinking U.S. Immigration Policy* (Brookings Institution Press, 2010); Joseph H. Carens, *Immigrants and the Right to Stay* (MIT Press, 2010); Julian L. Simon, *The Economic Consequences of Immigration*, 2nd ed. (University of Michigan Press, 1999) and *Immigration: The Demographic and Economic Facts* (Cato Institute, 1995). Sources that argue that immigrants have more negative than positive impacts include Mark Krikorian, *The New Case Against Immigration: Both Legal and Illegal* (Sentinel, 2008); Robert E. Koulish, *Immigration and American Democracy: Subverting the Rule of Law* (Routledge, 2010); George Borjas, *Heaven's Door: Immigration Policy and the American Economy* (Princeton University Press, 1999); Roy Beck, *The Case Against Immigration* (W. W. Norton, 1996); Patrick Buchanan, *The Death of the West: How Dying Populations and Immigrant Invasions Imperil Our Country and Civilization* (Thomas Dunne Books, 2002); and Otis L. Graham Jr., *Unguarded Gates: A History of America's Immigration Crisis* (Rowman & Littlefield, 2004). For a more even-handed discussion, see Sarah Spencer, *The Migration Debate* (Policy Press, 2011); Örn B. Bodvarsson, *The Economics of Immigration: Theory and Policy* (Springer, 2009); Peter Kivisto and Thomas Faist, *Beyond the Border: The Causes and Consequences of Contemporary Immigration* (Pine Forge Press, 2010); Philip L. Martin, *Importing Poverty?: Immigration and the Changing Face of Rural America* (Yale University Press, 2009);

Nancy Foner, ed., *Not Just Black and White: Historical and Contemporary Perspectives on Immigration, Race, and Ethnicity in the United States* (Russell Sage Foundation, 2004); and Frank D. Bean and Gilian Stevens, eds., *America's Newcomers and the Dynamics of Diversity* (Russell Sage Foundation, 2003). On the issue of Mexican immigration, see Douglas S. Massey, Jorge Durand, and Nolan J. Malone, *Beyond Smoke and Mirrors: Mexican Immigration in an Era of Economic Integration* (Russell Sage Foundation, 2003), and Victor Davis Hanson, *Mexifornia: A State of Becoming* (Encounter Books, 2003). Works that focus on attitudes toward immigrants and their rights include Peter Schrag, *Not Fit for Our Society: Nativism and Immigration* (University of California Press, 2010); Armando Navarro, *The Immigration Crisis: Nativism, Armed Vigilantism, and the Rise of a Countervailing Movement* (AltaMira Press, 2009); Michael Sobczak, *American Attitudes Toward Immigrants and Immigration Policy* (LFB Scholarly Publishing, 2010); Dorothee Schneider, *Crossing Borders: Immigration and Citizenship in the Twentieth-Century United States* (Harvard University Press, 2011); Christian Joppke, *Citizenship and Immigration* (Polity, 2010); and Kim Voss and Irene Bloemraad, eds., *Rallying for Immigrant Rights: The Fight for Inclusion in 21st Century America* (University of California Press, 2011).

An overview of the history of U.S. immigration and policy is found in Aristide R. Zolberg, *A Nation by Design: Immigration Policy in the Fashioning of America* (Harvard University Press, 2008). A group that favors fewer immigrant is the Center for Immigration Studies at www.cis.org. Taking a positive view of immigration and immigrants is the National Immigration Forum at www.immigrationforum.org.

Internet References . . .

Sociology—Study Sociology Online

http://edu.learnsoc.org/

Sociology Web Resources

www.mhhe.com/socscience/sociology/resources
/index.htm

Sociosite

www.topsite.com/goto/sociosite.net

Socioweb

www.topsite.com/goto/socioweb.com

ISSUE

Selected, Edited, and with Issue Framing Material by:
Kurt Finsterbusch, *University of Maryland, College Park*

Is Humankind Dangerously Harming the Environment?

YES: John Harte and Mary Ellen Harte, from "Alarmism Is Justified," *Foreign Affairs* (September/October 2012)

NO: Ramez Naam, from "How Innovation Could Save The Planet," *The Futurist* (March/April 2013)

Learning Outcomes

After reading this issue, you will be able to:

- Discern the trends or issues that greatly concern many environmentalists.
- Identify what has been done to address the environmental issues and estimate what still needs to be done.
- Assess the accuracy of the information on which you depend to understand environmental issues.
- Begin to explore the potential consequences of environmental problems on societies and lifestyles.
- Identify the information that you need to acquire a pretty good understanding of the environmental issues that are facing us today.

ISSUE SUMMARY

YES: John Harte, professor of ecosystem sciences at the University of California, Berkeley, and Mary Ellen Harte, a biologist and columnist who writes on climate change and population, argue against those that deny that there are limits to growth that expected technologies could not easily take care of. They claim that environmental and resource optimists ignore massive evidence of environmental problems and risks and belittle the concerns of thousands of scientists.

NO: Ramez Naam, a computer scientist, author, and former Microsoft executive, argues that innovations will deal with the serious issues of population growth, peak oil, resources depletion, climate change, and limits to growth. After reviewing some of the recent great accomplishments and some of the risks facing the planet, he shows how ideas and innovations have solved similar crises in the past and then gives reasons for being optimistic about the future.

Much of the literature on socioeconomic development in the 1960s was premised on the assumption of inevitable material progress for all. It largely ignored the impacts of development on the environment and presumed that the availability of raw materials would never be a problem. The common belief was that all societies would get richer because all societies were investing in new equipment and technologies that would increase productivity and wealth. Theorists recognized that some poor countries were having trouble developing, but they blamed those problems on the deficiencies of the values and attitudes of those countries and on inefficient governments and organizations.

In the late 1960s and early 1970s, an intellectual revolution occurred. Environmentalists had criticized the growth paradigm throughout the 1960s, but they were not taken very seriously at first. By the end of the 1960s, however, marine scientist Rachel Carson's book *Silent Spring* (Alfred A. Knopf, 1962) had worked its way into the public's consciousness. Carson's book traces the noticeable loss of birds to the use of pesticides. Her book made the middle and upper classes in the United States realize that pollution affects complex ecological systems in ways that put even the wealthy at risk. In 1968, Paul Ehrlich, a professor of population studies, published *The Population Bomb* (Ballantine Books), which states that overpopulation is the major problem facing mankind. This means that population has to be controlled or the human race might cause the collapse of the global ecosystems and the deaths of many humans. Ehrlich explained why he thought the devastation of the world was imminent: Because the human population of the planet is about five times too large, and we're managing to support all these people at today's level of misery only by spending our capital, burning our fossil fuels, dispersing our mineral resources, and turning our fresh water into salt water. We have not only overpopulated but overstretched our environment. We are poisoning the ecological systems of the earth upon which we are ultimately dependent for all of our food, for all of our oxygen, and for all of our waste disposal. In 1973, *The Limits to Growth* (Universe) by Donella H. Meadows et al. was published. It presents a dynamic systems computer model for world economic, demographic, and environmental trends. When the computer model projected trends into the future, it predicted that the world would experience ecological collapse and population die-off unless population growth and economic activity were greatly reduced. This study was both attacked and defended, and the debate about the health of the world has been heated ever since.

Let us examine the population growth rates for the past, present, and future. At about A.D. 1, the world had about one-quarter billion people. It took about 1,650 years to double this number to one-half billion and 200 years to double the world population again to 1 billion by 1850. The next doubling took only about 80 years, and the last doubling took about 45 years (from 2 billion in 1930 to about 4 billion in 1975). The world population may double again to 8 billion sometime between 2020 and 2025. At the same time that population is growing, people are trying to get richer, which means consuming more, polluting more, and using more resources. Are all these trends threatening the carrying capacity of the planet and jeopardizing the prospects for future generations? In the following selections, John Harte and Mary Ellen Harte warn that the population growth and the sevenfold expansion of the economy in the past half century is placing demands on the environment that exceed the Earth's natural capacity. As a result we face many environmental problems. They focus on refuting the critiques of their pessimistic view. They point out that the critics can find a false fact or an exaggerated statement of the pessimists here or there, but do not refute the strong evidence supporting the pessimist view. Ramez Naam presents and acknowledges both the positive and negative trends in the planet but focuses on the miraculous coming results of innovations which will adequately address the environmental problems and most other problems. Environmental collapse and die-off will not occur. Ideas will save the planet.

YES ↵

John Harte and Mary Ellen Harte

Alarmism Is Justified

In his essay, Bjørn Lomborg begins by criticizing the notion that the primary constraint on economic growth is the finiteness of resources, as if that remains the belief of the scientific community. Environmental scientists have long recognized, however, that the main limit to growth is not running out of resources but rather running out of space for the byproducts of that growth. Humans are filling the world's atmosphere with greenhouse gases, tainting its aquifer and surface water with deadly pollutants, eroding its soils, and allowing damaging toxics to build up in human bodies.

Obsessed with the numerical accuracy of projections made decades ago in *The Limits to Growth*, Lomborg ignores the importance of that study's qualitative insights, still valid today, concerning the interconnections between humanity and the natural world. The book illustrated the many ways in which increases in the human population and consumption levels undermine the sustainability of human society, including through pollution, the depletion of both renewable and nonrenewable resources, and industrial production. Lomborg also ignores some of the study's accurate quantitative insights: recent analyses by scientists show that *The Limits to Growth* was eerily correct in at least some of its most important projections. In a reexamination of the study, the ecologists Charles Hall and John Day showed that if a timeline were added to the book's predictions with 2000 at the halfway point, "then the model results are almost exactly on course some 35 years later in 2008."

The Limits to Growth countered the blissful ignorance of many economists and business magnates who wanted to believe in the convenient pipe dream of unlimited growth, denying the finiteness of the natural environment. Many policymakers did understand the value of the study, however, and tried to inculcate its basic concepts into our civilization, but without success. The scientific community thus still has educational work to do, and finishing it is essential to securing a future for our civilization.

What the Science Says

Lomborg promotes numerous misconceptions in his essay. Bemoaning *The Limits to Growth's* results as neither "simple nor easy to understand," Lomborg fails to grasp what many reputable scientists and policymakers have long

known: that predicting the details of complex phenomena is difficult. In that light, *The Limits to Growth* was just a first stab at analyzing the elaborate dynamics that cause continued economic growth to threaten the sustain ability of human society.

Lomborg further displays scientific ignorance when he talks about pesticides. His estimate of 20 U.S. deaths annually from pesticides ignores both the ecological harm they cause and the human health problems, including cancer, hormone disruption, and neurological effects, associated with pesticide exposure. His argument that DDT is a cheap, effective solution to malaria overlooks the ability of mosquitoes, like other pests, to evolve resistance. Pesticides can be valuable tools when used as scalpels, but when they are used as bludgeons, the evolution of resistance often undoes their efficacy. This is why many epidemiologists fear that society is regressing from the happy era of working antibiotics.

Lomborg also perpetuates the denial of the multiple ways in which civilization is underpinned by a healthy environment. Yes, we can continue to expand into previously untapped arable land, but only at the cost of undermining the giant planetary ecosystems that assure humanity will have clean air, clean water, and a sustainable and benign climate. Yes, we can forgo recycling and grow plantations for paper, but only at the expense of biodiversity. Indeed, as increasing population growth and overconsumption degrade the environment, none of the economic growth that Lomborg hopes for will be possible. Moreover, the capacity of society and its institutions to maintain, let alone improve, the quality of life—a capacity that Lomborg takes for granted—will be at risk.

Lomborg retells the story of how the biologist Paul Ehrlich, the physicist John Holdren, and one of us lost a bet in 1990 after the economist Julian Simon wagered that the prices of a number of commodities would drop over a ten-year period. But had the bet been extended a few more years, the scientists would have won, because the prices of those commodities had, on average, risen. Simon later challenged ecologists to a new set of bets on the future; Ehrlich and the climatologist Stephen Schneider accepted the challenge and picked 15 environmentally significant trends, such as the concentration of greenhouse gases in the atmosphere and the amount of biodiversity on the planet. To our surprise, once he recognized the trends, Simon saw the writing on the wall and promptly backed out of the bet; he would have lost more than $10,000.

Indeed, the limitations on the human enterprise extend beyond minerals. World hunger is increasing, as is the cost of basic food staples. The temporary advances of the environmental movement, such as the creation of more ecological reserves to protect biodiversity, are proving less and less effective faced with the sheer weight of further population growth and increasing consumption.

The Right Kind of Innovation

Lomborg is correct that innovation is an important tool. Yet he seems to display a curious lack of confidence in human ingenuity when it comes to solving the environmental problems that science has identified to be of most concern to the future of humanity. He praises the very actions that cause climate disruption and pollution, such as offshore oil drilling, but has no such confidence that technological achievements can sharply reduce the world's dependence on fossil fuels. He revels in a food-production system that is awash in overused fertilizers, harmful pesticides, herbicides, and antibiotics, and is a major destroyer of the biodiversity on which it depends, but sees no hope for new inventions that could bring down the cost of organically produced food. Unfortunately, Lomborg seems to support ingenuity only in the cause of the trends he likes, rather than in the cause of technologies that could create a more sustainable future.

In fact, the scientific community knows how to transition to renewable clean energy to create a safer, more politically stable world and prevent destructive climate change without decreasing the quality of life. We know how to stem the problem of overpopulation by supplying family-planning knowledge and contraceptives to the more than 100 million women who lack them in developing countries. Where the world most needs the ingenuity that Lomborg assures us exists is in replacing an economic system hooked on perpetual growth and overconsumption by the rich with one that is much more equitable and sustainable.

Unlike Lomborg, most scientists understand the pernicious exponential effects of overpopulation on the environment. In 1993, 58 academies of science stated that "continuing population growth poses a great risk to humanity," and it now looks like the population could roughly double from its 1993 size by the end of this century. Other recent scientific statements have sounded an equally "alarmist" note, and with good reason. In March, for example, the participants at the "Planet Under Pressure" meeting, a gathering of climate-change scientists, declared that "the continued functioning of the Earth system as it has supported the well-being of human civilization in recent centuries is at risk. Without urgent action, we face threats to water, food, biodiversity and other critical resources: these threats risk intensifying economic, ecological and social crises, creating the potential for a humanitarian emergency on a global scale." To translate the warnings of the scientific community into action, the world desperately needs courageous political leadership to counter the powerful interest groups that continue to deny the unsustainability of humanity's current existence.

The Limits to Growth helped educate a generation, and now more than ever, those concerned for humanity need to promote the solutions that can make society more sustainable. The denial of science is a perfectly harmless activity done in the privacy of one's own home, but when scientific misconceptions are laid out in the pages of the public media, as in Lomborg's essay, it is a threat to the world's well-being.

JOHN HARTE, professor of ecosystem sciences at the University of California, Berkeley, has authored over 200 scientific publications, including eight books. His research focuses on climate change, biodiversity, and maintaining ecosystem services for humanity.

MARY ELLEN HARTE is a biologist and columnist who writes on climate change and population issues. She coauthored the downloadable book, *Cool the Earth, Save the Economy*, and produces the weekday "Climate Change Report," 90-second audio newscasts, as well as the Climate Change Reports blog for *The Huffington Post*.

Ramez Naam    **NO**

How Innovation Could Save The Planet

Ideas may be our greatest natural resource, says a computer scientist and **futurist**. He argues that the world's most critical challenges—including population growth, peak oil, climate change, and limits to growth—could be met by encouraging innovation.

The Best of Times: Unprecedented Prosperity

There are many ways in which we are living in the most wonderful age ever. We can imagine we are heading toward a sort of science-fiction Utopia, where we are incredibly rich and incredibly prosperous, and the planet is healthy. But there are other reasons to fear that we're headed toward a dystopia of sorts.

On the positive side, life expectancy has been rising for the last 150 years, and faster since the early part of the twentieth century in the developing world than it has in the rich world. Along with that has come a massive reduction in poverty. The most fundamental empowerer of humans—education—has also soared, not just in the rich world, but throughout the world.

Another great empowerer of humanity is connectivity: Access to information and access to communication both have soared. The number of mobile phones on the planet was effectively zero in the early 1990s, and now it's in excess of 4 billion. More than three-quarters of humanity, in the span of one generation, have gotten access to connectivity that, as my friend Peter Diamandis likes to say, is greater than any president before 1995 had. A reasonably well-off person in India or in Nigeria has better access to information than Ronald Reagan did during most of his career.

With increased connectivity has come an increase in democracy. As people have gotten richer, more educated, more able to access information, and more able to communicate, they have demanded more control over the places where they live. The fraction of nations that are functional democracies is at an all-time high in this world—more than double what it was in the 1970s, with the collapse of the Soviet Union.

Economically, the world is a more equal place than it has been in decades. In the West, and especially in the United States, we hear a lot about growing inequality, but on a global scale, the opposite is true. As billions are rising out of poverty around the world, the global middle classes are catching up with the global rich.

In many ways, this is the age of the greatest human prosperity, freedom, and potential that has ever been on the face of this planet. But in other ways, we are facing some of the largest risks ever.

The Worst of Times: The Greatest Risks

At its peak, the ancient Mayan city of Tikal was a metropolis, a city of 200,000 people inside of a civilization of about 20 million people. Now, if you walk around any Mayan city, you see mounds of dirt. That's because these structures were all abandoned by about the mid-900s AD. We know now what happened: The Mayan civilization grew too large. It overpopulated. To feed themselves, they had to convert forest into farmland. They chopped down all of the forest. That, in turn, led to soil erosion. It also worsened drought, because trees, among other things, trap moisture and create a precipitation cycle.

When that happened, and was met by some normal (not human-caused) climate change, the Mayans found they didn't have enough food. They exhausted their primary energy supply, which is food. That in turn led to more violence in their society and ultimately to a complete collapse.

The greatest energy source for human civilization today is fossil fuels. Among those, none is more important than oil. In 1956, M. King Hubbert looked at production in individual oil fields and predicted that the United States would see the peak of its oil production in 1970 or so, and then drop. His prediction largely came true: Oil production went up but did peak in the 1970s, then plummeted.

Oil production has recently gone up in the United States a little bit, but it's still just barely more than half of what it was in its peak in the 1970s.

Hubbert also predicted that the global oil market would peak in about 2000, and for a long time he looked very foolish. But it now has basically plateaued. Since 2004, oil production has increased by about 4%, whereas in the 1950s it rose by about 4% every three months.

We haven't hit a peak; oil production around the world is still rising a little bit. It's certainly not declining, but we do appear to be near a plateau; supply is definitely rising more slowly than demand. Though there's plenty of oil in the ground, the oil that remains is in smaller fields, further from shore, under lower pressure, and harder to pump out.

Water is another resource that is incredibly precious to us. The predominant way in which we use water is through the food that we eat: 70% of the freshwater that humanity uses goes into agriculture.

The Ogallala Aquifer, the giant body of freshwater under the surface of the Earth in the Great Plains of the United States, is fossil water left from the melting and the retreat of glaciers in the end of the last Ice Age, 12,000–14,000 years ago. Its refill time is somewhere between 5,000 and 10,000 years from normal rainfall. Since 1960, we've drained between a third and a half of the water in this body, depending on what estimate you look at. In some areas, the water table is dropping about three feet per year.

If this was a surface lake in the United States or Canada, and people saw that happening, they'd stop it. But because it's out of sight, it's just considered a resource that we can tap. And indeed, in the north Texas area, wells are starting to fail already, and farms are being abandoned in some cases, because they can't get to the water that they once did.

Perhaps the largest risk of all is climate change. We've increased the temperature of the planet by about 2°F in the last 130 years, and that rate is accelerating. This is primarily because of the carbon dioxide we've put into the atmosphere, along with methane and nitrous oxide. CO_2 levels, now at over 390 parts per million, are the highest they've been in about 15 million years. Ice cores go back at least a million years, and we know that they're the highest they've been in that time. . . .

Over the next century, the seas are expected to rise about 3 to 6 feet. Most of that actually will not be melting glaciers; it's thermal expansion: As the ocean gets warmer, it gets a little bit bigger.

But 3 to 6 feet over a century doesn't sound like that big a deal to us, so we think of that as a distant problem. The reality is that there's a more severe problem with climate change: its impact on the weather and on agriculture.

In 2003, Europe went through its worst heat wave since 1540. Ukraine lost 75% of its wheat crop. In 2009, China had a once-in-a-century level drought; in 2010 they had another once-in-a-century level drought. That's twice. Wells that had given water continuously since the fifteenth century ran dry. When those rains returned, when the water that was soaked up by the atmosphere came back down, it came down on Pakistan, and half of Pakistan was under water in the floods of 2010. An area larger than Germany was under water.

Warmer air carries more water. Every degree Celsius that you increase the temperature value of air, it carries 7% more water. But it doesn't carry that water uniformly. It can suck water away from one place and then deliver it in a deluge in another place. So both the droughts are up and

flooding is up simultaneously, as precipitation becomes more lumpy and more concentrated.

In Russia's 2010 heat wave, 55,000 people died, 11,000 of them in Moscow alone. In 2011, the United States had the driest 10-month period ever in the American South, and Texas saw its worst wildfires ever. And 2012 was the worst drought in the United States since the Dust Bowl—the corn crop shrank by 20%. . . .

Ideas as a Resource Expander, Resource Preserver, and Waste Reducer

. . . Ideas can reduce resource use. I can give you many other examples. In the United States, the amount of energy used on farms per calorie grown has actually dropped by about half since the 1970s. That's in part because we now only use about a tenth of the energy to create synthetic nitrogen fertilizer, which is an important input.

The amount of food that you can grow per drop of water has roughly doubled since the 1980s. In wheat, it's actually more than tripled since 1960. The amount of water that we use in the United States per person has dropped by about a third since the 1970s, after rising for decades. As agriculture has gotten more efficient, we're using less water per person. So, again, ideas can reduce resource use. . . .

One more thing that ideas can do is transform waste into value. In places like Germany and Japan, people are mining landfills. Japan estimates that its landfills alone contain 10-year supplies of gold and rare-earth minerals for the world market. Alcoa estimates that the world's landfills contain a 15-year supply of aluminum. So there's tremendous value.

When we throw things away, they're not destroyed. If we "consume" things like aluminum, we're not really consuming it, we're rearranging it. We're changing where it's located. And in some cases, the concentration of these resources in our landfills is actually higher than it was in our mines. What it takes is energy and technology to get that resource back out and put it back into circulation.

Ideas for Stretching the Limits

So ideas can reduce resource use, can find substitutes for scarce resources, and can transform waste into value. In that context, what are the limits to growth?

Is there a population limit? Yes, there certainly is, but it doesn't look like we're going to hit that. Projections right now are that, by the middle of this century, world population will peak between 9 billion and 10 billion, and then start to decline. In fact, we'll be talking much more about the graying of civilization, and perhaps underpopulation—too-low birthrates on a current trend.

What about physical resources? Are there limits to physical resource use on this planet? Absolutely. It really is a finite planet. But where are those limits?

To illustrate, let's start with energy. This is the most important resource that we use, in many ways. But when we consider all the fossil fuels that humanity uses today—all the oil, coal, natural gas, and so on—it pales in comparison to a much larger resource, all around us, which is the amount of energy coming in from our Sun every day.

The amount of energy from sunlight that strikes the top of the atmosphere is about 10,000 times as much as the energy that we use from fossil fuels on a daily basis. Ten seconds of sunlight hitting the Earth is as much energy as humanity uses in an entire day; one hour of sunlight hitting the Earth provides as much energy to the planet as a whole as humanity uses from all sources combined in one year.

This is an incredibly abundant resource. It manifests in many ways. It heats the atmosphere differentially, creating winds that we can capture for wind power. It evaporates water, which leads to precipitation elsewhere, which turns into things like rivers and waterfalls, which we can capture as hydropower.

But by far the largest fraction of it—more than half—is photons hitting the surface of the Earth. Those are so abundant that, with one-third of 1% of the Earth's land area, using current technology of about 14%-efficient solar cells, we could capture enough electricity to power all of current human needs.

The problem is not the abundance of the energy; the problem is cost. Our technology is primitive. Our technology for building solar cells is similar to our technology for manufacturing computer chips. They're built on silicon wafers in clean rooms at high temperatures, and so they're very, very expensive.

But innovation has been dropping that cost tremendously. Over the last 30 years, we've gone from a watt of solar power costing $20 to about $1. That's a factor of 20. We roughly drop the cost of solar by one-half every decade, more or less. That means that, in the sunniest parts of the world today, solar is now basically at parity in cost, without subsidies, with coal and natural gas. Over the next 12–15 years, that will spread to most of the planet. That's incredibly good news for us.

Of course, we don't just use energy while the Sun is shining. We use energy at night to power our cities; we use energy in things like vehicles that have to move and that have high energy densities. Both of these need storage, and today's storage is actually a bigger challenge than capturing energy. But there's reason to believe that we can tackle the storage problem, as well.

For example, consider lithium ion batteries—the batteries that are in your laptop, your cell phone, and so on. The demand to have longer-lasting devices drove tremendous innovations in these batteries in the 1990s and the early part of the 2000s. Between 1991 and 2005, the cost of storage in lithium ion batteries dropped by about a factor of nine, and the density of storage—how much energy you can store in an ounce of battery—increased by a little over double in that time. If we do that again, we would be at the point where grid-scale storage is affordable and we can store that energy overnight. Our electric vehicles have ranges similar to the range you can get in a gasoline-powered vehicle.

This is a tall order. This represents perhaps tens of billions of dollars in R&D, but it is something that is possible and for which there is precedent.

Another approach being taken is turning energy into fuel. When you use a fuel such as gasoline, it's not really an energy source. It's an energy carrier, an energy storage system, if you will. You can store a lot of energy in a very small amount.

Today, two pioneers in genome sequencing—Craig Venter and George Church—both have founded companies to create next-generation biofuels. What they're both leveraging is that gene-sequencing cost is the fastest quantitative area of progress on the planet.

What they're trying to do is engineer microorganisms that consume CO_2, sunlight, and sugar and actually excrete fuel as a byproduct. If we could do this, maybe just 1% of the Earth's surface—or a thirtieth of what we use for agriculture—could provide all the liquid fuels that we need. We would conveniently grow algae on saltwater and waste water, so biofuel production wouldn't compete for freshwater. And the possible yields are vast if we can get there.

If we can crack energy, we can crack everything else: . . .

* Food. Can we grow enough food? Between now and 2050, we have to increase food yield by about 70%. Is that possible? I think it is. In industrialized nations, food yields are already twice what they are in the world as a whole. That's because we have irrigation, tractors, better pesticides, and so on. Given such energy and wealth, we already know that we can grow enough food to feed the planet.

Another option that's probably cheaper would be to leverage some things that nature's already produced. What most people don't know is that the yield of corn per acre and in calories is about 70% higher than the yield of wheat. Corn is a C_4 photosynthesis crop: It uses a different way of turning sunlight and CO_2 into sugars that evolved only 30 million years ago. Now, scientists around the world are working on taking these C_4 genes from crops like corn and transplanting them into wheat and rice, which could right away increase the yield of those staple grains by more than 50%.

Physical limits do exist, but they are extremely distant. We cannot grow exponentially in our physical resource use forever, but that point is still at least centuries in the future. It's something we have to address eventually, but it's not a problem that's pressing right now.

* Wealth. One thing that people don't appreciate very much is that wealth has been decoupling from physical resource use on this planet. Energy use per capita is going up, CO_2 emissions per capita have been going up a little bit, but they are both widely outstripped by the amount of wealth that we're creating. That's because we

can be more efficient in everything—using less energy per unit of food grown, and so on.

This again might sound extremely counterintuitive, but let me give you one concrete example of how that happens. Compare the ENIAC—which in the 1940s was the first digital computer ever created—to an iPhone. An iPhone is billions of times smaller, uses billions of times less energy, and has billions of times more computing power than ENIAC. If you tried to create an iPhone using ENIAC technology, it would be a cube a mile on the side, and it would use more electricity than the state of California. And it wouldn't have access to the Internet, because you'd have to invent that, as well.

This is what I mean when I say ideas are the ultimate resource. The difference between an ENIAC and an iPhone is that the iPhone is embodied knowledge that allows you to do more with less resources. That phenomenon is not limited to high tech. It's everywhere around us.

So ideas are the ultimate resource. They're the only resource that accumulates over time. Our store of knowledge is actually larger than in the past, as opposed to all physical resources.

Challenges Ahead for Innovation

Today we are seeing a race between our rate of consumption and our rate of innovation, and there are multiple challenges. One challenge is the Darwinian process, survival of the fittest. In areas like green tech, there will be hundreds and even thousands of companies founded, and 99% of them will go under. That is how innovation happens. . . .

RAMEZ NAAM is a computer scientist, author, and former Microsoft executive whose latest book, *The Infinite Resource: The Power of Ideas on a Finite Planet*, looks at the power of innovation to overcome natural resource and environmental challenges.

EXPLORING THE ISSUE

Is Humankind Dangerously Harming the Environment?

Critical Thinking and Reflection

1. What is the evidence that food production is inadequate for the current world population and probably will become even less adequate in the next two decades?
2. What current trends are worsening world agriculture's ability to keep total food production in pace with world population and increasingly rich (more meat) diets?
3. How are the world's major biosystems declining over the past four decades: croplands, grasslands, forests, and oceans?
4. The Hartes write about severe economic and social crises if appropriate steps are not taken soon. On what grounds do they make such scary statements?
5. What are the likely impacts of global warming over the next half century? What are the possible but debatable impacts of global warming?
6. What factors are holding back the changes that would make us a sustainable society according to the Hartes?

Is There Common Ground?

There is common ground in the belief that the environment is worsening in many ways. The disagreement is about how serious these problems are and whether market responses to higher prices along with technological innovations will largely take care of them. Most environmentalists, however, cannot believe these problems can be taken care of so easily. In general, conservation actions cost three times the value of the benefits they bring. This inhibits their application if market forces determine actions. Government regulations can force actions that polluters and other environmental abusers would resist. But powerful people and the corporations do a good job of preventing tough regulations and policies. So far this train of thought suggests that even if solutions are available, they may be difficult to institute, so the problems are likely to worsen.

The Hartes warn that the world has had 30–40 years to make the needed changes and has done little. Now it must act at wartime speed or environmental crises are possible. Naam is not worried about current problems because he believes that new ideas and technologies will deal with the problems, save the planet, and bring worldwide affluence.

Create Central

www.mhhe.com/createcentral

Additional Resources

The issue of the state of the environment and prospects for the future has been hotly debated for over 40 years,

with little chance of ending soon. Two key issues define this debate. First, what are the potential impacts of global warming? Second, what are the net effects of future agricultural technologies? Will they be able to feed the world even as increasing millions will demand richer diets (more meat)?

For works that argue that global warming is a major world problem, see: Al Gore, *An Inconvenient Truth: The Planetary Emergency of Global Warming and What We Can Do about It* (Rodale Press, 2006); William Antholis and Strobe Talbott, *Fast Forward: Ethics and Politics in the Age of Global Warming* (Brookings Institution Press, 2010); Mark Hertsgaard, *Hot: Living Through the Next Fifty Years on Earth* (Houghton Mifflin Harcourt, 2011); Brian M. Fagan, *The Great Warming: Climate Change and the Rise and Fall of Civilizations* (Bloomsbury Press, 2008); David Archer, *The Long Thaw: How Humans Are Changing the Next 100,000 Years of Earth's Climate* (Princeton University Press, 2009); Mark Lynas, *Six Degrees: Our Future on Hotter Planet* (National Geographic, 2008); Tim F. Flannery, *Now or Never: Why We Must Act Now to End Climate Change and Create a Sustainable Future* (Atlantic Monthly Press, 2009); Charles Derber, *Greed to Green: Solving Climate Change and Remaking the Economy* (Paradigm Publishers, 2010); and Gabrielle Walker and Sir David King, *The Hot Topic: What We Can Do about Global Warming* (Harcourt, 2008).

Antagonists to the global warming thesis that human activities are a major cause of global warming include: S. Fred Singer and Dennis T. Avery, *Unstoppable Global Warming: Every 1,500 Years* (Rowman & Littlefield, 2007); Roy W. Spencer, *The Great Global Warming Blunder: How Mother Nature Fooled the World's Top Climate Scientists* (Encounter Books, 2010); Ian R. Plimer, *Heaven* and *Earth: Global Warming, the Missing Science* (Taylor Trade, 2009); Patrick J. Michaels and Robert C. Balling Jr., *Climate of Extremes: Global Warming Science They Don't Want You to Know* (Cato Institute, 2009); Christopher Booker, *The Real Global Warming Disaster: Is the Obsession with Climate Change Turning Out to Be the Most Costly Scientific Blunder in History?* (Continuum, 2009); Garth W. Paltridge, *The Climate Caper: Facts and Fallacies of Global Warming* (Quartet Books, 2009); and Ronald Bailey, ed., *Global Warming and Other Eco-Myths: How the Environmental Movement Uses False Science to Scare Us to Death* (Prima, 2002).

For the political side of the global warming issue, see: Raymond S. Bradley, *Global Warming and Political Intimidation: How Politicians Cracked Down on Scientists as the Earth Heated Up* (University of Massachusetts Press, 2011).

Two works that focus on what to do about global warming are: Robert K. Musil, *Hope for a Heated Planet: How Americans Are Fighting Global Warming and Building a Better Future* (Rutgers University Press, 2009) and William D. Nordhaus, *A Question of Balance: Weighing the Options on Global Warming Policies* (Yale University Press, 2008).

On food production issues and agriculture technologies, see: Lester R. Brown, *On the Edge: How to Prevent Environmental and Economic Collapse* (Earth Policy Institute, 2011) and *Plan B 4.0: Mobilizing to Save Civilization* (W. W. Norton, 2009); and Bread for the World Institute, *Are We on Track to End Hunger? 14th Annual Report on the State of World Hunger* (Bread for the World Institute, 2004).

On agricultural technologies, see: Vaclav Smil, *Feeding the World: A Challenge for the Twenty-First Century* (MIT Press, 2000).

Publications that are optimistic about the health of the environment and the availability of resources include: Bjørn Lomborg, *The Skeptical Environmentalist: Measuring the Real State of the World* (Cambridge University Press, 2001); Ronald Bailey, ed., *The True State of the Planet* (Free Press, 1995); and Gregg Easterbrook, *A Moment on the Earth: The Coming Age of Environmental Optimism* (Viking, 1995).

Publications by some who believe that population growth and human interventions in the environment have dangerous consequences for the future of mankind include: Richard Krooth, *Gaia and the Fate of Midas: Wrenching Planet Earth* (University Press of America, 2009); Richard A. Matthew, ed., *Global Environmental Change and Human Society* (MIT Press, 2010); Hans Gunter Brauch et al., *Facing Global Environmental Change: Environmental, Human, Energy, Food, Health and Water Security Concepts* (Springer, 2009); Tim Jackson, *Prosperity Without Growth: Economics for a Finite Planet*

(Earthscan, 2009); Joseph Wayne Smith, Graham Lyons, and Gary Sauer-Thompson, *Healing a Wounded World* (Praeger, 1997); Douglas E. Booth, *The Environmental Consequences of Growth* (Routledge, 1998); Kirill Kondratyev et al., *Stability of Life on Earth: Principal Subject of Scientific Research in the 21st Century* (Springer 2004); and James Gustive Speth, *Red Sky at Morning: America and the Crisis of the Global Environment* (Yale University Press, 2004).

Several works relate environmental problems to very severe political, social, and economic problems, including: Joseph Wayne Smith and Sandro Positano, *The Self-Destructive Affluence of the First World: The Coming Crisis of Global Poverty and Ecological Collapse* (Edwin Mellen Press, 2010); Joel Kovel, *The Enemy of Nature: The End of Capitalism or the End of the World?* (Zed Books, 2007); Michael Renner, *Fighting for Survival* (W. W. Norton, 1996); Michael N. Dobkowski and Isidor Wallimann, eds., *The Coming Age of Scarcity: Preventing Mass Death and Genocide in the Twenty-First Century* (Syracuse University Press, 1998) and *On the Edge of Scarcity: Environment, Resources, Population, Sustainability, and Conflict* (Syracuse University Press, 2002); and one with a long time frame, Sing C. Chew, *World Ecological Degradation: Accumulation, Urbanization, and Deforestation, 3000 B.C.–A.D. 2000* (Roman & Littlefield, 2001).

Since environmental changes could have such devastating effects, many have proposed solutions to these problems. The major term for these changes is "sustainability." The following works suggests paths to sustainability, most of which require dramatic changes: Eric F. Lambin, *The Middle Path: Avoiding Environmental Catastrophe* (University of Chicago Press, 2007); James Gustave Speth, *The Bridge at the Edge of the World: Capitalism, the Environment, and Crossing from Crisis to Sustainability* (Yale University Press, 2008); Charles J. Kibert et al., *Working Toward Sustainability: Ethical Decision Making in a Technological World* (Wiley, 2012); Russ Beaton and Chris Maser, *Economics and Ecology: United for a Sustainable World* (CRC Press, 2012); Robin Hahnel, *Green Economics: Confronting the Ecological Crisis* (M. E. Sharpe, 2011); Ian Chambers and John Humble, *Developing a Plan for the Planet: A Business Plan for Sustainable Living* (Gower Publishing, 2011); Jennifer Clapp and Peter Dauvergne, *Paths to a Green World: The Political Economy of the Global Environment* (MIT Press, 2011); Costas Panayotakis, *Remaking Scarcity: From Capitalist Inefficiency to Economic Democracy* (Fernwood, 2011); and Milissa Leach et al., *Dynamic Sustainabilities: Technology, Environment, Social Justice* (Earthscan, 2010).

Worldwatch Institute publishes an important series on environmental problems, which includes two annuals: *State of the World* and *Vital Signs*.

Internet References . . .

Sociology—Study Sociology Online

> http://edu.learnsoc.org/

Sociology Web Resources

> www.mhhe.com/socscience/sociology/resources
> /index.htm

Sociosite

> www.topsite.com/goto/sociosite.net

Socioweb

> www.topsite.com/goto/socioweb.com

Selected, Edited, and with Issue Framing Material by:
Kurt Finsterbusch, *University of Maryland, College Park*

ISSUE

Is Economic Globalization Good for Both Rich and Poor?

YES: **IMF Staff**, from "Globalization: A Brief Overview," *International Monetary Fund* (May 2008)

NO: **Ravinder Rena**, from "Globalization Still Hurting Poor Nations," *Africa Economic Analysis* (January 2008)

Learning Outcomes

After reading this issue, you will be able to:

- Identify as complete a list as possible of the positive and negative impacts of globalization. Also identify what groups get the benefits and what groups get the harms.
- Understand the arguments that maintain that the majority of the benefits accrue to the developed nations and the majority of the harms accrue to the less developed nations. Also understand the arguments that maintain that the less developed nations obtain more benefits from globalization than harms.
- Ascertain what aspects of international relations are included in the concept of globalization. Do commentators on different sides of this debate use different dimensions of globalization and how does that affect their arguments?
- Determine what are the advantages for less developed nations to invite foreign corporate investments into their country and what are the disadvantages.
- Identify the differences between the forms of globalization today compared to several decades ago.
- Deduce the main reasons why many people have protested globalization and evaluate how factual their perspective is.

ISSUE SUMMARY

YES: IMF Staff examine both positive and negative effects of globalization and conclude that economic globalization contributes greatly to world prosperity.

NO: Ravinder Rena, an associate professor of economics at the Eritrea Institute of Technology, argues that globalization produces many benefits but also produces many negative impacts. The poor and poorer countries are the most harmed by globalization.

A really big issue of today is globalization, which stands for worldwide processes, activities, and institutions. It involves world markets, world finance, world communications, world media, world religions, world popular culture, world rights movements, world drug trade, etc. The focus of most commentators is on the world economy, which today spreads financial crisis from the United States to the rest of the world. Many believe, however, that globalization promises strong growth in world wealth in the long run. Critics focus on the world economy's negative impacts on workers' wages, environmental protections and regulations, national and local cultures, and vulnerability to economic crises. One thing everyone agrees on

is that the impacts of globalization are gigantic. The statistics are mind boggling. Global trade has grown over 2,000 percent since 1950 and now is over $15 trillion annually. Total international investment exceeds $25 trillion. Multinational corporations dominate global commerce and the 500 largest corporations account for annual sales of over $15 trillion. Another fact that all agree on is that America and its businesses, media, and culture are at the center of the globalized world. This normally ensures that America gains more than its proportional share of the benefits. But the real debate is whether or not globalization benefits all mankind. When the whole world is considered, there may be far more minuses to be weighed against the pluses. It is hard to settle this debate because so many different and incomparable dimensions must be included in the calculation of the costs relative to benefits.

Let's identify some benefits that people around the world seem to enjoy. People are communicating by cell phones and the Internet around the world. TV and the Web bring events from all corners of the world into our living rooms or on our iPods. As a result we feel much more interconnected. Furthermore, we have an abundance of goods at low prices. So each of us personally enjoy many benefits. On the other hand, workers lose jobs to cheap foreign workers as companies relocate or invest abroad. World interconnectedness makes us feel more vulnerable to foreign enemies. I have several times had foreigners try to scam money from me. My telephone number has been used for fraudulent international calls. Businesses and government agencies are terrified about the potential damage that hackers can cause. Terrorism experts now believe that cyber attacks could be far more dangerous to us than attacks with weapons of mass destruction, and cyber attacks can be launched from anywhere in the world. Many other problems seem to have their roots in globalization. Therefore, we are both thankful for and fearful of globalization.

The lists of benefits and costs could go on for many pages. I have no idea how to sum all of them up into a net score. Instead I will turn that task over to the two readings presented below. In the following selections, staff members of IMF argue that the benefits far exceed the costs, even for the poor. IMF is well positioned to know what is happening and it has conducted high-quality research on this issue. They conclude that as nations globalize, their citizens benefit because they gain "access to a wider variety of goods and services, lower prices, more and more better-paying jobs, improved health, and higher overall living standards." These benefits, however, are very unevenly distributed both within and between nations. This problem is the backbone of Ravinder Rena's argument against globalization. He criticizes globalization for increasing the gap between rich and poor.

YES ↙

IMF Staff

Globalization: A Brief Overview

A perennial challenge facing all of the world's countries, regardless of their level of economic development, is achieving financial stability, economic growth, and higher living standards. There are many different paths that can be taken to achieve these objectives, and every country's path will be different given the distinctive nature of national economies and political systems. The ingredients contributing to China's high growth rate over the past two decades have, for example, been very different from those that have contributed to high growth in countries as varied as Malaysia and Malta.

Yet, based on experiences throughout the world, several basic principles seem to underpin greater prosperity. These include investment (particularly foreign direct investment) [owning foreign companies or real estate], the spread of technology, strong institutions, sound macroeconomic policies, an educated workforce, and the existence of a market economy. Furthermore, a common denominator which appears to link nearly all high-growth countries together is their participation in, and integration with, the global economy.

There is substantial evidence, from countries of different sizes and different regions, that as countries "globalize" their citizens benefit, in the form of access to a wider variety of goods and services, lower prices, more and better-paying jobs, improved health, and higher overall living standards. It is probably no mere coincidence that over the past 20 years, as a number of countries have become more open to global economic forces, the percentage of the developing world living in extreme poverty—defined as living on less than $1 per day—has been cut in half.

As much as has been achieved in connection with globalization, there is much more to be done. Regional disparities persist: while poverty fell in East and South Asia, it actually rose in sub-Saharan Africa. The UN's Human Development Report notes there are still around 1 billion people surviving on less than $1 per day—with 2.6 billion living on less than $2 per day. Proponents of globalization argue that this is not because of too much globalization, but rather too little. And the biggest threat to continuing to raise living standards throughout the world is not that globalization will succeed but that it will fail. It is the people of developing economies who have the greatest need for globalization, as it provides them with the opportunities that come with being part of the world economy.

These opportunities are not without risks—such as those arising from volatile capital movements. The International Monetary Fund works to help economies manage or reduce these risks, through economic analysis and policy advice and through technical assistance in areas such as macroeconomic policy, financial sector sustainability, and the exchange-rate system.

The risks are not a reason to reverse direction, but for all concerned—in developing and advanced countries, among both investors and recipients—to embrace policy changes to build strong economies and a stronger world financial system that will produce more rapid growth and ensure that poverty is reduced.

The following is a brief overview to help guide anyone interested in gaining a better understanding of the many issues associated with globalization.

What Is Globalization?

Economic "globalization" is a historical process, the result of human innovation and technological progress. It refers to the increasing integration of economies around the world, particularly through the movement of goods, services, and capital across borders. The term sometimes also refers to the movement of people (labor) and knowledge (technology) across international borders. There are also broader cultural, political, and environmental dimensions of globalization.

The term "globalization" began to be used more commonly in the 1980s, reflecting technological advances that made it easier and quicker to complete international transactions—both trade and financial flows. It refers to an extension beyond national borders of the same market forces that have operated for centuries at all levels of human economic activity—village markets, urban industries, or financial centers.

There are countless indicators that illustrate how goods, capital, and people have become more globalized.

- The value of trade (goods and services) as a percentage of world GDP [gross domestic product: the value of all goods and services produced within an economic unit] increased from 42.1 percent in 1980 to 62.1 percent in 2007.
- Foreign direct investment increased from 6.5 percent of world GDP in 1980 to 31.8 percent in 2006.

- The stock of international claims (primarily bank loans), as a percentage of world GDP, increased from roughly 10 percent in 1980 to 48 percent in 2006.
- The number of minutes spent on cross-border telephone calls, on a per-capita basis, increased from 7.3 in 1991 to 28.8 in 2006.
- The number of foreign workers has increased from 78 million people (2.4 percent of the world population) in 1965 to 191 million people (3.0 percent of the world population) in 2005.

The growth in global markets has helped to promote efficiency through competition and the division of labor—the specialization that allows people and economies to focus on what they do best. Global markets also offer greater opportunity for people to tap into more diversified and larger markets around the world. It means that they can have access to more capital, technology, cheaper imports, and larger export markets. But markets do not necessarily ensure that the benefits of increased efficiency are shared by all. Countries must be prepared to embrace the policies needed, and, in the case of the poorest countries, may need the support of the international community as they do so. The broad reach of globalization easily extends to daily choices of personal, economic, and political life. For example, greater access to modern technologies, in the world of health care, could make the difference between life and death. In the world of communications, it would facilitate commerce and education, and allow access to independent media. Globalization can also create a framework for cooperation among nations on a range of non-economic issues that have cross-border implications, such as immigration, the environment, and legal issues. At the same time, the influx of foreign goods, services, and capital into a country can create incentives and demands for strengthening the education system, as a country's citizens recognize the competitive challenge before them.

Perhaps more importantly, globalization implies that information and knowledge get dispersed and shared.

Innovators—be they in business or government—can draw on ideas that have been successfully implemented in one jurisdiction and tailor them to suit their own jurisdiction. Just as important, they can avoid the ideas that have a clear track record of failure. Joseph Stiglitz, a Nobel laureate and frequent critic of globalization, has nonetheless observed that globalization "has reduced the sense of isolation felt in much of the developing world and has given many people in the developing world access to knowledge well beyond the reach of even the wealthiest in any country a century ago."

International Trade

A core element of globalization is the expansion of world trade through the elimination or reduction of trade barriers, such as import tariffs. Greater imports offer consumers a wider variety of goods at lower prices, while providing strong incentives for domestic industries to remain competitive. Exports, often a source of economic growth for developing nations, stimulate job creation as industries sell beyond their borders. More generally, trade enhances national competitiveness by driving workers to focus on those vocations where they, and their country, have a competitive advantage. Trade promotes economic resilience and flexibility, as higher imports help to offset adverse domestic supply shocks. Greater openness can also stimulate foreign investment, which would be a source of employment for the local workforce and could bring along new technologies—thus promoting higher productivity.

Restricting international trade—that is, engaging in protectionism—generates adverse consequences for a country that undertakes such a policy. For example, tariffs raise the prices of imported goods, harming consumers, many of which may be poor. Protectionism also tends to reward concentrated, well-organized and politically-connected groups, at the expense of those whose interests may be more diffuse (such as consumers). It also reduces the variety of goods available and generates inefficiency by reducing competition and encouraging resources to flow into protected sectors.

Developing countries can benefit from an expansion in international trade. Ernesto Zedillo, the former president of Mexico, has observed that, "In every case where a poor nation has significantly overcome its poverty, this has been achieved while engaging in production for export markets and opening itself to the influx of foreign goods, investment, and technology."

And the trend is clear. In the late 1980s, many developing countries began to dismantle their barriers to international trade, as a result of poor economic performance under protectionist polices and various economic crises. In the 1990s, many former Eastern bloc countries integrated into the global trading system and developing Asia—one of the most closed regions to trade in 1980—progressively dismantled barriers to trade. Overall, while the average tariff rate applied by developing countries is higher than that applied by advanced countries, it has declined significantly over the last several decades.

The Implications of Globalized Financial Markets

The world's financial markets have experienced a dramatic increase in globalization in recent years. Global capital flows fluctuated between 2 and 6 percent of world GDP during the period 1980–95, but since then they have risen to 14.8 percent of GDP, and in 2006 they totaled $7.2 trillion, more than tripling since 1995. The most rapid increase has been experienced by advanced economies, but emerging markets and developing countries have also become more financially integrated. As countries have strengthened their capital markets they have attracted more investment capital, which can enable a broader entrepreneurial class to develop, facilitate a more efficient allocation of capital, encourage international risk sharing, and foster economic growth. Yet there is an energetic debate underway, among leading academics and policy experts, on the precise impact of financial globalization. Some see it as a catalyst for economic growth and stability. Others see it as injecting dangerous—and often costly—volatility into the economies of growing middle-income countries.

A recent paper by the IMF's Research Department takes stock of what is known about the effects of financial globalization. The analysis of the past 30 years of data reveals two main lessons for countries to consider.

First, the findings support the view that countries must carefully weigh the risks and benefits of unfettered capital flows. The evidence points to largely unambiguous gains from financial integration for advanced economies. In emerging and developing countries, certain factors are likely to influence the effect of financial globalization on economic volatility and growth: countries with well-developed financial sectors, strong institutions, sound macroeconomic policies, and substantial trade openness are more likely to gain from financial liberalization and less likely to risk increased macroeconomic volatility and to experience financial crises. For example, well-developed financial markets help moderate boom-bust cycles that can be triggered by surges and sudden stops in international capital flows, while strong domestic institutions and sound macroeconomic policies help attract "good" capital, such as portfolio equity flows and FDI.

The second lesson to be drawn from the study is that there are also costs associated with being overly cautious about opening to capital flows. These costs include lower international trade, higher investment costs for firms, poorer economic incentives, and additional administrative/monitoring costs. Opening up to foreign investment may encourage changes in the domestic economy that eliminate these distortions and help foster growth.

Looking forward, the main policy lesson that can be drawn from these results is that capital account liberalization should be pursued as part of a broader reform package encompassing a country's macroeconomic policy framework, domestic financial system, and prudential regulation. Moreover, long-term, non-debt-creating flows, such as FDI, should be liberalized before short-term, debt-creating inflows. Countries should still weigh the possible risks involved in opening up to capital flows against the efficiency costs associated with controls, but under certain conditions (such as good institutions, sound domestic and foreign policies, and developed financial markets) the benefits from financial globalization are likely to outweigh the risks.

Globalization, Income Inequality, and Poverty

As some countries have embraced globalization, and experienced significant income increases, other countries that have rejected globalization, or embraced it only tepidly, have fallen behind. A similar phenomenon is at work within countries—some people have, inevitably, been bigger beneficiaries of globalization than others.

Over the past two decades, income inequality has risen in most regions and countries. At the same time, per capita incomes have risen across virtually all regions for even the poorest segments of populations, indicating that the poor are better off in an absolute sense during this phase of globalization, although incomes for the relatively well off have increased at a faster pace. Consumption data from groups of developing countries reveal the striking inequality that exists between the richest and the poorest in populations across different regions.

As discussed in the October 2007 issue of the *World Economic Outlook*, one must keep in mind that there are many sources of inequality. Contrary to popular belief, increased trade globalization is associated with a decline in inequality. The spread of technological advances and increased financial globalization—and foreign direct investment in particular—have instead contributed more to the recent rise in inequality by raising the demand for skilled labor and increasing the returns to skills in both developed and developing countries. Hence, while everyone benefits, those with skills benefit more.

It is important to ensure that the gains from globalization are more broadly shared across the population. To this effect, reforms to strengthen education and training would help ensure that workers have the appropriate skills for the evolving global economy. Policies that broaden the access of finance to the poor would also help, as would further trade liberalization that boosts agricultural exports from developing countries. Additional programs may include providing adequate income support to cushion, but not obstruct, the process of change, and also making health care less dependent on continued employment and increasing the portability of pension benefits in some countries.

Equally important, globalization should not be rejected because its impact has left some people unemployed. The dislocation may be a function of forces that have little to do with globalization and more to do with inevitable technological progress. And, the number of people who "lose" under globalization is likely to be outweighed by the number of people who "win."

Martin Wolf, the *Financial Times* columnist, highlights one of the fundamental contradictions inherent in those who bemoan inequality, pointing out that this charge amounts to arguing "that it would be better for everybody to be equally poor than for some to become significantly better off, even if, in the long run, this will almost certainly lead to advances for everybody."

Indeed, globalization has helped to deliver extraordinary progress for people living in developing nations. One of the most authoritative studies of the subject has been carried out by World Bank economists David Dollar and Aart Kraay. They concluded that since 1980, globalization has contributed to a reduction in poverty as well as a reduction in global income inequality. They found that in "globalizing" countries in the developing world, income per person grew three-and-a-half times faster than in "non-globalizing" countries, during the 1990s. In general, they noted, "higher growth rates in globalizing developing countries have translated into higher incomes for the poor." Dollar and Kraay also found that in virtually all events in which a country experienced growth at a rate of two percent or more, the income of the poor rose.

Critics point to those parts of the world that have achieved few gains during this period and highlight it as a failure of globalization. But that is to misdiagnose the problem. While serving as Secretary-General of the United Nations, Kofi Annan pointed out that "the main losers in today's very unequal world are not those who are too much exposed to globalization. They are those who have been left out." . . .

Myths about Globalization

No discussion of globalization would be complete without dispelling some of the myths that have been built up around it.

Downward pressure on wages: Globalization is rarely the primary factor that fosters wage moderation in low-skilled work conducted in developed countries. As discussed in a recent issue of the *World Economic Outlook,* a more significant factor is technology. As more work can be mechanized, and as fewer people are needed to do a given job than in the past, the demand for that labor will fall, and as a result the prevailing wages for that labor will be affected as well.

The "race to the bottom": Globalization has not caused the world's multinational corporations to simply scour the globe in search of the lowest-paid laborers. There are numerous factors that enter into corporate decisions on where to source products, including the supply of skilled labor, economic and political stability, the local infrastructure, the quality of institutions, and the overall business climate. In an open global market, while jurisdictions do compete with each other to attract investment, this competition incorporates factors well beyond just the hourly wage rate.

According to the UN Information Service, the developed world hosts two-thirds of the world's inward foreign direct investment. The 49 least developed countries—the poorest of the developing countries—account for around 2 percent of the total inward FDI stock of developing countries. Nor is it true that multinational corporations make a consistent practice of operating sweatshops in low-wage countries, with poor working conditions and substandard wages. While isolated examples of this can surely be uncovered, it is well established that multinationals, on average, pay higher wages than what is standard in developing nations, and offer higher labor standards. . . .

The shrinking state: Technologies that facilitate communication and commerce have curbed the power of some despots throughout the world, but in a globalized world governments take on new importance in one criti-cal respect, namely, setting, and enforcing, rules with respect to contracts and property rights. The potential of globalization can never be realized unless there are rules and regulations in place, and individuals to enforce them. This gives economic actors confidence to engage in business transactions. Further undermining the idea of globalization shrinking states is that states are not, in fact, shrinking. Public expenditures are, on average, as high or higher today as they have been at any point in recent memory. And among OECD [Organization of Economic Cooperation and Development is composed of 30 mostly high-income countries] countries, government tax revenue as a percentage of GDP increased from 25.5 percent in 1965 to 36.6 percent in 2006.

The Future of Globalization

Like a snowball rolling down a steep mountain, globalization seems to be gathering more and more momentum. And the question frequently asked about globalization is not whether it will continue, but at what pace.

A disparate set of factors will dictate the future direction of globalization, but one important entity—sovereign governments—should not be overlooked. They still have the power to erect significant obstacles to globalization, ranging from tariffs to immigration restrictions to military hostilities.

Nearly a century ago, the global economy operated in a very open environment, with goods, services, and people able to move across borders with little if any difficulty. That openness began to wither away with the onset of World War I in 1914, and recovering what was lost is a process that is still underway. Along the process, governments recognized the importance of international cooperation and coordination, which led to the emergence of numerous international organizations and financial institutions (among which the IMF and the World Bank, in 1944).

Indeed, the lessons included avoiding fragmentation and the breakdown of cooperation among nations. The world is still made up of nation states and a global marketplace. We need to get the right rules in place so the global system is more resilient, more beneficial, and more legitimate. International institutions have a difficult but indispensable role in helping to bring more of globalization's benefits to more people throughout the world. By helping to break down barriers—ranging from the regulatory to the cultural—more countries can be integrated into the global economy, and more people can seize more of the benefits of globalization.

IMF Staff began on December 27, 1945, in an effort to stabilize exchange rates and assist with the reconstruction of the world's international payment system.

Ravinder Rena

→ **NO**

Globalization Still Hurting Poor Nations

Globalization is a buzzword gaining increasing importance all over the world. Today, the world appears radically altered. A very significant feature of the global economy is the integration of the emerging economies in world markets and the expansion of economic activities across state borders. Other dimensions include the international movement of ideas, information, legal systems, organizations, people, popular globetrotting cuisine, cultural exchanges, and so forth.

However, the movement of people, even in this post-1970s era of globalization, is restricted and strictly regulated in the aftermath of the 9/11 attacks. More countries are now integrated into a global economic system in which trade and capital flow across borders with unprecedented energy. Nonetheless, globalization has become painful, rather than controversial, to the developing world. It has produced increasing global economic interdependence through the growing volume and variety of cross-border flows of finance, investment, goods, and services, and the rapid and widespread diffusion of technology.

A World Bank study, "Global Economic Prospects: Managing the Next Wave of Globalization," succinctly discusses the advantages of globalization. Driven by 1974-onward globalization, exports have doubled, as a proportion of world economic output, to over 25 percent, and, based on existing trends, will rise to 34 percent by 2030.

World income has doubled since 1980, and almost half-a-billion people have climbed out of poverty since 1990. According to current trends, the number of people living on less than 1-purchasing power-dollar-a-day will halve from today's 1 billion by 2030. This will take place as a result of growth in Southeast Asia, whose share of the poor will halve from 60 percent, while Africa's will rise from 30 percent to 55 percent.

The scale, benefits, and criticism of globalization are often exaggerated. On the contrary, compared to the immediate post-war period, the average rate of growth has steadily slowed during the age of globalization, from 3.5 percent per annum in the 1960s to 2.1 percent, 1.3 percent, and 1.0 percent in the 1970s, 1980s, and 1990s, respectively.

The growing economic interdependence is highly asymmetrical. The benefits of linking and the costs of de-linking are not equally distributed. Industrialized countries—the European Union, Japan, and the United States—are genuinely and highly interdependent in their relations with one another. The developing countries, on the other hand, are largely independent from one another in terms of economic relations, while being highly dependent on industrialized countries. Indeed, globalization creates losers as well as winners, and entails risks as well as opportunities. An International Labor Organization blue-ribbon panel noted in 2005 that the problems lie not in globalization per se but in the deficiencies in its governance.

Some globalization nay-sayers have vouched that there has been a growing divergence, not convergence, in income levels, both between countries and peoples. Inequality among, and within, nations has widened. Assets and incomes are more concentrated. Wage shares have fallen while profit shares have risen. Capital mobility alongside labor immobility has reduced the bargaining power of organized labor. The rise in unemployment and the accompanying "casualization" of the workforce, with more and more people working in the informal sector, have generated an excess supply of labor and depressed real wages.

Globalization has spurred inequality—both in the wealthiest countries as well as the developing world. China and India compete globally, yet only a fraction of their citizens prosper. Increasing inequality between rural and urban populations, and between coastal and inland areas in China, could have disastrous consequences in the event of political transition. Forty of the poorest nations, many in Africa, have had zero growth during the past 20 years. Their governments followed advice from wealthy nations and World Bank consultants on issues ranging from privatization to development, but millions of people suffer from poverty. Ironically, the wealthiest people benefit from the source of cheap labor. Western policies reinforce the growing divide between rich and poor.

Nearly three-quarters of Africa's population live in rural areas in contrast with less-than-10-percent in the developed world. Globalization has driven a wedge between social classes in the rich countries, while among the world's poor, the main divide is between countries—those that adapted well to globalization and, in many areas, prospered, and those that maladjusted and, in many cases, collapsed.

As the Second World [the Soviet Union and the communist countries of Eastern Europe] collapsed and globalization took off, the latter rationale evaporated and a few countries, notably India and China, accelerated their growth rates significantly, enjoying the fruits of freer trade and larger capital flows. Although the two countries adapted well to globalization, there is little doubt that their newfound relative prosperity opened many new fissure lines. Inequality between coastal and inland provinces, as well as between urban and rural areas, skyrocketed in China.

Another large group of Third World countries in Latin America, Africa, and former Communist countries experienced a quarter-century of decline, or stagnation, punctuated by civil wars, international conflicts, and the onslaught of AIDS. While rich countries grew on average by almost 2 percent per capita annually from 1980 to 2002, the world's poorest 40 countries had a combined growth rate of zero. For large swaths of Africa, the income level today is less than 1-dollar-per-day.

For these latter countries, the promised benefits of globalization never arrived. Social services were often taken over by foreigners. Western experts and technocrats arrived on their jets, stayed in luxury hotels, and hailed the obvious worsening of economic and social conditions as a step toward better lives and international integration.

Indeed, for many people in Latin America and Africa, globalization was merely a new, more attractive label, for the old imperialism, or worse—for a form of re-colonization. The left-wing reaction sweeping Latin America, from Mexico to Argentina, is a direct consequence of the fault lines opened by policies designed to benefit Wall Street, not the people in the streets of Asmara [capital of Eritrea] or Kampala [capital of Uganda].

The rapid growth of global markets has not seen the parallel development of social and economic institutions to ensure their smooth and efficient functioning; labor rights have been less diligently protected than capital and property rights; and the global rules on trade and finance are unfair to the extent that they produce asymmetric effects on rich and poor countries.

The deepening of poverty and inequality has implications for the social and political stability among, and within, nations. It is in this context that the plight and hopes of developing countries have to be understood in the Doha Round of trade talks. Having commenced in 2001, the Doha Round was supposed to be about the trade-led and trade-facilitated development of the world's poor countries. After five years of negotiations, the talks collapsed because of unbridgeable differences among the EU [European Union], the US, and developing countries led by India, Brazil, and China. [The Doha Round is the latest and continuing series of negotiations under the aegis of the World Trade Organization to reduce restrictions on trade and other forms of international economic interchange. The Doha Round began in 2001 and is at a virtual standstill because of, among other things, disagreements between the wealthier and poorer countries.]

From the developing world's perspective, the problem is that the rich countries want access to poor countries' resources, markets, and labor forces at the lowest possible price. Some rich countries were open to implementing deep cuts in agricultural subsidies, but resisted opening their markets, others wanted the reverse. Developing countries like India, China, and Eritrea, among other[s], are determined to protect the livelihood of their farmers. In countries like India, farmer suicide has been a terrible human cost and a political problem for India's state and central governments for some time, as well as a threat to rural development. Protecting farmers' needs, therefore, is essential for social stability as well as the political survival of governments in the developing world.

The rich countries' pledges of flexibility failed to translate into concrete proposals during the Doha negotiations. Instead, they effectively protected the interests of tiny agricultural minorities. By contrast, in developing countries, farming accounts for 30 to 60 percent of the Gross Domestic Product [GDP] and up to 70 percent of the labor force. This is why labor rights protection is at least as critical for developing countries as intellectual property rights protection is for the rich.

Developing countries were promised a new regime that would allow them to sell their goods and trade their way out of poverty through undistorted market openness. This required generous market access by the rich for the products of the poor, and also reduction-cum-elimination of market-distorting producer and export subsidies, with the resulting dumping of the rich world's produce on world markets.

Thus, Europe launched its "Everything but Arms" initiative whereby it would open its markets to the world's poorest countries. The initiative foundered on too many non-tariff barriers, for example in the technical rules of origin. The US seemed to offer so-called EBP—Everything But what they Produce. Under its proposals, developing countries would have been free to export jet engines and supercomputers to the US, but not textiles, agricultural products, or processed foods.

Elimination of rich country production and export subsidies, and the opening of markets, while necessary, would not be sufficient for developing countries to trade their way out of underdevelopment. They also have a desperate need to institute market-friendly incentives and regulatory regimes and increase their farmers' productivity, and may require technical assistance from international donors to achieve this through investment in training, infrastructure, and research.

The failure of the Doha Round is also, finally, symptomatic of a much bigger malaise, namely the crisis of multilateral governance in security and environmental matters, as well as in trade. In agriculture, as in other sectors, problems-without-passports require solutions-without-borders.

To convince Africans about the benefits of globalization, we must take a more enlightened view of liberalizing trade, services, and labor-intensive manufacturing in which African countries are competitive. Trade is not only a means to prosperity, but also a means of peace-building. We need to devise an enlightened approach in negotiations over the reduction of harmful gas emissions, intellectual property rights, lifesaving drugs, and the transfer of technologies toward combating poverty. Ultimately, globalization broadens the gap between rich and poor. It also creates distortions in the global economy. Therefore, it is not a panacea for world economic development.

Ravinder Rena is coordinator of the Joint African Masters Programme in Local Development (JAMP) at the Harold Pupkewitz Graduate School of Business, Polytechnic of Namibia. Rena has written and published six research books, four textbooks, 18 book chapters, and more than 90 refereed journal articles.

EXPLORING THE ISSUE

Is Economic Globalization Good for Both Rich and Poor?

Critical Thinking and Reflection

1. How can one compare different types of impacts? For example, how does one compare profits from corporate investments abroad to jobs lost in America for the same globalization action?
2. The communication revolution, which enables people throughout the world to communicate by phone and Internet, is bringing the world closer together. What specific benefits result from this and what specific harms result from this? What policies or changes could improve the benefits and what policies or changes could reduce the harms?
3. Have you benefited from globalization? If so, how?
4. Does globalization increase inequalities in the world? What changes might produce more equality in the world, both between countries and within countries?
5. Is there an alternative to globalization? Is it inevitable? Can globalization be significantly modified?

Is There Common Ground?

One thing that has been demonstrated by the above debate is that globalization has so many sides to it and so many impacts that any assessment of it can be easily challenged. The focus here is on economic globalization but that cannot be isolated from other aspects. In fact, many believe that economic integration will spawn greater political integration and cultural integration to the benefit of mankind. Others believe that it will destroy some of the protections that people need and undermine their value systems. There is evidence on both sides, but little can be determined now. Both sides are predicting the future state of affairs, so until the future declares one view the winner neither can be disproved. Finally, how do we predict the future when the current world economic crisis has contradicted many previous judgments about globalization?

Create Central

www.mhhe.com/createcentral

Additional Resources

There has been an explosion of books on globalization recently. Any analysis of globalization should begin with Thomas Friedman's best selling *The Lexus and the Olive Tree* (Farrar, Straus and Giroux, 1999), which strongly advocated for globalization for the prosperity it brings. He continues his advocacy in *The World Is Flat: A Brief History of the Twenty-First Century* (Picador, 2007) and *Hot, Flat and Crowded* (Farrar, Straus and Giroux, 2008). Friedman sees the United States as the nation that is best able to capitalize on that global economy, so it has the brightest

future. Other notable pro-globalization books include Jagdish N. Bhagwati, *In Defense of Globalization* (Oxford University Press, 2007) and Pankaj Ghemawat, *World 3.0: Global Prosperity and How to Achieve It* (Harvard University Press, 2011).

Attacks on globalization are prolific, as are the evils attributed to globalization. The attacks include William Grieder's *One World Ready or Not: The Manic Logic of Global Capitalism* (Simon & Schuster, 1997); David Korten's *When Corporations Rule the World* (Kumarian Press, 1996); Robert Went, *Globalization: Neoliberal Challenge, Radical Responses* (Pluto Press, 2000); William K. Tabb, *The Amoral Elephant: Globalization and the Struggle for Social Justice in the Twenty-First Century* (Monthly Review Press, 2001); Gary Teeple, *Globalization and the Decline of Social Reform* (Humanity Books, 2000); Noreena Hertz, *The Silent Takeover: Global Capitalism and the Death of Democracy* (Free Press, 2002); Alan Tomelson, *Race to the Bottom: Why a Worldwide Worker Surplus and Uncontrolled Free Trade Are Sinking American Living Standards* (Westview, 2000); Robert A. Isaak, *The Globalization Gap: How the Rich Get Richer and the Poor Get Left Further Behind* (Prentice-Hall, 2005); Joseph E. Stiglitz, *Making Globalization Work* (W. W. Norton, 2006); Gabor Steingart, *The War for Wealth: The True Story of Globalization or Why the Flat World Is Broken* (McGraw-Hill, 2008); and Rhoda E. Howard-Hassmann, *Can Globalization Promote Human Rights?* (Pennsylvania State University Press, 2010).

For relatively balanced discussions of globalization see Arthur P. J. Mol, *Globalization and Environmental Reform: The Ecological Modernization of the Global Economy* (MIT Press, 2001), which points to the environmental degradation that results from globalization but also actions that retard degradation and improve environmental quality; Kamal Dervis, *Better Globalization: Legitimacy, Governance and Reform* (Brookings, 2005); *Globalization and Anti-globalization: Dynamics of Change in the New World*, edited by Henry Veltmeyer (Ashgate, 2004); Dilip K. Das, *Two* *Faces of Globalization: Munificent and Malevolent* (Edward Elgar, 2009); and Alfred E. Eckes, *the Contemporary Global Economy: A History Since 1980* (Wiley-Blackwell, 2011).

Internet References . . .

Sociology—Study Sociology Online

http://edu.learnsoc.org/

Sociology Web Resources

www.mhhe.com/socscience/sociology/resources
/index.htm

Sociosite

www.topsite.com/goto/sociosite.net

Socioweb

www.topsite.com/goto/socioweb.com

Selected, Edited, and with Issue Framing Material by:
Kurt Finsterbusch, *University of Maryland, College Park*

ISSUE

Should Government Intervene in a Capitalist Economy?

YES: Joseph E. Stiglitz, from "Government Failure vs. Market Failure: Principles of Regulation," paper prepared for the conference "Government and Markets: Toward a New Theory of Regulation," February 1–3, 2008, Yulee, Florida (2009)

NO: Walter Williams, from "Future Prospects for Economic Liberty," *Imprimis* (September 2009)

Learning Outcomes

After reading this issue, you will be able to:

- Understand why many believe that intervention is necessary to address many problems and why many others believe that almost always the government will cause more harm than good.
- Identify a number of specific problems that seem to require government interventions.
- Identify a number of specific adverse consequences that government interventions could cause.
- Conduct a simple qualitative risk assessment of government interventions in a capitalist economy. This method would list possible positive and negative consequences of a specific potential government intervention and estimate whether each of the possible consequences are very likely, likely, 50/50, unlikely, or very unlikely. On the basis of the results, draw your conclusion as to whether the government should intervene or not in the case that you were considering. Perhaps this method would allow you to tentatively identify when government intervention would be good and when it would be bad.
- Evaluate the type and strength of the support that is provided for each side of this debate. Is the argument based mainly on a few stories, on ideology, on theories, on carefully selected cases, or on a large number of cases.
- Figure out how you or your family have been hurt or helped by government intervention in the economy.

ISSUE SUMMARY

YES: Joseph E. Stiglitz, University Professor at Columbia University, argues that the government plays an essential role in enabling the market to work properly. Capitalism runs amok if it is not regulated to protect against abuse and ensure fairness.

NO: Walter Williams, professor of economics at George Mason University, argues that the founders defined a small role for government in the Constitution and protected the freedom of individuals. Now the role of government is increasing and individual freedoms are declining. The free market has achieved great prosperity for America and the intervention of government has had net negative impacts.

The expression "That government is best which governs least" sums up a deeply rooted attitude of many Americans. From early presidents Thomas Jefferson and Andrew Jackson to America's most recent leaders, Ronald Reagan, George Bush, Bill Clinton, and George W. Bush, American politicians have often echoed the popular view that there are certain areas of life best left to the private actions of citizens.

One such area is the economic sphere, where people make their living by buying, selling, and producing goods and services. The tendency of most Americans is to regard direct government involvement in the economic sphere as both unnecessary and dangerous. The purest expression of this view is the economic theory of laissez-faire, a French term meaning "let be" or "let alone."

The seminal formulation of laissez-faire theory was the work of eighteenth-century Scottish philosopher

Adam Smith, whose treatise *The Wealth of Nations* appeared in 1776. Smith's thesis was that each individual, pursuing his or her own selfish interests in a competitive market, will be "led by an invisible hand to promote an end which was no part of his intention." In other words, when people single-mindedly seek profit, they actually serve the community, because sellers must keep prices down and quality up if they are to meet the competition of other sellers.

Laissez-faire economics was much honored (in theory, if not always in practice) during the nineteenth and early twentieth centuries. But as the nineteenth century drew to a close, the Populist Party sprang up. The Populists denounced eastern bankers, Wall Street stock manipulators, and rich "moneyed interests," and they called for government ownership of railroads, a progressive income tax, and other forms of state intervention. The Populist Party died out early in the twentieth century, but the Populist message was not forgotten. In fact, it was given new life after 1929, when the stock market collapsed and the United States was plunged into the worst economic depression in its history.

By 1932, a quarter of the nation's workforce was unemployed, and most Americans were finding it hard to believe that the "invisible hand" would set things right. Some Americans totally repudiated the idea of a free market and embraced socialism, the belief that the state (or "the community") should run all major industries. Most stopped short of supporting socialism, but they were now prepared to welcome some forms of state intervention in the economy. President Franklin D. Roosevelt, elected in 1932, spoke to this mood when he pledged a "New Deal" to the American people. "New Deal" has come to stand for a variety of programs that were enacted during the first eight years of Roosevelt's presidency, including business and banking regulations, government pension programs, federal aid to the disabled, unemployment compensation, and government-sponsored work programs. Side by side with the "invisible hand" of the marketplace was now the very visible hand of an activist government.

Government intervention in the economic sphere increased during World War II as the government fixed prices, rationed goods, and put millions to work in government-subsidized war industries. After the war the government's role in the economy declined dramatically, but the government continued to be fairly active during the 1950s. During the late 1960s and early 1970s, however, the role of the government in the economy increased greatly. It launched a variety of new welfare and regulatory programs: the multibillion-dollar War on Poverty; new civil rights and affirmative action mandates; and new laws protecting consumers, workers, disabled people, and the environment. These, in turn, led to a proliferation of new government agencies and bureaus, as well as shelves and shelves of published regulations. Proponents of the new activism like Stiglitz conceded that it was expensive, but they insisted that activist government was necessary to protect Americans against pollution, discrimination, dangerous products, and other effects of the modern marketplace. Critics of government involvement like Williams called attention not only to its direct costs but also to its effect on business activity and individual freedom.

YES ↵

Joseph E. Stiglitz

Government Failure vs. Market Failure: Principles of Regulation

The subject of regulation has been one of the most contentious, with critics arguing that regulations interfere with the efficiency of the market, and advocates arguing that well-designed regulations not only make markets more efficient but also help ensure that market outcomes are more equitable. Interestingly, as the economy plunges into a slowdown, if not a recession, with more than 2 million Americans expected to lose their homes (unless the government intervenes), there is a growing consensus: there was a need for more government regulation. Responding to these calls—as if to close the barn door after all the horses have gotten out—the Federal Reserve has tightened some regulations. If it is the case that better regulations could have prevented, or even mitigated, the downturn, the country, and the world, will be paying a heavy price for the failure to regulate adequately. And the social costs are no less grave—as hundreds of thousands of Americans will not only have lost their homes but their lifetime savings. Home ownership has long been thought of as contributing to the strength of communities; with the share of home ownership falling, communities too will be weaker. The foreclosures will exacerbate the decline in housing prices, and property tax bases will erode—a further knock on effect of inadequate regulation.

When Upton Sinclair's novel *The Jungle* depicted the terrible sanitary conditions in America's stock yards, Americans turned away from meat; and the meat packing industry asked for government food safety regulation to restore confidence. When the Enron/WorldCom scandal eroded confidence in America's financial markets and accounting firms, there was again a demand for stronger regulation to restore confidence. Whether Sarbanes-Oxley went too far or not far enough may be debated; but what is not debatable is that such regulations were viewed, at least by many Americans, as essential for restoring confidence in America's markets, where scandal had touched every accounting firm, most of the major investment banks, and many of its leading corporations.

Today, America's air and water is cleaner—and Americans are living longer—because of environmental regulations. No one can imagine a world today without food, safety, and environmental regulations. The debate is only whether we have gone too far, and whether we could have gotten the desired results at lower costs.

The General Theory of Regulation

The general theory of regulation begins with a simple question: Why is regulation needed? [The answer is] . . . market failures. Adam Smith (it is widely believed) argued that markets by themselves are efficient. Arrow and Debreu established the sense in which that was true (Pareto efficiency, i.e., no one could be made better off without making someone else worse off), and the conditions under which it was true (perfect competition, no externalities, no public goods). Subsequently, Greenwald and Stiglitz showed that whenever information is imperfect or markets incomplete—that is, always—there is a presumption that markets are not (constrained) Pareto efficient. Thus, the notion that markets, by themselves, lead to efficient outcomes has, today, no theoretical justification: no one believes that the conditions under which that statement is true are satisfied.

Some advocates of free markets take it as a matter of faith that the magnitude of the inefficiencies are small (though no one has suggested how one might prove that); but more commonly advocates of free markets take it as a matter of faith that government attempts to correct market failures by and large make things worse. To be sure, there are examples of badly designed government regulations, but the disasters associated with unfettered markets at least provide a prima facie case for the desirability of *some* regulation.

Regulations can thus play an important role in addressing market failures.

There are several particular categories of market failures to which I want to call attention. We have regulations designed to mitigate the extent of *externalities*. These include, for instance, zoning restrictions and environmental regulations. We have regulations designed to maintain competition (restrictions on anti-competitive practices), and to ensure that natural monopolies do not abuse their monopoly position (utilities regulations). We have a large set of regulations aimed at protecting consumers (ensuring that the banks where they deposit their money are sufficiently sound, that food and products are safe, or that they are not taken advantage of by unscrupulous merchants, advertising, or lenders). In several of these cases, as we shall note, disclosure is important; but the regulations go well beyond disclosure, for reasons which I explain below.

There are two further categories on which I want to comment, both related to *information problems*. The first concerns insurance. Private sector contractual arrangements often have what would appear to be "regulatory" structures. A fire insurance firm requires that the insured install sprinklers. Sometimes, insurance companies use the price system, i.e., they give a discount if sprinklers are installed. But sometimes they simply will not write the insurance policy if sprinklers are not installed. Many government regulations are similarly motivated: government absorbs risk, and to reduce its risk exposure, imposes constraints; it provides flood and earthquake insurance (explicitly in some cases and implicitly in others—if an earthquake occurs, it knows that it cannot deny assistance to anyone) and demands that houses be constructed so as to reduce the risk of loss. Because of moral hazard—or even because of a failure to perceive accurately the magnitude of the risk—individuals will take insufficient care.

The second category concerns what might be called certification. The meatpackers wanted certification that their products were produced in a safe and humane manner. They also knew that the only credible source of such certification was the government—if the meatpackers paid the certifiers directly, there would be a conflict of interest.

Recent troubles in accounting and rating agencies highlight the problems of private certification. The Enron scandal highlighted that the accounting firms' incentives were distorted; and while Sarbanes-Oxley improved matters, it did not fully resolve them. Similarly, with the rating agencies being paid by the financial firms to rate the complex products they were creating, it is perhaps no surprise that they gave AAA ratings to highly risky products.

Information is a public good. All individuals want to be assured that if they put money in a bank, the bank will be there when it comes time to withdraw the money. Government bank regulation is in part certification: it sets certain standards that a bank must satisfy—and inspects that it fulfills those standards. It could, of course, stop there, allowing individuals to deposit their money in "uncertified" banks (and in a sense, it does that—there are many non-certified financial institutions). But it goes beyond that: it does not allow banks to operate unless they satisfy certain conditions. And that, in part, is because it knows that if a bank fails, it may have to be bailed out. As one astute observer put it: there are two kinds of governments—those who provide deposit insurance and know it; and those who do so and don't know it. This in turn means that in order to mitigate the moral hazard problem, restrictions on banks have to be imposed.

Irrationality

The market failure approach growing out of an analysis of the standard assumptions required to establish the Pareto efficiency of the economy (the First Fundamental Theorem) is, however, only one of at least three strands of analysis underlying the demand for regulation. A second focuses on *market irrationality*. The standard competitive equilibrium model assumed that all individuals were rational; it explained why rational individuals (households) interacting with profit (or value) maximizing firms in a competitive marketplace might not result in Pareto efficient allocations. But individuals may not be rational and may deviate from rationality in systematic ways. Individuals (and even more so societies) have to be saved from themselves. Markets suffer from irrational exuberance and irrational pessimism. Individuals may not save adequately for their retirement.

Until the recent work on behavioral economics, economists typically looked askance at such paternalistic arguments for government intervention. Why, it was argued, should there be any presumption that governments are more rational or better informed than individuals? Who are we to impose our beliefs of what is rational on others? Part of the answer was provided by the classic theory of market failure: one might argue that so long as the individual only harms himself, there is no reason for government intervention. But individual actions may adversely affect others (there are, in effect, externalities). Regulation may reduce the likelihood of these adverse effects occurring and their impacts when they do. There is a special category of externalities that arises in democratic societies. Society cannot stand idly by when it sees someone starving—even if it is a result of the individual's own mistakes, say, not saving enough. Society will bail out the individual (or a bank which is too big to fail). Knowing that, individuals have an incentive to save too little (or banks to take too much risk). Knowing that, government should impose regulations to ensure that individuals do save enough (or banks do not undertake excessive risk).

But the new behavioral economics puts a new perspective on these issues: individuals may, in some sense, be better off if they are compelled to undertake some actions or are circumscribed from undertaking others. A potential alcoholic or drug addict may realize that he may be tempted to consume these toxic products and then become addicted. He knows *before he becomes addicted* that he will regret getting the addiction, but once he is addicted, will not be able to change his behavior. He therefore wants the government (or someone else) to make it impossible, or at least more difficult, to become addicted. (Matters are made worse by the fact that there are firms, such as those in the tobacco industry, who profit by taking advantage of addiction. By increasing the addictive properties of their products, they reduce the elasticity of demand and increase profitability.)

Similarly, individuals may know that they can easily be induced to save very little or a great deal, simply on the basis of the default set by the employer in choosing the fraction of income to put into a savings account. Accordingly, they might want the government to force the firm to undertake a kind of analysis that sets the default rate in ways which enable the individual to have a reasonably comfortable retirement, without sacrificing excessively current levels of consumption.

A formal welfare analysis of such regulations within the traditional welfare economics paradigm is, of course, difficult: Do we evaluate the impacts of the policy intervention using individuals' *ex ante* expected utility (their incorrect beliefs, for instance, about the consequences of their actions), or using *ex post* realized (average) utility?

Distributive Justice

There is a third category of rationale for government interventions: the best that can be said for the market economy is that it produces *efficient* outcomes; there is no presumption that it produces outcomes that are viewed as socially just. Regulations may be an important instrument for achieving distributive objectives, especially when governments face tight budgetary constraints (or other administrative constraints). CRA (Community Reinvestment Act) lending requirements or health insurance mandates may be an effective way of helping poor individuals when the government cannot afford other ways of helping them.

Some advocates of free markets appeal to Coase's conjecture (sometimes called Coase's theorem) that, even in the presence of externalities, individuals can bargain themselves to an efficient outcome, so long as there are clearly defined property rights. But such claims cannot be supported so long as there is imperfect information (e.g., concerning individuals' valuation of the external costs) or transactions costs, as there always are. Indeed, one of the standard arguments for regulation is that it economizes on transactions costs.

A variant of Coase's argument is that those injured should (be entitled to) sue those who are doing the injury. With a good tort legal system (including class action suits), individuals will have appropriate incentives. Interestingly, conservatives (like those in the Bush Administration) argue both for less regulation and reduced capacity to recover damages. They sometimes have a valid argument against the legal system: as currently constituted, in many areas it provides "excessive" recovery—providing excessive incentives for care—at the same time that in other areas it provides insufficient incentives (without class actions, the transactions costs are so large that recovery of damages is impossible).

More generally, sums required to compensate for damage done to individuals may not provide appropriate incentives; by linking the two together, incentives are not in general optimized. Moreover, in many cases, there is no adequate monetary incentive: someone whose child has died as a result of lead poisoning can never really be adequately compensated. *Ex post* compensation is not enough. We have to stop the bad behavior *ex ante,* if we can.

Other forms of market mechanisms, it is now realized, also are insufficient—reputation mechanisms help but do not ensure efficiency.

Regulations vs. Other Forms of Intervention

Critics of regulation argue the objectives of regulation can be achieved better at lower costs by using "market based" interventions, i.e., taxes and subsidies. If smoking gives rise to an externality, tax smoking. If greenhouse gases give rise to global warming, tax greenhouse gas emissions. Price interventions have much to commend them: they are general, simple, and often have low transaction costs. But research over the last quarter century has clarified an important set of limitations. Indeed, the very conditions (such as imperfect and asymmetric information) that imply that markets by themselves do not in general lead to (constrained) Pareto efficient outcomes also imply that price interventions by themselves will not suffice.

i. Imperfect information and incomplete contracting

Most importantly, in the presence of imperfect information and incomplete contracting, optimal incentive schemes typically are highly non-linear (they do not take the form of a price intervention) and may even impose constraints (like rationing and terminations). In a sense, most regulations can be recast as (typically simple) forms of non-linear price schedules; but few price schedules, used in the private or public sector, are in fact anywhere near the complexities of those that emerge from optimal incentive schemes. Whether a particular regulatory structure is better or worse than a particular simplified non-linear price system may be hard to ascertain; and in any case, viewed through lens, the distinction between regulatory systems and (non-linear) price systems is more a matter of semantics than anything else.

There is, of course, a literature contrasting polar forms: a pure price system or a pure quantity (regulatory) system. But there is seldom reason to resort to such extremes, and in many cases, the standard formulation is simply not relevant.

Prices vs. Quantities

Nonetheless, much of the literature has been couched in exactly these extremes. It has been argued, for instance, that, depending on the nature of the shocks (to the demand and supply curves), quantity interventions (regulations) may lead to a higher level of expected utility than price interventions. Consider, for instance, the problem of greenhouse gases. Some have suggested that this is a classic case where quantity regulation is to be preferred. With price interventions, the level of greenhouse gas emissions is uncertain; a change in the demand or supply curve will mean that we will have less or more emissions than is desirable.

But the argument is hardly persuasive: global warming is related to the level of concentration of greenhouse gases in the atmosphere, and what matters for this is not the level of emissions in any particular year. There is, in fact, even some uncertainty about the relationship between emission levels and changes in concentration levels and about the relationship between the level of concentration of greenhouse gases and the (precise) change in climate. There will have to be, in any case, adjustments to the allowable levels of emissions over time. Using prices (emission taxes), there will have to be adjustments too, with one additional factor of uncertainty: the relationship between taxes and emissions. But provided that adjustments are made in a relatively timely way, there is little additional risk in the variables of concern, the level of concentration of greenhouse gases, and climate change.

But there are contexts in which regulations may be better than price interventions. If import supply functions are highly variable but domestic demand and supply conditions do not vary, then setting a tariff leads to high variability in price, domestic output, and production; setting a quota eliminates this costly source of "imported" risk. Tariffication (shifting from quotas to tariffs) may, accordingly, not be welfare enhancing. In general, with imperfect information (and incomplete contracting) it is optimal to use a complex set of "controls" which entail both (generalized) incentives and constraints.

JOSEPH E. STIGLITZ is an economist and a professor at Columbia University. In 2001, he received the Nobel Memorial Prize in Economic Sciences. He is a former senior vice president and chief economist of the World Bank, and is a former member and chairman of the Council of Economic Advisers. In 2000, Stiglitz founded the Initiative for Policy Dialogue (IPD), a think tank on international development based at Columbia University.

Walter Williams   ➡ **NO**

Future Prospects for Economic Liberty

One of the justifications for the massive growth of government in the 20th and now the 21st centuries, far beyond the narrow limits envisioned by the founders of our nation, is the need to promote what the government defines as fair and just. But this begs the prior and more fundamental question: What is the legitimate role of government in a free society? To understand how America's Founders answered this question, we have only to look at the rule book they gave us—the Constitution. Most of what they understood as legitimate powers of the federal government are enumerated in Article 1, Section 8. Congress is authorized there to do 21 things, and as much as three-quarters of what Congress taxes us and spends our money for today is nowhere to be found on that list. To cite just a few examples, there is no constitutional authority for Congress to subsidize farms, bail out banks, or manage car companies. In this sense, I think we can safely say that America has departed from the constitutional principle of limited government that made us great and prosperous.

On the other side of the coin from limited government is individual liberty. The Founders understood private property as the bulwark of freedom for all Americans, rich and poor alike. But following a series of successful attacks on private property and free enterprise—beginning in the early 20th century and picking up steam during the New Deal, the Great Society, and then again recently—the government designed by our Founders and outlined in the Constitution has all but disappeared. Thomas Jefferson anticipated this when he said, "The natural progress of things is for liberty to yield and government to gain ground."

To see the extent to which liberty is yielding and government is gaining ground, one need simply look at what has happened to taxes and spending. A tax, of course, represents a government claim on private property. Every tax confiscates private property that could otherwise be freely spent or freely invested. At the same time, every additional dollar of government spending demands another tax dollar, whether now or in the future. With this in mind, consider that the average American now works from January 1 until May 5 to pay the federal, state, and local taxes required for current government spending levels. Thus the fruits of more than one-third of our labor are used in ways decided upon by others. The Founders favored the free market because it maximizes the freedom of all citizens and teaches respect for the rights of others. Expansive government, by contrast, contracts individual freedom and teaches disrespect for the rights of others. Thus clearly we are on what Friedrich Hayek called the road to serfdom, or what I prefer to call the road to tyranny.

As I said, the Constitution restricts the federal government to certain functions. What are they? The most fundamental one is the protection of citizens' lives. Therefore, the first legitimate function of the government is to provide for national defense against foreign enemies and for protection against criminals here at home. These and other legitimate public goods (as we economists call them) obviously require that each citizen pay his share in taxes. But along with people's lives, it is a vital function of the government to protect people's liberty as well—including economic liberty or property rights. So while I am not saying that we should pay no taxes, I am saying that they should be much lower—as they would be, if the government abided by the Constitution and allowed the free market system to flourish.

And it is important to remember what makes the free market work. Is it a desire we all have to do good for others? Do people in New York enjoy fresh steak for dinner at their favorite restaurant because cattle ranchers in Texas love to make New Yorkers happy? Of course not. It is in the interest of Texas ranchers to provide the steak. They benefit themselves and their families by doing so. This is the kind of enlightened self-interest discussed by Adam Smith in his *Wealth of Nations*, in which he argues that the social good is best served by pursuing private interests. The same principle explains why I take better care of my property than the government would. It explains as well why a large transfer or estate tax weakens the incentive a property owner has to care for his property and pass it along to his children in the best possible condition. It explains, in general, why free enterprise leads to prosperity.

Ironically, the free market system is threatened today not because of its failure, but because of its success. Capitalism has done so well in eliminating the traditional problems of mankind—disease, pestilence, gross hunger, and poverty—that other human problems seem to us unacceptable. So in the name of equalizing income, achieving sex and race balance, guaranteeing housing and medical care, protecting consumers, and conserving energy—just to name a few prominent causes of liberal government these days—individual liberty has become of secondary or tertiary concern.

Imagine what would happen if I wrote a letter to Congress and informed its members that, because I am fully capable of taking care of my own retirement needs, I respectfully request that they stop taking money out of my paycheck for Social Security. Such a letter would be greeted with contempt. But is there any difference between being forced to save for retirement and being forced to save for housing or for my child's education or for any other perceived good? None whatsoever. Yet for government to force us to do such things is to treat us as children rather than as rational citizens in possession of equal and inalienable natural rights.

We do not yet live under a tyranny, of course. Nor is one imminent. But a series of steps, whether small or large, tending toward a certain destination will eventually take us there. The philosopher David Hume observed that liberty is seldom lost all at once, but rather bit by bit. Or as my late colleague Leonard Read used to put it, taking liberty from Americans is like cooking a frog: It can't be done quickly because the frog will feel the heat and escape. But put a frog in cold water and heat it slowly, and by the time the frog grasps the danger, it's too late.

Again, the primary justification for increasing the size and scale of government at the expense of liberty is that government can achieve what it perceives as good. But government has no resources of its own with which to do so. Congressmen and senators don't reach into their own pockets to pay for a government program. They reach into yours and mine. Absent Santa Claus or the tooth fairy, the only way government can give one American a dollar in the name of this or that good thing is by taking it from some other American by force. If a private person did the same thing, no matter how admirable the motive, he would be arrested and tried as a thief. That is why I like to call what Congress does, more often than not, "legal theft." The question we have to ask ourselves is whether there is a moral basis for forcibly taking the rightful property of one person and giving it to another to whom it does not belong. I cannot think of one. Charity is noble and good when it involves reaching into your own pocket. But reaching into someone else's pocket is wrong.

In a free society, we want the great majority, if not all, of our relationships to be voluntary. I like to explain a voluntary exchange as a kind of non-amorous seduction. Both parties to the exchange feel good in an economic sense. Economists call this a positive sum gain. For example, if I offer my local grocer three dollars for a gallon of milk, implicit in the offer is that we will both be winners. The grocer is better off because he values the three dollars more than the milk, and I am better off because I value the milk more than the three dollars. That is a positive sum gain. Involuntary exchange, by contrast, means that one party gains and the other loses. If I use a gun to steal a gallon of milk, I win and the grocer loses. Economists call this a zero sum gain. And we are like that grocer in most of what Congress does these days.

Some will respond that big government is what the majority of voters want, and that in a democracy the majority rules. But America's Founders didn't found a democracy, they founded a republic. The authors of *The Federalist Papers*, arguing for ratification of the Constitution, showed how pure democracy has led historically to tyranny. Instead, they set up a limited government, with checks and balances, to help ensure that the reason of the people, rather than the selfish passions of a majority, would hold sway. Unaware of the distinction between a democracy and a republic, many today believe that a majority consensus establishes morality. Nothing could be further from the truth.

Another common argument is that we need big government to protect the little guy from corporate giants. But a corporation can't pick a consumer's pocket. The consumer must voluntarily pay money for the corporation's product. It is big government, not corporations, that have the power to take our money by force. I should also point out that private business *can* force us to pay them by employing government. To see this happening, just look at the automobile industry or at most corporate farmers today. If General Motors or a corporate farm is having trouble, they can ask me for help, and I may or may not choose to help. But if they ask government to help and an IRS agent shows up at my door demanding money, I have no choice but to hand it over. It is big government that the little guy needs protection against, not big business. And the only protection available is in the Constitution and the ballot box.

Speaking of the ballot box, we can blame politicians to some extent for the trampling of our liberty. But the bulk of the blame lies with us voters, because politicians are often doing what we elect them to do. The sad truth is that we elect them for the specific purpose of taking the property of other Americans and giving it to us. Many manufacturers think that the government owes them a protective tariff to keep out foreign goods, resulting in artificially higher prices for consumers. Many farmers think the government owes them a crop subsidy, which raises the price of food. Organized labor thinks government should protect their jobs from non-union competition. And so on. We could even consider many college professors, who love to secure government grants to study poverty and then meet at hotels in Miami during the winter to talk about poor people. All of these—and hundreds of other similar demands on government that I could cite—represent involuntary exchanges and diminish our freedom.

This reminds me of a lunch I had a number of years ago with my friend Jesse Helms, the late Senator from North Carolina. He knew that I was critical of farm subsidies, and he said he agreed with me 100 percent. But he wondered how a Senator from North Carolina could possibly vote against them. If he did so, his fellow North Carolinians would dump him and elect somebody worse in his place. And I remember wondering at the time if it is reasonable to ask a politician to commit political suicide for the sake of principle. The fact is that it's unreasonable of us to expect even principled politicians to vote against things like crop subsidies and stand up for the Constitution. This presents us with a challenge. It's up to us to ensure that it's in our representatives' interest to stand up for constitutional government.

Americans have never done the wrong thing for a long time, but if we're not going to go down the tubes as a great nation, we must get about changing things while we still have the liberty to do so.

WALTER WILLIAMS is the John M. Olin Distinguished Professor of Economics at George Mason University. He holds a BA from California State University at Los Angeles and an MA and a PhD in economics from UCLA. He has received numerous fellowships and awards, including a Hoover Institution National Fellowship and the Valley Forge Freedoms Foundation George Washington Medal of Honor. A nationally syndicated columnist, his articles and essays have appeared in publications such as *Economic Inquiry, American Economic Review, National Review, Reader's Digest, Policy Review,* and *Newsweek.* Williams has authored six books, including *The State Against Blacks* (later made into a PBS documentary entitled *Good Intentions*) and *Liberty versus the Tyranny of Socialism.*

EXPLORING THE ISSUE

Should Government Intervene in a Capitalist Economy?

Critical Thinking and Reflection

1. What role does the government already play in the economy and how successful has it been?
2. Would you say that the removal or weakening of government regulations was a primary cause of the recent financial crisis?
3. Are American businesses at a disadvantage compared to European businesses and if so, why?
4. Could regulations have prevented the depression and other failures of the market?
5. Have regulations noticeably slowed economic growth in the United States? Have they hindered American businesses in their competition with international companies?
6. If American businesses have the dominant influence over the government, they would have the regulations that would help them and not have the regulations that would hinder them. Is that the way things are? If not, why?
7. In 2011 a GOP candidate publicly declared that he would eliminate three departments if elected president because that would appeal to many voters. Can you explain this appeal?

Is There Common Ground?

As with most good debates, the issue of the rightness of government intervention is difficult to decide. Part of the difficulty is that it involves the trade-off of values that are in conflict in real situations, and part of the difficulty is that it involves uncertain estimations of the future consequences of policy changes. Both experts and interested parties can differ greatly on value trade-offs and estimations of impacts. Government regulations and other interventions cost money for both administration and compliance. Nevertheless, Stiglitz argues that certain government actions will provide benefits that greatly exceed the costs, and Williams argues the contrary view, that the costs will be far greater than Stiglitz expects and probably will have net negative results. Part of the strength of Williams's argument is that regulations often fail to do what they are designed to do. Part of the strength of Stiglitz's argument is that there are many observable problems that need to be addressed, and for some of these government action seems to be the only viable option. Possibly the best solution is to intervene as little as possible. This avoids the extreme positions that all interventions are bad or that beneficial interventions can address almost all problems of the market. Of course, the debate would continue over where the tipping point is between good and bad interventions.

Create Central

www.mhhe.com/createcentral

Additional Resources

One aspect of the issue is the morality of businesses. Most commentators have a low opinion of business ethics and the way corporations use their power, and point to the recent corporate scandals as confirmation. Many works criticize capitalism for a variety of reasons and these criticisms support the idea that corporations need to be regulated. Since they will not do what is right, they must be made to do what is right. For support of this view, see Frank Partnoy, *Infectious Greed: How Deceit and Risk Corrupted the Financial Markets* (PublicAffairs, 2009); Matthew Robinson and Daniel Murphy, *Greed Is Good: Maximization and Elite Deviance in America* (Rowman & Littlefield, 2009); Paul Mattick, *Business as Usual: The Economic Crisis and the Failure of Capitalism* (Reaktion Books, 2011); Robert H. Parks, *The End of Capitalism: Destructive Forces of an Economy Out of Control* (Prometheus Books, 2011); R. P. Bootle, *The Trouble with Markets: Saving Capitalism from Itself* (Nicholas Brealey Publishing, 2011); Joel Bakan, *The Corporation: The Pathological Pursuit of Profit and Power* (Free Press, 2004); Claude V. Chang, *Aggressive Capitalism: The Overleveraging of America's Wealth, Integrity, and Dollar* (University Press of America, 2010); Ha-Joon Chang, *23 Things They Don't Tell You about Capitalism* (Bloomsbury Press, 2010); John Bellamy Foster, *The Ecological Rift: Capitalism's War on the Earth* (Monthly Review Press, 2010); Chris Harman, *Zombie Capitalism: Global Crisis and the Relevance of Marx* (Bookmarks, 2009); John Weeks, *Capital, Exploitation, and Economic Crisis* (Routledge, 2010); David McNally, *Monsters of the Market: Zombies, Vampires, and Global Capitalism* (Brill, 2011); George Liodakis, *Totalitarian Capitalism and Beyond* (Ashgate, 2010); Justin O'Brien, *Wall Street on Trial: A Corrupted State?* (Wiley, 2003); Steve Tombs and Dave Whyte, *Unmasking the Crimes of the Powerful: Scrutinizing States and Corporations* (P. Lang, 2003); Jamie Court, *Corporateering: How Corporate Power Steals Your Personal Freedom— And What You Can Do about It* (Jeremy P. Tarcher/Putnam, 2003); Kenneth R. Gray et al., *Corporate Scandals: The*

Many Faces of Greed: The Great Heist, Financial Bubbles, and the Absence of Virtue (Paragon House, 2005); and Victor Perlo, *Superprofits and Crisis: Modern U.S. Capitalism* (International Publishers, 1988).

Some commentators, however, defend businesses in a competitive capitalistic market. Philosopher Michael Novak contends that the ethos of capitalism transcends mere moneymaking and is (or can be made) compatible with Judeo-Christian morality. See *The Spirit of Democratic Capitalism* (Madison Books, 1991) and *The Catholic Ethic and the Spirit of Capitalism* (Free Press, 1993). Two other defenses of capitalism on moral grounds are Peter Wehner and Arthur C. Brooks, *Wealth and Justice: The Morality of Democratic Capitalism* (AEI Press, 2011), and Andrew Bernstein, *Capitalism Unbound: The Incontestable Moral Case for Individual Rights* (University Press of America, 2010). Another broad-based defense of capitalism is Peter L. Berger's *The Capitalist Revolution: Fifty Propositions about Prosperity, Equality and Liberty* (Basic Books, 1988). For a feminist critique of capitalism, see J. K. Gibson-Graham, *The End of Capitalism (As We Know It): A Feminist Critique of Political Economy* (Blackwell, 1996). Two works that want to save capitalism through reforms are Roger Bootle, *The Trouble with Markets: Saving Capitalism from Itself* (Nicholas Brealey Publishing, 2011), and Matthew Bishop and Michael Green, *The Road from Ruin: How to Revive Capitalism and Put America Back on Top* (Crown Business, 2010). Howard K. Bloom argues that one of the positive features of capitalism is that it constantly revises itself in *The Genius of the Beast: A Radical Re-Vision of Capitalism* (Prometheus books, 2010). For a mixed view of capitalism, see Ann E. Cudd and Nancy Holmstrom, *Capitalism For and Against: A Feminist Debate* (Cambridge University Press, 2010), and Charles Wolf Jr., *Markets or Governments: Choosing Between Imperfect Alternatives* (MIT Press, 1993). A strong attack on government interventions in the market is Jonathan Rauch, *Demosclerosis: The Silent Killer of American Government* (Times Books, 1994). For an in-depth understanding of the way that markets work and the role that institutions maintained by the state, including property rights, function to maintain markets, see Neil Fligstein, *The Architecture of Markets: An Economic Sociology of Twenty-First Century Capitalist Societies* (Princeton University Press, 2001). An interesting role of government is its bailing out failed corporations. See *Too Big to Fail: Policies and Practices in Government Bailouts* edited by Benton E. Gup (Praeger, 2004), and David G. Mayes et al., *Who Pays for Bank Insolvency?* (Palgrave Macmillan, 2004). Often self-regulation is better than government regulation. See Virgina Haufler, *A Public Role for the Private Sector: Industry Self-Regulation in a Global Economy* (Carnegie Endowment for International Peace, 2001).

Internet References . . .

Sociology—Study Sociology Online

http://edu.learnsoc.org/

Sociology Web Resources

www.mhhe.com/socscience/sociology/resources/index.htm

Sociosite

www.topsite.com/goto/sociosite.net

Socioweb

www.topsite.com/goto/socioweb.com